PSALMS

This text introduces the book of Psalms and provides an exposition of each psalm with attention to genre, liturgical connections, societal issues, and the psalm's place in the book of Psalms as a whole. The treatments of the psalms feature a close look at particular issues raised by the text and the encounters between the world of the psalm and the world of contemporary readers. The exposition of each psalm provides a reader's guide to the text in conversation with relevant theological issues.

Walter Brueggemann is Professor Emeritus at Columbia Theological Seminary. He is an ordained minister in the United Church of Christ and was formerly president of the Society of Biblical Literature. His most recent books include *Disruptive Grace: Reflections on God, Scripture, and the Church* and *Journey to the Common Good.*

William H. Bellinger, Jr., is W. Marshall and Lulie Craig Chairholder in Bible, Chair of the Department of Religion, and Professor of Religion at Baylor University. He is author of *Psalms: A Guide to Studying the Psalter*, now in its second edition, and *Psalmody and Prophecy*, among other books. Professor Bellinger currently chairs the Steering Committee for the Book of Psalms Section of the Society of Biblical Literature and serves on the editorial board of the *Catholic Biblical Quarterly.*

NEW CAMBRIDGE BIBLE COMMENTARY

GENERAL EDITOR: Ben Witherington III

HEBREW BIBLE/OLD TESTAMENT EDITOR: Bill T. Arnold

The *New Cambridge Bible Commentary* (NCBC) aims to elucidate the Hebrew and Christian scriptures for a wide range of intellectually curious individuals. While building on the work and reputation of the *Cambridge Bible Commentary*, popular in the 1960s and 1970s, the NCBC takes advantage of many of the rewards provided by scholarly research over the last four decades. Volumes utilize recent gains in rhetorical criticism, social scientific study of the Scriptures, narrative criticism, and other developing disciplines to exploit the growing advances in biblical studies. Accessible, jargon-free commentary, annotated Suggested Readings lists, and the entire New Revised Standard Version (NRSV) text under discussion are the hallmarks of all volumes in the series.

PUBLISHED VOLUMES IN THE SERIES

Matthew, Craig A. Evans
Genesis, Bill T. Arnold
Exodus, Carol Meyers
Judges and Ruth, Victor H. Matthews
1–2 Corinthians, Craig S. Keener
The Gospel of John, Jerome H. Neyrey
James and Jude, William F. Brosend II
Revelation, Ben Witherington III

FORTHCOMING VOLUMES

Deuteronomy, Brent Strawn
Joshua, Douglas A. Knight
1–2 Chronicles, William M. Schniedewind
Isaiah 1–39, David Baer
Jeremiah, Baruch Halpern
Hosea, Joel, and Amos, J. J. M. Roberts
The Gospel of Luke, Amy-Jill Levine and Ben Witherington III
The Letters of John, Duane F. Watson

Psalms

Walter Brueggemann
Columbia Theological Seminary

William H. Bellinger, Jr.
Baylor University

CAMBRIDGE
UNIVERSITY PRESS

CAMBRIDGE
UNIVERSITY PRESS

One Liberty Plaza, 20th Floor, New York, NY 10006, USA

Cambridge University Press is part of the University of Cambridge.

It furthers the University's mission by disseminating knowledge in the pursuit of education, learning, and research at the highest international levels of excellence.

www.cambridge.org
Information on this title: www.cambridge.org/9780521600767

© Walter Brueggemann and W. H. Bellinger, Jr., 2014

First published 2014
5th printing 2019

Printed in the United Kingdom by TJ International Ltd. Padstow Cornwall

A catalog record for this publication is available from the British Library.

Library of Congress Cataloging in Publication Data
Brueggemann, Walter.
Psalms/Walter Brueggemann, William H. Bellinger, Jr.
    p.   cm. – (New Cambridge Bible commentary)
Includes bibliographical references and index.
ISBN 978-0-521-84092-7 (hardback) – ISBN 978-0-521-60076-7 (paperback)
1. Bible. O.T. Psalms – Commentaries.   I. Bellinger, W. H.   II. Title.
BS1430.53.B784   2013
223'.207–dc23   2012019716

ISBN 978-0-521-84092-7 Hardback
ISBN 978-0-521-60076-7 Paperback

Additional resources for this publication at www.cambridge.org/9780521840927

Contents

viii   *Contents*

Supplementary Sections

Preface

The biblical text has in it no indication of emphases for reading. In a number of texts quoted herein, we have italicized certain words in order to assist the reader in noting the rhetorical force of the text. In each case, such underscoring is our own work and of course coheres with our own sense of the text. When emphasis appears in a reference other than the Bible, the emphasis is ours unless stated otherwise. When a verse is cited without a book or chapter reference (e.g., v. 1), it is understood to refer to the psalm presently under discussion.

The authors thank the editors and publishers of the *New Cambridge Bible Commentary* for the opportunity to work on the book of Psalms. Special thanks also go to Libby Ballard, B. J. Parker, Anna Sieges, and Kim Williams Bodenhamer. May these comments on the Psalms help today's readers and hearers embrace these ancient texts in transforming ways.

A Word about Citations

All volumes in the *New Cambridge Bible Commentary* (NCBC) include footnotes, with full bibliographical citations included in the note when a source is first mentioned. Subsequent citations include the author's initial or initials, full last name, abbreviated title for the work, and date of publication. Most readers prefer this citation system to endnotes that require searching through pages at the back of the book.

The Suggested Readings lists, also included in all NCBC volumes after the Introduction, are not a part of this citation apparatus. Annotated and organized by publication type, the self-contained Suggested Readings lists are intended to introduce and briefly review some of the most well-known and helpful literature on the biblical text under discussion.

Abbreviations

BASOR	*Bulletin of the American Schools of Oriental Research*
BJRL	*Bulletin of the John Rylands University Library of Manchester*
BN	*Bible Review*
BTB	*Biblical Theology Bulletin*
BWANT	*Beiträge zur Wissenschaft vom Alten und Neuen Testament*
BZ	*Biblische Zeitschrift*
BZAW	*Beihefte zur Zeitschrift für die alttestamentliche Wissenschaft*
CB	*Cultura bíblica*
CBQ	*Catholic Biblical Quarterly*
CJT	*Canadian Journal of Theology*
EvQ	*Evangelical Quarterly*
Ex Aud	*Ex Auditu*
FAT	Forschungen zum Alten Testament
HBT	*Horizons in Biblical Theology*
HTR	*Harvard Theological Review*
HUCA	*Hebrew Union College Annual*
JAOS	*Journal of the American Oriental Society*
JBL	*Journal of Biblical Literature*
J Preachers	*Journal for Preachers*
JQR	*Jewish Quarterly Review*
JSOT	*Journal for the Study of the Old Testament*
JSOTSup	Journal for the Study of the Old Testament, Supplement Series
JTS	*Journal of Theological Studies*
OTL	Old Testament Library
SBLDS	Society of Biblical Literature Dissertation Series
SBLSP	*Society of Biblical Literature Seminar Papers*
SBT	Studies in Biblical Theology
SJT	*Scottish Journal of Theology*
TGUOS	*Transactions of the Glasgow University Oriental Society*

TZ	*Theologische Zeitschrift*
VT	*Vetus Testamentum*
WBC	Word Biblical Commentary
ZAW	*Zeitschrift für die alttestamentliche Wissenschaft*
ZTK	*Zeitschrift für Theologie und Kirche*

I. Introduction

When people of faith gather around the Hebrew scriptures, the focus is often the book of Psalms. This collection of songs has powerfully influenced worship, theology, ethics, and piety for centuries.[1] The book continues to influence contemporary readers with its eloquent poetic language, which communicates directly to the life circumstances of contemporary readers even though the language originated from the ancient Near East. The book undercuts private and simplistic forms of piety and yet it has been appropriately labeled the "Prayer Book of the Bible."[2] Luther has even given it the title of the "little Bible" because it encapsulates so much of the message of the Scriptures. He says the Psalter "might well be called a little Bible. In it is comprehended most beautifully and briefly everything that is in the entire Bible … so that anyone who could not read the whole Bible would have anyway almost an entire summary of it, comprised in one little book."[3] This central biblical book continues to capture the imaginations of readers today as they seek to pray and live faithfully.

MATTERS OF ORGANIZATION

The context of the book of Psalms can provide clues for readers, and so it may be helpful to discuss a number of introductory matters. The title "Psalms," which indicates songs accompanied by stringed instruments, comes from the title of the book in the Greek version of the Hebrew scriptures. The title "Psalter" in the Latin version refers to the stringed instrument. The Hebrew title aptly categorizes the book as "praises." The book is structured in five sections, or books, each of which concludes

---

1   See Susan Gillingham, *Psalms Through the Centuries: Volume One* (Blackwell Bible Commentaries; Oxford: Blackwell, 2008).
2   Dietrich Bonhoeffer, *Psalms: The Prayer Book of the Bible*, 2nd edition, trans. J. H. Burtness (Minneapolis: Augsburg, 1979).
3   Martin Luther, "Preface to the Psalter," in Martin Luther, *Luther's Works*, trans. C. M. Jacobs and Rev. E. T. Bachman (Philadelphia: Muhlenberg, 1960), 254.

with a benediction (Pss 41:13; 72:18–20; 89:52; 106:48; 145:21). Psalms 146–150 conclude the Psalter with a fivefold doxology. Psalms 1 and 2 introduce the collection.

Five Books of Psalms

Book I	Psalms 1–41
Book II	Psalms 42–72
Book III	Psalms 73–89
Book IV	Psalms 90–106
Book V	Psalms 107–150

The Psalter is a collection of collections that have come together to make up the five books. A number of these collections are related to the titles or superscriptions written as headings to many of the psalms (usually verse 1 in the Hebrew text but written as a heading in English translations).

Collections in the Psalter

Davidic Collections	Psalms 3–41; 51–72; 138–145
Korahite Collections	Psalms 42–49; 84–85; 87–88
Elohistic Collection	Psalms 42–83
Asaphite Collection	Psalms 73–83
Songs of Ascents	Psalms 120–134

The most common label is associated with David. Through the centuries a number of readers have taken those references to David as indications of authorship, but the preposition used with the famous royal name carries a wide variety of meanings, such as "dedicated to," "on behalf of," or "belonging to." It is best to take these references and other texts in the Hebrew scriptures that connect David with the Psalms in terms of a tradition of David as the patron or primary sponsor of psalmody in ancient Israel and the royal figure who authorized worship and its use of psalms in Jerusalem. A helpful analogy is the connection of King James I to the King James Version of the Bible. Some of the Davidic psalms are also part of the Elohistic Psalter (Psalms 42–83), given that title because of the preference for *Elohim* (God) rather than *YHWH* (Lord) when referring to the deity. Some psalms occur twice in the Psalter – once in the Elohistic Psalter and once elsewhere – and highlight the difference in divine name:

Ps 14:2: *The Lord (YHWH)* looks down from heaven on humankind …
Ps 53:2: *God (Elohim)* looks down from heaven on humankind …

The overlapping of collections in the Psalter indicates something of the process of its compilation. We do not know the whole story of how the Psalter came together, and we will return to this issue later in the Introduction, but it is fair to say that the Davidic collections form the core of the book of Psalms, and these psalms are primarily prayers of individuals. The psalms of the Korahites and of Asaph add community prayers and begin the move toward more psalms of praise, a move that continues in Books IV and V. The Psalter apparently arose from a lengthy process that shaped the book in a purposeful way.

Most of the psalms (116 out of 150 in the Hebrew Psalter) include superscriptions. Most interpreters agree that the superscriptions were added later, during the process of the compilation of the Psalter, but they are still part of the text and provide helpful clues to readers.[4] These headings often include three elements:

1. *Liturgical Collections.* Psalms of David or psalms of Asaph, for example, indicate the liturgical collection from which the psalm derived.
2. *Worship Terms.* Some of these terms are obscure, but "with stringed instruments" in Psalm 67 refers to the performance of the text in worship. "According to the lilies" in Psalm 69 apparently indicates the hymn tune to be used for this text in worship.
3. *Historical Notes.* The superscription of Psalm 57 includes the following: "Of David. A Miktam [golden poem], when he fled from Saul in the cave." In a heuristic move, the compilers of the Psalter suggest that readers consider Psalm 57 along with the narrative in 1 Samuel 22 where Saul pursues David as a competitor for the throne and in particular along with 1 Sam 22:1.

Psalm 59 includes all three of these elements: "To the leader: Do Not Destroy [worship terms]. Of David [liturgical collection]. A Miktam, when Saul ordered his house to be watched in order to kill him [historical note]."

MATTERS OF POETRY

The Psalms take the form of Hebrew poetry. The poetic form is somewhat different from traditional English poetry. Although a kind of meter may have characterized Hebrew poetry, we know little about that. What interpreters do often discern is the central presence of parallel structures – in words, poetic lines, and groups of

---

4 See, for example, B. S. Childs, "Psalms Titles and Midrashic Exegesis," *JSS* 16 (1971): 137–150; John J. Collins, *Introduction to the Hebrew Bible* (Minneapolis: Fortress Press, 2004), 461–462; and James L. Mays, *Psalms* (Interpretation; Louisville, KY: John Knox, 1994), 11–13, 53–54.

poetic lines. Parallel relations between lines of Hebrew poetry often come across in English translations as echoes. At times the echo suggests similarity of meaning:

The heavens are telling the glory of God;
and the firmament proclaims his handiwork. (Ps 19:1)

At other times, the echo is one of contrast:

For the Lord watches over the way of the righteous,
but the way of the wicked will perish. (Ps 1:6)

The nature of the echo between lines varies, but readers are well advised to note the relationships between the lines of verses in the Psalms.[5]

Poetry is highly structured and complex language that demands much of its readers. In addition to the parallel structures already mentioned, the Psalms also make use of repetition and poetic images. The particular vocabulary used also carries much freight; note the use of "righteous" and "wicked" in Psalm 1 quoted earlier. Scholars have begun to pay closer attention to these characteristics of the poetry in the Psalter. When readers follow the poetic sequencing and relationships in a psalm and pay close attention to the metaphors and language used, it becomes possible to plot the psalm's movement and to sense the text's poetic structure and purpose.[6]

MATTERS OF METHOD

This commentary will approach the Psalms by way of several of the methods of modern scholarship on the Psalter.

First, attention to matters of genre will be important. The inventor of the modern study of the Psalms is Hermann Gunkel, and his central contribution has to do with analyzing the Psalms according to type. Gunkel thought previous interpretations of the Psalms that centered on questions of authorship and historical events behind the texts did not take sufficient account of the poetic language of the Psalms themselves. He considered psalms found in texts from ancient Near Eastern peoples surrounding Israel and psalms that are found in the Bible in places other than the Psalter (for example, Exod 15:1–18; Jgs 5:1–31; 1 Sam 2:1–10; Jer 20:7–18). He carefully compared all these songs and those in the Hebrew Psalter and categorized

---

5   For helpful treatments of Hebrew poetry, see J. L. Kugel, *The Idea of Biblical Poetry: Parallelism and Its History* (New Haven, CT: Yale University Press, 1981); Robert Alter, *The Art of Biblical Poetry* (New York: Basic Books, 1985); and A. Berlin, *The Dynamics of Biblical Parallelism* (Bloomington: Indiana University Press, 1985).

6   See W. Brueggemann, *The Message of the Psalms: A Theological Commentary* (Minneapolis: Augsburg, 1984). Particularly helpful in envisioning the poetic imagery of the Psalms is William P. Brown, *Seeing the Psalms: A Theology of Metaphor* (Louisville, KY: Westminster John Knox, 2002).

them into literary groupings. Vocabulary, poetic structure, and religious tone were the criteria he used. Gunkel's work was widely influential in the twentieth century and continues to bear important fruit in the study of the Psalms.[7] Gunkel's work provides a way to organize one's study of the Psalter and a comparative basis for studying individual psalms as part of a category. Most works on the Psalms in the twentieth century began with a classification of the Psalms in the tradition of Gunkel's method. Questions of genre continue to carry import in Psalms study. Attention to genre can help readers follow the poetic sequence and see connections with other psalms.

The treatments of psalms in this commentary will pay attention to questions of genre. It may be helpful to list the primary types of psalms that will be discussed.

1. *Individual and Community Laments.* These psalms derive from a crisis either of a person of faith (such as illness or false accusation) or of the community of faith (such as war or famine). The prayers address Israel's God and portray the crisis and call for help. Most often the prayers come to a positive conclusion.

2. *Hymns of Praise.* These psalms offer adoration and praise to God as creator and redeemer. They begin with a call to the congregation to offer praise and often conclude with a very similar renewed call. The body of the psalm articulates reasons why the community should offer praise to God.

3. *Individual and Community Thanksgiving Psalms.* These texts narrate the story of how a person of faith or the community has been delivered from a crisis, put in the context of praise and gratitude to the God who delivers. Westermann understands these texts to be a particular kind of psalm of praise.[8]

4. *Royal Psalms.* These texts find their origin in various events in the life of the Davidic King in Jerusalem, such as battle or a royal coronation. This group of psalms is distinguished by that background more than by literary characteristics.

5. *Wisdom Psalms.* A number of interpreters identify some psalms as deriving from the wisdom circles in ancient Israel and reflecting their perspectives as seen in the book of Proverbs.

---

7   See H. Gunkel, *The Psalms: A Form-Critical Introduction* (Facet Books, Biblical Series 19; Philadelphia: Fortress Press, 1967); and H. Gunkel with Joachim Begrich, *An Introduction to the Psalms: The Genres of the Religious Lyric of Israel*, trans. James D. Nogalski (Macon, GA: Mercer University Press, 1998) [German original, 1933]. R. E. Clements, *One Hundred Years of Old Testament Interpretation* (Philadelphia: Westminster, 1976), 76–98, provides a helpful account of the form-critical approach to the Psalms.
8   Claus Westermann, *Praise and Lament in the Psalms*, trans. Keith R. Crim and Richard N. Soulen (Atlanta: John Knox, 1981).

Second, attention to matters of cultic setting will come to the fore in some of the psalm treatments. Ancient Israel's cult – their organized worship primarily in the Jerusalem temple – provides the religious and social setting from which many of the psalms derive. Gunkel began the emphasis on worship as the background of the Psalms, but it was his student Sigmund Mowinckel who took the matter to its logical conclusion.[9] For Mowinckel, the Psalms and their categories were tied to their use in worship. The language of the Psalms is liturgical language, reflecting actual worship practice. Leaders associated with the cultic establishment composed many of the texts for liturgical settings. Mowinckel understood that in ancient Israel the personal religion often sensed by readers of the Psalms and the religion of corporate worship are not mutually exclusive but are two dimensions of ancient Israel's religion. So the central interpretive question for Mowinckel is the function of the psalm in worship, in particular the identification of a festival or ritual setting that gave birth to the psalm. For Mowinckel, worship was a dramatic event that included sights and sounds as it brought to expression the relationship between the congregation and its deity. Processions and rituals with a variety of movements and offerings provide the context in which the Psalms were performed. The dramatic event of worship in Jerusalem was also tied to ancient Israel's faith narrative. In worship, the community reenacted its story of faith so that each generation might participate in the story and envision its great events. The reenactment of the Exodus from Egypt or of the kingship of the creator YHWH would have been part of the festival worship celebrations. Prayer rituals for healing or for pleas for deliverance were also important worship events. Such liturgical settings had implications for theology and ethics. For Mowinckel, the cult was central to ancient Israel's religion, and the Psalms were the songs set in that worship. So attention to this background provided the most basic information for interpreters.

Not all interpreters today would emphasize the cultic setting of the Psalms in the totalizing way Mowinckel did, especially the tie to the preexilic Jerusalem cult he extols. The understanding of setting is broader and more flexible. Still, most interpreters would agree that cult stands in the background of many psalms, and often this generative cult relates to the Jerusalem temple. The temple was sacred space for ancient Israel because it was seen to be a special place of the life-giving presence of YHWH.[10] A number of the psalms appear to relate to rituals and festivals in that context and, where warranted, this commentary will explore how those settings can inform interpretation.

9   See Sigmund Mowinckel, *The Psalms in Israel's Worship* (2 vols., Nashville, TN: Abingdon Press, 1962).
10 See Fredrik Lindström, *Suffering and Sin: Interpretations of Illness in the Individual Complaint Psalms* (Coniectanea Biblica; Stockholm: Almqvist and Wiksells, 1994), 192–193.

Third, the matter of a psalm's relationship to societal issues as part of its broader setting can provide interpretive clues. Claus Westermann's interaction with Gunkel's emphasis on genre provides a helpful starting point.[11] He has seen that the Psalms move from plea to praise and that lament is resolved into thanksgiving. Lament psalms often end positively with praise, and thanksgiving psalms fulfill the vow to offer gratitude upon the occasion of deliverance from the crisis. These thanksgiving psalms are related to the powerful hymnic praise in the Psalter. Walter Brueggemann has translated this perspective into relational terms: "In these psalms, Israel moves from *articulation* of hurt and anger, to *submission* of them to God, and finally to *relinquishment*.... Only when there is relinquishment can there be praise and acts of generosity."[12] Also relevant is Erhard Gerstenberger's understanding of the lament psalms as important pastoral texts related not to the cult of the Jerusalem temple but to extended family settings in which life crises from birth to death become part of prayer rituals.[13] What Brueggemann has seen from these studies of genre and setting is that the faith to which the Psalms bear witness is concerned with the dynamics of power. Petitioners in the Psalms plead with God to redress societal and relational wrongs as the covenant God who brings justice, and so the portrayal of YHWH in these texts is of a God who is engaged with this community – a God in the fray. Petitioners in the Psalms boldly address YHWH; such prayer speech is taken seriously and preserved as central to the covenant faith in the Psalter. These psalms also often seek a redress of human power relations. Forceful enemies attack the speakers in these psalms, and the speakers complain to the deity with the expectation that God will deal with such unjust attacks. The treatment of many of the psalms in this commentary will explore ways that these prayers reflect social oppression and seek a redress of power.

Fourth, a psalm's context in the Psalter carries import. The interpretive approaches described earlier most often deal with each psalm as a discrete text, but many recent interpreters suggest that the shape of the Hebrew Psalter as a whole

---

11 C. Westermann, *Praise and Lament in the Psalms* (1981).
12 W. Brueggemann, "The Costly Loss of Lament," in Patrick D. Miller (ed.), *The Psalms and the Life of Faith* (Minneapolis: Fortress Press, 1995), 100; see also W. Brueggemann, *Israel's Praise: Doxology Against Idolatry and Ideology* (Philadelphia: Fortress Press, 1988). Brueggemann's influential faith typology of the Psalms in terms of orientation, disorientation, and new orientation also connects to the relational dimension of psalmody; see W. Brueggemann, "Psalms and the Life of Faith: A Suggested Typology of Function," in P. D. Miller (ed.), *Psalms and the Life of Faith* (1995), 3–32.
13 See Erhard S. Gerstenberger, *Psalms, Part 1, with an Introduction to Cultic Poetry* (Forms of the Old Testament Literature; Grand Rapids, MI: Eerdmans, 1988); and Erhard S. Gerstenberger, *Psalms, Part 2, and Lamentations* (Forms of the Old Testament Literature; Grand Rapids, MI: Eerdmans, 2001).

can give helpful clues to readers. Gerald Wilson's work provides important starting points.[14] He argues that Books I–III of the Psalter have a different editorial history than Books IV–V. The first three books reflect the experience of the Davidic kingdom, initiated with the coronation of the king in Psalm 2 and concluding with the demise of Jerusalem at the end of Psalm 89. Books IV–V respond to the exile that originated from this crisis by reasserting the reign of YHWH as a basis for the community's future. Some have questioned this articulation of the macrostructure of the Hebrew Psalter because of the presence of Davidic elements in Books IV–V, but a number of scholars emphasize the centrality of divine kingship for the book.[15] This commentary will on occasion explore a particular psalm's place in the Psalter as a whole or its place in a collection of psalms. The other dimension of these recent interpretations of the Psalms has to do with microstructures; that is, the connections between individual psalms.[16] Most readers of Psalm 23, for example, do not account for its position and relationship with Psalms 22 and 24. The commentary will at times explore such relationships. Scholarship of recent decades has made it clear that there is a purposeful shape to the Hebrew Psalter, and readers can gain much by attending to this dimension of Psalms study.

The commentary will also attend to ancient Near Eastern connections to the Psalms and to the poetic dimensions already noted, though the dominant approaches are the four articulated here.

CONCLUSION

Contemporary readers continue to find the Psalms to be vibrant expressions of prayer and faith as well as vibrant portrayals of the divine and human encounter for faith communities. This commentary seeks to give context and color for those readers of the text in the hope that interpretive communities will interact with the Psalms, be formed by them, and embrace their life-giving impact.

14 G. H. Wilson, *The Editing of the Hebrew Psalter* (SBLDS 76; Chico, CA: Scholars Press, 1985); see also B. S. Childs, *Introduction to the Old Testament as Scripture* (Philadelphia: Fortress Press, 1979), 504–525. See James L. Crenshaw, *The Psalms: An Introduction* (Grand Rapids, MI: Eerdmans, 2001), as an illustration of the shift from beginning with genre in studying the Psalms to beginning with the compilation of the Psalter.
15 See, for example, James L. Mays, *The Lord Reigns: A Theological Handbook to the Psalms* (Louisville, KY: Westminster John Knox, 1994); and J. Clinton McCann, Jr., *A Theological Introduction to the Book of Psalms: The Psalms as Torah* (Nashville, TN: Abingdon Press, 1993). For a different view, see David C. Mitchell, *The Message of the Psalter: An Eschatological Programme in the Book of Psalms* (JSOTSup; Sheffield: Sheffield Academic, 1997).
16 See David M. Howard, *The Structure of Psalms 93–100* (Winona Lake, IN: Eisenbrauns, 1997); and Frank-Lothar Hossfeld and Erich Zenger, *Psalms 2: A Commentary on Psalms 51–100*, trans. Linda M. Maloney (Hermeneia; Minneapolis: Fortress Press, 2005).

PSALM COLLECTIONS AND PSALM TYPES

1	Book 1		Wisdom
2	1–41		Royal
3		David	Individual Lament
4		3–41	Individual Lament
5			Individual Lament
6			Individual Lament
7			Individual Lament
8			Creation
9			Individual Lament
10			Individual Lament
11			Individual Lament
12			Community Lament
13			Individual Lament
14			Community Lament
15			Entrance Liturgy
16			Individual Lament
17			Individual Lament
18			Royal
19			Creation
20			Royal
21			Royal
22			Individual Lament
23			Trust Psalm
24			Entrance Liturgy
25			Individual Lament
26			Individual Lament
27			Individual Lament
28			Individual Lament
29			General Hymn
30			Individual Psalm of Thanksgiving
31			Individual Lament
32			Wisdom
33			General Hymn
34			Individual Psalm of Thanksgiving
35			Individual Lament
36			Individual Lament
37			Wisdom
38			Individual Lament
39			Individual Lament
40			Individual Lament
41			Individual Psalm of Thanksgiving

42	Book 2	Korah	Elohistic	Individual Lament
43	42–72	42–49	42–83	Individual Lament
44				Community Lament
45				Royal
46				Zion Psalm
47				Enthronement
48				Zion Psalm
49				Wisdom
50		Psalm of Asaph		Hymn with Prophetic Warning
51		David		Individual Lament
52		51–72		Individual Lament
53				Community Lament
54				Individual Lament
55				Individual Lament
56				Individual Lament
57				Individual Lament
58				Community Lament
59				Individual Lament
60				Community Lament
61		Of Solomon		Individual Lament
62				Individual Lament
63				Individual Lament
64				Individual Lament
65				Creation
66				Individual Psalm of Thanksgiving
67				Community Psalm of Thanksgiving
68				General Hymn
69				Individual Lament
70				Individual Lament
71				Individual Lament
72				Royal
73	Book 3	Asaph		Wisdom
74	73–89	73–83		Community Lament
75				Community Psalm of Thanksgiving
76				Zion Psalm
77				Individual Lament
78				Wisdom
79				Community Lament
80				Community Lament
81				Hymn with Prophetic Warning
82				Hymn with Prophetic Warning
83				Community Lament

84		Korah		Zion Psalm
85		84–85		Community Lament
86		Of David		Individual Lament
87		Korah		Zion Psalm
88		87–88		Individual Lament
89				Royal
90	Book 4	Of Moses		Community Lament
91	90–106			Trust Psalm
92		For the Sabbath		Individual Psalm of Thanksgiving
93			Kingship	Enthronement
94			of God	Individual Lament
95			93–100	Enthronement
96				Enthronement
97				Enthronement
98				Enthronement
99				Enthronement
100				General Hymn
101		Of David		Royal
102				Individual Lament
103		Of David	Psalms of	General Hymn
104			Praise	Creation
105			103–107	General Hymn
106				Community Lament
107	Book 5			Community Psalm of Thanksgiving
108	107–150	Of David		Community Lament
109		Of David		Individual Lament
110		Of David		Royal
111			Hallelujah	Individual Hymn of Thanksgiving
112			111–118	Wisdom
113				General Hymn
114				General Hymn
115				General Hymn
116				Individual Psalm of Thanksgiving
117				General Hymn
118				Individual Psalm of Thanksgiving
119				Wisdom
120		Songs of Ascents		Individual Lament
121		120–134		Trust Psalm
122		Of David		Zion Psalm
123		Of David		Community Lament
124		Of Solomon		Community Psalm of Thanksgiving
125		Of David		Trust Psalm
126				Community Lament

127			Wisdom
128			Wisdom
129			Community Psalm of Thanksgiving
130			Individual Lament
131			Trust Psalm
132			Royal
133			Wisdom
134			General Hymn
135			General Hymn
136			Community Psalm of Thanksgiving
137			Community Lament
138	David		Individual Psalm of Thanksgiving
139	138–145		General Hymn
140			Individual Lament
141			Individual Lament
142			Individual Lament
143			Individual Lament
144			Royal
145			General Hymn
146		Hallelujah	General Hymn
147		146–150	General Hymn
148			Creation
149			General Hymn
150			General Hymn

Note: A color version of this table is available at www.cambridge.org/9780521840927.

II. Suggested Readings on the Psalms

The Hebrew Psalter has received extensive attention in the secondary literature. This section on suggested readings provides several sources that should prove helpful for readers of the Hebrew Psalter. The list is by no means exhaustive, but it does contain commentaries, books, and articles. These sources contain extensive bibliographies themselves that can act as guides for further reading.

COMMENTARIES

Leslie Allen, *Psalms 101–150* (WBC 21; Waco, TX: Word Books, 1983).

A. Anderson, *The Book of Psalms* (The New Century Bible Commentary; 2 vols., Grand Rapids, MI: Eerdmans, 1972).

W. E. Barnes, *The Psalms* (WC; London: Methuen and Co., 1931).

Charles A. Briggs and Emilie Briggs, *Psalms* (2 vols., Edinburgh: T. and T. Clark, 2000).

Craig C. Broyles, *Psalms* (New International Biblical Commentary. Old Testament 11; Peabody, MA: Hendrickson, 1999).

Moses Buttenwieser, *The Psalms Chronologically Treated, with a New Translation* (Hoboken, NJ: Ktav, 1969).

Richard J. Clifford, *Abingdon Old Testament Commentary* (2 vols., Nashville, TN: Abingdon Press, 2002).

Peter C. Craigie, *Psalms 1–50* (WBC 19; Waco, TX: Word Books, 1983).

Mitchell Dahood, *Psalms* (Anchor Bible; 3 vols., Garden City, NY: Doubleday, 1970).

Robert Davidson, *The Vitality of Worship: A Commentary on the Book of Psalms* (Grand Rapids, MI: Eerdmans, 1998).

Franz Delitzsch, *Biblical Commentary on the Psalms* (3 vols., Edinburgh: T. and T. Clark, 1908).

J. Durham, *Psalms* (Broadman Bible Commentary; Nashville, TN: Broadman
Press, 1971).

J. H. Eaton, *Psalms* (Torch Bible Commentary; London: SCM Press, 1967).

John Goldingay, *Psalms*, Tremper Longman III (ed.) (Baker Bible Commentaries;
3 vols., Grand Rapids, MI: Baker Academic, 2006).

Hermann Gunkel, *Einleitung in Die Psalmen Die Gattungen Der Religiösen
Lyrik Israels* (Handkommentar Zum Alten Testament 2; Göttingen:
Vandenhoeck and Ruprecht, 1933).

Frank-Lothar Hossfeld and Erich Zenger, *Die Psalmen* (Neue Echter Bibel.
Altes Testament 29; Würzburg: Echter Verlag, 1993).

Frank-Lothar Hossfeld, Erich Zenger, Klaus Baltzer, and Linda M. Maloney,
Psalms (Hermeneia; Minneapolis: Fortress Press, 2005).

A. F. Kirkpatrick, *Book of Psalms* (Grand Rapids, MI: Baker, 1982).

Edward J. Kissane, *The Book of Psalms* (Dublin: Browne and Nolan Limited,
1953).

Rudolf Kittel and Ernst Sellin, *Die Psalmen* (5. und 6. Auflage. Kommentar Zum
Alten Testament, Bd. 13; Leipzig: Deichertsche Verlagsbuchhandlung,
1929).

Hans-Joachim Kraus, *Psalms* (A Continental Commentary; 2 vols., Minneapolis:
Augsburg Fortress, 2000).

James Luther Mays, *Psalms* (Interpretation; Louisville, KY: Westminster John
Knox Press, 1994).

J. Clinton McCann, "Psalms," in Robert Doran, Leander Keck, J. Clinton
McCann, and Carol A. Newsom (eds.), *New Interpreter's Bible: 1 & 2
Maccabees, Job, Psalms* (Nashville, TN: Abingdon Press, 1996).

J. W. Rogerson and J. W. McKay, *Psalms* (2 vols., Cambridge: Cambridge
University Press, 1977).

Konrad Schaefer, *Psalms*, David W. Cotter and Jerome T. Walsh (eds.) (Berit
Olam; Collegeville, MN: Liturgical Press, 2001).

Marvin E. Tate, *Psalms 51–100* (WBC 20; Dallas: Word Books, 1991).

Artur Weiser, *Psalms* (OTL; Louisville, KY: Westminster John Knox Press,
2000).

INTRODUCTORY VOLUMES ON THE PSALMS

Wayne Ballard, Jr. and Dennis Tucker, Jr., *An Introduction to Wisdom Literature
and the Psalms: Festschrift Marvin E. Tate* (Macon, GA: Mercer University
Press, 2000).

W. H. Bellinger, Jr., *Psalms: Reading and Studying the Book of Praises* (Peabody,
MA: Hendrickson, 1990).

Psalms: A Guide to Studying the Psalter, 2nd edition (Grand Rapids, MI: Baker Academic, 2012).

James. L. Crenshaw, *The Psalms: An Introduction* (Grand Rapids, MI: Eerdmans, 2001).

John Day, *Psalms* (Old Testament Guides; Sheffield: JSOT, 1992).

Nancy L. DeClaisse-Walford, *Introduction to the Psalms: A Song from Ancient Israel* (St. Louis: Chalice Press, 2004).

Alfons Diessler, *Die Psalmen* (Dusseldorf: Patmosverlag, 1984).

Denise Dombkowski Hopkins, *Journey Through the Psalms* (St. Louis: Chalice Press, 2002).

E. S. Gerstenberger, *Psalms: Part 1, with an Introduction to Cultic Poetry* (Grand Rapids, MI: Eerdmans, 1988).

Psalms: Part 2, and Lamentations (Forms of the Old Testament Literature; Grand Rapids, MI: Eerdmans, 2001).

Hermann Gunkel, *Introduction to the Psalms*, trans. James D. Nogalski, completed by Joachim Begrich (Mercer Library of Biblical Studies; Macon, GA: Mercer University Press, 1998).

J. Hayes, *Understanding the Psalms* (Valley Forge, PA: Judson, 1976).

S. Mowinckel, *Psalmenstudien* (4 vols., Amsterdam: P. Schippers, 1961).

N. Ridderbos, *Die Psalmen* (Berlin: de Gruyter, 1972).

Leopold Sabourin, *The Psalms: Their Origin and Meaning* (2 vols., Staten Island, NY: Alba House, 1966).

Nahum M. Sarna, *Songs of the Heart: An Introduction to the Book of Psalms* (New York: Schocken, 1993).

K. Seybold, *Introducing the Psalms*, trans. R. Graeme Dunphy (Edinburgh: T. and T. Clark, 1990).

Carroll Stuhlmueller, *Psalms: Old Testament Message*, vols. 21–22 (Wilmington, DE: Michael Glazier, 1983).

SPECIAL STUDIES: LITERARY EMPHASIS

The categories used in the remaining suggested readings reflect an attempt to discern the major emphasis of a work. The literary study of the book of Psalms takes many guises. Some volumes attend to the background and composition of these poetic texts, others attend to the technical dimensions of Hebrew poetry, and still others comment on the reception history of the poems or how they fit together in the Psalter as a whole. The following list reflects these various literary approaches.

Robert Alter, *The Art of Biblical Poetry* (New York: Basic Books, 1985).

Pierre Auffret, *The Literary Structure of Psalm 2* (JSOTSup 3; Sheffield: JSOT, 1977).

Que seulement de tes yeux tu regardes … : Etude Structurelle de Treize Psaumes (Berlin: de Gruyter, 2003).

Egbert Ballhorn, *Zum Telos des Psalters: der Textzusammenhang des Vierten und Fünften Psalmenbuches (Ps 90–150)* (Berlin: Philo, 2004).

Joachim Becker, *Wege der Psalmenexegese* (Stuttgarter Bibelstudien 78; Stuttgart: KBW Verlag, 1975).

William H. Bellinger, *Psalmody and Prophecy* (JSOTSup 27; Sheffield: JSOT, 1984).

A Hermeneutic of Curiosity and Readings of Psalm 61 (Studies in Old Testament Interpretation; Macon, GA: Mercer University Press, 1995).

Adele Berlin, *The Dynamics of Biblical Parallelism* (Bloomington: Indiana University Press, 1985).

Donald K. Berry, *The Psalms and Their Readers: Interpretive Strategies for Psalm 18* (JSOTSup 153; Sheffield: JSOT, 1993).

Walter Beyerlin, *Die Rettung der Bedrängten in den Feindpsalmen der Einzelnen auf institutionelle Zusammenhange untersucht* (Gottingen: Vandenhoeck and Ruprecht, 1970).

Werden und Wesen des 107. Psalms (Berlin: de Gruyter, 1979).

We Are Like Dreamers: Studies in Psalm 126, trans. Dinah Livingstone (Edinburgh: T. and T. Clark, 1982).

Wider die Hybris des Geistes: Studien zum 131. Psalm (Stuttgart: Verlag Katholisches Bibelwerk Gmb.H., 1982).

Weisheitlich-kultische Heilsordnung: Studien zum 15. Psalm (Biblisch-Theologische Studien 9; Neukirchen Vluyn: Neukirchener, 1985).

William P. Brown, *Seeing the Psalms: A Theology of Metaphor* (Louisville, KY: Westminster John Knox Press, 2002).

Joel S. Burnett, W. H. Bellinger, and W. Dennis Tucker, *Diachronic and Synchronic: Reading the Psalms in Real Time: Proceedings of the Baylor Symposium on the Book of Psalms* (New York: T. and T. Clark, 2007).

Robert L. Cole, *The Shape and Message of Book III (Psalms 73–89)* (JSOTSup 307; Sheffield: Sheffield Academic, 2000).

Jerome F. D. Creach, *Yahweh as Refuge and the Editing of the Hebrew Psalter* (JSOTSup 217 ; Sheffield: JSOT, 1996).

The Destiny of the Righteous in the Psalms (St. Louis: Chalice Press, 2008).

Steven J. L. Croft, *The Identity of the Individual in the Psalms* (JSOTSup 44; Sheffield: JSOT, 1987).

F. Crüsemann, *Studien zur formgeschichte von Hymnus und Danklied in Israel* (WMANT 32; Neukirchen-Vluyn: Neukirchener Verlag, 1969).

R. C. Culley, *Oral Formulaic Language in the Biblical Psalms* (Toronto: University of Toronto Press, 1967).

L. Delekat, *Asylie und Schutzorakel am Zionheiligtum: Eine Untersuchung zu den Privaten Feindpsalmen* (Leiden: Brill, 1967).

P. Drijvers, *The Psalms, Their Structure and Meaning* (New York: Herder and Herder, 1965).

Peter W. Flint, *The Dead Sea Psalms Scrolls and the Book of Psalms* (Studies on the Texts of the Desert of Judea; Leiden: Brill, 1997).

Peter W. Flint and Patrick D. Miller, Jr., *The Book of Psalms: Composition and Reception* (Leiden: Brill, 2005).

Susan Gillingham, *Psalms Through the Centuries: Volume One* (Blackwell Bible Commentaries; Oxford: Blackwell, 2008).

M. D. Goulder, *The Psalms of the Sons of Korah: A Study in the Psalter* (JSOTSup 20; Sheffield: JSOT, 1982).

The Prayers of David: Psalms 51–72 (JSOTSup 102; Sheffield: JSOT, 1990).

The Psalms of Asaph and the Pentateuch (JSOTSup 233; Sheffield: JSOT, 1996).

The Psalms of the Return (Book V, Psalms 107–150) (JSOTSup 258; Sheffield: JSOT, 1998).

Jamie A. Grant, *The King as Exemplar: The Function of Deuteronomy's Kingship Law in the Shaping of the Book of Psalms* (Atlanta: SBL, 2004).

Harvey Guthrie, *Israel's Sacred Songs* (New York: Seabury Press, 1978).

John W. Hilber, *Cultic Prophecy in the Psalms* (Berlin: de Gruyter, 2005).

William L. Holladay, *The Psalms Through Three Thousand Years* (Minneapolis: Fortress Press, 1993).

Rolf A. Jacobson, *Many Are Saying: The Function of Direct Discourse in the Hebrew Psalter* (London: T. and T. Clark, 2004).

Hans Joachim Kraus, *Theology of the Psalms* (Minneapolis: Augsburg, 1986).

James L. Kugel, *The Idea of Biblical Poetry: Parallelism and Its History* (New Haven, CT: Yale University Press, 1981).

Gert Kwakkel, *According to My Righteousness: Upright Behaviour as Grounds for Deliverance in Psalms 7, 17, 18, 26, and 44* (Leiden: Brill, 2002).

Martin Leuenberger, *Konzeptionen des Königtums Gottes im Psalter: Untersuchungen zu Komposition und Redaktion der theokratischen Bücher IV–V i Psalter* (Zurich: Theologischer Verlag Zürich, 2004).

F. Lindström, *Suffering and Sin: Interpretations of Illness in the Individual Complaint Psalms* (Stockholm: Almqvist and Wiksells, 1994).

Oswald Loretz, *Psalmstudien: Kolometrie, Strophik und Theologie: Ausgewählter Psalmen* (Berlin: de Gruyter, 2002).

Marko Marttila, *Collective Reinterpretation in the Psalms: A Study of the Redaction History of the Psalter* (Tübingen: Mohr Siebeck, 2006).

J. Clinton McCann (ed.), *The Shape and Shaping of the Psalter* (Sheffield: JSOT, 1993).

Matthias Millard, *Die Komposition des Psalters: Ein formgeschiclthicher Ansatz* (FAT; Tübingen: Mohr Siebeck, 1994).

Patrick D. Miller, *Interpreting the Psalms* (Philadelphia: Fortress Press, 1986).

David C. Mitchell, *The Message of the Psalter: An Eschatological Programme in the Book of Psalms* (JSOTSup 252; Sheffield: Sheffield Academic Press, 1997).

Harry P. Nasuti, *Tradition History and the Psalms of Asaph* (SBLDS; Atlanta: Scholars Press, 1988).

M. O'Connor, *Hebrew Verse Structure* (Winona Lake, IN: Eisenbrauns, 1980).

David L. Petersen and Kent Harold Richards, *Interpreting Hebrew Poetry* (Old Testament Series; Minneapolis: Augsburg, 1992).

J. David Pleins, *The Psalms: Songs of Tragedy, Hope, and Justice* (Maryknoll, NY: Orbis Books, 1993).

P. R. Raabe, *Psalm Structures: A Study of Psalms with Refrains* (Sheffield: JSOT, 1990).

J. Sanders, *The Dead Sea Psalms Scroll* (Ithaca, NY: Cornell University Press, 1967).

Markus Saur, *Die Königspsalmen: Studien zur Entstehung und Theologie* (Berlin: de Gruyter, 2004).

K. Seybold, *Das Gebet den Kranken in Alten Testament* (BWANT 99; Stuttgart: Kohlhammer, 1973).

Poetik der Psalmen (Stuttgart: Kohlhammer, 2003).

Claudia Süssenbach, *Der elohistische Psalter: Untersuchungen zur Komposition und Theologie von Ps 42–83* (Tübingen: Mohr Siebeck, 2005).

Samuel L. Terrien, *The Psalms: Strophic Structure and Theological Commentary* (Grand Rapids, MI: Eerdmans, 2003).

John S. Vassar, *Recalling a Story Once Told: An Intertextual Reading of the Psalter and the Pentateuch* (Macon, GA: Mercer University Press, 2007).

C. J. A. Vos, *Theopoetry of the Psalms* (London: Protea Book House, 2005).

Robert E. Wallace, *The Narrative Effect of Book IV of the Hebrew Psalter* (New York: Peter Lang, 2007).

Gunther Wanke, *Die Zionstheologie der Korachiten in ihrem traditionsgeschichlichen Zusammenhang* (BZAW 97; Berlin: Töpelmann, 1966).

W. G. E. Watson, *Classical Hebrew Poetry: A Guide to Its Techniques* (JSOTSup 26; Sheffield: JSOT, 1986).

James W. Watts, *Psalm and Story: Inset Hymns in Hebrew Narratives* (JSOTSup 139; Sheffield: JSOT, 1992).

Claus Westermann, *The Psalms: Structure, Content, and Message* (Minneapolis: Augsburg, 1980).

Praise and Lament in the Psalms (Atlanta: John Knox Press, 1981).

The Living Psalms (Grand Rapids, MI: Eerdmans, 1989).
Norman Whybray, *Reading the Psalms as a Book* (JSOTSup 222; Sheffield: JSOT, 1996).
Gerald Henry Wilson, *The Editing of the Hebrew Psalter* (SBLDS; Chico, CA: Scholars Press, 1985).

SPECIAL STUDIES: THEOLOGICAL EMPHASIS

The following works emphasize theological perspectives on the Hebrew Psalter.

Bernhard W. Anderson, *Out of the Depths*, 3rd edition (Louisville, KY: Westminster John Knox, 2000).
S. Balentine, *The Hidden God* (Oxford Theological Monographs; Oxford: Oxford University Press, 1983).
Craig C. Broyles, *The Conflict of Faith and Experience in the Psalms: A Form-Critical and Theological Study* (JSOTSup 52; Sheffield: JSOT, 1989).
Walter Brueggemann, *Praying the Psalms* (Winona, MN: Saint Mary's Press, 1982).
  The Message of the Psalms: A Theological Commentary (Minneapolis: Augsburg, 1984).
  Israel's Praise: Doxology Against Idolatry and Ideology (Philadelphia: Fortress Press, 1988).
  Abiding Astonishment: Psalms, Modernity, and the Making of History (Literary Currents in Biblical Interpretation; Louisville, KY: Westminster John Knox, 1991).
  The Psalms and the Life of Faith, Patrick D. Miller (ed.) (Minneapolis: Fortress Press, 1995).
E. Dalglish, *Psalm Fifty-One in the Light of Ancient Near Eastern Patternism* (Leiden: Brill, 1962).
Nancy L. DeClaisse-Walford, *Reading from the Beginning: The Shaping of the Hebrew Psalter* (Macon, GA: Mercer University Press, 1997).
Harvey Guthrie, *Theology as Thanksgiving* (New York: Seabury Press, 1981).
Rolf A. Jacobson, *Soundings in the Theology of Psalms: Perspectives and Methods in Contemporary Scholarship* (Minneapolis: Fortress Press, 2010).
Herbert J. Levine, *Sing Unto God a New Song: A Contemporary Reading of the Psalms* (Indiana Studies in Biblical Literature; Bloomington: Indiana University Press, 1995).
Oswald Loretz, *Psalmstudien: Kolometrie, Strophik und Theologie: Ausgewählter Psalmen* (Berlin: de Gruyter, 2002).
James L. Mays, *The Lord Reigns: A Theological Handbook to the Psalms* (Louisville, KY: Westminster John Knox, 1994).

J. Clinton McCann, Jr., *A Theological Introduction to the Book of Psalms: The Psalms as Torah* (Nashville, TN: Abingdon Press, 1993).

Patrick D. Miller, *Interpreting the Psalms* (Philadelphia: Fortress Press, 1986).

Stephen Breck Reid (ed.), *The Psalms and Practice: Virtue, Authority, Worship* (Collegeville, MN: Liturgical Press, 2001).

H. Ringgren, *The Faith of the Psalmists* (Philadelphia: Fortress Press, 1963).

Samuel L. Terrien, *The Psalms: Strophic Structure and Theological Commentary* (Grand Rapids, MI: Eerdmans, 2003).

Erich Zenger, *A God of Vengeance? Understanding the Psalms of Divine Wrath*, trans. Linda Maloney (Louisville, KY: Westminster John Knox, 1996).

SPECIAL STUDIES: HISTORICAL EMPHASIS

Many of the studies that concentrate on the historical side of interpreting the book of Psalms focus on the background from which these texts originated.

Richard J. Bautch, *Developments in Genre between Post-Exilic Penitential Prayers and the Psalms of Communal Lament* (Academia Biblica; Atlanta: Society of Biblical Literature, 2003).

J. Becker, *Israel Deutet seine Psalmen* (Stuttgart: Verlag Katholisches Bibelwerk, 1966).

Ronald Clements, *God and Temple* (Philadelphia: Fortress Press, 1965).

Loren D. Crow, *The Songs of Ascents (Psalms 120–134): Their Place in Israel's History and Religion* (SBLDS; Atlanta: Scholars Press, 1996).

J. H. Eaton, *Kingship and the Psalms* (SBT 32 Second Series; London: SCM Press, 1976).

Ivan Engnell, *Studies in Divine Kingship in the Ancient Near East*, 2nd edition (Oxford: Blackwell, 1967).

John W. Hilber, *Cultic Prophecy in the Psalms* (Berlin: de Gruyter, 2005).

Aubrey Rodway Johnson, *The Cultic Prophet in Ancient Israel* (Cardiff: University of Wales, 1962).

   Sacral Kingship in Ancient Israel (Cardiff: University of Wales Press, 1967).

   The Cultic Prophet and Israel's Psalmody (Cardiff: University of Wales Press, 1979).

Othmar L. Keel, *The Symbolism of the Biblical World: Ancient Near Eastern Iconography and the Book of Psalms* (New York: Seabury Press, 1978).

Hans Joachim Kraus, *Worship in Israel: A Cultic History of the Old Testament*, trans. Geoffrey Buswell (Richmond, VA: John Knox Press, 1966).

H. H. Rowley, *Worship in Ancient Israel* (Philadelphia: Fortress Press, 1967).

ARTICLES

Finally, readers may find helpful a list of a variety of article-length publications on the Psalms.

G. W. Anderson, "Israel's Creed: Sung, Not Signed," *SJT* 16 (1963): 277–285.
  "Enemies and Evildoers in the Book of Psalms," *BJRL* 48 (1965–1966): 18–29.
Pierre Auffret, "Étude structurelle du Psaume 2," *Estudios Biblicos* 59, nos. 2–3 (2001): 307–323.
Samuel E. Balentine, "Turn, O Lord! How Long?" *Review & Expositor* 100, no. 3 (2003): 465–481.
J. Begrich, "Die Vertrauensausserungen im israelitischen Klageliede des Einzelnen und in seinem babylonischen Gegenstuck," *ZAW* 46 (1928): 221–260.
  "Das priesterliche Heilsorakel," *ZAW* 52 (1934): 81–92.
William H. Bellinger, "The Interpretation of Psalm 11," *Ev Q* 56 (1984): 95–101.
  "Psalms of the Falsely Accused: A Reassessment," *SBLSP* 25 (1986): 463–469.
  "Psalm 26: A Test of Method," *VT* 43 (1993): 452–461.
  "The Psalms as a Place to Begin for Old Testament Theology," *Psalms and Practice* (2001): 28–39.
William H. Bellinger, Jr. and Andrew E. Arterbury, "Returning to the Hospitality of the Lord: A Reconsideration of Psalm 23.5–6," *Biblica* 86, no. 3 (2005): 387–395.
Walter Beyerlin, "Die toda der Heilsverkundigung in der Klageliedern des Einzelnen," *ZAW* 79 (1967): 208–224.
  "Innerbiblische Aktualisierungsversuche: Schichten im 44. Psalm," *ZTK* 73 (1976): 446–460.
Marc Z. Brettler, "Images of YHWH the Warrior in Psalms," *Semeia* 61 (1993): 135–165.
Joel S. Burnett, "Forty-two Songs for Elohim: An Ancient Near Eastern Organizing Principle in the Shaping of the Elohistic Psalter," *JSOT* 31, no. 1 (2006): 81–101.
M. J. Buss, "Psalms of Asaph and Korah," *JBL* 82 (1963): 381–392.
Anthony R. Ceresko, "The ABC's of Wisdom in Psalm 34," *VT* 35 (1985): 99–104.
B. S. Childs, "Psalm 8 in the Context of the Christian Canon," *Interpretation* 23 (1969): 20–31.
  "Psalm Titles and Midrashic Exegesis," *JSS* 16 (1971): 137–150.

Richard J. Clifford, "Creation in the Psalms," in R. Clifford et al. (eds.), *Creation in the Biblical Traditions* (Washington, DC: Catholic Biblical Association of America, 1992), 57–69.

D. J. A. Clines, "Tree of Knowledge and the Law of Yahweh; Psalm 19," *VT* 24 (1974): 8–14.

Robert Alan Cole, "An Integrated Reading of Psalms 1 and 2," *JSOT* 98 (2002): 75–88.

Terence Collins, "'Decoding the Psalms: A Structural Approach to the Psalter," *JSOT* 37 (1987): 41–60.

Jerome Creach, "The Shape of Book Four of the Psalter and the Shape of Second Isaiah," *JSOT* 80 (1998): 63–76.

Loren D. Crow, "The Rhetoric of Psalm 44," *ZAW* 104 (1992): 394–401.

Robert Culley, "Psalm 102: A Complaint with a Difference," *Semeia* 62 (1993): 19–35.

Adrian H. W. Curtis, "Subjugation of the Water Motif in the Psalms: Imagery or Polemic?" *JSS* 23 (1978): 245–256.

G. H. Davies, "The Ark in the Psalms," in F. F. Bruce (ed.), *Promise and Fulfillment, S. H. Hooke Festschrift* (Edinburgh: T. and T. Clark, 1963), 51–61.

"Psalm 95," *ZAW* 85 (1973): 183–195.

Ellen F. Davis, "Exploding the Limits: Form and Function in Psalm 22,"*JSOT* 53 (1992): 93–105.

B. De Pinto, "Torah and Psalms," *JBL* 86 (1967): 154–174.

Katharine J. Dell, "I Will Solve My Riddle to the Music of the Lyre (Psalm xlix 4 [5]): A Cultic Setting for Wisdom Psalms?" *VT* 54, no. 4 (2004): 445–458.

J. Eaton, "The Psalms and Israelite Worship," in G. W. Anderson (ed.), *Tradition and Interpretation* (Oxford: Clarendon, 1979), 238–273.

Göran Eidevall, "Images of God, Self, and the Enemy in the Psalms: On the Role of Metaphor in Identity Construction," *Metaphor in the Hebrew Bible* (BETL 187; Dudley, MA: Peeters, 2005), 55–65.

B. Feininger, "A Decade of German Psalm-Criticism," *JSOT* 20 (1981): 91–103.

Peter W. Flint, "The Book of Psalms in the Light of the Dead Sea Scrolls," *VT* 48 (1998): 453–472.

Terence Fretheim, "Psalm 132: A Form-Critical Study," *JBL* 86 (1967): 289–300.

E. Gerstenberger, "Psalms," in J. Hayes (ed.), *Old Testament Form Criticism* (San Antonio, TX: Trinity University Press, 1974), 179–223.

"Enemies and Evil Doers in the Psalms: A Challenge to Christian Preaching," *HBT* 4 (1982–1983): 61–77.

"Where Is God? The Cry of the Psalmist," in C. Duquoc and C. Floristan (eds.), *Where Is God?* (London: SCM Press, 1992), 11–22.

John E. Goldingay, "Repetition and Variation in the Psalms." *JQR* 68 (1977–1978): 146–151.

"The Dynamic Cycle of Praise and Prayer in the Psalms," *JSOT* 20 (1981): 85–90.

M. D. Goulder, "The Fourth Book of the Psalter," *JTS* 26 (1975): 269–289.

"David and Yahweh in Psalms 23 and 24," *JSOT* 30, no. 4 (2006): 463–473.

D. R. Hillers, "Ritual Procession of the Ark and Ps. 132," *CBQ* 30 (1968): 48–55.

J. Holman, "Structure of Psalm 139," *VT* 21 (1971): 298–310.

Stefan Holtmann, "Die Asafpsalmen als Spiegel der Geschichte Israels: Überlegungen zur Komposition von Ps 73–83. Teil 1," *Biblische Notizen* 122 (2004): 44–79.

Walter Houston, "David, Asaph and the Mighty Works of God: Theme and Genre in the Psalm Collections," *JSOT* 68 (1995): 93–111.

David M. Howard, "Recent Trends in Psalms Study," in D. W. Baker and B. T. Arnold (eds.), *The Face of Old Testament Studies: A Survey of Contemporary Approaches* (Grand Rapids, MI: Baker, 1999), 329–368.

Avi Hurvitz, "Wisdom Vocabulary in the Hebrew Psalter: A Contribution to the Study of 'Wisdom Psalms," *VT* 38 (1988): 41–51.

C. F. Hyland, "Psalm 29: A Structural Analysis," *HTR* 66 (1973): 237–256.

F. N. Jasper, "Early Israelite Traditions and the Psalter," *VT* 17 (1967): 50–59.

Ernst Jenni, "Zu den Doxologischen Schlussformeln des Psalter," *ThZ* 40 (1984): 114–120.

J. Jeremias, "Lade und Zion," in H. W. Wolff (ed.), *Probleme Biblischer Theologie: für Gerhard von Rad* (Munich: Kaiser, 1971), 183–198.

David Jobling, "Deconstruction and the Political Analysis of Biblical Texts: A Jamesonian Reading of Psalm 72," *Semeia* 59 (1992): 95–127.

S. Kelley, "Psalm 46: A Study in Imagery," *JBL* 89 (1970): 305–312.

Helen A. Kenik, "Code of Conduct for a King: Psalm 101," *JBL* 95 (1976): 391–403.

Reuven Kimelman, "Theme, Structure, and Impact," *JBL* 113 (1994): 37–58.

Melody D. Knowles, "The Flexible Rhetoric of Retelling: The Choice of David in the Texts of the Psalms," *CBQ* 67, no. 2 (2005): 236–249.

Klaus Koch, "Der Psalter und seine Redaktionsgeschichte," in K. Seybold and E. Zenger (eds.), *Neue Wege des Psalmenforschung: für Walter Beyerlin* (Freiberg: Herder, 1994), 243–277.

Heinz Kruse, "Psalm 132 and the Royal Zion Festival," *VT* 33 (1983): 279–297.

John S. Kselman, "Psalm 72: Some Observations on Structure," *BASOR* 220 (1975): 77–81.

"Psalm 3: A Structural and Literary Study," *CBQ* 49 (1987): 572–580.

J. Kenneth Kuntz, "The Canonical Wisdom Psalms of Ancient Israel: Their Rhetorical, Thematic and Formal Dimensions," in J. Jackson and M. Kessler (eds.), *Rhetorical Criticism* (Pittsburgh Theological Monograph Series I; Pittsburgh: Pickwick Press, 1974), 186–222.

"Retribution Motif in Psalmic Wisdom," *ZAW* 89 (1977): 223–233.

"Psalm 18: A Rhetorical-Critical Analysis," *JSOT* 26 (1983): 3–31.

"Wisdom Psalms and the Shaping of the Hebrew Psalter," in R. Argall, B. Bow, and R. Werline (eds.), *For a Later Generation* (Harrisburg, PA: Trinity Press International, 2000).

Antti Laato, "Psalm 132 and The Development of the Jerusalemite/Israelite Royal Ideology," *CBQ* 54 (1992): 49–66.

Henk Leene, "The Coming of YHWH as King: The Complementary Character of Psalms 96 and 98," in K. Deurloo and J. Dyk (eds.), *Unless Someone Guide Me ... Festschrift for Karel A. Deurloo* (Maastricht: Shaker, 2000), 211–228.

Andrew A. Macintosh, "Consideration of the Problems Presented by Psalm 2:11 and 12," *JTS* 27 (1976): 1–14.

Rick R. Marrs, "A Cry from the Depths (Ps 130)," *ZAW* 100 (1988): 81–90.

James Luther Mays, "Worship, World, and Power: An Interpretation of Psalm 100," *Interpretation* 23 (1969): 315–330.

"The David of the Psalms," *Interpretation* 40 (1986): 143–155.

"The Place of the Torah-Psalms in the Psalter," *JBL* 106 (1987): 3–12.

"Maker of Heaven and Earth: Creation in the Psalms," in W. Towner, S. McBride, Jr., and W. Brown, *God Who Creates* (Grand Rapids, MI: Eerdmans, 2000), 75–86.

J. Clinton McCann, "The Psalms as Instruction," *Interpretation* 46 (1992): 117–128.

John W. McKay, "Psalm of Vigil [Daybreak]," *ZAW* 91 (1979): 229–247.

Jorge Mejia, "Some Observations on Psalm 107," *BTB* 5 (1975): 56–66.

A. L. Merrill, "Psalm XXIII and the Jerusalem Tradition," *VT* 15 (1965): 354–360.

J. Maxwell Miller, "'Korahites of Southern Judah," *CBQ* 32 (1970): 58–68.

Patrick D. Miller, Jr., "Poetic Ambiguity and Balance in Ps 15," *VT* 29 (1979): 416–424.

"Synonymous-Sequential Parallelisms in the Psalms," *Biblica* 61 (1980): 256–260.

"Psalm 127: The House That Yahweh Builds [With Discussion of Ps 128]," *JSOT* 22 (1982): 119–132.

"Trouble and Woe; Interpreting the Biblical Laments," *Interpretation* 37 (1983): 32–45.

"Enthroned on the Praises of Israel: The Praises of God in Old Testament Theology," *Interpretation* 39 (1985): 5–19.

"When the Gods Meet: Psalm 82 and the Issue of Justice," *J Prech* 9 (1986): 2–5.

"The Poetry of Creation: Psalm 104," in W. Towner, S. McBride, Jr., and W. Brown (eds.) *God Who Creates* (Grand Rapids, MI: Eerdmans, 2000), 87–103.

David C. Mitchell, "Lord, Remember David: G. H. Wilson and the Message of the Psalter," *VT* 56, no. 4 (2006): 526–548.

J. Muilenburg, "Form Criticism and Beyond," *JBL* 88 (1969): 1–18.

R. Murphy, "The Faith of the Psalmist," *Interpretation* 34 (1980): 229–239.

"The Psalms and Worship," *Ex Auditu* 8 (1992): 23–31.

Harry P. Nasuti, "Historical Narrative and Identity in the Psalms," *HBT* 23, no. 2D (2001): 132–153.

James Nogalski, "Reading David in the Psalter: A Study in Liturgical Hermeneutics," *HBT* 23, no. 2D (2001): 168–191.

Graham S. Ogden, "Prophetic Oracles Against Foreign Nations and Psalms of Communal Lament: The Relationship of Psalm 137 to Jeremiah 49:7–22 and Obadiah," *JSOT* 24 (1982): 89–97.

"Psalm 60: Its Rhetoric, Form, and Function," *JSOT* 31 (1985): 83–94.

J. David Pleins, "Death and Endurance: Reassessing the Literary Structure and Theology of Psalm 49," *JSOT* 69 (1996): 19–27.

G. von Rad, "The Royal Ritual in Judah," in Gerhard von Rad (ed.), *The Problem of the Hexateuch and Other Essays* (New York: McGraw-Hill, 1966), 221–231.

J. J. M. Roberts, "Religio-political Setting of Psalm 47," *BASOR* 221 (1976): 129–132.

"God's Imperial Reign According to the Psalter," *HBT* 23, no. 2D (2001): 211–221.

"The Enthronement of YHWH and David: The Abiding Theological Significance of the Kingship Language of the Psalms," *CBQ* 64, no. 4 (2002): 675–686.

R. A. Rosenberg, "Yahweh Becomes King," *JBL* 85 (1966): 297–307.

W. H. Schmidt, "Gott und Mensch in Ps 130: Formgeschichtliche Erwaegungen," *TZ* 22 (1966): 241–253.

Lewis Alonso Schokel, "The Poetic Structure of Psalm 42–43" [Replies M. Kessler and H. Ridderbos], *JSOT* 2 (1976): 4–11. Rejoinder in *JSOT* 3 (1977): 61–65.

Stefan Schreiner, "Erwaegungen zur Struktur des 90 Psalms," *Biblica* 59 (1978): 80–90.

Ruth Scoralick, "Hallelujah für einen gewalttätigen Gott? Zur Theologie von Psalm 135 und 136," *BZ* 46, no. 2 (2002): 253–272.

Klaus Seybold, "Die Redaction der Wallfahrtspsalmen," *ZAW* 91 (1979): 247–268.

"Psalm 58: Ein Loesungsversuch," *VT* 30 (1980): 53–66.

"Psalm 104 im Spiegel seiner Unterschrift," *TZ* 40 (1984): 1–11.

Elieser Slomovic, "Toward an Understanding of the Formation of Historical Titles in the Book of Psalms," *ZAW* 91 (1979): 350–380.

Samuel Terrien, "Wisdom in the Psalter," in L. Perdue et al., *In Search of Wisdom* (Louisville, KY: Westminster John Knox, 1994), 51–72.

Walter Vogels, "A Structural Analysis of Ps 1," *Biblica* 60 (1979): 410–416.

Gerhard Wallis, "Psalm 8 und die Ethische Fragestellung der Modernen naturwissenschaft," *TZ* 34 (1978): 193–201.

J. M. Ward, "The Literary Form and the Liturgical Background of Psalm LXXXIX," *VT* 11 (1961): 321–339.

John T. Willis, "The Juxtaposition of Synonymous and Chiastic Parallelism in Tricola in Old Testament Hebrew Psalm Poetry," *VT* 29 (1979): 465–480.

"Psalm 1: An Entity," *ZAW* 91 (1979): 381–401.

Timothy M. Willis, "A Fresh Look at Psalm 23:2a," *VT* 37 (1987): 104–106.

Gerald H. Wilson, "Evidence of Editorial Division in the Hebrew Psalter," *VT* 34 (1984): 336–352.

"The Use of 'Untitled' Psalms in the Hebrew Psalter," *ZAW* 97 (1985): 404–412.

"The Use of Royal Psalms at the 'Seams' of the Hebrew Psalter," *JSOT* 35 (1986): 85–94.

"The Shape of the Book of Psalms," *Interpretation* 46 (1992): 129–142.

"A First Century CE Date for the Closing of the Book of Psalms," *Jewish Bible Quarterly* 28 (2000): 102–110.

H. Wolff, "Der Aufruf zun Volksklage," *ZAW* 76 (1964): 48–56.

W. I. Wolverton, "Psalmists' Belief in God's Presence," *CJT* 9 (1963): 82–94.

Erich Zenger, "Komposition and Theologie des 5. Psalmenbuchs 107–145," *BN* 82 (1996): 97–116.

H. J. Zobel, "Das Gebet um Abwendung der Not und seine Erhörung in den Klageliedern des Alten Testaments und in der Inschrift des Königs Zakir von Hamath," *VT* 21 (1971): 91–99.

III. Commentary

PSALM 1

[1] Happy are those
  who do not follow the advice of the wicked,
or take the path that sinners tread,
  or sit in the seat of scoffers;
[2] but their delight is in the law of the LORD,
  and on his law they meditate day and night.
[3] They are like trees
  planted by streams of water,
which yield their fruit in its season,
  and their leaves do not wither.
In all that they do, they prosper.

[4] The wicked are not so,
  but are like chaff that the wind drives away.
[5] Therefore the wicked will not stand in the judgment,
  nor sinners in the congregation of the righteous;
[6] for the LORD watches over the way of the righteous,
  but the way of the wicked will perish.

Psalm 1 introduces the whole Psalter. We have textual evidence suggesting that in some later traditions Psalm 1 stood as a preamble, without a number, to the book of Psalms. For example, Acts 13:33 quotes a portion of Psalm 2 and identifies it as "the second psalm." But one early manuscript of that citation in Acts 13:33 refers to Psalm 2 as the "first psalm."[1] Most interpreters suggest that Psalm 2 is also part of

---

[1]   All uncials of Acts 13:33 have "the second psalm" except D (Bezae Cantabrigiensis), which has instead "the first psalm." See Nancy L. deClaissé-Walford, *Reading from the Beginning: The Shaping of the Hebrew Psalter* (Macon, GA: Mercer University Press, 1997), 37–41.

the introduction to the Psalter. As an introductory poem, Psalm 1 urges a lifestyle centered on meditating on divine instruction, or *torah*.

The psalm begins with a beatitude announcing that those who live in line with God's instruction are "blessed" or "happy," the most common translations of the psalm's opening word, *'ašrê*. This literary form, often associated with ancient Israel's wisdom teachers, passes on observations about how life is best lived. A beatitude announces the blessings of a lifestyle in order to encourage readers and hearers to follow this commended lifestyle. The form is used several times in the Psalter (e.g., Pss 32:1–2; 33:12; 41:1; 112:1; 119:1–3) and most famously in the New Testament (Matt 5:3–11). The beginning of Proverbs 3, though lacking the introductory term, illustrates both the connection with wisdom and the purpose of the opening psalm: living in line with God's instruction results in a long life characterized by "abundant welfare" (Prov 3:2). Psalm 1 is a poetic affirmation of the fruitfulness of a lifestyle attuned to God's instruction.

A Closer Look: Hebrew Poetic Devices

One of the characteristic features of Hebrew poetry is parallel structure. Psalm 1 is built on an antithetic parallel between the righteous and the wicked. Contrasting structures between these two lifestyles are central to the structure of the text. John Willis's account of the psalm's structure illustrates the antithesis:

A 1:1–3 The character and success of the righteous ones
    B 1:4–5 The character and success of wicked ones

A' 1:6a The reason for the success of righteous ones: God's care and concern
    B' 1:6b The announcement of the fate of the wicked ones.[2]

The psalm's concluding verse illustrates especially well the contrasts so central to this structure:

For the Lord watches over the way of the righteous,
But the way of the wicked will perish. (v. 6)

The psalm also uses a favorite framing device of Hebrew psalmists called an envelope structure, or *inclusio*. The poem begins and ends with the same topic – the wicked. In a device characteristic of wisdom writers, the psalm's first word begins with the first letter of the Hebrew alphabet and the last word of the psalm begins with the last letter of the alphabet, giving the psalm's perspective on life a totalizing effect.

---

2   John T. Willis, "Psalm 1: An Entity," *ZAW* 91 (1979): 399.

Verses 1–3. The psalm begins, "Blessed or happy is the person." Recent translations have rendered the opening word as "happy" rather than the traditional "blessed" in order to distinguish this word (*'ašrê*) from *bārûk*, which suggests a blessing pronounced in a liturgical setting. Psalm 1 begins not in a liturgical setting but with a celebration of the fruitfulness of a style of living. The psalm's opening Hebrew term (*'ašrê*) comes from a root word related to walking or journeying through life, and so this opening section of the psalm concerns the character and conduct of this life. Contemporary readers will need to be cautious with the translation "happy," for the term does not connote pleasing external circumstances in life but rather a deeper joy about the fruitfulness of the way of living urged on the readers of the psalm. The opening phrase is a kind of exclamation: How joyful is the person! The poem then portrays this joyful person, beginning with the negative. The person who is happy or blessed does not take the advice of the wicked as a guide for living. The three lines of verse 1 after the introductory phrase indicate a progression in movement. The happy person does not walk, stand, or sit with the wicked and thus avoids the counsel of the wicked, the way of sinners, and the seat of scoffers. The person who engages in this kind of constant movement of walking, standing, and sitting ends up in the circle of the foolish. The psalm commends a style of living that resists such influences. In the context of Psalm 1, the wicked are those who oppose God's instruction and the righteous are those who live according to that instruction. The psalm commends a life that is not self-determined but one that finds a home in God's teaching.

The second verse moves to the positive in this contrasting portrayal of faithful ones and makes explicit what is to guide a faithful person – the *torah* of YHWH. Twice the verse names YHWH's *torah* as the delight and subject of meditation for faithful ones. The contrast is with the death-giving advice of the wicked, whereas YHWH's instruction guides one to wholeness of life. *Torah* is commonly translated as "law," but the Hebrew term does not connote what "law" will for many contemporary readers. The Psalms celebrate YHWH's *torah* as a gift that provides a way to respond to the God who has given new life and as a means of response to God's granting new life to the community. More fitting renderings of the term are "guidance," "teaching," or "instruction." YHWH's *torah* gives direction for full living. The term can refer to particular commands, to the Pentateuch (the first section of the Hebrew canon), or to all of God's instruction. The last option appears to be most fitting in Psalm 1. The book of Psalms, which our poem introduces, becomes part of that *torah*, perhaps as a poetic response in five books to the five books of Moses in the Torah. A text that helps with the understanding of Ps 1:2 is Jo 1:8, in which Moses' successor is urged to meditate on the Torah. That text ties meditation to lifestyle. The verb (*hgh*) has to do with a low murmuring sound as if one were constantly chanting God's *torah*. That meditation provides a basis for full living.

Psalm 1:3 compares the faithful person to a tree "planted by streams of water." Such a tree is rooted, grounded, and nourished by the streams of water, and so bears fruit. The image is a strong poetic assurance that life according to *torah* prospers. Righteous ones bear fruit in the proper season and continue to do so. Joyous persons are rooted and grounded in YHWH's *torah* and are thus fruitful; YHWH "prospers" them.

Verses 4–6. The second half of Psalm 1 contrasts those who are faithful with those who are wicked, and begins with a contrast to the image in verse 3. If faithful ones are like a tree rooted and nourished in YHWH's *torah*, the wicked are like chaff. In the harvest practices of the day, grain was tossed into the air, and the wind separated the light chaff, the outer husk, and blew it away. The heavier grain fell to the threshing floor. The chaff is the trash that gets discarded, blown away. The contrast is a powerful one – a tree rooted and grounded, in contrast to wind-blown chaff. Verses 4 and 5 are strongly negative. Verse 5 articulates that the consequence of a life like chaff, driven away by the wind, is judgment. The second line of the verse interprets the first. It suggests that the wicked have no place to stand when the community makes judgments in the assembly of the righteous. The wicked are rootless and have no connection to the source of life, so when the community comes to make a legal judgment, the wicked have no place to stand and are blown away like chaff.

In the final verse of the psalm, the contrasts come to full flower. God becomes the subject of the verbs; God knows the way or path, the lifestyle of the community of faithful ones. The verb "to know" (*yd'*) suggests an intimate knowledge and thus connotes YHWH's care for the life of the righteous. God watches over or even embraces such a life. In a crowning contrast, the way or life path of the wicked disappears.

Bridging the Horizons: The Way of Righteousness

Psalm 1 is about the most basic decision of how to live. The poem crafts a world of contrasts in order to encourage its readers to live in the fruitful way of the righteous rather than the barren way of the wicked. The portrayals of the two lifestyles serve that rhetorical end. The psalm artistically presses the defining questions of life. To what is one devoted in life? How does one move forward in hope? What gives the most basic direction for living? With vivid poetic imagery, the poem invites readers to give attention to YHWH's teaching and instruction in the Psalms, in all of Scripture, and in God's continuing presence and activity. "Righteousness" suggests seeking to work out the divine–human relationship in all the relationships of life. The most basic decision is which advice to follow: that of those determined to rule the world or that of the creator. The most basic decision to follow God's direction makes it possible to be rooted, grounded, and fruitful. The wisdom teacher in Psalm 1 operates from the belief that God created a moral order to life and has observed that openness to divine instruction brings the possibility for full living. What directs life – how people live – matters.

Thus the poet places before hearers and readers the most basic decision about living. The psalm's hope is that readers and hearers will choose life in connection with God and God's *torah*, and so embrace life's fruitful possibilities. In 1835, Alexis de Tocqueville studied how Americans lived, and he observed, "Each citizen is habitually engaged in the contemplation of a very puny object, namely himself."[3] One way to appropriate Psalm 1 is to think of the basic decision of whether life comes from self-determination or from embracing the tradition of God's instruction.

Psalm 1 as a preamble to the Psalter urges a lifestyle that finds its source in the creator. The psalm speaks of life as a path or way, and of divine instruction as nourishment for the way. With the reference to YHWH's *torah* in verse 2, this introductory poem suggests that the Psalter is now part of that divine instruction. Much of its instruction is on prayer, a central aspect of the path of faith. The psalms that follow will portray prayer as the honest dialogue of faith carried on in the community that worships God. This introductory psalm suggests that the book will instruct its readers. The well-ordered world of YHWH and the well-being found in following YHWH's *torah* may not always be explicit in the psalms to follow, but all of these poems operate from the most basic decision so artistically urged in Psalm 1.[4] Readers will want to take a word of caution. One of the functions of the beginning of a text is to gather the participants for the textual journey. Psalm 1 does that with the major characters of YHWH, the righteous (psalmists), and the wicked (enemies). Although the well-ordered world of Psalm 1 urges assurance about living according to *torah*, readers will quickly see in the psalms to follow that the wicked persist in contesting life and its basis.

PSALM 2

[1] Why do the nations conspire,
   and the peoples plot in vain?
[2] The kings of the earth set themselves,
   and the rulers take counsel together,
   against the LORD and his anointed, saying,
[3] 'Let us burst their bonds asunder,
   and cast their cords from us.'

---

[3] Alexis de Tocqueville, *Democracy in America* (Washington, DC: Regnery, 2002), 450.
[4] For a delightful exposition of Psalm 1, see R. Alter, *Art of Biblical Poetry* (1985), 114–117.

⁴ He who sits in the heavens laughs;
  the Lᴏʀᴅ has them in derision.
⁵ Then he will speak to them in his wrath,
  and terrify them in his fury, saying,
⁶ 'I have set my king on Zion, my holy hill.'

⁷ I will tell of the decree of the Lᴏʀᴅ:
He said to me, 'You are my son;
  today I have begotten you.
⁸ Ask of me, and I will make the nations your heritage,
  and the ends of the earth your possession.
⁹ You shall break them with a rod of iron,
  and dash them in pieces like a potter's vessel.'

¹⁰ Now therefore, O kings, be wise;
   be warned, O rulers of the earth.
¹¹ Serve the Lᴏʀᴅ with fear,
   with trembling ¹² kiss his feet,
or he will be angry, and you will perish in the way;
   for his wrath is quickly kindled. Happy are all who take refuge in him.

Psalm 2, like Psalm 1, is part of the introduction to the book of Psalms. Psalm 1 begins with a beatitude and Psalm 2 concludes with one, indicating that the two poems are to be read together. Neither psalm has a superscription, which is unusual in Book I of the Psalter (Psalms 1–41). Psalm 2 is distinct in that it is a royal psalm, finding its ancient setting in an important occasion in the life of Jerusalem's Davidic monarchy. Most interpreters place Psalm 2 in the coronation festivities for the king (see 2 Kgs 11:12). Perhaps anniversaries of this coronation or other significant events in a king's rule could also have brought forth this text for the ancient community.

Readers can imagine this poem as part of a coronation ritual in ancient Israel. The text falls into four parts. The first three verses set the stage. Vassal nations are fomenting revolt, and a prime time for that move would be the change of rulers and transfer of power to a new king. The vassal nations and their rulers plot to rebel against the new Davidic king chosen by YHWH. In verses 4–6, YHWH, the divine king, who supports the Davidic monarchy in Jerusalem, laughs in the face of this revolt and strongly supports the chosen monarch. In verses 7–9, the king takes the floor and proclaims the divinely sanctioned decree central to the coronation rite. YHWH is the real power behind the Jerusalem throne. The concluding verses warn the vassal nations and their rulers of the serious consequences to those who rebel against YHWH and YHWH's anointed king. Peace is found in living under this ruling authority.

The first and last sections of the poem (vv. 1–3 and 10–12) concern the nations, whereas the two middle sections (vv. 4–6 and 7–9) attend to YHWH and YHWH's anointed. This kind of structure (ABB'A') is often labeled as chiastic. The additional artful device noticeable in the poetry is the intensification of the noisy and tumultuous plotting of the vassal nations and the movement to the divine promise of royal blessing in defeat of the nations along with the move in the poem's last line to refuge and blessing in YHWH. YHWH's blessing of the Davidic ruler is the key poetic affirmation.

Verses 1–3 portray the setting. The psalm begins with a rhetorical question, the surprised question that begins with "Why?" The question of why the vassal nations plot together in rebellion against YHWH and YHWH's anointed king covers the first two verses and sets the stage for the poem's dramatic action. The view of these nations is uttered in verse 3 as they proclaim their desire for liberation from dominance inflicted by the Davidic monarchy. The attentive reader will already realize that this rebellion is "in vain" (v. 1).

Those who read Psalm 2 along with the previous psalm as constituting the introduction to the Hebrew Psalter will also note that the enemies introduced in Psalm 1 as the wicked now take the form of vassal nations who oppose God and God's chosen ruler. A provocative connection between the poems is the use of the root word *hagah* in Ps 1:2 and Ps 2:1. In the first psalm, the term is translated as "meditate," and in the second as "plot." The contrast is between those who meditate on YHWH's *torah* and the futility of those who conspire together against YHWH and YHWH's anointed. Rather than considering the vassal nations' action as rebellion against the empire, Psalm 2 views the action as a conspiracy against divine sovereignty and against YHWH's co-regent. The psalm portrays the Davidic king as YHWH's chosen ruler in Zion/Jerusalem; it is YHWH who guarantees the Davidic monarchy. The issue in the psalm is whether the peoples live in relation to YHWH and YHWH's anointed.

Verses 4–6, in contrast, shift attention to the divine response to this conspiracy. The one who sits in the heavens is enthroned there as the divine king, and this king laughs in the face of this rebellion. The picture of YHWH heartily laughing in the face of rebellion is not unusual in the Psalms (Pss 37:13; 59:8). "Then," at the proper time, YHWH will terrify these rebels. Verse 3 is put emphatically in Hebrew, with the pronoun "my" in reference to both Zion and the Davidic king. It is YHWH who authorizes the rule of the Davidic kings in Jerusalem.

In verses 7–9, the speaking part in the drama falls to the chosen Davidic king. The king addresses the coronation audience and reads from "the decree of the Lord," the divine word that legitimizes the king as God's chosen ruler.[5] The Davidic king

---

5   For examples of other divine protocols from the ancient Near East, see Hans-Joachim Kraus, *Psalms 1–59: A Commentary*, trans. Hilton C. Oswald (Minneapolis: Augsburg, 1988), 129–133.

quotes YHWH: "You are my son; today I have begotten you." The "I" is emphatic; the choice of ruler is clearly from YHWH. The "today" refers to the day of coronation, and so the sonship affirmed is usually taken to be an adopted one. This beginning of the royal decree emphasizes the intimate relationship between YHWH and the chosen ruler in ancient Jerusalem/Zion. The affirmation is of the divine right of this ruler, so YHWH's adopted son may ask for dominion over the nations. It is often suggested that verse 9 reflects the custom of using the royal scepter, as a symbol of the royal office, to smash a piece of pottery to indicate the fate of those who do not bow to this chosen royal dominion. The emphasis is on the divine guarantee of Davidic rule.

The psalm's final three verses return to the rebellious kings of the earth and address them with the warning that it is wise to serve God; dire consequences await those who rebel against this divine monarch. Well-being in life is found in one's relationship with this YHWH, who is creator and giver of life.[6] The central issue is living under YHWH's life-giving authority. Psalm 2 concludes with a beatitude: Blessed or happy are those who take refuge in YHWH. The call is for trust in the divine monarch rather than rebellion. The concluding line brings readers back to the connection with Psalm 1, which begins with the form of the beatitude. Interestingly, those who oppose YHWH in this final section of Psalm 2 will "perish in the way" just as the "way of the wicked will perish" in the last line of Psalm 1. Royal blessings in Psalm 2 are tied to YHWH's sovereignty.

A Closer Look: The Messiah of Psalm 2

The term used to refer to the Davidic king in Psalm 2 is *māšîaḥ*, messiah, one chosen by YHWH. The term often refers to the king of the Davidic dynasty, but not always. Isaiah uses it in reference to Cyrus, the Persian ruler. Psalm 2 distinctly refers to the Davidic king as messiah and son of God. A number of interpreters have suggested that the description of the Davidic Empire in this and other psalms is idealistic.[7] The account of the size of the kingdom and the account of the kingdom's history are somewhat different in historical texts in the Hebrew canon. The Deuteronomic evaluation of the kings is less positive than the Psalms might suggest.

Although the portrayal of Davidic rule in the Psalms is not without historical basis, it does partake of ancient Near Eastern patterns for describing kings and their kingdoms and therefore is idealized. History records that in the sixth century the Davidic kingdom was defeated by Babylon. After the experience of

---

6   On the well-known textual difficulty in verses 11–12, see Peter C. Craigie, *Psalms 1–50*, 2nd edition (WBC 19; Dallas: Word Books, 2004), 64.

7   For an expansive view of the place of Davidic kingship in the Psalter, see John H. Eaton, *Kingship and the Psalms*, 2nd edition (Sheffield: JSOT, 1986).

defeat and exile, second-temple Judaism apparently included a variety of hopes for the return of Davidic rule, but major struggles for the Jewish community continued instead. Some came to apply the royal hopes to the community as a whole, whereas others came to look forward to a future in which one would come who would fulfill an ideal that had come to be seen as a messianic promise. In the Christian canon, the New Testament proclaims that Jesus of Nazareth came to fulfill the messianic promise and complete the line of David. The New Testament alludes to Psalm 2 in that proclamation (Matt 3:17; 17:5; Acts 13:33; Heb 1:5; 5:5) and incorporates the psalm's tradition of opposition to messianic rule (Acts 4:23–31; Rev 2:26–29).

A Closer Look: Covenant Renewal Ritual

The ritual reflected in Psalm 2 is a renewal of the Davidic covenant initiated, according to the biblical narrative, by the prophecy of Nathan in 2 Samuel 7. The psalm uses the father–son language of 2 Sam 7:13–15, which is also found in 1 Chr 28:6 and Ps 89:26–27. The newly crowned king in Psalm 2 is a successor in the line of Davidic rulers, whose covenant is renewed before the people in ancient Jerusalem. The covenant reflects the royal ideal of the Davidic dynasty. YHWH was ancient Israel's divine king; their earthly king could not take the place of YHWH. The kings of the line of David are human and enjoy a special relationship with YHWH. They represent God in ruling over the people in Jerusalem and in speaking to them. They also represent the people before God and thus are portrayed as mediating figures. The kings have special rights and responsibilities, and the royal psalms speak to those. Psalms 72 and 101, for example, attend to the central royal task of guaranteeing justice. The emphasis in Psalm 2 is that the king is YHWH's chosen one; the divine ruler has established the Davidic kingdom.

Bridging the Horizons: Life with YHWH

Psalm 2 speaks of royal blessings for the Davidic king, an important plank in ancient Israel's faith. It also affirms that behind Davidic rule is divine rule, and so an affirmation of divine sovereignty underlies the poem. The psalm's concluding line also suggests that it provides instruction for the lives of peoples. Those who take refuge in YHWH will find blessing or happiness. The concluding beatitude brings readers back to the opening beatitude in Psalm 1 and the call to delight in YHWH's *torah*. As part of the introduction to the Psalter, Psalm 2 treats topics central to the book: God's choice of a king, the place of Zion, conflict with the nations (enemies), and refuge in God. Psalms 1 and 2 persuasively invite readers and hearers to basic decisions for living in relationship with or in opposition to

YHWH. Psalm 1 addresses individuals; Psalm 2 addresses nations. The contrast between relationship with YHWH and opposition to YHWH persists in the psalms to follow. This invitation at the beginning of the book arouses interest in readers and communities for further instruction in the poems to follow.

PSALM 3 – A PSALM OF DAVID, WHEN HE FLED FROM HIS SON ABSALOM

¹ O Lᴏʀᴅ, how many are my foes!
  Many are rising against me;
² many are saying to me,
  'There is no help for you in God.'
      Selah

³ But you, O Lᴏʀᴅ, are a shield around me,
  my glory, and the one who lifts up my head.
⁴ I cry aloud to the Lᴏʀᴅ,
  and he answers me from his holy hill.
      Selah

⁵ I lie down and sleep;
  I wake again, for the Lᴏʀᴅ sustains me.
⁶ I am not afraid of tens of thousands of people
  who have set themselves against me all around.

⁷ Rise up, O Lᴏʀᴅ!
  Deliver me, O my God!
For you strike all my enemies on the cheek;
  you break the teeth of the wicked.

⁸ Deliverance belongs to the Lᴏʀᴅ;
  may your blessing be on your people!
      Selah

After the introduction of the book of Psalms in Psalms 1 and 2, we first encounter a cluster of five lament psalms: Psalms 3, 4, 5, 6, and 7. The location of this unit of five psalms of lament at the beginning of the Psalter is astonishing because this articulation of need and petition is jarringly in tension with the assurances offered at the beginnings of Psalms 1 and 2. As we have seen, Psalm 1 assumes that, in the well-ordered world of YHWH, Torah-keepers are assured of well-being (prosperity). But in these five psalms we hear the voice of the pious who have not received the promised prosperity. Thus these psalms immediately introduce a note of realism into the symmetrical "Torah piety" of Psalm 1. All five psalms, moreover, are "Psalms of David"; that is, somehow linked to the royal environs and assumptions of Jerusalem. But we have just seen, in Psalm 2, that God has promised the anointed king only well-being. Insofar as these five psalms are royal, they attest to the historical vagaries that face everyone, including kings who live under divine promise.

Thus, on both counts of *Torah assurance* in Psalm 1 and the *royal promises* of Psalm 2, these five psalms voice a note of realism that is pervasive in the Psalter. They acknowledge real trouble and real suffering. They do more than that, however; they also attest that in such a world of trouble, where neither Torah assurance nor divine promise makes one immune from threats, there is a God to whom one may turn in hope. In the purview of Israel's faith, the reality of God is as palpable as the reality of suffering and trouble. It is precisely the task of such psalms to keep closely connected the reality of troubled life and the reality of an available, responsive God. The faithful are able to "take to the Lord in prayer" all of their troubles.

The key element in the lament psalm is the petition that asks YHWH to move into a situation of trouble with transformative power in order to rectify the unbearable situation. For that reason, the place to begin in this psalm is with the double imperative of verse 7: "Arise ... deliver." The two verbs reflect a conviction that when activated YHWH has ample capacity to overcome every adversary. The verb "arise" of course suggests, in Christian reading, an appeal to the "resurrection" (coming to life) of a God who has been passive or dormant. Clearly, Israel believes that the prayers of the pious may so activate YHWH.

Verses 1–6 are a characteristic preparation for the imperative petition. These verses open with the threefold use of "many" that is answered by the same term rendered as "ten thousand" in verse 6. The fourfold usage is a hyperbolic utterance that voices the measure of a threat felt and the fact that the speaker by himself is helpless in the face of that threat. That acknowledgment of countless threats, however, is more than matched by the assertion of confidence in YHWH in verse 3 introduced by "but you." That particle is an adversative that moves our thought in a reverse direction, away from threats and toward YHWH, who is more than an adequate resource against threats. Thus the speaker puts his life down in confidence in YHWH, and in such serenity is able to sleep and rest in a state of well-being.

The appeal of this desperate speaker summons YHWH to help; the speaker reckons YHWH to be "my God." YHWH is the one who *answers* so that Israel can accept its life with YHWH as a dialogic transaction on which everything depends. It is noteworthy that YHWH's answer is "from his holy hill"; that is, from the temple.

This psalm is not an act of private piety; the speaker is a member of the worshiping community who knows that the temple is YHWH's characteristic place of residence from which help comes.

After the imperative petition in verse 7, the psalm articulates a conviction that YHWH is able and willing to "strike" and to "break"; that is, to engage in forceful, even violent action for the sake of the speaker, who is a member of the covenant community. The psalm concludes with a formal description of praise in verse 8. The term "deliverance" is reiterated from the imperative of verse 7. The prayer is a request in this particular circumstance that YHWH should add one more marvelous rescue to the long inventory of miracles that constitutes Israel's memory of faith. By alluding to such "deliverances" as the Exodus, the speaker is able to imagine that he himself is heir to that entire history of miracles, to which one more miracle may be added in the present circumstance.

The juxtaposition of "deliverance" and "blessing" in the final description moves Israel's praise from *concrete miracle* to *systemic well-being*, a move congruent with the God who presides from the temple over all creation in order to make it fruitful, productive, and sustaining. Thus the final "blessing" nicely alludes to the verb "sustain" in verse 5. The creator who sustains all of life may now sustain this particular person in distress.

A Closer Look: The Role of the Superscription

The superscription of the psalm connects it to the deep crisis in David's life when his son Absalom sought to seize his throne (2 Samuel 15–19). It is commonly thought that such superscriptions do not reflect actual historical reality. Rather, the superscription is an interpretive clue, a hint about how the psalm might be read in the canonical tradition. Connection to the Absalom rebellion portrays a speaker – any speaker – whose life is deeply in jeopardy and who lacks resources to cope on his own. The specificity of the superscription permits hearing the psalm in many specificities of extreme threat when subsequent speakers of the psalm are also in deep jeopardy and without resources. Like David, every person of faith may, in the midst of jeopardy, appeal through this psalm to the God of deliverance.

A Closer Look: The Temple – Where God Dwells

In the ancient world, all power for life was situated in the sanctuary (temple) wherein the divine presence dwelt. Thus even the most individual and seemingly private psalms proceed on the assumption that the God addressed inhabits the temple. The petition "arise" is the urging that YHWH should leave the temple and enter into the fray of trouble on behalf of the petitioner. Fredrik Lindström has shown that the mobilization from the temple assured rescue. In commenting on verse 5, Lindström writes:

The final goal on the way into the divine presence is YHWH's altar [Hebrew, 43:4a], a *pars pro toto* (Lam 2:7) of the symbolic world which the sanctuary makes visible and offers to the one who seeks the protective presence of YHWH from evil. The idea of the altar as the symbol of YHWH's protective presence, possibly has two aspects: on the one hand, the concept of a secure place (Ps 84:4) where the individual, like one seeking asylum by his contact with the holy is "infected" by it (Exod 29:37) and through it becomes inviolable (1 Kgs 1:50f, 53; 2:28f), on the other hand, the thought of this place as a place the innocent person seeks (Ps 26:6), like an (innocently) accused person of an unproven crime, in order to be justified (1 Kgs 8:31f).[8]

Bridging the Horizons: Petition

The purpose of the prayer is the petition, the act of seeking help from one competent to address the crisis faced. Such a petition is a recognition that the speaker is not self-sufficient but is characteristically dependent and must refer life to a "Higher Power" who is known in the tradition of Israel. Thus the psalm is distinctly "antimodern" in its acknowledgment both of needful dependency and of confidence in the fidelity of this "Holy Other." Perhaps such faith is exactly the alternative to the self-sufficiency of modernity that is visible in many forms of self-serving power, money, sexuality, and eventually violence.

PSALM 4 – TO THE LEADER: WITH STRINGED INSTRUMENTS. A PSALM OF DAVID

1 Answer me when I call, O God of my right!
You gave me room when I was in distress.
Be gracious to me, and hear my prayer.

2 How long, you people, shall my honor suffer shame?
How long will you love vain words, and seek after lies?
Selah

---

8 F. Lindström, *Suffering and Sin* (1994), 192–193.

³ But know that the Lord has set apart the faithful for himself;
  the Lord hears when I call to him.

⁴ When you are disturbed, do not sin;
  ponder it on your beds, and be silent.
      Selah
⁵ Offer right sacrifices,
  and put your trust in the Lord.

⁶ There are many who say, 'O that we might see some good!
  Let the light of your face shine on us, O Lord!'
⁷ You have put gladness in my heart
  more than when their grain and wine abound.

⁸ I will both lie down and sleep in peace;
  for you alone, O Lord, make me lie down in safety.

Psalm 4 is the second in this group of five lament psalms that open the Psalter. Like Psalm 3, this psalm is nicely linked to the two introductory psalms. The identity of "the faithful" in verse 3 plus the mention of "my right" in verse 1 correlate with Psalm 1, and the Davidic superscription relates to the royal promise of Psalm 2. This psalm, even in its brevity, sounds the most familiar cadences of Israel's prayer.

Verse 1 is a petition with three imperatives, all of which are roughly synonymous: "answer, be gracious, hear." The imperatives are supported by the statement of memory in the second line. In times past, YHWH gave broad space to those who were "squeezed" (in distress). The initial address to YHWH as "God of my right" indicates that the speaker is in a crisis and anticipates that YHWH will be the speaker's advocate and protector. Thus even in complaint the speaker voices hope and faith in YHWH.

Verse 2 is a very different complaint, now addressed not to God but to the people who are the speaker's tormenters. Although the double "How long" has the tone of complaint, in fact the verse is an accusation against those who have created the "distress" (narrow place) that is the locus of the complaint. Those addressed are accused of causing shame to one who has been respected; they are glad for "vanity" and "lies." The terms portray a complete lack of a moral norm that permits damage to the speaker, who is of that group in the community that continues to have anticipation of a properly ordered life. The words suggest a social context of disorder in which none of the old social realities now count for anything.

Verse 3. The vexation of verse 2 is sharply countered in verse 3, wherein the name of YHWH is invoked for the first time. Indeed, the deep trouble of verses 1 and 2 is exactly constituted by the absence of YHWH from life, just as YHWH is absent from the verses of the poem. When YHWH is invoked, the speaker can enact hope even amid dismay. YHWH has called out (set apart) the faithful, the Torah-keepers who faithfully keep the covenant. The verb "set apart" is a pivotal term in the Old Testament, referring to the chosen people. (The term is difficult; it is usually taken as *pl'*, on which see Exod 9:4. Israel as Torah-keeper, this speaker among them, are regarded by YHWH as "distinctive.") Here the speaker identifies himself among the chosen, and so affirms that YHWH is still attentive to those allied to YHWH. For that reason, the speaker is confident that YHWH will hear and answer prayers. The assurance that YHWH *hears* corresponds to the imperative of "hear" in verse 1. The psalmist knows that if prayer can secure the attention of YHWH, then YHWH will come and make all things well.

Verses 4 and 5. Now speaks a different voice that interrupts the aggrieved complainer of verses 1–3. As Carleen Mandolfo has shown, the Psalms characteristically permit a dialogic exchange between voices of grief and voices of instruction that seek to bring the aggrieved back into the world of coherent, disciplined faith.[9] Whereas the complainer of verses 1–3 must, perforce, give voice to need and eventually hope, the instructor counsels submissive silence (v. 4). The way through trouble, says the teacher, is dutiful performance of religious practices that exhibit trust in YHWH. It is likely that such performance of duty is not only public evidence that one has not given up on YHWH; the act itself is also a way of "acting oneself" back into trust. The term "trust" becomes key for the psalm and invites the complainer back into a simple confidence in YHWH that remains undisturbed by the troubles of verses 1 and 2.

Verses 6–8. The remainder of the psalm is an articulation of that trust in YHWH. The speaker here is now repositioned among the "many." The great throng of the glad congregation who count on, trust in, and wait for the goodness and light of YHWH; that is, for signs and assurances of YHWH's presence. The phrasing of the second line of verse 6 includes the familiar cadence of the Aaronide blessing of Numbers 6:

The Lord bless you and keep you;
the Lord make his face to shine upon you,
    and be gracious to you;
the Lord lift up his countenance upon you,
    and give you peace. (Num 6:24–26)

Here the "light" likely refers to divine presence in the temple. That phrase is matched in verse 1 by a petition to "be gracious," also an echo of the priestly blessing. Thus the quoted refrain of the congregation in verse 6 seeks to draw the disconsolate complainer back to liturgical solidarity and coherence. The outcome of such effort is a

---

9   Carleen Mandolfo, *God in the Dock: Dialogic Tension in the Psalms of Lament* (JSOTSup 357; New York: Sheffield Academic Press, 2002).

restoration of joy, the kind of exultant well-being that an agricultural community knows in the abundance of harvest season.

The instruction extends into verses 4–7. Then verse 8 may be the response to the instructor by the complainer of verses 1–3. Now the speaker, having returned to communal practices, is peaceable and at rest, exactly the antithesis of "disturbance" in verse 4. Through the intervention of the instructor, the complainer has turned attention away from trouble to focus on *YHWH alone*, the only source of comfort and strength in this age and in the age to come.[10] It is YHWH who gives "safety"; the final term of the psalm is the same term as "trust" in verse 5. Thus the teacher invites the hearer to trust, and now the complainer arrives back at trust. We are not told how the grievance has been resolved, but it clearly has been redefined and repositioned by the overriding positive reality of YHWH, who is both temple presence and pastoral assurance.

Bridging the Horizons: Faith in Dialogue

The dialogic interaction of voices – *the complainer-become-truster* and the *instructor* is characteristic of Israel's faith. It is possible to understand this *dialogical structure* of Israel's faith in terms of the contemporary theory of Mikhail Bakhtin, who proposed that dialogic transaction is a prime mark of great novels. This view has been made pertinent to the Bible by Barbara Green, Carleen Mandolfo, and Carol Newsom.[11] It is possible, however, to go behind such contemporary theory to recognize that such dialogue is intrinsic to human experience and is particularly evident in the self-understanding and practice of Israel's faith.

In this psalm, the dialogue is between *settled, confident faith* and the *restless protest* that is grounded in troubled experience. The interaction features human honesty down to the bottom of reality. But that interaction in candor is more than psychological interplay. It is a theological practice in ancient Israel, for YHWH is the *God of peaceable well-being* but also the *God of disputatious interaction*. In Israel's faith – so congruent with lived reality – neither impulse is permitted to veto or overcome the other. It is this quality of courage that makes this psalm and others like it perennially pertinent to living that is both self-knowing and God-acknowledging.

---

10 The familiar phrase is from the first answer to the *Heidelberg Catechism*.
11 C. Mandolfo, *God in the Dock* (2002); Barbara Green, *Mikhail Bakhtin and Biblical Scholarship: An Introduction* (Atlanta: Society of Biblical Literature, 2000); and Carol Newsom, *The Book of Job: A Contest of Moral Imaginations* (Oxford: Oxford University Press, 2003).

A Closer Look: Job's Similarities to the Psalmist

The accents of this psalm are more fully and boldly articulated in the poem of Job, who is a dramatic formulation of Israel's dialogic faith.[12] Like this psalm, Job complains and counts on YHWH. Like this psalmist, Job is beset by adversaries who demean his reputation. Like this psalmist, Job has friends who instruct him in normative faith. And like this psalmist, Job, in the end, arrives at *shalom* as a gift of God.

PSALM 5 – TO THE LEADER: FOR THE FLUTES. A PSALM OF DAVID

¹ Give ear to my words, O LORD;
   give heed to my sighing.
² Listen to the sound of my cry,
   my King and my God,
   for to you I pray.

³ O LORD, in the morning you hear my voice;
   in the morning I plead my case to you, and watch.
⁴ For you are not a God who delights in wickedness;
   evil will not sojourn with you.
⁵ The boastful will not stand before your eyes;
   you hate all evildoers.
⁶ You destroy those who speak lies;
   the LORD abhors the bloodthirsty and deceitful.

⁷ But I, through the abundance of your steadfast love,
   will enter your house,
I will bow down toward your holy temple
   in awe of you.
⁸ Lead me, O LORD, in your righteousness
   because of my enemies;
   make your way straight before me.

---

[12]   C. Newsom, *The Book of Job* (2003), has shown with great care and in great detail the way in which the book of Job serves the interests of dialogic faith that undermines all settled certitudes. Thus the form of the book matches its theological intentionality.

⁹ For there is no truth in their mouths;
  their hearts are destruction;
their throats are open graves;
  they flatter with their tongues.
¹⁰ Make them bear their guilt, O God;
  let them fall by their own counsels;
because of their many transgressions cast them out,
  for they have rebelled against you.

¹¹ But let all who take refuge in you rejoice;
  let them ever sing for joy.
Spread your protection over them,
  so that those who love your name may exult in you.
¹² For you bless the righteous, O Lord;
  you cover them with favor as with a shield.

The language of Psalm 5, the third in this opening group of five psalms of lament, is the rhetoric of legal dispute. The psalm seems to reflect an actual social dispute before YHWH in the temple. Or if not an actual dispute, then such language is a metaphor for social conflict that purports to imitate a judicial case. The conflict is between *the speaker*, a member of a subcommunity of intense Torah piety, and *his adversaries*, who are polemically characterized as "evil" and "wicked" and are arrayed against the entire enterprise of Torah obedience. The psalm is easily divided into five rhetorical units, each of which voices a characteristic note of Israel's practice of prayer.

It is likely that the petition of verse 8 is the pivot point of the entire psalm. Although the verse – containing echoes of the more familiar Psalm 23 – purports to be a petition, in fact it is a pledge of devotion to YHWH, and a readiness to live a life of "righteousness" as an appropriate response to the steadfast love of YHWH in verse 7. "Righteousness" here and elsewhere in the Psalter bespeaks a fully functioning relationship with YHWH in which the life of the righteous person is completely congruent with the character and will of YHWH. The entire psalm proceeds on the claim that the speaker is passionately among the righteous, and so deserving of YHWH's attentiveness (see the assurance to "the righteous" in Psalm 1). By contrast, the "wicked" who trouble the speaker are also presented – in the mouth of the righteous – as adversaries of YHWH. The entire argument is designed to align YHWH with the speaker and against his opponents.

Verses 1–3 voice a characteristic petition that YHWH should hear "my case," apparently a case presented in the temple. As in every part of this psalm, the rhetoric is laden with an oversupply of wording, here a long series of verbs. Notably, YHWH is addressed as "my king and my God," thus combining intimate relational language and formal address to a sovereign.

Verses 4–6 offer a characterization of YHWH that attests to YHWH that YHWH is on the side of the "righteous" (here the speaker) and against his opponents. These verses function as a motivation to YHWH, giving abundant reasons why YHWH should side with the speaker in the dispute at hand. Again a cluster of descriptive words is used, this time to characterize the adversaries as those who are inimical to God: wickedness, evil, boastful, evildoers, lies, bloodthirsty, deceitful. In this presentation, the adversaries of the speaker have no chance of meriting any positive characterization; consequently, YHWH must inescapably be on the side of the righteous and against them.

Verses 7–8 offer an abrupt contrast between the speaker (introduced as "But I") and those on the other side of the case. The speaker is rooted in YHWH's covenant love; because that relationship is enacted in temple worship, this statement amounts to a public attestation of commitment to YHWH. Here is yet another case in which personal piety and temple practice are deeply connected to each other. Because the speaker rests in covenantal love and attends to temple worship, the speaker bids for "paths of righteousness"; that is, patterns of Torah obedience that make life in the presence of YHWH possible.

Verses 9–10. Whereas verses 4–6 characterize YHWH as neither connected to nor inclined toward the wicked, here the wicked are directly characterized and critiqued. They are those who have no grounding in covenant and so live a life of normlessness that is an affront to YHWH and destructive of human community.

Verses 11–12. The prayer concludes with a petition for YHWH's gift of grace and protection, for well-being that only YHWH can give. The concluding verse is a thankful affirmation that YHWH gives blessings to the righteous. Thus the single covenantal assurance is consistent with the trajectory of Psalm 1. Here speaks a righteous person who anticipates receiving blessings of well-being from the God who cares for the Torah-keepers and, conversely, who is repelled by those who disregard the expectations of Torah.

A Closer Look: Zion Torah

The address of YHWH as "my king and my God" draws the speaker intimately to God but also situates the speaker in the temple cult where YHWH is celebrated as king. The Jerusalem temple was the place in which the kingship of YHWH was not only celebrated but also enacted, as is evident in Psalms 93 and 96–99. This title for YHWH of course bespeaks YHWH's sovereignty and evidences the appeal of biblical faith to political imagery, imagery that is carried into the New Testament with reference to "The Kingdom of God." Although the psalmist is clearly a Torah-keeper, the locus of this poem is in the environs of monarchic Jerusalem, thus bringing together *the memories of Moses at Sinai* and *the Davidic establishment in Jerusalem*. It is perhaps evident in this combination that the

Torah, as Hartmut Gese has suggested, has gravitated from Sinai to Jerusalem so that we may now speak of a "Zion Torah":

The Torah therefore describes the state of *shalom* in a more comprehensive manner, and this revelation is given, not at Sinai, but on Mount Zion. We can state it briefly by saying the Sinai revelation has become the eschatological Zion revelation, and the Torah of Sinai and that of Zion are different.

In the light of the dynamic development of Torah which we have observed, it is not surprising that the Zion Torah is more than just a quantitative expansion of the Sinai Torah. The Old Testament provides illustrations of a qualitative change in Torah.[13]

Bridging the Horizons: The Righteousness of God

This psalm, like so much of the Psalter, appeals to God's righteousness as the grounds of life. In verse 5, the speaker counts on that righteousness of God:

The righteousness of God, therefore, in this passage, as in many others, is to be understood of his faithfulness and mercy, which he shows in defending and preserving his people.[14]

It is precisely this understanding of God's righteousness as God's generous graciousness that Luther identified in the Psalter and that became the key insight of a Reformation theology of grace. In verse 12, the speaker is among the righteous; that is, among those who derive their life and their conduct from God's own righteous fidelity. It is clear that concerning God's righteousness and the derivative righteousness of the speaker, what matters is a relationship of responsible fidelity and not measuring up to particular commandments.

Bridging the Horizons: Adversaries and Allies

The poem is constituted in a dialectical fashion so that verses 1–3, 7–8, and 11–12 concern the speaker's attachment to YHWH and verses 4–5 and 9–10 are a counterpoint that speaks negatively of the adversary.[15] This movement in the psalm shows the speaker seeking YHWH as ally and protector against the adversary. When read in the categories of "systems analysis," this dramatic point and

[13] Hartmut Gese, *Essays on Biblical Theology* (Minneapolis: Augsburg, 1981), 81–82.
[14] John Calvin, *Commentary on The Psalms* (Grand Rapids, MI: Baker, 1979), 59.
[15] See Samuel Terrien, *The Psalms: Strophic Structure and Theological Commentary* (Grand Rapids, MI: Eerdmans, 2003), 104.

counterpoint is an attempt to "triangle" with YHWH against the enemy, so that it will be "two versus one."[16] It is most remarkable that the psalmist is unembarrassed about this dramatic strategy, indicating the tough-minded realism of this piety. This speaker needs all the allies he is able to muster in the face of the threat of his adversaries; he knows, moreover, that YHWH is the quintessential ally.

PSALM 6 – TO THE LEADER: WITH STRINGED INSTRUMENTS; ACCORDING TO THE SHEMINITH. A PSALM OF DAVID

¹ O Lord, do not rebuke me in your anger,
  or discipline me in your wrath.
² Be gracious to me, O Lord, for I am languishing;
  O Lord, heal me, for my bones are shaking with terror.
³ My soul also is struck with terror,
  while you, O Lord – how long?

⁴ Turn, O Lord, save my life;
  deliver me for the sake of your steadfast love.
⁵ For in death there is no remembrance of you;
  in Sheol who can give you praise?

⁶ I am weary with my moaning;
  every night I flood my bed with tears;
  I drench my couch with my weeping.
⁷ My eyes waste away because of grief;
  they grow weak because of all my foes.

⁸ Depart from me, all you workers of evil,
  for the Lord has heard the sound of my weeping.
⁹ The Lord has heard my supplication;
  the Lord accepts my prayer.
¹⁰ All my enemies shall be ashamed and struck with terror;
  they shall turn back, and in a moment be put to shame.

---

16   On the process of "triangling" in any system of interrelatedness, see Murray Bowen, *Family Therapy in Clinical Practice* (Lanham, MD: Rowman and Littlefield, 2004).

Of the five lament psalms that comprise the beginning of the Psalter (Psalms 3–7), Psalm 6 is the fullest in exhibiting the key elements of the genre and in "performing" the drama of lament that moves from plea to praise. It is readily evident that the utterance of the psalm is a process whereby the needful life of the speaker is drawn toward the defining reality of YHWH. This process is unmistakable in this psalm, as the name of YHWH clusters and dominates at the beginning and at the conclusion of the psalm.

At the outset, the speaker in profound need utters the name! YHWH is addressed three times in an attempt to secure the attention and assistance of YHWH:

YHWH, do not rebuke. (v. 1)
Be gracious YHWH. (v. 2)
YHWH, heal me. (v. 2)

Each utterance of the divine name is attached to an imperative petition, so that the aim of the imperative in each case is the mobilization of YHWH. It is fair to say that in the horizon of Israel YHWH is the proper and only addressee of such a petition, because only YHWH can be gracious and heal. The first negative petition, "do not rebuke," is matched by a second, "do not discipline," though the divine name is not uttered in the second negative petition. The petitions are reinforced by three motivational clauses to give YHWH reason to act, two of them introduced by the characteristic particle "for" (or because).

The threefold utterance of the divine name culminates in verse 3 with a quite remarkable fourth use, "You … O Lord … how long?" The phrasing is an emotional ejaculation rather than a complete sentence. It not only summons but confronts YHWH with an urgency that reminds YHWH of YHWH's role as savior. The "how long," moreover, is a conventional phrase of lament that asserts that the pain just described is no longer bearable, and the speaker is at the breaking point. The intent of the entire phrase is to mobilize YHWH in a moment of desperate need.

Verse 4 is something of a reprisal of verses 1–3 that reiterates the primary points. Again YHWH is named in the vocative, in the midst of three large imperatives, "turn, save, deliver," reinforced by two motivational clauses. The first, in verse 4c, attests that the grounds of both Israel's hope and YHWH's initiative is YHWH's covenant love that binds YHWH to Israel in its need. The second motivational clause in verse 5 is curious because it appeals to YHWH's vanity. It assumes that YHWH delights in being remembered and praised; it notes that the dead cannot do such remembrance or praise. The point of such an observation is that if the speaker – already in dire straits – dies, the speaker will no longer be able to participate in praise and remembrance, and YHWH will be deprived of one witness. The purpose of the motivational clause is to assert that the trouble just described not only concerns the speaker but is of immediate interest to YHWH as well.

The lament (description of trouble) continues in verses 6–7. It is noteworthy that after so much preoccupation with YHWH in verses 1–4 – with the divine name uttered five times – in these verses of complaint, the first-person singular pronoun dominates:

I am weary. (v. 6)
I flood my bed. (v. 6)
I drench my couch. (v. 6)
My eyes. (v. 7)
My foes. (v. 7)

The description of trouble exhibits the speaker boldly proceeding on the claim that the condition of the speaker is of immense importance to YHWH. There is no restraint in self-announcement before YHWH.

The statement of verse 7 with reference to "foes" is surprising because we have not heretofore been alerted that the speaker was in a socially conflicted context. We do not know who the foes are, but they clearly (a) cause trouble and (b) are enemies of YHWH. Thus the very sounding of the name of YHWH constitutes an act of resistance against the enemies.

The psalm concludes in verses 8–10 with another threefold utterance of the divine name that stands as a counterpoint to the multiple utterances of the divine name in verses 1–4:

YHWH has heard. (v. 8)
YHWH has heard. (v. 9)
YHWH has accepted. (v. 9)

The concluding verses are addressed to "workers of evil," who have caused the trouble. These "workers of evil" are no doubt the same folks as "the foes" in verse 7 and the "enemies" in verse 10. The threefold utterance of the divine name alongside the threefold mention of the adversaries reveals that the speaker is in a confrontational situation that is beyond the speaker's own capacity. Thus the conclusion gladly acknowledges that the active engagement of YHWH readily overrides whatever constituted the threat of the adversary.

These concluding verses are addressed defiantly to the adversary in verse 7. The speaker sounds a scornful dismissal of the enemy, who has now been rendered powerless by the active engagement of YHWH. The address to the adversary, however, is clearly a rhetorical device. The final declarative affirmation of the psalm assured that the God petitioned in verses 1–4 is the God who has answered, responded, and acted decisively for the sake of the speaker who has issued the imperatives.

The speaker who prayed the prayers of need is able to affirm that YHWH has heard the prayer, that YHWH has heard the supplication, and that YHWH has "taken" these prayers with seriousness. And that of course means that everything is now changed. The threat of the adversary has been held in check by YHWH or overcome. The enemies are defeated and humiliated by the power of YHWH. Consequently, the speaker (and Israel) now has uncontested room for life.

The dramatic form and structure of this psalm are especially important for our understanding of the faith of Israel that is enacted in such prayer. The prayer is bounded by reference to YHWH:

Verses 1–4	YHWH
	YHWH
	YHWH
	YHWH
	YHWH
Verses 8–10	YHWH
	YHWH
	YHWH

The first five mentions are *petitionary*; the last three are *celebrative* of a new circumstance caused by YHWH. Between the two foci on YHWH, the speaker can state the neediness of self, a needy self fully enwrapped in the powerful, transformative reality of YHWH. The enemies appear in this drama to be only marginally important, mentioned only in order to be dismissed.

It is evident in this structure of

verses 1–4 concerning YHWH,
verses 5–7 concerning self, and
verses 8–10 concerning YHWH

that something decisive has happened in the circumstances of the speaker between the plea of verses 6–7 and the affirmation of verses 8–10. The most likely hypothesis is that, in the dramatic performance of this psalm, an assurance of YHWH was uttered by some trustworthy speaker. It is an utterance of YHWH that changes everything because it assures the needy of YHWH's attentive presence and engagement. It is the case, given this structure, that YHWH has turned, saved, and delivered. We are left to believe, moreover, that YHWH's new initiative, evoked by serious prayer, is grounded in YHWH's own fidelity (v. 4). YHWH acts toward the petitioner who is needy on the basis of YHWH's own true character, which has long been known, celebrated, and trusted in Israel.

A Closer Look: Who Are the Enemies?

It is clear that the speakers who address YHWH in complaint psalms are regularly aware of being under threat from "enemies." In this psalm they are variously named as "foes" (v. 7), "workers of evil" (v. 8), and "enemies" (v. 10).[17] It

---

[17]   See Patrick D. Miller, *They Cried to the Lord: The Form and Theology of Biblical Prayer* (Minneapolis: Fortress Press, 1994), 81–86.

is possible that the adversary is sometimes a foreign threat, an intruding ruler
or army. More often, the adversary would seem to be another member of the
community in which the speaker stands. This may be especially the case in the
later community of emerging Judaism, where there were important disputes
between the self-styled "righteous" and the pejoratively labeled "wicked," the
classic case of "in group and out group." The threat of the adversary sometimes seems to be one of physical force, but more often the threat takes the
form of speech, slander, or perhaps testimony in court. A peculiar hypothesis of
Sigmund Mowinckel, a great Norwegian psalm scholar, pertains to the phrase
"workers of evil" in verse 8. Mowinckel proposes that this phrase pertains to
those who speak powerful words that cause destructive effects in the social
group and so unleash hostile social powers, before which the speaker is helpless, save for appeal to YHWH:

All such words were considered to be powerful and fatal "curses," and were even
used by the ancients in war, or before a battle, in order to strike the enemy in a
way just as effective as the use of sword or spear. That was why, before a war, they
would send for the seer or the *nābhî'*, that his powerful words might enervate the
enemy, so that the army might defeat him, as we hear for instance in the story
about the seer Balaam. In the eyes of those who are the objects of such words,
they are naturally looked upon as *evil* curses, unlawful supernatural harmful
words and operations, "sorcery" and "devilry". This is what is meant by words like
"guile", "falsehood", "delusion", "mischievous words" and the like, and especially
by the word *'āwen*. It indicates the evil "power", or power used for evil ends, and
its effects, and the means of starting it; but also the things and beings filled with
this evil "power". Above all *'āwen* is used of *words* having such power and such
effects. It need not have anything to do with "sorcerers" and "magic words" in a
technical and, so to speak, professional sense, with people who themselves know
that they are practicing sorcery, and have established themselves as masters of
that art, so to say. According to ancient opinion, *all* words were powerful in proportion to the "power" of the speaker; evil words, curses, abuse, threats, sneers,
evil wishes, "the evil eye", jealous thoughts, scornful or threatening gestures and
looks and symbols – in the eyes of the Israelites and of all other ancient orientals
all such things were powerful, and would do harm to the soul and happiness of
those against whom they were directed. All the powerful means of the gentile
enemies, their plans and threats and sneers, the "curses" of their prophets and
priests, and all their accompanying ceremonies, in short all their religious and
cultic measures and acts and words, in the eyes of the Israelites seemed to be
sorcery, *'āwen*; when used for the gods of the gentiles the word actually means
"demons", "devils", "trolls". What to one person is cultus, to the person on the
other side appears as sorcery. Such powerful words on the part of the enemy are
"falsehoods", "deceitful words", because they call up the "false", pernicious power

in life, "the curse", draining and laying waste blessing and happiness. But they are also "falsehoods", because they will make righteous people "scoundrels", and because, by Yahweh's help, they shall turn out to be unreal and of no effect, injuring only the mischief-maker.[18]

The psalm thus reflects a dangerous world in which recourse to YHWH is urgent. The speaker has no alternative source of rescue or well-being.

Bridging the Horizons: The Drama of Prayer

The shift between verse 7 and verse 8 poses the difficult question: Does the prayer of Israel in fact change YHWH and mobilize YHWH to act? In conventional scholastic theology that takes God to be omniscient and immutable, that question is answered negatively. No, YHWH cannot be changed in this way, because YHWH already knows everything. The psalm, however, does not practice such faith. Rather, it reflects a *dramatic* theology in which the speaker and YHWH, who is addressed, engage in a dynamic transaction in which both partners are under way in response to the other. Thus the prayers are not play-acting or psychological games of self-improvement. They are real exchanges that are taken to be effective in importuning YHWH:

This becomes an article of faith for D. Robertson, who declares that "the Israelite community knows what Shelley knows, that no petition from them is going to lead God to make human life basically different." This is *not* what the Israelite community knows; it knows that, mysterious though the ways of God are, there is still a potency in prayer, a power not to be rigidly separated from outer events in the "world" – "this poor man cried and the Lord heard, and saved him out of all his troubles" (34:6).... Against the purity of the inner dialogue, or rather in addition to it, we have the emphasis repeated here, as in many other psalms, on the comforts of the Temple worship, where the well-tried and well-established forms of ritual observance bring to the dialogue with God an institutional basis and framework.[19]

This prayer and many others like it are real prayers of genuine engagement. We may notice that for those who find settled, static theology adequate, such a dialogic note makes little sense. Those who are in great distress, however, are drawn, intuitively and perhaps against a more sober judgment, to engage in such dialogic utterance as a court of last resort. Such speech may be regarded by the

18 S. Mowinckel, *Psalms in Israel's Worship*, vol. 1 (1962), 199–200.
19 Harold Fisch, *Poetry with a Purpose: Biblical Poetics and Interpretation* (Bloomington: Indiana University Press, 1998), 110–111.

settled as "regressive," but it becomes necessary and credible in the context of immense need that is matched by a deep sense of powerlessness.

Bridging the Horizons: A Penitential Psalm?

This psalm is identified in long-standing Christian tradition as one of the "seven penitential psalms." This is a curious notation, even if long established in the tradition, because the speaker nowhere voices penitence. Samuel Terrien makes the shrewd suggestion that the penance here undertaken is "in the strange and secret imitation of God's eventual 'return,' 'change of course,' or 'repetition.'"[20] Terrien has referenced particularly verse 4 and the verb "turn." That the speaker can summon YHWH to "turn" of course testifies to the intense dialogic intention of the prayer.

PSALM 7 – A SHIGGAION OF DAVID, WHICH HE SANG TO THE LORD CONCERNING CUSH, A BENJAMINITE

¹ O LORD my God, in you I take refuge;
 save me from all my pursuers, and deliver me,
² or like a lion they will tear me apart;
 they will drag me away, with no one to rescue.

³ O LORD my God, if I have done this,
 if there is wrong in my hands,
⁴ if I have repaid my ally with harm
 or plundered my foe without cause,
⁵ then let the enemy pursue and overtake me,
 trample my life to the ground,
 and lay my soul in the dust.
  Selah

⁶ Rise up, O LORD, in your anger;
 lift yourself up against the fury of my enemies;

20 S. Terrien, *Psalms* (2003).

awake, O my God; you have appointed a judgment.
7 Let the assembly of the peoples be gathered around you,
   and over it take your seat on high.
8 The LORD judges the peoples;
   judge me, O LORD, according to my righteousness
   and according to the integrity that is in me.

9 O let the evil of the wicked come to an end,
   but establish the righteous,
you who test the minds and hearts,
   O righteous God.
10 God is my shield,
   who saves the upright in heart.
11 God is a righteous judge,
   and a God who has indignation every day.

12 If one does not repent, God will whet his sword;
   he has bent and strung his bow;
13 he has prepared his deadly weapons,
   making his arrows fiery shafts.
14 See how they conceive evil,
   and are pregnant with mischief,
   and bring forth lies.
15 They make a pit, digging it out,
   and fall into the hole that they have made.
16 Their mischief returns upon their own heads,
   and on their own heads their violence descends.

17 I will give to the LORD the thanks due to his righteousness,
   and sing praise to the name of the LORD, the Most High.

This final lament psalm of the opening set (Psalms 3–7) is situated formally in the judicial framework of "Torah piety" that we have seen already in Psalm 1 (vv. 5–6). At the center of Psalm 7, in verse 8, it is affirmed that YHWH holds court and adjudicates between the righteous and the wicked; that is, those whose lives are ordered according to YHWH's will and those who are not. This imagery likely reflects liturgical practice in Israel, and certainly reflects the sociological reality of "insiders and outsiders" in a community under Torah commitments. Everything in the psalm revolves around this judicial imagery; the voice that speaks here is one confident of divine acquittal and so is eager for adjudication. That confidence, moreover, becomes the grounds for petition to YHWH, for the speaker makes a claim for rescue to which he is entitled through a Torah-keeping righteousness.

Each part of the psalm refers to this adjudication and confidence about the outcome of the judgment. Verses 1–2 address YHWH in a petition governed by two imperatives, "O Lord my God … save me, deliver me." The complaint seeks to establish with YHWH that only rescue of YHWH can save. Without that divine intervention, all will be lost for the speaker. But then, this is exactly the function of the judiciary, to intervene so that disputants are not left to their own savage devices with each other.

The second appeal to the "Lord my God" is an assertion of innocence and therefore an implied merit that rightly expects rescue (vv. 3–5). The claim is organized around three "if" clauses followed by a "then." Although the rhetoric would seem to suggest that the speaker leaves the verdict open and wants YHWH to do whatever is appropriate, in fact the "if-then" formulation is a declaration of innocence, insisting that the "ifs" are not true and therefore the "then" of punishment does not apply. The same "if-then" structure is elaborately utilized in Job's grand self-defense in Job 31. In both cases, the innocence of the speaker is profoundly assured.

On the basis of the *petition* (vv. 1–2) and a *statement of innocence* (vv. 3–5), the speaker issues a powerful *imperative* to YHWH: "rise up, lift, awake!" (v. 6). The first two imperatives assume that the petition in verses 1–2 has evoked YHWH's defense of the speaker and YHWH's commensurate anger against those who would save the speaker. The entire movement of verses 1–6 assumes that YHWH is completely committed to the safety, well-being, and innocence of the speaker. Without the intervention of YHWH, the speaker is helpless before the "pursuers." With the intervention of YHWH, the speaker will be well protected. The imperatives ask YHWH, who has apparently been dormant and passive, to be active and mobilized, and assumes that the urgent petitions of the speaker are sufficient for that mobilization. The initial imperative, "rise up," may reflect an old pattern of seasonal gods who hibernate; in Christian reading, however, the imperative verb evokes Easter's hope and anticipation.

The last line of verse 6 and the verses that follow indicate why the speaker is full of hope. The God to whom petition is made is a judge who will assemble a court and make a ruling in the dispute between the speaker and his adversaries. The urgency of such a trial is made more vivid and detailed in Psalm 82, but here the appellation of "judge" assumes such a venue of adjudication. The judge is known to be "righteous" (that is, committed to a just ruling), and since the speaker is "righteous" and filled with "integrity," a good outcome is assured. Thus the speaker does not appeal to God's mercy and compassion but to the innocence already claimed in verses 3–5. The appeal to one's own virtue bespeaks the Torah piety of Israel that assumes the Torah can indeed be fully kept. Such rhetoric is of course distant from the rhetoric of the Protestant Reformation, which threw itself completely on the "righteousness

of God" because "human righteousness" in itself would fail. The Psalter variously
counts on human and/or divine righteousness; in this case, however, the speaker
is confident of his own qualification, a confidence that comes to be writ large in
the person of Job. "Integrity" bespeaks a singleness of vision and purpose, and the
speaker attests to undivided loyalty to YHWH.

The issue, as in Psalm 1, is clearly put in verse 9: the judge will give verdicts concerning "the wicked" (those who are adversaries to the speaker) and the "righteous"
(the speaker). These categories are large and inclusive in the Psalter, and reflect the
two ways of life that live for or against YHWH in the world. Carleen Mandolfo has
demonstrated that in verse 8a and then later in verses 11–16 a different voice that is
explanatory speaks in the psalm. It attests to the either/or that is normative in the
faith of the Psalter, an ethic intimately connected to the tradition of Deuteronomy
(see Deut 30:15–20).[21] Thus the Psalter, in this reading, is a dialogue between *normative teaching* and the *appropriation of normative teaching* by the speaker in the
interest of receiving vindication from YHWH.

The concluding verses of the psalm are a rumination on YHWH as "righteous judge"
with powerful implications for the two parties in the psalm (v. 11). YHWH is filled
with "indignation" toward the adversary and, conversely, is committed to the righteous
speaker. Things will go very badly for the wicked who do not repent and who conceive
evil (vv. 12–16). It is no wonder that the psalm concludes in verse 17 with a grand utterance of thanks and praise. Now the speaker relies not on "my righteousness," as in verse
8, but on "his righteousness," which yields well-being for Torah-keepers:

God does not shut up or conceal his righteousness from our view in the secret
recesses of his own mind, but manifests it for our advantage when he defends us
against all wrongful violence, delivers us from oppression, and preserves us in
safety, although wicked men make war upon us and persecute us.[22]

A Closer Look: A Temple Setting

There is much scholarly speculation about the social setting of this psalm and
others like it. Although much of the speculation is not persuasive, attention
should be given to 1 Kgs 8:31–32, which seems to reflect an actual temple setting whereby guilt and innocence are adjudicated. The double verbs in that
text of "condemn" (*rs'*) and "acquit" (*sdq*) are the same words as "wicked" and
"righteous" in this psalm. Apparently the adjudication by YHWH, so directly
affirmed in the psalm, was performed through priestly office.

---

[21] C. Mandolfo, *God in the Dock* (2002), 35–41.
[22] John Calvin, *Commentary on The Book of Psalms*, vol. 2 (Grand Rapids, MI: Baker,
1979), 92.

Bridging the Horizons: Whose Righteousness?

The speaker of the psalm variously appeals to "my righteousness" (v. 8) and "his righteousness" (v. 17). Such a tension has been problematic in Protestant Reformation thought, which depends completely on "God's righteousness." From that perspective, any appeal to "my righteousness" would seem utterly presumptuous. Although the accent in the two usages is different, it surely is the case that the significance of "my righteousness" is situated completely in the context of, and is encompassed by, God's righteousness. Thus, even given different accents, this likely is not a contradiction.

This reliance on YHWH's capacity to acquit is evident in Rom 8:33–34, but that text reflects the remarkable affirmation of Isa 50:9:

It is the Lord God who helps me;
    who will declare me guilty? (Isa 50:9a)

The matter of God's righteousness as ultimate assurance is immediately pertinent in contemporary life. The attempt to establish one's own righteousness in an anxious consumer society may take the form of excessive productivity, excessive patriotism, or even excessive self-indulgence, each an effort to exhibit a full, whole self. The psalmist knew – long before Paul or Luther – that such "self-righteousness" is never sufficient, except by submission of the self to the fidelity of God, who makes our own efforts at wholeness always penultimate.

PSALM 8 – TO THE LEADER: ACCORDING TO THE GITTITH. A PSALM OF DAVID

¹ O Lᴏʀᴅ, our Sovereign,
   how majestic is your name in all the earth!

You have set your glory above the heavens.
² Out of the mouths of babes and infants
you have founded a bulwark because of your foes,
   to silence the enemy and the avenger.

³ When I look at your heavens, the work of your fingers,
   the moon and the stars that you have established;
⁴ what are human beings that you are mindful of them,
   mortals that you care for them?

⁵ Yet you have made them a little lower than God,
   and crowned them with glory and honor.
⁶ You have given them dominion over the works of your hands;
   you have put all things under their feet,
⁷ all sheep and oxen,
   and also the beasts of the field,
⁸ the birds of the air, and the fish of the sea,
   whatever passes along the paths of the seas.

⁹ O Lord, our Sovereign,
   how majestic is your name in all the earth!

Psalm 8 is the first hymn of praise readers of the Psalter encounter; the hymn follows the introductory Psalms 1 and 2 and an initial set of lament psalms. The concluding verse of Psalm 7 vows to sing praise to the name of YHWH, and Psalm 8 fulfills that promise. The psalm is the first hymn of praise in the book, but it is still related to the laments preceding it. While praising God, the psalm portrays YHWH, who is addressed in the first seven psalms and characterizes the relationship between those offering the prayers and their God.

Psalm 8 is somewhat distinct as a hymn of praise. First, the poetic voice is that of an individual rather than a community, though the "I" is not likely autobiographical but representative. Second, the psalm in its entirety addresses God in the second person. The form of the hymn is the standard three-part structure of hymns of praise, with an introduction followed by the body of the hymn – here with a focus on creation – and a conclusion that repeats the introduction. The variation of the form in Psalm 8, however, is that the introduction and conclusion do not call the community to praise but begin and end the psalm with sudden exclamations of praise.

YHWH, our Lord,
how majestic is your name in all the earth! (v. 1)

The beginning and ending of the psalm constitute a fine example of an envelope structure, setting off the poem. The psalm is a creation hymn that centers on the place of humans in God's creation.

The opening line of the psalm is awkward to put in English because it begins with YHWH, who is characterized as "our Lord." As the proper Hebrew name for God, YHWH is often translated into English as "Lord." YHWH's name is celebrated as glorious throughout all creation. For the ancient psalmist, the name was more than a mere label; it also spoke of one's character. Therefore the psalm's opening line claims that YHWH is the majesty or glory of creation. This beginning of the psalm in its ancient Near Eastern context has royal connotations, reminiscent of the enthronement psalms that celebrate the kingship of YHWH. For example, Ps 99:3 calls for praise of YHWH's "great and awesome name," and Ps 97:9 describes YHWH as "most high over all the earth." The concluding line of verse 1 includes a textual difficulty.

The theme following the opening line concerns the praise of YHWH even in the heavenly realms. For many readers, verse 2 seems not to fit in this psalm, but the ancient Near Eastern setting and literary context can help readers at this point. In addition, the psalm's creation theme may also be part of this verse. Ancient Near Eastern creation texts often include the building of a fortress or citadel for the creator after the work of creation is complete. In Ps 8:2, the fortress is built after the defeat of enemies representative of chaos; this fortress or bulwark comes even from "the mouths of babes and infants." The verse thus fits the psalm's focus on creation and illustrates a common theme in the Hebrew Bible of weakness turned into strength. In so doing, the verse anticipates the psalm's central affirmation of humanity's place in creation. Readers of the first eight psalms will also note that even a hymn of praise attends to enemies, following a series of lament psalms saturated with enemies.

In verse 3, the human activity of seeing comes to the fore, and it is the night sky as representative of creation that is the object of human seeing. Creation is established as the work of YHWH's fingers; it is vast and incomprehensible. The contrast comes quickly with the reference to "mere mortals" in verse 4. Given the vastness of creation, why would this God bother to pay attention to humans, who are but tiny particles in the grand scheme of creation? The terms used for humans in verse 4 are *ĕnôš* and *bēn ādām*. The first is often associated with human frailty. The second refers to descendants of *ādām*, who came from *ădāmāh*, earth or ground. The poet marvels at the divine care for and attention to these human creatures that seem to be so insignificant. Verses 3–4 constitute a remarkable piece of biblical faith and raise questions about the place of humans in relationship with God.

The footnote in the NRSV's rendering of verse 5 refers to the debate about the translation of *ĕlōhîm*. The term can mean God, gods, or divine beings. A number of scholars suggest that Psalm 8 is a poetic reflection on Genesis 1. The rendering in Genesis 1 is "God," and thus that rendering would be most appropriate in Psalm 8. The psalm further alludes to the Bible's opening creation account. Psalm 8 asks how God – creator of the amazing universe – cares about the insignificant creatures called humans. Genesis 1:26–31 suggests that God created women and men in the image and likeness of God, "crowned them with glory and honor." Just as Genesis 1 and Psalm 8 speak of God with royal overtones, Ps 8:5 describes humans with royal overtones. Humans are God's likeness, God's representatives in having dominion over the works of the divine fingers. Dominion here does not indicate permission to exhaust the creation's resources but suggests that God grants to humans the honor of representing God in caring for all of creation. Humans receive the gift of caring for the creation as the shepherd king cares for the kingdom. "Glory and honor" suggest divine presence and activity in the world, demonstrated in human care for the creation. The poet then articulates the works of God's hands and comes to a sudden stop. Then the psalm ends as it began, with the poetic affirmation that all of creation displays God's majesty.

A Closer Look: What Is Man that You Should Note Him?

Robert Alter has attended to the poetic dimensions of Psalm 8. He notes the envelope structure created by the refrain that begins and ends the poem:

A perfect circle is closed: the majesty of God, affirmed at the beginning, is restated verbatim at the end, but with the sense accrued through the intervening eight lines of what concretely it means for His name to be majestic throughout the earth.[23]

Alter notes the monosyllabic word for "all" (*kōl*) that draws attention to that central motif in the poem. "All" things are put under human feet, "all" sheep and oxen (vv. 6–7). The use of earth and heaven in verse 1 also suggests "all" of creation. The place of women and men in all of God's creation is at the center of this psalm. Alter also comments on the psalm's central affirmation:

The famous cry of amazement over God's singling out of man (line 5) is a particularly striking instance of the intuition of counterpoint that often guided biblical poets in their occasional use of static semantic parallelism. In every other line of the poem, there is dynamic movement between the versets: specification, focusing, heightening, or sequentiality. Here, by contrast, at the exact thematic center and in the fifth of the poem's ten lines, semantic movement is slowed to allow for the strong, stately emphasis of virtual synonymity, noun for noun and verb for verb in the same syntactical order: "What is man that You should note him,/human creature, that You pay him heed?"[24]

Bridging the Horizons: Power and Praise

The structure of Psalm 8 provides a beneficial way to think about the psalm's significance. The envelope of the psalm is about God, whereas the body of the text is about human dominion. God (theology), humanity (anthropology), and creation (ecology) are intertwined, but the perspective of the psalm is theocentric

---

[23] R. Alter, *Art of Biblical Poetry* (1985), 119.
[24] R. Alter, *Art of Biblical Poetry* (1985), 120.

rather than anthropocentric. Human dominion is a gift from God the creator. Human dominion in the body of the psalm and the praise of God at the edges of the psalm must be held together.[25] An attitude that only sees life as praise of God is not what the psalm imagines. The use of human power without the praise of God is to exploit creation and corrupt the psalm's hope:

> It is not naïve to say that the first step in addressing the environmental crisis is to praise God, for praising God is that act of worship and mode of existence that reminds us that we human beings are not free to do whatever our science and technology enable us to do. Praise flies in the face of our culture's tendency to unrestrained exploitation.[26]

It is also helpful to remember that Psalm 8 follows seven psalms full to the brim with enemies, and more will follow after our psalm. Humans suffer in the first seven psalms, and yet Psalm 8 depicts humans as crowned "with glory and honor." Suffering does not diminish the royal place and vocation of humanity to care for God's creation. Psalm 8 is filled with wonder and awe. The psalm meditates on God's amazing creation and marvels that God cares for women and men and entrusts them with the care of creation. The text praises God as creator of the universe and as giver of life lived to the fullest.

A Closer Look: Psalm 8 in Other Biblical Texts

Other biblical texts allude to Psalm 8. Job 7:17 quotes Ps 8:4 with a negative connotation. Job describes his suffering as the loss of glory. By the end of his struggle, however, he returns to the perspective of Psalm 8 and its vision for human beings.[27] Brevard Childs has considered the allusions in the New Testament.[28] Matthew 21:16 quotes Ps 8:2 in a polemic against opposing authorities and says that babes and infants are closer to the praise of God. Hebrews 2 reads Ps 8:4–6 from a Christological perspective. In addition, Psalm 8 has spawned much beneficial midrash.

---

[25] Walter Brueggemann, *The Message of the Psalms: A Theological Commentary* (Minneapolis: Augsburg, 1984), 37–38.

[26] J. C. McCann, Jr., *Theological Introduction to the Book of Psalms* (1993), 59.

[27] J. Clinton McCann, Jr., "The Book of Psalms: Introduction, Commentary, and Reflections," in Leander E. Keck et al. (eds.), *The New Interpreter's Bible*, vol. 4 (Nashville: Abingdon Press, 1996), 712–713.

[28] Brevard Springs Childs, "Psalm 8 in the Context of the Christian Canon," *Interpretation* 23 (1969): 20–31.

PSALMS 9 AND 10 – TO THE LEADER: ACCORDING TO MUTH-LABBEN. A PSALM OF DAVID

¹ I will give thanks to the LORD with my whole heart;
  I will tell of all your wonderful deeds.
² I will be glad and exult in you;
  I will sing praise to your name, O Most High.

³ When my enemies turned back,
  they stumbled and perished before you.
⁴ For you have maintained my just cause;
  you have sat on the throne giving righteous judgment.

⁵ You have rebuked the nations, you have destroyed the wicked;
  you have blotted out their name for ever and ever.
⁶ The enemies have vanished in everlasting ruins;
  their cities you have rooted out;
  the very memory of them has perished.

⁷ But the LORD sits enthroned for ever,
  he has established his throne for judgment.
⁸ He judges the world with righteousness;
  he judges the peoples with equity.

⁹ The LORD is a stronghold for the oppressed,
  a stronghold in times of trouble.
¹⁰ And those who know your name put their trust in you,
  for you, O LORD, have not forsaken those who seek you.

¹¹ Sing praises to the LORD, who dwells in Zion.
  Declare his deeds among the peoples.
¹² For he who avenges blood is mindful of them;
  he does not forget the cry of the afflicted.

¹³ Be gracious to me, O LORD.
  See what I suffer from those who hate me;
  you are the one who lifts me up from the gates of death,
¹⁴ so that I may recount all your praises,
  and, in the gates of daughter Zion,
  rejoice in your deliverance.

¹⁵ The nations have sunk in the pit that they made;
   in the net that they hid has their own foot been caught.
¹⁶ The Lord has made himself known, he has executed judgment;
   the wicked are snared in the work of their own hands.
      Higgaion. Selah

¹⁷ The wicked shall depart to Sheol,
   all the nations that forget God.

¹⁸ For the needy shall not always be forgotten,
   nor the hope of the poor perish for ever.

¹⁹ Rise up, O Lord! Do not let mortals prevail;
   let the nations be judged before you.
²⁰ Put them in fear, O Lord;
   let the nations know that they are only human.
      Selah

Most interpreters treat Psalms 9 and 10 together, following the view that the two texts were initially one psalm. Psalm 10 is one of the few poems in Book I of the Psalter without a superscription, and Psalm 9 unusually concludes with the term *selah*. Both of those indicators suggest that the two psalms were originally one. Together the texts constitute a reasonably complete alphabetic acrostic, and the Greek version includes them as one psalm. The two texts also exhibit similarities in style and vocabulary. For example, the terms "the poor" (Pss 9:12, 13, 18; 10:2, 9, 17) and "the oppressed" (Pss 9:9; 10:18), as descriptions of those who are persecuted, run throughout the two psalms. We will consider the psalms together since it appears that they initially were one poem. Psalm 9 emphasizes thanksgiving, and Psalm 10 emphasizes lament. Perhaps the compiler(s) of Book I was influenced by this distinction in form and divided the psalms. There also is some textual corruption, and that could have been part of the history of the text that led to the division into Psalms 9 and 10. It is difficult to sustain a clear reading of the two psalms together. Perhaps the best way forward is to think of thanksgiving as a prelude to lament. The rehearsal of God's mighty acts in thanksgiving could suggest the plea that God will enact such salvation again.[29]

A crisis lies behind this text, and the nature of the crisis is best understood as that of social oppression within the faith community. That kind of crisis is commonly reflected in Hebrew prophetic texts. Readers today are not in a position to be more specific about the crisis involved. The structure of the psalm begins with

---

[29]   S. Mowinckel, *Psalms in Israel's Worship*, vol. 1 (1962), 95.

thanksgiving and moves to petition. Lament then leads to further petition followed by a positive conclusion.

The psalm opens in verses 1–2 with a characteristic introductory statement of the purpose of the psalm to offer praise and thanksgiving. The language is reminiscent of the vow of praise that concludes Psalm 7 (v. 17) with the use of *Elyon*, Most High. The reference to the divine name also brings to mind the introductory word of praise in Psalm 8. It is typical of thanksgiving texts in the Hebrew Psalter to begin with an expression of the intent to give thanks to God. The thanksgiving psalms typically recount the mighty acts of deliverance accomplished by God. The rehearsal in Psalm 9 is a kind of summary of God's mighty acts rather than a description of God's deliverance of the speaker from a particular crisis.

Verses 3–12 carry out the announced thanksgiving. These verses recall that God deals with those who persecute the faithful. That perspective will be familiar to readers of the first ten psalms. This psalm exhibits connections with lament psalms that come before it in Book I, especially Psalm 7, but also with other psalms (Psalms 3, 5, 6). The portrayal of YHWH in verses 3–12 is of the divine judge enthroned in Zion who has accomplished the defeat of the enemies. The psalmist describes these enemies as nonspecific adversaries, but also as nations who oppose the divine judge. This judge has "blotted out" the evil enemies. Verses 5–6 suggest that the enemies have been devastated; no one can even remember them. The righteous judge has enacted deliverance for the oppressed and also defeated the enemies. The reference to the divine name in verse 10 strikes a contrast with the destruction of the name of the enemies in verse 5. YHWH rules from the throne of justice and brings hope for those who are persecuted with deeds of violence. YHWH does not forget but hears the cry of the afflicted and brings hope out of a crisis by defeating the enemies. Because of these mighty acts, the psalmist gives praise and thanksgiving to God.

The remainder of Psalm 9 moves to petition. Based on this recounting of what God has done in the past, our poet crafts a plea for help. For the one persecuted at the "gates of death," the plea is that the divine judge will lift that one from one gate to another, from the "gates of death" to the "gates of the daughter Zion." Then this one who has been delivered can recount YHWH's mighty act of deliverance in worship that includes praise and thanksgiving. Verse 15 engages the imagery of hunting. The oppressors have dug a pit in an effort to catch the unsuspecting faithful ones, but the surprise reversal of fortunes is that God will bring hope from this setting of social oppression. The divine judge will see the plight of the oppressed and lift them up while the oppressors sink down into a pit of their own making. Perhaps this sinking down suggests their descent into Sheol, the underworld. The evil of the enemies has rebounded onto their own heads. God has remembered and brought hope for the poor. Further petitions conclude this portion of the text and anticipate what will come in Psalm 10. The hope is that God will defeat the oppressors and lift up the persecuted.

¹ Why, O Lord, do you stand far off?
   Why do you hide yourself in times of trouble?
² In arrogance the wicked persecute the poor –
   let them be caught in the schemes they have devised.

³ For the wicked boast of the desires of their heart,
   those greedy for gain curse and renounce the Lord.
⁴ In the pride of their countenance the wicked say, 'God will not seek it out';
   all their thoughts are, 'There is no God.'

⁵ Their ways prosper at all times;
   your judgments are on high, out of their sight;
   as for their foes, they scoff at them.
⁶ They think in their heart, 'We shall not be moved;
   throughout all generations we shall not meet adversity.'

⁷ Their mouths are filled with cursing and deceit and oppression;
   under their tongues are mischief and iniquity.
⁸ They sit in ambush in the villages;
   in hiding-places they murder the innocent.

Their eyes stealthily watch for the helpless;
⁹ they lurk in secret like a lion in its covert;
they lurk that they may seize the poor;
   they seize the poor and drag them off in their net.

¹⁰ They stoop, they crouch,
   and the helpless fall by their might.
¹¹ They think in their heart, 'God has forgotten,
   he has hidden his face, he will never see it.'

¹² Rise up, O Lord; O God, lift up your hand;
   do not forget the oppressed.
¹³ Why do the wicked renounce God,
   and say in their hearts, 'You will not call us to account'?

¹⁴ But you do see! Indeed you note trouble and grief,
   that you may take it into your hands;
the helpless commit themselves to you;
   you have been the helper of the orphan.

¹⁵ Break the arm of the wicked and evildoers;
     seek out their wickedness until you find none.
¹⁶ The Lord is king for ever and ever;
     the nations shall perish from his land.

¹⁷ O Lord, you will hear the desire of the meek;
     you will strengthen their heart, you will incline your ear
¹⁸ to do justice for the orphan and the oppressed,
     so that those from earth may strike terror no more.

Verses 1–11 of Psalm 10 take readers back to lament and a description of the crisis at hand, with an emphasis on the opponents. The opening verse is in the form of a rhetorical question about God's apparent absence ("you stand afar off"). What makes this divine absence so pressing is the oppression of the wicked. These enemies are arrogant and do not believe that God will hold them accountable for their actions, and so they do not believe they are vulnerable. These enemies are described as practical atheists. They would not deny the existence of God, but they do not find God to be relevant or present in a way that impinges on their actions. These wicked ones are arrogant scoffers who hide in ambush and lurk to pounce on the unsuspecting poor like a lion pouncing on its prey, and there is no one to deliver. By their words and actions, these arrogant evil ones oppose God and the faithful. This contrast of oppressed and oppressor is central to the rhetoric of the prayer in Psalms 9–10.

Lament leads to petition in verse 12. The plea is for YHWH the righteous judge to rise up and intervene in the oppression at hand by protecting the oppressed. Central to the rhetorical strategy of the prayer is the characterization of the opponents as evil oppressors. If YHWH is the divine judge who upholds the moral order of the universe, then the one to whom the prayer is addressed will powerfully help the persecuted and bring down the arrogant enemies who dismiss this divine judge. Verse 14 is a strong statement of faith: God breaks the power of the oppressors and brings hope to the oppressed. Power is central to this section of the psalm, with "the arm of the wicked" in verse 15 and the divine hand in verses 12 and 14. The hope is both for refuge for the poor and defeat for the wicked.

The psalm concludes in a hopeful way. It begins with a confession of faith that YHWH is king and thus the one who brings justice. "The nations" are the oppressors, who are characterized throughout the psalm. The concluding verses express the faith that God hears the cry of the oppressed, encourages them, and brings justice. "The orphan and the oppressed" are the powerless in society. The powerless find justice in refuge; the oppressors find justice in their wickedness rebounding on them.

Bridging the Horizons: An Appeal against Injustice

The faith of ancient Israel affirmed that God is the divine king who brings justice, but Psalms 9 and 10 reflect an experience of injustice. Broyles comments, "Psalm 9–10 presents a powerful appeal to God. It neither retreats from reality, using God as a security blanket, nor rejects God's promises in view of the lamentable reality. Rather, it sets the contradictions side by side and leaves their resolution to God."[30] The prayer articulates both lament and thanksgiving, both of which are constitutive of the human experience. The poet persists in pleading with the divine judge and holds on until reaching a hopeful conclusion based on the kingship of YHWH. Lessons learned in the thanksgiving at the beginning of the prayer became a basis of the plea. The psalm resists the temptation to give in to the oppressors and their arrogant denial of YHWH's justice.

The psalm reflects a socioeconomic crisis, and its prayer is a political act of rhetoric giving a strong voice to the oppressed in contrast to the arrogant oppressors.[31] The hope is that YHWH will intervene as a third party in the face of dismissal from those characterized as socially and economically destructive. The prayer persistently hopes in the justice of God in the face of social oppression. In the first ten psalms of the Hebrew Psalter, enemies abound, but the psalmist persists in coming to a hard-won faith in God as the just judge. In the triangle of relationships between God, psalmist, and enemies, God takes the side of the oppressed psalmist, who candidly speaks persuasive prayer in the midst of trouble and woe.

A Closer Look: An Acrostic Psalm

Psalms 9 and 10 are in the form of an alphabetic acrostic. Every other verse begins with the next letter of the Hebrew alphabet. This highly formal poetic pattern served as both a mnemonic device and an organizing principle for the poet. The pattern may also be a symbol for completeness. The psalm has covered everything on the topic from A to Z, only in Hebrew! Four acrostic psalms occur in Book I of the Psalter (Psalms 9, 10, 25, and 34) and four in Book V (Psalms 111, 112, 119, and 145).

---

[30] Craig C. Broyles, *Psalms* (NIBC 11; Peabody, MA: Hendrickson, 1999), 78.
[31] Walter Brueggemann, "Psalms 9–10: A Counter to Conventional Social Reality," in Patrick D. Miller (ed.), *The Psalms and the Life of Faith* (Minneapolis: Fortress Press, 1995), 217–234.

PSALM 11 – TO THE LEADER. OF DAVID

¹ In the LORD I take refuge; how can you say to me,
  'Flee like a bird to the mountains;
² for look, the wicked bend the bow,
  they have fitted their arrow to the string,
  to shoot in the dark at the upright in heart.
³ If the foundations are destroyed,
  what can the righteous do?'

⁴ The LORD is in his holy temple;
  the LORD's throne is in heaven.
  His eyes behold, his gaze examines humankind.
⁵ The LORD tests the righteous and the wicked,
  and his soul hates the lover of violence.
⁶ On the wicked he will rain coals of fire and sulphur;
  a scorching wind shall be the portion of their cup.
⁷ For the LORD is righteous;
he loves righteous deeds;
  the upright shall behold his face.

This psalm articulates two motifs that are familiar in the expression of lament and complaint. At the beginning of the psalm, the speaker voices trust in YHWH, a statement that counts on the protective care of YHWH (v. 1). This entrustment of self to YHWH is supported in verses 2–3 by a characterization of the destructive power of the wicked that renders the righteous vulnerable and helpless, and in need of YHWH's protection. Although the presentation of these verses is somewhat different from the conventional "motivational clause," they in fact function precisely as a motivational clause. They imply that YHWH's protective care in verse 1 is indispensable because the righteous have no support other than YHWH and cannot protect themselves.

The second line of verse 1 is quite obscure. The rendering offered in the NRSV suggests that the speaker has been told (by friends) to fly away to safety.[32] The speaker, however, rejects such a suggestion, and is unable to flee in such a way. The inability to flee in the face of the threat of the wicked becomes the reason for trust in YHWH as the only source of comfort and well-being. Calvin offers two alternative reasons why the petitioner cannot flee at the behest of this advice: (a) "It would be

32   S. Terrien, *Psalms* (2003), 148.

a sign of distrust were he to place his safety in flight" and perhaps unlawful; (b) The counsel to flee "tended only to make him yield to utter despair. But it would have been wrong for him to yield to these fears."[33]

The second familiar motif in this psalm is the assertion in verses 5–7 that YHWH is a judge who will sort the "righteous" and "the wicked," those who keep Torah and those who defy Torah. Clearly the speaker is to be reckoned among the keepers of Torah and thus congruent with the Torah piety of Psalm 1. The verbs for YHWH's designation of various cases are "hate" and "love," referring respectively to the wicked and the righteous. YHWH hates the wicked, who are subjected to punishment because of their "violence," their damage done to the community. Conversely, YHWH loves righteous deeds; that is, actions congruent with Torah because YHWH himself is aligned with communal well-being. The reward for the righteous is the capacity to "see God." It is likely that the rhetoric of punishment is hyperbolic and is not to be taken in terms of "eternal torment." It is clear here, as in many psalms, that YHWH's adjudication sorts out the human community – or better the community of Israel – in terms of compatibility with YHWH's will for the world.

Both the initial statement of trust (vv. 1–3) and the concluding statement about YHWH's judgment (vv. 5–7) are introduced by the utterance of the name of YHWH. What distinguishes this psalm, however, is verse 4, which is situated between the two units already identified; it also is introduced by the utterance of the divine name. This verse attests YHWH's character, purpose, and activity, offered in three parallel statements. The first two statements situate YHWH "in his holy temple" and on his "throne that is in heaven." The close parallelism suggests that the "holy temple" refers to a heavenly temple. We may, however, suggest that the two parallel lines at the same time offer a characteristic juxtaposition about the *temple in Jerusalem* and the *dwelling of YHWH in heaven* as a way of making a claim for Solomon's temple, and acknowledge that divine residence is not in the temple in Jerusalem but in heaven, beyond human patronage and domestication.

This same careful juxtaposition of temple and heavenly dwelling is voiced in the temple theology of 1 Kgs 8:30:

Hear the plea of your servant and of your people Israel when they pray toward this place; O hear in heaven your dwelling place; heed and forgive.

This way of reading the poetic parallelism would affirm that the appeal to YHWH as "refuge" refers to the safety of the Jerusalem sanctuary (v. 1) and lets the divine judgment take place in the Jerusalem temple, where YHWH sits in court to adjudicate between the guilty and the innocent of the community.

---

[33] J. Calvin, *Commentary on the Book of Psalms*, vol. 1 (1979), 160–161.

The third line of verse 4 characterizes YHWH's judicial activity in the temple; namely, to keep all humanity under scrutiny for the purpose of dispensing blessings and curses. The attentiveness of YHWH toward the temple is congruent with the temple theology of 1 Kings 8:

That your eyes may be open night and day toward this house, the place of which you said, "My name shall be there," that you may heed the prayer that your servant prays toward this place. (1 Kgs 8:29)

In this latter text, YHWH's *eye* is on the temple "day and night" to hear prayer, and YHWH's *ear* is attentive to the temple in order to "hear and forgive." To be sure, the divine attentiveness in 1 Kings 8 would seem to be more benign than the divine attentiveness in this psalm, which is for the purpose of adjudication. But the judicial act of reward and punishment and the priestly act of forgiveness are not remote from each other; the judge can indeed pardon the righteous, who depend on the righteousness of YHWH.

The locus of "refuge" (vv. 1–3) and adjudication (vv. 5–7) in the temple, more-over, is reinforced by the final phrase of the psalm, "behold his face." It is most likely that this phrase refers to cultic presence and access to the life-giving altar where YHWH's presence can dispense the gift of life. The face of YHWH is indeed a source of life. When the "face" refers to cultic presence, then access to the altar is a gift of life, as in the Aaronide blessing that articulates *the face of YHWH* as a source of blessing (see Num 6:24–26). Thus YHWH "gazes" on humanity, and in turn the righteous among humanity are privileged to "behold the face." The temple is a vehicle for face-to-face encounter that yields for the qualified the gift of life. It is surely of immense importance that the *gaze* of YHWH in verse 4 and the *behold* of the righteous in verse 7 use the same verb, *hzh*. Face-to-faceness is a gift to the righteous (withheld from the wicked) that makes them safe in a world of threat. Whereas the temple as "refuge" may be taken as a metaphor, the psalm surely makes an offer of Real Presence of the "God who dwells in heaven" and who graciously meets the righteous in direct, albeit mediated ways. It is no wonder that this temple community is glad indeed when it is said,

Let us go to the house of the Lord. (Ps 122:1)

The house of the Lord as a place of presence is an antidote to all the threatening powers of death. This speaker is confronted with an unbearable situation of anxiety and risk. He cannot cope with it himself, but he courageously refuses to flee from danger. It is precisely appeal to YHWH – here named five times – that makes it possible to remain in the trouble instead of flight or instead of succumbing to despair. The speaker appeals to the resilient institutional force of presence that stands at the center of his community. He is, in the end, not disappointed. It is the very fidelity of YHWH that lets him bask in a presence he thus far has only anticipated.

Bridging the Horizons: Holy Other, Wholly Other

The anticipation of beholding "his face" is an invitation to reflect on the teaching of Emmanuel Lévinas, who ponders the holy "other" character of God yet knows that access to this "other" – when God shows God's face – is the source of life.[34] In such "beholding," Israel is aware that God is radically and deeply different from us, thus compelling a rejection of every idol made in our own image. It is, so Lévinas knows, the face of the other who threatens that is the very source of life. This double reality of divine face *as threat* and *as source* is no doubt why the psalm must "double" the divine residence in heaven and in the temple.

Bridging the Horizons: Real Presence

The psalm concerns confidence in divine presence as an assurance in the face of every threat. Israel knows exactly in such assurance, however, that the face is the presence of an awesome sovereign God. Thus divine presence, direct as it is, is mediated in temple forms, practices, and procedures. Such a guarded Real Presence is an adumbration of the entire struggle of Christian sacramental theology with Real Presence. In subsequent Christian tradition, the struggle concerning the Real Presence in sacrament simply continues the problematic that Israel had known from the outset.

PSALM 12 – TO THE LEADER: ACCORDING TO THE SHEMINITH. A PSALM OF DAVID

¹ Help, O Lord, for there is no longer anyone who is godly;
    the faithful have disappeared from humankind.
² They utter lies to each other;
    with flattering lips and a double heart they speak.

³ May the Lord cut off all flattering lips,
    the tongue that makes great boasts,
⁴ those who say, 'With our tongues we will prevail;
    our lips are our own – who is our master?'

---

34 Emmanuel Lévinas, *Totality and Infinity: An Essay on Exteriority* (Pittsburgh: Duquesne University Press, 1969).

⁵ 'Because the poor are despoiled, because the needy groan,
  I will now rise up,' says the LORD;
  'I will place them in the safety for which they long.'
⁶ The promises of the LORD are promises that are pure,
  silver refined in a furnace on the ground,
  purified seven times.

⁷ You, O LORD, will protect us;
  you will guard us from this generation for ever.
⁸ On every side the wicked prowl,
  as vileness is exalted among humankind.

As with many lament psalms, this one is preoccupied with speech that sounds in several voices. This is highly contested speech concerning life-or-death matters for the psalmist.

The voice that forms and shapes this psalm is that of the suppliant in the psalm. He speaks twice, at the beginning and at the conclusion. In his initial speech, the psalmist utters a petition to YHWH, beginning with a strong imperative, "save," followed by the divine name as a vocative (v. 1). This stark imperative is followed by a motivational clause characterizing the threat that evokes the petition. On the one hand, there is a lack of supportive human community (v. 1). What is missing for the speaker is a community of *hesed* and *amunah*, steadfast love and faithfulness. This word pair is a characteristic mark of those who practice neighborly covenant. On the other hand, the social void is filled by others, who speak with a double heart. (The Hebrew is literally "heart and heart.") These adversaries speak the sort of false-hood that is damaging to the psalmist.

The second speech of the psalmist is in the conclusion of verses 7–8. Verse 7 is the direct affirmative address to YHWH: "You, O Lord." The speaker affirms that YHWH is indeed responsive to need, has answered the opening petition, and has indeed "saved." Verse 8 is a curious acknowledgment that the wicked still persist and have not been "cut off" by YHWH as was promised in verse 3. Nonetheless, YHWH has dealt decisively with the threat in a way that permits the psalmist to speak with great confidence.

These utterances by the psalmist, the *petition-complaint* at the beginning (vv. 1–3) and the *statement of confidence* at the end (vv. 7–8), indicate the radical dramatic development of the psalm.

It remains to consider the intervening verses in order to see how the speaker has moved from urgent petition to confidence. The space between in verses 3–6 features two voices in contest, to each of whom the psalmist attributes a decisive utterance. Concerning the adversary, we have already seen in verse 2 the indict-ment that "they" utter lies, have "flattering lips" that go with a "double heart"; that is, they speak destructive nonsense, apparently in a public venue where such speech is lastingly destructive.

In verses 3–4, the characterization of the adversary reiterates the phrase of "flattering lips" and attributes to them highly cynical speech with boasting tongues that articulate their arrogant autonomy: "Who is our master?" The implication is that they have no master, are accountable to no one, and can do whatever they like without measuring up to any norm of honesty or neighborliness. They are, it appears, a living embodiment of Dostoyevsky's aphorism, "Without God everything is possible." What is possible here is destructive speech against the psalmist that has no basis in reality. It is plausible that this dismissive characterization of the autonomous adversary also is cast as a petitionary notification to YHWH, who will hardly countenance such defiant autonomy.

In response to the utterance attributed to the adversary, now an utterance attributed to YHWH serves as a decisive antidote to the speech of the adversary (v. 5). The decisive utterance is "Now I will arise" (v. 5). The verb suggests that YHWH has been dormant and inactive, but now, in response to petition, YHWH is mobilized to decisive intervention. Here YHWH acts in a way congruent with the urgent petition of Ps 7:6. The needy who lack resources of their own rightly ask YHWH to intervene on their behalf. Here YHWH resolves to act; YHWH, moreover, gives the reasons for such action. YHWH acts in response to the poor and needy. The situation of need and response here is quite parallel to the normative account of Exod 3:23–25 with a closely paralleled verb for "groan." In both cases, voiced need mobilizes YHWH. In addition to a resolve to "rise," YHWH vows to "save," the same verb as in the initial petition of verse 1. (The NRSV renders the verb "place in safety.") But the repetition of the verb (a repetition lost in the NRSV) indicates the precise correlation of petition and response.

In verse 6, the text reflects on the utterance of YHWH in verse 5. Whereas the NRSV speaks twice of "promise," the Hebrew term is "utterance" (*'mr*), utterances that are, of course, promissory. Thus the utterance of YHWH, with its substantive force, is quite contrasted with the speech of "flattering lips" and "boasting tongues." Indeed, YHWH's own speech in verse 3 mentions "flattering lips" as part of the dismissive judgment.

Thus the psalmist's speeches of *petition* and *assurance* bracket the attributed speeches of *adversary* (v. 4) and *YHWH* (v. 5). These two verses have attached to them verses 3 and 6, which are reflective of the two speeches. It is clear that YHWH's promissory speech is an exact counterpoint to that of the adversary. As the adversary asks defiantly, "Who is our master?" YHWH in verse 5 answers exactly that question. It is YHWH who is master of the adversary and who will override the false speech of the adversary. Or perhaps the psalmist's concluding "You YHWH" is an answer to the question of verse 4. The psalmist knows, and the drama of the psalm confirms, that the speaker lives in a world well and protectively governed by YHWH. The psalmist has always known and trusted, but the adversaries did not know and so harbor illusions about their own autonomy.

This is a psalm that offers three voices, those of *the psalmist, the adversary,* and YHWH. Scholars have attempted to construct a social-judicial-liturgical venue for such interaction. It may be that there really was such a procedure that allowed YHWH to have a decisive word. Or it could be that we are to take this three-voiced interaction as a characteristic field of imagination in Israel, for Israel always understands itself as situated between the adversary and YHWH. Or perhaps in the heart and on the tongue of the psalmist, this interaction is an internal drama as the psalmist adjudicates between voices alive and surging in his own life. The speaker, like everyone, knows the internal voices that threaten to undo us. It is fortunate that the speaker also has available the victorious counterpoint of the assuring voice of YHWH.

A Closer Look: Israel's Spirituality

In his study of lament psalms, Claus Westermann has noted that the complaint psalms are regularly a triangular interaction between the speaker, God, and the adversary.[35] This psalm is an epitome of that ongoing drama that characterizes Israel's spirituality. It is clear that this spirituality is a judicial rather than a therapeutic model; Israel knows that space and resources for life are always highly contested. Israel characteristically has confidence that solidarity with YHWH is a more than adequate response to the threat of the adversary. Israel, however, can never escape the triangle.

Bridging the Horizons: Divine Truth

With reference to this psalm, attention should be paid to the exposition of Martin Buber. Buber sees this psalm as an explication of "the big lie" that makes life delusional. Such an acknowledgment of the big lie and a faithful antidote to it is surely germane in a culture of toxic euphemisms that seek to disguise barbaric reality by "flattering lips." Buber writes:

God will preserve him, as each time of need comes, from the power of the lie, by setting in freedom and salvation him who is devoted to the truth. The truth is God's alone, but there is a human truth, namely, to be devoted to the truth. The lie is from time and will be swallowed up by time; the truth, the divine truth, is from eternity and in eternity, and this devotion to the truth, which we call human truth, partakes of eternity.[36]

---

35 Claus Westermann, *The Praise of God in the Psalms* (Richmond, VA: John Knox Press, 1965).
36 Martin Buber, *Right and Wrong: An Interpretation of Some Psalms* (London: SCM Press, 1952), 17.

Bridging the Horizons: Hearing the Victim's Cry

In the horizon of the faith of Israel it is YHWH's most characteristic action to respond in compassionate and transformative ways to the needs of the poor and needy. James Kugel, in commenting on this theme, writes:

> hearing the victim's cry is a god's duty and God's duty.... Yet here, in Exodus, this cliché is presented as revelation, God's ultimate self-revelation to Moses. I am by nature *ḥannum* and *raḥum* (despite all evidence to the contrary). I hear the cry of the victim; I can't help it.[37]

PSALM 13 – TO THE LEADER. A PSALM OF DAVID

¹ How long, O LORD? Will you forget me for ever?
  How long will you hide your face from me?
² How long must I bear pain in my soul,
  and have sorrow in my heart all day long?
How long shall my enemy be exalted over me?

³ Consider and answer me, O LORD my God!
  Give light to my eyes, or I will sleep the sleep of death,
⁴ and my enemy will say, 'I have prevailed';
  my foes will rejoice because I am shaken.

⁵ But I trusted in your steadfast love;
  my heart shall rejoice in your salvation.
⁶ I will sing to the LORD,
  because he has dealt bountifully with me.

Of all the many psalms of lament and complaint, Psalm 13 is the clearest, purest example of the genre. Its larger movement "from plea to praise" is unmistakably marked.[38] Within that large dramatic movement, the specific rhetorical elements that constitute the genre are readily evident. Indeed, if one wants either to study the genre in order to understand its dramatic power or learn to pray in such a vigorous, candid way, Psalm 13 is the preferred beginning point.

---

37 James Kugel, *The God of Old: Inside the Lost World of the Bible* (New York: Free Press, 2003), 124, 126.
38 See C. Westermann, *Praise and Lament in the Psalms* (1981), 68–69.

The psalm turns on the strange, freighted gap between verses 1–4 and verses 5–6 when something decisive and transformative has occurred. What happened at that point is a matter of hypothesis. The most popular guess is that, at this point in the dramatic articulation of the psalm, a divine oracle of assurance ("salvation oracle") was declared by an authorized pastoral/liturgical speaker as a response to the petition of verses 1–4. Although that is a plausible explanation for the movement of the psalm, it is not a necessary conclusion. It may just as well be that as the cry of need is articulated, the urgency is spent. The speaker may fall back on a more elemental assurance of faith. Whatever happened "in between," the movement permits us to work both *backward to petition* and *forward to doxology*.

The psalm begins with the characteristic elements of "plea." The fourfold "how long" of verses 1–2 amounts to a complaint that communicates to the deity that the impatient speaker is in an unbearable situation that the speaker fully expects God to remedy. The phrase "how long" is not a request for data concerning a timetable; rather it is a statement of impatient hope. Not only is the present circumstance unbearable; it cannot be endured, and it need not last if YHWH will simply pay attention. The statement of the fourfold protest includes an accusation against YHWH, who has forgotten and hidden from the speaker; such forgetting and hiding amounts to a violation of YHWH's promised attentive fidelity to Israelites. The "hidden face" of YHWH contrasts with the expectation of "seeing God's face" in Ps 11:7. The third usage of the phrase characterizes the unbearable pain, and the fourth reports on the humiliation suffered because of taunting adversaries. Although the adversaries taunt, there is no doubt that it is YHWH's neglect that has created the situation.

In verse 3, the poem moves to petition; YHWH is addressed intimately as "my God," from whom the speaker has legitimate expectation. YHWH is addressed with three urgent verbs: "look, answer, give light." The sequence of the three is appropriate. The initial verb summons YHWH to notice the plight of the petitioner. If YHWH notices, then YHWH may answer. But the third verb, "give light," suggests a specific answer. "Light" here is the power of life, for the speaker in present circumstances is about to sink into oblivion and is without resources.

Perhaps the most interesting element of the psalm is the introduction of three motivational clauses introduced by the double "lest." The purpose of such utterances is to give YHWH a reason (motivation) for engaging the trouble of the speaker and answering the petition. Here the threefold motivation (perhaps designed to match the threefold petition) is that, unless YHWH acts, (a) the speaker will die; (b) the enemy will gloat, which is already a problem in verse 2b; and (c) the enemy will be glad that the psalmist is "destabilized." The first motivation clearly concerns the destiny of the speaker, but the second and third motivations draw YHWH into the issue and make clear that there is as much at stake for YHWH as there is for the petitioner. If the enemy can "prevail" (see also Ps 12:4), this will represent a defeat for YHWH, who has not "prevailed." Thus YHWH must act for the speaker in order to exhibit YHWH's own sovereign power evidenced in YHWH's capacity to sustain the life of the petitioner. The same motivation is voiced in the narrative account of Num 14:13–18.

Then we have a pause. When the speaker continues, everything has been changed, perhaps because of the divine oracle. The prayer now comes to resolution. It is evident that YHWH has seen, has answered, and has acted to sustain the life of the desperate one. Now the elated speaker issues three parallel statements of affirmation, the three elements corresponding to the three petitions of verse 3 and the three motivations of verses 3–4. The turn now accomplished through some form of divine response and intervention is an exhibit of YHWH's "steadfast love," which is the grounds of all of Israel's hope, indeed the grounds of the petition in verse 3. Perhaps Israel prays, hopes, and demands because it trusts completely that YHWH's steadfast love will prevail over every threat of death, darkness, and instability. Given that effective steadfast love of YHWH, the speaker can respond and sing, referring all of one's life back "to the Lord." The prayer that began in dismay now concludes in full and glad praise, thanksgiving, and buoyant trust in YHWH. It is, however, the case that the trust so evident in the conclusion was in fact the same trust that permitted the lament in the first place:

When he saw not a single ray of good hope to whatever quarter he turned, so far as human reason could judge, constrained by grief, he cries out that God did not regard him; and yet by this very complaint he gives evidence that faith enabled him to rise higher, and to conclude, contrary to the judgment of the flesh, that his welfare was secure in the hand of God.[39]

In both plea and praise, the speaker places all trust in YHWH. In this case, the prayer of the faithful is not disappointed.

A Closer Look: Plea-Praise

The rhetorical movement of this prayer, so characteristic in Israel, is from "plea to praise." The wonder of these prayers is that the prayers *move*, so that everything is different at the end from what it was at the beginning. Although the form of rhetoric accomplishes this move, we should not miss that it is the power and transformative agency of YHWH that makes the dramatic movement possible. The issue finally is not literary or rhetorical but theological.

---

[39]   J. Calvin, *Commentaries on The Book of Joshua* (1979), 182.

A Closer Look: The "Fear Not" of YHWH

The hypothesis of a divine oracle of salvation occurring between the two parts of the prayer has been classically articulated by Joachim Begrich.[40] The examples he finds of such an oracle are the texts that articulate the "fear not" of YHWH in the exilic prophetic corpus as in Isa 41:8–13, 14–16; 43:1–7; 44:8; Jer 30:10–11. Edgar Conrad, to the contrary, has argued that Begrich's influential proposal cannot be sustained.[41]

A Closer Look: Ask, Search, Knock

The structure of "plea-praise" articulates the quintessence of biblical prayer. In his instruction to his disciples, Jesus offered a threefold teaching that corresponds to this structure:

ask … and it will be given to you;
search … and you will find;
knock … and the door will be opened to you. (Matt 7:7)

In this psalm, verses 1–4 constitute the acts of "ask, search, knock." The resolution of verses 5–6 indicates that the petition has yielded *answering, finding*, and *having opened*. Jesus' teaching is a summary of the practice of prayer that is so clearly evidenced in this psalm.

Bridging the Horizons: How Long?

The repeated phrase "How long?" is an important address to God amid trouble, an impatient hope that expects God to redress the trouble promptly. This phrase has been a staple of African American preaching: "How long? How long must I work in the vineyard?" (For arousing the audience, "How long?" is like placing a match to gasoline.)[42] That rhetorical practice was famously taken up by Martin Luther King, Jr. In a sermon preached in Montgomery, Alabama, on March 25, 1965, King said:

---

[40] See P. D. Miller, *They Cried to the Lord* (1994), 135–177. See citation of Begrich, p. 395, n. 25.

[41] Edgar W. Conrad, *Fear Not Warrior: A Study of 'al tira' Pericopes in the Hebrew Scripture* (Brown Judaic Studies 75; Chico, CA: Scholars Press, 1985).

[42] William H. Pipes, *Say Amen, Brother! Old-Time Negro Preaching: A Study in American Frustration* (Detroit: Wayne State University Press, 1992), 42.

How long? Not long, because no lie can live forever. How long? Not long, because you still reap what you sow. How long? Not long, because the arm of the moral universe is long but it bends toward justice. How long? Not long, 'cause mine eyes have seen the glory of the coming of the Lord.[43]

King's usage is a clear example of the way in which lament itself is an act of fervent hope.

PSALM 14 – TO THE LEADER. OF DAVID

1 Fools say in their hearts, 'There is no God.'
They are corrupt, they do abominable deeds;
there is no one who does good.

2 The LORD looks down from heaven on humankind
to see if there are any who are wise,
who seek after God.

3 They have all gone astray, they are all alike perverse;
there is no one who does good,
no, not one.

4 Have they no knowledge, all the evildoers
who eat up my people as they eat bread,
and do not call upon the LORD?

5 There they shall be in great terror,
for God is with the company of the righteous.
6 You would confound the plans of the poor,
but the LORD is their refuge.

7 O that deliverance for Israel would come from Zion!
When the LORD restores the fortunes of his people,
Jacob will rejoice; Israel will be glad.

---

43   See James Melvin Washington (ed.), *A Testament of Hope: The Essential Writings of Martin Luther King, Jr.* (San Francisco: Harper and Row, 1986), 230; and Richard Lischer, *The Preacher King: Martin Luther King, Jr. and the Word That Moved America* (Oxford: Oxford University Press, 1995), 128.

This psalm has traces of complaint, but it is cast as an instruction. There is no direct address to God, no direct complaint, and no petition. It does, quite like the lament genre, champion "the righteous" (v. 5) and cast "fools" as the antagonists to the righteous poor (vv. 1, 6). It presents YHWH, moreover, as the great champion of the righteous poor, who are helpless before the destructive fools, the evildoers. Thus the social map of "fools-evildoers" versus the "righteous poor" is not unlike the social grid of many lament psalms. The rhetoric in this psalm, however, is not the language of appeal but is perhaps an instruction to the young. That instruction, however, is at the same time a voice of advocacy.

The psalm is a critical reflection on the nature of "fools" and their destructive behavior (vv. 1–4). The category of "fool" brings us into the world of sapiential instruction, or specifically to the book of Proverbs. In that teaching, emphasis is on the conduct of fools, whereas here that conduct is rooted in a mistaken theological orientation that imagines autonomy without accountability to God. Verse 1 nicely links *thought* ("say in the heart") of autonomy with the *act* of social destructiveness. The rhetoric is dominated by a fourfold use of the negative particle "no" (*'in*): "no God, no one (does good), no one (does good), no." The attitudes and actions of this group of destructive people negate everything on which life depends. They do not *love God* (seek God), and they do not love their neighbor. Their theological-moral lack of accountability leads to conduct and policies that "eat" the poor. This perverse theological substructure produces disastrous economic conduct. In verse 4, the link between *social destructiveness* and *theological indifference* is clearly made.

But, says this teaching voice, the Lord who seeks the wise (and finds none) (v. 2) is the same God who will work havoc among the foolish (v. 5). The language of punishment here is quick and terse. It is likely that in such a rhetorical environment the teacher does not intend an invasive "supernatural" punishment but rather a social situation that arises as a consequence of avarice, which will impact the foolish who are greedy. Thus verse 5 does not assert that God will act but only that God is in solidarity with the righteous to see that the long-term intention of the creator God is enacted. The juxtaposition of the *righteous* in verse 5 and the *poor* in verse 6 suggests that this psalm is a teaching that reflects a social circumstance dominated by those who overturn established communal mores for the sake of big profits. The culminating judgment is that the poor who are exposed and vulnerable in an aggressive economy nonetheless are under the safety and protection of the God who makes such aggressive economic policy at best penultimate.

Verse 7 strikes one as a curious addendum that disregards the social destructiveness and conflicts of the foregoing and treats the entire community as unified. The particular phrase "restores the fortune" is used most often to refer to restoration of Israel after the exile, as in Jer 31:18; 32:44; and 33:26 (see Job 42:10). If that is the usage reflected here, then verse 7 offers a quite new and different reading of verses 1–6 wherein the "who" would be a foreign oppressor (Babylon) and the righteous poor would be the entire community of Israel, which is devoured by international threats.

Bridging the Horizons: Wealth at the Expense of Others

Erhard Gerstenberger concludes that the psalm may be against the rich Jewish upper class, which makes big profits under the protection of a foreign administration.[44] Thus it is plausible that the psalm reflects a socioeconomic crisis in which some in the community suffer at the hands of others who have become cynically autonomous (see Nehemiah 5). Viewed broadly, it is no stretch to think that the psalm might well illuminate the current economic crisis of "globalization," in which high-powered economic forces, in the interest of immense profits, run roughshod over normal social relations by implementing destructive social policies. The psalm of course not only offers a diagnosis of such a crisis but dares to assert that such cynical exploitation contains within itself the seeds of its own destruction. The reality of God is asserted as a curb against self-serving rapaciousness. Although the phrase "evildoer" in verse 4 is often taken to have connotations of "magical manipulation," such an understanding may be remote from contemporary "evildoers" who are able to manipulate in hidden ways the course of the market for some at the expense of others.

PSALM 15 – A PSALM OF DAVID

[1] O LORD, who may abide in your tent?
Who may dwell on your holy hill?

[2] Those who walk blamelessly, and do what is right,
and speak the truth from their heart;
[3] who do not slander with their tongue,
and do no evil to their friends,
nor take up a reproach against their neighbors;
[4] in whose eyes the wicked are despised,
but who honor those who fear the LORD;
who stand by their oath even to their hurt;
[5] who do not lend money at interest,
and do not take a bribe against the innocent.

Those who do these things shall never be moved.

---

[44]   E. S. Gerstenberger, *Psalms, Part 1* (1988), 220.

The classic exposition of Psalm 15 understands the psalm as an entrance liturgy or entrance torah: pilgrims ask a question about entrance into the holy place, and a liturgist provides an answer. John Day suggests that entrance liturgies have three parts:[45]

1. question about who may be admitted to the temple;
2. answer, setting out the ethical requirement;
3. word of blessing with regard to those who are qualified to enter the temple.

Readers can imagine the scene: a group of pilgrims makes its way to the entrance to the temple in ancient Jerusalem and asks a question about who may enter to worship, and the priest gives an answer in the form of a priestly *torah*. Psalm 24; Isa 33:14–16; Mi 6:6–8; and Zechariah 7 have a similar question-and-answer style and a similar emphasis on ethics. The psalm likely originated in connection with the pre-exilic temple in Jerusalem. The psalms treat the Jerusalem temple as sacred space and as a place of the divine presence. Preparation to encounter the divine presence is central in the Hebrew scriptures. Leviticus 10, for example, warns the community to take considerable care in approaching worship in sacred space. It is noteworthy that Psalm 15 appears to envision worshipers entering the sanctuary; the key is preparation. Informing the psalm is the understanding of God as both holy and accessible (see the exposition for Psalm 11). To enter the holy place is both risky and life-giving.

Also inherent in this picture of a liturgical setting is the reality that the psalm instructs its hearers and readers. Some interpreters would emphasize the didactic nature of the text in addition to the liturgical setting. The psalm instructs the community in the moral implications of worship and so urges openness to God's instruction. The psalm is both liturgy and instruction. Two perspectives on the psalm's instruction relate the text to other parts of the Hebrew canon. One is that there are ten entrance requirements in the psalm, and thus they should be considered as part of the Decalogue tradition in the Pentateuch. The list of ten serves as a quick reference for students and portrays morality as a whole for life. Peter Craigie suggests the following structure.[46]

Positive Conditions (v. 2)	Negative Conditions (v. 3)
1. Walking blamelessly	4. No falsity
2. Doing Right	5. No evil
3. Speaking Truth	6. No reproach
Positive Conditions (v. 4)	Negative Conditions (v. 5)
7. Despise reprobates	9. No usury
8. Swear to do good	10. No bribery

45 John Day, *Psalms* (Old Testament Guides; Sheffield: JSOT, 1992), 60.
46 P. C. Craigie, *Psalms 1–50* (2004), 150–151. The problem is that verse 4 appears to state three conditions.

Psalm 15 also relates to those who are described as faithful in the preceding psalms. Those who take refuge in God (Pss 2:12; 5:11; 7:1; 11:1; 14:6), the poor (Pss 9:9, 12; 10:2, 9, 12; 12:5), and the righteous (Pss 1:5–6; 11:3, 5; 14:5) are pilgrims open to God's instruction. Their struggles are reflected in these first psalms; at the conclusion of Psalm 15, they find the hope of stability. We will read Psalm 15 with both its liturgical setting and its instruction in view.

Verse 1 articulates the question to which the remainder of the psalm responds. Imagine the scene. Worshipers come to the entrance to the temple and submit a question. The question is about who may come into the sanctuary to worship and is addressed to God. The response comes in the form of priestly instruction. The two lines of the question are close parallels, asking the question in echoes. The terms "tent" and "holy hill" refer to the Jerusalem sanctuary; "tent" derives from the tabernacle traditions. Both verbs suggest temporary presence in the temple. Good translations would be "sojourn" and "tabernacle." Behind the question is the understanding of sanctuary/temple as a place of divine presence that is both threat and promise of life, so the question is about who might receive the gift of hospitality from this powerful, life-giving presence. The question emphasizes the interrogative "Who?" and so suggests that it is about identity issues. Identity issues stretch all the way back to Psalm 1 and its portrayal of the faithful as those who follow not the advice of the wicked but God's *torah*. A sample of God's *torah* follows in the answer to the question beginning Psalm 15.

The remainder of the psalm responds to the question about who is prepared to enter the temple to worship. Verse 2 uses participial verb forms, indicating continuous action, to craft a response in terms of lifestyle. Those who may enter to worship are those with lives characterized by walking blamelessly, doing right, and speaking truth. The whole of life is in view, and the issue is integrity. The parts of life fit together, including speech. Of particular note is the second phrase in the verse: "and do what is right" (NRSV). The term indicates a doer of righteousness (*pō'ēl ṣedeq*), a clear contrast to the doers of evil (*pō'ălê 'āwen*), the common characterization of the enemies in the Psalter (Pss 5:5; 6:8; 14:4). Those who are prepared for worship act and speak in a manner in line with their connection to YHWH. The central concern in verse 2 is not so much about individual acts as it is about ethical living, especially in terms of human relationships.

Verses 3–5 give a more specific response. Those who are prepared for worship do not verbally abuse others; verses 2 and 3 make it clear that speech is part of a faithful lifestyle. The contrast again is with the evildoers in the Psalms (Pss 5:9; 12:4). This person who is prepared for worship understands that there are both faithful and wicked people in the world, and the contrast between the two groups undergirds the psalm. The conclusion of verse 4 is obscure. A common rendering follows the Greek version: "He swears to the [his] neighbor and does not change," suggesting integrity of speech. The concluding verse affirms that the faithful person does not practice usury or bribery. Such practices were problematic in ancient Near Eastern society. Pentateuchal instructions allow for the lending of money (Exod 22:25–27; Lev 25:35–38; Deut 16:19–20) but for the purpose of helping those in need rather than to earn interest. The positive ideals are justice and mercy. There is demand in entering the holy place for worship; it connotes ethical living as preparation.

The other side of the matter is that, for the faithful, entering the holy place brings security, for the place of the divine presence is the secure place of the rock. YHWH and the temple are solid and do not move. The wicked shall be moved (Ps 10:6), and even the faithful fear that they will be moved or shaken (Ps 13:4), but YHWH and the sanctuary are stable. It is the divine presence that provides protection and stability. The portrait of the holy place in these first psalms is as a place of refuge. God's presence is both demanding and life-giving. The hope of temple worship and its encounter with the life-giving God make possible faithful and vibrant days for ancient Israel as a community.

Bridging the Horizons: The Righteous Worshiper

Psalm 15 understands YHWH to be both holy and available, and to be one who gives guidance in preparing for worship and in living in Israel's covenant community. The hope at the end of the psalm is a hope based on God's life-giving presence in worship in the sanctuary. The psalm is important for the Psalter's emphasis on worship. Another perspective on the psalm is that it paints a picture of the righteous worshiper. It is not a legalistic prescription for behavior but is a characterization of the one who is living faithfully in covenant relationship with YHWH. It articulates goals for faithful and vibrant living in the covenant community. The psalm suggests that there is a rhythm to life and worship. Living in line with the covenant instruction revealed by YHWH prepares the pilgrims for worship, and powerful worship renews by way of encounter with the life-giving deity and so sustains faithful covenant living.

The psalm emphasizes ethics and so has a strong prophetic tone. Perhaps ancient Israel's prophets learned their faith with this kind of emphasis in worship and in that way such worship influenced their preaching, as seen in Mi 6:6–8 and Isa 1:12–17. Preparation for true worship is ethical in nature.

PSALM 16 – A MIKTAM OF DAVID

[1] Protect me, O God, for in you I take refuge.
[2] I say to the LORD, 'You are my LORD;
I have no good apart from you.'

³ As for the holy ones in the land, they are the noble,
in whom is all my delight.

⁴ Those who choose another god multiply their sorrows;
their drink-offerings of blood I will not pour out
or take their names upon my lips.

⁵ The LORD is my chosen portion and my cup;
you hold my lot.
⁶ The boundary lines have fallen for me in pleasant places;
I have a goodly heritage.

⁷ I bless the LORD who gives me counsel;
in the night also my heart instructs me.
⁸ I keep the LORD always before me;
because he is at my right hand, I shall not be moved.

⁹ Therefore my heart is glad, and my soul rejoices;
my body also rests secure.
¹⁰ For you do not give me up to Sheol,
or let your faithful one see the Pit.

¹¹ You show me the path of life.
In your presence there is fullness of joy;
in your right hand are pleasures for evermore.

One of the themes that surfaces in the first poems of the Hebrew Psalter is that of refuge, especially refuge associated with the temple. Psalms 5, 7, 11, and 15 emphasize the theme. Psalm 15 articulates qualifications for entering the temple to worship, and Psalm 16 is often interpreted in terms of refuge in the temple or sanctuary. The psalm clearly begins with that concern. In that sense, readers of the Psalter are in familiar territory with Psalm 16. The text reflects a crisis, either past or present. Whereas the opening prayer is for refuge, much of the psalm constitutes either praise or confession of trust. The movement of the poem is from an opening plea, to a recounting of God's actions on the speaker's behalf, to a closing confession of trust.

When interpreters make the attempt to see through the poetic language to the ancient setting, the picture becomes murkier, however. Hans-Joachim Kraus interprets the prayer in terms of refuge in the sanctuary. The psalm is a confession of trust in God, who provides refuge for the faithful in ancient Israel.[47] He understands

---

[47] H.-J. Kraus, *Psalms 1–59* (1988), 234.

the language of verses 5–6 to suggest that the psalm's speaker is a Levite reflecting on the distinctive Levite privilege of receiving land from God (Lev 25:32–33; Num 35:8; Jo 14:4). A variation on this view would be to read the prayer in terms of temple refuge but to take the language in verses 5–6 in the broader sense of being included in the ancient Israelite community of faith. Refuge in the temple would include receiving a portion in that community and so confessing trust in YHWH the God of Israel, who has given that portion, in contrast to other gods.

Peter Craigie takes a different interpretive route.[48] He understands the prayer to be spoken by a person of faith who stands in contrast to syncretists, those who speak the name of YHWH but also worship other gods in various cults throughout the land. He interprets verses 2–3 as words of the syncretists that contrast with the psalmist's confessions of trust in Israel's God.[49] These attempts to construct the ancient setting of Psalm 16 demonstrate the difficulty of deciphering an original setting for poetic language that is adaptable for worshipers in various contexts. However, they also remind contemporary readers that these psalms came from real ancient worship settings rather than some general conceptual or spiritual framework.

The psalm's opening section (vv. 1–4) begins with a plea for refuge that sets the tone of the prayer. We have already noted that this theme is a common one in the first part of the Psalter. The opening verse suggests that the speaker has an intimate relationship with the God of ancient Israel and so pleads with God for protection. The relationship between the speaker and God is also on display in verse 2 and constitutes the context of the prayer. The verse also declares that the speaker is faithful to the one true and living God. We have already indicated that the rendering of verses 2–3 is debatable and that Craigie interprets these words as a quotation from syncretists. He suggests that the syncretists affirm God and still delight in other gods, "the holy ones" of verse 3. The verses thus exhibit the mixing of loyalties in syncretism. We have also seen that Kraus understands "the holy ones" as Levitical priests who are faithful to God and who serve God.

Perhaps the language could also refer more broadly to those who are faithful. The speaker is one who is faithful to YHWH and delights in those in the community of faith who are loyal to YHWH. Syncretists are causing trouble in the community (v. 4). They chase after idols while still confessing the name of YHWH. This theological and social setting would be similar to that envisioned in the book of the prophet Hosea. Psalm 16:1–4 contrasts the faithful petitioner and those who attempt to mix faith in YHWH with faith in the idols worshiped in the surrounding culture. The speaker of the psalm consistently confesses trust in the living God who gives life, and rejects the other false gods.

---

[48] P. C. Craigie, *Psalms 1–50* (2004), 155–159.
[49] Verses 2–4 exhibit some textual problems, and decisions about those issues have interpretive consequences.

The psalmist's affirmation of faith continues in verses 5–8. The terms used in verses 5–6 – "chosen portion," "lot," "boundary lines," and "heritage" – are those related to the possession of land (see Jo 13:23; 14:4; 15:3; 17:5). We have already noted Kraus's view that this language relates to the Levites and God's provision of land and livelihood for them. The inheritance of land here is closely associated with YHWH. We have also suggested an alternative view that, in the midst of a crisis and conflict, the speaker expresses confidence in YHWH. These verses show that the one praying has experienced YHWH's gifts of land and provision for life by way of a casting of lots to distribute land. Ron Clements has shown that there is a connection between the privilege of dwelling in the land given by God and the privilege of worship.[50] The language of verses 5–6 then suggests that YHWH has included the petitioner in the worshiping community that lives in the land and thus the language about land heritage. The speaker continues by recognizing divine instruction that informs "my heart." That is another way of affirming the education of the conscience of faith. Verse 8 affirms that the speaker is confident that God will provide deliverance from the crisis at hand and will provide for a vibrant life; all of that is in contrast to the syncretists in the first part of the psalm. The phrase "I shall not be moved" is reminiscent of the conclusion of Psalm 15, indicating that the faithful shall not be shaken, a contrast to the fear that the faithful will be moved or shaken in Ps 13:4. The poetic voice in Psalm 16 is confident in YHWH.

The psalm's concluding verses (vv. 9–11) sing of trust in the God who delivers. The language is characteristic of those psalms that narrate God's deliverance from the power of death. YHWH preserves the faithful one from death, and the psalmist looks forward to the path of fullness of life. The speaker is preserved from Sheol, or the Pit, the realm of the dead, the underworld characterized by separation from the life-giving God and from the worshiping community. The protection God provides brings rest (vv. 1, 9). The language of presence in verse 11 suggests temple refuge, as does the psalm's opening plea. The prayer confesses faith in YHWH's protection, and so its purpose is to engender trust in YHWH from readers.

Bridging the Horizons: An Expression of Loyalty

Psalm 16 is a prayer to YHWH and an expression of confidence in YHWH's protection and provision for life. The psalm's conclusion uses language typical of the way lament psalms speak of divine deliverance from the power of death. The poet imagines God's continuing protection and a life based on trust in that God, the only living God. That kind of trust makes life possible in the midst of difficulty. History includes many such examples – Martin Luther and Martin

---

[50]   Ronald E. Clements, "Temple and Land: A Significant Aspect of Israel's Worship," *TGUOS* 19 (1963): 16–28.

Luther King, to name only two. Divine loyalty and a response of human loyalty craft a way forward. Temple refuge and its divine presence become an image of hope in the midst of despair. To put the matter another way, the psalm includes the three characters typical of the prayers in the first part of the Psalter – the faithful psalmist, the enemies, and YHWH. In the triangulation characteristic of these prayers, divine help is on the side of the psalmist. The poem moves from a plea to be counted among the faithful, to affirmation of divine instruction, and then to confidence in God, who provides "fullness of joy." The poem characterizes the enemies as syncretists, those who name the name of YHWH and still follow other deities. That label might help contemporary readers think about the enemies in the prayers of the Psalter. Readers will likely identify with the faithful psalmists, but could we also think of how we are like the enemies? The culture around us can easily corrupt our image of the divine and of faithfulness. In what ways are we loyal to the militant consumerism that dominates our culture? What does faithfulness to the living God mean in such a culture?

A Closer Look: Psalm 16 and Peter's Speech

Those reading in the Christian tradition may recognize that Psalm 16 appears in the New Testament in Acts 2:24–31 as part of Peter's speech. There the last four verses of the Greek text of the psalm are used to support the view that the Davidic messiah would be resurrected, and since David was not resurrected, the text must refer to Jesus. The interpretation is in continuity with the sense of the psalm in ancient Israel, but also differs from it. In ancient Israel, the concluding section of the psalm relates to deliverance from the danger of death; the New Testament interpretation relates to the resurrection of Messiah Jesus from the tomb.

PSALM 17 – A PRAYER OF DAVID

1 Hear a just cause, O LORD; attend to my cry;
   give ear to my prayer from lips free of deceit.
2 From you let my vindication come;
   let your eyes see the right.

3 If you try my heart, if you visit me by night,
   if you test me, you will find no wickedness in me;

my mouth does not transgress.
⁴ As for what others do, by the word of your lips
   I have avoided the ways of the violent.
⁵ My steps have held fast to your paths;
   my feet have not slipped.

⁶ I call upon you, for you will answer me, O God;
   incline your ear to me, hear my words.
⁷ Wondrously show your steadfast love,
   O saviour of those who seek refuge
   from their adversaries at your right hand.

⁸ Guard me as the apple of the eye;
   hide me in the shadow of your wings,
⁹ from the wicked who despoil me,
   my deadly enemies who surround me.
¹⁰ They close their hearts to pity;
   with their mouths they speak arrogantly.
¹¹ They track me down; now they surround me;
   they set their eyes to cast me to the ground.
¹² They are like a lion eager to tear,
   like a young lion lurking in ambush.

¹³ Rise up, O Lord, confront them, overthrow them!
   By your sword deliver my life from the wicked,
¹⁴ from mortals – by your hand, O Lord –
   from mortals whose portion in life is in this world.
May their bellies be filled with what you have stored up for them;
   may their children have more than enough;
   may they leave something over to their little ones.

¹⁵ As for me, I shall behold your face in righteousness;
   when I awake I shall be satisfied, beholding your likeness.

One of the themes at the center of a study of the first psalms in the Hebrew Psalter is the centrality of the sanctuary (temple) as a place of refuge. Psalms 3, 5, 7, 11, 15, and 16 all reflect this perspective, as does Psalm 17. Psalm 16 concludes with the hope born from the divine presence, at the right hand of God. That language suggests temple and cult. This psalm brings the speaker's crisis and the place of enemies in the crisis into the context of a petition for protection. Divine presence found in the sanctuary offers this protection.

The most common interpretation of Psalm 17 ties it to an ancient social setting akin to 1 Kgs 8:31–32, which is Solomon's prayer of dedication of the temple. This prayer includes the provision for the divine judge to decide conflicts and vindicate "the righteous by rewarding them according to their righteousness." Psalm 17 bears the marks of the kind of setting in which the speaker has been falsely accused and seeks the protection of the temple precincts, urging the divine judge to declare the speaker innocent of the accusation. Powerful oppressors have brought on the crisis, and an innocent verdict would indicate acceptance into the divine presence. The background is certainly plausible for this cry for refuge.

The poetic language of the text is sufficiently open, however, for the prayer to have significance for people of faith in a variety of crises. The canonical language is adaptable for life. Psalms are worship poems without the stage instructions. They intimate cultic settings but do not describe them, and so speculations about ancient cultic settings often outrun the evidence. In ancient Israel, the poem makes clear that the divine presence centered in the sanctuary is requisite for a full life to continue. The psalm moves from an opening petition and affirmation of innocence to a prayer for refuge, and then to a focus on the enemies, followed by a positive conclusion.[51]

The psalm begins with a petition from one who is characterized as innocent. The claim in verse 1 is that the speaker is honest and without deception and in the midst of a dispute seeks vindication. Any vindication will come from the divine judge, for YHWH is the one who sees to the core character of both the psalmist and the enemies. The senses of hearing, seeing, and speaking come to the fore in the initial petition and continue through the poem. The term for righteousness (*şedek*) is translated in verse 1 with "just cause" in the NRSV. That term is a loaded one in the Psalter. It is shorthand for a right relationship with YHWH, a relationship initiated by God and in that sense a gift from God. So the speaker of the petition claims that this prayer grows out of a relationship with YHWH, and that the speaker is faithful to that relationship.

The speaker's self-affirmation of innocence or integrity continues in verses 3–5. The verbs in the Hebrew perfect tense suggest that the speaker has been tried, visited, and tested, and the result of the trial is that the petitioner follows a lifestyle of righteousness rather than wickedness. The petitioner has not engaged in acts of violence but has followed the path of faithfulness in word and deed. The claim is one of loyalty to a right relationship with YHWH that is demonstrated in right relationships with other people. These opening verses plead for a judgment from

---

51 The text of the psalm includes a variety of textual problems, especially in verses 4, 11, and 14. J. C. McCann, Jr., "Book of Psalms," in L. E. Keck et al. (eds.), *The New Interpreter's Bible*, vol. 4 (1996), 740–741, includes a reasonable description of the issue. We generally move in a similar direction and in the direction of the NRSV. See the NIV for a different view of verse 14.

God, and the speaker claims to be transparent in this plea. So the speaker operates from a vantage point of confidence in requesting a divine verdict. Verses 3–5 are not quite the same form, but they function much like the protestation of innocence in Ps 7:3–5, which probably reflects a similar background.

Verses 6–7 push the psalm forward with an additional plea for YHWH to hear and answer this plea for refuge in the face of oppressors. Hearing, seeing, and speaking continue to come to the fore in this prayer. The plea is that God will hear, answer, and help. The prayer from its beginning depends on the righteousness of God and now pleads for that righteousness to be shown in the life of the community. The beginning of verse 7 urges that YHWH demonstrate a wondrous or extraordinary act of *hesed*, God's loyal love for the faithful petitioner, which does not change with the circumstances of the conflict at hand. The language of the verse calls to mind Exodus 15 and the celebration of the Exodus deliverance from slavery in Egypt and the crossing of the sea. The petitioner makes use of the faith tradition of ancient Israel as a point of contact for the worshiping community. The deliverance at the sea is part of the root metaphor of the deliverance from Egypt for this community, so the plea in Psalm 17 is that God will again demonstrate divine righteousness by delivering this one who is oppressed. The hope of the petitioner is to take the journey of a personal exodus from oppression to refuge, as indicated in the remainder of verse 7. The petition is in line with the perspective of the first psalms in the Psalter – that refuge is found in the divine presence – and fits with the reality of temple refuge. Some contemporary readers will identify needs for refuge or sanctuary.

The petition for protection continues in verses 8–12 and emphasizes the place of the opponents. The petition in verse 8 uses imagery familiar to contemporary readers. "The apple of the eye," apparently referring to the pupil of the eye, and the shelter of the divine wings connote God's tender and close care as the hope of the petitioner. The shadow of the wings may have originally referred to the wings of the cherubim guarding the Ark of the Covenant in the most holy place of the temple, or more broadly to temple refuge, but the same imagery is used in Deut 32:10–11 in the Song of Moses to speak of God's gracious provision and care for the covenant community throughout its history. In the Deuteronomy text, the image is tied to the mother bird's wing, so with the apple of the eye and the shadow of the wing the petitioner again marshals the community's historical traditions in crafting a poetic case for this petition for refuge in the midst of the current conflict. The rhetoric accentuates the contrast between the petitioner and the opponents described in the following verses. The petitioner pleads for God's tender care while the enemies are viciously attacking the speaker. They are malicious, arrogant, and relentless in their secretive pursuit of this oppressed person.

They are like a lion eager to tear,
like a young lion lurking in ambush. (v. 12)

The contrast to the protection of the mother bird's wing is striking. This pejorative portrayal of the enemies provides further motivation for the righteous YHWH to intervene and protect this faithful petitioner. The petition's characterizations of YHWH, enemies, and petitioner are typical of the prayer for help in the Psalter.

Verses 13–14 continue to emphasize the opponents in the context of a petition that the divine judge will bring a verdict against them in no uncertain terms. The petition calls to mind the beginning of the psalm. It calls for protection for the petitioner, and it calls for hard justice for the oppressive accusers. The language carries a military tone, with the overthrow of enemies by the sword. Apparently verse 14 suggests that destruction will come to the oppressors with such force that there will be some of it left even for the next generation. The petitioner claims to be a victim of social oppression and calls for a full measure of divine destruction on the perpetrators of injustice. It is important to note that the plea is again addressed to the divine judge who determines the verdict. The psalm's concluding verse appears to make a sudden change to an expression of confidence that the petitioner will encounter the divine presence. Beholding "your face" and "your likeness" connotes divine presence or theophany in the temple. Looking YHWH fully in the face would bring the vindication urged in the psalm's opening plea.

Bridging the Horizons: Crisis and Covenant

Psalm 17 is a fully developed example of a petitioner crafting an ironclad case to present to the divine judge. The prayer calls on imagery of hearing, seeing, and speaking, and on a rhetoric of contrast with the malicious opponents, to shape a persuasive petition for protection. The prayer especially calls on the theological traditions of covenant. YHWH initiated a covenant relationship with ancient Israel by way of the Exodus from Egyptian oppression, and so the psalmist has learned that YHWH is the God who delivers. In Psalm 17, the psalmist pleads with YHWH to act like the covenant God who delivers and bring protection for the faithful petitioner in this dispute. So the poet brings this crisis within the community into the covenant traditions and urges YHWH to act like the covenant God and deliver the faithful petitioner. Contemporary readers of the Psalms may be more accustomed to thinking of covenant and righteousness in terms of divine calls for the community to live faithfully. Here the petitioner calls on YHWH to be faithful to the covenant relationship initiated in the Exodus from Egypt.

This psalm, and a number of other psalms like it, is an important part of the covenant dialogue of faith in the Hebrew canon. It is the part of the dialogue initiated on the human side and holding YHWH accountable in the covenant relationship. That kind of straightforward dialogue with the divine judge may be surprising to contemporary readers, who may also be troubled by the claim of righteousness on the part of the petitioner. It is important to remember, however, that the claim is not an arrogant self-righteousness but has to do with living faithfully in a relationship initiated by the covenant God. The book of Psalms rolls out more prayers of innocence like Psalm 17 than it does prayers of penitence. These petitions are part of the intimate opening relationship with the divine judge that deepens a covenant relationship. Psalm 17 seeks to bring the experience of the crisis at hand into the faith carried on in the covenant community and so calls on the covenant God to demonstrate faithfulness to the covenant relationship, even in this crisis. The petition calls to mind the book of Job and Job's case calling for a just verdict from the divine judge. As with Job, the concluding verse of Psalm 17 suggests hope found in the encounter with the divine. The powerful refuge of the divine presence makes life possible even in the midst of chaotic conflict.

PSALM 18 – TO THE LEADER. A PSALM OF DAVID THE SERVANT OF THE LORD, WHO ADDRESSED THE WORDS OF THIS SONG TO THE LORD ON THE DAY WHEN THE LORD DELIVERED HIM FROM THE HAND OF ALL HIS ENEMIES, AND FROM THE HAND OF SAUL

He said:
¹ I love you, O LORD, my strength.
² The LORD is my rock, my fortress, and my deliverer,
    my God, my rock in whom I take refuge,
    my shield, and the horn of my salvation, my stronghold.
³ I call upon the LORD, who is worthy to be praised;
    so I shall be saved from my enemies.

⁴ The cords of death encompassed me;
    the torrents of perdition assailed me;
⁵ the cords of Sheol entangled me;
    the snares of death confronted me.

⁶ In my distress I called upon the LORD;
    to my God I cried for help.
From his temple he heard my voice,
    and my cry to him reached his ears.

 7 Then the earth reeled and rocked;
    the foundations also of the mountains trembled
    and quaked, because he was angry.
 8 Smoke went up from his nostrils,
    and devouring fire from his mouth;
    glowing coals flamed forth from him.
 9 He bowed the heavens, and came down;
    thick darkness was under his feet.
10 He rode on a cherub, and flew;
    he came swiftly upon the wings of the wind.
11 He made darkness his covering around him,
    his canopy thick clouds dark with water.
12 Out of the brightness before him
    there broke through his clouds
    hailstones and coals of fire.
13 The LORD also thundered in the heavens,
    and the Most High uttered his voice.
14 And he sent out his arrows, and scattered them;
    he flashed forth lightnings, and routed them.
15 Then the channels of the sea were seen,
    and the foundations of the world were laid bare
at your rebuke, O LORD,
    at the blast of the breath of your nostrils.

16 He reached down from on high, he took me;
    he drew me out of mighty waters.
17 He delivered me from my strong enemy,
    and from those who hated me;
    for they were too mighty for me.
18 They confronted me in the day of my calamity;
    but the LORD was my support.
19 He brought me out into a broad place;
    he delivered me, because he delighted in me.

20 The LORD rewarded me according to my righteousness;
    according to the cleanness of my hands he recompensed me.
21 For I have kept the ways of the LORD,
    and have not wickedly departed from my God.
22 For all his ordinances were before me,
    and his statutes I did not put away from me.

²³ I was blameless before him,
   and I kept myself from guilt.
²⁴ Therefore the Lord has recompensed me according to my righteousness,
   according to the cleanness of my hands in his sight.

²⁵ With the loyal you show yourself loyal;
   with the blameless you show yourself blameless;
²⁶ with the pure you show yourself pure;
   and with the crooked you show yourself perverse.
²⁷ For you deliver a humble people,
   but the haughty eyes you bring down.
²⁸ It is you who light my lamp;
   the Lord, my God, lights up my darkness.
²⁹ By you I can crush a troop,
   and by my God I can leap over a wall.
³⁰ This God – his way is perfect;
   the promise of the Lord proves true;
   he is a shield for all who take refuge in him.

³¹ For who is God except the Lord?
   And who is a rock besides our God? –
³² the God who girded me with strength,
   and made my way safe.
³³ He made my feet like the feet of a deer,
   and set me secure on the heights.
³⁴ He trains my hands for war,
   so that my arms can bend a bow of bronze.
³⁵ You have given me the shield of your salvation,
   and your right hand has supported me;
   your help has made me great.
³⁶ You gave me a wide place for my steps under me,
   and my feet did not slip.
³⁷ I pursued my enemies and overtook them;
   and did not turn back until they were consumed.
³⁸ I struck them down, so that they were not able to rise;
   they fell under my feet.
³⁹ For you girded me with strength for the battle;
   you made my assailants sink under me.
⁴⁰ You made my enemies turn their backs to me,
   and those who hated me I destroyed.

⁴¹ They cried for help, but there was no one to save them;
    they cried to the Lᴏʀᴅ, but he did not answer them.
⁴² I beat them fine, like dust before the wind;
    I cast them out like the mire of the streets.

⁴³ You delivered me from strife with the peoples;
    you made me head of the nations;
    people whom I had not known served me.
⁴⁴ As soon as they heard of me they obeyed me;
    foreigners came cringing to me.
⁴⁵ Foreigners lost heart,
    and came trembling out of their strongholds.

⁴⁶ The Lᴏʀᴅ lives! Blessed be my rock,
    and exalted be the God of my salvation,
⁴⁷ the God who gave me vengeance
    and subdued peoples under me;
⁴⁸ who delivered me from my enemies;
    indeed, you exalted me above my adversaries;
    you delivered me from the violent.

⁴⁹ For this I will extol you, O Lᴏʀᴅ, among the nations,
    and sing praises to your name.
⁵⁰ Great triumphs he gives to his king,
    and shows steadfast love to his anointed,
    to David and his descendants for ever.

Psalm 18 is the second royal psalm in the book of Psalms. In the first royal psalm, Psalm 2, the Davidic king is installed as YHWH's anointed and promised ruler over the nations. The superscription to Psalm 18 and its conclusion tie the text to the Davidic king; the psalm expresses thanksgiving for the victories YHWH gives to the Davidic ruler. At the same time, the pressing presence of those who oppose both God and the speaker, as well as the speaker's claims of a faithful relationship with God, relate the psalms to most of the petitions that precede it in the Psalter. So perhaps the psalm has a broader application in the community of faith.

The text is fairly characterized as a royal psalm of thanksgiving. It includes the elements of a thanksgiving psalm of an individual; in this case, the individual is the king. The poem is of particular textual interest because it also appears in 2 Samuel 22, as suggested by the psalm's superscription. In 2 Samuel, the poem appears in a narrative context after David has been rescued in battles with the Philistines. In its setting in the Psalter, the poem takes on a more adaptable tone. The psalm's heading is similar to 2 Sam 22:1, though it begins with the address to the chief musician, thus suggesting a cultic setting. David is characterized as "the servant of the Lord," and the context includes royal enemies exemplified in Saul. The psalm would likely have been used to celebrate Davidic victories and a variety of such occasions. It could have become a part of ancient Israelite festivals celebrating the hope of royal victories. Much of the psalm's language is applicable more broadly to the community of faith and could fit a variety of settings. Gerstenberger suggests a postexilic setting in the synagogue "to keep hope alive for hard-pressed Jewish communities."[52] The song is lengthy; we will consider it in sections.

Verses 1–6 introduce the thanksgiving song with praise. Westermann characterized this kind of praise as narrative or declarative praise. The psalm narrates God's deliverance of the speaker and in so doing declares thanksgiving to God. The purpose of the song of thanksgiving is to draw the congregation into the narrative so that the whole community can encounter the God who brings about the salvation. The psalm's opening word is unique in the Psalms; the use of *rḥm* ("love") with a human subject is rare. The suggestion is that YHWH has loved this singer of thanks with the love of a mother who has given birth by rescuing the singer from enemies, and so the singer loves YHWH intimately. The introductory section of praise centers on epithets, titles, or descriptions of YHWH as the one who protects the king: my strength, rock, fortress, deliverer, shield, and stronghold. The characterization of YHWH in verses 2–3 as the one who saves the king provides a striking contrast to verse 41, where no one saves the opponents. These first verses suggest that the divine presence in the midst of opposition from enemies has shaped an intimate relationship between YHWH and the Davidic ruler, so that these epithets carry the first-person singular pronoun: my strength and my salvation. Verses 4–6 use the typical language of lament and thanksgiving songs in the Psalter. God has delivered the ruler from the constricting powers of Sheol, the realm of the dead. God has rescued the ruler from the place of no return, the snares and torrents of death. The Davidic kings faced historical enemies such as the Philistines in the Samuel narrative. The song of thanksgiving characterizes these enemies as powers of chaos and evil and the crisis as urgent. The king cried for divine help, and YHWH heard and answered from the Jerusalem temple. Psalm 18 is the king's praise and thanksgiving to YHWH for this salvation.

Verses 7–19 narrate the deliverance in terms of a theophany, an appearance of God. The standard description of a theophany for ancient Israel was on Mount Sinai, with the divine presence manifested in earthquakes, thunder, clouds, and lightning. In this psalm, God is pictured as making quite an entrance in a mysterious chariot on the wings of the wind. YHWH comes powerfully because of the attack on the anointed Davidic ruler. The description of theophany in verses 7–15 is classic for the Hebrew scriptures; the creator and sovereign of the universe has appeared in full

---

[52] E. S. Gerstenberger, *Psalms, Part 1* (1988), 100.

majesty. And the purpose of the divine appearance is to reach down and deliver the king from the overwhelming powers of enemies and death. The king was at the edge of the place of no return, but the powerful one who comes in theophany plucked him from the deluge and put him in a broad place for life itself. God delivered this chosen one from the powers of death.

Verses 20–30 articulate a rationale for this divine deliverance in terms of the relationship between God and king. The king's claim is one of righteousness in verses 20–24. Those who are reading the book of Psalms in order will be familiar with such a claim; it is in line with those in previous psalms (Psalms 1, 5, 7, 15, and 17, for example). "Righteousness" in the Psalms is not a self-righteousness that claims to be perfect. It is rather a claim to faithful living in a relationship initiated by God and characterized by faithfulness to God's instruction. This section of the psalm talks about living in line with God's *torah*. Importantly, the king's faithfulness reflects God's faithfulness, and so the remainder of the section portrays God as a God of steadfast love and integrity (v. 25). Verses 25–30 operate on contrasts between God and the king on the one hand and the evil enemies on the other. God brings light in the midst of darkness, and protection in the midst of battles that the king faces. The affirmation is a trust in divine refuge for the Davidic ruler. The promise in verse 30 reminds one of the promise of royal victory in Psalm 2 and perhaps remembers David's victories in battle.

Verses 31–45 sing a song of victory as a demonstration of the characteristics of God articulated in the opening praise of Psalm 18. Complete victory in battle is possible because of God's preparation of the king. The preparation and victory belong to God. The defeat is complete; the enemies are reduced to dust and mud. With poetic imagery characteristic of the Psalter, the song celebrates God as the complete victor over opponents. Verses 43–45 call to mind King David's victories narrated in the Deuteronomistic History. The psalm makes clear that God is faithful to the promise of royal victories for the Davidic king articulated in Psalm 2. The song praises and thanks God for delivering the king from enemies in battle.

Verses 46–50 bring the psalm to a close with a vibrant hymn of praise for the God who delivers, called "the God of salvation" in verse 46, and the hymnic description of the God who delivers continues in verses 47–48. The section begins with the exclamation "The Lord lives!" The other ancient Near Eastern idols are not the deities who act to save; it is ancient Israel's YHWH who acts to deliver. The concluding verses vow renewed praise and thanksgiving to the God who makes victory possible as a demonstration of loyal love to the chosen Davidic ruler, God's anointed one. The term is "messiah," God's anointed or chosen one, usually the Davidic king in the Psalms. Interestingly, by the time the first three books of the Hebrew Psalter came to a final form, there was no king in ancient Israel. The anointed one in Psalm 18, described in the psalm's heading as YHWH's servant, faces defeat but is delivered by YHWH. The psalm is a part of the Davidic tradition in the Hebrew scriptures. Its setting in the Hebrew Psalter attests to the view that Davidic hopes continued to feed hope in the ancient community even after the fall of the Davidic kingdom. The focus of the psalm, however, is on YHWH as the one who delivers in the midst of trouble. The figure of the king in the psalm demonstrates faith in this God in line with the royal ideal in Deut 17:14–20.

Bridging the Horizons: In the Fray

The captivating poetry of Psalm 18 crafts a stunning confession of faith in the living God. As creator of the universe, this God hears the cry of a petitioner hard-pressed by enemies and intervenes with a powerful display of divine presence. YHWH reaches down into the very depths of death to rescue the Davidic ruler, who faces defeat. YHWH fulfills the royal promise of rule over the nations. The psalm reflects the powerful cries for help in the lament traditions; the thanksgiving offered to God in Psalm 18 is equally extravagant.

The psalm's powerful portrayal of God as victor will strike some contemporary readers as problematic. This God is powerful but also violent and warring. The focus in the context of the Psalms is a covenant theology in which God relates to the faithful and the oppressed as the one who comes to deliver. The description of God certainly partakes of its ancient Near Eastern setting, but the focus of the psalm is on YHWH as the one who fulfills the promise of salvation for David and his descendants as well as the faithful who cry to YHWH for help. This God is in the fray. We have already noted that the psalm has implications beyond the Davidic line. The king is representative of the person journeying in faith, and the petition calls readers of the psalm to faith in this God who delivers, perhaps even to join this God in the fray on behalf of those in need. Such a faith affirmation flies in the face of contemporary empirical evidence, but the psalm's faith is a persistent one, even if troubling.

A Closer Look: Two Approaches to Hebrew Poetry

Treatments of Psalm 18 provide a look at two different approaches to the Hebrew poetry of the Psalms. Hans-Joachim Kraus constructs an original text with the aid of 2 Samuel 22 and with the assumption that the meter of the psalm usually exhibits three beats in each line.[53] In contrast, Robert Alter considers the relationships between the lines of the poem for the purpose of constructing a sense of the psalm as a whole, the narrative impulse of the text. Alter measures an artful poem, often with the use of catchwords, which confesses powerful faith.[54]

---

[53] H.-J. Kraus, *Psalms 1–59* (1988), 254–256.
[54] R. Alter, *Art of Biblical Poetry* (1985), 29–38.

PSALM 19 – TO THE LEADER. A PSALM OF DAVID

¹ The heavens are telling the glory of God;
   and the firmament proclaims his handiwork.
² Day to day pours forth speech,
   and night to night declares knowledge.
³ There is no speech, nor are there words;
   their voice is not heard;
⁴ yet their voice goes out through all the earth,
   and their words to the end of the world.

In the heavens he has set a tent for the sun,
⁵ which comes out like a bridegroom from his wedding canopy,
   and like a strong man runs its course with joy.
⁶ Its rising is from the end of the heavens,
   and its circuit to the end of them;
   and nothing is hidden from its heat.

⁷ The law of the LORD is perfect,
   reviving the soul;
the decrees of the LORD are sure,
   making wise the simple;
⁸ the precepts of the LORD are right,
   rejoicing the heart;
the commandment of the LORD is clear,
   enlightening the eyes;
⁹ the fear of the LORD is pure,
   enduring for ever;
the ordinances of the LORD are true
   and righteous altogether.
¹⁰ More to be desired are they than gold,
   even much fine gold;
sweeter also than honey,
   and drippings of the honeycomb.

¹¹ Moreover by them is your servant warned;
   in keeping them there is great reward.
¹² But who can detect their errors?
   Clear me from hidden faults.

¹³ Keep back your servant also from the insolent;
   do not let them have dominion over me.
Then I shall be blameless,
   and innocent of great transgression.

¹⁴ Let the words of my mouth and the meditation of my heart
   be acceptable to you,
   O LORD, my rock and my redeemer.

"I take this to be the greatest poem in the Psalter and one of the greatest lyrics in the world."[55] The history of critical scholarship on Psalm 19 is not in line with those words of C. S. Lewis, for many scholars have divided the psalm into two with the suggestion that verses 1–6 form a creation psalm and verses 7–14 a psalm on *torah*. The exposition that follows will treat the two parts of the psalm, but the approach here will suggest that the psalm is an artistic unit and at least proceed in dialogue with Lewis's response to the poem. The opening verse announces the theme of Psalm 19 – the revelation of God – seen first in creation and then in divine instruction. In that sense, the psalm is thematically unified and offers readers appetizing food for thought. It may well be that the poet has taken up readily available poetic elements in praise of the sun god to show that ancient Israel's God is the creator of the sun. The Babylonian sun god is Shamash; the Hebrew for sun is *šemeš*. The words use the same root consonants. At that level, the poem engages in polemic and articulates praise to the living God as creator. The two parts of the psalm share vocabulary, and it is commonly suggested that the sun, so prominent in the first part of the psalm, is in the ancient Near East associated with order and justice, themes that accord well with the second part of the psalm. The psalm begins with divine revelation in creation and narrows to greater specificity with the sun. The revelation becomes even more specific with YHWH's *torah*. The psalm then reaches a climax with a concluding prayer, especially in its familiar last verse. The description suggests that the psalm is a structure of intensification and thus a remarkable unit. This description suggests the possibility of considering the psalm in three parts rather than two. The movement is from the skies of creation to the divine instruction and finally to the worshiper. The heavens display knowledge; God reveals the *torah* that brings wisdom; and the speaker petitions that spoken words will be pleasing to God. The movements are paralleled with the psalm's allusions to the divine as El (God), then YHWH, and then "my rock and my redeemer." The psalm's poetic imagery is also of one piece. God gives the sun that makes light, and God's instruction gives light (v. 8). The sun rejoices, and divine instruction also brings rejoicing. Nothing can hide from the sun's heat, and

---

⁵⁵ C. S. Lewis, *Reflections on the Psalms* (New York: Harcourt, 1958), 63.

the concluding prayer seeks forgiveness from "hidden faults." We will consider the poem in terms of a journey in divine revelation.

The psalm is a hymn of praise, though with a rather distinctive form. It begins with praise of the creator and then the giver of *torah*, and concludes with a petition. Psalm 19 is the second hymn of praise in the Psalter; Psalm 8 is also a creation hymn. Our psalm is placed among royal psalms (Psalms 18, 20, and 21), perhaps suggesting that the king attend to the divine revelation in creation and *torah*.

Verses 1–6 of the psalm focus on creation. The opening verse pictures the heavens and the firmament (sky) as revealing the divine glory and handiwork. The term used for God is El, an ancient Near Eastern term for the high god. The glory of God has to do with a manifestation of divine presence and activity in the world. In Psalm 18, the divine revelation came through a theophany. In Psalm 19, the revelation is by way of creation. The first verse is a fine example of Hebrew poetic structure, with the second line echoing the first, only with more specificity. The lines exhibit a chiastic relationship.

> The heavens – are telling – the glory of God;
> and the work of God's hands – proclaims – the sky. (v. 1)

This divine revelation covers both day and night. Verses 3–4 suggest an interesting paradox. The heavens proclaim God, but there is no sound. This "unheard sound" persists through all of creation and is open for all. The poetic language in verses 1–4 could be described as excited. The verses provide food for the lively imagination in confessing that the sky reveals God to all.

The imagery continues through verse 6 and becomes more specific with a personification of the sun. The picture is of the sun rising and leaving a tent. The sun comes out like a bridegroom coming from the wedding tent and running the course of the day like a hero. The sun covers the whole of creation and joyfully so; nothing can hide from its heat. Even if one cannot see God's revelation in the sky, one can feel the heat of the sun. The sun is a part of God's creation; indeed the sun as part of the creation proclaims the glory of God.

The second part of the psalm moves to the glory of God in *torah*. Verses 7–9 consist of six poetic lines portraying God's instruction and its benefits. The reader gets an extensive and varied view of God's instruction. The effect of verses 1–6 also suggests that the *torah* has a universal dimension reaching to all of creation, as does the sun. This second part of the psalm suggests that divine revelation becomes more specific in relating to the human community. The term in the first line of verse 7 is *torah*, divine instruction, guidance, or direction for living. *Torah* is here characterized as whole or complete ("perfect" in the NRSV). *Torah* renews or restores life. Divine decrees are also trustworthy and teach wisdom and maturity. God's upright precepts bring joy, and God's commandment brings light. Verse 9 speaks of the enduring "fear of the Lord." The term suggests awe and reverence for YHWH;

whom one reveres, one obeys. That is how the term fits in this poetic celebration of the divine instruction. The characterization of "the fear of the Lord" is in terms of purity, a term used to describe the priestly declaration of purity in Leviticus. The second line of verse 9 speaks of God's just instructions as true and righteous. God's instruction becomes a means to righteousness – right relationship with God worked out in right human relationships. The imagery continues in verse 10 with the comparison of divine instruction to what is of utmost value and sweetness. Later in the Psalter, Psalm 119 greatly expands this poetic meditation on *torah*.

The final four verses of the psalm conclude with a tone of meditation on the divine instruction. The just decrees of YHWH warn the servant; the term "your servant" suggests a close relationship. Attention to the divine instruction has consequences for the life of faith. This warning brings to mind for the poet "hidden faults" and the hope that they can be forgiven. The petitioner here at the conclusion of the psalm hopes for forgiveness and a journey toward maturity, and so prays that arrogant enemies will not lead the petitioner astray. That is the common interpretation of the first part of verse 13, though a translation in terms of arrogant acts of rebellion against God is also possible. The concluding verse prays that the psalmist's words and meditations will be "acceptable," the term frequently used of sacrifices (Lev 22:17–20). These words and meditations become a sacrifice to YHWH, "my rock and my redeemer." In the Holiness Code, the redeemer is the next of kin who redeems a person out of dire circumstances. In Psalm 19, the creator of the universe is in the end the petitioner's next of kin, who makes possible a direction for living.

Bridging the Horizons: The Gift of Creation, the Gift of Torah

Psalm 19 begins with praise of the creator of the creation. In an age of ever-increasing technology in the Western world, the attitude of many is how to exploit nature for human convenience. The militant consumerism of contemporary society feeds off of that attitude. The psalm imagines the world as a divine creation and so suggests the question of how humans can best be stewards of this gift. In that sense, the psalm carries an environmentalist tone. In the poetic imagination of this psalm, both creator and creation relate to humans. The poetic movement is from the creation, to divine instruction, to a concluding petition. Women and men are created to be part of God's creation and not independent from it. With the sequence of creation-*torah*-petition, the poetic model suggests that readers live in response to divine direction. Poetic meditation on divine instruction leads to prayer. The poetic model is not unlike the narrative in Genesis 2–3 in which YHWH creates woman and man and provides instruction. The human response is of considerable consequence. The divine instruction purposes life, healthy community life in hope. In that sense, *torah* is a delightful gift, part of the creator's provision for full living.

PSALM 20 – TO THE LEADER. A PSALM OF DAVID

¹ The LORD answer you in the day of trouble!
  The name of the God of Jacob protect you!
² May he send you help from the sanctuary,
  and give you support from Zion.
³ May he remember all your offerings,
  and regard with favor your burnt sacrifices.
      Selah

⁴ May he grant you your heart's desire,
  and fulfil all your plans.
⁵ May we shout for joy over your victory,
  and in the name of our God set up our banners.
May the LORD fulfil all your petitions.

⁶ Now I know that the LORD will help his anointed;
  he will answer him from his holy heaven
  with mighty victories by his right hand.
⁷ Some take pride in chariots, and some in horses,
  but our pride is in the name of the LORD our God.
⁸ They will collapse and fall,
  but we shall rise and stand upright.

⁹ Give victory to the king, O LORD;
  answer us when we call.

This psalm, commonly grouped among the "royal psalms," divides into two main parts, with an additional petition in the concluding verse. The longer, opening section of the psalm consists of a series of statements that could be rendered in the optative or in the simple indicative future (vv. 1–5). When rendered in the optative (as in the NRSV), the statements amount to wishes or petitionary prayers, perhaps uttered in temple liturgy. If rendered in simple indicatives, the statements function as a series of assurances. Either way, they concern the king mentioned as "anointed" in verse 6; such statements anticipate the success of the king's venture when supported by the power of YHWH.

This series of statements in verses 1–5 mentions the "Lord" and "the name of the God of Jacob" in verse 1 as the addressees of wish or prayer. This double address is echoed in characteristic fashion at the conclusion of the section, with mention of "name of our God" and "Lord." The statements in between in verses 2–4 rely on divine promises, and they clearly refer to the God identified in verses 1 and 5. The petitions, wishes, or assurances (depending on the translation) appeal to a series of strong verbs identifying YHWH's characteristic actions of rescue and solidarity. The lead verb "answer" recurs in the second section of the psalm (v. 6) as well as in the concluding praise (v. 9). Thus we may take "answer" as a leitmotif of the psalm. It is the prayer of a people (or a king) that articulates need with an expectation that YHWH will respond to need and to the petition in decisive and saving ways.

Between the twofold mention of YHWH in verse 1 and verse 5, we may identify two motifs. In verses 2–3, the petition is grounded in temple theology. It is understood that divine help will come from Zion, YHWH's royal residence. In that residence, moreover, the God of the regime is mindful of the king's public acts of piety and will respond on that basis; see Amos 1:2. The second motif in verses 4–5 suggests that the theme of the psalm is war. The king is off to battle; this is a temple liturgy mobilizing YHWH's aid to Israel's military. The dual theme of *temple and war* suggests the way in which this psalm is a characteristic "God and country" utterance that assures YHWH's readiness on behalf of Israel's armies.

It is on the basis of this series of wishes or prayers that we come to the second section of the psalm, a more intense and confident assertion of divine help for the king in Jerusalem (vv. 6–8). This section begins with "now" (*attah*), as though the previous petitions have evoked this second voice in the psalms; or perhaps we are to hypothesize that after verse 5 there is a divine oracle of assurance to which verse 6 is the response.

In any case, the speaker is now confident, a confidence reflected in some manuscripts by the absolute infinitive, "I really know." The new certitude concerns royal victory (*ys'*), a term already used in verse 6. In verse 2, the speaker imagines that divine help will come "from Zion"; here help is from "his holy heaven" (v. 6). This dual usage reflects the ongoing difficulty in Israel's temple theology about the place of divine presence. But, either way, the God present and holy is available to help in decisive ways.

The confident asseveration of verse 6 is reinforced in verses 7–8. In verse 7, the contrast is between "our pride" in "the name of YHWH"; thus an appeal to the divine name on the one hand and pride in armaments on the other. The contrast is between those who count on YHWH and those – "unlike us" – who rely solely on human arms and weapons. This contrast between faith and armaments, which is stated in absolutist terms, is reflected in the theology of the book of Isaiah as well as Israel's wisdom tradition:

> For thus said the Lord God, the Holy One of Israel:
> In returning and rest you shall be saved;
> in quietness and in trust shall be your strength.
> But you refused and said,

"No! We will flee upon horses" –
therefore you shall flee!
and, "We will ride upon swift steeds" –
therefore your pursuers shall be swift! (Isa 30:15–16)

No wisdom, no understanding, no counsel,
can avail against the Lord.
The horse is made ready for the day of battle,
but the victory belongs to the Lord. (Prov 21:30–31; see Zech 4:6)

Verse 8 in the psalm draws a conclusion that contrasts "we" and "they," *we* who follow the king messiah and trust in the name of YHWH and *they* who trust in armaments. Each subject receives two verbs: "we" rise and stand; "they" collapse and fall. These verses thus contain a critique of military self-sufficiency and offer an alternative in faith that does not seek to master history by force.

The final verse offers a concluding petition. It addresses YHWH on behalf of the king (anointed) and reiterates the dual accent on *answer* (see vv. 1, 6) and *victory* (vv. 5, 6). The "day of trouble" in verse 1 is answered in verse 9 by "day of our calling"; that is, the day of prayer is directly the day of trouble and need beyond the king's own resources. It is because the king (and Israel) have chosen reliance on YHWH rather than on self that Israel can be confident of divine help in this state emergency. Read in a jingoistic way, this psalm can be heard as an appeal to God to support the "war effort" of the Jerusalem establishment. Read more carefully, however, it may be exactly a protest against such an easy equation of God and war. The God who inhabits the temple and who answers from Zion is a transcendent God, not one domesticated to "reasons of state."

Bridging the Horizons: Thinking about Power

Writing about this psalm in the midst of the U.S. military occupation of Iraq suggests that the psalm may be immediately contemporary. There is no doubt that the psalm is a petition, a hope, and a wish that God's power will assure the victory of the political-military leader in Jerusalem. Of course, there is no obvious parallel between ancient Israel and the contemporary hegemonic power of the United States. It is the case, however, that verse 7 may be a chastening for military power that is exercised in the interest of political and economic autonomy.

It is of course possible, as in some other hermeneutical stances, that the occupation of Iraq is understood as a holy crusade sanctioned by the God of the Bible. The military dimension of political leadership invites acute interpretive questions about the interface between the power of God and human power exercised through the state. There is no doubt that this psalm lives close to jingoistic patriotism, but is sobered by the choice between "pride" here and "pride" in verse 7.

Bridging the Horizons: Piety

Whereas the psalm reflects a *royal context* with a *military threat*, the piety that permeates this psalm is an awareness that petition when in need is a proper stance of faith before God. The prayer is not offered in anxiety or desperation, but in confidence that YHWH's "victory" will be decisive in the real world. This is the piety that trusts in the assurance, "Ask and it will be given."

Bridging the Horizons: Watchful Waiting?

The contrast in verse 7 between those who are proud of weapons and those who boast in the name of YHWH calls to mind the famous exchange between H. Richard Niebuhr and Reinhold Niebuhr in the 1930s. H. Richard Niebuhr warned against an overzealous Christian activism in the public affairs of the world and urged a "watchful waiting" that is rooted in God's hidden, providential governance.[56] Such "inactive Christianity" urged by Niebuhr is not to be confused with the inactivity of frustration and moral indignation. Of the kind of inactive Christianity that Niebuhr commends, he writes, "While it does nothing, it knows that something is being done, something that is divine both in its threat and in its promise."[57] This judgment would, we have no doubt, be accepted by the voice of verse 7, which trusts in the decisive power of the divine name.

In answer to H. Richard Niebuhr, Reinhold Niebuhr agrees with much of that verdict,[58] except in his response Reinhold Niebuhr resists any romantic or Utopian passivity in an ethic of pure love. Reinhold Niebuhr would be more inclined than the psalmist to put some faith in military capacity. We cite the exchange of the Niebuhrs to indicate that the stark either/or of the psalmist persists as an urgent question even among us today.

PSALM 21 – TO THE LEADER. A PSALM OF DAVID

1 In your strength the king rejoices, O Lord,
  and in your help how greatly he exults!
2 You have given him his heart's desire,

---

56 H. Richard Niebuhr, "The Grace of Doing Nothing?" *Christian Century* (March 30, 1932), 378–380.
57 H. R. Niebuhr, "The Grace of Doing Nothing?" *Christian Century* (March 30, 1932), 379.
58 Reinhold Niebuhr, "Must We Do Nothing?" *Christian Century* (March 30, 1932), 415–417.

and have not withheld the request of his lips.
>   *Selah*
3 For you meet him with rich blessings;
>   you set a crown of fine gold on his head.
4 He asked you for life; you gave it to him –
>   length of days for ever and ever.
5 His glory is great through your help;
>   splendour and majesty you bestow on him.
6 You bestow on him blessings for ever;
>   you make him glad with the joy of your presence.
7 For the king trusts in the LORD,
>   and through the steadfast love of the Most High he shall not be moved.

8 Your hand will find out all your enemies;
>   your right hand will find out those who hate you.
9 You will make them like a fiery furnace
>   when you appear.
The LORD will swallow them up in his wrath,
>   and fire will consume them.
10 You will destroy their offspring from the earth,
>   and their children from among humankind.
11 If they plan evil against you,
>   if they devise mischief, they will not succeed.
12 For you will put them to flight;
>   you will aim at their faces with your bows.

13 Be exalted, O LORD, in your strength!
>   We will sing and praise your power.

This psalm is bracketed by references to the "strength of YHWH" in verses 1 and 13. The psalm is a celebration and affirmation of YHWH's strength as it is exhibited in the public affairs of Israel and as it is acknowledged in the Jerusalem temple. The strength of YHWH, however, is brought into play much more concretely by reference to the king in verses 1 and 7. In verses 8–12, moreover, the repeated pronoun "you" apparently refers to the human king and the ferocious military actions of which the king is capable. This psalm nicely juxtaposes a series of "you" verbs in verses 1–7 referring to YHWH and in verses 8–12 referring to the king. That juxtaposition focuses on the military agenda of the king but situates that royal agenda amid the splendor, power, and sovereignty of YHWH, who is the ultimate source of strength. This human enterprise (in the person of the king) is vigorously subordinated to the power of YHWH, who is grandly celebrated in the final doxology of verse 13. J. Clinton McCann can say, "everything that can be said about the king begins and ends with God's strength."[59]

The initial doxology of YHWH in verses 1–7 celebrates the initiative YHWH has taken toward the king in giving the king everything necessary for secure and majestic life in Jerusalem. The pronoun "you" (referring to YHWH), coupled with active verbs, constitutes the substance of these verses. The recital amounts to an extended expression of thanksgiving for YHWH's generous, life-giving support of the king and the royal establishment. The psalm is deeply and gratefully moved by YHWH's capacity in making royal power in Jerusalem what it is:

> You have given ...
> You have not withheld ...
>   You meet ...
>   You set ...
>   You gave ...
>   You bestow ...
>   You bestow ...
>   You make ...

The king is clearly the recipient, not the agent, of all things good. The request of the king in verse 4 likely is reminiscent of Solomon's dream petition (1 Kgs 3:11), and even the king's glory is derived from YHWH's action (v. 5). These verses altogether imagine a flourishing, impressive royal establishment, but all is gift and not royal achievement. The unit culminates in verse 7 with a cluster of important terms. The king's role is to trust YHWH and rely on YHWH's support and help. The basis of royal trust is YHWH's abiding fidelity (*ḥesed*). That old covenantal term, however, is juxtaposed with the divine appellation Elyon, perhaps a generic title linked to older Jerusalem traditions (see Gen 14:19–20). The outcome of the whole is that the royal establishment in Jerusalem, because of divine fidelity, will not be threatened or destabilized.

The psalm shifts tone and address abruptly in verse 8. Now the "You" is apparently the king, who is now celebrated as a fierce and effective military leader:

> Your hand will find your enemies ...
> Your right hand will find out ...
> You make ...
> You destroy ...
> You put to flight ...
> You aim.

---

[59]   J. C. McCann, Jr., "Book of Psalms," in L. E. Keck et al. (eds.), *The New Interpreter's Bible*, vol. 4 (1996), 757.

All of these actions refer to military prowess and success. The recital is interrupted only twice. In verse, YHWH is mentioned once in a way that suggests YHWH's decisiveness in and through royal activity, so that even when the king succeeds, it is YHWH who "swallows in anger." The other interruption in verse 11 is quite incidental, for the reference to "they," the enemy, is only a counterpoint to royal success.

The most interesting issue in this psalm is the relationship between the two parts, verses 1–7 featuring YHWH and verses 8–12 celebrating the king. A prominent hypothesis is that between verses 7 and 8 there was the announcement of a divine oracle in the temple that gave assurance of victory to the king. This would account for the shift and fits with what we know elsewhere of divine oracles. It also illuminates why the psalm, after the affirmation of the king, returns in verse 13 to celebrate YHWH's muscular power (*geborah*). The imperative verb of verse 11 is a bid for new divine intervention in a military context:

One should not translate, "Be thou exalted!" The emphatic form of the imperative transforms the request into a rude command. The psalmist pronounces a military order of critical urgency.[60]

This psalm is focused on military success by the Jerusalem government and readily assures that the enemies of Jerusalem are the enemies of YHWH. Read as military cant, the psalm effectively draws YHWH into Davidic military adventure. Read as political critique, the psalm decisively makes the king penultimate and dependent on divine initiative. Either way, the psalm shows how an intense and convinced liturgical community can connect the awesome rule of YHWH with the "facts on the ground." There is a long-standing practice of giving the psalm a Christological reading, wherein Christ is the victor over the demonic powers of death:

The doctrine of the everlasting duration of the kingdom of Christ is, therefore, here established, seeing he was not placed upon the throne by the favour or suffrages of men, but by God, who, from heaven, set the royal crown upon his head with his own hand.[61]

This particularly applies to the kingdom of Christ, which is never without enemies in this world. True, it is not always assailed by open war, and there is sometimes granted to it a period of respite; but the ministers of Satan never lay aside their malice and desire to do mischief, and therefore they never cease to plot and to endeavour to accomplish the overthrow of Christ's kingdom.[62]

There is denounced against the enemies of Christ a destruction like that which God in old time sent upon Sodom and Gomorrah. That punishment was a striking and memorable example above all others of the judgment of God against all the wicked, or rather it was, as it were, a visible image upon earth of the eternal fire of hell which

60 S. Terrien, *Psalms* (2003), 223.
61 J. Calvin, *Commentary on the Book of Psalms*, vol. 1 (1979), 346.
62 J. Calvin, *Commentary on the Book of Psalms*, vol. 1 (1979), 350–351.

is prepared for the reprobate: and hence this similitude is frequently to be met with in the sacred writings.[63]

Such a reading, well established in the church, is a considerable stretch for the reiterated military accents of the psalm itself.

A Closer Look: Trust and Steadfast Love

It is likely that the psalm focuses theologically in verse 7, wherein the *trust* of the king is responsive to the *steadfast love* of the Lord. The word "trust" (*bth*) means to rely on YHWH's power in circumstances of threat and anxiety. Reference will usefully be made to Isaiah 36, wherein Hezekiah is under assault from the Assyrian armies. The taunting speech of the Assyrians in Isa 36:4–10 revolves around the word *batah*, which is variously translated in the NRSV as "confidence" and "rely." In the end, Hezekiah is vindicated as a king who does indeed place utter confidence in YHWH even in a situation of military danger. Josiah, the grandson of Hezekiah, moreover, is celebrated as the one who does indeed trust in YHWH. In 2 Kgs 23:25, he is saluted as the one who kept the Torah of Moses and as the one who trusted YHWH with all of his heart. It may well be that Psalm 21 was particularly appropriate during the reigns of Hezekiah and/or Josiah, kings who seriously engaged the Yahwistic dimension of their power.

PSALM 22 – TO THE LEADER: ACCORDING TO THE DEER OF THE DAWN. A PSALM OF DAVID

1 My God, my God, why have you forsaken me?
  Why are you so far from helping me, from the words of my groaning?
2 O my God, I cry by day, but you do not answer;
  and by night, but find no rest.

3 Yet you are holy,
  enthroned on the praises of Israel.
4 In you our ancestors trusted;
  they trusted, and you delivered them.
5 To you they cried, and were saved;
  in you they trusted, and were not put to shame.

---

63 J. Calvin, *Commentary on the Book of Psalms*, vol. 1 (1979), 353.

⁶ But I am a worm, and not human;
  scorned by others, and despised by the people.
⁷ All who see me mock at me;
  they make mouths at me, they shake their heads;
⁸ 'Commit your cause to the Lord; let him deliver –
  let him rescue the one in whom he delights!'

⁹ Yet it was you who took me from the womb;
  you kept me safe on my mother's breast.
¹⁰ On you I was cast from my birth,
   and since my mother bore me you have been my God.
¹¹ Do not be far from me,
   for trouble is near
   and there is no one to help.

¹² Many bulls encircle me,
   strong bulls of Bashan surround me;
¹³ they open wide their mouths at me,
   like a ravening and roaring lion.

¹⁴ I am poured out like water,
   and all my bones are out of joint;
my heart is like wax;
   it is melted within my breast;
¹⁵ my mouth is dried up like a potsherd,
   and my tongue sticks to my jaws;
   you lay me in the dust of death.

¹⁶ For dogs are all around me;
   a company of evildoers encircles me.
My hands and feet have shrivelled;
¹⁷ I can count all my bones.
They stare and gloat over me;
¹⁸ they divide my clothes among themselves,
   and for my clothing they cast lots.

¹⁹ But you, O Lord, do not be far away!
   O my help, come quickly to my aid!
²⁰ Deliver my soul from the sword,
   my life from the power of the dog!
²¹ Save me from the mouth of the lion!

From the horns of the wild oxen you have rescued me.

²² I will tell of your name to my brothers and sisters;
in the midst of the congregation I will praise you:
²³ You who fear the LORD, praise him!
All you offspring of Jacob, glorify him;
stand in awe of him, all you offspring of Israel!
²⁴ For he did not despise or abhor
the affliction of the afflicted;
he did not hide his face from me,
but heard when I cried to him.

²⁵ From you comes my praise in the great congregation;
my vows I will pay before those who fear him.
²⁶ The poor shall eat and be satisfied;
those who seek him shall praise the LORD.
May your hearts live for ever!

²⁷ All the ends of the earth shall remember
and turn to the LORD;
and all the families of the nations
shall worship before him.
²⁸ For dominion belongs to the LORD,
and he rules over the nations.

²⁹ To him, indeed, shall all who sleep in the earth bow down;
before him shall bow all who go down to the dust,
and I shall live for him.
³⁰ Posterity will serve him;
future generations will be told about the LORD,
³¹ and proclaim his deliverance to a people yet unborn,
saying that he has done it.

Because of the citation of Ps 22:1 in the Passion narrative of Matt 27:46 and Mk 15:34, this psalm is the best-known lament among Christians. Indeed, for many it is the only lament psalm known or used at all. Before we consider the citation of the psalm in the Passion narrative of Jesus, we must consider it in its Old Testament venue.

This psalm, a classic example of a psalm of lament, is readily divided into two parts: the complaint of the speaker in trouble (vv. 1–21a) and praise and thanksgiving after the resolution of the trouble (vv. 21b–31). We shall consider each section in turn.

The lament of verses 1–21a moves through the highly stylized elements of that most characteristic of all of Israel's prayers. It begins with a statement of intimacy: "My God, my God." Such prayers of complaint and petition are characteristically prayed not by strangers but by those with a long history of positive interaction with YHWH. Indeed, in this case that long history has likely included promises of fidelity on the part of YHWH to the psalmist and his community. For that reason, the initial address of verse 1 is immediately followed in verses 1 and 2 with an accusation that YHWH, who promised to stand in solidarity with Israel, has in fact abandoned it. The first part of the psalm proceeds on the assumption of divine abandonment and aims, in ways that are characteristic in Israel, to mobilize YHWH to re-engage on behalf of this helpless petitioner. Calvin, among many interpreters, has seen how this double phrase, "My God, my God … why hast thou forsaken me?" contains a remarkable contradiction; Calvin, however, suggests that although the psalmist comes close to despair, in the end this is corrected by faith:

Faith, lest he should when so severely tried sink into despair, put into his mouth a correction of this language, so that he boldly called God, of whom he thought he was forsaken, his God. Yea, we see that he has given the first place to faith. Before he allows himself to utter his complaint, in order to give faith the chief place, he first declares that he still claimed God as his own God, and betook himself to him for refuge.[64]

Through verses 3–21, we are able to identify three conventional rhetorical maneuvers: *motivation, complaint,* and *petition.* They are conventional in Israel's prayer and are uttered, moreover, in the conviction that when YHWH reengages the life of the petitioner, all will be well.

Verses 3–5 offer a motivation to YHWH, a reason why YHWH should pay attention to this desperate petitioner. YHWH is reminded of times past when Israel (amid which this petitioner is located) was in need and trusted YHWH; and YHWH was seen to be trustworthy. This motivation appeals to precedent and asks YHWH to do now yet again what YHWH has done in times past. The assumption of the petition is that YHWH can be motivated out of dormancy by appeals to YHWH's own trustworthy past to do YHWH's characteristically faithful action yet one more time.

After the motivation, verses 6–7 offer a complaint, a portrayal of the desperate situation of the speaker. Informed by three derogatory terms – scorned, despised, mocked – the speaker is abased and ashamed, and reduced in terms of social identity to a subhuman condition. In that condition of shame, the petitioner is helpless in the face of ridicule. The hyperbolic rhetoric is, on the one hand, a candid self-portrayal without restraint. On the other hand, it is assumed that such a portrayal may move YHWH to act, for YHWH does not want any of YHWH's people to be

---

[64]   J. Calvin, *Commentary on the Book of Psalms,* vol. 1 (1979), 359.

ridiculed. The petition assumes that YHWH has a stake in the rescue and so is humiliated alongside the humiliation of the petitioner.

The psalm reverts to motivation in verses 9–10, only this time the case is made that the life of the speaker was at YHWH's initiative and therefore YHWH has continuing responsibility for that life. This divine obligation is matched by the speaker's complete attachment to YHWH, who is "my God," the one accusatorily addressed in verses 1–2. In both verses 3–5 and verses 9–10, the motivation draws YHWH into the trouble and states in demanding ways that YHWH is implicated in the crisis and is required by previous commitments to act for the well-being of the speaker.

Only now, in verse 11, do we come to the first petition of the psalm. The psalm has delayed this long in asking anything specific of YHWH. The petition is only one brief phrase: "Do not be far from me." The remainder of the verse is an additional reinforcing motivation that underscores the urgency of the request. The petition for nearness suggests that it is YHWH's remoteness and detachment that have permit-ted the trouble to occupy the void left by divine absence. From such a verdict of *absence*, clearly it is the sought-after *nearness* of YHWH that will turn a circum-stance of trouble to one of well-being. Fredrik Lindström has shown in persuasive ways that the absence of YHWH and the hoped-for presence of YHWH are deeply related to temple theology.[65] It is in the temple that the saving presence of YHWH is known and where the void of absence is most acutely felt. Lindström moreover has noted that in the petition of verse 11, as in the later petition of verse 19, the plea for *presence* is linked to the possibility of *help*. Thus help is mediated through, and known primarily in, temple presence.[66]

After the initial petition of verse 10, the psalm offers a long complaint charac-terizing an acute jeopardy articulated in astonishingly hyperbolic language (vv. 12–18). In verses 12–13, this extended complaint characterizes the adversaries as bulls, or alternatively as lions, in either case as aggressive, rapacious agents of destructiveness. Verses 14–15 describe physical deterioration of the speaker, the "I" of the speaker afflicted in bones, heart, breast, mouth, tongue, and jaws. As Aubrey Johnson has shown in his demarcation of "synecdoche," each element of the body signifies the whole of the self, so that each item in the biological inventory is yet another mark of the loss of the self.[67] A culmination of these verses in the last line is a direct address of accusation against "you" (=YHWH), who causes death to the speaker. This accusation echoes the initial charge of abandonment in verse 1. The failure of YHWH's fidelity alleged here exposes the unprotected psalmist to the disintegrating powers of death.

---

[65]   F. Lindström, *Suffering and Sin* (1994), 75–80.
[66]   F. Lindström, *Suffering and Sin* (1994), 77.
[67]   Aubrey Johnson, *The Vitality of the Individual in the Thought of Ancient Israel* (Cardiff: University of Wales Press, 1949), 40 and passim.

In verses 16–18, the complaint continues, naming the adversary as a company of evildoers, denigrating them as "dogs." In this utterance, the trouble is not caused by YHWH in verse 15; it is, however, the inattentive absence of YHWH that permits the "dogs" to work their destructiveness. This band of adversaries already imagines the speaker as dead (see v. 15) and is busy dividing up among themselves what is left by the deceased.

These three quite distinct images of rapacious adversaries (vv. 12–13), personal, physical disintegration (vv. 14–15), and social treatment "as good as dead" (vv. 16–18) in sum portray a condition of misery, helplessness, and complete social failure. The psalmist voices desperate need for a life exposed, unprotected, and in acute jeopardy.

In verses 19–21a, the psalmist issues a final petition that echoes verse 10. Remarkably but characteristically, Israel in jeopardy addresses YHWH, the very same YHWH who has been accused of absence (vv. 1–2) and destructiveness (v. 15). Indeed Israel has nowhere to turn except to that God it has found fickle, in the deep and insistent hope that the fickle God can yet again be summoned to fidelity; it is only YHWH's faithful, intrusive action that can turn deathly jeopardy back to life. Thus the address in all its abruptness is demanding: "But you YHWH" (v. 19). This is the same direct pronoun already employed in parallel in verse 3 ("Yet you") and in verse 9 ("Yet it was you"). The independent pronoun "you" (*attah*) evidences Israel's daring to name, identify, and address YHWH, calling YHWH to account and affirming that the God known to be fickle is the God nonetheless capable of transformative intervention. It is this God who is "my help," indeed my only help. So also in verse 11, "There is no one to help"; no one, that is, except YHWH, who may yet be mobilized to act. The petition features four imperatives and contrasts YHWH with "the power of the dog" (see v. 16) and "the mouth of the lion" (see v. 13):

Do not be far away (see v. 10),
    for it is YHWH's remoteness that permits dogs, bulls, and lions to operate
  in their destructiveness;
Come quickly,
    from where you have been in remoteness;
Deliver … from the power of the dog;
Save … from the mouth of the lion.

The speaker, even in shame, misery, and disarray, can still muster large and demanding imperatives: "Do not be far from me. Come quickly, deliver, save!" Now the complaint is ended, a massive appeal with ample motivation that encompasses both accusation and hope. The entire utterance of verses 1–21a is the exercise of intense candor, surely with immense risk to be so exposed at the throne of the holy one.

But then, in midverse, the psalm changes abruptly. Something decisive has happened, for now the speaker voices no more distress but only amazement and gratitude. Whatever one may make of the psalm, one cannot avoid the conclusion of a deep break in the rhetoric, reflecting a changed and restored relationship. As elsewhere in the Psalter, the most plausible explanation is that an authorized divine oracle has been uttered, giving assurance of YHWH's attentive concern for the speaker. Such an explanation is given cogency by the statement in verse 21b, "from the horns of wild oxen you have answered me." (In the NRSV, the verb is translated as "rescued.") Thus it is most plausible that *a divine answer* has been given to the freighted complaint just completed.

The outcome of the transformation caused by divine response is a new situation about which the speaker will gladly "tell" (v. 22). The verb "tell" means to narrate, and can sometimes positively mean "narrate the good news," which in Christian parlance amounts to "reiterate the gospel." Thus the narration that follows is the witness the speaker bears to a situation of need that is now completely transformed by YHWH's new manifestation of fidelity, which effectively turns death to life.

This speaker, like every person who receives an inexplicable new start in well-being, cannot keep silent but must share with others "the good news." Ellen Davis has shrewdly noted that the audience for such news is moved in ever-expanding concentric circles from the smallest to the largest imaginable.[68]

Initially the "telling" is to "my brothers" (and sisters), perhaps the most intimate circle of family. This is in parallel to "the assembly," perhaps the most immediate community of worship. That community is invited by the speaker to share the wonder and amazement of the speaker and to join in praise of YHWH. Verse 24 specifies (as if we did not already know) the reason for all to praise. YHWH has heard and answered. YHWH did not reject the petitioner or remain hidden as in verses 1–2. Praise celebrates YHWH's effective fidelity and solidarity.

The circle of praise is expanded in verse 25 to "the great congregation," perhaps a larger or more socially significant assembly. Praise and thanks characteristically are not only verbal but also include "a payment of vows." Probably it was usual in seasons of distress to pledge a special offering or contribution to YHWH upon deliverance, and now the speaker remembers the pledge and gladly meets the obligation. Such a vow paid "in kind" here is utilized for a great festival meal to which the poor are invited (see Deut 14:28–29):

This substrophe looks forward to a feast in which the famished shall eat and be sated. Not only shall the poor be fed, but a eucharistic meal shall go beyond the succor offered to the homeless: the race of Israel will no longer exclude the *goyim*. The holy people, even at the extremities of the earth, will be, outside of genealogy or ritual conversion, "those who seek the Lord" (v. 27). It will include "all the families of nations."[69]

---

68   Ellen Davis, "Exploding the Limits: Form and Function in Psalm 22," *JSOT* 53 (1992): 93–105.

69   S. Terrien, *Psalms* (2003), 234.

This gratitude and praise addressed to YHWH has concrete expression in "neighbor love," so that others may also benefit from the divine miracle of restoration.

The circle of praise and thanks is extended "to the ends of the earth" (v. 27), well beyond Israel. Here the speaker imagines that all people everywhere will take this concrete miracle of deliverance as a sign and assurance of YHWH's sovereignty. In this doxological phrasing, the particular and intimate miracle of rescue is transposed into a hymn of enthronement, the sort of rhetorical formula found in the great temple liturgies (see Psalm 96; Ps 145:13).

In verses 29–31, finally, the scope of praise encompasses all those *already dead* who now fully acknowledge YHWH's rule (v. 29) and those *not yet born* in all coming generations (vv. 30–31). Thus the sweep of praise and gratitude is as all-inclusive as the poet can possibly imagine. But that of course is characteristic of Israel's liturgical logic, in which the most *concrete act of YHWH's goodness* becomes a source of *cosmic joy* and well-being.

The sweep of this psalm as a characteristic drama of faith in the life of Israel is astonishing. It begins in *abandonment* (vv. 1–2) and ends in *resounding doxology* (v. 25), a transposition made possible by an *answer of rescue* from the God who is no longer absent. Everything turns, so it seems, on the candor of the psalmist and on the relentless insistence of the psalmist (a) that the present circumstance is unacceptable and (b) that YHWH is capable of transformation if and when YHWH is mobilized. The entire community of humanity – even the dead and the yet-to-be-born – gather around the speaker to attest that neither the speaker nor the world is ever left to its own resources. Finally, it is YHWH and not circumstance that constitutes the substance of reality to which Israel gladly attests.

It is not difficult to trace the movement of the psalm or to identify its several rhetorical elements. Finally, however, our interpretive energy should be on the parts, as they constitute a dramatic whole, for the entire drama poses the deepest interpretive *questions* and offers the richest *affirmations* of faith.

Two questions arise from the drama of this psalm. First, is it true that YHWH can come and go, can be present and then absent, and consequently be with people and then abandon them? Of course, conventional theology, in its appeal to the metaphysics of the classical tradition, refuses such a characterization of YHWH. It is clear nonetheless that in the Psalter an account is given of lived reality that takes place through a dangerous drama of give and take in which YHWH is a player in the entire tension of fidelity and infidelity. Israel is thereby free to attest to its *experience* of divine abandonment and to take it at face value as a theological point. Conventional theology is wont to say that God "seems" to abandon, but Israel will not allow YHWH that luxury, knowing that such a "seems" immediately introduces the pretend theology of Docetism. Israel trusts its experience, from which grows its theological attestation; Israel will not curb that attestation to its own experience of abandonment, even in defense of YHWH.

Second, is Israel free and unrestrained in its capacity to voice its conviction of divine abandonment? This psalm, among others, makes clear that Israel uses no-holds-barred rhetoric to attest its conviction about YHWH. Orthodoxy places no curbs on Israel's rhetoric. Such utterances, moreover, not only characterize such a reality of divine absence but do so in an accusatory tone, assuming that Israel is entitled to richer fidelity from YHWH than it readily experiences.

Alongside such questions, two affirmations are central to this faith. First, Israel trusts that serious, engaged petition will indeed mobilize YHWH to salvific action that YHWH would not otherwise undertake. Thus the petition of verses 1–21a does evoke some divine response, apparently an oracle of salvation. Such prayer is not play-acting but is life-or-death engagement with YHWH, who is thereby summoned from infidelity to fidelity, from absence to presence.

The second affirmation is that YHWH, the God who has been absent, can be again present in decisive, transformative, life-giving ways. The psalmist has no other source of help (v. 10) and needs none; YHWH is fully able and sufficient even to "the dust of death" (v. 15). Thus the dramatic movement of the psalm is not only a rhetorical pattern but a normative theological affirmation for Israel concerning the God who comes into circumstances of death and gives new life. It is because of this God that sorrow is turned to joy:

Very truly, I tell you, you will weep and mourn, but the world will rejoice; you will have pain, but your pain will turn into joy. (Jn 16:20)

The psalm begins in abandonment, where many prayers in Israel begin, an experience of divine abandonment that gives rise to passionate prayer. A loss of Jerusalem and the sixth-century displacement become for Israel the quintessential moment of divine abandonment, and we imagine this and many psalms like it in such a context. In its massive lament over Jerusalem, Israel can conclude:

Why have you forgotten us completely?
Why have you forsaken us ['*azav*] these many days? (Lam 5:20)

That assault on YHWH is, to be sure, countered in a prophetic oracle that quotes Lam 5:20 in order to refute it:

But Zion said, "The Lord has forsaken me,
    my Lord has forgotten me."
Can a woman forget her nursing child,
    or show no compassion for the child of her womb?
Even these may forget,
    yet I will not forget you. (Isa 49:14–15)

In this oracle, YHWH refuses the accusation and asserts divine innocence and fidelity. Alongside that claim, however, the same poetry offers an acknowledgment on the part of YHWH:

For a brief moment I abandoned you. (Isa 54:7)
In overflowing wrath for a moment
I hid my face from you. (Isa 54:8)

Here divine abandonment is acknowledged out of YHWH's own mouth, though it is asserted that compassion and not abandonment is the final divine intent. Thus our psalm is best understood in a larger context as part of a deep issue that preoccupied Israel concerning divine fidelity.

A Closer Look: "My God, My God, Why Have You Forsaken Me?"

This psalm is of special interest for Christian readers because Jesus quotes verse 1 from the cross (Matt 27:46; Mk 15:34). Scholarship is divided on the question of whether the words derived from Jesus are from early church tradition, but in the text itself they are given as Jesus' own words. Taken as the gospel text stands, the quotation is a measure of the total abandonment known by Jesus on the cross. The quotation permits no sugar-water triumphalism about the crucifixion of Jesus, for Jesus is the righteous sufferer who knows divine abandonment. It is often proposed that the quotation of verse 1 permits us to infer that the gospel tradition intends us to reckon here with the entire poem and not just verse 1. Such an inference thus would read verses 1–21a as a full articulation of *the crucifixion of Jesus* and verses 21b–31 as a move in the drama toward *the resurrection of Jesus*. Such an inference is legitimate as long as it is not used to tone down the raw aloneness of verse 1, a raw aloneness essential to any serious "theology of the cross." Thus the bereftness of Jesus must be given full voice, just as the culmination in praise must not in the psalm itself be permitted to subvert the raw candor of verses 1–21a. This psalm, in its Old Testament usage and on the lips of Jesus, concerns real suffering, real abandonment, and real death. That there is more is the surprise of the rhetoric and a miracle of YHWH.

Bridging the Horizons: Righteous Suffering and *The Crucified God*

This abandonment of Jesus on the cross – given voice through the psalm – is congruent with the bereftness of every righteous sufferer. For a Christian understanding of the crucifixion of Jesus, the cry from the cross is to be understood as a defining theological point. For that reason, Jürgen Moltmann, in *The Crucified God*, has made the quotation of verse 1 central to his theme. Following Luther, Moltmann sees that the cry on the cross, in the words of Psalm 22, yields a theology of the cross that is centered on the father's abandonment of the son.[70] Moltmann, however, insists that the cry must be taken

---

[70] Jürgen Moltmann, *The Crucified God: The Cross of Christ as the Foundation and Criticism of Christian Theology* (New York: Harper and Row, 1974), 208.

in Trinitarian fashion so that the abandonment of the son extends to the father as well:

What is Ps. 22 lamenting, and what in his turn is the dying Jesus lamenting? The prayer of the Old Testament itself is not lamenting the speaker's own fate in a mood of self-pity, but in the words of the psalm is calling upon the faithfulness of God, which as a righteous man he is defending. Psalm 22 is a legal plea. Jesus is not calling for the compassion of God upon his own person, but for the revelation of the righteousness of the God who promised "not to forsake the work of his hands." Abandoned by God, the righteous man sees God's deity itself at stake, for he himself is the faithfulness and honour of God in the world. And therefore the prayer of Ps. 22 calls upon the faithfulness of God for God's sake. Likewise, the cry of Jesus, as interpreted by Ps. 22, is not one of self-pity and an expression of personal distress, but is once again a call upon God for God's sake, a legal plea. However, unlike the speaker in Ps. 22, Jesus is not just making a claim upon the faithfulness of the God of Israel to his covenant, as he had promised to the whole people; in a special way he is laying claim upon the faithfulness of his Father to himself, the Son who has taken his part. In the words "My God, why hast thou forsaken me?" Jesus is putting at stake not only his personal existence, but his theological existence, his whole proclamation of God.[71]

The only way past protest atheism is through a theology of the cross which understands God as the suffering God in the suffering of Christ and which cries out with the godforsaken God, "My God, why have you forsaken me?" For this theology, God and suffering are no longer contradictions, as in theism and atheism, but God's being is in suffering and the suffering is in God's being itself, because God is love.[72]

To understand what happened between Jesus and his God and Father on the cross, it is necessary to talk in trinitarian terms. The Son suffers dying, the Father suffers the death of the Son. The grief of the Father here is just as important as the death of the Son. The Fatherlessness of the Son constituted himself as the Father of Jesus Christ, then he also suffers the death of his Fatherhood in the death of the Son.[73]

It is clear that the citation becomes a central piece in the mystery of evangelical faith whereby *the abandonment of Friday* becomes the venue for *the new life of Easter Sunday*. That move from Friday to Sunday, definitional for Christian faith, reflects precisely the dramatic movement and structure of the psalm itself.

---

[71]   J. Moltmann, *The Crucified God* (1974), 150–151.
[72]   J. Moltmann, *The Crucified God* (1974), 227.
[73]   J. Moltmann, *The Crucified God* (1974), 243.

PSALM 23 – A PSALM OF DAVID

¹ The LORD is my shepherd, I shall not want.
² He makes me lie down in green pastures;
he leads me beside still waters;
³ he restores my soul.
He leads me in right paths
  for his name's sake.

⁴ Even though I walk through the darkest valley,
  I fear no evil;
for you are with me;
  your rod and your staff –
  they comfort me.

⁵ You prepare a table before me
  in the presence of my enemies;
you anoint my head with oil;
  my cup overflows.
⁶ Surely goodness and mercy shall follow me
  all the days of my life,
and I shall dwell in the house of the LORD
  my whole life long.

This most familiar and most beloved psalm invites us to a rich play of imagery. The predominant metaphor of the psalm is, of course, God as shepherd. Although some scholars believe that the metaphor of shepherd is carried through the entire psalm, it seems more plausible to us that in the latter part of the psalm the imagery shifts from God as shepherd to God as generous host and giver of hospitality. In between the imagery of the good shepherd in verses 1–3 and the conclusion with hospitality in "the house of the Lord," verses 4–5 suggest protection during dangerous travel. It is of course possible, as Terrien suggests, that the dangerous traveler is a flock of sheep who are at risk in narrow ravines and dangerous pathways. All of these images converge into a statement of the buoyant trustworthiness of YHWH in the face of every circumstance, so that the speaker of the psalm is confident and serene in the face of every threat.

The imagery of shepherd-sheep is featured clearly in verses 1–3, with the sheep giving testimony about the good shepherd. While the metaphor is carried out in some detail, it is important to recognize that "shepherd" is a term used in the ancient world to refer to a king whose task it is to protect and provide for the subjects of the realm. It is likely that the psalm is not idyllic and romantic as is often interpreted; rather, the psalmist speaks out of a context of deep danger and articulates confidence in YHWH as the one who will keep the flock safe and protected in the face of every danger.

The imagery is pervaded by political nuance. The sheep as subject gladly attest exclusive loyalty and exclusive reliance on YHWH and then tell why. Calvin observes that the sheep are presented as those "who willingly abide in his sheepfold and surrender themselves to be governed by him."[74] Calvin's comment on this claim stresses not the role of the shepherd but the immense faith of the sheep. The generous provision of YHWH as shepherd means that there are no needs, deficits, or deficiencies, as these words from the hymn "Great Is Thy Faithfulness" testify:

All that I've needed thy hand hath provided;
Great is thy faithfulness, Lord unto me.

The shepherd provides for the sheep good pasture grass; safe, secure water; and safe, protected paths. That of course is all a sheep could ever need. The opening line of verse 3 is a bit curious and seems to affirm that YHWH "revives my life." Terrien translates the verse as "He causes me to come back," the statement of a victim of exhaustion as a result of the vicissitudes of dangerous territory.[75] We may picture a sheep living without water or grass, exposed to wild animals, and therefore at risk. This protective, attentive shepherd changes all of that, and the sheep is given a life of well-being. The rendering "soul," familiar as it is, introduces a religious motif that seems alien to the imagery itself. The final phrase of verse 3, "for his namesake," means that by such care for the sheep the shepherd establishes a good reputation as a reliable shepherd. He will be well thought of by other shepherds, and no doubt the word will get around to other sheep, who will want to be under his care. When this is taken as a theological affirmation, the text seems to assert that YHWH's attentiveness to Israel will be so attractive that it will draw other nations to the worship of YHWH as well.

The imagery shifts somewhat in verses 4–5, though it is not impossible that the sheep still speaks. More likely, the voice is that of a traveler in a culture where roads were not at all safe (see, for example, the risks of Ps 90:11–13 and Ps 123:3–8); entry into "death valley" is indeed ominous. The phrase, which has been variously translated, clearly refers to a high-risk exposure that makes the traveler exceedingly vulnerable. The imagery likely does not refer in the first instance to hidden powers of death, though of course it can be heard that way in belated pastoral circumstances. The remarkable conviction of the psalmist is that the protective presence of YHWH

---

[74]   J. Calvin, *Commentary on the Book of Psalms*, vol. 1 (1979), 392.
[75]   S. Terrien, *Psalms* (2003), 392.

overrides every threat along the way. This central statement of confidence is given us in two terse lines:

> I will fear no evil
> because you are with me. (v. 4)

This affirmation would seem to be a transposition of a familiar salvation oracle also present in Psalm 22. Such oracles regularly state, as in Isaiah:

> Do not fear,
> for I am with you. (Isa 41:10)

That oracle is characteristically on the lips of YHWH; in the psalm, however, it has moved to the lips of the speaker, but the assurance is the same. YHWH vetoes every threat and every fear, and thereby makes life safe.

This core affirmation is followed in quick order by four explanatory comments that tell why there is no fear on the part of the speaker:

- The tools of the shepherd (rod and staff) give comfort and assurance by providing strength and protection for the vulnerable sheep.
- The protective God feeds the trusting subject, even in a hostile environment.
- Oil may be used as a healing ointment for wounds that are acquired on the dangerous paths.
- The subject experiences luxurious extravagance in a context of threat, danger, and death.

On all counts, this generous, trustworthy portrayal of YHWH is more than a match for every threat and every adversity. The assurance of divine presence and protection is perhaps not unlike another context of potential anxiety in the teaching of Jesus:

> For it is the Gentiles who strive for all these things; and indeed your heavenly Father knows that you need all these things. (Matt 6:32)

In the last verse of this psalm, the traveler perhaps arrives at a safe destination, which turns out to be "the house of the Lord"; that is, the Jerusalem temple. In retrospect, the psalmist is able to recognize that "goodness and fidelity" have been "in pursuit of him"; this remarkable verb suggests that the subject thought he was being pursued by dangers and threats, but in fact it was the providential goodness of God that was what had been following him and chasing after him. The alternative life made possible by such divine pursuit concerns the generous God of creation (goodness) and the faithful God of covenant (fidelity), who has been the subject's companion all along the way. On reflection, the traveler is able to conclude that to sojourn in the safe environment of the table, the place of YHWH's most intense presence, is the fulfillment of life. The sheep who "lack nothing" in verse 1 is the traveler in verse 6, who sees that YHWH is fully satisfying and nothing else is needed or desired:

> Whom have I in heaven but you?
>   And there is nothing on earth
>   that I desire other than you. (Ps 73:25)

The sense of the entire psalm is that of a calm assurance and abiding trust, all the while alert to the reality of threat that is kept in check by the faithful God. This poem is a clear statement of how the God of Israel functions decisively to counter all circumstances. It is this faith that permits Paul to assert:

> If God is for us,
> who is against us? (Rom 8:31)

And the vigorous answer of faith is: nobody of any consequence is against us!

A Closer Look: The King-Shepherd

The fullest exposition of the imagery of the shepherd is offered in the prophetic discourse of Ezekiel 34. It is asserted in verses 2–6 that it is the failure of kings in Jerusalem to exercise the protective care of a shepherd that has produced the exile in Israel. Given the failure of the monarchy, YHWH then resolves to exercise "direct rule" in the place of the monarch. The resolution of YHWH provides an inventory of what a good king-shepherd will do. That inventory is not unlike the assurance given in this psalm:

> For thus says the Lord God: I myself will search for my sheep, and will seek them out.... I myself will be the shepherd of my sheep, and I will make them lie down, says the Lord God. I will seek the lost, and I will bring back the strayed, and I will bind up the injured, and I will strengthen the weak, but the fat and the strong I will destroy. I will feed them with justice. (Ezek 34:11, 15–16)

It is remarkable that after the divine assertion of direct rule, YHWH proposes a new David as shepherd:

> I will set up over them one shepherd, my servant David, and he shall feed them; he shall feed them and be their shepherd. And I, the Lord, will be their God, and my servant David shall be prince among them; I, the Lord, have spoken. (Ezek 34:23–24)

This belated promise in its original context perhaps anticipates the restoration of the monarchy. More broadly, it permits the expectation of a "coming shepherd," an expectation that Christian interpretation has readily connected to Jesus.

A Closer Look: The Sheep of His Hand

The imagery of the shepherd-sheep was available for Israel's liturgy. Psalm 95:1–7a likely reflects a liturgical entry into a place of worship. The community gathers willingly and gladly identifies itself as the "sheep of his hand":

> O come, let us worship and bow down,
>   let us kneel before the Lord, our Maker!
> For he is our God,
>   and we are the people of his pasture,
>   and the sheep of his hand. (Ps 95:6–7)

Worship thus is an exercise of finding safety, nurture, and well-being as gifts of YHWH; conversely, worship is an opportunity to reflect on the claim that nothing is lacking for the community that trusts the good shepherd.

Bridging the Horizons: The Shepherd and the Pastor

The move from Ezekiel 34 and Psalm 23 into the New Testament is readily made in John 10 (see also Luke 15:3–6). Thus the entire imagery of YHWH as "good shepherd" is here redeployed as a characterization of Jesus. On the one hand, it is Jesus as shepherd who assures abundant life (v. 10). One can see that the ministry of Jesus in healing and feeding is a replication of the provision of grass, water, safe paths, and life in the psalm.

   Conversely, the sheep that belong to this shepherd "know his voice" (v. 4), trust him, rely on him, and obey him.

   The imagery of the shepherd provides a fresh way to think about the work of a "pastor" as shepherd of the flock, one who nurtures, feeds, and protects. The office of pastor in Christian tradition is authorized by Jesus and is urgent in a world filled with many "valleys of the shadow of death."

PSALM 24 – OF DAVID. A PSALM

1 The earth is the Lord's and all that is in it,
   the world, and those who live in it;
2 for he has founded it on the seas,
   and established it on the rivers.

³ Who shall ascend the hill of the LORD?
  And who shall stand in his holy place?
⁴ Those who have clean hands and pure hearts,
  who do not lift up their souls to what is false,
  and do not swear deceitfully.
⁵ They will receive blessing from the LORD,
  and vindication from the God of their salvation.
⁶ Such is the company of those who seek him,
  who seek the face of the God of Jacob.
      Selah

⁷ Lift up your heads, O gates!
  and be lifted up, O ancient doors!
  that the King of glory may come in.
⁸ Who is the King of glory?
  The LORD, strong and mighty,
  the LORD, mighty in battle.
⁹ Lift up your heads, O gates!
  and be lifted up, O ancient doors!
  that the King of glory may come in.
¹⁰ Who is this King of glory?
   The LORD of hosts,
   he is the King of glory.
      Selah

The crucial interpretive move for readers of Psalm 24 is to find a way to relate the three parts of the psalm. The psalm begins with characteristic hymnic praise (vv. 1–2) and then moves to an entrance liturgy reminiscent of Psalm 15 (vv. 3–6). The psalm concludes with a question-and-answer litany that many interpreters associate with a procession of the Ark of the Covenant (vv. 7–10). Imaginative readers often construct an ancient cultic setting for the psalm and in that way find the poem's unity. Often the setting begins with a procession that includes entering the sanctuary as well as the initial confession of faith in the form of praise. The celebration of both creation and divine kingship are combined with an emphasis on the place of the sanctuary. Such attempts to construct an ancient setting for the psalm are helpful in the interpretive task.

The poem's theological perspective is also instructive. The beginning of the psalm (vv. 1–2) and the concluding part (vv. 7–10) both celebrate the divine victory over chaos. The middle section of the poem (vv. 3–6) addresses the question of who may enter into this celebration. A connection between creation and sanctuary also suggests thematic unity in the psalm. Characteristic of ancient Near Eastern creation texts, Genesis and Exodus tie the completion of the tabernacle to the completion of creation. The two are also connected in Psalm 24. This psalm also continues a theme from Psalm 23: the hospitality and provision of YHWH. In Psalm 24, YHWH provides life and a sanctuary for the community.

The psalm begins in the first two verses with the hymnic affirmation that the world belongs to YHWH. The word order suggests an emphasis on YHWH and no other. It was this God and no other who created the world and did so by subjugating the powers of chaos, represented by the seas and rivers (v. 2) in the ancient Near Eastern context. Craig C. Broyles names them Prince Sea and Judge River.[76] No other idol or power has conquered these powers of chaos but YHWH. That is the emphasis of the opening word of praise. It is YHWH – and not chaos or the Baals – who is sovereign over the creation, and YHWH has tamed chaos and brought order to the world. Such words of praise suggest that neither idols nor human rulers absolutize their authority. It is YHWH who has created the world in an orderly way. The poetic form of these opening verses is also noteworthy. The first line of verse 1 affirms that the world and everything in it belong to the creator. The second line affirms a parallel of greater specificity by affirming that the people who inhabit the world belong to the creator. The lines of verse 2 echo each other; the first line begins with the emphatic personal pronoun and thus continues the emphasis on YHWH. Psalm 24 thus begins with a vibrant word of praise, with each line contributing to the affirmation of faith in the creator.

The second part of the psalm (vv. 3–6) ties the opening affirmation of creation to the sanctuary. "The hill of the Lord" and "his holy place" indicates the sanctuary or temple. The Jerusalem temple was symbolic of the Creation and the order YHWH brought to it. The ancient setting of these verses is similar to that reflected in Psalm 15. Pilgrims on the way to the sanctuary ask in verse 3 who is qualified to enter the holy place to worship. The response comes in verses 4–6, with instructions about who is prepared for worship. The response gives a prophetic tone to the psalm, for the qualifications for entering the sanctuary are ethical rather than ritual. Verse 4 puts those moral qualities in the positive first – "clean hands and pure hearts." Both actions and intentions are part of the equation that is based on integrity rather than deception. The second part of the verse puts the matter in the negative – avoiding commitment "to what is false" and avoiding oaths motivated by deception. "What is false" may refer to false gods, so the instruction is for good and not evil, for a life of integrity. Worship and other dimensions of life are to match. So within the first four verses of the psalm, the movement is from creation to sanctuary and from order, rather than chaos, in creation to moral order. The instruction continues with the observation in verse 5 that those who match their lives of worship and integrity experience God as the one who is present to bless; that is, the one who makes possible the power to grow and thrive in the world. They also experience God as the

76   C. C. Broyles, *Psalms* (1999), 128.

one who comes to deliver and so initiate a right divine–human relationship (righteousness) as part of the worshiping community. Such a relationship is a divine gift. Verse 6 summarizes this section as a characterization of those who worship God; they are people of moral integrity. To seek God and to seek the face of God are terms indicating worship. Such a community of those who worship the mysterious creator is characterized by moral integrity.

When readers reflect on the relationship of the middle section of the psalm (vv. 3–6) to the psalm's opening word of praise (vv. 1–2), the middle section envisions a community shaped by the creator praised in the psalm's opening words. On that basis, the community relates to both God and neighbor in ways characterized by integrity. That same perspective characterizes the Decalogue (Exodus 20) and so fits the ethical tradition of the Hebrew scriptures. In Psalm 24, the ethical character of the community is set as preparation for entering the sanctuary, the special place of divine presence. Again, the tie between worship and ethics is significant.

Interpreters often connect the concluding section of the psalm (vv. 7–10) with the Ark of the Covenant and David's bringing the Ark to Jerusalem in festive procession (2 Samuel 6). Some suggest that this part of the psalm is a reenactment of that event. Apparently the procession of worshipers addresses the gates and doors of the sanctuary. The gates and doors are addressed so that "the King of glory may come in." The lifting up is a sign of victory, and so the hope is that the King will enter with splendor, majesty, and power. Then comes the question, "Who is the King of glory?" The answer is King YHWH, the mighty warrior. Then, in powerful fashion, the litany is repeated with the address to the doors and gates and the question and answer to bring a climactic end to the poem: the victorious YHWH of armies; he (with the emphatic personal pronoun) is the King of glory! "The Lord of hosts" is a familiar divine title. Who are the hosts? They could be the angelic heavenly hosts or the heavenly hosts of the sun, moon, and stars. The preceding rendering of YHWH of armies suggests the hosts of the armies of ancient Israel as appropriate for a battle context. The psalm thus concludes with the powerful and victorious King YHWH, who is able to deliver, having begun with God as creator (vv. 1–2). In the concluding section of the psalm (vv. 7–10), the victorious one enters the palace, the temple, the sacred place of divine presence in the psalms. The middle section of the psalm (vv. 3–6) attends to the worshiping community of this sovereign God.

Bridging the Horizons: A Confession that Transforms Life

The poetic voices in Psalm 24 praise YHWH as creator and king. This God is powerfully present in the sanctuary in Jerusalem. The opening and closing sections of the psalm sandwich verses 3–6, which relate to a human community of faith and worship. This God who tames chaos and is present in Zion in life-giving ways offers a life of integrity, most fully nurtured in the worship at the sanctuary. Another way to put the matter is that the confessions in the first and last parts of the psalm affirm that YHWH is creator and sovereign. That confession transforms life for the community that worships YHWH. In response, the community is called to wholeness and integrity. King YHWH establishes life with its order and its hope, and gives life to the community. The psalm sings of the connotations of that confession. In a sense, the community sings itself toward faith; the song makes it possible to imagine life differently. Christian tradition has used the psalm to celebrate the advent of God in the triumphal entry of Jesus into Jerusalem and in the triumph over death, especially on Ascension Day.

PSALM 25 – OF DAVID

¹ To you, O Lord, I lift up my soul.
² O my God, in you I trust;
   do not let me be put to shame;
   do not let my enemies exult over me.
³ Do not let those who wait for you be put to shame;
   let them be ashamed who are wantonly treacherous.

⁴ Make me to know your ways, O Lord;
   teach me your paths.
⁵ Lead me in your truth, and teach me,
   for you are the God of my salvation;
   for you I wait all day long.

⁶ Be mindful of your mercy, O Lord, and of your steadfast love,
   for they have been from of old.
⁷ Do not remember the sins of my youth or my transgressions;
   according to your steadfast love remember me,
   for your goodness' sake, O Lord!
⁸ Good and upright is the Lord;
   therefore he instructs sinners in the way.
⁹ He leads the humble in what is right,
   and teaches the humble his way.
¹⁰ All the paths of the Lord are steadfast love and faithfulness,
   for those who keep his covenant and his decrees.

¹¹ For your name's sake, O LORD,
   pardon my guilt, for it is great.
¹² Who are they that fear the LORD?
   He will teach them the way that they should choose.

¹³ They will abide in prosperity,
   and their children shall possess the land.
¹⁴ The friendship of the LORD is for those who fear him,
   and he makes his covenant known to them.
¹⁵ My eyes are ever toward the LORD,
   for he will pluck my feet out of the net.
¹⁶ Turn to me and be gracious to me,
   for I am lonely and afflicted.
¹⁷ Relieve the troubles of my heart,
   and bring me out of my distress.
¹⁸ Consider my affliction and my trouble,
   and forgive all my sins.

¹⁹ Consider how many are my foes,
   and with what violent hatred they hate me.
²⁰ O guard my life, and deliver me;
   do not let me be put to shame, for I take refuge in you.
²¹ May integrity and uprightness preserve me,
   for I wait for you.

²² Redeem Israel, O God,
   out of all its troubles.

This psalm is a characteristic psalm of petition, seeking YHWH's intervention in a circumstance of need and jeopardy. Its primary point of interest is its acrostic form; thus its twenty-two verses move through the alphabet, each verse beginning with the next letter of the alphabet. It is likely the psalm's acrostic structure that gives it a rather diffuse and disconnected quality.

At the beginning (vv. 1–3) and at the end (vv. 16–21), the psalm is a characteristic utterance of need and petition, permeated with imperatives that address YHWH. In between, as a counterpoint (vv. 4–15), is a more reasoned reflection on faith, marked by sapiential themes and cast in an instructional tone. We may identify five themes in the psalm:

1. The speaker is in a dire emergency but relies completely and confidently on YHWH's capacity and willingness to intervene to rescue him. The tag

word for this *confidence* is the term "wait" (vv. 3, 5, 21), which bespeaks eager longing and powerful expectation. The psalmist fully anticipates that YHWH answers prayer and is capable of wondrous rescue.

2. The grounds for hope in the psalm is confidence in *YHWH's steadfast love*, YHWH's readiness to be reliable for the sake of the petitioner and his ilk in Israel. The term steadfast love (*ḥesed*) occurs three times (vv. 6, 7, 10); in verse 6, the term is coupled with "mercy," and in verse 10 it is paired with a characteristic word partner, "faithfulness." The three terms together – mercy, steadfast love, faithfulness – refer to YHWH's deep promises to Israel and to the house of David, which gave Israel a basis for well-being, even in a world of threat. (See Lam 3:22–23 for the same triad and Ps 89:24, 33 for the recurring word pair bespeaking YHWH's commitment to Israel.)

3. The speaker attests that he is an *eager covenant-hoper who is fully devoted to YHWH* and to YHWH's commands. Thus YHWH's goodness is toward covenant-keepers (vv. 10, 14). The conclusion of the appeal in verse 21, moreover, echoes the word for "integrity and righteousness," which were the terms that characterized Job as the quintessential pious man (see Job 1:9; 2:3). The speaker is among those who "fear YHWH" (vv. 12, 14), who closely adhere to YHWH, and who therefore rightly anticipate a good future of well-being in the land as a consequence of that covenant status.

4. It is curious that this assertion of commitment to YHWH is matched, or perhaps countered, by a *confession of sin and an acknowledgment of way-wardness* (vv. 7, 8, 11, 18). Thus the psalmist not only attests to faith but acknowledges failed faith and sees pardon and forgiveness. A declaration of integrity and a confession of sin constitute no debilitating contradiction in the life of faith.

5. Thus *the themes of fidelity and failure are juxtaposed*; together they indicate the thick and complex relationship that believers have with YHWH. In context, it is likely that both the themes of human fidelity and human failed faith are motivations offered to YHWH for YHWH's intervention. For the faithful, YHWH has pledged protection and well-being. For the failed, YHWH is a gracious God who restores relationships when they have failed. It is not necessary – or even possible – for the psalmist to claim a one-dimensional default on covenant, because the covenant is filled with all the trickiness of a genuine candid relationship. The intention of this psalm, in any case, is that this ambivalent attachment to YHWH is indeed voiced as an appeal to YHWH. The psalmist counts on YHWH's fidelity, which moves past the human reality of fidelity-cum-

failure. Thus the psalm voices "the human condition" but knows in powerful ways that the "human condition" can never compromise or place in question YHWH's fidelity and YHWH's resolve to save.

The hopeful petitions of verses 1–3 and 16–21 sandwich an instructional motif. It is not enough for the faithful to be in dialogue with the God who outstrips human ambiguity. It is equally urgent to inculcate others, no doubt the young, into the reality of YHWH's fidelity.

This psalm thus offers what in Christian tradition are the characteristic marks of evangelical faith. On the one hand, that faith consists in a full acknowledgment of human need, hope, and dependence. On the other hand, it affirms the full, unqualified mercy of YHWH toward the faithful. This mismatch between human ambiguity and divine singularity is the hallmark of biblical faith. It is this complete confidence in YHWH that invites the generic conclusion of verse 22. In the final utterance of the psalm, the faith of the psalmist, grounded in profound piety, is extended to the entire community, whereas the petition is to a particular circumstance, the conclusion for "all the troubles." The particular prayer of the psalmist becomes standing ground for the entire congregation of faith in all its need. The God addressed here is fully adequate for the entire spectrum of faithful life in the world.

PSALM 26 – OF DAVID

¹ Vindicate me, O Lord,
  for I have walked in my integrity,
  and I have trusted in the Lord without wavering.
² Prove me, O Lord, and try me;
  test my heart and mind.
³ For your steadfast love is before my eyes,
  and I walk in faithfulness to you.

⁴ I do not sit with the worthless,
  nor do I consort with hypocrites;
⁵ I hate the company of evildoers,
  and will not sit with the wicked.

⁶ I wash my hands in innocence,
  and go around your altar, O Lord,
⁷ singing aloud a song of thanksgiving,
  and telling all your wondrous deeds.

⁸ O Lᴏʀᴅ, I love the house in which you dwell,
  and the place where your glory abides.
⁹ Do not sweep me away with sinners,
  nor my life with the bloodthirsty,
¹⁰ those in whose hands are evil devices,
   and whose right hands are full of bribes.

¹¹ But as for me, I walk in my integrity;
   redeem me, and be gracious to me.
¹² My foot stands on level ground;
   in the great congregation I will bless the Lᴏʀᴅ.

The poem consists of five sections in a pattern common in the psalms. The opening (vv. 1–3) and concluding sections (vv. 11–12) present the petition for help, which comes to a positive resolution. Sections two (vv. 4–5) and four (vv. 9–10) relate to the enemies. Section three (vv. 6–8) stands in the central position and emphasizes the protection of the sanctuary. The psalm is a characteristic plea that YHWH will declare a verdict in favor of the petitioner rather than the opponents. The triangle of deity, petitioner, and enemies so characteristic of many of the psalms in Book I of the Psalter is on full display in this prayer, with an emphasis on the tie between YHWH and the petitioner. In the plot of the psalm, the covenant relationship between the speaker and YHWH is at stake. Verses 1, 9, and 11 suggest that the speaker faces the possibility of death itself as a result of being clumped together with those who oppose the covenant God. Some would suggest that the psalmist has been accused of some covenant-breaking offense and so faces the threat of a fearful fracture in the life-giving covenant relationship with YHWH. The psalm is thus an urgent plea for God to restore the full order of things for life rather than for death.

Psalm 26 exhibits a number of connections with previous psalms (Psalms 1, 7, 15, 17, 24) and to Psalms 27 and 28. Connections to Psalm 25 are particularly noteworthy. "Integrity" is important in both psalms (Pss 26:1 and 25:21), along with the petitioner's trust in God (Pss 26:1 and 25:2). God's steadfast love and faithfulness are central to both texts (Pss 26:3 and 25:10), along with divine grace (Pss 26:11 and 25:16) and redemption (Pss 26:11 and 25:22). Psalm 26 is a prayer for justice (v. 1), and Psalm 25 confesses that YHWH leads in just ways (v. 9). Psalm 26 is a fervent prayer, and yet in it readers of Book I of the Psalter will find themselves in familiar territory.

The opening plea in verses 1–3, set off with the verb "walk," is a double plea, with each plea followed by motivation. The opening verse introduces the entire psalm, with its prayer for justice and its unwavering confession of faithfulness by the petitioner. The first-person singular pronoun is pronounced in these verses. First the petitioner pleads for vindication from YHWH in the first person. The motivation for the plea is the life of integrity and trust the speaker ("I") has persistently pursued. The vocabulary of the prayer is both striking and characteristic of the psalms that plead for divine aid. The petitioner seeks justice on the basis of a life of integrity and trust. The plea is from a stance of righteousness, right relationship with the covenant God, a life of covenant loyalty and faith. The speaker is devoted to the covenant God and lives based on that relationship. This covenant devotion to YHWH is in response to divine constancy and trustworthiness, as verse 3 implies. The second plea partakes of the image of divine inspection of the speaker's "heart and mind." The image comes from the refining, testing, and purifying of metal. The speaker stands fully transparent to the covenant God. The core of the person stands to be tested before God; the "heart and mind" suggest the seat of the will and thus the most basic decisions for living. God's steadfast love and fidelity are ever before the petitioner; such a life of faithful living becomes the motivation for the plea that God test that life and as a result of the test bring justice to this faithful covenant partner.

With verse 4, the petitioner turns to the enemies for the sake of contrast. This section presents the other side of the confession of faithfulness claimed by the speaker in verses 1 and 3. The petitioner has nothing to do with the deceitful and wicked and their gatherings, so the contrast that is articulated is between the faithful psalmist and the enemies, who are portrayed as opposing both the psalmist and God. These enemies are characterized by emptiness and hypocrisy. The psalmist claims to have made a lifestyle decision never to participate in the gatherings of those who oppose God; the psalmist is the faithful one. The section begins and ends with this rejection of assembling with the evildoers. The chiastic structure is characteristic of Hebrew poetry:

> I do not sit with false people and with dissemblers I do not associate.
> I hate the company of evildoers and with the wicked I do not sit. (vv. 4–5)

These claims of faithfulness serve as further motivation for the psalmist's plea for justice. In the triangle of God, enemies, and psalmist, the psalmist is with God and pleads for God to acknowledge that faith.

The psalm's central section (vv. 6–8) focuses on the sanctuary and what takes place there, though the contrast with the enemies is still in view. First there is the washing of the hands to show innocence (note the reference to clean hands in Ps 24:4), followed by the procession around the altar. The procession is an opportunity to sing a *tôdāh*, a "song of thanksgiving," confessing divine activity on behalf of the covenant people. The song is a rehearsal of the mighty acts of God for salvation. Verse 8 continues with the confession of faith that the sanctuary is a place of divine presence; this confession also provides further support for the petitioner's plea. This faithful psalmist loves the sanctuary of YHWH as "the place where your glory abides," the place where divine presence and activity are seen.

The next section (vv. 9–10) furthers the prayer by returning to the enemies. These verses, along with verses 4–5, focus on the contrast between the psalmist and the wicked. The petitioner fears being counted among the wicked and thus being swept away. The psalmist's case argues for being counted among the righteous rather than the wicked, who are guilty of shedding blood and of using all manner of evil, including bribes. The portrayal of the enemies serves to heighten the contrast with the petitioner and so supports the case before the divine judge.

The psalm's concluding verses also begin with that contrast: "But as for me." In contrast to the enemies of verses 9–10, our petitioner is not guilty of the charge of breaking the covenant with YHWH. This concluding section of the psalm brings readers back to the poem's beginning and the psalmist's claim of walking or living "in integrity." The plea in verse 11 seeks release from all suspicion of evil. The contrast between the psalmist and the enemies undergirds the entire prayer, including this closing petition. The petitioner seeks to avoid the fate of the wicked. Divine grace or mercy is the basis of the hope behind the petition (v. 11). The final verse is an image of the petitioner's foot standing firm rather than slipping or stumbling, or becoming enmeshed in the traps of the wicked. The psalmist lives not among the wicked but among the gathering of those faithful to the covenant relationship with YHWH. The psalm thus ends on a hopeful note with the picture of the psalmist among the congregation of the righteous singing praise and thanksgiving to YHWH. The psalm's concluding line takes readers back to the *tôdāh*, or thanksgiving song (v. 7). The faithful worshiper will confess the greatness and presence of the covenant God as part of public worship; that is, "bless the Lord." The psalmist in these concluding verses indicates a dependence on the covenant God, a characteristic of the righteous in the psalms. The enemies or evildoers are those who assert autonomy from God. That contrast runs throughout this poem and is ever present in Book I of the Psalter. The psalmist is counted not among the wicked but among the faithful congregation worshiping YHWH and enjoying the life of faith and refuge in the sanctuary.

Bridging the Horizons: Questioning Loyalty

Psalm 26 centers on the question of loyalty to the congregation of the righteous or the gathering of evildoers. One's community shapes life. The psalm's plea is for justice, and the psalmist claims fierce loyalty to YHWH and the covenant community. The petitioner prays boldly and comes to the hope of being able to sing a song of thanksgiving, a song declaring God's saving help for the petitioner. The psalmist hopes for a life-giving encounter with the covenant God. The speaker pleads on the basis of integrity but makes it clear that the verdict is dependent on divine grace. The boldness of the prayer will trouble some readers, who might even characterize the petitioner as self-righteous. A careful reading of the psalm suggests that it is about a particular crisis and is not a claim of sinlessness. The psalmist's claim of integrity is in the end based on divine initiative in a covenant relationship. That relationship makes possible a life of integrity, a life of wholeness that is integrated rather than fragmented. Putting life together is possible for this petitioner because of the covenant relationship initiated by the covenant God. In the end, the psalmist's claim of integrity is based on a divine gift rather than on earnings from proper acts. This bold petition exhibits an intimate relationship with YHWH. The petitioner's hope is to continue in YHWH's covenant community rather than in the community of evildoers; that verdict determines life.

A Closer Look: A Liturgy for the Falsely Accused

Scholarly imaginations have constructed ancient settings for Psalm 26. The most common suggestion is that the petition comes from a setting of false accusation akin to that envisioned in 1 Kgs 8:31–32. The petitioner would come to the temple to plead a case before God and seek acquittal. E. Vogt has proposed to read Psalm 26 as an entrance liturgy along with Psalms 15 and 24, with the purpose of gaining admission to the temple in contrast to the evildoers.[77] Paul Mosca proposes that the speaker is a priest, who must wash his hands before ascending the altar or face death.[78] Although the psalm came from a particular life setting, within the Psalter it has a broader significance for the life of faith.

PSALM 27 – OF DAVID

[1] The LORD is my light and my salvation;
   whom shall I fear?
The LORD is the stronghold of my life;
   of whom shall I be afraid?

[2] When evildoers assail me
   to devour my flesh –
my adversaries and foes –
   they shall stumble and fall.

---

[77] E. Vogt, "Psalm 26, Ein Pilgergebet," *Biblica* 43 (1962): 328–337.
[78] Paul G. Mosca, "Psalm 26: Poetic Structure and the Form-Critical Task," *CBQ* 47 (1985): 223–225.

³ Though an army encamp against me,
   my heart shall not fear;
though war rise up against me,
   yet I will be confident.

⁴ One thing I asked of the Lord,
   that will I seek after:
to live in the house of the Lord
   all the days of my life,
to behold the beauty of the Lord,
   and to inquire in his temple.

⁵ For he will hide me in his shelter
   in the day of trouble;
he will conceal me under the cover of his tent;
   he will set me high on a rock.

⁶ Now my head is lifted up
   above my enemies all around me,
and I will offer in his tent
   sacrifices with shouts of joy;
I will sing and make melody to the Lord.

⁷ Hear, O Lord, when I cry aloud,
   be gracious to me and answer me!
⁸ 'Come,' my heart says, 'seek his face!'
   Your face, Lord, do I seek.
⁹ Do not hide your face from me.

Do not turn your servant away in anger,
   you who have been my help.
Do not cast me off, do not forsake me,
   O God of my salvation!
¹⁰ If my father and mother forsake me,
   the Lord will take me up.

¹¹ Teach me your way, O Lord,
   and lead me on a level path
   because of my enemies.
¹² Do not give me up to the will of my adversaries,

for false witnesses have risen against me,
and they are breathing out violence.

¹³ I believe that I shall see the goodness of the LORD
in the land of the living.
¹⁴ Wait for the LORD;
be strong, and let your heart take courage;
wait for the LORD!

Psalm 27 is an example of the honest dialogue of faith characteristic of the psalm-ists in the face of opposition. The temple and its worship are also central to the psalm, as is the case with Psalms 15, 22, 23, 24, and 26. The sanctuary is both a place of refuge and a place of renewing worship. Psalm 27 has a number of con-nections with the psalms preceding it. It exhibits military language (Psalms 18, 20, and 21) and imagery of light (Psalm 19), asks for instruction (Psalms 19 and 25), and may relate to false accusation (Psalms 17 and 26). The reference to false wit-nesses in verse 12 would support an ancient setting of a ritual brought on by false accusations. Witnesses were an important part of ancient Israel's hopes for justice. Others have suggested that the psalm is a royal liturgy. It is not unusual for several ancient settings to be constructed for such a prayer. What is noteworthy about the psalm is that its poetry resists the attempt to restrict the prayer to any one setting. The psalmist's enemies take on the quality of archetype. The open poetic language of Psalm 27 makes it appropriate for any number of settings in which believers face opposition. The psalm begins with an expression of trust and, based on that trust, petitions God for help.

1. Verses 1–3 establish the basis of the psalm in terms of *trust*. The first verse consists of two parallel affirmations followed by rhetorical questions. The verse puts before readers two alternatives for life – fear or faith. Fear, and not doubt, is cast as the alternative to faith. The two faith affirmations suggest why the poet chooses faith. YHWH is light that dispels darkness, and the one who brings wholeness (salvation) to life. The second image of the divine is "stronghold," refuge, or defense. In spite of life-threatening opponents, who appear quickly in verse 2, trust is the order of the day. The enemies are described as wild beasts who would devour their prey and then as an army rising up against the psalmist. In the face of armies and war and the onslaught of evil, the psalmist embraces trust in the mighty fortress who is the saving and protecting God. God is worthy of trust.

2. Verses 4–6 shift to imagery associated with the *temple*. Verse 4 is central to the poem in that it confirms the single-minded commitment of the psalmist; "one thing" is what is asked, and that one thing is "to live in the

house of the Lord all the days of my life." It may well be that the Jerusalem temple was a place of asylum in the face of pursuers that intend harm. Living in the house of the Lord is not a hope for permanent residence in the temple but of continuing to return to the temple to worship and "behold the beauty of the Lord"; that is, the divine presence. To inquire in the temple may refer to a request for direction in living or may refer more specifically to seeking a divine word of protection in the current crisis. Inquiring in the temple, beholding the beauty of God, and dwelling in the temple are taken to be one request: encountering the life-giving divine presence. The images of "shelter," "tent," and "rock" continue the temple imagery as a place of protection in the face of opposition. In verse 6, the lifting of the head is an indication of victory, celebrated with temple sacrifices. The sacrifice is a celebration of joy and thanksgiving accompanied by songs telling the story of God's victory, a clear confession of the psalmist's trust.

3.   Verses 7–10 are a *prayer for help* in the midst of trouble and woe. The imperatives state the petition succinctly: "hear," "be gracious," "answer," "turn not," and "cast me not off." The petition is for the hope that the divine salvation and protection in verses 1–6 will come to pass in the current crisis. The psalmist seeks the protecting divine presence (YHWH's face). The seeking of YHWH's face is worship language; it is also an indication of the intimate relationship between the petitioner and YHWH. Exodus 33:20 brings the response to Moses' request that no one may see the face of YHWH, and yet that is precisely the request of the speaker in Psalm 27. The prayer for help comes to a climax in addressing YHWH as "God of my salvation," an allusion to verse 1. The prayer is that this God will protect the petitioner even if family will not.

4.   Verses 11–14 also center on imperatives ("teach," "lead," "do not give me up") but move in a new direction with the *request that God give direction* to the poet. The imperative translated "teach" is the root word for *torah* and has to do with giving direction. This petition brings to mind the description of *torah* as a guide for the righteous in Psalm 1. The hope is that this teaching of *torah* will lead the petitioner to "a level path" in the face of enemies. The speaker seeks the same broad place of deliverance described in Ps 26:12 as "level ground." The petitioner's hope is to live by *torah* and so be included in the community of *torah* rather than the community of falsehood characteristic of the enemies, for the power of life stems from YHWH. Verse 12 characterizes the enemies as false accusers and their acts as violence. The Hebrew covenant community depended on reliable witnesses. Bearing false witness (Exod 20:16) was

taken seriously as a threat to the integrity of the community. The psalm comes to a hopeful conclusion with a further affirmation of trust in divine protection. The concluding verse is addressed to the congregation with the imperatives "wait," "be strong," and "take courage" in the hope that the community can join in trusting YHWH.

A Closer Look: One Poem or Two?

Many treatments of Psalm 27 begin with the question of whether the text is one poem or two. Verses 1–6 comprise a confession of trust and confidence and refer to God in the third person. Verses 7–14 address God in the second person in a prayer for help. Most recent commentators suggest that the psalm is a unit. There are a number of connections between the parts: "salvation" in verses 1 and 9; "adversaries" in verses 2 and 12; "heart" in verses 3, 8, and 14; "rise" in verses 3 and 12; "seek" in verses 4 and 8; and "life" in verses 4 and 13. The reading here has taken the expression of trust in the first part of the psalm as the context for the prayer in the second part.

Bridging the Horizons: An Era of Anxiety

The urgent threat in Psalm 27 makes it a good text to reflect on *anxiety or fear*. Many in our day live anxious or fearful lives, so our era has been characterized as an era of anxiety. In contrast to what some in our society would say, the contrast to fear in the psalm is not autonomy but rather *trust* in God. The poem calls on various images to urge trust: light, salvation, refuge, and shelter coming from YHWH in the face of threats. The psalm urges an alternative to the fear and anxiety so present in our age. It is not an alternative to denial, for the presence of trouble and woe are front and center in the psalm. Rather, the alternative is trust in the face of trouble and opposition. Such trust is nurtured in worshiping communities. Psalm 27 concludes with the imperative "wait for the Lord." This waiting is not a passive, anxious waiting but an active waiting. Perhaps we could paraphrase it as hoping and believing that the covenant God will act as the one who delivers and blesses in the present troubling crisis and thus makes possible a way forward. That faith is the kind of trust Psalm 27 commends, and it is nurtured in *worship*. The psalm time and again comes back to the temple and the divine presence there as central to its affirmation of trust. In worship, the community of faith is shaped and molded. In worship, the encounter with the life-giving divine presence brings renewal that makes it possible to face opposition. That is the kind of trust commended in the Hebrew covenant traditions. The

threat in Psalm 27 is from enemies, but a loss of trust is also a threat. The psalm
suggests the nurturing of trust. Trust is not a private affair but needs the renewal
and the nurture that comes from the encounter of the divine in liturgy.

Psalm 27 recognizes the power of language in nurturing trust and also in nurturing fear or anxiety. In one sense, the question the psalm presents is, in which
language will we put our trust – the language of trust or the language of fear? The
false accusers feed anxiety and fear. The true worshiping community embraces
the psalm's first verse and, in the face of opposition, confesses trust in the Lord
as "my light and my salvation."

PSALM 28 – OF DAVID

¹ To you, O Lord, I call;
    my rock, do not refuse to hear me,
for if you are silent to me,
    I shall be like those who go down to the Pit.
² Hear the voice of my supplication,
    as I cry to you for help,
as I lift up my hands
    toward your most holy sanctuary.

³ Do not drag me away with the wicked,
    with those who are workers of evil,
who speak peace with their neighbors,
    while mischief is in their hearts.
⁴ Repay them according to their work,
    and according to the evil of their deeds;
repay them according to the work of their hands;
    render them their due reward.
⁵ Because they do not regard the works of the Lord,
    or the work of his hands,
he will break them down and build them up no more.

⁶ Blessed be the Lord,
    for he has heard the sound of my pleadings.
⁷ The Lord is my strength and my shield;

in him my heart trusts;
so I am helped, and my heart exults,
  and with my song I give thanks to him.

⁸ The LORD is the strength of his people;
  he is the saving refuge of his anointed.
⁹ O save your people, and bless your heritage;
  be their shepherd, and carry them for ever.

Psalm 28 is structured as a prayer in verses 1–5 and comes to a positive conclusion in verses 6–9. Those verses express confidence that God will hear the prayer. The poem is skillfully composed. The language of prayer in verse 2 reappears in verse 6 and the beginning of the conclusion. The repetition of a variety of forms of "works" in verses 3–5 heightens the contrast between works of evil and "the works of the Lord." The opening and closing verses of the conclusion speak of blessing. In addition, the psalm exhibits continuity with the preceding psalm. Although Psalm 28 begins with a petition rather than a confession of trust, the petition is set in a context of trust, and the concluding section of Psalm 28 calls on imagery similar to that in the descriptions of YHWH in the previous psalm. The psalm is also similar to its predecessor on the question of its ancient setting. A variety of proposals for that setting include the suggestions that the speaker faces false accusation or sickness or that the speaker is the king who faces such a crisis. It is also possible that the psalm is part of the liturgy for entering the sanctuary. The temple is important in the poem. As is the case with Psalm 27 and other petitions in the Psalter, the poetic language makes it difficult to be precise about the ancient crisis behind the prayer. There may have been some accusation; there are certainly enemies. The text we now read is adaptable for life, however, and can be used in a variety of times of trouble. The best way forward is to consider the psalm as a prayer for help that comes to a hopeful resolution, with its expression of certainty that God has heard. With that judgment about genre in view, readers can contemplate the poetic imagery in four parts.

The prayer begins urgently in verses 1–2 in language fraught with loaded terms. The immediate beginning of the prayer is "to you" even prior to the invocation of the divine name YHWH. The plea is for a divine hearing; without it comes death. The divine presence is essential for a full life. Central to this opening plea is the contrast between God as "my rock" and a pit. A pit would be like a narrow cistern dug into the ground, in which the speaker could be lowered and isolated in the miry muck of a cramped hole. That is a striking contrast to the rock as a strong protecting place of hope. In the lament psalms, the pit carries a further connotation as a symbol of Sheol, the realm of the dead. Sheol is the place of no return, a place of divine absence, the underworld, the place of death. The opening prayer is that

God will hear this petition and respond with divine presence and therefore life. The current crisis is a sojourn in the power of Sheol, the characteristic description of trouble and woe in the lament psalms. For this reason, the psalmist lifts up the voice of petition and also the hands. To lift the hands toward the presence of God was the ancient posture of supplication. Perhaps the hands were lifted toward the most holy place of the sanctuary, the place of the Ark of the Covenant, the powerful symbol of divine presence. This opening prayer vibrates with a sense of urgency; the context is one of life and death.

The prayer continues in verses 3–5 with the petition that the speaker not be included among the wicked, for they surely will land in Sheol. The contrast between the psalmist and the enemies underlies these verses. The enemies are hypocritical in speaking peaceably to neighbors while plotting violence. Verse 3 characterizes them as workers of iniquity, which is the central description of the wicked in the lament psalms. They are practitioners of what is false. Their words and actions are in conflict with their inner lives. The "work" of these evildoers dominates these verses. The enemies are obsessed with the wicked work of their hands and so do not attend to God or the covenant community. Their work is in contrast to "the works of the Lord" in verse 5. The psalmist's petition is that the enemies' work will come to its predictable end and rebound on their heads. The conclusion of verse 5 leads to the psalm's next section.

Verses 6–7 give a clear example of the sudden change of mood in a lament psalm. The petitioner is now certain that God heard the prayer: "He has heard the sound of my pleadings." The Hebrew indicates a clear response to "Hear the voice of my supplication" in verse 2. The covenant God is not silent but hears the petition, so the speaker offers praise and thanksgiving to YHWH in the sanctuary. God has brought life and blessing, and the psalmist now returns the favor with praise. The imagery and the confession of faith in verses 6–7 bring to mind Psalm 27 and its context of trust. In contrast to the evildoers, who depend on their own scheming, the poet trusts in God as "my strength and my shield." The language is reminiscent of the beginning of Exodus 15 and the song of celebration at the deliverance from Pharaoh. The faith tradition of ancient Israel is now again proven true in the midst of trouble and woe. The petitioner has found divine aid and so sings a *tôdāh*, a song of thanksgiving performed in the worshiping community as a confession of how God has come to deliver.

Verses 8–9 shift attention explicitly to the congregation gathered for worship. The images of YHWH as "strength" and "refuge" are again front and center, now in relation to the community. The parallelism of verse 8 suggests that "his anointed" may be God's chosen people rather than a royal or priestly figure. At issue is God's blessing and deliverance for the community. The concluding verse's petition is for deliverance from crises and for blessing, the power to grow and thrive in the world. The plea is that God will provide life for this worshiping community. The final plea is that God will carry the people as a shepherd, meaning to care for them as creator and ruler. The community is characterized as God's "heritage," a community that God created and that personifies the divine witness. This concluding prayer for the community suggests that crisis is still in view, even if the crisis is now in the context of trust in the confession that God hears.

A Closer Look: A Lamenter's Mood Swing

Psalm 28 presents a clear example of one of the central structural motifs of lament psalms – the move from petition to certainty that God hears the prayer. Scholars have made a number of suggestions about how that sudden change of mood might occur. Some would suggest that verses 6–9 were added after the crisis was resolved or that this poetic pattern is simply the ancient cultic custom. It is more likely that the petitioner appropriates the historical memory of the faith community that YHWH is the God who delivers or that the prayer reflects the movement of faith in the petitioner. The explanation most popular among scholars is the suggestion that a worship leader delivers a hopeful oracle and the speaker responds in gratitude in verses 6–9. The psalms are worship texts without the stage directions, so certainty on how the sudden change of mood comes to pass is not possible. The structural move of petition to assurance and thanksgiving, however, is central to the literary and theological import of these prayers.

Bridging the Horizons: Community and the Dialogue of Faith

The structure of Psalm 28 suggests that the movement to hope in the face of trouble is not a private affair. It is a relational issue with the covenant God in the context of the faith community. The petitioner comes to trust that God hears and is thus able to see life in the context of faith and a worshiping community. This fervent prayer is in the context of public worship.

Psalm 28 also affirms that life is a gift from the creator. The enemies in this psalm are absorbed with the power to possess and control life. The speaker understands that life is a gift and is able to move to trust in the creator as a way forward. The speaker is not moved by the powerful influence of the enemies but holds to the honest dialogue of faith and leaves the outcome to YHWH, the giver of life. The psalm boldly addresses God from a genuine pastoral crisis and comes to hope in the faith tradition that God is not silent but hears the prayer. The psalm affirms the petitioner's faithfulness, a sign of hope for the whole community.

PSALM 29 – A PSALM OF DAVID

¹ Ascribe to the LORD, O heavenly beings,
  ascribe to the LORD glory and strength.
² Ascribe to the LORD the glory of his name;
  worship the LORD in holy splendour.

³ The voice of the LORD is over the waters;
  the God of glory thunders,
  the LORD, over mighty waters.
⁴ The voice of the LORD is powerful;
  the voice of the LORD is full of majesty.

⁵ The voice of the LORD breaks the cedars;
  the LORD breaks the cedars of Lebanon.
⁶ He makes Lebanon skip like a calf,
  and Sirion like a young wild ox.

⁷ The voice of the LORD flashes forth flames of fire.
⁸ The voice of the LORD shakes the wilderness;
  the LORD shakes the wilderness of Kadesh.

⁹ The voice of the LORD causes the oaks to whirl,
  and strips the forest bare;
  and in his temple all say, 'Glory!'

¹⁰ The LORD sits enthroned over the flood;
   the LORD sits enthroned as king for ever.
¹¹ May the LORD give strength to his people!
   May the LORD bless his people with peace!

Psalm 29 is a hymn of praise with the characteristic three parts. Verses 1–2 call to praise, and the body of the hymn provides the reason for praise in verses 3–9. The conclusion, in verses 10–11, comes back to the praise of God and its implications. The hymn is unusual in that the addressees appear to be divine, so the action of the hymn seems to take place in the heavenly realm. The discussion that follows will suggest a kind of echo effect between worship in the heavenly realm and worship in the Jerusalem temple. The poetic form and imagery of the hymn will bring an immediate response from readers. Repetition brings the poem to a climax in verse

9, but even the call to praise uses repetition and parallel structures to intensify the opening of the psalm. The continuing repetition of "the voice of the Lord" in the main section of the hymn brings the poem to a climax with the shout of "Glory!" in verse 9. The final two verses continue the theme.

One of the issues that has fascinated scholars is the connection between this psalm and Canaanite religion. The Hebrew scriptures and the book of Psalms reflect the social setting of ancient Israel in the ancient Near East, and Psalm 29 is a text that indicates that cultural context. It is often suggested that this psalm is one of the older texts in the Psalter, and that it derived from Canaanite religion and was appropriated for use in the Jerusalem cult by YHWH worshipers. Thunderstorms were often taken by ancient peoples to be indications of divine revelation, and this text uses thunderstorm imagery in portraying divine power. It may be that portraying YHWH as the divine king with authority over all of creation provided a kind of polemic against Canaanite deities.

A Closer Look: A Canaanite Hymn

Interpreters often suggest that Psalm 29 was originally a Canaanite hymn to the storm god that has been adapted to fit the faith of ancient Israel. Several commentators note connections to Baal texts. Connections to Baal imagery may well be in the background of the psalm, but the issue becomes more difficult when one tries to establish the details. John Day makes the following suggestion:

So great are the similarities between Psalm 29 and Canaanite Baal mythology that it has often been supposed that the psalm has simply appropriated a Canaanite Baal hymn and substituted the name Yahweh for Baal. However, this is probably going too far, since v. 11 sounds more Yahwistic than Baalistic ... while v. 8 sounds like an allusion to Yahweh's theophany at Sinai.[79]

Day suggests that Psalm 29 was modeled on Baal texts. We have suggested that an anti-Baal polemic could be at work.

The psalm's opening call to praise is unusual in that it addresses "sons of gods" (*běnê ʾēlîm*). These who are called to praise are to "ascribe" or give to YHWH praise reflecting divine majesty and strength, the kind of worship that can only be conducted in splendor. The NRSV rendering of "heavenly beings" reflects the common interpretation of the addressees in terms of an assembly of the divine council in the throne room of God, where the members of that council, the heavenly messengers, are called to the praise of YHWH. McCann proposes, however, that the opening

---

[79]   John Day, *Psalms* (T. and T. Clark Study Guides; New York: T. and T. Clark, 1999; previous edition, Sheffield: JSOT, 1992), 42–43.

call to praise is addressed to "the deposed gods of the Canaanite pantheon."[80] These gods previously praised Marduk but are now called to the praise of YHWH. The call to praise is in intense poetic form.

Repetition is central to the body of the psalm in verses 3–9. "The voice of the Lord" occurs seven times in the main section of the psalm. The imagery of the psalm seems to derive from thunderstorms, and it may be that the repetition of *qôl YHWH*, "the voice of the Lord," suggests the sound of approaching thunder in the storm. There is a good bit of evidence that this imagery was associated with Baal. In the Ugaritic texts, Baal worshipers said that the voice of Baal was heard in the thunderstorm. The psalm refers to thunder, lightning, damage to trees, the earth shaking, and thus the power of a mighty thunderstorm. This imagery in the Hebrew scriptures brings to mind the powers of chaos. The waters represent the powers of chaos and disorder that oppose YHWH's creation. "The flood" in verse 10 reminds informed readers of the waters of chaos in the story of the flood in Genesis 6–9. The poetic proclamation of the psalm is that the thundering voice of YHWH rules over the powers of chaos. That divine voice is so powerful that it breaks the cedars of Lebanon, a symbol of great strength. Sirion in verse 6 is likely a synonym for Mount Hermon. YHWH also controls both lightning and the wilderness (vv. 7–8). "The voice of the Lord" is no standard thunderstorm; verse 8 suggests an accompanying earthquake as well. The power is both overwhelming and majestic.

The imagery of Psalm 29 falls squarely in the tradition of theophanies in the Hebrew scriptures. A theophany is an appearance of God to humans. Verse 9 concludes with the worshipers' response to the divine presence with the shout "Glory!" The term suggests a manifestation of King YHWH's presence and activity in the world, which causes worshipers to shout exclamations of honor and majesty to the living God. Verse 9 brings readers back to the question of the identity of the worshipers. The psalm's opening addressed "heavenly beings." Perhaps the word "temple" includes some ambiguity and could refer to both a heavenly setting and an earthly setting. The tension and connections between the Jerusalem temple and the heavenly throne room are reflected in a number of psalms. In Psalm 29, heavenly worship is to be echoed in the worship of YHWH in the Jerusalem temple.

Verses 10–11 conclude the hymn with a summary reaffirming divine rule over the powers of chaos as "the Lord sits enthroned as king." Ancient Near Eastern creation traditions typically include the celebration of the creator king in the palace or temple at the completion of the Creation and the taming of the powers of chaos. Psalm 29 emphasizes that YHWH rules over the powers of nature as well as ruling in the human realm. The benediction in verse 11 invites YHWH to channel the great power imagined in this psalm toward granting *shalom*, peace, to the faith community. The hope is that YHWH will bring the same order both to life and to

---

80   J. C. McCann, Jr., "Book of Psalms," in L. E. Keck et al. (eds.), *The New Interpreter's Bible*, vol. 4 (1996), 792.

creation. The terms "strength" and "bless" connect the conclusion to the two previous psalms, which emphasize trust (Pss 27:14; 28:6–9).

Bridging the Horizons: Opposing Baal Worship

Psalm 29 makes daring use of poetic imagery. Baal worship was always seductive for the ancient Israelites, as suggested in prophetic texts such as the book of Hosea. Our poem uses imagery associated with Baal to praise YHWH and thus oppose Baal worship. Throughout history, congregations have adopted and adapted music and imagery of the day for worship. Psalm 29 fully incorporates ancient Near Eastern imagery into the worship of YHWH as lord of history and nature.

If Psalm 29 opposes Baal worship, what would constitute such Baalism in contemporary culture? Taking a clue from the creation imagery in the hymn, one suggestion would be the prevailing view that nature is a part of life to be explained and exploited for human desires, as something to be reduced to the control of human reason for the benefit of humans. That view underlies the militant consumerism that is the original sin of Western society. That view sees humans as the center of life, as those who dictate and control the path of life. The praise of God in Psalm 29 rejects that view and proclaims that it is the living God who is lord of all creation and life. And so God is universally to be praised.

PSALM 30 – A PSALM. A SONG AT THE DEDICATION OF THE TEMPLE. OF DAVID

¹ I will extol you, O Lord, for you have drawn me up,
  and did not let my foes rejoice over me.
² O Lord my God, I cried to you for help,
  and you have healed me.
³ O Lord, you brought up my soul from Sheol,
  restored me to life from among those gone down to the Pit.

⁴ Sing praises to the Lord, O you his faithful ones,
  and give thanks to his holy name.
⁵ For his anger is but for a moment;
  his favor is for a lifetime.
Weeping may linger for the night,
  but joy comes with the morning.

⁶ As for me, I said in my prosperity,
  'I shall never be moved.'
⁷ By your favor, O LORD,
  you had established me as a strong mountain;
you hid your face;
  I was dismayed.

⁸ To you, O LORD, I cried,
  and to the LORD I made supplication:
⁹ 'What profit is there in my death,
  if I go down to the Pit?
Will the dust praise you?
  Will it tell of your faithfulness?
¹⁰ Hear, O LORD, and be gracious to me!
  O LORD, be my helper!'

¹¹ You have turned my mourning into dancing;
  you have taken off my sackcloth
  and clothed me with joy,
¹² so that my soul may praise you and not be silent.
  O LORD my God, I will give thanks to you for ever.

Israel's prayer characteristically begins in petition. This is what we have witnessed in the several psalms of lament, complaint, and protest that we have considered thus far. Israel prays in a variety of death-threatening circumstances. Israel prays with urgency, but nonetheless with confidence in YHWH; in its prayer, Israel is sure that YHWH has the capacity to intervene in its most dire circumstances and turn any near-death condition to life and well-being.

In a corresponding way, Israel's prayer characteristically culminates in thanksgiving to YHWH in glad acknowledgment that YHWH has heard, intervened, and decisively transformed the situation of the petitioner. The articulation (and enactment) of thanks is a final response to YHWH's gracious attentiveness and so confirms the vitality and effectiveness of the relationship that the thanks-giver has with YHWH. As Claus Westermann has made clear, thanksgiving (in contrast to praise) concerns a concrete, nameable gift from YHWH.[81]

It is characteristic of Israel's expression of thanks to YHWH to narrate the initial petition in the context of thanks and to describe the circumstances of need that had initially evoked the petition. Thus Westermann rightly calls these psalms of

81 C. Westermann, *Praise and Lament in the Psalms* (1981), 25–30.

thanksgiving "narrative Psalms" because they do, characteristically, relate the entire drama of faith from *need* and *petition* through *rescue* and finally to *gratitude*.[82] Thus the narrative articulation regularly attests to the "before" of need and the "after" of gratitude, placing at the center of the dramatic narrative the miracle of YHWH's intervention.

In this psalm, the narrative of *need-rescue-thanks* is offered, first of all, in verses 1–3. YHWH is named three times: the God now "extolled" (v. 1), the God addressed in trouble (v. 2), and the God who rescued (v. 3). These verses identify the "before" of foes, Sheol, and the Pit, all signs of powerless desperation. The "after" is that the speaker is "brought up" and "restored to life" by YHWH.

The same narrative account of *need-petition-rescue-thanks* is more fully articulated in verses 6–12. Only here the psalmist, in narrative mode, goes one step further back to describe the life of *complete stability and well-being* prior to any threat (vv. 6–7a). That initial state of total well-being, however, is abruptly shattered in verse 7c,d; the absence of YHWH's life-giving face leads to dismay and disarray. Because God's "face" often signifies cultic presence, Fredrik Lindström has rightly suggested that it is the divine absence in the temple that matters here.[83] The petitioner has found the temple absent of saving presence. This absence of "face," of course, contrasts with the assurance of a saving face in the familiar benediction of Num 6:22–26. It is remarkable that these two brief lines are all that are offered concerning the condition of need. More important is the remembered petition in which the psalmist quotes himself and remembers what he said to YHWH (vv. 8–10). In these verses, YHWH is addressed four times. Verse 10 features three synonymous imperatives, all of which urge rescue by YHWH. That petition, moreover, is reinforced by the motivation in verse 9. This "supplication" mentioned in verse 8 is quoted in verse 9. In a series of four questions, YHWH is reminded that if the speaker is allowed to die (go down into the Pit), there will be one less voice to sing praise to YHWH. Thus YHWH has a vested interest in keeping the petitioner alive as a witness to YHWH's faithfulness:

Like Job in his rebellious tirades, a man who endures the memory of his physical pain and his cosmic solitude carries his boldness to near blasphemy. Or did he think a macabre bit of wit would soften the sovereign Judge? *Humour noir* can be fitting in a cry for pity (v. 9).

Here is an example of the psalmist's candor. Like the mystics of other cultures and times, the devotee of the Lord begged for grace at the exact time he played the game of seeming to be disrespectful of the Most High. Sliding into

82 Claus Westermann, *The Psalms; Structure, Content & Message* (Minneapolis: Augsburg, 1980), 73–83.
83 F. Lindström, *Suffering and Sin* (1994), 65–128 and passim.

the persiflage of comradeship, he unconsciously demonstrated the authenticity of his faith.[84]

After a pause at the end of verse 10 – during which time we are invited to imagine a divine initiative that restores – the speaker attests that YHWH has indeed acted to cause restoration and well-being (vv. 11–12). The three verbs characterizing YHWH's action – turn, take off, clothe – are perhaps parallel to the three imperatives of verse 10. These three verbs assigned to YHWH signify a radical transformation enacted by YHWH. The two verbs "take off" and "put on" bespeak a total reconfiguration of the petitioner, perhaps not unlike the baptismal formula of Eph 4:22–24, wherein one is made wholly new. That is like taking off the *old self* and putting on the *new self*. This is a transformation that evokes praise and thanks, for only YHWH could have effected such a change. Thus verses 6–12 narrate, in greater length, the same narrative drama given in verses 1–3.

Both scenarios of "before-after" are articulated in the first-person singular (vv. 1–3, 6–12). These two units, however, bracket verses 4–5, which break beyond the intimate personal mode to a more generic communal aspect of praise. Here the summons of praise is addressed to the congregation of the faithful, the assembly that joins the individual voice of thanks. Now the entire community celebrates the particular transformation of the individual petitioner. In verse 5, the community of covenant-keepers contrasts the "before" of anger and the long, durable "after" of divine favor, the brevity of weeping and the durability of joy. Thus the contrast of

anger/favor
weeping/joy

reflects the drama from petition to thanksgiving. The juxtaposition of weeping and joy is perhaps echoed in the teaching of Jesus in Luke 6:21, 24. In each case in these contrasts, the final condition of well-being will persist. The trouble is short-term because YHWH does come and intervenes to positive effect. In the end, both the individual petitions (vv. 2, 8–10) and the reflective commentary (vv. 4–5) become grounds for gratitude (vv. 4, 12). The psalm thus reflects the *experience* and *the faith* of Israel. It is worth observing, however, that there is some tension between the large communal faith claim of verse 5 and the lived reality of verse 7, for the petitioner in verse 7 has found YHWH to be, at least short-term, less than reliable. The power of the general affirmation of YHWH, however, seems to overcome that lived reality, so that in the end it is confidence in YHWH that persists. There is no doubt for this psalmist that YHWH will override trouble and make all things new. It is Israel's task to sound the petition, to watch for the rescue, and then to acknowledge that rescue with thanksgiving.

---

[84]   S. Terrien, *Psalms* (2003), 283.

Israel's faith is concrete and concerns "the facts on the ground." One of those "facts" is YHWH's anger, which is known to cause trouble. Without flinching from this reality, Israel has deep confidence in YHWH, which goes beyond Israel's anger. Israel knows that divine anger is not defining for YHWH; it is rather always YHWH's purpose to move beyond anger to restorative favor and rescue. Thus the psalm, without flinching from candor, holds candor about trouble to the deeper reality of YHWH's attentive fidelity. YHWH's favor is as sure as the rising of the sun when morning breaks. Israel's thanks are a precise and appropriate counterpoint to YHWH's generous care. In its receptivity to YHWH's newness, Israel is not able to keep silent; rather Israel must sing and say its gratitude for life as a gift against every debilitating circumstance.

A Closer Look: The Material Side of Thanksgiving

In this psalm, the thanks to be rendered by the petitioner and by Israel appear to be verbal; that is, retelling the narrative of rescue in the midst of the congregation. In many other contexts, however, the rendering of thanks is not only verbal but material as well. Thus thanks in Ps 50:23 and Ps 116:17–18 has to do with bringing a material offering that is visible and no doubt has something of a sacramental quality to it. It may be that such material offering is implied in our psalm, but there is no explicit reference to that aspect of thanks in this context.

Bridging the Horizons: YHWH's Short-Term Anger

The conviction expressed in verse 5 that YHWH will not stay angry forever is paralleled in Ps 103:9–10. Although this is a common conviction in Israel, perhaps the most acute statement concerning the momentary impact of YHWH's anger is articulated in Isa 54:7–8:

For a brief moment I abandoned you,
  but with great compassion I will gather you.
In overflowing wrath for a moment I hid my face from you,
  but with everlasting love I will have compassion on you,
  says the Lord, your Redeemer. (Isa 54:7–8)

In both verses, the same word, "moment" (*re'*), is cited as the brief duration of YHWH's anger. This "moment" in Isaiah 54 refers to the length of time that Israel was in exile in Babylon. Thus it is not an exact measure of time but rather a figurative device to contrast *short-term anger* and *long-term fidelity*. The exile is simply Israel's most acute experience of this characteristic reality concerning YHWH's fidelity.

Bridging the Horizons: A Response to Grace

George Stroup, following Karl Barth, exposits gratitude as the key impetus and practice for a human life of obedience in response to the goodness and graciousness of God:

> Barth described a "closed circle of the relationship between divine grace and human gratitude" with four propositions, two concerning God and two concerning human beings (p. 169). First, only God deserves human thanks. There are various forms of gratitude, but "true and essential gratitude," Barth argued, is directed only to God. Second, only human beings can thank God. Indeed, that is a human being's vocation, what human beings are summoned or called to do – to be grateful. It follows, therefore, that "any action of man which is not basically an expression of gratitude is inadequate in the face of God" (p. 170). Third, God's revelation of his grace toward human beings is the "objective and receptive aspect" of human being. The "subjective and spontaneous" aspect is that a human being is truly and fully human only in giving thanks to God, "because it is in this action alone that he does justice to that in which his being is rooted, to the Word of God which declares that God is gracious to him" (p. 171). Fourth, although we do not know what relationship God has to nonhuman creatures, we do not know of any creature other than the human whose calling is to give thanks to God and who is responsible for fulfilling his calling by giving God thanks.[85]

Barth traced the link between God's grace on the one hand and the human act of gratitude or thanksgiving on the other. Particularly important is his claim that human beings only begin to fulfill their humanity in the particular act of gratitude to God for God's grace in Jesus Christ. Gratitude is rooted in and an expression of human subjectivity, and insofar as gratitude is also a human responsibility, a response to God's summons, it is an act that human beings can choose or refuse. But in turning away from gratitude toward God, human beings turn away from who they truly are, what they are called to be and to do, and become something less.

PSALM 31 – TO THE LEADER. A PSALM OF DAVID

¹ In you, O Lᴏʀᴅ, I seek refuge;
  do not let me ever be put to shame;
  in your righteousness deliver me.

---

85   George W. Stroup, *Before God* (Grand Rapids, MI: Eerdmans, 2004), 145–146.

² Incline your ear to me;
   rescue me speedily.
Be a rock of refuge for me,
   a strong fortress to save me.

³ You are indeed my rock and my fortress;
   for your name's sake lead me and guide me,
⁴ take me out of the net that is hidden for me,
   for you are my refuge.
⁵ Into your hand I commit my spirit;
   you have redeemed me, O Lord, faithful God.

⁶ You hate those who pay regard to worthless idols,
   but I trust in the Lord.
⁷ I will exult and rejoice in your steadfast love,
   because you have seen my affliction;
   you have taken heed of my adversities,
⁸ and have not delivered me into the hand of the enemy;
   you have set my feet in a broad place.

⁹ Be gracious to me, O Lord, for I am in distress;
   my eye wastes away from grief,
   my soul and body also.
¹⁰ For my life is spent with sorrow,
   and my years with sighing;
my strength fails because of my misery,
   and my bones waste away.

¹¹ I am the scorn of all my adversaries,
   a horror to my neighbors,
an object of dread to my acquaintances;
   those who see me in the street flee from me.
¹² I have passed out of mind like one who is dead;
   I have become like a broken vessel.
¹³ For I hear the whispering of many –
   terror all around! –
as they scheme together against me,
   as they plot to take my life.

¹⁴ But I trust in you, O Lord;
   I say, 'You are my God.'

¹⁵ My times are in your hand;
   deliver me from the hand of my enemies and persecutors.
¹⁶ Let your face shine upon your servant;
   save me in your steadfast love.
¹⁷ Do not let me be put to shame, O Lord,
   for I call on you;
let the wicked be put to shame;
   let them go dumbfounded to Sheol.
¹⁸ Let the lying lips be stilled
   that speak insolently against the righteous
   with pride and contempt.

¹⁹ O how abundant is your goodness
   that you have laid up for those who fear you,
and accomplished for those who take refuge in you,
   in the sight of everyone!
²⁰ In the shelter of your presence you hide them
   from human plots;
you hold them safe under your shelter
   from contentious tongues.

²¹ Blessed be the Lord,
   for he has wondrously shown his steadfast love to me
   when I was beset as a city under siege.
²² I had said in my alarm,
   'I am driven far from your sight.'
But you heard my supplications
   when I cried out to you for help.

²³ Love the Lord, all you his saints.
   The Lord preserves the faithful,
   but abundantly repays the one who acts haughtily.
²⁴ Be strong, and let your heart take courage,
   all you who wait for the Lord.

The first book of the Psalter is dominated by prayers from ancient Israel that were used for petition in crises. Psalm 31 provides yet another example of such a prayer, with a distinct alternation of petition and confession of trust. The prayer arose from a setting of crisis, but the expressions of trust color the psalm with a sense of confidence in God. This hopeful tone also characterizes Psalms 26–30. Readers of Book I of the Psalter are on familiar ground with this prayer, which also exhibits linguistic connections with the preceding psalms. The prayer reflects a genuine pastoral crisis. It is not a generalized formula so much as it is a prayer from a particular crisis in the life of the covenant community. At the same time, the text's open poetic language makes the psalm adaptable for life and various crises worshipers may face. The language is similar to that of other lament psalms and so suggests persecution, depression, grief, and sickness. Verses 18 and 20 make it clear that the petitioner faces verbal opposition, so some would suggest that the problem is false accusation by enemies, but the language appears to be too open-ended to support a legal setting for the prayer. Another possibility would be that the petitioner faces a crisis of malicious gossip, false words that would carry considerable force and would lead to shame. The crisis is not one to be solved by standard institutional procedures in society, so the speaker comes to the divine judge to seek help in a cultic context. The kind of conflict that brings about the prayer would not be uncommon in daily life; its import in the language of the psalm, however, bears considerable freight.

The prayer consists of two petitions, each moving from petition to trust (vv. 1–8 and 9–20) and including common vocabulary. The concluding section in verses 21–24 brings the entire prayer to completion. The treatment that follows will consider each petition in turn.

Verses 1–8 articulate a prayer beginning in verses 1–2 with a petition for refuge, which is characteristic of many of the first psalms. The opening verse suggests that the alternative to refuge from YHWH is shame. Contemporary readers will likely associate shame with embarrassment and grief, but in the ancient Near East, shame was a more powerful force, a life of dishonor. It was associated with death and destruction, a broken life with no hope. The psalm indicates that this possibility of shame comes from the powerful words of opponents, and the poetic imagery portrays a profound crisis. The petition to YHWH is for refuge and a reversal of the crisis. The petitioner appeals to YHWH's righteousness early in the prayer. This God took the risk of initiating a relationship with the covenant community, and that includes the speaker. The expectation of that relationship is that God is the one who comes to deliver. The petitioner thus pleads for God to act like the righteous covenant God and deliver him from the crisis at hand. The imagery in the first part of the psalm portrays God as the one who protects. The last line of verse 3 brings to mind the language of Psalm 23 with the hope that God will carry the petitioner out of the current persecution. The next verse uses the imagery of hunting and pleads for escape from the hunter's trap. Verse 5 makes the transition to an expression of trust that begins with a contrast with idol worshipers and moves to a hymnic expression of love that does not change with external circumstances. YHWH is the God who sees, hears, and embraces the pain of the petitioner and comes to deliver him from it. In language familiar from previous psalms, deliverance is compared to liberation that brings the petitioner into a broad and open place where there is no persecution. It is YHWH who brings about this salvation.

Verses 9–20 articulate a renewed prayer for help, beginning again with strong petition. The language of the petition will be familiar to readers of the laments in the first part of the Psalms; the language echoes other petitions. Verses 9–10 use personal imagery to characterize a crisis that involves all of life: eye, body, strength, and bones. Sorrow and grief define all of life. Verses 11–13 characterize the crisis in terms of isolation from both enemies and friends. The speaker has been shamed and so is shunned as a broken life, as one gripped by the power of death. The image at the end of verse 12 is powerful. The petitioner is an ancient Humpty Dumpty, a shattered pot never to be put back together again. Enemies' malicious words endlessly surround this outcast as one who is on the edge of death. The language of verse 13 calls to mind the prophet Jeremiah and the persecution he encountered as a prophetic messenger. With verse 14, there is a change in the prayer to an expression of trust. Although it seems that enemies surround the petitioner, God is still worthy of trust: "I say, 'You are my God.'" That simple and profound articulation of the I–Thou relationship makes it clear that the petitioner's future is in divine hands, the power of the covenant God rather than the power of the enemies. The prayer continues to articulate petition, but now in the context of trust in the divine presence ("your face") and so of hope for deliverance and a change of fortune in life. The hope is that YHWH will demonstrate the hoped-for steadfast love and bring renewed life. Such a reversal of fortune would bring silence, shame, and trouble for the opponents who speak falsely. The contrast between the petitioner and the malicious opponents is on full display in verses 15–18 with the characterization of the enemies in terms of "lying lips," insolence, pride, and contempt. This second petition of Psalm 31 comes to completion in verses 19–20 with a full expression of trust in YHWH as the one who gives refuge to the faithful and does so publicly. The refuge is from malicious gossip and the shame it brings. God is the one who gives refuge.

Verses 21–24 bring the psalm to a positive conclusion. It is the characteristic expression of certainty that God hears the petitions of the covenant community. It is in the style of a celebratory hymn with a call to praise followed by the reason for the praise. The petitioner has found renewed faith in the midst of this struggle. These verses complete both articulations of petition in the psalm and bring the whole poem to a fitting conclusion. God's answer to the petition is characterized as a demonstration of *ḥesed*, unflinching fidelity, alluding to both petition and expression of trust in verses 7 and 16. The petitioner's fear was that the shame resulting from malicious enemies would lead to even more troubling isolation, but the covenant God has now heard the prayer. Perhaps a priest or prophet has proclaimed a favorable oracle for the petitioner. Verse 21 compares the crisis to a city under siege, an image in contrast to the characterization of YHWH as rock and refuge at the beginning of the psalm. The poem comes to a conclusion with the petitioner addressing the covenant congregation. "His saints" are those who encounter the divine *ḥesed* and live faithfully to that. So the call to the congregation is to enter the narrative articulated in the petition and so in trust anticipate the salvation of the covenant God with love, courage, and strength. The conclusion implies that the petitioner has found a renewed faith and perspective even though the crisis is still present. The speaker has been able through trust in the divine promise to imagine life differently. The divine promise stands even in the face of oppression.

Bridging the Horizons: An Enduring Faith

Psalm 31 models faith in the face of trouble and woe. We indicated earlier connections with the prophet Jeremiah. Jeremiah lived as a faithful prophet in the midst of both good and bad times in ancient Jerusalem. Such faith is at times characterized by brutal honesty in the dialogue with the giver of faith. Even raw petitions such as those recorded from Jeremiah in the midst of great anguish suggest an intimate relationship with the covenant God. Through such difficulty and hope, trust was central to Jeremiah's pilgrimage of enduring faith. He actively "waited upon the Lord," anticipating the demonstration of God's unfailing loyalty. Trust in that hope makes it possible for one to take strength and courage (v. 24). The Psalms and the book of Jeremiah make it clear that those who are faithful will face opposition. The force of malicious words and alienation can overwhelm in this world; one of the keys to faithful living is trust in the God who brings all refuge. The petitioner depends on the righteousness of YHWH, that this covenant God initiates a relationship to set things right, and Psalm 31 proclaims that great is God's faithfulness to that promise. Thus believers can trust in the face of malicious opposition.

Verse 5 is familiar in Christian tradition because Jesus quotes it from the cross (Luke 23:46) as an expression of trust in the providence of God in the severest of moments. This tradition of committing one's life into divine power and authority became a tradition for saints who died with those words on their lips – Polycarp, Jerome, Luther, and John Knox. The psalm has been a model for living and dying faithfully.

PSALM 32 – OF DAVID. A MASKIL

¹ Happy are those whose transgression is forgiven,
  whose sin is covered.
² Happy are those to whom the Lord imputes no iniquity,
  and in whose spirit there is no deceit.

³ While I kept silence, my body wasted away
  through my groaning all day long.
⁴ For day and night your hand was heavy upon me;

my strength was dried up as by the heat of summer.
  Selah

5 Then I acknowledged my sin to you,
  and I did not hide my iniquity;
I said, 'I will confess my transgressions to the LORD',
  and you forgave the guilt of my sin.
  Selah

6 Therefore let all who are faithful
  offer prayer to you;
at a time of distress, the rush of mighty waters
  shall not reach them.
7 You are a hiding-place for me;
  you preserve me from trouble;
  you surround me with glad cries of deliverance.
  Selah

8 I will instruct you and teach you the way you should go;
  I will counsel you with my eye upon you.
9 Do not be like a horse or a mule, without understanding,
  whose temper must be curbed with bit and bridle,
  else it will not stay near you.

10 Many are the torments of the wicked,
  but steadfast love surrounds those who trust in the LORD.
11 Be glad in the LORD and rejoice, O righteous,
  and shout for joy, all you upright in heart.

Though an unfortunate misnomer, this psalm, in Christian tradition, has been identified as a "penitential psalm." In fact, there is nothing in this psalm about "penitence" of any conventional kind. Rather, the psalm is an affirmation about the miracle of God's forgiveness that requires none of the discipline or work of penitence:

Divine forgiveness resembles a miracle; God re-creates life, just like the first autumnal rain that generally accompanies the New Year.... When God forgives, he brings rebirth.[86]

---

86   S. Terrien, *Psalms* (2003), 293.

The emphasis is completely on God's readiness to forgive and the capacity of the psalmist to *tell the truth* in a simple, direct way that makes divine forgiveness possible.

The primal drama of forgiveness is narrated in verses 3–5, which trace in a simple way the move from *sin concealed* to *sin confessed and forgiven*. The psalmist first describes the silence of denial that fuses confession and the resultant psychosomatic disability that follows from such denial (vv. 3–4). Then abruptly, in verse 5, the psalmist breaks the silence and blurts out the admission of sin and guilt. The key term is "I acknowledged," meaning said out loud; the speaker no longer hid ("covered") the sin but articulated it (v. 5). The verse is laden with three characteristic terms for sin in the Old Testament, variously rendered "sin, iniquity, transgression." The fullness of the vocabulary bespeaks the readiness of the psalmist to conceal nothing of the distorted self. At the end of verse 5, with an emphatic pronoun "you," it is affirmed that immediately on confession YHWH forgave ("lifted") the guilt. One is struck by the immediacy of forgiveness upon confession, with no intermediate rebuke or discipline of any kind. All that is required is unguarded truth-telling. YHWH wants only the truth moved beyond the falseness of silence; forgiveness is immediately at the ready from the God of all mercy.

This simple transaction is reflected in the narrative form by David's confession to Nathan after the Uriah-Bathsheba episode (2 Sam 12:13):

David: I have sinned against the Lord.
Nathan: Now the Lord has put away your sin.

This is a remarkably prompt resolution of a quintessential act of defiance against YHWH, against YHWH's Torah, and against YHWH's prophet. We might, however, notice two caveats in the narrative that do not appear in the direct forgiveness of the psalm. First, in the very next verse, verse 14, Nathan assesses a harsh penalty against David, namely the death of the son born out of this sordid affair. Second, Saul has a like confrontation with Samuel in 1 Samuel 15. Like David, Saul confesses sin and asks forgiveness (vv. 24–25), but in this narrative Saul remains unforgiven (vv. 26–29). Thus this psalm is a model for forgiveness, but forgiveness is not without complexity in other testimonies of Israel's faith.

This remarkable drama of confession and forgiveness in verses 3–5 is now encapsulated in instructional material in verses 1–2 and 6–11 that seeks to draw others into the drama of reconciliation:

As in Psalm 51, which is another penitential psalm, the forgiven sinner teaches God's ways to others (see 51:13). This educational ministry is not presumptuous, for the psalmist witnesses not to his or her own righteousness but to divine grace – God's willingness and God's ability to set things and persons right. Thus "the way you should go" (v. 8) points to the psalmist's example of breaking silence to confess sin (vv. 3, 5) and to his or her conviction of God's willingness to forgive and restore (vv. 7, 10). The psalmist's witness in vv. 6–11 is in essence an invitation to others, including the readers of Psalm 32, to confess their own sinfulness and to live in dependence upon the grace of God.[87]

Verses 1–2, which introduce the psalm, offer proverbial sayings about the way to good fortune ("happiness") – the foundation of happiness is forgiveness. Two points may be noted in this verse. In verse 1, the term "covered," which here refers to sins forgiven, is the same word as "hide" in verse 5. Whereas verse 1 uses the term to refer to God's forgiveness, the term in verse 5 refers to human denial. The double use of the term is intentional and refers to the "two ways" of managing guilt, either grace rooted in YHWH or denial rooted in self-sufficiency.

Second, the term rendered "impute" in the NRSV renders the Hebrew *ḥšv*. This same term is used in Gen 15:6 concerning Abraham's righteousness, and this verse became crucial for Paul's argument concerning justification of sinners.[88] The term in verse 2 of the psalm suggests that YHWH *assigns* a state of "no iniquity" not to one who is sinless but to one who has sinned but is forgiven. It is the state of forgiveness that determines one's standing before YHWH.

Verses 6–7 are an invitation to others to entrust themselves fully to the "Rock of Ages" to whom we pray, "Let me hide myself in thee." In these verses, the problem is not guilt but rather chaos; "the rush of many waters" refers to the threat of chaos that may or may not be rooted in guilt. As the speaker in verses 3–5 has found, YHWH is the only sure, *safe place* for human life. The teacher, in verses 8–9, urges an open responsiveness to YHWH and warns against stubborn autonomy. The final verses outline the characteristic distinction between "wicked" and "righteous" that permeates the Psalter, which we have seen already in Psalm 1 (vv. 10–11). It is most likely, however, that in this contest the terms righteous and wicked do not refer to pure torah-keepers but to those who resolve their sin and failure by turning to YHWH in confession. The hope for Israel – and for all humanity – is not in sinlessness but in forgiveness by YHWH, which is freely offered.

Bridging the Horizons: Forgiveness

Verses 1–2 of this psalm are quoted in Rom 4:7–8 just after the citation of Gen 15:6 in Rom 4:3 (see also Rom 4:9, 22). Using verses 1–2, Paul makes the argument that forgiveness is the grounds for new life, and any "moral qualification" (such as circumcision) is irrelevant. Everything depends on God's generous forgiveness. Thus Paul faithfully renders this psalm in his own context of divine mercy and forbearance as the truth of human life.

---

[87]   J. Clinton McCann, Jr., *The New Interpreter's Bible*, vol. 4 (Nashville, TN: Abingdon Press, 1996), 806.

[88]   See Gerhard von Rad, *The Problem of the Hexateuch and Other Essays* (New York: McGraw-Hill, 1966), 125–130.

Bridging the Horizons: Silence Kills

The need for articulation of guilt that overruns denial and repression is an elemental truth of all modern psychotherapy that is rooted in the insight of Sigmund
Freud. Clearly the ancient Israelites had already understood the truth that "silence
kills" long before Freud reintroduced this Jewish insight into the modern world.[89]
It is surely noteworthy that the most prominent studies of silence that kills are by
women. We think it likely that it is precisely male-oriented, authoritarian societies that have been the primary sponsors of silence that kills.

PSALM 33

1 Rejoice in the LORD, O you righteous.
  Praise befits the upright.
2 Praise the LORD with the lyre;
  make melody to him with the harp of ten strings.
3 Sing to him a new song;
  play skilfully on the strings, with loud shouts.

4 For the word of the LORD is upright,
  and all his work is done in faithfulness.
5 He loves righteousness and justice;
  the earth is full of the steadfast love of the LORD.

6 By the word of the LORD the heavens were made,
  and all their host by the breath of his mouth.
7 He gathered the waters of the sea as in a bottle;
  he put the deeps in storehouses.

8 Let all the earth fear the LORD;
  let all the inhabitants of the world stand in awe of him.
9 For he spoke, and it came to be;
  he commanded, and it stood firm.

[89] See Walter Brueggemann, "Voice as Counter to Violence," *Calvin Theological Journal*
36, no. 1 (April 2001): 22–23, which provides a bibliography on contemporary studies of
silence that kills and the recovery of life through speech with reference to the work of
Rebecca Chopp, Carol Gilligan, Judith Lewis Hermann, Alice Miller, and Elaine Scarry.

¹⁰ The Lord brings the counsel of the nations to nothing;
  he frustrates the plans of the peoples.
¹¹ The counsel of the Lord stands for ever,
  the thoughts of his heart to all generations.
¹² Happy is the nation whose God is the Lord,
  the people whom he has chosen as his heritage.

¹³ The Lord looks down from heaven;
  he sees all humankind.
¹⁴ From where he sits enthroned he watches
  all the inhabitants of the earth –
¹⁵ he who fashions the hearts of them all,
  and observes all their deeds.
¹⁶ A king is not saved by his great army;
  a warrior is not delivered by his great strength.
¹⁷ The war horse is a vain hope for victory,
  and by its great might it cannot save.

¹⁸ Truly the eye of the Lord is on those who fear him,
  on those who hope in his steadfast love,
¹⁹ to deliver their soul from death,
  and to keep them alive in famine.

²⁰ Our soul waits for the Lord;
  he is our help and shield.
²¹ Our heart is glad in him,
  because we trust in his holy name.
²² Let your steadfast love, O Lord, be upon us,
  even as we hope in you.

The final verse of Psalm 32 (v. 11) summoned Israel to praise after forgiveness. Psalm 33 now delivers the praise of YHWH called for in Psalm 32. The enactment of praise through song, instrument, and narrative is to celebrate "the kingdom, the power, and the glory of YHWH" in an exuberant mode of self-abandonment. The aim of the praise of YHWH is to focus completely on YHWH's character and actions, for which the worshiping congregation of Israel is unreservedly grateful. Such praise is a powerful antidote to every temptation to autonomy and self-sufficiency.

Verses 1–5 exhibit the two characteristic elements of praise. First, verses 1–3 are a summons to praise in a series of imperatives that mobilize the "righteous" congregation to praise. Second, verses 4–5 introduce reasons for praise, here an acknowledgment of YHWH's powerful word and YHWH's character, which is marked by faithfulness, righteousness, justice, and steadfast love. This sequence of four words summarizes Israel's affirmation of YHWH as an utterly reliable presence on the lips of Israel and in the life of the world. Verse 4 suggests that YHWH, like a great, powerful sovereign, accomplishes divine purposes by utterance: the issuance of an order, a decree, or a dictum that is promptly enacted by subordinates.

The leitmotif in verse 4 is developed in verses 6–7 in order to refer to the creation of the world by utterance as in Genesis 1. In verse 8, the psalm turns from the wonder of *creation* to the reality of *history*, which is also accomplished by divine speech (v. 9). Verses 10 and 11 focus on YHWH's sovereignty over all the nations, a point accented by the enthronement psalms, and verse 12 moves more specifically to YHWH's governance over Israel, a governance that assures Israel of "happiness."

The imagery of royal governance is reinforced and reiterated in verses 13–15 by reference to "enthronement" in verse 14. From that high and lifted-up throne, this attentive king keeps all of creation under surveillance. The watchfulness of YHWH the sovereign is voiced in verse 14 and is resounded in verse 18 concerning YHWH's "eye." YHWH keeps "all inhabitants" under surveillance, aware of their "hearts" (thought) and actions. Particularly, YHWH is watchful concerning YHWH's obedient subjects. In verse 8, all are to fear and stand in awe, and in verse 18 it is more likely Israel that is to practice hope. Thus the psalm moves back and forth between the specificity of covenant and the more generic category of creatureliness. In terms of both *creation* and *covenant*, YHWH governs in attentive ways.

The proverbial teaching of verses 16–17 appears to be an addendum that attests in insistent and practical ways to YHWH's sovereignty. In these verses, it is asserted, as in Psalm 20, that military prowess cannot save; it is only YHWH who can rescue and deliver. These verses thus refute any claim of self-securing autonomy. This negative dismissal of autonomous power in verses 16–17 is matched by the affirmation in verses 18–19 concerning the God-fearers (Torah-keepers) who fear YHWH and hope in YHWH. These are the ones who believe that both creation and history are in YHWH's good hands and who, by Torah obedience, align themselves with YHWH's rule in the world. In verse 19, the psalm touches the concrete realities of death and famine, two characteristic exemplars of the negation of life. Such realities are palpable in the world, but the hopers know that beyond such realities is the promissory power of YHWH, who sustains the future of the world.

The conclusion of verses 20–22 is curious in its beginning with the phrase "our soul." The phrase joins a plural possessive pronoun to a singular noun, thus exhibiting the community of faith in its unity, all of one mind. The phrase bespeaks the confident trusting faith of Israel. In the end, Israel can be "glad" because it has complete confidence in YHWH, counts on YHWH's name, and relies on YHWH's "fidelity," the same term as in verse 5.

The psalm begins in praise and ends in trust. Both the first more exuberant articulation and the final note, which is more quietly durable, witness to Israel's readiness to trust its life and its world to the rule of YHWH. Although this psalm concerns the creative power and the governance of YHWH, in the end it is a song of hope. Israel sings its confidence that the world will hold in the face of chaos and that history will hold in the face of military threat, because the creator-king finally will defeat all rival powers and all threats to good governance. This psalm of confidence, in a daring but characteristic statement, voices reassurance in the face of deep threats to political and environmental orders. In hymnic form, this psalm attests to Israel's singular confidence in YHWH and its characteristic refusal to trust in any form of church, state, army, economic system, or any other human capacity. That hope in YHWH is lean, but it is intensely focused on the one who has spoken and who continues to speak the word of life.

A Closer Look: The Word of YHWH

It is usual to notice in this psalm that there is a focus on the word of YHWH that creates the world and that governs nations, a word that is marked by steadfast fidelity. Indeed Hans-Joachim Kraus has offered a full exposition of such a "theology of the word" that is evident already in the traditions of ancient Egypt.[90] In the Old Testament, moreover, this psalm has clear connections to the theme of creation by the word in Genesis 1.

In our judgment, however, this singular focus on creation by word usually given to this psalm is unfortunate, for it begins with YHWH's governance of creation and history and finally governance of the life of Israel, but it then moves to speak of Israel's *response* to that governing word, response in "fear" (v. 18), hope (v. 18), waiting (v. 20), trust (v. 21), and finally yet again in hope (v. 22). That is, the ruling word of YHWH evokes a response in faith so that the logic of the psalm concerns both *divine address* and *human response in faith*. Israel trusts in the rule of YHWH. The two parts of the psalm are nicely held together in the following aphorism of Gerhard Ebeling: "Faith, however, is at bottom nothing else but praise of the creator."[91]

Bridging the Horizons: Trust As an Act of Courage

This psalm moves from divine rule to Israel's trust. The culminating statement of trust (*bṭḥ*) in verse 2 is well illuminated by the narrative theology of 2 Kgs 18:19–26. In that text that exposits the term "trust," the Assyrian diplomat challenges King Hezekiah not to "rely" on YHWH. The term "rely" in verses 20, 21, and 24 renders our term *bṭḥ*. The challenge given to the Jerusalem king is to trust

90   H.-J. Kraus, *Psalms 1–59* (1988), 376–378.
91   Gerhard Ebeling, *Word of Faith* (Philadelphia: Fortress Press, 1963), 385.

YHWH in dangerous public circumstances. The belated prophetic response to
the Assyrian challenge in 2 Kgs 19:21–28 and the resulting deliverance of the city
of Jerusalem vindicated trust in YHWH (2 Kgs 19:35–37). Both this psalm and
the narrative of 2 Kings make evident that "trust" is no pious attitude; it is rather
an act of courage that matters decisively in a genuinely risky circumstance.

PSALM 34 – OF DAVID, WHEN HE FEIGNED MADNESS BEFORE ABIMELECH, SO THAT HE DROVE HIM OUT, AND HE WENT AWAY

¹ I will bless the LORD at all times;
   his praise shall continually be in my mouth.
² My soul makes its boast in the LORD;
   let the humble hear and be glad.
³ O magnify the LORD with me,
   and let us exalt his name together.

⁴ I sought the LORD, and he answered me,
   and delivered me from all my fears.
⁵ Look to him, and be radiant;
   so your faces shall never be ashamed.
⁶ This poor soul cried, and was heard by the LORD,
   and was saved from every trouble.
⁷ The angel of the LORD encamps
   around those who fear him, and delivers them.
⁸ O taste and see that the LORD is good;
   happy are those who take refuge in him.
⁹ O fear the LORD, you his holy ones,
   for those who fear him have no want.
¹⁰ The young lions suffer want and hunger,
    but those who seek the LORD lack no good thing.

¹¹ Come, O children, listen to me;
    I will teach you the fear of the LORD.
¹² Which of you desires life,
    and covets many days to enjoy good?

¹³ Keep your tongue from evil,
   and your lips from speaking deceit.
¹⁴ Depart from evil, and do good;
   seek peace, and pursue it.

¹⁵ The eyes of the LORD are on the righteous,
   and his ears are open to their cry.
¹⁶ The face of the LORD is against evildoers,
   to cut off the remembrance of them from the earth.
¹⁷ When the righteous cry for help, the LORD hears,
   and rescues them from all their troubles.
¹⁸ The LORD is near to the broken-hearted,
   and saves the crushed in spirit.

¹⁹ Many are the afflictions of the righteous,
   but the LORD rescues them from them all.
²⁰ He keeps all their bones;
   not one of them will be broken.
²¹ Evil brings death to the wicked,
   and those who hate the righteous will be condemned.
²² The LORD redeems the life of his servants;
   none of those who take refuge in him will be condemned.

Psalm 34 is an alphabetic acrostic and is thus often compared to Psalm 25, another acrostic with similar characteristics. McCann points to another literary device in the poem, in which the first letters of verses 1, 11, and 22 at the beginning, middle, and end of the psalm spell *'alep*, the first letter of the Hebrew alphabet.[92] Such playfulness is often associated with wisdom, as is the acrostic form. This psalm betrays a didactic tone that is often compared to Proverbs. The psalm appears to be a studied literary creation unified with the acrostic form and the repetition of terms throughout the poem. The psalm combines instruction with thanksgiving. A narrative of deliverance and the subsequent thanksgiving become a means of instructing the congregation, in a style similar to Psalm 32. In this way, Psalm 34 continues the hopeful tone that characterizes several of the psalms preceding this one and combines that with a didactic purpose. The psalm begins in the style of a bold thanksgiving psalm from an individual, though the congregation comes into view quickly in verse 3. Congregational involvement in the text is clear, though the

---

92   J. C. McCann, Jr., "Book of Psalms," in L. E. Keck et al. (eds.), *The New Interpreter's Bible*, vol. 4 (1996), 813.

nature of the trouble narrated in the thanksgiving dimension of the psalm is no longer identifiable through the open-ended language of the poem.

The psalm begins with bold language in the characteristic style of thanksgiving psalms in verses 1–3 by expressing the purpose of offering praise and thanksgiving to YHWH, the God who comes to deliver. The promise is of praise and thanksgiving without ceasing. The verbs indicate the purpose: to bless, magnify, and exalt YHWH. The implication is that YHWH has brought hope to this worshiper, who now in response acknowledges greatness. The exaggerated poetic language contrasts God, who is magnified or made great, and the congregation, described as "the humble." So the focus of this introductory section is not the psalmist but the purpose of praise and thanksgiving to God that comes from a divine rescue from trouble, as indicated in the next part of the psalm. This opening expression of purpose is characteristic of thanksgiving psalms; verse 3 calls for the congregation to participate in these acts and so join the experience of deliverance and gratitude and thus learn.

Verses 4–10 narrate the rescue at the base of this expression of thanksgiving. The same root word sets off the section with "I sought the Lord" in verse 4 and "those who seek the Lord" in verse 10. The verbs used to characterize divine action are also noteworthy: God "answered," "delivered," "heard," and "saved." The psalm's purpose of thanksgiving derives from such divine acts of deliverance. Seeking the Lord suggests cultic activity, and it may well be that the speaker went to the temple to pray in the midst of crisis. There the speaker sought a divine word of hope and received an oracle of salvation such as is often suggested was part of the sudden change of mood from crisis to hope.

The psalms in Book I of the Psalter make it clear that the temple is a place of salvation and divine presence. By the time readers of Psalm 34 reach verse 5, it is already clear that one of the characteristics of the poem is the connection between thanksgiving and instruction of the congregation. Along with the narrative of the crisis and deliverance, the psalmist calls the assembly to look to God as the one who protects and sustains. The call is to trust in the refuge God provides, refuge that brings joy to life. The call to "taste and see that the Lord is good" is the language of experiment, to try out the divine protection and see if God is faithful. Divine protection is here associated with the fear of the Lord, or reverence for God, which implies trust. "The young lions" (v. 10) are the examples of self-sufficiency. Even these lords of the jungle will go without food and will suffer, but those who fear YHWH receive protection from YHWH, who is good.

This emphasis on the fear of the Lord (vv. 7 and 9) leads in verses 11–14 to a section of instruction on "the fear of the Lord." The narrative of verses 4–10 calls on the congregation to "taste and see" that God is trustworthy. Having thus called the community to faith, the psalmist moves to the position of the wisdom teacher and expands on the fear of the Lord. Fear here has to do with being in awe of the divine or revering or respecting God. The wisdom teacher addresses students ("children" in v. 11) so that they will learn the lesson of the narrative of verses 4–10: God is faithful to deliver. It would be easy to take the life of faith for granted, and so the psalmist urges the community to keep both gratitude and reverence for God ever in view. The most familiar use of "the fear of the Lord" is in the motto of the book of Proverbs (Prov 1:7) that teaches that such reverence for YHWH is the beginning of wisdom. In line with such wisdom teaching, verse 12 of this psalm ties the fear of the Lord to life and enjoying good life. This section of the psalm makes clear that the good life is the good, moral life. Verse 13 makes it clear that speech is a central part of morality. Evil and deceitful speech can bring about great crises; history is replete with examples of wars started with words. The concluding verse of the section summarizes the instruction about the fear of the Lord.

> Depart from evil, and do good;
> seek peace, and pursue it. (v. 14)

Verses 15–22 continue to instruct while focusing on the characterization of God. God sees all and is especially attentive to the righteous and hears their cry. The portrayal of the righteous is also important in the final section of the psalm. In contrast to the doers of evil, who will be entirely cut off, God rescues the righteous. The term is here associated with crying out to God for help, with "the brokenhearted," "the crushed in spirit" (v. 18), and God's servants (v. 22). It is YHWH, and not the powerful of society, who provides help for the righteous. Societal structures can afflict and crush spirits; YHWH hears the cries of the afflicted. The implication of this portrayal of the righteous is that they are not those who earn their way by doing morally correct deeds. Rather, the righteous are those who live out of fidelity to their relationship with YHWH with just human relationships. YHWH protects the righteous, and in response they live in faith and justice. The portrayal of the life of the righteous in these last verses makes it clear that such a life is often found in the midst of suffering. The promise of YHWH is not a promise of undisturbed happy circumstances but a promise of divine presence and hope in all of life. Verse 20 expresses this presence in a powerful way with the image of divine protection of "all their bones." The conclusion of the psalm is in a proverbial style affirming that those who take refuge in YHWH will find redemption rather than condemnation. The conclusion of Psalm 34 is yet another reminder to readers that divine refuge in the face of enemies and trouble is central to the first part of the Hebrew Psalter.

A Closer Look: Naming Philistine Kings

The superscription of Psalm 34 includes a historical note from the life of David. The allusion is apparently to the narrative in 1 Sam 21:10–15 in which David "feigned madness" before the King of Gath and thereby escaped. The narrative names the king as Achish, however, whereas the superscription to Psalm 34 names the king Abimelech. Craigie suggests that "Abimelech" ("my father is king") could be a title for the Philistine ruler.[93] The significance of the superscription is more interpretive than historical, however. Reading the psalm with the narrative provides a real-life setting in which readers can imagine the use of the psalm.

Bridging the Horizons: Naive Generalization or Robust Faith?

The poetry of Psalm 34 has a totalizing effect. The word for "all" occurs in verses 1, 4, 6, 17, and 19; "continually" in verse 1; "never" in verse 5; "nothing" in verse 9; "no good thing" in verse 10; "not one" in verse 20; and "none" in verse 22. Is the psalm naive in its sweeping generalizations about life? Three points are worth considering. First, verse 19 makes it clear the righteous will suffer:

Many are the afflictions of the righteous,
but the Lord rescues them from them all. (v. 19)

The psalm characterizes God not as one who protects the speaker from all harm but as one who comes to deliver the speaker from crises. Second, the portrayal of YHWH in this text is not simply theory. It is based on the speaker's experience of rescue from trouble. Third, this psalm reminds readers of the persistent presence of evil and enemies in Psalms 1–34. Craigie notes:

The fear of the Lord ... may mend the broken heart, but it does not prevent the heart from being broken; it may restore the spiritually crushed, but it does not crush the forces that may create oppression. The psalm, if fully grasped, dispels the naiveté of that faith which does not contain within it the strength to stand against the onslaught of evil.[94]

Bridging the Horizons: Joy

The search for joy in life motivates many people in our day. Psalm 34 affirms that such joy is a gift from God rather than earnings from individual achievement or from happy life circumstances. The psalmist expresses gratitude for the gift rather than the desire for more of the "stuff" of life. The psalm is a witness against a culture's commitment to consumerism and the acquisition of things. Verse 8 is often used with the Christian Eucharist, and that is an appropriate use for it has to do with gratitude for the God who redeems. The psalm urges that such gratitude be expressed by departing from evil, doing good, and pursuing peace (v. 14).

---

[93] P. C. Craigie, *Psalms 1–50* (2004), 278.
[94] P. C. Craigie, *Psalms 1–50* (2004), 282.

PSALM 35 – OF DAVID

¹ Contend, O Lord, with those who contend with me;
  fight against those who fight against me!
² Take hold of shield and buckler,
  and rise up to help me!
³ Draw the spear and javelin
  against my pursuers;
say to my soul,
  'I am your salvation.'

⁴ Let them be put to shame and dishonor
  who seek after my life.
Let them be turned back and confounded
  who devise evil against me.
⁵ Let them be like chaff before the wind,
  with the angel of the Lord driving them on.
⁶ Let their way be dark and slippery,
  with the angel of the Lord pursuing them.

⁷ For without cause they hid their net for me;
  without cause they dug a pit for my life.
⁸ Let ruin come on them unawares.
And let the net that they hid ensnare them;
  let them fall in it – to their ruin.

⁹ Then my soul shall rejoice in the Lord,
  exulting in his deliverance.
¹⁰ All my bones shall say,
  'O Lord, who is like you?
You deliver the weak
  from those too strong for them,
  the weak and needy from those who despoil them.'

¹¹ Malicious witnesses rise up;
  they ask me about things I do not know.
¹² They repay me evil for good;
  my soul is forlorn.
¹³ But as for me, when they were sick,

I wore sackcloth;
I afflicted myself with fasting.
I prayed with head bowed on my bosom,
¹⁴ as though I grieved for a friend or a brother;
I went about as one who laments for a mother,
    bowed down and in mourning.

¹⁵ But at my stumbling they gathered in glee,
    they gathered together against me;
ruffians whom I did not know
    tore at me without ceasing;
¹⁶ they impiously mocked more and more,
    gnashing at me with their teeth.

¹⁷ How long, O Lord, will you look on?
    Rescue me from their ravages,
    my life from the lions!
¹⁸ Then I will thank you in the great congregation;
    in the mighty throng I will praise you.

¹⁹ Do not let my treacherous enemies rejoice over me,
    or those who hate me without cause wink the eye.
²⁰ For they do not speak peace,
    but they conceive deceitful words
    against those who are quiet in the land.
²¹ They open wide their mouths against me;
    they say, 'Aha, Aha,
    our eyes have seen it.'

²² You have seen, O Lord; do not be silent!
    O Lord, do not be far from me!
²³ Wake up! Bestir yourself for my defense,
    for my cause, my God and my Lord!
²⁴ Vindicate me, O Lord, my God,
    according to your righteousness,
    and do not let them rejoice over me.
²⁵ Do not let them say to themselves,
    'Aha, we have our heart's desire.'
Do not let them say, 'We have swallowed you up.'

²⁶ Let all those who rejoice at my calamity
   be put to shame and confusion;
let those who exalt themselves against me
   be clothed with shame and dishonor.

²⁷ Let those who desire my vindication
   shout for joy and be glad,
   and say evermore,
'Great is the LORD,
   who delights in the welfare of his servant.'
²⁸ Then my tongue shall tell of your righteousness
   and of your praise all day long.

This psalm is a characteristic prayer of lamentation. It largely consists of three recurring speech patterns of Israel's lament:

1. *Complaint* in hyperbolic language seeks to communicate to YHWH as fully as possible the grievance of present circumstances (vv. 7, 11–16, 20–21).
2. *Petition* seeks to draw YHWH into the fray, fully confident that when YHWH is mobilized all will be well. Thus YHWH is addressed with vigorous, compelling imperatives (vv. 1–3, 17, 22–25).
3. *Imprecation* is the dark side of petition. In this speech, the psalmist asks YHWH to punish the adversary, to bring on the adversary dismay commensurate with the trouble the adversary has caused (vv. 4–6, 8, 26). The psalmist characteristically believes that the salvific intervention of YHWH is not complete until those who impose trouble are made to bear the weight of YHWH's determined sovereignty.

There has been scholarly speculation about the precise circumstances of this psalmist, but such speculation is futile. The psalm is expressed in juridical language addressing a judge who metes out punishment and well-being, but the rhetoric of the psalm is open enough to relate, over time, to many circumstances for those who continue to use the psalm in changing venues.

Two particular dimensions of the psalm may be noted that are to some extent distinctive, even though the psalm is fairly stereotypical. First, in verses 9–10, 18, and 27–28, the psalmist makes a promise to offer praise and thanks to YHWH when deliverance is enacted. In the NRSV, each of these three promises of thanks is introduced by "then," that is, upon deliverance. In the Hebrew text, however, the introduction of these rhetorical elements is grammatically less clear. In verses 9 and 28, the promise is introduced by the conjunction *waw*, and in verse 18 there is no introductory particle at all. The move toward thanks in all three cases nonetheless is noteworthy because promised praise and thanks indicate that the petition is offered in deep hope that YHWH will indeed respond. The speaker, representative of Israel's faith, prays in deep confidence to YHWH. The "then" of the phrase, either stated or implicit, suggests a quid pro quo of deliverance and thanks. That is, the speaker withholds thanks and praise, and will not offer them for YHWH until there is a deliverance. In the latter two cases, moreover, the promised thanks and praise will engage "the great congregation." It is plausible, as Patrick Miller suggests, that the petition is a quite personal, even private, matter, but praise is public and requires the engagement of the entire community, which will join in celebration once deliverance is enacted by YHWH.

Second, such a dramatic transaction is accomplished in this psalm in a dialogic way concerning speech and response. We may identify four characters in the drama to whom lines of speech are assigned, even though all of the suggested utterances are, in the first instant, on the lips of the psalmist:

1. It is urged and hoped that YHWH will deliver an oracle that gives assurance to the speaker:

    I am your salvation. (v. 3)

This hoped-for utterance from YHWH is a characteristic divine intervention that decisively alters circumstances.

2. *The speaker* anticipates a time to come when he will deliver a sweeping doxology that will celebrate and enhance YHWH:

    O Lord, who is like you?
    You deliver the weak
       from those too strong for them,
       the weak and needy from
         those who despoil them. (v. 10)

This promised doxology celebrates YHWH's incomparability and locates that divine incomparability in YHWH's engagement on behalf of the weak.[95]

3. *The cynical detractors* who abuse and taunt the speaker, the one against whom petition is made, are also permitted to speak their most characteristic mock:

    Aha! aha! (v. 21)

This particle of speech in context appears to be a dismissive comment; the term itself is perhaps an onomatopoeia, a sound like that of a mocking animal. The point

---

[95] Walter Brueggemann, *Theology of the Old Testament: Testimony, Dispute, Advocacy* (Minneapolis: Fortress Press, 1997), 139–144.

apparently is that the adversary makes light of the speaker, who is thereby made vulnerable and socially exposed. This utterance of the adversary is reinforced by the imagined statement of verse 25 where the same particle is repeated:

> Do not let them say to themselves,
>   "Aha, we have our heart's desire."
> Do not let them say, "We have swallowed you up." (v. 25)

4. The fourth speech is the culminating doxological address of *the community of faith* in which the speaker is gladly embedded. At the end of the poem, the community joins the speaker in praise to the God who has given *shalom* to the speaker. YHWH's act is celebrated as an act of putting the world right.

These four speakers, in the imagination of the poet, sketch out the interactive tension of the drama whereby the promissory oracle of YHWH, the anticipated praise of the delivered speaker, the taunt of the adversary, and the supportive doxology of the community are all outlined. This pattern of interaction, taken as a whole, enacts the drama of faith from *need* to *joy* and *well-being*. The entire drama is advanced and accomplished by the rhetorical exchange in which subsequent Psalm-users may participate.

A Closer Look: Everything in God's Hands

The imprecation against the adversary is vicious and relentless (vv. 4–6, 8, 26). This sort of utterance, so characteristic of Israel's laments, no doubt poses problems for a belated theological interpretation, either Jewish or Christian. The most helpful treatment of this issue in the Psalter is by Erich Zenger, who understands such speech as an act of faith that God, in the end, will prevail over evil and those who do evil:

As poetic prayers, the psalms of vengeance are a passionate clinging to God when everything really speaks *against* God. For that reason they can rightly be called *psalms of zeal*, to the extent that in them passion for God is aflame in the midst of the ashes of doubt about God and despair over human beings. These psalms are the expression of a longing that evil, and evil people, may not have the last word in history, for this world and its history belong to God. Thus, to use theological terminology, these psalms are realized theodicy: They affirm God by surrendering the last word *to God*. They give *to God* not only their lament about their desperate situation, but also the right to judge the originators of that situation. They leave *everything* in God's hands, even feelings of hatred and aggression.

These psalms do not arise from the well-tempered psychological state of people from whom every scrap of sensitivity and emotion has been driven out. On the contrary, they are serious about the fundamental biblical conviction that in prayer we may say everything, literally everything, if only we say it to "GOD," who is our father and mother.[96]

PSALM 36 – TO THE LEADER. OF DAVID, THE SERVANT OF THE LORD

¹ Transgression speaks to the wicked
  deep in their hearts;
there is no fear of God
  before their eyes.
² For they flatter themselves in their own eyes
  that their iniquity cannot be found out and hated.
³ The words of their mouths are mischief and deceit;
  they have ceased to act wisely and do good.
⁴ They plot mischief while on their beds;
  they are set on a way that is not good;
  they do not reject evil.

⁵ Your steadfast love, O LORD, extends to the heavens,
  your faithfulness to the clouds.
⁶ Your righteousness is like the mighty mountains,
  your judgments are like the great deep;
  you save humans and animals alike, O LORD.

⁷ How precious is your steadfast love, O God!
  All people may take refuge in the shadow of your wings.
⁸ They feast on the abundance of your house,
  and you give them drink from the river of your delights.
⁹ For with you is the fountain of life;
  in your light we see light.

¹⁰ O continue your steadfast love to those who know you,
  and your salvation to the upright of heart!

96   Erich Zenger, *A God of Vengeance? Understanding the Psalms of Divine Wrath* (Louisville, KY: Westminster John Knox Press, 1994), 79.

¹¹ Do not let the foot of the arrogant tread on me,
   or the hand of the wicked drive me away.
¹² There the evildoers lie prostrate;
   they are thrust down, unable to rise.

This psalm is a prayer of trust in YHWH by one who has experienced betrayal and alienation from other members of the community. The psalm is divided into two primary parts, verses 1–4 concerning *the destructive behavior of the wicked* and verses 5–9 concerning *the steadfast fidelity of YHWH*, which contrasts with the way of the wicked. These two contrasting themes are brought together in the concluding petitionary prayer of verses 10–12.

The opening section is a rumination on the destructive conduct of the adversaries of the psalmist, the wicked who live in devious, destructive, and arrogant ways. The psalmist portrays them as alienated from God ("no fear of God"), but it is destructiveness in social relationships in which the speaker is involved. The opening line of the psalm is odd and not without problems. The NRSV translation suggests that "transgression" (rebellion) is a substantive force that addresses the wicked and sets them on their disobedient way. The Hebrew text has a first-person pronoun, "speak in my heart," suggesting that the speaker spends much time pondering being preoccupied by the adversary. Either way, these verses attest to an acute social disorder in the community.

After such an extended characterization of the wicked, verse 5 turns abruptly from that portrayal. Now the name of YHWH is uttered for the first time; YHWH is celebrated as a faithful creator-redeemer God who saves all creatures. In verses 5–6, four most characteristic terms are employed in order to fully bear witness to YHWH. In verse 5, the most defining covenantal word pair is employed, "grace and truth" (*ḥesed we' amunah*). In verse 6, a second word pair is used to signify covenantal rectitude, righteousness-judgment (*ṣedeqah-mišpat*). The four terms together constitute a summary of YHWH's profound responsibility known in the saving memory of Israel and in the sustenance of all creation. The full phrasing of verse 6, "humans and animals," suggests a focus on the goodness and reliability of all creation, though creation is here subsumed in the category of "save."

The meditation on YHWH's fidelity is continued in verses 7–9 with a reiteration of the prime category *ḥesed* (steadfast love). These verses then exposit God's fidelity in some specificity. The reference to "shadow of your wings" and "abundance of your house" is likely a reference to the Jerusalem temple, where the extravagance of YHWH is fully exhibited and experienced. Appeal to the temple, in this construe, is apparently in terms of creation theology and not the "salvation history" of Israel. Thus the characterization of extravagance speaks of "rivers of delight," in which the word "delight" is "Eden," thus alluding to creation (see Gen 2:10–14). The imagery of creation is reinforced in verse 9 with reference to a fountain and light. These images pertain to the life-giving power of the creator that is vested in the Jerusalem temple.

That life-giving power stands in deep contrast to the death-dealing wickedness of verses 1–4. The psalm leaves no doubt that YHWH's abiding fidelity will override the destructiveness of "transgression."

This note of profound trust in YHWH's goodness is the basis for the prayer in verses 10–12. In verse 10, the term *hesed* (steadfast love) is repeated now for the third time in a petition that seeks YHWH's fidelity for YHWH's "covenant-keepers." It is likely that "those who know you" now refers not to all creatures or all human creatures but to those who stand in the Sinai or Zion covenant. The positive petition of verse 10 is matched in verses 11–12 by a final plea asking protection from the wicked we already encountered in verses 1–4. In this final utterance, that group of troublemakers is now characterized as "arrogant, wicked, evil-doers," a reprise on the statement of verses 1–4. The conclusion is a comment dismissive of that group of despised people who are now "unable to rise," that is, without power and therefore without power to hurt. They are, in the end, adversaries, in contrast with the ones who have known YHWH and are therefore safe, fed, watered, cared for, and surrounded in the well-being that YHWH can give and the wicked cannot negate.

A Closer Look: The Temple and Creation

There is no doubt that verses 5–9 praise YHWH in categories that are resonant with creation theology. The psalmist witnesses to God's fidelity on a cosmic scale. Given that, the mention of "your house" in verse 8 is curious because it seems to refer to the Jerusalem temple. The phrase is so odd in context that J. Clinton McCann believes it cannot refer literally to the temple.[97]

If, however, we remember that the Jerusalem temple is a replica and miniature of creation, then the mention of the temple with reference to "rivers of delight," fountains of life, and light is with some precision linked to the good, life-giving order of creation. In commenting on the correlation of Genesis 1 and the tabernacle in Exodus 25–31, 35–40, Jon Levenson can conclude:

Collectively, the function of these correspondences is to underscore the depiction of the sanctuary as a world, that is, an ordered, supportive, and obedient environment, and the depiction of the world as a sanctuary, that is, a place in which the reign of God is visible and unchallenged, and his holiness is palpable, unthreatened, and pervasive. Our examination of the two sets of Priestly texts, one at the beginning of Genesis and the other at the end of Exodus, has developed powerful evidence that, as in many cultures, the Temple was conceived as a microcosm, a miniature world. But it is equally the case that in Israel (and probably also in the other cultures), the world – or, as I should say, the ideal or

---

97 J. C. McCann, Jr., "Book of Psalms," in L. E. Keck et al. (eds.), *The New Interpreter's Bible*, vol. 4 (1996), 823.

protological world, the world viewed *sub specie creationis* – was conceived, at least in Priestly circles, as a macro-temple, the palace of God in which all are obedient to his commands.[98]

Given such a cosmic vision experienced quite locally, we are able to see that the "wicked" and "evil-doers" not only threaten the psalmist, but by their arrogance they jeopardize the order of creation that is sustained by YHWH's fidelity.

This linkage of creation and temple is also indicated by the fact that the "rivers of delight" in Gen 2:10–14 are in the priestly tradition of Ezekiel resituated in the temple:

Then he brought me back to the entrance of the temple; there, water was flowing from below the threshold of the temple toward the east (for the temple faced east); and the water was flowing down from below the south end of the threshold of the temple, south of the altar. Then he brought me out by way of the north gate, and led me around on the outside to the outer gate that faces toward the east; and the water was coming out on the south side. (Ezek 47:1–2)

Bridging the Horizons: Light, Water, and Bread

The gifts of life expressed as water, light, and the food of the feast are taken up as defining images in the fourth gospel: light (Jn 1:9), water (Jn 4:14), and bread (food) (Jn 6:33–35). What is adumbrated in the psalm is given, in Christian articulation, full play in John's gospel. Where the rule of God is visible, the gifts that sustain life are fully and palpably present.

PSALM 37 – OF DAVID

[1] Do not fret because of the wicked;
do not be envious of wrongdoers,
[2] for they will soon fade like the grass,
and wither like the green herb.

[3] Trust in the LORD, and do good;
so you will live in the land, and enjoy security.

[98] Jon D. Levenson, *Creation and the Persistence of Evil: The Jewish Drama of Divine Omnipotence* (San Francisco: Harper and Row, 1988), 86.

4 Take delight in the LORD,
     and he will give you the desires of your heart.

5 Commit your way to the LORD;
     trust in him, and he will act.
6 He will make your vindication shine like the light,
     and the justice of your cause like the noonday.

7 Be still before the LORD, and wait patiently for him;
     do not fret over those who prosper in their way,
     over those who carry out evil devices.

8 Refrain from anger, and forsake wrath.
     Do not fret – it leads only to evil.
9 For the wicked shall be cut off,
     but those who wait for the LORD shall inherit the land.

10 Yet a little while, and the wicked will be no more;
      though you look diligently for their place, they will not be there.
11 But the meek shall inherit the land,
      and delight in abundant prosperity.

12 The wicked plot against the righteous,
      and gnash their teeth at them;
13 but the LORD laughs at the wicked,
      for he sees that their day is coming.

14 The wicked draw the sword and bend their bows
      to bring down the poor and needy,
      to kill those who walk uprightly;
15 their sword shall enter their own heart,
      and their bows shall be broken.

16 Better is a little that the righteous person has
      than the abundance of many wicked.
17 For the arms of the wicked shall be broken,
      but the LORD upholds the righteous.

18 The LORD knows the days of the blameless,
      and their heritage will abide for ever;

¹⁹ they are not put to shame in evil times,
   in the days of famine they have abundance.

²⁰ But the wicked perish,
   and the enemies of the Lord are like the glory of the pastures;
   they vanish – like smoke they vanish away.

²¹ The wicked borrow, and do not pay back,
   but the righteous are generous and keep giving;
²² for those blessed by the Lord shall inherit the land,
   but those cursed by him shall be cut off.

²³ Our steps are made firm by the Lord,
   when he delights in our way;
²⁴ though we stumble, we shall not fall headlong,
   for the Lord holds us by the hand.

²⁵ I have been young, and now am old,
   yet I have not seen the righteous forsaken
   or their children begging bread.
²⁶ They are ever giving liberally and lending,
   and their children become a blessing.

²⁷ Depart from evil, and do good;
   so you shall abide for ever.
²⁸ For the Lord loves justice;
   he will not forsake his faithful ones.

The righteous shall be kept safe for ever,
   but the children of the wicked shall be cut off.
²⁹ The righteous shall inherit the land,
   and live in it for ever.

³⁰ The mouths of the righteous utter wisdom,
   and their tongues speak justice.
³¹ The law of their God is in their hearts;
   their steps do not slip.

³² The wicked watch for the righteous,
   and seek to kill them.

³³ The LORD will not abandon them to their power,
   or let them be condemned when they are brought to trial.

³⁴ Wait for the LORD, and keep to his way,
   and he will exalt you to inherit the land;
   you will look on the destruction of the wicked.

³⁵ I have seen the wicked oppressing,
   and towering like a cedar of Lebanon.
³⁶ Again I passed by, and they were no more;
   though I sought them, they could not be found.

³⁷ Mark the blameless, and behold the upright,
   for there is posterity for the peaceable.
³⁸ But transgressors shall be altogether destroyed;
   the posterity of the wicked shall be cut off.

³⁹ The salvation of the righteous is from the LORD;
   he is their refuge in the time of trouble.
⁴⁰ The LORD helps them and rescues them;
   he rescues them from the wicked, and saves them,
   because they take refuge in him.

Readers of Book I of the Hebrew Psalter will find themselves in familiar territory with the contrast between the righteous and the wicked undergirding Psalm 37. Psalms 1 and 2 introduce the theme at the very beginning of the book. A concern with the wicked is central to Psalms 35 and 36 and continues in this psalm. Psalm 37 is in the form of an alphabetic acrostic; each section, usually two verses, begins with successive letters of the Hebrew alphabet. The acrostic is an anthology of proverbial sayings. The purpose of the psalm is similar to that of the book of Proverbs – practical instruction for living.

In this psalm, the problem is the prosperity of the wicked. The contrast between the righteous and the wicked is central to this text, which is a kind of meditation on the problem that the wicked seem to be doing well in life. The psalm puts the question in terms of a faith choice: Do you believe in the prosperity of the wicked or in the providence of YHWH? Contemporary readers need to tread carefully, however. The psalm is not a piece of theory that articulates a universal structure of reality. It is rather a pragmatic homily on how to live in the face of the observation that the wicked seem to prosper. In parts of the psalm (vv. 25–26 and 35–36), the speaker looks back on experience and, using an autobiographical form, gives advice from that experience.

The psalmist also speaks of the faithful inheriting the land. It is likely that this is to be interpreted not in a literal sense but as a symbol of a full life. In living faithfully one finds wholeness. The psalm may be an educational tool for the young to urge youth to live faithfully as the psalm urges. The contrast between the righteous or wise and the wicked or foolish paths of life and their consequences provides the poet with a properly ordered universe, but the sayings in the psalm, like those in Proverbs, do not attempt to describe a universal and guaranteed theory for success in life, nor do they detail how to interpret events as clear determinants of whether a person is righteous or wicked. The sayings instead have the purpose of instruction for the community.

A Closer Look: A Wisdom Psalm?

The genre and purpose of Psalm 37 are important for its interpretation. Many interpreters would classify the text as a wisdom psalm, as suggested by the preceding comparison with the book of Proverbs. The use of wisdom in recent scholarship as a category in Psalms study has been controversial. James Crenshaw, in his introductory volume, has argued against the category and against the view that there is wisdom influence in the book of Psalms.[99] He suggests that there is lack of clarity in defining wisdom and its characteristics, and thus the category is finally confusing. The preceding comments focus on the psalm's didactic purpose.

The exposition of this psalm will consider it in four parts. In verses 1–11, the poem instructs in the imperative mode. The psalmist begins with the assumption of divine providence, and that leads to a hope that pervades life and leads to the imperative instruction in the first part of the poem. The poem calls its readers to trust in divine providence and thus live faithfully, therein finding health for life. Then a sense that the wicked are prospering will not be threatening; the success of evil opponents will not bring anxiety or hostility. The view of the psalmist is also that such prosperity of the wicked is transitory; it will fade like the drought-stricken grass. The psalm's opening verses suggest the familiar contrast between the wicked, who oppose God and the community of faith, and the righteous, who depend on divine providence. Verses 5 and 6 use images of light to suggest that YHWH brings justice and wholeness in life; compare Ps 36:9. That needs to be the focus for the faithful. Obsession with the apparent success of evil opponents is unproductive and can be debilitating. That seems to be the psalmist's concern for the community; note the imperatives in verse 8: "Refrain from anger," "forsake wrath," and "do not fret."

---

[99] J. L. Crenshaw, *Psalms* (2001), 87–95.

With verses 12–20, the psalm moves from instruction in the imperative mode to observations about life. Verses 12–15 imagine divine laughter at the foolish attempts of the wicked to scheme against the righteous. To take the matter further, the evil of the wicked will roll back on their own heads in a kind of boomerang effect. The familiar contrast between the righteous and wicked is central to this part of the psalm and takes the form of contrasting poetic lines or antitheses. Verses 12 and 13 provide contrasts, as do the two lines of verse 17. Verses 18 and 19 also contrast with verse 20. Perhaps these verses suggest a societal context behind the psalm, one in which the wicked are in power and the righteous struggle with that reality. Such contexts lead to many of the petitions in the Psalter. The verses are also rich with poetic imagery portraying the wicked as both hunters in verse 14 and as beasts in verse 12. The demise of the wicked is also stated in no uncertain terms in verses 15, 17, and 20.

Verses 21–29 characterize the lifestyles of the righteous and wicked and their consequences. The righteous live out of a relationship initiated by divine grace and thereby contribute to the community in generous and gracious ways; they are givers rather than takers. YHWH delights in the righteous path of life and therefore holds such people by the hand, but it is important to notice that the righteous stumble. The carefully put perspective of the psalm becomes clear in verses 23–24. The righteous stumble, but YHWH is present:

> though we stumble, we shall not fall headlong,
> for the Lord holds us by the hand. (v. 24)

Verses 25–26 take an autobiographical form as the psalmist looks back over a long life and affirms that the righteous operate out of a generous spirit and still do not suffer from want. The psalm consistently argues that God sustains those who are faithful. In living faithfully, they encounter hope. The "faithful ones" in verse 28 are those who have encountered divine fidelity and are thus able to live generously. The faith relationship makes full and complete living possible. The faithful are the ones who can "depart from evil and do good" (v. 27).

The psalm's concluding reflections in verses 30–40 include both instructions in the imperative and observations about life. The body imagery of verses 30–31 of mouth, tongue, heart, and step portray the righteous as those who meditate on the *torah*, as suggested in Ps 1:2, and so speak wisdom and justice. Life for the righteous is a divine gift. The wicked, in contrast, will try every trick available to plot against the righteous. The imperative instruction in verse 34 is to "wait for the Lord and keep to his way," an instruction familiar to readers of the Psalms. The call is to hope in YHWH, who is worthy of trust. Verses 34–35 paint a scene in which the wicked are no more. They are compared to a powerful and oppressive tree, and in this autobiographical reflection, the psalmist looks for the tree but can no longer find it. The righteous or peaceable, in contrast, are like a flourishing tree, as suggested in Psalm 1, and so find a future (v. 37). Divine refuge crafts a future for the faithful in times of prosperity and in times of oppression. Such refuge is a divine gift.

Bridging the Horizons: Imperatives Based on Indicatives

At the beginning of the exposition on the psalm's parts, we suggested that the psalmist assumes divine providence. Based on that affirmation of faith, the psalmist urges the community of faith toward a clear path of life. The psalm's purpose is educational. In a similar way, in the New Testament, the epistles with imperatives urge the community toward faithful living with imperatives based on the indicative of divine work to bring about right relationships. Similarly, in the gospels, Jesus announces the kingdom of God and, based on that, calls for faithful living. An interesting and rather different appropriation of the psalm occurs in the eschatological Qumran community, which thinks more of the apocalyptic end of the wicked and the triumph of the Qumran community and its leaders.

Some readers may be tempted to dismiss Psalm 37 as naive or even misleading in portraying life as just. The preceding exposition has suggested that the poem is more nuanced, however. The psalm admits that one can observe life and see the wicked succeed. It admits that an honest view of life brings troubling questions and does not advance all the answers. At the same time, the poem believes, based on life experience, that God is trustworthy. The justice (vv. 6 and 28) and faithfulness of God are at the heart of this meditation. The psalm does not exhibit a triumphalist tone, but it tenaciously holds onto the trustworthiness of God in the long view.

PSALM 38 – A PSALM OF DAVID, FOR THE MEMORIAL OFFERING

¹ O LORD, do not rebuke me in your anger,
  or discipline me in your wrath.
² For your arrows have sunk into me,
  and your hand has come down on me.

³ There is no soundness in my flesh
  because of your indignation;
there is no health in my bones
  because of my sin.
⁴ For my iniquities have gone over my head;
  they weigh like a burden too heavy for me.

⁵ My wounds grow foul and fester
  because of my foolishness;

⁶ I am utterly bowed down and prostrate;
  all day long I go around mourning.
⁷ For my loins are filled with burning,
  and there is no soundness in my flesh.
⁸ I am utterly spent and crushed;
  I groan because of the tumult of my heart.

⁹ O LORD, all my longing is known to you;
  my sighing is not hidden from you.
¹⁰ My heart throbs, my strength fails me;
  as for the light of my eyes – it also has gone from me.
¹¹ My friends and companions stand aloof from my affliction,
  and my neighbors stand far off.

¹² Those who seek my life lay their snares;
  those who seek to hurt me speak of ruin,
  and meditate treachery all day long.

¹³ But I am like the deaf, I do not hear;
  like the mute, who cannot speak.
¹⁴ Truly, I am like one who does not hear,
  and in whose mouth is no retort.

¹⁵ But it is for you, O LORD, that I wait;
  it is you, O LORD my God, who will answer.
¹⁶ For I pray, 'Only do not let them rejoice over me,
  those who boast against me when my foot slips.'

¹⁷ For I am ready to fall,
  and my pain is ever with me.
¹⁸ I confess my iniquity;
  I am sorry for my sin.
¹⁹ Those who are my foes without cause are mighty,
  and many are those who hate me wrongfully.
²⁰ Those who render me evil for good
  are my adversaries because I follow after good.

²¹ Do not forsake me, O LORD;
  O my God, do not be far from me;
²² make haste to help me,
  O LORD, my salvation.

This psalm, clearly a poem of lament, is reckoned in classical Christian interpretation among the seven penitential psalms. Alongside Psalm 51, it makes the most direct statement concerning guilt, repentance of guilt, and awareness of punishment because of the "indignation" of YHWH. The great body of the psalm is a complaint that describes the suffering of the psalmist, which is taken as divine punishment. In verses 3–8, there is a detailed description of bodily illness and a lack of "soundness" (vv. 3, 7). This condition is a result "of my sin," "my iniquities," "my foolishness." In verses 10–14, the poet continues a descriptive statement; here alongside physical illness are social alienation and vulnerability before adversaries who place his life in jeopardy. The same characterization of unbearable misery is voiced in verses 17–20, again with a heavy accent on sin. All three sections, verses 3–8, 10–14, and 17–20, describe the trouble, but only the first and third units of text make a direct connection to sin.

It is fair to say that the main line of argument here offers a direct connection between *sin and suffering*, a simplistic connection that persists in many popular forms of contemporary faith. Attention should be given, however, to verse 19, which seems to speak against such a connection, for it is asserted that social abuse is "without cause," thus breaking that simplistic connection. The same qualifying language is used in Pss 35:19 and 65:9, where abuse is also "without cause." In Lam 3:52, moreover, the same qualification would seem to undermine the accent on guilt in that long poem. The recurrence of this qualification suggests, so it seems, that Israel's critical reflection wavered between a systemic direct connection of sin and suffering and an awareness that such a tight correlation is not sustainable.

In any case, the clue to reading this psalm as a voice of faith is to notice where the divine name occurs; that is, where YHWH is directly addressed in petition. As a start, we note that in the three extended sections already cited, the name of YHWH does not occur (vv. 3–8, 10–14, and 17–20). And indeed, since these sections are descriptive complaints, there is no reason that the divine name should occur, though in verse 3 the pronoun "you" refers to YHWH.

It is most important that this long, descriptive complaint is interrupted or countered by the invocation of the name of YHWH, which, in each case, is an act of hope that suffering, even if it is as punishment, is not the final outcome of this life. In verses 1–2, YHWH is addressed in a petition with two imperatives. In verse 9, the term "Lord" is not the proper name YHWH but the divine title *'adon*; in this address, the psalmist states a longing and a sighing for new life. Clearly, the longing and sighing are profound acts of hope that life could be otherwise if only YHWH would intervene.

The third use of the divine name is in the fullest petition in verses 15–16, where YHWH is named twice, with the appellation "my God." YHWH moreover is addressed with a strong independent pronoun of direct address: "It is you...." YHWH is the powerful hope of the psalmist in trouble, the one to whom prayer is addressed. Verse 16 even quotes the prayer that is a characteristic response to the trouble already described. Most important, the psalmist accents, "It is you who will answer"; and the divine answer will be intervention that will terminate the suffering. The sin–suffering connection voiced in the psalm may be impersonal and even mechanistic in a way that knows that certain *deeds* do indeed produce certain *outcomes*. But if that logic is simplistic and reductionist, the appeal against it in these petitions is intimate and relational, grounded in a deep covenantal conviction. Thus the prayer appeals beyond and outside any conventional, stereotypical notion of punishment to the fidelity of YHWH, who will be the advocate and rescuer of the psalmist. The power of the psalm is missed unless we see how the petition overrules the condition of complaint. That expectation that YHWH will "override" such mechanistic punishment is indeed the substance of Israel's faith, the subject of Israel's prayer, and the grounds of Israel's future. In this prayer, Israel refuses to be fated to the consequences of its action and relies completely on the reality of the God who intervenes to save.

In the conclusion of verses 21–22, YHWH is addressed a fourth time, now not only as "my God," as in verse 15, but also as "my salvation." In the complaints, the speaker has used first-person pronouns many times as a self-reference in order to describe the circumstances. In these verses, however, the promise is an expression of intense communion and fidelity, now no longer focused on the "I" of the psalmist. The conclusion voices three imperatives: "Do not forsake ... Do not be far from me ... Make haste." The prayer summons YHWH to come where YHWH has not been. The language of "abandonment" (*'azav*) and "far" (*raḥoq*) echo the more familiar Psalm 22. The psalmist, set deep in Israel's faith, trusts in the interpersonal reality of YHWH, who can and surely will override unbearable circumstances.

A Closer Look: Sin and Suffering

This psalm poses in acute form the question of the relationship between sin and suffering, perhaps the ultimate and certainly a recurring pastoral question. Taken in the most simplistic fashion, it is popularly assumed that sin and suffering have a one-to-one correlation, a view embraced by some forms of retribution theology in the Old Testament. Such a tight correlation cannot be sustained, however, as is made clear in the poem of Job. In a much more sophisticated mode, however, the question persists. If

- congruity with the will of the creator fashions well-being, and if
- sin violates the will of the creator,
- then sin does indeed produce suffering.

In the end, this psalm affirms that it is *relationship to YHWH* and not performance of a required code that breaks the connection of sin and suffering.

The issue is sharply voiced in the healing narrative of Jesus in Mk 2:1–12. The "holy people" object that Jesus proposes to forgive sin; Jesus, however, refuses to quit as healer. It is clear in this narrative that Jesus proceeds on the assumption

that sin has disabled this man. For that reason, *forgiveness* and *healing* are intimately connected if not equated. Both forgiveness and healing break the vicious
cycle of deathliness that is set in motion by disregarding YHWH's given order of
life. The issue pertains peculiarly to concerns for health and self-care, and probably the issue of environmental abuse. God's order is not mocked with impunity!
But beyond the quid pro quo of God's ordering, there is the ability and readiness
of YHWH to make all things new. It is on this ability and readiness of YHWH to
enact a newness that the psalmist stakes his future.

PSALM 39 – TO THE LEADER: TO JEDUTHUN. A PSALM OF DAVID

¹ I said, 'I will guard my ways
   that I may not sin with my tongue;
I will keep a muzzle on my mouth
   as long as the wicked are in my presence.'
² I was silent and still;
   I held my peace to no avail;
my distress grew worse,
³ my heart became hot within me.
While I mused, the fire burned;
   then I spoke with my tongue:

⁴ 'LORD, let me know my end,
   and what is the measure of my days;
   let me know how fleeting my life is.
⁵ You have made my days a few handbreadths,
   and my lifetime is as nothing in your sight.
Surely everyone stands as a mere breath.
      Selah
⁶ Surely everyone goes about like a shadow.
Surely for nothing they are in turmoil;
   they heap up, and do not know who will gather.

⁷ 'And now, O LORD, what do I wait for?
   My hope is in you.
⁸ Deliver me from all my transgressions.

Do not make me the scorn of the fool.
⁹ I am silent; I do not open my mouth,
  for it is you who have done it.
¹⁰ Remove your stroke from me;
  I am worn down by the blows of your hand.

¹¹ 'You chastise mortals
  in punishment for sin,
consuming like a moth what is dear to them;
  surely everyone is a mere breath.
    Selah

¹² 'Hear my prayer, O LORD,
  and give ear to my cry;
  do not hold your peace at my tears.
For I am your passing guest,
  an alien, like all my forebears.
¹³ Turn your gaze away from me, that I may smile again,
  before I depart and am no more.'

The social context of Psalm 39 reflects a number of similarities to Psalm 38. Psalm 39 is a prayer for help, and enemies are present. Readers are confronted with both silence and hope in the face of what might be illness. At the same time, the psalm is rather distinct from other prayers for help that readers will find in Book I of the Hebrew Psalter. Robert Alter suggests, "The speaker flounders in a world of radical ambiguities where the antithetical values of speech and silence, existence and extinction, perhaps even innocence and transgression, have been brought dangerously close together."[100] The psalm attends to human transience along with silence and speech, as well as sin and suffering. Scholarly imaginations have been at work to construct an ancient setting from which the psalm arose. It may be that a setting of major illness is behind the prayer along with the aggravation of insensitive opponents and a sense of floundering for a way forward in life. The psalm does have the sense of a reflection on life and struggling to make sense of it all and consider it all. In this prayer, the transient and troubling sense of life seems to be more important than any particular crisis. In terms of structure, the poem makes a turn at verse 7 and moves toward a strong conclusion. The exposition that follows will consider four sections of verses: 1–3, 4–6, 7–11, and 12–13.

---

[100] R. Alter, *Art of Biblical Poetry* (1985), 69.

1. *Verses 1–3.* The psalm does not begin in the Psalter's traditional way for peti-
    tions. Rather, it begins with a self-quotation articulating the psalmist's intent
    to remain silent. The psalm makes it clear that the petitioner has a question
    to ask YHWH, but that the presence of enemies is also a focus of atten-
    tion. It may be that the petitioner does not want to give the mockers any
    ammunition by giving the impression of accusing YHWH in any way. The
    petitioner thus says, "I will keep a muzzle on my mouth." The problem is
    that the enemies stand ready to say that the crisis at hand is deserved, and so
    the petitioner does not want to aid their cause in any way. The enemies rep-
    resent the common view that there is a certain connection between sin and
    suffering. The setting is akin to that in the book of Job. Initially, Job is silent,
    but then fervent prayer and strong protest flow forth in his speeches. As the
    trouble continues in this psalm, "the fire burned" within the psalmist and
    speech came forth. The need to speak trumped the efforts to remain silent.
    These opening verses are also akin to the setting of the prophet Jeremiah,
    who determined to be silent when his preaching caused such trouble, but
    the fire began to burn within him. These first three verses intensify as the
    pressure builds for the reader: "my distress grew worse," and the burning
    within came to the surface. Like a geyser, the fire came forth and the speech
    began to flow. The content of the speech follows.

2. *Verses 4–6.* The speech that follows is a petition, but it does not give the
    sense of an eruption. It rather has more of a sense of a reflection on the
    transience of life. It does not give the sense of "sin with my tongue" (v. 1).
    Verses 4–6 do, however, give the sense of intensifying as they proceed.
    The psalmist's first question is about the length of this troublesome path
    of life: How long will it last? Verse 4 sets the questions, and verses 5–6
    intensify the issue with images of the transience of human life. The first
    image is that life is but "a few handbreadths." A handbreadth is the small-
    est of measures, the measure of the four fingers of a hand held together.
    A life is nothing but a vapor. People are like shadows in the midst of
    turmoil and know nothing of the end. The images seem to pile on one
    another, intensifying the psalmist's question about the end of this tran-
    sient human life. The repetition of sounds in the poetry adds to this effect
    of poetry heaping up. Life is fleeting (*ḥādēl* – v. 4); a lifetime (*ḥeldî* – v.
    5) is nothing, a mere breath (*hebel* – v. 5), the word Qoheleth uses to
    portray human transience. Three consecutive lines in verses 5–6 begin
    with *'ak*, "surely." The question presses on the exasperated psalmist. The
    term rendered "shadow" in verse 6 can also carry the sense of "image"
    and is one of the terms used in Gen 1:26–27 to portray the creation of
    woman and man in the image of God. When one reads the texts together,
    the suggestion is that finite, human life is not insignificant. In Genesis 1,

these images of God are called to exercise dominion in the creation. In Psalm 38, the petitioner continues with human initiative in addressing God with troubling and articulate questions. These verses are in the form of a question, but implicit in them is a cry for YHWH to answer.

3.   *Verses 7–11.* The psalm makes a turn with verse 7 and the question of where hope is to be found. To "wait" is to hope or expect. Immediately the psalmist affirms that any hope is to be found in YHWH rather than in the opponents or any other component of human life. On that basis, the psalmist moves to matters of confession and forgiveness, and petition comes to the surface. Now the speaker suggests that the oppressing blows of life originate from YHWH, and the silence articulated at the beginning of the psalm returns. Most interpreters understand verse 10 in terms of illness. The speaker is clearly at the lowest point and returns to the theme of the transience of life in verse 11. Life is but a vapor, and the oppressive divine presence takes a severe toll. The themes from earlier in the psalm of silence and human transience and a fear of the scorn of enemies return in these verses, which explicitly cry for deliverance "from all my transgressions."

4.   *Verses 12–13.* The concluding verses of the psalm begin with a petition for hearing characteristic of the lament psalms. The following lines, however, depart from that tradition. The psalmist's tears become motivation for YHWH to respond to the petition. The striking self-portrait in the last line of verse 12 as a sojourner, a resident alien who is passing through the land, as are the people of Israel, brings to mind Lev 25:23 and 1 Chr 29:15. In the latter text, David reflects at the end of life on its transience in a way similar to Psalm 39. Life is transient for the psalmist and for all humans. The concluding petition comes as a surprise to readers when it asks for YHWH to turn away. Up to this point, the psalmist has been pleading for YHWH to come and deliver him from transgressions and troubles. Now the petition is for the oppressive divine presence to turn away so that a smile may be possible before the end. The concluding petition is again reminiscent of Job, in which God is both the real trouble and the only hope. The conclusion is both poignant and a weary end, the hope for a smile before I "am no more."

A Closer Look: Jeduthun

The superscription to Psalm 39 provides the first reference to Jeduthun, identified in 1 Chr 16:41 as one of David's important musicians. The heading suggests a tie between Jeduthun and the leader of worship and associates the psalm with Israel's corporate worship.

Bridging the Horizons: The Ambiguity of Life

Psalm 39 is not the standard petition in the book of Psalms. At its center is the ambiguity of life. Psalm 38 assumed a connection between sin and suffering but opened the door to questions; Psalm 39 walks through the door and lives with the great mix of questions life brings:

Psalm 39 articulates despair and hope *simultaneously*. In so doing, it portrays the way life really is: terrifyingly short, yet awesomely wonderful. And it represents the tension inevitably involved in our response to life – that is, both hopeful awe and nearly unspeakable despair that finally cannot be silenced.[101]

The psalm reflects on the transience and troubles of life, of an oppressive divine presence, and of a connection between sin and suffering. The psalm also speaks of hope and petitions for help and forgiveness. The psalmist searches for a hope beyond a mechanistic connection between acts and consequences. The psalm moves beyond an oversimplified theology that is common in contemporary society. Life is ambiguous, and the psalmist strains toward a theology of a hopeful divine presence in that life. The poem brings to mind both Job and Ecclesiastes. The psalm articulates silence and speech, hope and despair, all in just thirteen verses. The movement is from speech to hope, and that seems to subvert the despair, but the concluding verse is ambiguous at best. Still, as in Job's experience, address of YHWH continues. Is that a significant sign of hope in despair? All are sojourners and resident aliens in a world and life created and sustained by God. The psalmist searches for a way forward with the persistent troubles of life; the beginning point is a relational one in verse 7: "My hope is in you."

PSALM 40 – TO THE LEADER. OF DAVID. A PSALM

¹ I waited patiently for the LORD;
  he inclined to me and heard my cry.
² He drew me up from the desolate pit,
  out of the miry bog,
and set my feet upon a rock,
  making my steps secure.

---

[101] J. C. McCann, Jr., "Book of Psalms," in L. E. Keck et al. (eds.), *The New Interpreter's Bible*, vol. 4 (1996), 837.

³ He put a new song in my mouth,
  a song of praise to our God.
Many will see and fear,
  and put their trust in the LORD.

⁴ Happy are those who make
  the LORD their trust,
who do not turn to the proud,
  to those who go astray after false gods.
⁵ You have multiplied, O LORD my God,
  your wondrous deeds and your thoughts toward us;
  none can compare with you.
Were I to proclaim and tell of them,
  they would be more than can be counted.

⁶ Sacrifice and offering you do not desire,
  but you have given me an open ear.
Burnt-offering and sin-offering
  you have not required.
⁷ Then I said, 'Here I am;
  in the scroll of the book it is written of me.
⁸ I delight to do your will, O my God;
  your law is within my heart.'

⁹ I have told the glad news of deliverance
  in the great congregation;
see, I have not restrained my lips,
  as you know, O LORD.
¹⁰ I have not hidden your saving help within my heart,
  I have spoken of your faithfulness and your salvation;
I have not concealed your steadfast love and your faithfulness
  from the great congregation.

¹¹ Do not, O LORD, withhold
  your mercy from me;
let your steadfast love and your faithfulness
  keep me safe for ever.
¹² For evils have encompassed me
  without number;
my iniquities have overtaken me,

until I cannot see;
they are more than the hairs of my head,
   and my heart fails me.

¹³ Be pleased, O Lᴏʀᴅ, to deliver me;
   O Lᴏʀᴅ, make haste to help me.
¹⁴ Let all those be put to shame and confusion
   who seek to snatch away my life;
let those be turned back and brought to dishonor
   who desire my hurt.
¹⁵ Let those be appalled because of their shame
   who say to me, 'Aha, Aha!'

¹⁶ But may all who seek you
   rejoice and be glad in you;
may those who love your salvation
   say continually, 'Great is the Lᴏʀᴅ!'
¹⁷ As for me, I am poor and needy,
   but the Lᴏʀᴅ takes thought for me.
You are my help and my deliverer;
   do not delay, O my God.

Readers of the Psalms are on familiar ground in Psalm 40 with a prayer in the midst of enemies, though the text's opening section clearly provides a contrast to the view in Psalm 39. Although much about Psalm 40 fits well with the petitions in the early part of the Psalter, its form is not the standard. Rather than moving from petition to thanksgiving, the psalm reverses the order and begins with thanksgiving and concludes with petition. The concluding prayer (vv. 13–17) also appears as the entirety of Psalm 70. The traditional form-critical solution has been to treat the two parts of the psalm as separate texts, but a number of recent interpreters have noted connections between the parts and pointed to the pattern of thanksgiving followed by petition in Psalms 9–10. There thanksgiving becomes a basis for renewed petition. There appears to be sufficient basis for reading Psalm 40 as a unit, and this treatment will follow that approach. It may be that the psalmist included an older petition as part of the psalm or that Psalm 70 is later and drew on the earlier text. The psalm reflects cultic usage, but the ancient setting from which it originated is lost in the mists of time. Scholarly suggestions include the views that the thanksgiving originated from recovery from sickness or from royal victory in battle.

   The opening section of the psalm (vv. 1–5) proceeds in a way characteristic of Israel's expression of thanksgiving by reporting the deliverance from a crisis that YHWH has accomplished on behalf of the psalmist. The familiar opening verse rendered "waited patiently" may give the impression of a passive psalmist, but an intense hope might be a better sense of the first line. The opening verses report that God delivered the speaker from the power of death, here portrayed in terms familiar to readers of the Psalms. The psalmist had encountered the power of Sheol invading life and diminishing life, and the poet compares that experience to a muddy pit with its muck and mire, its darkness and isolation. From "the miry bog," the speaker was delivered to a secure and solid rock. In response, the psalmist brings forth a new song of thanksgiving. The phrasing of verse 3 makes it clear that the song is a divine gift deriving from the divine act of moving the speaker from the miry pit to the secure rock. Verse 4 is in the form of a beatitude pronounced on those trusting YHWH rather than false idols. In contrast to the false idols, YHWH is the one who is able to deliver the trusting from the miry pit. Verse 5 envisions this act of deliverance as part of the extensive ("more than can be counted") salvation history of Israel. The *tôdāh*, or song of thanksgiving, narrates the divine deliverance from trouble in the congregation. The psalmist articulates this proclamation for the purpose of bringing others to trust in YHWH as the one who delivers.

Verses 6–10 continue the themes of thanksgiving by emphasizing the psalmist's response to the divine act of deliverance. The response desired by God is not sacrificial offerings but apparently an attitude of hearing and obeying. The sense of the middle part of verse 6 is a bit obscure, but the emphasis seems to be on hearing and obeying God rather than on sacrifice. Verse 6 is one of the texts often taken to express a negative view of sacrifice. That emphasis combined with verse 8 is reminiscent of the prophecies of a new covenant written on the heart in Jer 31:31–34 and Ezek 36:26–28. The psalm could well reflect concerns also found in exilic prophetic traditions in Jeremiah, Ezekiel, and Isaiah 40–55. In Psalm 40, offering thanksgiving is more important than sacrifice. Exilic traditions seem to suggest a relativization of the importance of sacrifice. Internal motivation for faithful living becomes more important than offerings of sacrifice:

> I delight to do your will, O my God;
> your law is within my heart. (v. 8)

The sense of the "scroll of the book" in verse 7 is obscure. Is it a book with the listing of those counted as righteous by YHWH, a "book of life"? Another possibility could be that the scroll is the narrative of divine deliverance from the psalmist. The emphasis of verses 6–8 is not so much a denigration of sacrifice as it is a full and faithful response to the divine act of deliverance. The psalmist continues to tell the story, declaring God's deliverance "in the great congregation" with the new song of verse 3. Verse 10 calls on many of the loaded terms from Israel's faith tradition in that song: God's "saving help," "faithfulness," "salvation," and "steadfast love." The thanksgiving song bears witness to the trust of Israel's confession of the fidelity of

YHWH as the God who comes to deliver and bring life to the covenant community. The psalmist's experience of finding hope has brought about a new song and a new obedience.

The thanksgiving in verses 1–10 provides a context for the last part of the psalm and its petition. The verbs in verse 11 could be taken as a plea, such as in the NRSV rendering, or they could be taken in the indicative as a confession of faith in divine mercy, steadfast love, and faithfulness. That ambiguity helps readers move to the context of petition. In verse 12, a crisis presses on the speaker. Troubles are both external and internal, and so strong that the petitioner cannot see a way forward. The remainder of the prayer emphasizes the part of enemies in this trouble. Perhaps their mocking has led the psalmist to concerns about "my iniquities" and numerous failings. Verses 13–17 articulate a strong and clear plea for help. The hope is that divine deliverance will come again, as the first part of the psalm suggests it has before. Opponents seek to dishonor the speaker and bring an end to life. The description of the opponents is of those who stand around and point at the suffering petitioner and make gloating sounds of mockery: "Aha, Aha!" The psalmist again hopes to sing a *tôdāh*, a song of joy and thanksgiving that indicates that God has again acted to deliver. The hope is to experience that again and to sing the song "in the great congregation." The prayer suggests hope, but it also suggests a major crisis. The psalm concludes with the petition that God will not delay but will act as recounted at the beginning of the text.

Bridging the Horizons: The Pilgrimage of Faith

The pattern of Psalm 40 fits the salvation history of ancient Israel. The covenant God delivered them from slavery in Egypt and they rejoiced. Trouble came again in the wilderness, and divine providence brought them into the land. There they faced further pressure from the Canaanites, and YHWH raised up leaders to show them ways forward. The fall of Jerusalem brought major catastrophe, but eventually the community found restoration. The pattern in this story of ancient Israel is that communities and people of faith are always waiting and hoping in divine providence. The pilgrimage of faith simultaneously includes renewal and trouble. In Psalm 40, trouble and woe come again following the newness enjoyed in the first part of the psalm. The sequence of the psalm is thus instructive: trouble and woe can always come. The psalm suggests that in the midst of this mix of life and faith, openness to divine instruction, singing of divine involvement in life, and trust in divine providence are commendable. The realistic faith of Psalm 40 urges hope that God will be involved in the midst of the pilgrimage.

PSALM 41 – TO THE LEADER. A PSALM OF DAVID

¹ Happy are those who consider the poor;
the Lord delivers them in the day of trouble.
² The Lord protects them and keeps them alive;
they are called happy in the land.
You do not give them up to the will of their enemies.
³ The Lord sustains them on their sickbed;
in their illness you heal all their infirmities.

⁴ As for me, I said, 'O Lord, be gracious to me;
heal me, for I have sinned against you.'
⁵ My enemies wonder in malice
when I will die, and my name perish.
⁶ And when they come to see me, they utter empty words,
while their hearts gather mischief;
when they go out, they tell it abroad.
⁷ All who hate me whisper together about me;
they imagine the worst for me.

⁸ They think that a deadly thing has fastened on me,
that I will not rise again from where I lie.
⁹ Even my bosom friend in whom I trusted,
who ate of my bread, has lifted the heel against me.
¹⁰ But you, O Lord, be gracious to me,
and raise me up, that I may repay them.

¹¹ By this I know that you are pleased with me;
because my enemy has not triumphed over me.
¹² But you have upheld me because of my integrity,
and set me in your presence for ever.

¹³ Blessed be the Lord, the God of Israel,
from everlasting to everlasting. Amen and Amen.

It is helpful to begin our study of this psalm in its middle portion (vv. 5–9). In these verses, we find the psalmist in the midst of life in trouble, the place from which Israel's prayer characteristically arises. In these verses, the speaker describes a social situation of alienation and illness that is caused by slander and a "whisper campaign." These verses begin with reference to "my enemies" and conclude with "my bosom friend." These two references that bracket the complaint suggest that all social relationships for this psalmist have become distorted and destructive. The psalmist is near total defeat, for his adversaries imagine that he is so down and out that he cannot "arise again."

That condition, however, does not evoke despair in Israel. Rather, it evokes an intense dialogical exchange with YHWH, the God of Israel. Thus the complaint of verses 5–9 is bracketed in verses 4 and 10 by the defining pronouns of dialogue. In verse 4, the psalmist says, "*I, I said.*" The speaker, even in dismay, is capable of enough self-announcement and self-assertion to risk an imperative petition of demand to YHWH. The psalmist quotes for us his own prayer, asking for healing and acknowledging sin. This self-announcement in verse 4 corresponds with the strong pronoun "*You*" in verse 10, addressed to YHWH. In verse 4, the two impera- tives are "be gracious, heal." In verse 10, the two imperatives are "be gracious, raise me up." Thus, in verses 4–10, the articulation of trouble that results in helplessness in verses 5–9 is bracketed by engagement with YHWH and by the deep hope that YHWH will act decisively to give life back to this nearly defeated speaker. Verses 4 and 10 are nearly symmetrical in one other regard. In verse 4, the supporting clause is a confession of sin. In verse 10, the hope is that "being raised" will apparently permit the speaker to retaliate against his adversaries, both "enemy" and "friend." It is possible that the last phrase rendered in the NRSV as "that I may repay them" may be given a different reading. Terrien reminds us that the word "repay" comes from the noun *shalom*, and it might indeed mean to "make sound or complete, to restore, to recompense, to reward."[102] Terrien suggests that such an "ethic of the wise" would heap coals of fire on the head of the enemy by feeding him. This is a possible alternative reading. The final petition of verse 10, "raise me up," is a direct response to the complaint of verse 8, "not rise again." Thus, verses 4 and 10 frame the complaint and anticipate the divine rescue whereby *the Thou of YHWH* attends to *the helpless I* of the psalmist.

As we move from the center of the psalm to its beginning and end, the rheto- ric of the poetry shifts. At the beginning, in verses 1–3, the psalm offers a criti- cal, somewhat didactic reflection. These verses do not say that YHWH delivers the poor (weak) but that YHWH delivers those who "consider the poor." It is as though the psalmist has reflected on his own rescue and has concluded that he is rescued because of his social engagement on behalf of the economically vulnerable. This is a curious, relayed concern, but it does, albeit indirectly, attest to "God's prefer- ential option for the poor." This attestation features a series of verbs concerning YHWH's powerful, decisive intervention: "Deliver, protect, not give up, sustain, heal." YHWH acts to enhance life for those who enact YHWH's compassion and justice in the world.

---

[102] S. Terrien, *Psalms* (2003), 346.

Verses 1–3 as a didactic introduction are matched in verses 11–12 by a concluding statement in which the speaker draws another conclusion. "By this," apparently
by being "raised up" to new life (v. 10), by being delivered, protected, sustained,
and healed (vv. 1–3), the speaker comes to a new certitude, namely that YHWH
is "pleased" with the psalmist, apparently because he "considered the poor." The
consequence of YHWH's "pleasure" in the psalmist is that YHWH has "upheld"
the psalmist in his integrity. YHWH has granted the psalmist abiding access to
YHWH's presence and has defeated the enemies characterized in verses 5–9. This
assurance in verses 11–12 thus suggests that the prayer in verses 4–10 has indeed
been answered by YHWH. The concluding doxology in verse 13 is a sweeping affirmation of YHWH, who has just been affirmed in the psalm. This verse, however,
draws a conclusion not only to Psalm 41 but to the entire Book I of the Psalms,
Psalms 1–41. The generic blessing of YHWH derives from the particularities of such
attestations as are offered in Psalm 41. Thus the psalm moves from the center both
forward and backward:

> The conclusion of the ground of rescue (vv. 1–3);
>> The I of dialogue and petition (v. 4);
> Complaint (vv. 5–9);
>> The Thou of dialogue and petition (v. 10);
> The conclusion of being a pleasure to YHWH (vv. 11–12).

The psalm thus offers a full characterization of the God who saves. Beyond that, it
traces the drama of transformation from "not rise" to "rise," effected by the God of
all resurrections. Whereas the speaker has confessed sin (v. 4), the stronger claim is
the integrity of the psalmist (v. 12), a oneness of purpose that has set the life of the
psalmist in complete congruity with the will of YHWH. The affirmation of integrity
is so strong that Lindström has drawn the conclusion that the confession of sin in
verse 4 is a late addendum to the psalm.[103] Lindström's judgment is that trouble
described in the psalm is understood not as a response to sin but as an attack from
the destructive powers of the kingdom of Death: the sick person has left the good
sphere of life, manifested by YHWH's temple, and finds himself already in Sheol (v.
9). The enemies who are present and the friends who are absent express the petitioner's anxiety that his "fall" is definite. The enemies are thus de facto representatives of this area, which is hostile to life and foreign to YHWH.[104]

The trouble that occupies the center of this psalm and the center of much of
Israel's life is encompassed and thereby redefined by the *dialogic transaction of
I-You* that results in well-being for the psalmist and "pleasure" for YHWH. The
psalm brings the speaker – and those who belatedly read the psalm – to a season of
well-being without at all denying the locus of trouble as the venue for new life.

[103] F. Lindström, *Suffering and Sin* (1994), 319–321.
[104] F. Lindström, *Suffering and Sin* (1994), 315–316.

Bridging the Horizons: Raise Me Up

The petition "raise me up" (v. 10) refers to restoration of life after deep threat and jeopardy. The verb is used to attest YHWH's power for life. In the Old Testament, such language is not yet concerned with resurrection "of the dead"; nonetheless, the phrase anticipates the power of resurrection that becomes central to the Easter faith of the church. Thus, in Luke 7:22, for example, the affirmation that the "dead are raised" is treated along with other characteristic acts of human rehabilitation. All of these acts of human rehabilitation belong together as wonders wrought by YHWH, the God of life.

A Closer Look: Integrity

The reference to "integrity" in verse 12 leads us to refer to the case of Job, a connection suggested by Calvin.[105] Like this psalmist, Job is a man of "integrity" (Job 27:5). Job is also celebrated for "having considered the poor" (Job 31:16–23). Thus Job, reflecting the piety of this psalm, could also anticipate rescue by YHWH. It is helpful to consider the poem of Job as a critical reflection on the confident piety of this psalm that in itself raises no question of theodicy.[106]

PSALMS 42 AND 43 – TO THE LEADER. A MASKIL OF THE KORAHITES

¹ As a deer longs for flowing streams,
   so my soul longs for you, O God.
² My soul thirsts for God,
   for the living God.
When shall I come and behold
   the face of God?
³ My tears have been my food
   day and night,
while people say to me continually,
   'Where is your God?'

---

105 J. Calvin, *Commentary on the Book of Psalms*, vol. 2 (1979), 113.
106 S. Terrien, *Psalms* (2003), 347.

⁴ These things I remember,
   as I pour out my soul:
how I went with the throng,
   and led them in procession to the house of God,
with glad shouts and songs of thanksgiving,
   a multitude keeping festival.
⁵ Why are you cast down, O my soul,
   and why are you disquieted within me?
Hope in God; for I shall again praise him,
   my help ⁶and my God.

My soul is cast down within me;
   therefore I remember you
from the land of Jordan and of Hermon,
   from Mount Mizar.
⁷ Deep calls to deep
   at the thunder of your cataracts;
all your waves and your billows
   have gone over me.
⁸ By day the LORD commands his steadfast love,
   and at night his song is with me,
   a prayer to the God of my life.

⁹ I say to God, my rock,
   'Why have you forgotten me?
Why must I walk about mournfully
   because the enemy oppresses me?'
¹⁰ As with a deadly wound in my body,
   my adversaries taunt me,
while they say to me continually,
   'Where is your God?'

¹¹ Why are you cast down, O my soul,
   and why are you disquieted within me?
Hope in God; for I shall again praise him,
   my help and my God.

¹ Vindicate me, O God, and defend my cause
   against an ungodly people;
from those who are deceitful and unjust

deliver me!
² For you are the God in whom I take refuge;
why have you cast me off?
Why must I walk about mournfully
because of the oppression of the enemy?

³ O send out your light and your truth;
let them lead me;
let them bring me to your holy hill
and to your dwelling.
⁴ Then I will go to the altar of God,
to God my exceeding joy;
and I will praise you with the harp,
O God, my God.

⁵ Why are you cast down, O my soul,
and why are you disquieted within me?
Hope in God; for I shall again praise him,
my help and my God.

Several Hebrew manuscripts preserve Psalms 42 and 43 as one psalm. The refrain that occurs in both psalms (Pss 42:5, 11; 43:5) is the clearest sign of unity; they also share common vocabulary and themes.[107] We will treat the text as one psalm. The poem is a prayer of an individual in crisis, a prayer in three parts marked off by the refrain. The refrain takes the unusual form of dialogue with the self as a way of expressing the impact of the crisis at hand and of expressing the way forward to a new orientation toward life. The parts move from complaint to petition with a hopeful conclusion. The background may be sickness or it may be exile from the life-giving sacred space of the temple. The text, along with a number of psalms in Book I, uses highly figurative language that could apply to a variety of life settings.

A Closer Look: Korah

The superscription of Psalm 42 ties the psalm to the Korahite collection of psalms (Psalms 42–49). Korah was a Levite and leader of a guild of psalmists (1 Chr 9:19; 2 Chr 20:19). The psalm also opens Book II of the Psalter (Psalms 42–72). Books II and III begin with a prayer of an individual followed by a prayer

---

[107] C. C. Broyles, *Psalms* (1999), 195, provides a good summary of the reasons for treating Psalms 42 and 43 as one psalm.

of the community. Although the crisis that gave rise to the psalm may be different, the extant literary context at the beginning of Book II of the Psalter may well
relate to the community's experience of exile and particularly reflect the anxiety
of separation from Zion as the central place of the divine presence.

Ps 42:1–5. The psalm begins with the striking image of a deer thirsting for water
and arriving at a streambed that is now only dry with sand. The deer cries out in
anguished thirst. Just as water is necessary for life and just as the deer's need is urgent,
so is God necessary for life and the speaker's need for the divine presence urgent. The
term translated "soul" in verses 1 and 2 in the NRSV would be better read as "self"
or "person." It is the same term (*nepeš*) used in the psalm's refrain in the dialogue
with the self (and in Ps 42:4, 6). Such repetition of terms is one of the ways in which
the poem coheres. Verse 2 suggests that the speaker yearns for the "face of God,"
connoting worship in the temple on Zion, the special place of the divine presence or
countenance. The yearning is for the life-giving presence of God. In contrast to that
hope is the present characterized by tears. Rather than drinking in the refreshing
water of worship, the speaker pours out the "water" of tears. Others wonder if this
petitioner has done something to cause the crisis and experience of divine absence,
and so they begin to ask questions. As tears flow and the speaker begins to "pour out
my soul," memories begin to flow and the speaker remembers past processions to
the temple to offer praise and thanksgiving to God in the congregation. The contrast
between then and now, between times of gladness and joy and the current spiritual
desert, makes the crisis more difficult and leads to the first refrain (Ps 42:5). In this
inner dialogue, the speaker asks the self: Why are you so troubled and so dispirited?
The dialogue suggests an inner struggle between the trouble at hand and the hope
seen in the praise of God in worship, the hope that might be found in pilgrimage to
Zion to worship. This first section of the psalm makes clear that it is the presence of
God that makes life possible and powerfully articulates the yearning to encounter
that presence in worship.

Ps 42:6–11. In repetition characteristic of this psalm, the first line of verse 6
repeats a line from the refrain to help readers with the transition to the second
part of the poem. Memory of the divine presence is still at the fore, but the setting
has changed. Water continues to be central to the psalm's imagery. The geography
is now in the area of the source of the Jordan River. The water is now related to the
great chaotic deep. This water is powerful and overwhelms the speaker as thunder-
ous waves crash on this self, who is already in the midst of trouble and woe. The
poetic imagery is strong and communicates that this self is pummeled by the suffering at hand. With verse 8, however, a shift occurs in which hope begins to surface.
The speaker remembers again the divine steadfast love. There is a history of God's
coming to deliver and being present to bless, but somehow that divine presence is
now absent and the crisis is urgent. The speaker addresses God to ask why God has

forgotten. Why are enemies oppressing this faithful one and mocking this one with the words of divine absence: "Where is your God?" This taunting makes the crisis even worse, leading to the image of a mortal wound. The speaker's prayer leads then to the second refrain with its inner dialogue. This dialogue holds out hope even in the midst of chaos, hope that God can again bring about praise in the midst of the great congregation.

Ps 43:1–5. The third section of the psalm moves from complaint to petition. The image in verse 1 calls for God to act as the speaker's defense attorney in the face of the enemies ("ungodly people"). These "deceitful and unjust" ones who taunt the petitioner are a persistent presence in Psalms 42–43. What can we say about their identity? These opponents are likely people who see the petitioner's crisis and take the view that the speaker has done something to cause the trouble. The enemies do not cause the crisis, but they make it worse by mocking the petitioner as one who is under divine judgment. Psalm 43:2 makes it clear that one of the bases of the prayer is the contrast between these oppressive enemies and the God who provides the refuge for which the psalm pleads. The petitioner seeks God's light and truth, again in contrast to the darkness of the crisis at hand. The petition operates in the hope that light and truth will bring this faithful one to the place of the divine presence that renews and makes possible the praise of God. Verse 4 articulates a vow of praise with the harp in the context of the great congregation. Such worship would indicate the satisfaction of the yearning for God with which the psalm began. The praise offered would narrate how God has come to deliver from trouble and woe. The chaotic and oppressive crisis does not have the last word in this psalm. The concluding verse is the final refrain and offers a final word of trust and hope. The use of the personal pronoun with the divine name in the psalm's last line ("my help and my God") suggests the concluding hope in relationship with the living God, the God who comes to deliver. It is that God whom this hopeful petition addresses.

Bridging the Horizons: Exile

Psalms 42–43 in the current literary context articulate faith in the middle of the experience of exile, whether that exile is geographical or spiritual. Contemporary readers of the Psalter will know such seasons of life, but contemporary Western culture often suggests that we depend on ourselves rather than God in such settings. The perspective of the Psalms is that such an approach leads to isolation, fear, and more trouble. Hope and help are found in the covenant God who continues to engage the world, communities, and persons, and makes it possible to take the journey toward wholeness in the context of a worshiping community:

The poet yearns to be surrounded by the believing and worshiping community: to participate in the worship services of the Temple and to celebrate with the people the presence of God in their midst. This is not the kind of private piety or spiritual individualism that is often manifest in churches today.[108]

In Christian tradition, the New Testament also speaks of thirst for God (Matt 5:6) and of God's quenching of the thirst (Jn 4:14; 6:35; Rev 21:6). Psalms 42–43 and this biblical theme offer a strong countercultural word of hope in our era of anxiety, isolation, and exhaustion.

The covenant God of this worshiping community continues to engage the world and make it possible to journey toward wholeness. The psalm makes it very clear that both despair and hope inhabit life, and both can lead to maturity. The poetic movement of the parts of this psalm takes the petitioner beyond a private grief to hope found in a worshiping community shaped by YHWH, so the psalm portrays the faithful person at prayer with the companions of both hope and despair, and, in the middle of this crisis, the faithful person remembers God's unswerving love and trustworthiness (Ps 42:8). Much of the hope the petitioner finds in this psalm is tied to liturgy. It is the liturgy that speaks to the wilderness of divine absence and moves the inner dialogue to God and to the divine presence in the temple. That worship makes possible the move from the poignant yearning in the psalm's first line to the hope in its last line. The hope is in the life-giving presence of God.

PSALM 44 – TO THE LEADER. OF THE KORAHITES. A MASKIL

[1] We have heard with our ears, O God,
   our ancestors have told us,
what deeds you performed in their days,
   in the days of old:
[2] you with your own hand drove out the nations,
   but them you planted;
you afflicted the peoples,
   but them you set free;
[3] for not by their own sword did they win the land,
   nor did their own arm give them victory;
but your right hand, and your arm,

---

[108] Bernhard Anderson, *Out of the Depths: The Psalms Speak for Us Today*, 3rd edition (Louisville, KY: Westminster John Knox, 2000), 66–67.

and the light of your countenance,
for you delighted in them.

⁴ You are my King and my God;
you command victories for Jacob.
⁵ Through you we push down our foes;
through your name we tread down our assailants.
⁶ For not in my bow do I trust,
nor can my sword save me.
⁷ But you have saved us from our foes,
and have put to confusion those who hate us.
⁸ In God we have boasted continually,
and we will give thanks to your name for ever.
Selah

⁹ Yet you have rejected us and abased us,
and have not gone out with our armies.
¹⁰ You made us turn back from the foe,
and our enemies have taken spoil for themselves.
¹¹ You have made us like sheep for slaughter,
and have scattered us among the nations.
¹² You have sold your people for a trifle,
demanding no high price for them.

¹³ You have made us the taunt of our neighbors,
the derision and scorn of those around us.
¹⁴ You have made us a byword among the nations,
a laughing-stock among the peoples.
¹⁵ All day long my disgrace is before me,
and shame has covered my face
¹⁶ at the words of the taunters and revilers,
at the sight of the enemy and the avenger.

¹⁷ All this has come upon us,
yet we have not forgotten you,
or been false to your covenant.
¹⁸ Our heart has not turned back,
nor have our steps departed from your way,
¹⁹ yet you have broken us in the haunt of jackals,
and covered us with deep darkness.

²⁰ If we had forgotten the name of our God,
  or spread out our hands to a strange god,
²¹ would not God discover this?
  For he knows the secrets of the heart.
²² Because of you we are being killed all day long,
  and accounted as sheep for the slaughter.

²³ Rouse yourself! Why do you sleep, O LORD?
  Awake, do not cast us off for ever!
²⁴ Why do you hide your face?
  Why do you forget our affliction and oppression?
²⁵ For we sink down to the dust;
  our bodies cling to the ground.
²⁶ Rise up, come to our help.
  Redeem us for the sake of your steadfast love.

This psalm is an extraordinary communal lament that grieves and protests over a national calamity, apparently a defeat in war. It divides into three parts, the second of which is dazzling and gut-wrenching in its daring.

The psalm begins in verses 1–8 with a celebrative memory of YHWH's "deeds" from ancient times. Of all of the inventory of miracles available to Israel, the one accented here is the gift of the promised land where Israel is "planted," accomplished by the military assertion of YHWH. The reference is to the strenuous military achievement of the book of Joshua, here credited completely to YHWH's "right hand." The outcome of YHWH's "victory" is that YHWH is declared to be "king and God," exercising sovereignty, to which the psalmist gladly and willingly responds. Israel, moreover, has faithfully fulfilled its obligation to YHWH by "boasting" (praising) YHWH in order to enhance YHWH at the expense of the other gods, who are defeated just as the previous inhabitants of the land have been defeated.

That covenantal act of remembering doxology, however, is only a foil for the stunning middle portion of the psalm (vv. 9–22). Although Israel is regularly capable of lament over loss, here the poetry goes beyond lament to a strident accusation against YHWH for having failed Israel and having carelessly handed it over to its enemies in a shameless military humiliation. The disjunctive particle introducing verse 9 – rendered in the NRSV as "yet" – serves to contrast in a sharp way the affirmation of verses 1–8 and the protest of verses 9–16. The disjunction shows that YHWH, who had been the powerful protector and advocate for Israel, has now failed Israel on all counts. But the juxtaposition of the two parts is more specific than that; it is exactly YHWH's *military effectiveness* that is celebrated in verses 1–8 and YHWH's *military failure* that is voiced in verses 9–16. Verses 9–12 describe the defeat of Israel with a series of "you" statements that fix the blame singularly on YHWH, from whom better had been expected. The defeat in verses 9–12 is followed in verses 13–16 with the enduring shame among the nations for being a failed, defeated people. These verses reflect on Israel's social circumstances but also on the character of YHWH, who is here seen to be unreliable. YHWH has abandoned Israel in its time of need!

The failure of YHWH is underscored by the assertion of Israel's fidelity to YHWH (vv. 17–22). These verses are dominated by the term "forget," which means to disregard covenantal obligations. In verse 17, the term is linked to covenant, and in verse 20 the term is connected to the first commandment ("no other gods"). Israel's steadfast obedience to YHWH exposes YHWH's failure in the starkest of terms. In verses like Lam 5:20 and Isa 49:14, the term "forget" is parallel to "forsake" ('azav), thus bespeaking complete abandonment of covenantal obligations and the covenant partner. This claim of fidelity on Israel's part is interspersed in verses 19 and 22 with a reiteration of the charge against YHWH.

The third section of the psalm, surprising and yet so characteristic of Israel's prayer, is a vigorous petition to YHWH, to the very God who has been accused and assaulted (vv. 23–26). These verses are bracketed by four imperative petitions, "rouse, awake" in verse 23 and "rise up, redeem" in verse 26. Between the two pairs of imperatives, in verse 24, are two questions "why?" In the second question addressed to YHWH, the term "forget" occurs a third time, this time with reference to YHWH's indifference to Israel's suffering. Israel ponders why the God of all fidelity should have been so fickle.

The shift to petition in verse 23 is the most spectacular feature of the psalm. In the end, Israel prays to the very God who has failed. The reason for that is that Israel believes its prayer can mobilize YHWH back to fidelity. Israel has no doubt that YHWH *can* make a decisive, positive difference in its life if only YHWH *will* answer prayer. This prayer to the God who has abandoned is typical in this remarkably dynamic faith. The last word of the psalm is *ḥesed*, steadfast love. Israel in the end counts on YHWH's fidelity and praise to the God of all fidelity to return to a proper covenantal relationship. This is Israel's only chance in the world. Israel's hope in YHWH is as strong and vigorous as Israel's accusation against YHWH is daring and candid. Israel believes its own prayer can decisively change the disposition of YHWH. The failure so evident in the psalm need not persist, because YHWH can indeed invert circumstance. This is the grounds for the daring reversal of tone in the psalm.

A Closer Look: Bilateral Covenant

This psalm turns on mutual covenantal obligation. The use of the term "covenant" (v. 17), the allusion to the first commandment (v. 20), and the reference to a covenant curse in verse 14 (see Deut 28:37) all attest to the genuinely bilateral character of Israel's covenant. Appeal to the Sinai tradition suggests that this psalmist is fully confident of Israel's *covenantal obedience* and fully convinced of YHWH's *covenantal default*. The final imperative suggests that YHWH can reenter a renewed covenant with Israel by performing covenantal obligations to Israel. Israel has the capacity to hold its partner to those obligations.

Bridging the Horizons: Critiquing God

In his courageous critique of God for having abused the Jews in the Holocaust, David Blumenthal utilizes Psalm 44 as a text pertinent to that critique. Blumenthal sounds the important bilateral quality of the covenant:

As God is a jealous God demanding loyalty from us in covenant, so we, in our searing humiliation, demand. We transform our anger, through the covenant, into our moral claim against God. As God is angry with us in covenant, so we are angry with Him in covenant. We experience a true anger, which becomes a true moral claim, rooted in our mutual covenantal debt.[109]

Beyond that, moreover, Blumenthal offers a contemporary shrill Jewish articulation that is likely congruent with the demanding mood of the psalm, which speaks out of humiliation and a sense of outrage:

Life is not a cup of tea with crumpets. Life is goring one's enemies, as an ox gores another ox or a person. Life is fierce loyalty to one's family and people. Life is also watching out for, and actively combatting, those who would do you in. Life is a jungle. Hatred and jealousy, not love, motivate life.

Why should I forgive my enemy?! Especially if he or she has done nothing to indicate any feeling of genuine remorse?! Better to be wary, to return hostility. People rarely grow spiritually, psychologically. Sibling jealousy, fear of death, economic envy, racial prejudice – these do not go away. Better to know and acknowledge one's enemies, to be ready to gore them. Christians often preach that the only way out of the jungle of life is love. Jews know that Christians have preached love but have not always practiced it. Almost twenty centuries of Christian persecution of Jews has convinced us that love is no way to act in the jungle of life. Living under the white Christian man's burden has convinced most of the rest of the non-Christian world, too, that Christian preaching and action are not always one, that Christian love is not effective in the jungle.[110]

[109] David R. Blumenthal, *Facing the Abusing God: A Theology of Protest* (Louisville, KY: Westminster John Knox Press, 1993), 107.
[110] D. R. Blumenthal, *Facing the Abusing God* (1993), 97.

A Closer Look: Genesis 9:15

In verse 24, YHWH is said to "forget" Israel in its need. Reference might be made to Gen 9:15, wherein the rainbow is a reminder to YHWH concerning the covenant of Noah. Unfortunately, the Sinai covenant offers YHWH no such rainbow of reminder, hence YHWH's amnesia about covenant.

PSALM 45 – TO THE LEADER: ACCORDING TO LILIES. OF THE KORAHITES. A MASKIL. A LOVE SONG

¹ My heart overflows with a goodly theme;
   I address my verses to the king;
   my tongue is like the pen of a ready scribe.

² You are the most handsome of men;
   grace is poured upon your lips;
   therefore God has blessed you for ever.
³ Gird your sword on your thigh, O mighty one,
   in your glory and majesty.

⁴ In your majesty ride on victoriously
   for the cause of truth and to defend the right;
   let your right hand teach you dread deeds.
⁵ Your arrows are sharp
   in the heart of the king's enemies;
   the peoples fall under you.

⁶ Your throne, O God, endures for ever and ever.
   Your royal sceptre is a sceptre of equity;
⁷ you love righteousness and hate wickedness.
Therefore God, your God, has anointed you
   with the oil of gladness beyond your companions;
⁸ your robes are all fragrant with myrrh and aloes and cassia.
From ivory palaces stringed instruments make you glad;
⁹ daughters of kings are among your ladies of honor;
   at your right hand stands the queen in gold of Ophir.

¹⁰ Hear, O daughter, consider and incline your ear;
forget your people and your father's house,
¹¹ and the king will desire your beauty.
Since he is your lord, bow to him;
¹² the people of Tyre will seek your favor with gifts,
the richest of the people ¹³ with all kinds of wealth.

The princess is decked in her chamber with gold-woven robes;
¹⁴ in many-coloured robes she is led to the king;
behind her the virgins, her companions, follow.
¹⁵ With joy and gladness they are led along
as they enter the palace of the king.

¹⁶ In the place of ancestors you, O king, shall have sons;
you will make them princes in all the earth.
¹⁷ I will cause your name to be celebrated in all generations;
therefore the peoples will praise you for ever and ever.

Psalm 45 is unusual in the Psalter and in the whole of the Hebrew scriptures. It is a wedding song on the occasion of the king's marriage. Psalms 2, 18, 20, and 21 in Book I of the Psalter are associated with the coronation or battle settings in the life of the Davidic king in Jerusalem. Psalm 45 is a song of celebration on the king's wedding day. It is impossible to know for which king the song was initially written, though scholars have made a variety of suggestions. A royal wedding would have been a significant political and religious occasion, and this song was likely used at a variety of such settings. It reflects the magnitude of the event and was likely composed for such occasions during the time of the Davidic monarchy in Jerusalem.

As befits such a royal setting, the king is portrayed as the ideal ruler, excellent in appearance and physical attributes as well as in wisdom and justice. Scholars often note that the psalm partakes of the ancient Near Eastern court style that praises the king in glowing terms. Some have suggested that the kind of exaggerated praise given to the king in Psalm 45 is commonly reserved for God in much of the Hebrew canon. It may even be that in verse 6 the king is addressed as *ĕlōhîm*, God. We will return to the various translation possibilities for that verse. The psalm does seem to press the limits when it comes to praising a mortal, even if he is the king, especially when ancient Israel struggled with the place of the king in a faith that declares that it has no other God besides YHWH. The deuteronomist warned the community that trust in the monarchy would lead to dire consequences. Hebrew narratives recount various contexts in which a confused Israel trusted the monarch rather than God, and seldom did the kings meet the royal ideal articulated for the community. The psalm makes it clear that the king is God's anointed one and is to be seen as a gift to the community. It is fitting to celebrate the king and queen on the occasion of marriage. Because of the story of ancient Israel, however, the fear of too much trust in the monarch always lurks in the background. We will consider this royal wedding song in two parts, the first focusing on the groom and the second on the bride.

The psalm is set off with a frame in the first and last verses, with the poet speaking in the first person. The opening verse speaks of the poet's inspiration in penning this song for the king – an uncommon beginning for a psalm – and returns to that theme in verse 17. The psalm's concluding line, "Therefore the peoples will praise you forever and ever," echoes the concluding line of verse 2, "Therefore God has blessed you forever." Verses 1–9 heap praise on the royal groom as "the most handsome of men" blessed by God. The king is portrayed as a great warrior who brings victory in battle for the community. The nations fall to this great military leader, as suggested in the coronation in Psalm 2. The king is also the one who brings justice to the community. That task is central to the royal ideal articulated in the royal psalms. The king stands for the cause of truth and righteousness, even in battle (v. 4), and the "royal scepter is a scepter of equity" (v. 6). The king loves righteousness (v. 7). Verses 6 and 7 are central in reflecting on the royal ideal in the Davidic line. The king is joyfully anointed with oil by God, signifying that God has chosen the king as an intermediary figure. The king represents God in ruling over the people in Jerusalem and speaking to them. The king also represents the people in speaking to God in prayer. The poet celebrates the ideal king, who has a special relationship with God and who brings justice and honor to the kingdom.

Perhaps in exuberance over the festive occasion, the psalm presses the limits of the ideal. The first line of verse 6 illustrates this. The rendering of the line is problematic. Various suggestions have been made, such as "Your throne is like God's forever and ever," "Your throne is God's forever and ever," or "Your throne, O God, is forever and ever." The last possibility is the most natural for the Hebrew and shows that the royal portrayal in this psalm is on the edge of divinity. Much of the Hebrew canon worries about covenant faithfulness to YHWH and fears that royal corruptions will lead the community down a deadly path.

With verses 8 and 9, the poem returns more specifically to the marriage celebration, with the wedding process and its fragrance, music, and beauty.

The bride is now at the royal groom's side, and the poem shifts to the queen at verse 10. The bride apparently comes from another people, and the poet urges her to change her loyalties from her family and people of origin to the king she is marrying, and perhaps to the king's faith. The beautiful bride will be showered with gifts from those of wealth and influence, from the people of power throughout the kingdom. The poet then moves again to the wedding procession, with an emphasis on the bride. She moves toward the marriage ceremony with lavishly colored, beautiful garments. Along with her attendants, she moves "with joy and gladness" into the palace for the wedding. The concluding verses pronounce a blessing on the royal marriage. The hope is for royal descendants to rule in the future, and for this poem to continue to bring joy and hope for the kingdom and its rulers in the future.

The royal ideology lying behind this text is troubling for two reasons. The first is that the poem's praise of the king is praise often attached to God; apparently verse 6 addresses the king as *ĕlōhîm*. This one psalm is little evidence to suggest, however, that ancient Israel viewed its king as divine. In Egypt, the royal figures were considered divine, and that is clear from many texts. In Psalm 45, the ideal is that the king serves as God's representative to bring justice and blessing to the community. It is God who is the author of these life-giving gifts. The king is God's representative and ruler, a channel of blessing for the kingdom, and the people's representative, so the king is a major figure in the community. Thus, important events in the king's life are community events, and a royal wedding would be a major celebration. A royal wedding in that setting related to the future of the dynasty and future rulers, so it is natural for this poet and the community to celebrate the occasion and the bride and groom with much hope. It is important not to lose in that perspective, however, that the text also calls the king to the task of justice and righteousness as a ruler.

The second issue is the loyalty required of the bride and of the king's subjects. They are all to serve and praise the queen. The psalm is conditioned by its ancient Near Eastern culture, a very different setting from modern democracies. In the midst of that royal ideology, however, readers can see that the psalm celebrates the hope of a gift from God of a leader and a future.

A Closer Look: A Korahite and Elohistic Psalter

Psalm 45 is, according to its superscription, one of the psalms of the Sons of Korah, a guild of temple singers in the second temple. The psalm follows two laments: an individual petition and a community petition. Psalm 45 carries a more hopeful tone that continues in the next three psalms. This first Korahite collection of psalms (Psalms 42–49) is also part of the Elohistic Psalter (Psalms 42–82). In these psalms, *ĕlōhîm* is the dominant name for God rather than YHWH. The second line of Ps 45:7 uses the phrase "God, your God." The more common phrase would be "YHWH, your God."

Bridging the Horizons: A Particular Setting

The particularity of Psalm 45 makes it difficult to view it as more than a cultural artifact. It arose as part of a dynamic faith and political setting. It came to be read in terms of messianic hope in Judaism and Christianity. Perhaps contemporary readers can see it as a celebration of hope and joy that can be found in other particular settings.

PSALM 46 – TO THE LEADER. OF THE KORAHITES. ACCORDING TO ALAMOTH. A SONG

¹ God is our refuge and strength,
  a very present help in trouble.
² Therefore we will not fear, though the earth should change,
  though the mountains shake in the heart of the sea;
³ though its waters roar and foam,
  though the mountains tremble with its tumult.
    Selah

⁴ There is a river whose streams make glad the city of God,
  the holy habitation of the Most High.
⁵ God is in the midst of the city; it shall not be moved;
  God will help it when the morning dawns.
⁶ The nations are in an uproar, the kingdoms totter;
  he utters his voice, the earth melts.
⁷ The LORD of hosts is with us;
  the God of Jacob is our refuge.
    Selah

⁸ Come, behold the works of the LORD;
  see what desolations he has brought on the earth.
⁹ He makes wars cease to the end of the earth;
  he breaks the bow, and shatters the spear;
  he burns the shields with fire.
¹⁰ 'Be still, and know that I am God!
  I am exalted among the nations,
  I am exalted in the earth.'
¹¹ The LORD of hosts is with us;
  the God of Jacob is our refuge.
    Selah

Psalm 46 is a hymn of praise of a particular kind. It does not begin with a call to praise but from the beginning offers praise to the God who is present in Zion, and so the psalm is usually considered among the Zion songs. Zion/Jerusalem was ancient Israel's sacred place of divine presence, a sacred place from which salvation and wholeness derive. The psalm likely came from cultic celebrations of the reign of God and God's choice of Zion as a sacred place of divine presence and hope. These celebrations may well have been part of the fall festival complex that looks toward a new year with an emphasis on the renewal of the kingship of YHWH. The psalm is in three parts (vv. 1–3, 4–7, and 8–11), with a refrain at the end of parts two and three. Shared vocabulary helps readers follow the progression of thought through the poem. "Earth" as the place of God's reign appears in each part of the psalm, three times in the third part. Common to the first two parts is the vocabulary of shaking, tottering, and roaring, as well as the term "help." "The nations" appears in parts two and three. We will consider the three stanzas of the psalm in order.

Book II of the Psalter begins with two lament psalms (Psalms 42–43 and 44); Psalm 45 introduces a hopeful tone with the celebration of the Davidic monarch in Zion on the occasion of a royal wedding. Psalm 46 continues that hopeful tone with a celebration of the divine presence in Zion; the emphasis on God's reign from Zion continues in Psalms 47 and 48. Readers of Book I (Psalms 1–41) will recall that YHWH as refuge is one of the significant themes in those psalms. With Psalm 46, that theme now surfaces in Book II.

The psalm begins with the affirmation that God is "our refuge and strength" and "help" in trouble and woe. This confession of faith opening the first stanza (vv. 1–3) nourishes courage in the face of disturbances in "the earth." The poetic image is of a world-threatening earthquake. The ground is moving and the mountains in the seas shake, causing waters to roar and foam. Verses 2 and 3 suggest a disaster of cosmic proportions. In the ancient Near East, the mountains "in the heart of the sea" are the pillars of the earth that also hold the sky in place. The thought of those mountains tottering suggests that the earth is about to collapse and the sky about to fall. Chaos is seeking to reassert itself and destroy the order of creation. In the midst of such a threat of chaos, the psalm confesses that God is refuge and strength. The God who is creator and remains sovereign over the creation is also the God who is present with the community in Zion/Jerusalem. The psalm urges faith in this divine presence in the midst of threats to the created order.

Verse 4 witnesses a remarkable transition at the beginning of the second stanza (vv. 4–7). The chaotic and destructive waters in the first stanza now become a nourishing stream, watering and nourishing Zion, the sacred place of divine presence. "Streams" is the same term used to portray the nurturing of the tree in Psalm 1; in Psalm 46, it is Zion that is nurtured. For centuries, interpreters puzzled over the reference to a river in verse 4 because there is no river in Jerusalem. The reference, however, is a poetic image of sacred places in the ancient Near East. Images of sacred places of divine presence often pictured rivers running through them, and Zion is the dwelling of YHWH. The streams of water flow from the divine presence and bring nourishment and hope to the community. The refreshing, cool waters coming from the divine presence bring joy to the city and thus to the community of faith. Verse 5 explicitly affirms the divine presence in the midst of the city of Zion. The mountains "in the heart of the sea" may totter, but God's dwelling will stand. God is "a very present help in trouble," for deliverance will come in the morning (v.

5). Verse 6 provides another picture of the opponent. It is now a historicized chaos that roars rather than the threatening waters in the first stanza. "The nations" (see Psalm 2) are now the makers of trouble. Zion as God's dwelling will stand firm, but the kingdoms that attack Zion will "totter." The powerful divine word will melt the enemies throughout the earth. Verse 7 is the first appearance of the refrain in the psalm. It affirms the presence of divine help and refuge. The poetic image is of a secure fortress high above the threat of chaos. It is YHWH who brings such hope and safety in the midst of crashing seas and warring nations, two pictures of chaos. "The Lord of hosts" could be rendered "YHWH of armies." The armies could be the angelic hosts or heavenly host of sun, moon, and stars, the armies of Israel, or some combination of those possibilities. The God who is creator and sovereign tames both cosmic and historical chaos and brings order out of disorder; this God is present in Zion in the midst of life for the community.

The third stanza (vv. 8–11) begins with a call to behold the works of YHWH in defeating the powers of chaos and disorder in "the earth." YHWH "makes wars cease to the end of the earth" and is "exalted in the earth." The reign of the one who has made the world and sustains it extends from Zion throughout all of creation. This divine warrior ironically does battle to defeat war and the weapons of war – bow, spear, and shield. It is in that context that the familiar opening line of verse 10 appears: "Be still and know that I am God." The call is not to a quiet spirituality and pietism but to see that God has destroyed war and trust in military solutions. This God is exalted over all the nations of war and over all the powers of chaos and disorder in creation. The call is to see these "works of the Lord." Where might that occur? The most likely place is in the Zion temple cult. There the mighty acts of God in defeating the powers of chaos and disorder are dramatically portrayed so that the community may see them and respond with enthusiastic praise of the God who reigns from Zion. In such worship, the community can appropriate the rule of YHWH. The psalm concludes with the refrain confessing again that the powerful YHWH is help and refuge in the midst of world-shattering threats.

A Closer Look: Kingship and Zion

Undergirding the poetry of Psalm 46 are two theological affirmations: the kingship of YHWH and the choice of Zion/Jerusalem as the place of the divine dwelling from which YHWH rules. The first emphasis is the divine presence as a source of protection and help. This God reigns over both creation and history, and has chosen to be present within this community. The psalm praises this God who brings order, refuge, and hope. This powerful God also works to bring about the peaceable kingdom and destroy the evils of war. YHWH ironically fights for peace but in so doing brings about complete refuge. The psalm praises God and expresses trust in God, but the place Zion is also central to the text, for here God is powerfully present in the midst of the community. The sacred place provided a center for the world as that community knew it; the revelation of the presence of YHWH came there. There one found salvation, hope, and protection in the midst of chaos and the courage to affirm the divine reign. There the congregation could witness the rehearsal of the mighty acts of God and so imagine the world differently as a world of order and peace in which God is present. In that sense, the temple was the center of the world.

Bridging the Horizons: A Mighty Fortress

The opening words of Psalm 46 were frequently heard in the United States following the events of September 11, 2001. The words provided comfort and hope in the God of refuge in the midst of what was for many a chaotic time. The psalm's opening confession of faith has been applied to many personal and communal crises and so has been woven into many lives. Martin Luther provided what are probably the most familiar words inspired by the psalm in the hymn "A Mighty Fortress." Generations of worshipers have sung the hymn. The martial language of the hymn and of the psalm will trouble some readers. The psalm's perspective is that there are powers of chaos, evil, and war in the world *and* that God is present to tame those principalities and powers and bring refuge and peace.

However, in turning to this and other psalms in times of personal and national crisis, there is a danger that readers will equate themselves or their nation with the ancient people of Israel. Readers might be inclined to see God as unequivocally fighting on their side against their enemies, justifying their own martial actions against other people. Readers must exercise caution and allow the psalm to provide comfort and hope in God, without appropriating it to justify violent action on the part of a group or a nation. The psalm is clear that YHWH, not any political entity, is our fortress.

PSALM 47 – TO THE LEADER. OF THE KORAHITES. A PSALM

[1] Clap your hands, all you peoples;
  shout to God with loud songs of joy.
[2] For the LORD, the Most High, is awesome,
  a great king over all the earth.

³ He subdued peoples under us,
  and nations under our feet.
⁴ He chose our heritage for us,
  the pride of Jacob whom he loves.
      Selah

⁵ God has gone up with a shout,
  the Lᴏʀᴅ with the sound of a trumpet.
⁶ Sing praises to God, sing praises;
  sing praises to our King, sing praises.
⁷ For God is the king of all the earth;
  sing praises with a psalm.

⁸ God is king over the nations;
  God sits on his holy throne.
⁹ The princes of the peoples gather
  as the people of the God of Abraham.
For the shields of the earth belong to God;
  he is highly exalted.

This psalm is sandwiched between the two songs of Zion in Psalms 46 and 48. Like them, it also concerns the theological claims and realities of the Jerusalem establishment. This psalm concerns the kingship of YHWH over all nations, over all creation. According to much scholarly speculation, the psalm reflects an actual liturgical event that was regularly reenacted whereby the theological claim of divine sovereignty was given dramatic replication in the temple; it is for that reason that several aspects of liturgical activity are delineated, such as "clap your hands" (v. 1), "shout, trumpet" (v. 5), and "sing, sing, sing" (v. 6). The invitation to clap hands is the sort of cheering that we still do at a time of victory. The trumpet, we know from 2 Sam 15:10 and 2 Kgs 9:13, was used at the enthronement of human kings; thus it is likely that the celebration of divine kingship replicates that of human kingship.

The kingship of YHWH, noted in verses 2, 6, 7, and 8, bespeaks the defeat of the other gods, perhaps accomplished in ritual drama (as well as in actual historical affairs), the subjugation of all peoples, and the right ordering of creation, wherein all nations and princes submit to the rule of YHWH. It is entirely plausible that the phrase "God is the king" in verse 11 might be translated as "God has just become king." That is, what is judged to be effected in the world is dramatically enacted in liturgical activity so that there is a match between *what is claimed for out there* in the world and *what is actually done in here* in the liturgy.

Perhaps the most interesting aspect of the psalm is the way in which the cosmic (or international or mythological) scope of YHWH's sovereignty articulated in verses 2–3 and 7–9 is held in tension with the special and particular claim of Israel (v. 4). This juxtaposition of the cosmic and particular is reflected as well in the names used for the deity. God is generically referred to as *ĕlōhîm* (God) but is also celebrated as "Most High," the one who presides over all of the other gods in a world of polytheism. Alongside this cosmic appellation, however, the specific name of the Israelite God, YHWH, is mentioned twice (vv. 2 and 5). The poetic parallelism juxtaposes a generic and particular divine name and therefore has the effect of asserting *the God of Israel* as *the sovereign of all of the earth.* Thus the particular Israelite liturgy of divine enthronement has in purview a governance that is very large and that transcends the particularities of Israel without compromising Israel's peculiar status as the people of YHWH.

This juxtaposition is most powerfully and peculiarly elaborated in verse 9. In that verse, "the princes of the people" preside over other peoples. But the next phrase is particularly Israelite, referring to "the people of the God of Abraham." It is not at all clear how these two phrases connect. The Hebrew, in a parataxic maneuver, sets the two phrases side by side without explicit connection. The NRSV inserts an "as" and thus suggests that the princes of the people become the people of the God of Abraham: "The logic of the entire poem from the beginning leads directly to this amazing statement, that the princes of the peoples are gathered as the people of the God of Abraham."[111] In the Septuagint (LXX), the connection is made between the two occurrences of "with" (*meta*), which lets a duality persist without equating the two.

The psalm in fact does not resolve this tension between the cosmic and particular, and indeed neither does the Bible more generally. There can nonetheless be no doubt that this divine sovereignty extends both in generic rule over the nations and particular chosenness concerning the status of Israel. The temple of Jerusalem apparently was open enough and focused enough to host both claims.

Bridging the Horizons: Divine Kingship

The language of divine kingship in our time is problematic, as it smacks of pretentious and hierarchical authority when it is twinned with political intentionality. Nevertheless such language is pervasive in the Bible. Martin Buber has seen that the theme is already defining for the old Sinai tradition:

The unconditioned claim of the divine Kingship is recognized at the point when the people proclaim JHWH Himself as King, Him alone and directly (Exodus 15:18), and JHWH Himself enters upon the kingly reign (19:6). He is not content to be "God" in the religious sense. He does not want to surrender to a man that

---

[111] James Muilenberg, "Psalm 47," in Thomas F. Best (ed.), *Hearing and Speaking the Word: Selections from the Works of James Muilenburg* (Chico, CA: Scholars Press, 1984), 94.

which is not "God's", the rule over the entire actuality of worldly life: this very rule He lays claim to and enters upon it; for there is nothing which is not God's. He will apportion to the one, for ever and ever chosen by Him, his tasks, but naked power without a situationally related task. He does not wish to bestow. He makes known His will first of all as constitution – not constitution of cult and custom only, also of economy and society – He will proclaim it again and again to the changing generations, certainly but simply as reply to a question, institutionally through priestly mouth, above all, however, in the freedom of His surging spirit, through every one whom His spirit seizes. *The separation of religion and politics which stretches through history is here overcome in real paradox.*

Is this – which takes its place beside the oriental conception of the divine kingship – only a doctrine, or is its core an experience? Is it historicizing theology or is it history that a confederation of half-nomadic Semitic tribes at some time, undoubtedly more than three thousand years ago, on their wanderings from Egypt to Canaan, instead, perhaps, as other Semitic peoples did in such an hour of unification and high-spirited onward advance, of elevating its human leader as *melekh* (although under divine authority with the same title), proclaimed its God, JHWH, as *melekh*? That, accordingly, this confederation of tribes which called itself Israel, dared as a people, first and once-for-all in the history of peoples, to deal seriously with exclusive divine rulership? As people – to be sure, in the unceasing dialectic of the divine conflict between subjects and rebels, between Gideons and Abimelechs, yet, even so, acting as people: proclaiming, obeying, following?[112]

The same theme stretches forward even into the New Testament. There, for example, the Lord's Prayer, so much prayed by the church, continues to hope and pray for the coming of this rule (Matt 6:10).

Bridging the Horizons: The People of Abraham

The juxtaposition of *Abraham* and *peoples* is pertinent in contemporary religious discussion. It is often agreed and widely recognized that the legacy of Abraham includes Jews, Muslims, and Christians. Thus it is a matter of calling things by their right name to link "princes of the people" to Abraham.[113]

---

[112] Martin Buber, *Kingship of God* (Atlantic Highlands, NJ: Humanities Press International, 1967), 119.
[113] See, for example, Bruce S. Feiler, *Abraham: A Journey to the Heart of Three Faiths* (New York: William Morrow, 2002).

Bridging the Horizons: Divine Enthronement

The concrete cultic act whereby the divine king is enthroned may sound odd to us. Such a claim is in tension with conventional metaphysical notions of divine authority. That is, if God is sovereign, why would there be a need for liturgical enactment of sovereignty? To that question we may answer that the church, in its celebration of the kingship of Jesus, does indeed enact that kingship in the great festivals of Christmas and Easter. It is for that reason that this psalm is particularly used in the church order for Ascension Day, the day when Jesus is said to have "ascended" in power to the throne of God. The pattern of enthronement recurs in the celebrative life of the church:

At the same time, the sacred writer, under that shadowy ceremony, doubtless intended to lead us to consider another kind of going up more triumphant – that of Christ when he "ascended up far above all heavens," (Eph. iv. 10), and obtained the empire of the whole world, and armed with his celestial power, subdued all pride and loftiness.[114]

PSALM 48 – A SONG. A PSALM OF THE KORAHITES

[1] Great is the LORD and greatly to be praised
   in the city of our God.
His holy mountain, [2] beautiful in elevation,
   is the joy of all the earth,
Mount Zion, in the far north,
   the city of the great King.
[3] Within its citadels God
   has shown himself a sure defense.

[4] Then the kings assembled,
   they came on together.
[5] As soon as they saw it, they were astounded;
   they were in panic, they took to flight;
[6] trembling took hold of them there,
   pains as of a woman in labor,

---

[114] J. Calvin, *Commentary on the Book of Psalms*, vol. 2 (1979), 211.

⁷ as when an east wind shatters
the ships of Tarshish.
⁸ As we have heard, so have we seen
in the city of the LORD of hosts,
in the city of our God,
which God establishes for ever.
Selah

⁹ We ponder your steadfast love, O God,
in the midst of your temple.
¹⁰ Your name, O God, like your praise,
reaches to the ends of the earth.
Your right hand is filled with victory.
¹¹ Let Mount Zion be glad,
let the towns of Judah rejoice
because of your judgments.

¹² Walk about Zion, go all around it,
count its towers,
¹³ consider well its ramparts;
go through its citadels,
that you may tell the next generation
¹⁴ that this is God,
our God for ever and ever.
He will be our guide for ever.

This song of Zion continues the high Jerusalem theology we observed in Psalm 46, a song of Zion, and in Psalm 47, a psalm of divine enthronement. Psalm 48 celebrates the Jerusalem temple, admires its artistic quality, recognizes its military invincibility, and celebrates the "Real Presence" of YHWH in the temple. This psalm and temple theology more generally have behind them the narrative account of 1 Kgs 8:1–13, wherein Solomon transported the "visible presence" of YHWH in the form of an ark into the temple in a grand liturgy. Once there, moreover, the God who takes up residence there is said to be a permanent resident, thereby making the temple and the city immune to every threat (see 1 Kgs 8:12–13).

The beginning of the psalm (vv. 1–3) and the conclusion (vv. 12–14) are nearly symmetrical. Both textual units attest to the splendor of "our God," and both affirm the wonder of the temple, nearly equating the God of the temple with the beauty and symmetry of it. In verses 1–2, Jerusalem is celebrated as Mount Zion "in the far north." This odd geographic reference likely confirms that an older temple song from a northern (perhaps non-Israelite) temple, with its mythic claims, has been taken over wholesale and transferred to the temple in Jerusalem. Thus it is evident that the high theology of divine presence in the Jerusalem temple partakes of a common Near Eastern theology of presence that is in considerable tension with the covenantal notion of presence placed in the tradition of Sinai and of Deuteronomy. That high theology of presence is particularly suggested in the odd phrasing of verses 13–14. Verses 12–13 speak of the temple, and then verse 14 says abruptly, "Surely this is our God." Manifestly, these verses cannot and do not mean that this, the temple, is "our God." The phrase refers to the God who inhabits the temple. Nonetheless, these lines are close to identifying *temple and God* so that God's presence is probably known and experienced in the beauty of the temple itself.

The second unit of the psalm (vv. 4–8) offers a scenario not unlike Psalm 2:1–6, in which the nations conspire against God in Jerusalem. In this psalm, the nations seem poised to conduct a military assault on Jerusalem but are put to flight when they sense how impregnable the city is. The cluster of terms describing the reaction of the nations to the city and to the temple make the point of invincibility: "astonished, panic, fled, trembling, shatter." The image of "a woman in labor," moreover, is designed to ridicule would-be challengers, who are completely immobilized and ineffective. In these verses, the panic of the adversary (vv. 5–6) is sharply in contrast to the solemn, self-assured claim made for YHWH in verse 8. This is indeed "the Lord of the troops," who is "forever," YHWH thus making the city safe. Jerusalem is indeed safe, as claimed in Psalm 46 and as attested in the Isaiah narratives concerning the "miraculous deliverance" of the city from the Assyrians (Isa 37:21–29, 30–35, 36–38). Such invincibility and certitude are not grounded in geography, aesthetics, or military advantage but in the reality of YHWH, who is beyond the challenge of feverish military forces.

In verses 9–11, the psalm sounds the accents of Israel's covenant, a tradition that is quite distinct from the more mythically articulated claims we have seen in verses 1–3. In verses 9–11, the accent is rather on YHWH's steadfast love (*ḥesed*), YHWH's victorious power (*ṣedeq*), and YHWH's judicial capacity (*mišpat*). This is a God who governs in fidelity, yielding saving and reliable verdicts that make Jerusalem safe and that order the world securely to the ends of the earth. It is evident that this psalm, surely rooted in the Jerusalem liturgy, deftly manages to bring together old covenant traditions and appropriated mythic traditions of presence. The outcome is a song for a worshiping congregation that may live in the real world and yet have complete confidence in the God attested in the liturgy. The rule of YHWH from the holy city is for all time and in every place. This God extends faithfulness to the ends of the earth.

A Closer Look: Divine Presence

It is evident that this high temple theology is one of several trajectories of theology in the Old Testament concerning the temple and YHWH's presence in it. Whereas that presence is here celebrated without qualification, the related text of

1 Kings 8 shows Israel's awareness that the issue of YHWH's presence in the sanctuary is a much more complex matter. The same high claim for divine presence is made in 1 Kgs 8:12–13, but it is asserted in 1 Kgs 8:9 that the Ark, totem of divine presence, is in fact empty; in verses 27–30, moreover, it is asserted that the temple is no adequate place of residence for the high God who resides in heaven.

It is evident that the matter of divine presence in this temple remained contested and unsettled in ancient Israel, even though this psalm holds to one view without apology or qualification. It is likely that this contest was not unlike the later Christian polemics in the Reformation period concerning Real Presence in the Eucharist.

A Closer Look: Real Presence

Real Presence is a claim made here and characteristically made in liturgical traditions. It is not to be imagined, however, that such claims are single-minded or one-dimensionally accepted. Those who offer this theological-liturgical articulation are concerned that while they assert Real Presence, they also affirm the transcendent freedom of God, who is not domesticated in any temple apparatus. Given that safeguard, however, there is no doubt that such a claim for palpable cultic presence is a source of immense pastoral reassurance and confidence. Thus, in the familiar Psalm 23, for example, there is no doubt that verse 6 calls to mind life lived in the Real Presence of YHWH. Such a high claim of divine presence sometimes tended to claim too much and evoked prophetic critique (see Isa 1:12–15; Jer 7:3–4; Amos 4:4–5). The claim of presence itself, however, is a crucial one for the delight and joy of worship and for the well-being of the worshiping community.

PSALM 49 – TO THE LEADER. OF THE KORAHITES. A PSALM

[1] Hear this, all you peoples;
   give ear, all inhabitants of the world,
[2] both low and high,
   rich and poor together.
[3] My mouth shall speak wisdom;
   the meditation of my heart shall be understanding.

⁴ I will incline my ear to a proverb;
   I will solve my riddle to the music of the harp.

⁵ Why should I fear in times of trouble,
   when the iniquity of my persecutors surrounds me,
⁶ those who trust in their wealth
   and boast of the abundance of their riches?
⁷ Truly, no ransom avails for one's life,
   there is no price one can give to God for it.
⁸ For the ransom of life is costly,
   and can never suffice,
⁹ that one should live on for ever
   and never see the grave.

¹⁰ When we look at the wise, they die;
   fool and dolt perish together
   and leave their wealth to others.
¹¹ Their graves are their homes for ever,
   their dwelling-places to all generations,
   though they named lands their own.
¹² Mortals cannot abide in their pomp;
   they are like the animals that perish.

¹³ Such is the fate of the foolhardy,
   the end of those who are pleased with their lot.
      Selah
¹⁴ Like sheep they are appointed for Sheol;
   Death shall be their shepherd;
straight to the grave they descend,
   and their form shall waste away;
   Sheol shall be their home.
¹⁵ But God will ransom my soul from the power of Sheol,
   for he will receive me.
      Selah

¹⁶ Do not be afraid when some become rich,
   when the wealth of their houses increases.
¹⁷ For when they die they will carry nothing away;
   their wealth will not go down after them.
¹⁸ Though in their lifetime they count themselves happy

– for you are praised when you do well for yourself –
¹⁹ they will go to the company of their ancestors,
   who will never again see the light.
²⁰ Mortals cannot abide in their pomp;
   they are like the animals that perish.

This psalm echoes the instructional style of the book of Proverbs. It voices the central reflection of one who has observed the aggressively rich and their inability to secure their future by their acquisitive practices. The psalm begins with a catalog of terms bespeaking didactic material that goes behind appearances to the "really real": "wisdom, proverb, riddle" (vv. 1–4). It is instructive that in this psalm the name of YHWH is not invoked and the generic term "God" occurs only in verses 7 and 15. For the most part, the psalm reflects on a God who guarantees governance and a moral order to which there are no exceptions.

The first instructional element of the psalm ponders in turn "those who trust in their wealth" (vv. 5–9) and the wise, who rely on their own discernment (vv. 10–11). The same conclusion is drawn for both: death is their future; neither wealth nor wisdom can "buy" (ransom) a different future. This critique and warning are apparently offered by one who is situated neither among the wealthy nor the wise but is affronted by their "pomp" and knows that their picture of success is transient and cannot be sustained. Verse 14 would seem to be a conclusion to the poetic unit, treating both the wealthy and wise as "fools" because they misperceive the world, misconstrue how it is ordered by God, and will come to a sorry death that they do not imagine. They are engaged in an illusion that cannot circumvent the divine givenness of the created order, namely that "you cannot take it with you."

The second part of the teaching reiterates the main point (vv. 16–19) and ends with the conclusion of verse 12 reiterated (v. 20). Here the inescapable end of the foolhardy is put more graphically: they are ushered into the place of the dead (v. 14, on which see Isa 14:9–11). The latter text describes the arrival of the powerful into the realm of the dead, now rendered weak and insignificant, even the ones who had relished their own "pomp."

Verse 15 is an especially interesting verse because it promises to the psalmist a future quite in contrast to that of the rich and the wise, who are in fact foolish. The term "ransom" has been used negatively in verse 8 to deny that there is any such rescue; here it is used positively to give hope to the nonrich and the nonwise speaker of the psalm. The verse seems to offer hope in the face of death, though that hope here is only inchoate and not at all developed. It is usual in this context to cite Enoch and Elijah as the ones who did not die but were "taken" by God, so now the psalmist – who does not trust wealth or wisdom – is himself among those who have hope beyond the death that awaits the acquisitive.

The psalmist in an instruction about right priorities sees that death is the great equalizer for the wealthy, who will also end up empty-handed, as must all creatures. All that will matter at that moment is the relationship with God.

A Closer Look: Foolishness

The declaration that reliance on *wealth and wisdom* is in the end *foolishness* invites attention to several other suggestive texts:

- The book of Ecclesiastes is a meditation precisely on such foolishness ("vanity"). On the futility of wisdom, see Eccl 1:12–14. On the vanity of wealth, see Eccl 5:10.
- Behind the tradition of Ecclesiastes stands the remembered figure of Solomon, the quintessential practitioner of wealth and wisdom. Although he is promised such gifts by God (1 Kgs 3:10–13), the sum of the narrative on Solomon exhibits his self-destructive foolishness and surely renders Solomon's achievements in an ironic way.[115]
- The contrast between a way of life marked by covenant fidelity ("steadfast love, justice, and righteousness") and self-indulgence ("wisdom, might, wealth") is precisely delineated in Jer 9:23–24.[116] The psalm plays on the same contrast that is characteristic in Israel's ethical reflection.

Bridging the Horizons: Rich in Things, Poor in Soul

This psalm is particularly important and surely pertinent in a contemporary society that is "rich in things and poor in soul." The psalm, faithful to proverbial teaching, has a sense of what is "better." It is better to rely on God than on any accumulated commodities. The point is an urgent one in a consumer society that seeks immediate gratification of artificially manufactured hungers and "needs."

The alternative to death is here given not as afterlife but only as a relationship with God. This psalm well anticipates the following Pauline affirmation:

For I am convinced that neither death, nor life, nor angels, nor rulers, nor things present, nor things to come, nor powers, nor height, nor depth, nor anything

---

[115] See Walter Brueggemann, *Solomon: Israel's Ironic Icon of Human Achievement* (Columbia: University of South Carolina Press, 2005).

[116] See Walter Brueggemann, "The Epistemological Crisis in Israel's Two Histories (Jeremiah 9:22–23)," in John G. Gammie et al. (eds.), *Israelite Wisdom: Theological and Literary Essays in Honor of Samuel Terrien* (Missoula, MT: Scholars Press, 1978), 85–105.

else in all creation, will be able to separate us from the love of God in Christ Jesus our Lord. (Rom 8:38–39)

Those who stay close to God are assured of a sustaining relationship, which the pursuit of commodities can never provide.

PSALM 50 – A PSALM OF ASAPH

¹ The mighty one, God the LORD,
   speaks and summons the earth
   from the rising of the sun to its setting.
² Out of Zion, the perfection of beauty,
   God shines forth.

³ Our God comes and does not keep silence,
   before him is a devouring fire,
   and a mighty tempest all around him.
⁴ He calls to the heavens above
   and to the earth, that he may judge his people:
⁵ 'Gather to me my faithful ones,
   who made a covenant with me by sacrifice!'
⁶ The heavens declare his righteousness,
   for God himself is judge.
      Selah

⁷ 'Hear, O my people, and I will speak,
   O Israel, I will testify against you.
   I am God, your God.
⁸ Not for your sacrifices do I rebuke you;
   your burnt-offerings are continually before me.
⁹ I will not accept a bull from your house,
   or goats from your folds.
¹⁰ For every wild animal of the forest is mine,
   the cattle on a thousand hills.
¹¹ I know all the birds of the air,
   and all that moves in the field is mine.

¹² 'If I were hungry, I would not tell you,
   for the world and all that is in it is mine.

¹³ Do I eat the flesh of bulls,
    or drink the blood of goats?
¹⁴ Offer to God a sacrifice of thanksgiving,
    and pay your vows to the Most High.
¹⁵ Call on me in the day of trouble;
    I will deliver you, and you shall glorify me.'

¹⁶ But to the wicked God says:
    'What right have you to recite my statutes,
    or take my covenant on your lips?
¹⁷ For you hate discipline,
    and you cast my words behind you.
¹⁸ You make friends with a thief when you see one,
    and you keep company with adulterers.

¹⁹ 'You give your mouth free rein for evil,
    and your tongue frames deceit.
²⁰ You sit and speak against your kin;
    you slander your own mother's child.
²¹ These things you have done and I have been silent;
    you thought that I was one just like yourself.
But now I rebuke you, and lay the charge before you.

²² 'Mark this, then, you who forget God,
    or I will tear you apart, and there will be no one to deliver.
²³ Those who bring thanksgiving as their sacrifice honor me;
    to those who go the right way
    I will show the salvation of God.'

A number of the psalms of the Korahites (Psalms 42–49) partake of a high Zion theology and emphasize the divine presence in Zion. In Psalm 50, that God now "shines forth" from Zion and addresses the community. This psalm's superscription associates it with Asaph the temple singer. The collection of the Asaphite psalms (Psalms 73–83) begins Book III of the Psalter. Our psalm provides a bridge between the Korahite collection and the collection of Davidic psalms that begins with Psalm 51. Following the initial summons to worship, Psalm 50 moves to a focus on traditions of the Sinaitic covenant, so most interpreters suggest that the background of the psalm was a covenant renewal festival with connections to the Sinai traditions in Exodus 19–24.[117] The psalm begins with the language of praise and worship

---

[117] J. Day, *Psalms* (1999), 82–85. J. L. Crenshaw, *Psalms* (2001), 25, in contrast, reads the psalm
      in terms of the beginnings of the synagogue and the substitution of prayer for sacrifice.

but then moves to direct divine speech beginning in verse 7. The psalm is a hymn but one that contains a prophetic warning. These divine speeches or oracles were spoken by a cultic leader in the context of worship. The oracle is a prophetic word from God and in this case is a word of warning. Sigmund Mowinckel popularized the view that such divine speeches would have been spoken by cultic prophets; that is, prophets who were members of the temple establishment.[118] It is not the temple functionary who determines the prophetic nature of the speech, however, but the content of the oracle. Priests also delivered oracles. One of the temple leaders, perhaps a priest, would have spoken the divine oracle as a sermonic word in the covenant renewal festival. The psalm begins with a summons to worship followed by two divine speeches (vv. 7–15 and 16–23).

The psalm's opening verses summon the community to worship to hear a divine revelation. Verses 1–2 partake of the same language and high Zion theology of the Korahite psalms, especially Psalms 46–48. YHWH, also described as "the mighty one" and *ĕlōhîm*, summons the whole world. The psalm partakes of the theophany tradition in ancient Israel in which God appears to humans as a means of divine revelation. The classic theophany in the Hebrew scriptures is the one at Sinai, and the "devouring fire" and "mighty tempest" in verse 3 may well reflect the thunderstorm imagery that was part of that tradition. In Psalm 50, however, God comes from Zion, "the perfection of beauty," the sacred place of the divine presence. Verses 3–6 make it clear that this one who comes to speak with authority will speak a prophetic word of critique. The psalm makes a shift of traditions here from the Korahite theology of the divine presence in Zion to a covenant theology and holds both traditions together. One way of reading the text is to see the theology of divine presence in Zion as the common ancient Near Eastern theology. The divine oracle in Psalm 50 pronounces a kind of check on that theology that makes clear that the covenant community will be accountable for both worship and behavior. God is the righteous judge who has initiated a covenant relationship with ancient Israel and now calls heaven and earth to witness this ceremony of covenant renewal that emphasizes the connections between covenant and ethical living. Heaven and earth – and not just Zion – as witnesses are part of the Deuteronomic covenant tradition (Deuteronomy 32), and verse 5 is replete with covenant terminology. Israel sealed a "covenant" with a "sacrifice" and is called God's "faithful ones." The term is from *ḥesed* and indicates those who respond to God's covenant loyalty or fidelity. God now comes in theophany to speak to this covenant community.

The first divine speech, in verses 7–15, begins with a call for the community to listen to this word from "your God." The pronoun suggests the covenant relationship. Verse 7 characterizes the speech as testimony against the people. The subject of the speech is sacrifice and its purpose. Verse 8 makes it clear that the issue is not whether the people sacrifice but their motivation. Various types of sacrifices from

[118] S. Mowinckel, *Psalms in Israel's Worship*, vol. 1 (1962), 55–58, 90–95.

herds, from flocks, and from birds are included. The punch line is that God is the creator of all these animals; they already belong to God, and thus God does not need them as sacrifices. God is not in need of sacrifice; it is rather an act of thanksgiving. The common theology of the ancient Near East suggested that the purpose of the sacrificial cult was to support the sanctuary and the priestly establishment and its deities. Sacrifice was food for the gods and for the priests. Psalm 50 moves against such a view by characterizing the temple and cult as avenues by which the covenant community thanks and worships God. God has created the entire world and all that is in it, and so is not dependent on the cultic establishment for food or drink, including meat from the herd or blood from the flock in verse 13. The psalm characterizes God as the one who delivers and in so doing makes a covenant with this community that praises and thanks God in worship. The psalm suggests that the proper context for understanding the sacrificial system is the context of covenant relationship with God. Sacrifice does not cause God to act but is a response of thanksgiving to the covenant God, who already hears the cry of the worshipers and embraces their pain.

The second divine speech begins in verse 16 and addresses the wicked, probably the wicked within the covenant community, and warns them about the connection between faith affirmations and lifestyle. In the covenant renewal festivities, the community would recite God's covenant instruction (v. 16). The concern is that some in the community will recite the instruction while living in contradiction to it. It is as if "the wicked" have forgotten the covenant God and put the covenant statutes out of sight, and so they are immune to any warning. They have turned to evil, stealing, adultery, false witness, and slander, and have been taken over by such a lifestyle. Danger is inherent in such a hypocritical lifestyle that confesses the covenant faith while living in ways that fracture the covenant relationship. God in Psalm 50 is not silent in the face of such evil but confronts it with a warning. Those addressed with this second divine oracle are not without hope, however. The charge is to turn and live in the covenant way, to live out faith in justice. The concern to match confessions in worship and actions in the rest of life is characteristic of the Hebrew prophets. Their affirmation also is that the covenant God worshiped on Zion is a God of social justice and ethical living. This oracle in Psalm 50 is a call to the community for repentance and change as a part of this ceremony of covenant renewal. The charge is to live in the way of the divine covenant instruction, to live out faith in justice, and to bring sacrifices to God as thanksgiving. Verses 22–23 offer both warning and hope as a summarizing conclusion.

Bridging the Horizons: Covenant Relationship

Covenant is one of the root metaphors for the Hebrew scriptures. The covenant God initiated a relationship with ancient Israel. The relationship is a gift – rather than being born of some divine need – that suggests a divine hope for the community to encounter wholeness in life. The sacrificial system is a gift in the context of the covenant relationship that is an avenue of worship rather than a way to manipulate the divine. Psalm 50 worries that the people have been confused by overly depending on the common theology of the ancient Near East, in which one does something for the gods and gets something in return; perhaps they have come to think of God as simply another person in the community, one like themselves (v. 21). The psalm articulates the classic view of the covenant from the Sinai narrative. The God who comes to deliver initiates a covenant relationship with the community and warns the community of the dangers of breaking the covenant. God gives the relationship and articulates the community's responsibilities; they ignore them to their own peril. The latter part of the psalm seems to have the second half of the Decalogue in view, but when readers put the two divine speeches together, the concern is that the people will craft God into another one of the idols and so deny both halves of the Decalogue. The danger persists for worshiping communities. Blindness to issues of social justice while conducting grandiose services still constitutes living "at ease in Zion."

PSALM 51 – TO THE LEADER. A PSALM OF DAVID, WHEN THE PROPHET NATHAN CAME TO HIM, AFTER HE HAD GONE IN TO BATHSHEBA

1 Have mercy on me, O God,
 according to your steadfast love;
according to your abundant mercy
 blot out my transgressions.
2 Wash me thoroughly from my iniquity,
 and cleanse me from my sin.

3 For I know my transgressions,
 and my sin is ever before me.
4 Against you, you alone, have I sinned,
 and done what is evil in your sight,
so that you are justified in your sentence
 and blameless when you pass judgment.
5 Indeed, I was born guilty,
 a sinner when my mother conceived me.

⁶ You desire truth in the inward being;
  therefore teach me wisdom in my secret heart.
⁷ Purge me with hyssop, and I shall be clean;
  wash me, and I shall be whiter than snow.
⁸ Let me hear joy and gladness;
  let the bones that you have crushed rejoice.
⁹ Hide your face from my sins,
  and blot out all my iniquities.

¹⁰ Create in me a clean heart, O God,
   and put a new and right spirit within me.
¹¹ Do not cast me away from your presence,
   and do not take your holy spirit from me.
¹² Restore to me the joy of your salvation,
   and sustain in me a willing spirit.

¹³ Then I will teach transgressors your ways,
   and sinners will return to you.
¹⁴ Deliver me from bloodshed, O God,
   O God of my salvation,
   and my tongue will sing aloud of your deliverance.

¹⁵ O Lord, open my lips,
   and my mouth will declare your praise.
¹⁶ For you have no delight in sacrifice;
   if I were to give a burnt-offering, you would not be pleased.
¹⁷ The sacrifice acceptable to God is a broken spirit;
   a broken and contrite heart, O God, you will not despise.

¹⁸ Do good to Zion in your good pleasure;
   rebuild the walls of Jerusalem,
¹⁹ then you will delight in right sacrifices,
   in burnt-offerings and whole burnt-offerings;
   then bulls will be offered on your altar.

This psalm is the best known and the most used of the seven "penitential psalms" in the classical Christian tradition. It is an extended *confession* of sin and an *anticipation* of new life grounded in divine forgiveness. The power of this psalm is further enhanced by the superscription, which in the tradition links the psalm to David's confession in 2 Sam 12:13 after the Uriah-Bathsheba episode. Although the theme of confession permeates the entire psalm, it is possible to see a movement from confession in verses 1–9 to anticipation in verses 10–19.

In the beginning, the interface of YHWH and the voice of Israel is stated in quite contrasting terms (vv. 1–2). YHWH is assigned three terms that characterize YHWH's generous fidelity: *mercy, steadfast love*, and abundant *mercy*. The terms allude to YHWH's deep commitment, on which the psalmist counts even in the midst of alienation. Indeed this triad of terms is the recurring and most important summary of YHWH's character as a faithful, covenant-keeping God (see Exod 34:6). The psalmist's condition of alienation is also characterized by three terms that constitute Israel's preferred vocabulary for separation from God: *sin, transgression,* and *iniquity*. It is the wager of the psalmist and the deep conviction of ancient Israel that YHWH's *mercy and steadfastness* will override and serve as a decisive alternative to *sin, transgression, and iniquity*.

Verses 3–5 pursue the defining, dialogical shape of the life of faith in Israel. The speaker is fully conscious of the self, but the speaker also knows that this self stands inescapably before God.[119] It is *life before God* that creates an awareness of sin that eventually leads to hope for life beyond sin. Thus the speaker can say, "Against you, you only...." The sin confessed is not specific, unlike many modern attempts at naming affronts. The double "you" suggests that the affront, whatever its specificity may be, is a violation of the first commandment. This is no groveling or chest-beating moralism but a deep awareness of the theological shape of life as life *before the God* who saves and who commands. Indeed the speaker concedes that all of life is permeated with alienation and recalcitrance but, as is always the case in the Psalter, the only hope is to turn in need to the one to whom allegiance has already been given.

In verses 6–7, the psalmist begins to think beyond guilt and alienation. There is critical reflection on what God desires: truth and wisdom. That divine desiring begins to be seen by this psalmist as an option for a new beginning beyond the failure already acknowledged. Thus the psalmist anticipates, by a cultic act of purgation, a move toward newness and the recovery of joy. The implication of the petition for joy in verse 8 is that guilt and alienation have precluded any joy in the life of the psalmist. Life apart from God or life against God is a joyless existence, and no amount of self-indulgence can be a persuasive substitute for God-given joy. This section of the psalm closes in verse 9 with two more petitions concerning sin and iniquity.

By verse 10, the poem moves from confession to petition in a series of imperatives addressed to the God of mercy and steadfast love; these petitions constitute an act of hope for a renewed, restored relationship with God. Thus the imperatives "create, put, do not cast, do not take, restore, sustain," followed in verse 14 by "deliver," articulate a confident conviction that God is fully able to move life beyond

---

[119] See G. W. Stroup, *Before God* (2004).

alienation. All that is required is an acknowledgment of need, and the psalmist can count fully on God's abiding fidelity. The use of the word "create" to begin this section is powerful and daring, for the psalmist has in mind an act of generativity that is fully as wondrous as the initial act of generativity in Genesis 1:

By employing the term *create*, he expresses his persuasion that nothing less than a miracle could effect his reformation, and emphatically declares that repentance is the gift of God.... David, by the word which he here uses, describes the work of God in renewing the heart in a manner suitable to its extraordinary nature, representing it as the formation of a new creature.[120]

The new gift anticipated by the psalmist is a *clean heart*, a *new and right spirit*; that is, a self that is wholly and unreservedly given over to the truth of obedience and to the wisdom of loyalty that are God's deep desires. In other words, the hope is that God will offer a fully constituted *new self* who can live freely and gladly *before God*. In response to such a gift, which must be given by God, the speaker promises to teach others about the possibility of new life (v. 13) and to sing aloud praise in the congregation (v. 14). The twofold response of *teach* and *praise* catches both a *liturgical responsiveness* championed in liturgical churches and the *didactic response* that is the hallmark of Calvinism. The two responses together provide grounds for ecumenism in the church that variously accents word or sacrament.[121]

By the end of verse 14, the speaker knows that praise is the proper response to the divine gift of new life, which overrides alienation. It is this voice of praise that yields the familiar response of Christian liturgy that even the praise of the glad community of faith is made possible by the action of God, who "opens lips" by restoring and sustaining new life. The psalmist reflects on the proper response to the gift of new life – joy, new heart, new spirit – and knows that a spirit and heart addressed wholly to God are appropriate (see Ezek 36:26). This characterization of heart and spirit in verse 17 does not refer to a groveling or excessively humble attitude; rather it anticipates a life wholly given over in gladness to God. That is, the relational aspects of genuine communion are what are now required. This relational practice of communion is contrasted with the practice of commodity in the form of sacrifices and burnt offerings (v. 16). The offer of commodity is too cheap and too surface for life with God, incongruent with the self-giving of God, who wants in return only a devoted self. This requirement of a devoted self rather than goods is a hard lesson anytime, certainly in a commodity-oriented society. The same contrast is made in

---

[120] J. Calvin, *Commentary on The Book of Psalms*, vol. 2 (1979), 298–299.
[121] The pairing of *teach* and *praise* calls to mind the dialectic of *proclamation* and *manifestation* proposed by Paul Ricoeur and exposited in David Tracy, *The Analogical Imagination: Christian Theology and the Culture of Pluralism* (New York: Crossroad, 1981), 202–218. Tracy develops the dialectic in *Word* and *Sacrament*, an extrapolation not far removed from the resolve of the psalmist.

Mi 6:8, wherein the oracle reviews all of the possible "commodities" that may be offered in sacrifice to God, and concludes that what is required is a relational commitment of fidelity. Indeed, to "walk humbly" with God is a close counterpoint to "broken spirit and contrite heart" in this psalm (see Mi 6:8).

Verse 17 may strike us as a conclusion for the psalm, whereby the speaker moves from alienation from YHWH to submission and glad trust in YHWH. For good reason, verses 18–19 are most often regarded as an addendum to the psalm, an institutional imposition on the prayer. In light of the foregoing and especially in light of Ps 50:8–13, which rejects such offerings, the mention of "sacrifices and burnt offerings" in these verses is curious except that the psalm, in its final form, recognizes that a new, glad commitment to YHWH must be given concrete, visible, public articulation, and that is what is accomplished in such sacrifices. These sacrifices, in context, are no substitute for or alternative to a right relationship; they are rather a public verification of a newly restored relationship.

In sum then, this psalm is an intense and honest tracing of the route from *an old life of alienation* to *a new life of glad relationship*. That restored relationship depends completely on the readiness of God to *create, restore, sustain,* and *deliver*. The psalmist does not doubt YHWH's readiness for such a relationship. What is required of the psalmist is complete candor and articulation of guilt; what is undertaken by the psalmist is a new beginning in song and thanks with glad lips of praise. This is indeed a drama of rehabilitation that is grounded in the covenant made possible by God's readiness to begin again.

A Closer Look: Nathan, David, and the Psalmist

The superscription of this psalm links the confession to the narrative of David in 2 Samuel 11–12. Although the superscription is not historically reliable, it nonetheless provides a clue for reading and hearing the psalm. The relationship of the psalm to the narrative of 2 Samuel is interesting on several counts. First, whereas the psalmist indicts himself in his confession in the narrative, the primary and extensive indictment is on the lips of Nathan (2 Sam 12:7–12). Second, whereas the psalmist confesses sin at great length, David's confession is a terse acknowledgment without any elaboration (2 Sam 12:13). Third and most important, the narrative permits Nathan to offer a pardon to David (2 Sam 12:13), whereas the confession of the psalmist in fact goes unanswered though the answer of forgiveness may be implied. Fourth, whereas the psalmist seems to move by candor and submissiveness to a new life of joy, David, in the narrative, only does so through the anguish of the death of his son, costly forgiveness indeed! (See 2 Sam 12:14, 15–23.) It is not important that the psalm in the narrative should closely or easily cohere, but the angular and awkward interface between the two is of immense heuristic value for the interpreter.

A Closer Look: God's Readiness to Forgive

To the extent that we may take this psalm as a Psalm of David, we should note God's readiness to forgive David ... and the psalmist. At the same time, it is useful to notice the parallel confession of King Saul, whose prayer of confession is much the same (1 Sam 15:25). In that exchange with Samuel, however, Saul is not forgiven; he is held in judgment and given a severe, dismissive punishment. The contrast may suggest that although the psalmist offers an invitation to reconciliation, it is not the case in the life of faith that every confession of sin "works." The counterpoint of the Saul narrative is a reminder that grace is costly and not readily available to all. Many in faith, like Saul, know the truth of sin unforgiven.

A Closer Look: An Absence of Assurance

When the psalm is compared to the narrative of 2 Samuel 11–12, we may be struck by the fact that there is in the psalm no divine response to the confession. What Christians call "an assurance of pardon" is not uttered or offered to the psalmist. This is especially curious when we recognize that many psalms appear to revolve around a divine utterance of a "salvation oracle." It may be that such an assurance is implied with the keen anticipation of joy, or it may be that such an assurance cannot be presumed. In either case, it appears that such an assurance is still anticipated by the psalmist, even if it is not yet given. Given Israel's broader conviction of divine forgiveness, such a deficiency may not be important, except to notice that in lived reality, as distinct from liturgical enactment, forgiveness is very often hoped for and awaited but not yet granted.

Bridging the Horizons: The Prodigal

The turn from *miserable alienation* to *joyous restoration* that is sketched in the psalm is given narrative specificity in the familiar parable of Luke 15:11–32. The narrative traces the life of a son from miserable alienation (vv. 16–17), to confession (vv. 18, 21), to the welcome by his father (vv. 22–24). The exchange of father and son replicates the cultic transaction of confession and assurance:

Son: Then the son said to him, "Father, I have sinned against heaven and before you; I am no longer worthy to be called your son." (Luke 15:21)
Father: But the father said to his slaves, "Quickly, bring out a robe – the best one – and put it on him; put a ring on his finger and sandals on his feet. And get the fatted calf and kill it, and let us eat and celebrate; for this son of mine

was dead and is alive again; he was lost and is found!" And they began to celebrate. (Luke 15:22–24)

The parallel may indicate that the parable arises from the long-established Jewish tradition of confession and pardon. In the psalm and the narrative, the faithful know:

The Lord is merciful and gracious,
    slow to anger and abounding in steadfast love.
He will not always accuse,
    nor will he keep his anger forever. (Ps 103:8–9)

PSALM 52 – TO THE LEADER. A MASKIL OF DAVID, WHEN DOEG THE EDOMITE CAME TO SAUL AND SAID TO HIM, 'DAVID HAS COME TO THE HOUSE OF AHIMELECH'

[1] Why do you boast, O mighty one,
    of mischief done against the godly?
    All day long [2]you are plotting destruction.
Your tongue is like a sharp razor,
    you worker of treachery.
[3] You love evil more than good,
    and lying more than speaking the truth.
        Selah
[4] You love all words that devour,
    O deceitful tongue.

[5] But God will break you down for ever;
    he will snatch and tear you from your tent;
    he will uproot you from the land of the living.
        Selah
[6] The righteous will see, and fear,
    and will laugh at the evildoer, saying,
[7] 'See the one who would not take
    refuge in God,
but trusted in abundant riches,
    and sought refuge in wealth!'

⁸ But I am like a green olive tree
  in the house of God.
I trust in the steadfast love of God
  for ever and ever.
⁹ I will thank you for ever,
  because of what you have done.
In the presence of the faithful
  I will proclaim your name, for it is good.

Psalm 51 movingly articulates the prayer of a contrite sinner. Psalm 52, in contrast, portrays an arrogant deceiver. The latter psalm fits its context well in this part of the Psalter. It relates to the theme of the prosperity of the wicked, as does Psalm 49, and to the theme of divine judgment, as does Psalm 50. Then there is the contrast with Psalm 51. Psalm 52 is brief and poses several challenges for readers. It does not fit most of the categories used for psalms.

Psalm 52 is addressed to an enemy, and so some interpreters tie the psalm to the prayers for help in the face of enemies so dominantly present in the first half of the Psalter. The psalm also focuses on the outcome of a foolish lifestyle, and so some interpreters associate it with wisdom reflections on wise and foolish lifestyles in the Hebrew scriptures. Contrasts are central to the poem, and the contrast of the prosperity of the wicked and the destruction of "workers of iniquity" is akin to Hebrew wisdom texts. Marvin Tate provides an alternative suggestion for reading the text.[122] He suggests reading the psalm as a prophetic judgment speech addressed to this opponent, such as the one in Isa 22:15–19. With this option in mind, one could read the first four verses as the accusation against this arrogant enemy and the remainder of the psalm as the announcement of judgment. Verses 5–7 articulate the divine response to the accusation followed by the response of the "righteous." Verses 8–9 contrast the place of the righteous "I" with the judgment of the evildoer. Adversative conjunctions ("but") at the beginning of verses 5 and 8 mark the sections of the poem.

The psalm begins with an accusing question addressed to "O mighty one." Perhaps "big shot" carries the sense of the Hebrew *gibbôr* or hero, often a military hero. The question seems to carry a sense of irony or even sarcasm. The translation of this first verse is debated and challenging. Again, Tate's suggestion provides a way forward that is faithful to the Hebrew text and preserves the contrast central to the psalm, a contrast between divine faithfulness and the treachery of the one addressed in this first section of the psalm.[123]

[122] Marvin E. Tate, *Psalms 51–100* (WBC 20; Dallas: Word Books, 1990), 35–39.
[123] M. E. Tate, *Psalms 51–100* (1990), 32–33.

> Why brag about evil, you hero!
> – God's loyal-love does not cease – (v. 1)

This "worker of treachery" is constantly wagging the tongue to plot destructive acts; the words of this "hero" are constantly in the service of destruction to be brought on the faithful. Deception and treachery are the hallmarks of the lifestyle of this one who loves evil more than good and deceit more than truth. The powerful use of language is central to this portrayal of the opponent, and the uses here are all destructive. The poet includes striking imagery about the tongue as "a sharp razor" that devours and destroys. The arrogant "hero" addressed in this first part of the psalm has chosen evil over good and uses language ("your tongue") to further those evil plans and uses people for that purpose and to attack people of faith.

The conjunction at the beginning of verse 5 features one of the contrasts central to the poem – "But God." Verses 5–6 announce God's judgment on the "worker of treachery." In strong contrast to the bragging of the one addressed in the psalm, God will perpetually break down that person. The announcement is severe and simple, and tells what will happen to this "hero." The deceitful one will be torn from the tent and uprooted "from the land of the living." The terms "tent" and "land of the living" could both have connections to the temple, especially given the language in the psalm's last two verses. If that is so, this deceiver will be torn from the worshiping community. Such a judgment would have serious consequences; it would be tantamount to being excluded from the community in every way. Verse 6 makes it clear that the righteous ones in the community will witness this judgment coming on the "hero" and respond with laughter and awe. God's response to the evildoer is made public in the judgment, and the faithful ones in the community will not miss the irony of this sudden reversal of fortune. This reversal of fortune is rich with irony, as demonstrated in the response of the faithful in verse 7. The deceiver trusted in self-procured possessions rather than "refuge in God," and so precisely what the enemy bragged about brought self-destruction. The Hebrew text at the end of verse 7 says that the enemy "sought refuge in his destruction." The assertion of self-sufficiency ironically will bring self-destruction. The righteous see the folly of the enemy's plots against the faithful and are both amused and take instruction. The evil of the "worker of treachery" will boomerang on the head of this "hero."

The opening adversative conjunction in verse 8 indicates that another contrast is at hand for readers of Psalm 52. The faithful psalmist now speaks in the first person ("But I") and contrasts the fate of the deceiver in verse 5 with the trust of the psalmist in verse 8. The psalmist is "like a green olive tree in the house of God." The contrast is between the braggadocious "worker of treachery" who is uprooted from the worshiping community and the psalmist, who is now firmly planted in the place of the life-giving divine presence ("refuge in God" in v. 7). In the ancient Near East, the olive tree – a thing of economic importance – symbolized life, fertility, and vitality, so the psalm confesses faith in the God who both uproots evil and nourishes faith. The second line of verse 8 is a simple and profound confession of faith. Refuge for life is found not in achievements one brags about but in trust in God's stead-fast love, *ḥesed*. That kind of trust forms persons and communities into faithful congregations. The psalm urges the community to follow this path of trust in God rather than the false path of deception and arrogance, contrasting the deceiver and the righteous. The psalm's concluding verse voices a vow of praise to be fulfilled in the congregation. In the place of divine presence and based on the demonstration of divine steadfast love, the psalmist is now flourishing like an olive tree rooted and grounded in God's refuge rather than in arrogance. This praise bears witness to the divine steadfast love, so the psalmist gives thanks in worship, for it is the good and right thing to do.

A Closer Look: David, Ahimelech, and Doeg

The psalm's superscription contains elements that will be familiar to readers of Book II of the Psalter (Psalms 42–72). It adds a note to associate the psalm with the incident narrated in 1 Samuel 21–22 as part of the David story and so sug-gests reading the psalm in tandem with that narrative. In the narrative, David flees from Saul and is assisted by Ahimelech. Doeg tells Saul where David is and also informs on those who have helped David. In the context of that narrative, Doeg would be the addressee of Psalm 52. His actions led to the execution of many priests at Nob, and so it is reasonable to think of his tongue as being "like a sharp razor."

Bridging the Horizons: Wisdom and Foolishness

Psalm 52 contains themes familiar to readers of the Psalms, though the form of the poem is rather distinctive. The poem focuses on the contrast between the wise and the foolish or the righteous and the wicked. At the heart of the folly is a sense of self-sufficiency or arrogance. The portrayal of the "worker of treachery" centers on deception. The psalm is reminiscent of Psalm 1, where the faithful are compared to a tree rooted and grounded in God's instruction. In Psalm 52, the foolish one is uprooted, whereas the faithful psalmist is firmly rooted in the place of divine presence and the worshiping community there. The psalm's contrasts also remind one of the entrance liturgies, Psalms 15 and 24, where the place of divine presence is also central. Transparency is a key for both Psalms 51 and 52. In Psalm 51, the contrition of the petitioner is transparent; in Psalm 52, the arrogance of a bragging deceiver is in full view. The foolish one opposes God and the faithful with deceitful practices and thus attracts divine judgment. The seeds of self-destruction are found in trust in self: How the mighty have fallen!

This psalm artfully imagines that lesson for the community and confesses that
true refuge is found in God's steadfast love (v. 8). That persistent confession of
faith characterizes the worshiping community of the Psalter.

PSALM 53 – TO THE LEADER: ACCORDING TO
MAHALATH. A MASKIL OF DAVID

¹ Fools say in their hearts, 'There is no God.'
  They are corrupt, they commit abominable acts;
  there is no one who does good.

² God looks down from heaven on humankind
  to see if there are any who are wise,
  who seek after God.

³ They have all fallen away, they are all alike perverse;
  there is no one who does good,
  no, not one.

⁴ Have they no knowledge, those evildoers,
  who eat up my people as they eat bread,
  and do not call upon God?

⁵ There they shall be in great terror,
  in terror such as has not been.
For God will scatter the bones of the ungodly;
  they will be put to shame, for God has rejected them.

⁶ O that deliverance for Israel would come from Zion!
  When God restores the fortunes of his people,
  Jacob will rejoice; Israel will be glad.

Psalm 53 is essentially a duplicate of Psalm 14; see the commentary on Psalm 14 for
further exposition. Each psalm portrays a corrupt society that will face divine judgment. Psalms 14 and 53 differ primarily at verse 5. The translation is difficult, but the
text appears to pronounce judgment on the wicked. In Psalm 14, the primary concern
is refuge for the poor, but in Psalm 53 the workers of iniquity are in the forefront.

They oppose God and the faithful, acts that bring consequences. The verse is a prophetic proclamation of judgment on those portrayed as foolish people. These enemies and their downfall are central to the verse. This theme continues from Psalm 52. The theme of deliverance from enemies continues in the psalms that follow. Psalms 14 and 53 each fit well with surrounding psalms and thus their literary contexts in the Psalter. The divergent text in Ps 53:5 fits the changed context in Book II especially well.

A Closer Look: Duplicate Psalms

Duplicate psalms likely reflect the growth of the Psalter as a collection of collections. Both psalms are labeled as Davidic in their superscriptions but apparently came into the Psalter from different Davidic collections. The superscription to Psalm 53 also applies the label *Maskil*, an instructive or artistic poem, and gives (apparently) a hymn tune (*Mahalath*) for performing the psalm. A difference between Psalms 14 and 53, in addition to verse 5, is that the latter psalm is in a collection known as the Elohistic Psalter (Psalms 42–83), suggesting a preference for the divine name *Elohim*, "God." Psalm 53:2, 4, 5, and 6 use this more generic divine name, whereas Ps 14:2, 4, 6, and 7 use YHWH, "Lord."

PSALM 54 – TO THE LEADER: WITH STRINGED INSTRUMENTS. A MASKIL OF DAVID, WHEN THE ZIPHITES WENT AND TOLD SAUL, 'DAVID IS IN HIDING AMONG US'

¹ Save me, O God, by your name,
   and vindicate me by your might.
² Hear my prayer, O God;
   give ear to the words of my mouth.

³ For the insolent have risen against me,
   the ruthless seek my life;
   they do not set God before them.
        Selah

⁴ But surely, God is my helper;
   the LORD is the upholder of my life.
⁵ He will repay my enemies for their evil.
   In your faithfulness, put an end to them.

⁶ With a freewill-offering I will sacrifice to you;
  I will give thanks to your name, O LORD, for it is good.
⁷ For he has delivered me from every trouble,
  and my eye has looked in triumph on my enemies.

Prayer in the face of persistent enemies is the regular staple of readers in this part
of the book of Psalms. Psalm 54 exemplifies this trend; the poem exhibits many of
the typical elements of individual lament psalms. It begins with an initial plea for
help and hearing supported by an appeal to oppression from enemies. At the center
of the psalm, in verse 4, comes a profound expression of confidence and trust in
God that leads to a further petition that God bring help for the faithful against the
evildoers. The psalm concludes with a vow of thanksgiving and sacrifice based on
God's deliverance from this oppression.

The question of the identity of the speaker in Psalm 54 has captured the attention
of a number of Psalms scholars. One possibility is that the speaker is the Davidic
king facing foreign armies in battle.[124] Another possibility is that the speaker comes
from among the poor in ancient Israel and has come, in the face of oppression, to
the temple to seek relief from the God who delivers. Some interpreters suggest that
the lamenter is facing false accusation and seeks relief in a judicial hearing in the
temple.[125] Such a temple trial is plausible as an explanation of the original setting
for which the prayer was composed, but the language of Psalm 54 could easily relate
to a number of different crises in life and has a kind of formulaic character to it.
The psalm is adaptable for life. Such poetic language is frustrating to scholars who
search for original settings in ancient Israel's social and religious life, but it makes
the prayer more germane to various settings and generations in life. So the basic
identity of the speaker is a faithful worshiper who is facing oppression and brings
this plea to the covenant God of ancient Israel, who delivers petitioners from such
trouble and woe.

Verses 1–3 constitute an opening petition characteristic of prayers for help in
the Psalter. The plea is that God will hear the prayer and deliver the petitioner
from the crisis at hand, and in so doing establish justice ("vindicate me"). Verse 3
offers a motivation or reason for God to answer the prayer: oppression from enemies of God and the faithful psalmist. The parallelism in verse 1 between "your
name" and "your might" suggest that in the ancient Near East a name is more
than an identifier. Rather, one's whole character or personality is bound up in
the name. To speak of God's name is to speak of God. In verse 1, the divine name
connotes the power of the God who is here petitioned, the power to deliver. That
deliverance from the crisis at hand would indicate that God has heard the prayer,

[124] J. H. Eaton, *Kingship and the Psalms* (1986), 73.
[125] H.-J. Kraus, *Psalms 1–59* (1988), 514.

has been revealed in life, and is the one who embraces the pain of this faithful petitioner. In these opening verses, the opponents of the psalmist are very present. The NRSV rendering of verse 3 characterizes them as "insolent" and "ruthless." An alternative understanding of the first term would see these opponents as strangers or foreigners, so some would suggest that the opponents are foreign military opponents of the king and thus that the speaker is the king. The parallel with "ruthless," however, emphasizes the portrayal of these oppressors as presumptuous and arrogant oppressors. These enemies also give homage to God, as indicated in the concluding line of verse 3. The opening petition is for divine help in the face of such oppression.

The opening word of verse 4 is an interjection that indicates a shift to what is the central faith affirmation of this poem. The verse confesses that God is the one who delivers and who sustains the life of the psalmist. The contrast is in the affirmation of trust and confidence in God in verse 4 as opposed to the enemies' rejection of God at the end of verse 3. These enemies are persistent, to judge from verses 3, 5, and 7, but in the midst of such powerful opposition the psalmist confesses the faith of the community that the covenant God is the one who embraces pain and will come to deliver them from such debilitating oppression. The enemies are those who lie in wait, looking to pounce on this faithful psalmist with intent to harm. The hope is that God will bring their evil acts back on them and so silence them and eradicate their oppression. With such an act of deliverance, God would demonstrate trustworthiness and faithfulness in the relationship with this faithful member of the worshiping community. In verses 4–5, the psalm confesses remarkable trust in the divine helper and sustainer in the face of oppressive troubles.

Verses 6–7 are made up of a vow of thanksgiving and sacrifice to this God who delivers. The concluding verse offers the reason for the vow in terms of the lamenter's deliverance and the enemies' defeat. The psalmist sees this defeat and thus enjoys justice or vindication from God as urged in the psalm's opening petition. The thanksgiving is also offered to "your name," echoing the hope in the opening line of verse 1 that God will save "by your name." The offering of thanksgiving to "your name" in verse 6 brings to mind the tradition of the temple as the place where God has made the divine name to dwell. The tradition affirms that God is present and active in a powerful way in the temple, though not limited to that place. This "name" tradition implies the power of the sacred place of worship and thus the praise and thanksgiving of worship there. God's deliverance comes from Zion, the temple mount. The temple as the place of divine presence is the place that sustains life for the faithful. At the same time, it is important to see that our poet lives in the already but not yet. The clear confession and confidence is that God is the one who delivers, but the context of the psalm suggests that the rescue has not yet come to pass. The psalm is thus a remarkable confession of hope in the midst of powerful opposition. The faith and hope of the psalm encourage readers in the midst of real life.

A Closer Look: A Prayer for Real Circumstances

The superscription to Psalm 54 suggests that stringed instruments should accompany the psalm when it is performed in worship. The heading also suggests that readers consider the psalm along with the narrative in 1 Sam 23:15–28 with the note "when the Ziphites went and told Saul, 'David is in hiding among us.'" Saul in that narrative was pursuing David, and those who preserved and passed on the psalm saw a parallel between Ps 54:3 ("the ruthless seek my life") and 1 Sam 23:15 ("Saul had come out to seek his life"). As is characteristic of the notes referring to incidents in David's life in the psalm superscriptions, David is the representative person of faith struggling with the perils of life, especially with enemies. The superscription refers to a life setting such that readers can envision using the prayer in such a real circumstance in the life of faith.[126]

Bridging the Horizons: To Pray This Text ...

The issues raised by Psalm 54 are typical of those raised by the prayers for help in this part of the Psalter. Contemporary readers could take the psalmist to be self-righteous and vindictive and thus not a model of faith to follow. That response, however, does not fit the framework of the prayer. The opening petition and the concluding affirmation of faith trumpet the psalm's purpose as a plea for God to intercede and bring justice. The psalm confesses a faith that God is worthy of trust and calls for God to bring about the deliverance that the covenant promises, so the speaker is one who is encountering oppression and seeking divine help. For contemporary readers, at least two extremes are dangerous in appropriating a prayer such as Psalm 54. One is the temptation to think that all the people a community of believers does not like are God's enemies. The poetic language of the psalm moves in the other direction; the beginning point for identifying "my enemies" is that they oppose God. For contemporary readers to pray this text faithfully, they will need to reflect on whether they oppose God or follow God ("set God before them," v. 3) and consider the question in the context of the whole of Scripture. A second extreme is that a contemporary community of faith could be so identified with its cultural context that they would not recognize evil in the world. Psalm 54 is painfully aware of evil and opposition, and suggests continuing resistance. The psalm thus prays for God to bring justice.

---

[126] Brevard Springs Childs, "Psalm Titles and Midrashic Exegesis," *JSS* 16 (1971): 148–150.

PSALM 55 – TO THE LEADER: WITH STRINGED INSTRUMENTS. A MASKIL OF DAVID

¹ Give ear to my prayer, O God;
   do not hide yourself from my supplication.
² Attend to me, and answer me;
   I am troubled in my complaint.
I am distraught ³by the noise of the enemy,
   because of the clamour of the wicked.
For they bring trouble upon me,
   and in anger they cherish enmity against me.

⁴ My heart is in anguish within me,
   the terrors of death have fallen upon me.
⁵ Fear and trembling come upon me,
   and horror overwhelms me.
⁶ And I say, 'O that I had wings like a dove!
   I would fly away and be at rest;
⁷ truly, I would flee far away;
   I would lodge in the wilderness;
      Selah
⁸ I would hurry to find a shelter for myself
   from the raging wind and tempest.'

⁹ Confuse, O LORD, confound their speech;
   for I see violence and strife in the city.
¹⁰ Day and night they go around it
   on its walls,
and iniquity and trouble are within it;
¹¹ ruin is in its midst;
oppression and fraud
   do not depart from its market-place.

¹² It is not enemies who taunt me –
   I could bear that;
it is not adversaries who deal insolently with me –
   I could hide from them.
¹³ But it is you, my equal,
   my companion, my familiar friend,

¹⁴ with whom I kept pleasant company;
    we walked in the house of God with the throng.
¹⁵ Let death come upon them;
    let them go down alive to Sheol;
    for evil is in their homes and in their hearts.

¹⁶ But I call upon God,
    and the LORD will save me.
¹⁷ Evening and morning and at noon
    I utter my complaint and moan,
    and he will hear my voice.
¹⁸ He will redeem me unharmed
    from the battle that I wage,
    for many are arrayed against me.
¹⁹ God, who is enthroned from of old,
        Selah
    will hear, and will humble them –
because they do not change,
    and do not fear God.

²⁰ My companion laid hands on a friend
    and violated a covenant with me
²¹ with speech smoother than butter,
    but with a heart set on war;
with words that were softer than oil,
    but in fact were drawn swords.

²² Cast your burden on the LORD,
    and he will sustain you;
he will never permit
    the righteous to be moved.

²³ But you, O God, will cast them down
    into the lowest pit;
the bloodthirsty and treacherous
    shall not live out half their days.
But I will trust in you.

This psalm, situated in a series of lament psalms, sounds the characteristic cadences of Israel's prayers *of lament and complaint*. We may identify three quite familiar motifs of the genre in this psalm:

1.   The speech of *complaint* is an exercise in candor in which the speaker describes a situation of alienation and violence; the voice of the psalm is one of candor and is given to us in hyperbolic form (vv. 9b–14, 17, 20–21, 26–28). As is usual in such descriptions, the language is quite specific to the speaker, but open enough that others may belatedly take the prayer as their own. The speaker finds himself in an unbearable context of threat, danger, and alienation. Not only is the speaker surrounded by adversaries, but he has been betrayed by his "familiar friend" (v. 13), who has violated a covenant through deceptive speech (vv. 20–21). The speaker is exceedingly vulnerable and wants to flee his social reality (vv. 6–8).

2.   The speaker addresses an urgent *petition* to YHWH that YHWH should intervene and transform the situation (vv. 1–2a, 9a, 15). The petition, whereby YHWH is addressed in imperatives, seeks not only rescue but also retaliation against the adversary and the friend who has betrayed the speaker. The urge to retaliate in verse 15 calls down a heavy judgment on the enemy; in the words of McCann,[127] the prayer is that the enemy should "go to hell." The speaker has great confidence that YHWH is able to act decisively if only YHWH will do so.

3.   Closely related to the petition is a series of *assurances* whereby the speaker expresses complete confidence in YHWH (vv. 16, 18–19, 23). The speaker is resilient about prayer and in verses 16–17 does indeed "pray without ceasing." The assurance is an affirmation that sooner or later the will of YHWH will override the destructive ways of human contemporaries. Thus the capacity and willingness of YHWH dominate the faith of Israel and make the prayer possible. The most direct assurance is the address to God in verse 23, wherein God is the powerful and undoubted antidote to the trouble. This assurance culminates in the final statement of verse 23: "I will trust you." The pronouns "I" and "you" indicate the intensely interactive quality of the relationship and of the prayer. The verb "trust," which binds the two parties to each other, voices the conviction that God is reliable in every circumstance, including this particular situation of misery.

Notice may be taken of verse 22, in which the speaker for an instant opts out of intense transactions with God and instructs others. This speaker knows, beyond any doubt, that God is powerful and faithful, and invites others to trust as he trusts. Thus praise turns to instruction because the news of God's reliability is too good to keep private. The community must know so that others can replicate the faith of this psalmist.

---

[127]   J. C. McCann, Jr., "Book of Psalms," in L. E. Keck et al. (eds.), *The New Interpreter's Bible*, vol. 4 (1996), 898.

Bridging the Horizons: Jeremiah 9:1–3

The description of unbearable trouble in verses 6–8 portrays the speaker as one who wishes to flee the trouble in order to find a safe place away from present circumstances. It is worth noting that these verses are parallel to Jer 9:1–3. Although the direction of dependence is not certain, it is probable that the prophetic tradition is derived from the liturgical tradition of the Psalms. In the prophetic tradition, Jeremiah is portrayed as the one who expresses a yearning to flee. It is, moreover, clear that Jeremiah – like the psalmist – lived in circumstances of deep trouble, alienated from both adversary and would-be friend. It is noteworthy that whereas the voice in the psalm culminates in affirmation, in the prophetic articulation the verses are turned to yet another prophetic indictment of Jerusalem. Given the parallelism, there is heuristic value in considering Jeremiah as the one who speaks in the psalm. The collection of "lamentations" in Jeremiah gives credence to such a reading of the psalm and helps to give a concrete locus for generic speech.[128] This theme of the *righteous sufferer* (see v. 22) pertains to Jeremiah; in Christian interpretation, it can also be heard with reference to Jesus, the voice of the righteous sufferer who is wrongly condemned and executed.

PSALM 56 – TO THE LEADER: ACCORDING TO THE DOVE ON FAR-OFF TEREBINTHS. OF DAVID. A MIKTAM, WHEN THE PHILISTINES SEIZED HIM IN GATH

¹ Be gracious to me, O God, for people trample on me;
 all day long foes oppress me;
² my enemies trample on me all day long,
 for many fight against me.
O Most High, ³when I am afraid,
 I put my trust in you.
⁴ In God, whose word I praise,
 in God I trust; I am not afraid;
 what can flesh do to me?

---

[128] See Walter Baumgartner, *Jeremiah's Poems of Lament*, trans. David E. Orton (Sheffield: Almond Press, 1988).

⁵ All day long they seek to injure my cause;
    all their thoughts are against me for evil.
⁶ They stir up strife, they lurk,
    they watch my steps.
As they hoped to have my life,
⁷ so repay them for their crime;
    in wrath cast down the peoples, O God!

⁸ You have kept count of my tossings;
    put my tears in your bottle.
    Are they not in your record?
⁹ Then my enemies will retreat
    on the day when I call.
    This I know, that God is for me.
¹⁰ In God, whose word I praise,
    in the Lord, whose word I praise,
¹¹ in God I trust; I am not afraid.
    What can a mere mortal do to me?

¹² My vows to you I must perform, O God;
    I will render thank-offerings to you.
¹³ For you have delivered my soul from death,
    and my feet from falling,
so that I may walk before God
    in the light of life.

The sequence of lament psalms in Psalms 54 and 55 continues in Psalm 56. The two dominant motifs of the lament genre are evident here in the first half of the psalm. The *complaint* describing trouble is voiced in verses 1b–2a, 5–7a. In these verses, the speaker is under assault, though the complaint lacks specificity. The *petition* is addressed to God in verses 1a and 7b. The psalmist appeals to God, who is capable of defeating the enemy. These two motifs are reinforced by a statement of *trust and assurance* in verses 2b–4. God is addressed as the "Most High," and thus supreme, sovereign God over all the powers at work in the world. In these verses, God is named three times, thus giving rhetorical intensity to conviction. The word "trust" is used twice, and the statement of trust moves in a remarkable way:

at the beginning,

    when I am afraid (v. 3);

at the end,

  I am not afraid (v. 11).

The reference to the Most High transforms *fear into fearlessness*!

  After verse 8, the cadences of lament are superseded by a statement of trust (vv. 8–11), a payment of vows (v. 12), and an affirmation of decisive deliverance already accomplished (v. 13). Thus the division of the psalm into two parts, verses 1–7 and verses 8–13, suggests that between verse 7 and verse 8 there was some word or gesture of divine intervention that permits an affirmation of confidence.

  The statement of trust in verses 8–11 offers echoes of verses 2a–4. At the center of this assurance is the simple, direct statement "God is for me" (v. 9). This defining conviction of course anticipates the Pauline affirmation of Romans:

No, in all these things we are more than conquerors through him who loved us. For I am convinced that neither death, nor life, nor angels, nor rulers, nor things present, nor things to come, nor powers, nor height, nor depth, nor anything else in all creation, will be able to separate us from the love of God in Christ Jesus our Lord. (Rom 8:37–39)

  The introduction of this statement is based on confidence that God has kept, treasured, and preserved "my tears"; that is, all the pain and suffering that the psalmist has experienced. God is the great rememberer who treasures pain so that the psalmist is free to move beyond that pain. The concluding statement of assurance again names God twice in acts of praise and culminates in trust. This freighted affirmation ends with a defiant statement, echoing verse 5: "What can a mere mortal do?" The answer of course is "nothing!" God is decisive, and all threats are thereby subverted and made innocuous. The speaker is now free of all those threats enumerated in the first part of the psalm.

  The proper response to such "unburdening" is the payment of vows and thank offerings (v. 12). There is a need to give material expression to the new "economy of well-being" already voiced in the psalm. Such unburdening is matched by a generous gratitude. The final verse, verse 13, articulates the outcome of the reality that "God is for me." A new life begins!

  In this speech, the psalmist testifies to the reality that the faithful God has intervened to deliver and to make a new life possible. Thus the psalmist reiterates yet again the narrative of miraculous deliverance that constitutes the center of Israel's faith, always the move from trouble to new well-being. Although the narrative is familiar, here it is given a particular expression, for only here is the image of "tears in a bottle" voiced. The grief of the speaker is kept and honored by the God of all grief, and so trust overrides fear and grief and arrives at newness!

A Closer Look: Risky Business

The superscription of the psalm relates to the episode in David's life in 2 Sam 21:10–15. In that episode, David is put at risk by being among the Philistines and, in particular, King [Achish] of Gath. This connection gives particularity to the psalm because the voice of the psalmist is that of one who is at great risk but who trusts in YHWH against the risk. Although such a superscription provides a clue to reading, it is not thought by critical scholars to have a historical foundation.

PSALM 57 – TO THE LEADER: DO NOT DESTROY. OF DAVID. A MIKTAM, WHEN HE FLED FROM SAUL, IN THE CAVE

¹ Be merciful to me, O God, be merciful to me,
   for in you my soul takes refuge;
in the shadow of your wings I will take refuge,
   until the destroying storms pass by.
² I cry to God Most High,
   to God who fulfils his purpose for me.
³ He will send from heaven and save me,
   he will put to shame those who trample on me.
      Selah
God will send forth his steadfast love and his faithfulness.

⁴ I lie down among lions
   that greedily devour human prey;
their teeth are spears and arrows,
   their tongues sharp swords.

⁵ Be exalted, O God, above the heavens.
   Let your glory be over all the earth.

⁶ They set a net for my steps;
   my soul was bowed down.
They dug a pit in my path,
   but they have fallen into it themselves.
      Selah

⁷ My heart is steadfast, O God,
  my heart is steadfast.
I will sing and make melody.
⁸ Awake, my soul!
Awake, O harp and lyre!
  I will awake the dawn.
⁹ I will give thanks to you, O Lord, among the peoples;
  I will sing praises to you among the nations.
¹⁰ For your steadfast love is as high as the heavens;
  your faithfulness extends to the clouds.

¹¹ Be exalted, O God, above the heavens.
  Let your glory be over all the earth.

Psalm 57 operates in a context of hope and voices a prayer for help. The psalm touts hope in the face of ongoing opposition. In that context, the prayer exhibits both *petition and complaint,* characteristic elements of ancient Israel's prayer. The psalm is found among a number of prayers from the Davidic hymnbook in which enemies are persistently present. Two comments become clear for readers of such prayers in this part of the Hebrew Psalter.

1. The prayers in the Psalter relate to real life and worship; they are more than abstract poems.
2. The prayers in the Psalter are adaptable for life and thus appropriate for various settings in the pilgrimage of faith.

The question of the ancient setting from which the prayer arose has attracted the attention of Psalms scholars. Based on the enemies' use of words in verse 4, some have argued that the psalm came from a setting in which the psalmist has been falsely accused and seeks a word of acquittal in the sanctuary of the temple.[129] Others understand the psalm as the prayer of the king who faces enemies.[130] The poetic language appears to be too open-ended to justify these ancient contexts. The voice of the psalmist does seek a divine judgment in the face of enemies who use "their tongues" as weapons. Perhaps the context is one of malicious gossip in which the psalmist seeks divine vindication in the life of prayer rather than in a judicial context.[131]

The literary shape of the prayer is marked by a refrain in verses 5 and 11. The first five verses focus on petition in a context of trust. The second part of the psalm

---

[129] H.-J. Kraus, *Psalms 1–59* (1988), 57.
[130] J. H. Eaton, *Kingship and the Psalms* (1986), 46–47.
[131] William H. Bellinger, Jr., *Psalmody and Prophecy* (JSOTSup 27; Sheffield: JSOT, 1984), 32–34, 53–55.

begins with a complaint about enemies and moves to hopeful expressions of confidence to conclude the prayer.

The psalm opens with a *petition* reminiscent of the beginning of Psalm 56, though emphasized with the repetition of "be merciful to me." In the face of the battering storms, the psalmist takes refuge in the God who delivers. The petitions in the first part of the psalm move quickly to expressions of trust in God's refuge in the storms. The reference to refuge in the shelter of God's wings in the first verse prefigures similar references in Psalms 61 and 63. The image of a mother bird protecting her young is a powerful metaphor and one that provides hope in the face of opposition. Refuge in the shelter of God's wings is also often associated with the sanctuary the temple could provide. Further, a number of interpreters take the wings to refer to the wings of the creatures guarding the Ark of the Covenant in the most holy place in the temple. The Ark is a visible symbol of the presence of the covenant God. It is this God whom the petitioner addresses, this God who, while addressed as "God Most High," is not distant but provides refuge in the midst of the storms at hand. The messengers of this God are "steadfast love" and "faithfulness." These terms, loyal love and trustworthiness, will be familiar to readers of the Psalter and are here personified as God's means of answering the petition for help in the conflict with opponents. The opponents are portrayed as roaring and ravenous lions (v. 4) whose teeth and tongues are sharp weapons as they "devour human prey." The first part of the psalm concludes with a refrain that petitions God to exercise rule over all creation and thus to be present to the psalmist.

The second part of the psalm returns to the enemies and portrays them with imagery from hunting. The hunters dig a pit in the path with the hope that the prey – in this case the psalmist – will fall into it. The psalmist is complaining that these opponents seek to destroy the psalmist, but hope and refuge are found in the sovereign one appealed to in the psalm's refrain. The conclusion of verse 6 envisions a reversal of fortune and thus a hope for justice. The enemies fall into the pit they have intended for the psalmist; their evil has rebounded against them. The image of the pit may suggest that the enemies will go down to Sheol, the realm of the dead. The vision of hope in verse 6 leads to exalted expressions of trust in the remainder of the prayer. The psalmist now trusts that God will deliver, expressed in verse 7 in terms of a trusting heart, and so calls the self to enthusiastic praise, even praise that "will wake the dawn!" Morning is often thought of in the Hebrew scriptures as the time of deliverance, and so the psalmist will begin early with "harp and lyre" to praise and thank God. The praise will also be voiced "among the peoples/nations." The pledge of thanksgiving in Psalm 57 is characteristic of ancient Israel's narrative or declarative praise. The worshiper will narrate how God has come to deliver Israel from the crisis, and this testimony is declared to the congregation. This confession of praise becomes part of ancient Israel's witness to God's involvement in the world on behalf of the faithful and thus part of the community's story of faith among the nations. The refrain in Psalm 57 is a call for God to be present (the sense of "glory") and to reign "over all the earth." The praise of God here derives from deliverance for the community from a present crisis. However, God's salvific action for the community echoes through the creation as an embodiment of the covenant, God's involvement in the world on behalf of the faithful, and so demonstrates the reign of God over all creation. Verse 10 puts the expansive conclusion of the prayer in terms of the divine "steadfast love" and "faithfulness," named as the divine messengers in verse 3. God can be trusted with life, and God's loyal love does not wither in the face of opposition. The psalm concludes with the repetition of the refrain. As a renewed petition, the refrain suggests that the deliverance has not yet come to pass but that the psalmist has found hope and trust in the midst of the crisis at hand. The prayer clearly operates in a context of hope.

A Closer Look: A Multipart Superscription

The psalm's superscription includes a variety of elements: the liturgical collection from which it comes (Davidic), instructions for use in worship ("Do Not Destroy" as the hymn tune for accompaniment), and a historical note. The allusion of the cave is likely 1 Samuel 22 or 24. The note is of heuristic importance as an indication of a life context for the use of the prayer: David's fleeing from Saul. As is consistently the case in psalm superscriptions, David is here not the grand and glorious king but a representative person of faith at prayer.

A Closer Look: Duplications

Psalm 57:7–11 also appears as the first five verses of Psalm 108, a composite of Psalms 57 and 60. Psalm 108 puts these verses in a different context. Such duplications in the Psalms are a result of the process of composing and collecting the texts that make up the Psalter.

Bridging the Horizons: Conclusions

Reading Psalm 57 brings several conclusions:

1. The psalm bears witness to the God who delivers. The psalm is not simplistic, however; it makes clear that there is evil opposition in the world. The psalmist confesses trust in the covenant God, who is both present and trustworthy.
2. The prayer has implications beyond this one petitioner and this particular crisis. The prayer is voiced among the community and among

the nations. Its confession of divine steadfastness is an act of faith that moves beyond local circumstances.

3. The faithful psalmist of Psalm 57 lives in the "already but not yet." To put that in broader terms, the Psalter affirms God's reign over all creation, but that reign is opposed. The psalm calls the congregation to trust the tradition's central confession of faith in divine steadfast love and faithfulness in the face of opposition. The Psalter and this psalm affirm that God is exalted (reigns) and plea for God to be exalted. The conviction of this psalmist is that God's unchanging love and trustworthiness are the most basic and enduring realities of life. That is a remarkable confession in the midst of persecution and is Israel's persistent confession in the Psalter. With that confession, the congregation can realistically face the darkness in the world with trust in a steadfast loyalty beyond themselves.

PSALM 58 – TO THE LEADER: DO NOT DESTROY. OF DAVID. A MIKTAM

¹ Do you indeed decree what is right, you gods?
  Do you judge people fairly?
² No, in your hearts you devise wrongs;
  your hands deal out violence on earth.

³ The wicked go astray from the womb;
  they err from their birth, speaking lies.
⁴ They have venom like the venom of a serpent,
  like the deaf adder that stops its ear,
⁵ so that it does not hear the voice of charmers
  or of the cunning enchanter.

⁶ O God, break the teeth in their mouths;
  tear out the fangs of the young lions, O Lord!
⁷ Let them vanish like water that runs away;
  like grass let them be trodden down and wither.
⁸ Let them be like the snail that dissolves into slime;
  like the untimely birth that never sees the sun.
⁹ Sooner than your pots can feel the heat of thorns,
  whether green or ablaze, may he sweep them away!

¹⁰ The righteous will rejoice when they see vengeance done;
   they will bathe their feet in the blood of the wicked.
¹¹ People will say, 'Surely there is a reward for the righteous;
   surely there is a God who judges on earth.'

Psalm 58 is a difficult text and one that is unusual in the Psalter. At the same time, the psalm has connections with surrounding psalms in this section of the book. This part of Book II (Psalms 42–72) of the Psalter is awash in enemies, who also dominate the perspective in Psalm 58. Enemies are ever present, but the deeper confession of faith in this psalm is the reign of God over all creation, including the enemies. Psalm 58 has many elements of the imprecatory psalms or psalms of vengeance, and so this exposition will provide an opportunity to consider that theme.

It may help readers to think about the question of how to classify Psalm 58. The psalm begins by addressing those who do evil and violence and describing them as a group (vv. 1–5). The next part of the psalm is a prayer for justice, including the destruction of the wicked (vv. 6–9). The final two verses provide assurance for the righteous and claim that God will bring justice. Prayer is central to the text, so a number of interpreters consider the text along with the lament psalms, either from individuals or from the community. That view also fits the setting in Book II of the Psalter, a book dominated by prayers for help in the face of enemies. Others would point to the opening of the psalm and consider its nature as a prophetic word of judgment aimed at the wicked, whether they are inside or outside the community of faith. Some have suggested viewing the psalm as the words of a temple prophet. The psalm as prayer and the psalm as judgment both deserve consideration; the treatment to follow emphasizes prayer as central to the text.

Verses 1–5. The psalm's textual difficulties begin with its first line. English translations vary. The word translated as "gods" in the NRSV (*ēlem*) in the Hebrew text is a word that suggests silence or muteness, perhaps indicating that those addressed are silent when they should be decreeing justice. Most interpreters suggest, however, that this word is a defective or shortened spelling of the word *ēlîm*, meaning "gods" or "mighty ones." That term is then interpreted in two ways. Some refer to Ps 82:1 and take the term to indicate divine beings, those subordinate to the living God. In this interpretation, the psalm begins with a rebuke to these divine beings who instigate evil, which is then embodied in the human community as portrayed in verses 3–5.[132] That interpretation is in line with the NRSV rendering. The other option would be to take the term "mighty ones" (*ēlîm*) to refer to human rulers or judges. McCann pursues this position, referring to Psalm 52 and appealing to context since human evildoers are in view beginning in verse 3.[133] Whether the opening question

---

132 See H.-J. Kraus, *Psalms 1–59* (1988), 535.
133 J. C. McCann, Jr., "Book of Psalms," in L. E. Keck et al. (eds.), *The New Interpreter's Bible*, vol. 4 (1996), 908.

in Psalm 58 is addressed to unjust divine beings or unjust humans, the psalm makes it clear that both wrongdoing and violence are woven into the very fabric of the human experience and that leaders, whether heavenly or earthly, encourage this evil and violence.

Verses 3–5 characterize the evildoers as those who from the very beginning of their lives spread lies throughout the human community. Poetic images pervade this psalm, and the first one is of the wicked as a poisonous snake. These snakes are so intent on spreading deception that even the music of the snake charmer does not stop them from spreading their venom. They are deaf to the snake charmer or the sorcerer, who might distract them from their evil deeds and remove the venom. They persist in conveying injustice and deception. This image is akin to the characterization of the enemies in the Psalms. Their intent is to do wrong and violence, as indicated in verse 2; they "go astray," "speaking lies" (v. 3).

Verses 6–11. The psalm's imagery continues with the move to the text's central prayer to seek divine justice in verse 6. The speaker in Psalm 58 begins by addressing those who "devise wrong" and pursue violence. The first part of the psalm describes the wicked and perhaps suggests that the origin of their deceiving ways is in the heavenly realm. Verse 6 comes at the center of the psalm and is a petition that God will destroy the weapons of the deceivers. The wicked are now portrayed as roaring lions who hunt the righteous to devour them. The petition is that God will smash the teeth of the lions and extract their fangs so that they have no weapons to harm the faithful. The striking imagery continues in the petition through verse 9. The first image is that the evildoers will vanish like water that evaporates. The image is likely that of a wadi with flowing water that suddenly disappears and what is left is a dry streambed of hot sand. The petition is for protection by removing the wicked. The next image is problematic. The NRSV rendering takes it to be grass on a path beaten down by those who trample on it. Others suggest that the treading is a reference to the bending of the bow with one's foot in order to prepare the weapon to shoot arrows but that here the arrows wither or fade and so are of no use; the weapons of the deceivers lose all effectiveness. The second option is reflected in the NIV rendering.

The imagery continues in verse 8 with the slug that dissolves into slime and disappears. The second image is that of the stillborn who never sees the light of day. The petition is that the evildoers and their injustice will be no more. The petition in verse 9 is that God will "sweep away" these evildoers, but the sense of the imagery is unclear. Perhaps it is the hope that God will sweep away the wicked quicker than pots can feel the heat of fire beneath them when the fuel for the fire is thorns. It is clear that the hope is for the complete defeat of the wicked. Verses 6–9 are in the form of prayer. They are not in the form of incantations or impersonal curses but are framed as petitions to God for the destruction of the evildoers.

The psalm's two concluding verses express the joy of the righteous and the coming of divine justice. "Vindication" is a better rendering in verse 10. The second line of verse 10 uses the terrible image of a bloodbath as the righteous "bathe their feet in the blood of the wicked." The final verse claims that observers will note that God brings justice for the righteous.

Bridging the Horizons: A Psalm of Vengeance

Psalm 58 and its stark imagery will be troubling to many readers. It is an example of what are often called the psalms of vengeance. Several comments may help put the psalm in context. First, the central part of the psalm is in the form of prayer. It is not in the form of a curse or of a call for human violence. It is rather addressed to God in the hope that God will bring justice. One way to think of the prayer is in terms of the model prayer: "Your will be done on earth as it is in heaven." The prayer assumes that God is the one who reigns over all life and prays for divine justice in the face of strong injustice, violence, and falsehood. The psalm is not so much about personal vengeance as it is about the hope for God's justice.[134]

Second, the psalm worries about persistent and violent evil. This theme is very present in the book of Psalms. Enemies who oppose both God and the faithful embody this evil. The psalm can remind readers to think of the many powerless victims of injustice in the world. The stunning poetic imagery portrays this persistent evil in troubling and pressing ways. In the New Testament, the imagery is akin to that in 2 Thess 1:5–12.

Third, and based on these first two comments, Psalm 58 is a brutally honest prayer that God will powerfully bring justice for the oppressed in this world. Read in such a theological context and with such oppression in mind, the psalm is a bold act of faith, taking the pain and anger of injustice to the one who can act powerfully. In the Hebrew tradition, the execution of justice is the divine prerogative. God is the one who knows and embraces pain, and the plea is that God will act on the side of the faithful. This comment suggests that the lively and intense dialogue of faith modeled in the Hebrew Psalter includes the arresting presence of evil in the world as part of the wrestling with faith and with God. Theodical issues are pressing. Faith in the Psalter is not idealistic but disturbingly realistic.

Fourth, it will be important for readers to reflect a great deal before identifying contemporary evildoers with those in the psalm. The evil portrayed in the text does not seem to reflect routine conflicts of everyday life but rather extreme embodiments of injustice. Appropriating Psalm 58 for contemporary believers will require considerable self-examination on the question of whether such injustice has been done to the reader. Those of us who read the Psalms may at times actually be the evildoers.

---

[134] D. Bonhoeffer, *Psalms* (1970), 57; Bonhoeffer's reflection on "The Enemies" (pp. 56–60) is one attempt to avoid the abusive misuse of the imprecatory psalms.

PSALM 59 – TO THE LEADER: DO NOT DESTROY. OF DAVID. A MIKTAM, WHEN SAUL ORDERED HIS HOUSE TO BE WATCHED IN ORDER TO KILL HIM

¹ Deliver me from my enemies, O my God;
  protect me from those who rise up against me.
² Deliver me from those who work evil;
  from the bloodthirsty save me.

³ Even now they lie in wait for my life;
  the mighty stir up strife against me.
For no transgression or sin of mine, O Lord,
⁴ for no fault of mine, they run and make ready.

Rouse yourself, come to my help and see!
⁵ You, Lord God of hosts, are God of Israel.
Awake to punish all the nations;
  spare none of those who treacherously plot evil.
    Selah

⁶ Each evening they come back,
  howling like dogs
  and prowling about the city.
⁷ There they are, bellowing with their mouths,
  with sharp words on their lips –
  for 'Who,' they think, 'will hear us?'

⁸ But you laugh at them, O Lord;
  you hold all the nations in derision.
⁹ O my strength, I will watch for you;
  for you, O God, are my fortress.
¹⁰ My God in his steadfast love will meet me;
  my God will let me look in triumph on my enemies.

¹¹ Do not kill them, or my people may forget;
  make them totter by your power, and bring them down,
  O Lord, our shield.
¹² For the sin of their mouths, the words of their lips,
  let them be trapped in their pride.

For the cursing and lies that they utter,
¹³ consume them in wrath;
   consume them until they are no more.
Then it will be known to the ends of the earth
   that God rules over Jacob.
         Selah

¹⁴ Each evening they come back,
   howling like dogs
   and prowling about the city.
¹⁵ They roam about for food,
   and growl if they do not get their fill.

¹⁶ But I will sing of your might;
   I will sing aloud of your steadfast love in the morning.
For you have been a fortress for me
   and a refuge on the day of my distress.
¹⁷ O my strength, I will sing praises to you,
   for you, O God, are my fortress,
   the God who shows me steadfast love.

The sequence of lament psalms continues from Psalms 54, 55, 56, 57, and 58. Psalm 59 includes the two primary points of the genre of lament, *complaint* and *petition*. The *complaint*, here as elsewhere, describes for YHWH in vivid language the trouble faced by the psalmist (vv. 3a, 6–7, 14–15). The petitioner is under assault from the "bloodthirsty" who "lie in wait." The pursuers are portrayed as hungry dogs who act as scavengers and who imagine they can operate with unrestrained viciousness. The poetic articulation is dazzling because the rhetoric is vivid and intense, yet lacking in any descriptive specificity. The *petition* offered to YHWH is as demanding as the description is vivid. The petitioner issues a remarkable set of imperatives to YHWH: "deliver, protect, deliver" (vv. 1–2), "raise, come, see" (v. 4), "awake, spare not" (v. 5), and then as a wish in verse 10 and as an imperative in verses 11–13, "make totter, bring down, consume, consume." The petitioner prays with immense confidence and with ferocious passion to match that confidence. Such prayer does indeed "tell God what to do," and prays for divine violence with a passion that hides nothing of the hate and vengeance from God, for this is indeed a God "from whom no secret can be hid." The *complaint* and *petition* are fairly predictable for the genre, even if expressed with poetic inventiveness.

Having observed the primary elements of the prayer, we may pay particular attention to the "I-Thou" faith assumptions and assertions that evidence the deep faith of the psalmist. These assumptions and assertions provide the relational matrix in which complaint can be candid – even hyperbolic – and in which petition can be direct and unrestrained.

The psalmist makes a remarkable statement about himself, namely that the petitioner is without fault (vv. 3b–4a). It is frequently the case that the trouble described in complaint is recognized as appropriate divine judgment on sin, but not here. Here the trouble is not punishment from God but the work of human adversaries. The punishment is, moreover, totally undeserved. The asserted innocence of the petitioner gives the one who prays to YHWH special entitlement. This entitled petitioner has a claim on God for a better deal than the trouble described. It is this innocence that gives the petition force and that especially claims and expects God's responsive attention.

Having spoken of his innocence, the petitioner then makes two direct assertions to God about God. In verse 5a, there is a direct address: "*You ... God of Israel.*" It is as though the trouble comes because God has been inattentive to Israel and to this Israelite in particular. The assertion thus is a reminder of divine responsibility and a summons to YHWH to act appropriately. The direct address of verse 5 is more fully developed in verses 8–9. Again it is "you." YHWH is reminded that YHWH is superior to and unfazed by assaulting enemies, and moreover is pledged to be "my fortress" and sure defense. Both direct addresses to "you" (v. 5, 8–9) summon YHWH back to a proper role as a partner; if YHWH acts responsibly, the "howling dogs" will evaporate in fear, for they are indeed held in divine derision.

The entire reassertion of I–Thou relatedness – through the candor of complaint and the vigor of petition – is an act of hope. The psalmist can indeed imagine a new state of existence for himself when YHWH has acted faithfully. A new state of well-being as a gift from YHWH in response to needful petition leads to exuberant praise. In verse 3b, God's rule over Israel will be known everywhere because Israel will sing and dance and give testimony. The motif of prayer that enhances the rule of YHWH, moreover, is the culminating point of verses 16–17. In these two verses, the term *ḥesed* occurs at the beginning (v. 16) and end (v. 17) as the last word of the psalm. In addition to these two uses of *ḥesed*, the term is also used in verse 10. It is YHWH's *ḥesed* that is the subject of Israel's true praise. In a world of jeopardy, risk, fear, and violence, it is YHWH's fidelity that makes new life possible. The work of prayer is to mobilize that fidelity of YHWH in specific contexts. Characteristically, Israel can readily imagine the new world wrought by YHWH's faithfulness. Indeed the central drama of Israel's faith is the regular and recurring movement from death to life, from trouble to well-being, from jeopardy to safety, from emptiness to fullness, each time accomplished by YHWH's faithfulness. This faithfulness is the grounds of the prayer and the guarantee of its joyous outcome.

A Closer Look: An Honest Prayer

Particular note may be taken of verse 11, which suggests that the adversaries of
the psalmist should not be killed immediately and directly by God, as God is
able to do. Rather, they should be made to totter and suffer over a long period
of time. In a psalm of trust, this is a surprising sentiment; it is a vicious wish for
the suffering of the enemy. The verse is to be noted precisely because even in its
most confident faith Israel can be honest about its resentments and its hope for
vengeance and retaliation.

PSALM 60 – TO THE LEADER: ACCORDING TO THE LILY OF THE COVENANT. A MIKTAM OF DAVID; FOR INSTRUCTION; WHEN HE STRUGGLED WITH ARAM-NAHARAIM AND WITH ARAM-ZOBAH, AND WHEN JOAB ON HIS RETURN KILLED TWELVE THOUSAND EDOMITES IN THE VALLEY OF SALT

¹ O God, you have rejected us, broken our defenses;
  you have been angry; now restore us!
² You have caused the land to quake; you have torn it open;
  repair the cracks in it, for it is tottering.
³ You have made your people suffer hard things;
  you have given us wine to drink that made us reel.

⁴ You have set up a banner for those who fear you,
  to rally to it out of bowshot.
    Selah
⁵ Give victory with your right hand, and answer us,
  so that those whom you love may be rescued.

⁶ God has promised in his sanctuary:
  'With exultation I will divide up Shechem,
  and portion out the Vale of Succoth.
⁷ Gilead is mine, and Manasseh is mine;
  Ephraim is my helmet;
  Judah is my sceptre.
⁸ Moab is my wash-basin;

on Edom I hurl my shoe;
over Philistia I shout in triumph.'

⁹ Who will bring me to the fortified city?
  Who will lead me to Edom?
¹⁰ Have you not rejected us, O God?
  You do not go out, O God, with our armies.
¹¹ O grant us help against the foe,
  for human help is worthless.
¹² With God we shall do valiantly;
  it is he who will tread down our foes.

This psalm is divided into two parts, a petition in verses 1–5 and a divine oracle in verses 6–8, with a reprise of disappointment, need, and hope in verses 9–12. The subject of the whole is the need for divine support in war, perhaps alluding to the military adventures of the Davidic government in Jerusalem. Whereas the psalm itself is generic in its articulation and might apply to any military emergency, the superscription more specifically pertains to the military efforts of David and Joab (2 Sam 8:1–14; 1 Chr 18:12–13). In these narrative reports, military victories are accomplished as "the Lord gave victory to David wherever he went" (2 Sam 8:14). The particulars of the superscription may pertain variously to the defeat of the Moabites (2 Sam 12:26–31), Edom (2 Sam 8:13–14), and the Philistines (2 Sam 5:17–25). The rhetorical effect of the connection between the narrative reports and the Psalms is to confirm that it is indeed God who will "tread down our foes" (Ps 60:12).

The petition in verses 1–5 revolves around three imperatives: "restore" (v. 1), "repair" (v. 2), and "give victory" (v. 5). The first two imperatives suggest a previous defeat for which there must now be redress. All three imperatives evidence complete confidence that YHWH is able to make Israel a winner if YHWH can be moved to act. These three imperatives are embedded, quite remarkably, in a series of accusations against YHWH that YHWH had abandoned Israel to its enemies and in doing so had reneged on the covenantal faithfulness due Israel. The harsh allegations against YHWH – offered in a series of "you" statements – are intended to exhibit YHWH's faithlessness in order to urge a renewed fidelity on YHWH's part toward Israel. It is acknowledged in verse 4 that YHWH has provided a rallying point for Israel, but now YHWH must complete what has begun. Only in verse 5 is the covenantal connection of YHWH to Israel mentioned, in the phrase "whom you love." These verses in a characteristic way exhibit Israel's readiness to be candid about YHWH and Israel's urgent insistence on its entitlement to YHWH's protection. Israel clearly has nowhere else to turn for help.

As the psalm develops, there must have been a long pause of waiting after verse 5. In due course, there is a divine response to the prayer, apparently given in the liturgical context in a divine oracle (vv. 5–8). Thus the prayer of verses 1–5 is decisively answered in the affirmative by a divine assurance of presence and help. These verses are of particular importance in the study of the Psalter because they evidence the way in which a divine oracular response in a cultic context is a reality in the practice of public prayer in Israel. Patrick Miller draws the following conclusions from his survey of oracular answers to prayers:

> This survey of the prayers of the Bible has made it clear that there are many indications, in the prayers themselves, in the songs of thanksgiving, and in the accounts of people praying, that God heard the prayers and responded in some fashion to help. One expects that would be so in the stories, for the record of the prayer is likely to be preserved precisely because the prayer was heard. But that, of course, is just the point. Time and again in the story, the people cried out to God and God responded. It is one of the primary threads binding the whole together. When the people, in one voice or in many, cry out for help, the ears of God are open, and God responds in ways to deal with their situation, to provide the help that is needed. The narrative contexts reveal what the psalm prayers suggest, that the prayer for help is often in a situation of such desperation that no other help is available or possible.[135]

The divine utterance makes three decisive claims. First, it is asserted in verses 6b–7a that YHWH possesses and governs all of the land that is in dispute and will manage it according to divine will. The implied counterpoint is that no challenge to this divine rule – according to the superscription a challenge from the Arameans and the Edomites – has any legitimate claim. The land belongs to YHWH, and that rule is not in question. Second, in verse 7b, the leading tribal groups in Israel – Judah and Ephraim – are staples of YHWH's rule and of YHWH's military capability. That is, YHWH's capacity to govern is intimately linked to the chosen people. It may well be that the reference to Judah and Ephraim in fact refers to the two kingdoms or it may be a reference to tribal groupings prior to the kingdoms. Third, in verse 8, the traditional enemies of Israel – Moab, Edom, and the Philistines – are dismissed and devalued in the eyes of YHWH, so that the enhancement of Judah and Manasseh and the diminishment of Moab, Edom, and the Philistines form a perfect contrast, a contrast between those "whom you love" and those who are of no account to YHWH. The designation of Moab as "washbasin" surely refers to a lowly and humiliating status, and the phrase "hurl my shoe" likely refers to preemptive ownership. Thus the oracle in sum assures the petitioning community of its special status with YHWH and the intimacy of its petition to YHWH.

Verses 9–10 form a curious communal (or royal) response to the divine oracle. The voice that speaks here has grave doubts and wonderments, suggesting that the divine support just promised does not seem to be forthcoming. Verse 11, moreover, reverts to the accusatory tone of the earlier verses. The concluding verse of the psalm

---

[135] P. D. Miller, *They Cried to the Lord* (1994), 140.

ushers in one more petition (v. 11) and one final statement of confidence in YHWH (v. 12). Thus the psalm voices Israel's characteristic modes of prayer, *immense need*, and *profound confidence in YHWH*. The whole of Israel's public life – political and military – is, in the psalm, outlined as a covenantal transaction. The psalm engages in no calculation about military strategy. It all comes down to YHWH, "our help is in no other save in thee alone." It is indeed *he!*, and that is enough!

A Closer Look: Salvation Oracles

This divine oracle in verses 6–8, reiterated in Psalm 108, is a specific case of the larger genre of salvation oracles.[136] The larger rubric for such assurances is "the salvation oracle" that has at its center the phrase "fear not" (see, for example, Isa 41:8–13, 43:1–5). It is plausible, as Gerhard von Rad urged long ago, that the "fear not" oracle has as one of its most vivid venues the threat of war. It is faith in YHWH in the context of huge risk that is reflected in YHWH's oracle and Israel's confidence in the oracle.

A Closer Look: An Enemy Triad

Clint McCann has noted that the enemies of YHWH listed in the divine oracle – Moab, Edom, and the Philistines – are also named in the victory song of Exod 15:14–15.[137] This outlining of traditional enemies suggests that the triad was a very old formulation in the celebrative liturgies of Israel. The mention in Exodus 15 also confirms that it is exactly appeal to the steadfast love of YHWH in that poem that is the characteristic antidote to fear and anxiety in Israel in the face of ominous threats.

PSALM 61 – TO THE LEADER: WITH STRINGED INSTRUMENTS. OF DAVID

1 Hear my cry, O God;
listen to my prayer.
2 From the end of the earth I call to you,
when my heart is faint.

---

[136] P. D. Miller, *They Cried to the Lord* (1994), 135–177.
[137] J. C. McCann, Jr., "Book of Psalms," in L. E. Keck et al. (eds.), *The New Interpreter's Bible*, vol. 4 (1996), 917.

Lead me to the rock
  that is higher than I;
³ for you are my refuge,
  a strong tower against the enemy.

⁴ Let me abide in your tent for ever,
  find refuge under the shelter of your wings.
    Selah
⁵ For you, O God, have heard my vows;
  you have given me the heritage of those who fear your name.

⁶ Prolong the life of the king;
  may his years endure to all generations!
⁷ May he be enthroned for ever before God;
  appoint steadfast love and faithfulness to watch over him!

⁸ So I will always sing praises to your name,
  as I pay my vows day after day.

This short psalm sounds Israel's characteristic motifs *of petition* (vv. 1–7) and *praise* (v. 8). The petition is in two parts. The first part is a characteristic statement of need that relies on YHWH as the only source of help (vv. 1–3). This particular articulation is distinctive on two counts.

First, the psalm uses no words or energy to describe the situation of need, a description that in many other psalms is quite long and detailed. Rather, the rhetorical energy of the psalm is in a doxology that characterizes YHWH in imaginative ways. The psalm anticipates new well-being and safety when YHWH answers the prayer in the same way as in the past. YHWH's anticipated deliverance is voiced in the psalm in three images. First, YHWH offers a "rock that is high" (v. 2). This figure, which may originally have referred to an actual safe place in a sanctuary, suggests the rising waters of chaos that jeopardize life; the rock is a safe, high place above the rising waters that threaten life. Second, YHWH is a tower of defense, suggesting a military haven in the face of a military threat (v. 3). Third, YHWH's sanctuary is a "shelter" (v. 4). Perhaps the "wings" refer to the carved cherubim in the temple. The sum of the three images envisions YHWH as an alternative to the threat of chaos or enemy and finds YHWH as a more than adequate antidote to the threat. It is moreover to be noted that these images characteristically refer to the temple as a safe haven where the threatened may find well-being and protection. With his accent on the divine presence in temple theology, Lindström comments on the imagery of this psalm:

This temple theology implies a "dualistic" understanding of life. The metaphors "rock, shelter, tower of strength" presuppose that human life is threatened and that the threat derives from a realm in competition with YHWH's sphere of power:

> … From the end of the earth
> … I call to you,
> … when my heart is faint, (v. 3a, b, c).

The anxiety (v. 3c), which in the individual complaint psalms is often a component in all kinds of bodily and mental affliction, is caused by an existence at "the ends of the earth." The petitioner thus finds himself in the twilight zone, in the foyer of the area of Death (cf. Ps 42:7). Therefore, it is likely that the enemy (v. 4b) from whom the petitioner is seeking refuge is the archenemy Death (e.g., Pss 7:6; 13:3–5; 30:2). This first and last enemy in the individual complaint psalms cannot be defeated by human effort.[138]

Second, verse 5 refers to vows, a not infrequent reference in the psalms. The vow apparently was a promise made at the time of petition that a specific offering of gratitude would be given to YHWH on rescue. Such a view could, of course, be taken as an attempt to bribe God, but when given in good faith it would be a token transaction in the covenant, an ongoing interaction of mutual loyalty marked by YHWH's graciousness and Israel's gratitude. The psalmist reckons that the declaration of vows has been noted by YHWH and that the vows may persuade YHWH to act according to the petition. It is clear that the address to YHWH is grounded in deep confidence and trust.

The fourfold petition in verses 7–8 comes as something of a surprise. Whereas the prayer in verses 1–5 is in the first person, here the king is referred to in the third person. It may be that these two verses are an intrusion into the psalm, so that one could read directly from verse 5 to verse 8. But there is no reason that a petitioner (vv. 1–5) could not voice an intercession for another, in this case for the king (vv. 6–7). Such a move in the prayer could indicate that the psalmist is able to think and pray beyond personal need in order to be concerned for the public realm over which the king presides. If such a prayer is offered in the temple, then it is not surprising that the king receives attention in the prayer, for the temple is indeed "the king's chapel" (see Amos 7:13).

These two latter verses are sandwiched as two jussive statements between two direct imperatives, all of which together seek the enduring well-being of the king through which the entire realm may prosper. The use of the adverb "forever" is typical hyperbolic language of the royal court (v. 7). The most crucial element of the prayer is the petition for YHWH's "steadfast love and faithfulness," a word pair bespeaking YHWH's fidelity that often pertains to the monarchy (see Ps 89:14, 33).

---

[138] F. Lindström, *Suffering and Sin* (1994), 403.

The conclusion of the psalm parallels the offer of praise and the payment of vows, two liturgical gestures of loyalty and gratitude (v. 8). It may be that this verse is parallel to verse 5 and only anticipates the payment of vows when the petition is answered (see Gen 28:20–22). Or it is possible that after verse 7 an oracle of divine assurance is offered that resolves the need of the psalmist, so that verse 8 is a response that is enacted and no longer anticipatory. The introduction of verse 8 with "so " (*ken*) might indicate such an oracle, for it may be understood as meaning "as a consequence." In any case, the general movement of the psalm, so characteristic in Israel, is a move from *need* to *restitution*, or in Claus Westermann's categories, from *plea* to *praise*. The whole of the prayer is performed in profound confidence in YHWH. The psalmist is confident that God will be a safe high rock, a strong tower, and a safe shelter. The offer of such protection is given to everyone who is able to "fear your name" (v. 5). As the assurance may include every Israelite, it certainly pertains to the king, who, like every Israelite, lives by this covenantal fidelity.

A Closer Look: A Grateful Response

The promise of an offering and a payment of vows may be taken in good faith as an act of gratitude in response to divine generosity. Israel, however, was not aware that the transaction could be reduced to a quid pro quo, an attempt to bribe YHWH. In that regard, particular reference should be made to Ps 50:9–13, wherein the divine oracle makes quite clear that YHWH is in need of nothing that Israel has or can offer. The reason that YHWH has no such need and does not need to respond to Israel's offering is because "the world and all that is in it is mine" (Ps 50:12).

PSALM 62 – TO THE LEADER: ACCORDING TO JEDUTHUN. A PSALM OF DAVID

¹ For God alone my soul waits in silence;
from him comes my salvation.
² He alone is my rock and my salvation,
my fortress; I shall never be shaken.

³ How long will you assail a person,
will you batter your victim, all of you,
as you would a leaning wall, a tottering fence?
⁴ Their only plan is to bring down a person of prominence.

They take pleasure in falsehood;
they bless with their mouths,
   but inwardly they curse.
      Selah

⁵ For God alone my soul waits in silence,
   for my hope is from him.
⁶ He alone is my rock and my salvation,
   my fortress; I shall not be shaken.
⁷ On God rests my deliverance and my honor;
   my mighty rock, my refuge is in God.

⁸ Trust in him at all times, O people;
   pour out your heart before him;
   God is a refuge for us.
      Selah

⁹ Those of low estate are but a breath,
   those of high estate are a delusion;
in the balances they go up;
   they are together lighter than a breath.
¹⁰ Put no confidence in extortion,
   and set no vain hopes on robbery;
   if riches increase, do not set your heart on them.

¹¹ Once God has spoken;
   twice have I heard this:
that power belongs to God,
¹² and steadfast love belongs to you, O Lᴏʀᴅ.
For you repay to all
   according to their work.

Psalm 62 constitutes an apt sequel to Psalm 61 and an apt prequel to Psalm 63. The three poems share a number of terms and images. The superscription to Psalm 62 refers to Jeduthun, who, along with his descendants, is associated with temple music and worship. The purpose of the psalm appears to be fostering in the congregation trust in the living God alone, even in crises. The poem operates from the basic experience of the speaker and instructs the congregation based on that; perhaps that experience was associated with the "sanctuary" function of the temple. The psalm's imagery emphasizes divine protection. The basis for the imagery could well be the asylum function of the temple, from which comes divine salvation.

Whereas the psalm's imagery and expression of trust are characteristic of the Psalter, the form of the poem is distinctive. Some type of crisis is in the picture, including enemies, but the psalm does not take the traditional form of the lament psalm or the thanksgiving psalm. It has some connections with wisdom, given its instructional dimensions. Most of the psalm speaks about God and trust in God. God is not addressed until the concluding verse with an expression of trust. The best way forward for readers of the text may well be to think of it as an expression of trust in God in the face of difficulty. The psalm's basic literary structure is tied to what appears to be a refrain in verses 1–2 and verses 5–6. Following the opening expression of trust, the psalm addresses the enemies. Verses 5–7, with the second use of the refrain, return to the expression of trust. The final verses (vv. 8–12) address the community based on the expressions of trust in the first seven verses. The psalm contains complaint, as is characteristic of ancient Israel's prayer, but there is no petition. The psalm addresses God at the end, but with an expression of trust. That appears to be the focus of the poem.

Verses 1–7. The psalm opens with a radical poetic assertion: it is God alone who can provide protection and wholeness in the face of crisis. The faithful psalmist waits for that salvation. The characteristic images of rock, salvation, and fortress reflect a crisis with enemies on the prowl. Only God is the one who provides a safe haven, a sure protection in the face of opponents. These images associated with the temple provide lasting assurance. The conclusion of verse 2 reminds readers of the conclusion of Psalm 15, a text closely tied to the temple.

With verse 3, the psalmist addresses the enemies with a question familiar to readers of the lament psalms: How long? But here the question is addressed to the enemies to ask, how long will they "batter your victim?" The image is of a fence that is about to fall, and yet these enemies keep pounding it until it falls to the ground and lies in total destruction. The speaker is apparently "a person of prominence" opposed by these hypocritical ones who delight in "falsehood." The imagery in verses 3–4 provides the precious little we know about these enemies. The poetic language is open-ended, and yet the lively imagery makes it possible for readers to imagine the types of people they are who press falsehood against this one who trusts in the God of salvation.

Verse 5 brings the psalm back to the initial confession of trust in God as rock, salvation, and fortress. In the sequence of the psalm, these expressions of trust "surround the address to and description of the enemies in vv. 3–4."[139] This interplay between the crisis centering on the enemies and the psalmist's confessions of trust is central to the psalm's import. Trust in the God who delivers provides the most basic context for the crisis. One shift from the refrain in verses 1–2 is noteworthy. In verse 1, "salvation" comes from God alone; in verse 5, "hope" comes from God. Hope

---

[139] J. C. McCann, Jr., "Book of Psalms," in L. E. Keck et al. (eds.), *The New Interpreter's Bible*, vol. 4 (1996), 922.

sustains the psalmist while waiting for the salvation of God to come to fruition. Verse 7 continues the imagery of divine deliverance in terms of rock and refuge. The "honor" of the psalmist, presumably some type of vindication, is dependent on God. Verses 1–7 offer strong expressions of trust in an exclusive way; only God brings hope and salvation. The confession of trust is the basis for the remainder of the psalm.

Verses 8–12. The concluding verses of the psalm address the community of faith ("people" in v. 8) and instruct them based on the first part of the psalm. In that sense, the psalm carries a hint of wisdom, as is also indicated with the image of the scales in verse 9 and the numerical saying in verse 11. Both literary devices are found in the book of Proverbs. The call is to trust in God and thus to pray in utter honesty; that is the lesson of this psalmist's experience. All humans come before God in full equality, those of "low estate" and those of "high estate." God judges all humans, and the corrupting efforts of extortion, robbery, and wealth in the end become bankrupt. *Only God* is worthy of complete trust. The numerical saying in verse 11 makes it clear that God is the one who determines life for all humans. Interestingly, "power" at the end of verse 11 is parallel to "steadfast love," both of which come only from God. God's refuge derives from that loyal love. The psalm's conclusion affirms the justice of this powerful and loving God. This conclusion implies bad news for the enemies characterized by "falsehood" (v. 4), but the focus of the conclusion of the psalm is the confession of ancient Israel's normative faith in the divine steadfast love. The psalm is realistic in grappling with the trouble and woe of life, but this confession of trust in God's trustworthiness trumps all that reality. The psalm's confession of trust is total and radical. Only God is refuge and hope. That is both the psalmist's confession and the lesson for the community.

Bridging the Horizons: In Whom Do We Trust?

The radical confession of God as refuge in Psalm 62 is a stunning minority report for most historical epochs in human history; few have followed the route of the psalm. So the question for communities encountering the psalm becomes: In whom or what do we place our trust? In much of contemporary Western culture, "It's about the economy, stupid," to quote from the Bill Clinton presidential campaigns, leading to a militant consumerism. Life is about the acquisition of things and financial success. The warnings in verses 9–10 seem to suggest a similar setting in ancient society. This psalm flies in the face of such militant consumerism and in a poetic confession of faith – seldom followed by the majority in any society – urges that it is God alone who brings hope and refuge in the face of the vicissitudes of life. The psalm rejects position, wealth, conniving, and oppression as means of salvation; only God provides refuge. Psalm 62:8–12 challenges the community to take up the radical confession of trust and try it as the pattern of

prayer and of everyday life. Only in trusting God is there hope. In Christian tradition, the psalm's plea is not unlike the call of Jesus in the beginning of Mark's
gospel to repent and believe in the good news.

PSALM 63 – A PSALM OF DAVID, WHEN HE WAS IN THE WILDERNESS OF JUDAH

¹ O God, you are my God, I seek you,
   my soul thirsts for you;
my flesh faints for you,
   as in a dry and weary land where there is no water.
² So I have looked upon you in the sanctuary,
   beholding your power and glory.
³ Because your steadfast love is better than life,
   my lips will praise you.
⁴ So I will bless you as long as I live;
   I will lift up my hands and call on your name.

⁵ My soul is satisfied as with a rich feast,
   and my mouth praises you with joyful lips
⁶ when I think of you on my bed,
   and meditate on you in the watches of the night;
⁷ for you have been my help,
   and in the shadow of your wings I sing for joy.
⁸ My soul clings to you;
   your right hand upholds me.

⁹ But those who seek to destroy my life
   shall go down into the depths of the earth;
¹⁰ they shall be given over to the power of the sword,
   they shall be prey for jackals.
¹¹ But the king shall rejoice in God;
   all who swear by him shall exult,
   for the mouths of liars will be stopped.

Psalm 63 continues an emphasis on the theme of trust in this section of the book of
Psalms. Psalms 61 and 62 confess confidence in the God who comes to deliver, and

Psalm 64 continues the theme. This look at Psalm 63 will consider the text a prayer of trust and look at the psalm in two parts: verses 1–8 constitute a confession of trust, and verses 9–11 turn to the issue of enemies.

This psalm has clear connections to the divine presence made visible in the temple. Two options have been proposed for identifying the speaker. One is that the speaker is the Davidic king in the midst of battle.[140] In this interpretation, the king confesses trust in the midst of a military conflict that is reflected in the subject of opponents in verses 9–10. The psalm's concluding verse speaks of the king. Other interpreters suggest that the speaker is a faithful worshiper who has been falsely accused and comes to the temple seeking refuge.[141] The concluding verse of the psalm identifies the enemies as liars. In this interpretation, the king is the one who guarantees the refuge in the temple and thus is mentioned in the concluding verse. Here the first part of the psalm becomes the expression of trust in the divine judge who will bring protection and hope in the midst of these accusations. Both interpretations suggest plausible readings of the psalm, but the most reasonable conclusion is that the poetic language does not provide enough evidence for readers to choose one option. At the same time, these proposals for the ancient worship setting in which the psalm was used remind interpreters that the poem is not some abstract set of lovely words floating along outside of space and time. The prayer originated in a cultural setting tied to worship. Verses 2–5 make it clear that the text is connected to the Jerusalem temple as a center of divine presence. Fredrik Lindström has shown the powerful import of the temple for that community: "Its theological profile is comprised of the temple theological experience that YHWH is the power who helps the threatened individual with his protection and care. These experiences of the petitioner of the central aspects of the character and activity of the present YHWH are manifested by the temple on Zion."[142] At the same time, the poetic language makes it possible for the text to adapt to a variety of settings and generations in the worship of God.

The first eight verses of the psalm articulate the speaker's *confession of trust*. The poetic imagery in verse 1 is probably the tie to the setting of David "in the Wilderness of Judah" in the psalm's heading. A specific wilderness time is not given; perhaps times in the wilderness fleeing from Saul as narrated in 1 Samuel were in view when scribes added the heading to this poem from the Davidic hymnbook. The psalm brings together a number of poetic images characteristic of the Psalter. The text begins with an arresting image of the psalmist's thirst to encounter the presence of

---

[140] S. Mowinckel, *Psalms in Israel's Worship*, vol. 1 (1962), 100; J. H. Eaton, *Kingship and the Psalms* (1986), 50–51.

[141] Walter Beyerlin, *Die Rettung der Bedrängten in den Feindpsalmen der Einzelnen auf institutionelle Zusammenhänge untersucht* (Gottingen: Vandenhoeck and Ruprecht, 1970), 135–138; and Hans-Joachim Kraus, *Psalms 60–150: A Commentary*, trans. Hilton C. Oswald (Minneapolis: Augsburg, 1988), 18.

[142] F. Lindström, *Suffering and Sin* (1994), 412.

God. The speaker seeks and thirsts, and faints as if in a wilderness with no water, "a dry and weary land." The confession of trust thus begins with this intense seeking after "my God," and the seeking leads to the sanctuary.

Verse 2 ties the sanctuary to the divine presence in terms of "power and glory," suggesting that God is decisively present and active in the world. It is in the sanctuary as a place of divine presence that the speaker's thirst can be fulfilled and life nurtured. In the sanctuary, the speaker encounters steadfast love in the midst of this wilderness time. Even with the hunger and thirst associated with the desert, the speaker comes to the praise of God because of the life-giving divine presence. The lifting up of the hands in verse 4 is the characteristic act of prayer for this ancient worshiping community. The feasting in verse 5 also speaks of fulfilling the needs of hunger and thirst. Leviticus 3:16 indicates that "All fat is the Lord's." Psalm 63 suggests that the fat (translated "rich feast" in the NRSV) is shared with this worshiper. The verse likely reflects the meals and celebrations around sacrifices as part of the sanctuary events. The use of "mouth" in verse 5 is in notable contrast with the use in the psalm's last verse, where the mouths of the lying opponents will be stopped. The faithful psalmist's mouth is open to give joyful praise. In the first part of the psalm, the psalmist's mouth hungers and thirsts for God, praises God, and prays to God. Perhaps the psalmist's open mouth indicates openness to God, which can bring life itself.[143] The confession in verse 3 is a notable one in the Psalter. It claims that God's *steadfast love* is even better than life and thus leads to praise. The psalmists often plead for divine help in trouble. This confession suggests that divine loyalty is a deeper reality than wilderness experiences and the opposition of evildoers. When one combines that confession with the use of the word *nepeš*, often translated as "soul" but more likely meaning "life" in a holistic sense, used in verses 1, 5, and 9, it becomes clear that the confession of trust becomes a hope for fullness of life that only the divine ḥesed, steadfast love, can bring. The first five verses make it clear that the sanctuary and the worshiping community are essential to that life.

The language in verses 1–5 is tied to the sanctuary and its worship, but with verse 6 it becomes clear that personal meditation is also part of the psalmist's confession of trust. Prayer and thanksgiving are also in the forefront for this psalmist during the night while in bed. The divine protection and nurture is still in mind. The image of help "in the shadow of your wings" in verse 7 also occurs in Psalm 61. It may relate to the shelter of the wings of a mother bird, and it may also relate to the protection of the temple. The wings may relate to the winged creatures in the most holy place with the Ark. "Your right hand" in verse 8 brings to mind the Exodus traditions of the God who comes to deliver. This same God upholds the psalmist. The confession of trust in verses 1–8 brings together a

---

[143]   J. C. McCann, Jr., "Book of Psalms," in L. E. Keck et al. (eds.), *The New Interpreter's Bible*, vol. 4 (1996), 928.

number of poetic images to express trust with public and personal dimensions, and yet the whole of the confession appears to be one nurtured in temple worship. In the Psalms, the temple as the place of divine presence is central to the hopes for salvation.

The adversative "But" at the beginning of verse 9 is a clue to readers that the psalm's last three verses provide a clear contrast for the first eight. *The enemies* are now in the forefront of concern, and they seek to destroy the psalmist's life (*nepeš*). The confession of trust in the first part of the psalm is still operative for the psalmist, however, for verse 9 affirms that the lying oppressors will go down to "the depths of the earth"; that is, to Sheol, the realm of death. They will also roam unprotected as prey for jackals. Their lying mouths will be stopped by utter and complete defeat. Verse 11 concludes the psalm with a reference to the king as rejoicing in God; compare again Psalm 61. The Davidic king as God's representative ruling in Jerusalem becomes the one who guarantees justice and thus protection for the psalmist and defeat for those spreading falsehood. When the king is rejoicing, there is justice and hope for the faithful psalmist.

Psalm 63 brings to words the desert experience of hungering and thirsting after God, an experience brought about by lying oppressors. The satisfying of hunger and quenching of thirst is found in the God who comes to deliver and is present to bless. The psalmist encounters that one in the sanctuary's worship and so confesses trust for life's journey. The faithful psalmist trusts that the God who delivers will embrace the pain of this wilderness time and bring hope. That is the task of the covenant God. The language and imagery of the psalm come from *the tradition of covenant*, and the encounter of worship leads the psalmist to express trust in the covenant God.

A Closer Look: A Boundless Optimist

Crenshaw writes:

The Sixty-third Psalm best exemplifies this boundless optimist. It voices the intensity of emotional intimacy between the psalmist and God, a love that rivals that of a man and a woman. Physical desire for water by a parched land provides the simile for the depth of intimacy enjoyed here. Indeed, the psalmist even considers God's love the highest good, better than life itself, and thinks such ardor will endure until his dying moment. In the shadow of divine wings the poet finds rest; the single comment about danger takes the form of confidence that foes will die. Here we encounter the only reference to a king in these psalms. David's sojourn in the wilderness of Judah seems an appropriate setting for this beautiful psalm.[144]

[144] J. L. Crenshaw, *Psalms* (2001), 15.

PSALM 64 – TO THE LEADER. A PSALM OF DAVID

¹ Hear my voice, O God, in my complaint;
 preserve my life from the dread enemy.
² Hide me from the secret plots of the wicked,
 from the scheming of evildoers,
³ who whet their tongues like swords,
 who aim bitter words like arrows,
⁴ shooting from ambush at the blameless;
 they shoot suddenly and without fear.
⁵ They hold fast to their evil purpose;
 they talk of laying snares secretly,
thinking, 'Who can see us?
⁶ Who can search out our crimes?
We have thought out a cunningly conceived plot.'
 For the human heart and mind are deep.

⁷ But God will shoot his arrow at them;
 they will be wounded suddenly.
⁸ Because of their tongue he will bring them to ruin;
 all who see them will shake with horror.
⁹ Then everyone will fear;
 they will tell what God has brought about,
 and ponder what he has done.

¹⁰ Let the righteous rejoice in the LORD
 and take refuge in him.
Let all the upright in heart glory.

Book II of the Psalter (Psalms 42–72), especially in its middle portion, includes a number of psalms that give attention to the persistent and oppressive presence of enemies. In Psalms 61–63, however, those enemies do not have the last say. The context is rather one of trust in God. The conclusion of Psalm 63 portrays the enemies as liars whose mouths "will be stopped." In Psalm 64, the enemies are again using words with evil intent, words aimed as weapons against the righteous, but the conclusion of the psalm calls for rejoicing on the part of the righteous, for whom God will intervene. The rejoicing continues in Psalm 65 and beyond.

Psalm 65 is a prayer for help from a person who is oppressed by enemies. Such individual lament psalms are characterized by *petition and complaint*, often beginning

with an introductory plea followed by a portrayal of the crisis that includes enemies. Psalm 64 is cast as a petition, with the complaint about the enemies providing
the context. The last part of the psalm moves to an expression of confidence; that is
also characteristic of the genre. The speaker has moved to a very different place at
the conclusion of the psalm. The movement is from the oppression of the enemies
as the experience of the power of death or the Pit to refuge in the shelter of divine
protection. That movement leads to rejoicing. Verses 1–6 articulate the introductory plea and the description of the enemies; verses 7–10 portray a vision of God's
intervention and conclude with the call for praise and thanksgiving to God. This
psalm may relate, as do a number of others, to the sanctuary the faithful found in
the Jerusalem temple, but the text concentrates on the enemies. Who are they? They
use words for evil intent; perhaps they are slanderers, or perhaps they are those who
spread malicious gossip. Such falsehood carried grave consequences in an ancient
society. This psalm marshals many images and descriptions in order to seek divine
assistance.

Verses 1–6. In line with the lament genre, the psalm begins with an introductory plea that characterizes the prayer as a "complaint" and moves quickly to "the
dread enemy." Imagery from the world of hunting provides the basic portrayal of
the opponents. These evildoers craft "secret plots" and schemes. The psalmist seeks
a hearing from God in the hope that God will preserve this faithful life and "hide
me" from the slings and arrows of these wicked opponents, especially from their
ambushes. The enemies shoot arrows and aim swords brazenly and quickly. They
arrogantly lurk about, seeking to trap their innocent victims with words characterized as swords and arrows. This faithful psalmist fears being blindsided by them.
The complaint then quotes the enemies as they lay secret traps for the psalmist to
portray their arrogance. They think they will get away with this ambush: "Who can
see us?" (v. 5) They trust in their own arrogance and shrewdness and think they will
continue to be able to operate in secrecy. These enemies operate with single-minded
and persistent intent.

The complaint portrays the enemies and the psalmist in clear contrast. The
psalmist is the innocent victim, and the enemies are the wicked who persistently
oppress and attack the faithful psalmist. Verse 3 makes it clear that the weapons
portrayed in this hunting imagery are words. The verbal weapons attack like swords
and arrows, and so the psalmist pleads for God to hear the petition for protection
from these unpredictable verbal assaults. In ancient society, considerable damage
could be done to a person's position and security by malicious gossip. The concluding line of verse 6 is striking. It is a kind of moan from the psalmist to the effect
that the oppression of the enemies is so thoroughly evil and so strong that it strains
credulity. These opening verses of the psalm urge divine intervention.

Verses 7–10. The adversative conjunction that begins verse 7 ("But") is a clue to
the contrast these verses establish between God's actions and those of the enemies.
The hunting imagery continues in this part of the psalm. There is a reversal, an

irony, to the imagery now; it is the mirror image of the first part of the psalm. Just as the enemies shot suddenly and fearlessly, so God will shoot the arrow of divine judgment and suddenly wound them. The irony continues with the divine use of "their tongues" as the means of judgment. These enemies who were so arrogant and self-assured with their verbal attacks will now be publicly humiliated. The psalmist narrates the response of the community, and so the sudden downfall of the enemies is seen in public. Those who see the fall of the enemies will shake their heads "with horror." The scheming of the evildoers has come to light for the community, and their evil has boomeranged on their own heads. The rest of the community response is that of reverence for God, who has intervened decisively and acted as the just sovereign of all creation. The community will also narrate this story of justice and continue to reflect on it.

The psalm's concluding verse is both a call to trust in God as refuge and a call to give thanks to the God who delivers. God's involvement in the human realm has now become clear to the community, and the words at the end of the psalm are words of praise and thanksgiving. The speakers at the end of the psalm are those who have seen the acts of God, and their speech is a considerable contrast to the vile speech of the evildoers in the first part of the psalm. The righteous now rejoice. Also noteworthy is the use of "heart" in verses 6 and 10. The contrast drawn is between "the upright in heart" who glory in God and the incredible evil of the human heart seen in "the dread enemy."

The imagery and language of Psalm 64 are stunning; the ironies and reversals are central to this brief but powerful text. The enemies placed great confidence in their verbal assaults ("their tongues" in v. 8), and yet it is because of them that they are defeated. The enemies who thought they were carrying out the ambush in secret are publicly humiliated. The enemies shoot arrows, and God shoots arrows at them in return. Their evil rolls back on them. Indeed, the downfall of the wicked at the hands of the divine judge is sudden; its narration is considerably shorter than the portrayal of the enemies and the trouble they cause. Human evil may be so strong as to strain credulity (v. 6), but God brings it to its knees suddenly. It is also noteworthy with all the hunting imagery in Psalm 64 that the response to the downfall of the enemies is not vengeful; rather it is tied in the conclusion of the psalm to reverence and thanksgiving for God, who brings justice and hope for the faithful.

Bridging the Horizons: The Power of Words

The words of Psalm 64 play on the power of words, a theme in several psalms. The enemies use words as powerful weapons, and their words bring about their downfall. The psalm concludes with words of thanksgiving and joy. We may say, "Sticks and stones may break my bones, but words will never hurt me," but this psalm begs to differ. Words are powerful in contemporary culture, both for good and ill. Some reflect the depth and power of human evil; others commend grace and care. The power of words provides a connection between Psalm 64 and today's culture. Evil and its words continue to be pervasive and powerful – words such as racism, cancer, or poverty. People continue to suffer under the power of such words, which become the slings and arrows of the chaos knocking at the door. Of remarkable importance is the reality that the final word of the psalm is not one of chaos but of praise and thanksgiving to the living God, who embraces the pain of those who trust.

PSALM 65 – TO THE LEADER. A PSALM OF DAVID. A SONG

¹ Praise is due to you,
   O God, in Zion;
and to you shall vows be performed,
² O you who answer prayer!
To you all flesh shall come.
³ When deeds of iniquity overwhelm us,
   you forgive our transgressions.
⁴ Happy are those whom you choose and bring near
   to live in your courts.
We shall be satisfied with the goodness of your house,
   your holy temple.

⁵ By awesome deeds you answer us with deliverance,
   O God of our salvation;
you are the hope of all the ends of the earth
   and of the farthest seas.
⁶ By your strength you established the mountains;
   you are girded with might.
⁷ You silence the roaring of the seas,
   the roaring of their waves,
   the tumult of the peoples.
⁸ Those who live at earth's farthest bounds are awed by your signs;
you make the gateways of the morning and the evening shout for joy.

⁹ You visit the earth and water it,
   you greatly enrich it;

the river of God is full of water;
    you provide the people with grain,
    for so you have prepared it.
¹⁰ You water its furrows abundantly,
    settling its ridges,
softening it with showers,
    and blessing its growth.
¹¹ You crown the year with your bounty;
    your wagon tracks overflow with richness.
¹² The pastures of the wilderness overflow,
    the hills gird themselves with joy,
¹³ the meadows clothe themselves with flocks,
    the valleys deck themselves with grain,
    they shout and sing together for joy.

This psalm revels in the recognition that God (referred to generically and never in this psalm by the name YHWH) is both creator and redeemer. The God who *orders the earth* (creator) and *who forgives sins and delivers* (redeemer) receives exuberant celebrative praise in the Jerusalem temple (v. 1). As always with praise, the acknowledgment of praise is itself an active *performance* of praise whereby YHWH is magnified.

God as redeemer is worthy of praise and receives praise, because it is God who answers prayers (v. 2), who forgives sin (v. 3), and who does deeds of deliverance (v. 5). God is celebrated as *hope* "for all flesh" (v. 2), all "the ends of the earth" (v. 5). Thus the temple in Jerusalem becomes the venue wherein the whole of creation joins Israel in praise of YHWH.

The more extensive part of the psalm centers on and offers praise for God's generous, generative power *as creator* (vv. 6–13). We may discern in this long doxology three rhetorical units. In verses 6–8, the praise of Israel acknowledges God's primordial curbing of the powers of chaos. Verse 7 is of special interest because the parallel lines of poetry refer to cosmic disorder ("roaring of the seas") and social disorder ("tumult of the peoples"), both being severe threats that jeopardize an ordered life for the world. God is the great enforcer and guarantor of order, which is indispensable for viable life in the world.

Second, verses 9–11 offer a series of verbs of which "you" (God) is the powerful subject. Whereas verses 6–8 are concerned with the curbing of *chaotic waters*, in these verses *life-giving water* essential to agriculture is celebrated. The verses have a special poignancy when it is remembered that the Bible is set in an arid climate, where any rain is taken as a defining gift of God. Verse 11 would seem to refer to a bountiful harvest, of course made possible by abundant rain. The curious phrase "your wagon tracks" perhaps imagines a cart hauling grain from the field at harvest time (v. 11).

In verses 12–13, the rhetorical pattern changes. God is no longer addressed; now the psalmist simply describes the luxuriant produce of the harvest and the consequent joy over the abundance. Of course God, the creator who authorizes "fruitfulness," is in every line to be inferred even though unmentioned.

The sum of this praise is that Israel can assert that in all parts of its life it is astonished and dazzled that the world works so well; Israel knows, of course, that a properly functioning world is not autonomous but is the gift of God. The song is offered in the temple, and the offering is given there because the temple is the place of *rhetorical extravagance* that corresponds to *the extravagance of God's world*. The temple is no place of stenic, descriptive language. It is rather a matrix for liturgical utterance that overreaches the mundane and in exalted joy contacts the self-giving of God. The performance of vows is a modest but crucial response of Israel to divine generosity (v. 1). The vows would seem to pertain both to answered prayer concerning forgiveness and to the teeming abundance of creation. On both counts, Israel can only offer praise, a capacity to move beyond description and explanation to exuberant affirmation of the one who stands behind the wondrous gifts of life.

Bridging the Horizons: Creator and Redeemer

This psalm holds creation and redemption together in praise. That of course is a fundamental claim of Christian teaching fully affirmed in the doctrinal traditions of the church and its creeds. Although that may be obvious in any Trinitarian setting, it is useful to recognize that the church has had to struggle to sustain this fundamental claim of faith. In the early church, it was the advocacy of Marcion that sought to break the two themes apart and to posit distinct Gods, creator and redeemer. In contemporary religious ferment, moreover, there are temptations in "New Age" religion and in various quasi-gnostic articulations to separate the two. Israel would not countenance such an interpretive split.

It is to be recognized, however, that much twentieth-century Old Testament interpretation, with its accent on "history" to the neglect of "nature," fell exactly into such a temptation. Here we are struck by the easy connection between creation and redemption that Israel voices and surely takes for granted. The pervasive affirmation of the Old Testament is that the God of Israel is the creator of the world. The cosmic claim and the particularity of Israel's rescue are held together. It is of course no different in the New Testament and in the Trinitarian articulations of the church that affirm that all persons of the Trinity (Father, Son, and Spirit) are the creator God and all persons of the Trinity (Father, Son, and Spirit) are the redeemer God. The church is regularly tempted to a modalism that designates different functions to different persons of the Trinity. But this is a disastrous misconstrual of the doctrinal conviction of the church.

PSALM 66 – TO THE LEADER. A SONG. A PSALM

¹ Make a joyful noise to God, all the earth;
² sing the glory of his name;
  give to him glorious praise.
³ Say to God, 'How awesome are your deeds!
  Because of your great power, your enemies cringe before you.
⁴ All the earth worships you;
  they sing praises to you,
  sing praises to your name.'
      Selah

⁵ Come and see what God has done:
  he is awesome in his deeds among mortals.
⁶ He turned the sea into dry land;
  they passed through the river on foot.
There we rejoiced in him,
⁷ who rules by his might for ever,
whose eyes keep watch on the nations –
  let the rebellious not exalt themselves.
      Selah

⁸ Bless our God, O peoples,
  let the sound of his praise be heard,
⁹ who has kept us among the living,
  and has not let our feet slip.
¹⁰ For you, O God, have tested us;
   you have tried us as silver is tried.
¹¹ You brought us into the net;
   you laid burdens on our backs;
¹² you let people ride over our heads;
   we went through fire and through water;
yet you have brought us out to a spacious place.

¹³ I will come into your house with burnt-offerings;
   I will pay you my vows,
¹⁴ those that my lips uttered
   and my mouth promised when I was in trouble.
¹⁵ I will offer to you burnt-offerings of fatlings,

with the smoke of the sacrifice of rams;
I will make an offering of bulls and goats.
    Selah

16 Come and hear, all you who fear God,
    and I will tell what he has done for me.
17 I cried aloud to him,
    and he was extolled with my tongue.
18 If I had cherished iniquity in my heart,
    the Lord would not have listened.
19 But truly God has listened;
    he has given heed to the words of my prayer.

20 Blessed be God,
    because he has not rejected my prayer
    or removed his steadfast love from me.

Psalm 66 is a complex poem, but its primary accent on *praise and thanks* is unmistakable. We may identify four rhetorical units concerning praise, each of which is introduced by an imperative summons to praise (vv. 1–4, 5–7, 8–12, and 16–19). Each of these units of imperative summons (except for vv. 5–7) is followed by a vocative that is quite inclusive: "all peoples" (v. 1), "O people" (v. 8), and "all you who fear God" (v. 16). Verses 13–15, with a series of "I" statements, constitute a response to the celebration of God's power and fidelity, and verse 20 is a statement by the praising subject expressing confidence in God.

The initial unit of doxology celebrates God's power, which evokes exuberant praise by all creation (vv. 1–4). The "awesome deed" of YHWH is not specified, though there is reference to the defeat of the enemies. In the context of temple worship, "your enemies" might refer to the historical enemies of Israel, or, conversely, the phrase might refer to the forces of chaos that destabilize creation. Either way, God is more than a match for every adversary who threatens an ordered life. All creatures are glad and grateful for such a guarantee of order.

The second rhetorical unit of praise begins with a second summons, though without any explicit vocative (vv. 5–7). We may assume that the initial vocative of verse 1 is still in force, so that again "all the earth" is called to witness to God's "awesome deeds." In this unit, the miracle wrought by God is explicitly the Exodus; it may be that in verse 3 we also have a reference to Exodus, but in that case it is not explicit. In verses 5–7, all are invited to notice the Exodus; in the Exodus narrative, Pharaoh is a rebellious subject of YHWH who exalts himself (see v. 7; Exod 5:2; Ezek 29:3). Thus the Exodus is cited as a case study for all victories concerning the sovereign rule of God that is sustained by wonders, and it concludes in verse 7 with a warning against recalcitrance against YHWH's rule: "There may have been one deliverance in particular, which the Psalmist celebrates here in the name of the Church, but he includes the many and various mercies which God had all along conferred upon his chosen people."[145]

The third unit of doxology, again with a vocative "O peoples," invites general celebration (vv. 8–12). It is not clear who the "us" of verse 9 may be. It is, however, most plausible, given the wording of verse 6, that the reference is to Israel and specifically to the Exodus. This rhetorical unit is distinguished by the series of "you" statements addressed directly to God. It is God who has tried, tested, snared, laid on burdens, and led the Israelites through fire and water (see Isa 43:2). This sequence is likely a general reference to Egyptian slavery, for that slavery is elsewhere a "fiery furnace" that tests and purifies (Dan 3:6–26). The reference to "burdens" and to being "rode over," plus the passage through waters, altogether characterizes the negativity of slavery. The final line of verse 12, moreover, uses the recurring exodus verb "bring out" ($y\ṣ'$). The NRSV translates the conjunction as "yet," which may be correct, though it is more emphatic in translation than it appears to be in the Hebrew text. The comment is that nations are to "bless God" for the wondrous rescue of Israel. Thus Israel invites into its doxology other nations who here come to know about the deliverance of Israel.

The sequence of doxological units is interrupted in verses 13–15 by a series of "I" statements that are the glad liturgical response of an individual to the wonders just named and celebrated. Whereas the doxologies focus on public events, these verses refer to quite intimate, personal experiences of rescue from "trouble." The paradigmatic event of Israel's slavery is easily and readily transposed into a host of more personal crises. In both public and personal venues, the God of Israel delivers and evokes grateful celebration. As is characteristic in songs of thanksgiving, the proper expression of gratitude here is a "thank offering" of an animal sacrifice that is commensurate with the pledge made to be paid upon deliverance by God. These verses bespeak *personal thanksgiving* in the midst of *public praise*. Whereas the *praise* is for great public events of deliverance that function in paradigmatic ways for Israel, *thanks* is intimate, personal, and concrete. Both praise and thanks, however, acknowledge that any appositive future is a gift of YHWH that can never be accomplished by human effort. Israel is so dazzled by such generous divine action that it invites others into the celebration.

In verses 16–19, the two components of *public theology* and *personal thanks* are nicely integrated. In verse 16, all the faithful (here all Israel and not other peoples) are invited to listen. What they are to hear is the first-person testimony of the "I" of verses 13–15. The same speaker now testifies in the assembly concerning what God has done. The verb "tell" in verse 16 is a standard term for recital and means the narrative announcement of the good news of God's deliverance. God has in fact listened and answered. On the way to this affirmation, the speaker also attests to his own innocence, which he takes as a precondition to God's answer to prayer (v.

[145] J. Calvin, *Commentary on The Book of Psalms*, vol. 2 (1979), 465.

18). Verse 20 celebrates God's steadfast love (*ḥesed*), which is the reason God has answered prayer. God is reliable! Consequently Israel and this speaker are confident. This speaker has found God to be utterly trustworthy. In its deepest memory – the Exodus – Israel has found God to be reliable and attentive; in the summons to praise, all the earth and all peoples on earth now have reason to celebrate God's abiding fidelity, a faithfulness expressed as transformative power.

The sum of this psalm is to attest to God's sovereignty and fidelity, which are made evident in concrete acts of transformation. The psalm witnesses to the character of the biblical God. The rhetorical strategy for such testimony is that quite concrete attestations of Israel, or of an individual Israelite, become grounds for recruiting all others in praise. Thus the doxology moves from Israel's *particularity* to *cosmic doxological generalization*. That maneuver is, of course, the one the church always risks; it begins with the specificity of Jesus of Nazareth and then invites into faith many who are remote from that concrete experience but who are invited to trust in and respond to quite particular testimony. Everything is rooted in nameable, known, remembered miracles!

A Closer Look: An All-Inclusive Psalm

Israel's doxological tradition, so well exemplified in this psalm, is a simple attestation by the community concerning a nameable miracle, the Exodus. In practice, however, Israel's praise is "thick" and multilayered on two counts. First, the singing of Israel is extended in imagination to "all creatures of our God and king." It is not only Israel who sings. Second, the citation of one crucial miracle is offered as an allusion to a myriad of miracles, or as McCann says, "recurring exoduses in new circumstances."[146] The praise of Israel is not understood in its defining force unless this "thickness" concerning participants and subject matter is recognized. In its worship, Israel knows and practices "the codes" that make temple singing an all-inclusive event commensurate with the majesty and grandeur of the creator God.

PSALM 67 – TO THE LEADER: WITH STRINGED INSTRUMENTS. A PSALM. A SONG

[1] May God be gracious to us and bless us
and make his face to shine upon us,
Selah

---

[146] J. C. McCann, Jr., in L. E. Keck et al. (eds.), *The New Interpreter's Bible*, vol. 4 (1996), 338.

² that your way may be known upon earth,
  your saving power among all nations.
³ Let the peoples praise you, O God;
  let all the peoples praise you.

⁴ Let the nations be glad and sing for joy,
  for you judge the peoples with equity
  and guide the nations upon earth.
      Selah
⁵ Let the peoples praise you, O God;
  let all the peoples praise you.

⁶ The earth has yielded its increase;
  God, our God, has blessed us.
⁷ May God continue to bless us;
  let all the ends of the earth revere him.

This psalm is a celebration of God's gracious blessing to Israel (vv. 1–2, 6–7) and a summons to other nations to join Israel in praise for God's abundant goodness to all creation (vv. 3–5). In each of the four small rhetorical units of the psalm, the name of God is uttered (vv. 1, 3, 5, 6), and the themes of blessing and praise dominate every element of the psalm. The sum of the entire poem is gladness for the life-giving, world-ordering power of God that makes a viable, shared life in the world possible.

The psalm begins with a familiar formula of blessing that is parallel to the priestly blessing of Num 6:24–26 (v. 1). In this case, however, the consequence of a blessing to Israel is that the life-giving power of God will be known beyond Israel in the world. It is not suggested in verse 2 how that blessing to Israel is to be known and celebrated elsewhere. In any case, as a result of that blessing, all the nations beyond Israel are to join in glad praise of God (vv. 3–5; see Gen 12:3). The reason given for that broad sweep of praise in verse 4 is that YHWH is a judge who will bring all nations to justice, well-being, and peace. The psalm attests that the double effect of God's goodness impinges on both Israel and the nations. That same doubling is evident, for example, in the interpretive comment of Joshua concerning the crossing of the Jordan into the land of promise:

For the Lord your God dried up the waters of the Jordan for you until you crossed over, as the Lord your God did to the Red Sea, which he dried up for us until we crossed over, so that all the peoples of *the earth may know* that the hand of the Lord is mighty, and so *that you may fear* the Lord your God forever. (Josh 4:23–24)

The miracle of the Jordan (which replicates the miracle of the Exodus) is *so that* (a) the *peoples* will know that YHWH is strong and (b) *Israel* will fear God forever.

The both/and of God toward Israel and toward the nations is structurally crucial in this psalm. In verses 6–7, the psalm returns to the initial accent of verse 1, a celebration of God's blessing to Israel; verse 7, however, relates the dual character of the response to God, which pertains to both Israel and "the ends of the earth."

This psalm is an articulation of *the work of YHWH in* creation and in history, the latter with reference to verse 4. That surely is the focus of the doxological tone of the whole poem. The most interesting rhetorical nuance, however, is the duality of Israel and the nations or Israel and creation. It is characteristic of the Old Testament that alongside the sustained commitment that YHWH has to Israel, the work of God cannot be contained in and for Israel but always spills over into the larger horizon of other peoples. These other peoples are the subject of God's goodness, which is rooted as deeply as God's call to Abraham (Gen 12:3). The accent is expressed in Paul as God's concern for Gentiles. Thus, in Galatians, Paul refers back to the mandate to Abraham:

And the scripture, foreseeing that God would justify the Gentiles by faith, declared the gospel beforehand to Abraham, saying, "All the Gentiles shall be blessed in you." (Gal 3:8)

That accent on the nations beyond Israel is critical to this psalm and perhaps reflects the Jerusalem liturgy that construes YHWH as king of all nations. Thus verse 4 seems to contain echoes of the liturgical expression of Psalm 96:

Say among the nations, "The Lord is king!" (Ps 96:10a)

This broad sweep invites us to wonder about the "us" in Psalm 67 (vv. 1, 6–7). It is conventional, on the basis of the blessing of Num 6:24–26, to take "us" as Israel. But here the rhetoric of the psalm seems to draw the nations into the blessed "us" of the creator God. To be sure, the important distinction between Israel and the nations is never blurred, but there is always more to Israel's affirmation of YHWH than just its own well-being. At the far edge of the Old Testament, the prophetic oracle can imagine that God, in times to come, will have many chosen peoples, others alongside Israel and given pet names as God's chosen peoples:

On that day there will be a highway from Egypt to Assyria, and the Assyrian will come into Egypt, and the Egyptian into Assyria, and the Egyptians will worship with the Assyrians. On that day Israel will be the third with Egypt and Assyria, a blessing in the midst of the earth, whom the Lord of hosts has blessed, saying, "Blessed be Egypt my people, and Assyria the work of my hands, and Israel my heritage." (Isa 19:23–25)

This psalm does not acknowledge any tension between the election of Israel and creation faith. Rather it entertains a large vision of God so that the blessing given to Israel is readily extended to all of God's beloved peoples.

Bridging the Horizons: Universalism and Particularism

Jon Levenson has written persuasively that the Hebrew Bible never (a) permits "the universal availability of God" to be displaced "by more particularistic theologies."[147] (b) Conversely, "Jewish chosenness" has its own claim to make, which is more than "instrumental." In the end, Levenson concludes, "Nothing is more delicate than the interplay of universalism and particularism in traditional Jewish theology." This point is most important in a church that is excessively complacent about being God's chosen community without an awareness that God is missionally at work elsewhere in the world. Mutatis mutandis, in a world dominated by U.S. "empire," this psalm attests that God is at work everywhere in the world and that this "empire" has no monopoly on God's blessing for the future.

PSALM 68 – TO THE LEADER. OF DAVID. A PSALM. A SONG

¹ Let God rise up, let his enemies be scattered;
  let those who hate him flee before him.
² As smoke is driven away, so drive them away;
  as wax melts before the fire,
  let the wicked perish before God.
³ But let the righteous be joyful;
  let them exult before God;
  let them be jubilant with joy.

⁴ Sing to God, sing praises to his name;
  lift up a song to him who rides upon the clouds
his name is the LORD –
  be exultant before him.

⁵ Father of orphans and protector of widows
  is God in his holy habitation.
⁶ God gives the desolate a home to live in;

147 Jon D. Levenson, "The Universal Horizon of Biblical Particularism," in Mark G. Brett (ed.), *Ethnicity and the Bible* (Leiden: Brill, 1996), 149, 157, 159.

he leads out the prisoners to prosperity,
but the rebellious live in a parched land.

7 O God, when you went out before your people,
  when you marched through the wilderness,
       Selah
8 the earth quaked, the heavens poured down rain
  at the presence of God, the God of Sinai,
  at the presence of God, the God of Israel.
9 Rain in abundance, O God, you showered abroad;
  you restored your heritage when it languished;
10 your flock found a dwelling in it;
   in your goodness, O God, you provided for the needy.

11 The Lord gives the command;
   great is the company of those who bore the tidings:
12 'The kings of the armies, they flee, they flee!'
The women at home divide the spoil,
13 though they stay among the sheepfolds –
the wings of a dove covered with silver,
   its pinions with green gold.
14 When the Almighty scattered kings there,
   snow fell on Zalmon.

15 O mighty mountain, mountain of Bashan;
   O many-peaked mountain, mountain of Bashan!
16 Why do you look with envy, O many-peaked mountain,
   at the mount that God desired for his abode,
   where the Lord will reside for ever?

17 With mighty chariotry, twice ten thousand,
   thousands upon thousands,
   the Lord came from Sinai into the holy place.
18 You ascended the high mount,
   leading captives in your train
   and receiving gifts from people,
even from those who rebel against the Lord God's abiding there.
19 Blessed be the Lord,
   who daily bears us up;

God is our salvation.
    Selah
²⁰ Our God is a God of salvation,
  and to God, the Lord, belongs escape from death.

²¹ But God will shatter the heads of his enemies,
  the hairy crown of those who walk in their guilty ways.
²² The Lord said,
  'I will bring them back from Bashan,
I will bring them back from the depths of the sea,
²³ so that you may bathe your feet in blood,
  so that the tongues of your dogs may have their share from the foe.'

²⁴ Your solemn processions are seen, O God,
  the processions of my God, my King, into the sanctuary –
²⁵ the singers in front, the musicians last,
  between them girls playing tambourines:
²⁶ 'Bless God in the great congregation,
  the Lord, O you who are of Israel's fountain!'
²⁷ There is Benjamin, the least of them, in the lead,
  the princes of Judah in a body,
  the princes of Zebulun, the princes of Naphtali.

²⁸ Summon your might, O God;
  show your strength, O God, as you have done for us before.
²⁹ Because of your temple at Jerusalem
  kings bear gifts to you.
³⁰ Rebuke the wild animals that live among the reeds,
  the herd of bulls with the calves of the peoples.
Trample under foot those who lust after tribute;
  scatter the peoples who delight in war.
³¹ Let bronze be brought from Egypt;
  let Ethiopia hasten to stretch out its hands to God.

³² Sing to God, O kingdoms of the earth;
  sing praises to the Lord,
    Selah
³³ O rider in the heavens, the ancient heavens;
  listen, he sends out his voice, his mighty voice.
³⁴ Ascribe power to God,

whose majesty is over Israel;
and whose power is in the skies.
35 Awesome is God in his sanctuary,
the God of Israel;
he gives power and strength to his people.

Blessed be God!

Interpreters have struggled with Psalm 68 because it contains a variety of elements and because interpreters have seen difficulty in connecting the poetry in the various parts of the composition. W. F. Albright's influential work suggests that the psalm is a collection of Hebrew poems.[148] Sigmund Mowinckel takes a decidedly different tack. He connects the psalm to the fall festival he envisions in Jerusalem that celebrates the enthronement of YHWH, and that allows him to interpret the psalm in one unified setting. Psalm 68 is one of the texts Mowinckel refers to in articulating his approach to the Psalms as cultic poetry.[149]

Psalm 68 does contain a variety of elements, but most interpreters understand the text as a whole in terms of a victory song. The text is the final of four psalms (Psalms 65–68) that are hymns; the cluster of psalms comes to an end with "Blessed be God" at the end of Psalm 68. Psalm 67 characterizes the living God as the one who is present to bless; Psalm 68 portrays God as the one who comes to deliver and then is present to bless the community from Zion. The text also implies its use in ritual in several places. The victory of God who rules in Zion is at the heart of the text, and it is likely that the community celebrated God's kingship in a variety of worship settings. Perhaps this psalm is tied to one of those. Beginning with verse 24, a cultic procession is in view, and there seem to be allusions to the Ark of the Covenant. Although we do not know all the specifics, the theme of praising this God and associations with Zion run through the text, and so there is a basis for reading it as a unit connected to a liturgical celebration of the kingship of YHWH. We will consider the psalm as a unit with four parts (vv. 1–6, 7–18, 19–27, and 28–35).[150] There is unity in the psalm's diverse elements.

1. *Verses 1–6.* The psalm begins with a call for God to "rise up" and for the enemies to "flee before him." This opening call alludes to Num 10:35 and the formula used when the Ark sets out: "Arise, O Lord, let your enemies be scattered, and your foes flee before you." The poetry in the opening call dramatically calls for God to bring about the utter downfall of the

---

[148] W. F. Albright, "A Catalogue of Early Hebrew Lyric Poems (Psalm LXVIII)," *HUCA* 23 (1950): 1–39.
[149] S. Mowinckel, *Psalms in Israel's Worship*, vol. 1 (1962), 5, 7, 11, 172–174.
[150] See C. C. Broyles, *Psalms* (1999), 282–283.

wicked. The contrast comes in verse 3, with the righteous, who will be in jubilation. The requests in the first three verses (in the "jussive" grammatical form – "Let God rise up") revel in the justice God will bring between the righteous and the wicked as a demonstration of the reign of God. The remainder of this first section of the psalm then calls the community to praise this divine judge, a theme that runs throughout the psalm. In verse 4, God is characterized as the Cloud Rider or the Wilderness Rider. Either translation is plausible. The first option suggests that YHWH rather than Baal is the rider on the clouds; the phrase is a Canaanite title for the god Baal. This rendering thus says that YHWH rather than Baal is the one who rides on the clouds or heavens to bring help to those who are vulnerable. The alternative rendering affirms that YHWH brought the people through the wilderness. Both renderings are part of the text. This God is the one who brings protection to the vulnerable in society – the orphans and widows. This God is present "in his holy habitation"; that is, in Zion, the Jerusalem temple. From there God enacts justice leading to shelter and means to live for those in need, in contrast to the desert that awaits the wicked.

2. *Verses 7–18.* This section of the psalm is a dramatic account of the journey of YHWH from Sinai through the wilderness to Zion. God "marched through the wilderness" and led the people throughout this journey. The quaking and storming in verse 8 allude to ancient Israel's fundamental experience of theophany at Mount Sinai, the special place of divine revelation in the wilderness. Judges 5:3–5 offers a similar description and refers to YHWH as "the One of Sinai." On this journey, the divine presence brought abundant rain and renewal for the people of God. Enemies flee before this pilgrim band, and they celebrate divine victories and divide the spoils of war. God defeated mighty enemies before them and provided for this needy flock. The journey is from Sinai through the wilderness to Zion. Even Bashan, the fertile and strong mountainous region to the north, becomes envious of Mount Zion, the special place of YHWH's presence. The final two verses of this section emphasize the military might and power of this YHWH who has made this journey. Even defeated enemies, enemies of great strength, bow down to this victorious one who ascends the throne on Zion. Psalm 68 calls for praise of the God of justice, who has journeyed from Sinai to Zion. The journey is narrated in terms of a remarkable theophany. The primary place of God's presence has moved from Sinai to Zion.

3. *Verses 19–27.* The call to praise is renewed in verse 19. The "God of our salvation" brings life even out of death. The God of ancient Israel's salvation

is the same God who brings defeat for the guilty. The arresting language in verses 21–23 comes from the ancient Near Eastern military culture. The language and imagery will be rather shocking for many readers, but the context in this psalm is the contrast between righteous and wicked. God provides for the righteous needy and shatters the enemies who have been oppressing the vulnerable. The defeat of the enemies is described in all its gruesome glory. Verses 24–27 conclude this section of the psalm by narrating the procession into the sanctuary on Zion as the place of life-giving divine presence. The scene is the great setting of worship and celebration with much music and joy. The poet delights in envisioning the tribal groups and their leaders in the procession that celebrates the presence in Zion of the one who brings life for this worshiping community. Exuberant liturgical praise marks much of Psalm 68.

4.   *Verses 28–35.* The psalm's concluding section once again calls on the living God to manifest strength. This psalm revels in the kingship of YHWH on Zion and here, as at the beginning of the poem, calls for the one who reigns on Zion to bring down those who are arrogant oppressors. The goal is for all, even the boastful enemies, to bow down to the giver of life. The hope is that gifts of reverence will come even from such powers as Egypt. The psalm's last four verses revert again to the call to praise, here for all kingdoms of the world to give honor to the majestic and powerful king on Zion. God has demonstrated power in the journey from Sinai to Zion and the defeat of evildoers, and now speaks from Zion to give life. In verse 33, YHWH is again named the Cloud Rider, as this majestic one who is worthy of praise and honor from all. God on Zion reigns and imparts life. The psalm ends with "Blessed be God!" (see vv. 19 and 26) and brings readers back to the theme of praise as called for in verse 4. The psalm praises the powerful God in Zion, who delivers and gives life. There certainly are obscurities in this text, but the main themes have become clear.

Bridging the Horizons: Puzzling Territory

Contemporary readers who seek a revelatory word in Psalm 68 may well find themselves in uncomfortable and puzzling territory. In addition to the obscurities in the text, there are other obstacles. First, the military imagery in the psalm will disturb some readers. That language comes from a particular cultural setting and also probably reflects a community that has suffered from military oppression. The intent of the divine king's action is central to the context. This God defeats enemies and in so doing protects the vulnerable orphans and widows, the desolate and the prisoners, and brings salvation to the community. In this psalm, the worshiping community of ancient Israel confesses that they belong to this God who reigns.

Second, contemporary readers may be uncomfortable and even puzzled by the particularity of the portrayal of God in Psalm 68. The poem celebrates in liturgy this life-giving YHWH, who has taken a remarkable journey from Sinai through the wilderness and on to the throne in Zion, where this divine judge gives just judgments and instruction for living. Every revelation of God comes from a particular time, place, and culture. Psalm 68 portrays a life-shaping memory of God for the faith community of ancient Israel. It is this divine king whom the community worships and in whom they confess faith. The celebration of the reign of God is not so much about triumphalism as it is about finding life that only this one can grant, as is indicated in the concluding verse. The poem is a way for the community to imagine a life of growth and vitality in which justice for all those in need is possible.

PSALM 69 – TO THE LEADER: ACCORDING TO LILIES. OF DAVID

¹ Save me, O God,
   for the waters have come up to my neck.
² I sink in deep mire,
   where there is no foothold;
I have come into deep waters,
   and the flood sweeps over me.
³ I am weary with my crying;
   my throat is parched.
My eyes grow dim
   with waiting for my God.

⁴ More in number than the hairs of my head
   are those who hate me without cause;
many are those who would destroy me,
   my enemies who accuse me falsely.
What I did not steal
   must I now restore?
⁵ O God, you know my folly;
   the wrongs I have done are not hidden from you.

⁶ Do not let those who hope in you be put to shame because of me,
  O Lᴏʀᴅ God of hosts;
do not let those who seek you be dishonored because of me,
  O God of Israel.
⁷ It is for your sake that I have borne reproach,
  that shame has covered my face.
⁸ I have become a stranger to my kindred,
  an alien to my mother's children.

⁹ It is zeal for your house that has consumed me;
  the insults of those who insult you have fallen on me.
¹⁰ When I humbled my soul with fasting,
  they insulted me for doing so.
¹¹ When I made sackcloth my clothing,
  I became a byword to them.
¹² I am the subject of gossip for those who sit in the gate,
  and the drunkards make songs about me.

¹³ But as for me, my prayer is to you, O Lᴏʀᴅ.
  At an acceptable time, O God,
  in the abundance of your steadfast love, answer me.
With your faithful help ¹⁴ rescue me
  from sinking in the mire;
let me be delivered from my enemies
  and from the deep waters.
¹⁵ Do not let the flood sweep over me,
  or the deep swallow me up,
  or the Pit close its mouth over me.

¹⁶ Answer me, O Lᴏʀᴅ, for your steadfast love is good;
  according to your abundant mercy, turn to me.
¹⁷ Do not hide your face from your servant,
  for I am in distress – make haste to answer me.
¹⁸ Draw near to me, redeem me,
  set me free because of my enemies.

¹⁹ You know the insults I receive,
  and my shame and dishonor;
  my foes are all known to you.
²⁰ Insults have broken my heart,
  so that I am in despair.

I looked for pity, but there was none;
  and for comforters, but I found none.
²¹ They gave me poison for food,
  and for my thirst they gave me vinegar to drink.

²² Let their table be a trap for them,
  a snare for their allies.
²³ Let their eyes be darkened so that they cannot see,
  and make their loins tremble continually.
²⁴ Pour out your indignation upon them,
  and let your burning anger overtake them.
²⁵ May their camp be a desolation;
  let no one live in their tents.
²⁶ For they persecute those whom you have struck down,
  and those whom you have wounded, they attack still more.
²⁷ Add guilt to their guilt;
  may they have no acquittal from you.
²⁸ Let them be blotted out of the book of the living;
  let them not be enrolled among the righteous.
²⁹ But I am lowly and in pain;
  let your salvation, O God, protect me.

³⁰ I will praise the name of God with a song;
  I will magnify him with thanksgiving.
³¹ This will please the Lord more than an ox
  or a bull with horns and hoofs.
³² Let the oppressed see it and be glad;
  you who seek God, let your hearts revive.
³³ For the Lord hears the needy,
  and does not despise his own that are in bonds.

³⁴ Let heaven and earth praise him,
  the seas and everything that moves in them.
³⁵ For God will save Zion
  and rebuild the cities of Judah;
and his servants shall live there and possess it;
³⁶ the children of his servants shall inherit it,
  and those who love his name shall live in it.

The first part of this psalm articulates the usual elements of the complaint prayer. Although the several elements cannot be clearly and cleanly sorted out, we may note four conventional elements in such a prayer:

1. The prayer issues a powerful series of *petitions* to YHWH, the sum of which assumes that the speaker is entitled to the caring, protective treatment of YHWH (vv. 1a, 6, 13–15, 16–18). These petitions seek rescue from YHWH when the speaker has no more resources for his own cause. These petitions are based partly on a description of need and partly on an acknowledgment of YHWH's gracious fidelity. In verses 13 and 16, the petitioner pleads with YHWH to answer in an effective and transformative way; these two petitions appeal to and are grounded in YHWH's *steadfast love*, which grounds all of Israel's hope. The circumstance of need is not clear, because the petition uses a variety of images. In any case, the psalmist is besieged by adversaries and requires deliverance by the powerful intervention of YHWH. The petition moreover slides into imprecation in verses 22–25 and 26–27, for the petitioner wills the death of his adversary. The imprecations are simply the backside of positive petition.

2. As is usual in such prayers, the petition is matched by a *complaint*, a hyperbolic description of the circumstance of need (vv. 1–4, 12–14, 19–21, 26). The trouble is connected to destructive speech that is uttered falsely against the petitioner. The context for such false speech may be the courtroom; in any case, the petitioner is placed in social jeopardy by such speech against him.

3. Conversely, verse 5 stands by itself as a *confession of guilt*. This verse is a very odd note in isolation here and no doubt functions as a motivation to God; that is, an attempt to motivate God to rescue "one sinner who repents" (Luke 15:7). Calvin takes the statement of guilt as ironic, as in fact referring to the guilt of his adversaries, and Gerstenberger takes the verse as a late intrusion in the psalm.[151]

Lindström follows Calvin and suggests that single isolated verse of confession "functions negatively":

Concerning our *main question* in this chapter, we emphasize that the mention of sin in Ps 69:6, consequently, does not function as a rational explanation of a pseudotheological nature of the reason for sickness and the removal of YHWH's saving presence. Even if we look away from the fact that the motif of sin in this case lacks every connection with suffering caused by sickness and that the passage is contextually related to the idea of false accusation for transgressions on the social plane, the conclusion remains this: Ps 69:6 is a well articulated protest against the idea of a visible context between personal guilt and suffering.[152]

---

[151] J. Calvin, *Commentary on the Psalms*, vol. 3 (1979), 50, 53; and E. S. Gerstenberger, *Psalms, Part 2 and Lamentations FOTL vol. XV*, 47.
[152] F. Lindström, *Suffering and Sin* (1994), 348; see also 341–343.

This judgment is congruent with Lindström's general hypothesis that a confession of guilt plays little or no role in the practice of lament in Israel's psalms.

4. This psalm offers a series of *motivations* that suggest reasons for YHWH's anticipated action (vv. 7–8, 9–10). The speaker describes the life of devoted discipline that is above reproach. It is all "for your sake." The phrase "zeal for your house" suggests the voice of one who is intensely involved in the cultic apparatus of YHWH, perhaps a priest who has been utterly devoted to YHWH. The appeal to YHWH is characteristically voiced as a statement *of profound need* on Israel's part that is matched by YHWH's *profound fidelity.*

By verse 30, the situation of trouble and need appears to have spent itself. In verse 30, the psalm turns toward celebrative affirmation, albeit as anticipation. The psalmist celebrates the new gift of life even before it has been enacted by YHWH. On the basis of the turn and rhetoric in verse 30, one may hypothesize that between verses 29 and 30 a "salvation oracle" is spoken, or some equivalent gesture is made that gives assurance to the speaker, an assurance so profound that circumstance in principle has already been altered.

The conclusion of verses 30–36 renders to YHWH appropriate thanks and praise. In verse 30, it is "I," the reassured speaker, who offers praise; the speaker knows that such praise pleases YHWH, the God who does not want commodities or sacrifices (see Ps 30:12–13). In what follows, the circle of celebration is expanded well beyond the speaker. It includes the "oppressed and needy," who take heart in their circumstances by the affirmation that YHWH can do acts to create a new social reality in which the oppressed are released and the needy are cared for (vv. 32–33). This affirmation of the oppressed and needy as recipients of YHWH's deliverance calls to mind Isa 58:6–7, which envisions well-being for exactly these social groups. If we juxtapose this psalm with Isaiah 58, we may suggest that deliverance by YHWH in the psalm is in fact accomplished by human activity of the kind urged in Isaiah 58.

But even beyond the *self who praises* and the *oppressed who seek God*, the circle of exuberant response extends to include "heaven and earth, the sea and all that is in them"; that is, the whole of creation (v. 34). Given that anticipation, verses 35–36 are not a good fit but can be understood in context. These verses apply the good news of YHWH's rescue to the city of Jerusalem, which is to be saved and rebuilt. If the temple of Jerusalem is the place of effective divine presence, as Lindström proposes, then it is fitting that the psalm ends in an affirmation that all will be well in Jerusalem, for if all is well at the epicenter of YHWH's creation, then all will be well everywhere else in creation.

The movement of the psalm, especially with reference to the turn in verse 30, presents the characteristic drama prayer in which Israel moves from *need and petition* to glad *celebration* because the petition is answered in divine response. The prayers of Israel do indeed evoke YHWH's attentiveness and result in fresh ways of well-being.

A Closer Look: A Psalm for a Righteous Sufferer

This psalm became an important reference point for Christian usage in interpreting the passion of Jesus with reference to Old Testament scripture: "No wonder that the first Christians – Jews most of them – applied Psalm 69 to the scandalous crucifixion of a just man, whom they held as their Lord and Master."[153]

Kraus provides a full account of the usages of this psalm in the New Testament, of which we may note three in particular. Psalm 69:4–5 is reflected in Jn 15:25, wherein Jesus is an object of scorn and hatred. Psalm 69 is reflected in Jn 2:17, Rom 15:3, and Heb 11:26 concerning zeal for the house of the Lord, and, especially, Ps 69:21 is reflected in all four Gospels about the serving of vinegar to Jesus on the cross (Matt 27:34, 48; Mk 15:36; Luke 23:36; Jn 18:29). Although Kraus himself is inclined to think that these allusions are evoked because of their actual happening in the life of Jesus, it is more likely that these psalm usages fit the imagination of the early church in developing its narrative memory about Jesus. Either way, it is clear that as Jeremiah from the Old Testament seems reflected in the suffering of this psalm, so the early church found the connection to Jesus as a righteous sufferer most compelling.

Beyond an appeal to either Jeremiah or Jesus, it is clear that this psalm is a reflection on suffering that cannot be contained in a simple taxonomy of suffering as punishment for sin. The critical judgment that verse 5 is a late confession of guilt means that suffering is to be understood on grounds other than guilt; the psalm is the prayer of a righteous sufferer who seeks to mobilize God to rescue. It is not difficult to see why the early church would have appealed to this psalm with reference to Jesus; nor is it difficult to see that the resurrection of Jesus may be taken as a divine response of power to such an articulation of undeserved suffering.

PSALM 70 – TO THE LEADER. OF DAVID, FOR THE MEMORIAL OFFERING

¹ Be pleased, O God, to deliver me.
O LORD, make haste to help me!
² Let those be put to shame and confusion
who seek my life.

---

[153] S. Terrien, *Psalms* (2003), 505. See Hans Joachim Kraus, *Theology of the Psalms* (Minneapolis: Augsburg, 1986), 191–193.

Let those be turned back and brought to dishonor
  who desire to hurt me.
³ Let those who say, 'Aha, Aha!'
  turn back because of their shame.

⁴ Let all who seek you
  rejoice and be glad in you.
Let those who love your salvation
  say evermore, 'God is great!'
⁵ But I am poor and needy;
  hasten to me, O God!
You are my help and my deliverer;
  O LORD, do not delay!

Psalm 70 is a brief prayer for help from a person who is oppressed by enemies. Kraus connects the prayer to the protection of the sanctuary and describes the psalm as having the effect of a sigh.[154] The psalm portrays the speaker as one who serves God and yet is in need. The language would fit a variety of crises in life, so attempts to date the psalm or to tie it to a well-defined crisis do not find much support in the text. The repetition in the first and last verses centering on the speaker's need to hasten divine help frame the poem and its plea. Following the opening plea, verses 1–3 focus on the enemies, whereas verses 4–5 focus on the faithful.

A Closer Look: An Adaptable Psalm

Psalm 70 also occurs, with minor variations, earlier in the Psalter in Ps 40:13–17. These verses stand alone in Psalm 70 but come at the end of a psalm of thanksgiving in the earlier text. The duplication of these verses in the Psalter indicates that they are adaptable for various settings in life and in the collections brought together in the Psalter. Psalm 70 appears as part of the Elohistic Psalter (Psalms 42–83), so one of the differences in the texts is the use of the divine name. In Ps 70:1, 4, the more generic *Elohim* is used, whereas YHWH is used in the corresponding places in Psalm 40. Psalm 70 does, however, use the special Hebrew title as a divine name in its first and last verses. Psalm 70 is thus a text that reflects some of the editorial process that produced the book of Psalms as a whole. The psalm is also closely connected to Psalm 71 on both verbal and thematic levels. Connections include "make haste" (Pss 70:1, 5; 71:12), "shame" (Pss 70:2, 3; 71:13, 24), "deliver" and "salvation" (Pss 70:1, 4, 5; 71:2, 4, 15), and "evermore" and "continually" (Pss 70:4; 71:6, 14). The enemies portrayed in Ps 70:2 as those "who seek

---

[154] H.-J. Kraus, *Psalms 60–150* (1988), 67.

my life" and "who desire to hurt me" are in Ps 71:13, 24, as accusers "who seek
to hurt me" and "who tried to do me harm." It is plausible that the shapers of
the book of Psalms intended for Psalms 70 and 71 to be read together; perhaps
Psalm 70 introduces the longer prayer to follow. Psalm 71 is without a heading.
The heading to Psalm 70 indicates that the text comes from the Davidic collection and gives instructions for its use in worship. Included is a term derived
from the root *zkr* (to remember), a term also found in the heading to Psalm 38.
The NRSV plausibly translates the term as "for the memorial offering." There are
times that the book of Leviticus indicates acts of worship for which the book of
Psalms provides accompanying words. The prayer could accompany the memorial portion of the sacrifice in Leviticus 2 and Lev 5:11–13. The term could also be
literally translated as "to cause to remember" as a reference to the hope that the
prayer will bring God to remember the covenant with ancient Israel and so act
to deliver the Israelites.

Psalm 70 is brief but characteristic of the prayers in the Psalter in including petition and complaint. The poem opens (v. 1) with a succinct but intense prayer that
YHWH will "make haste" to deliver this one who is in crisis. The prayer then moves
quickly (vv. 2–3) to the enemies that are ever present in the prayers for help in the
Psalter. The complaint about enemies here is consistently made in the context of
petition. The plea is for a reversal of fortune. The psalm seems to have in clear view
a group of opponents who seek the petitioner's life and "desire to hurt me." The
speaker hopes that the evil of these enemies will boomerang on their own heads.
Language of shame and honor is important in this plea; the speaker hopes that
the enemies will encounter the shame and humiliation they seek for the petitioner.
Verse 3 suggests that the enemies pile scorn and mockery on the speaker. The psalm
envisions two identifiable groups – the righteous and the wicked – and the speaker
urgently seeks to be included among the righteous, whom God helps. Those who
oppose God and the faithful do not enjoy God's help and blessing, so the speaker
fervently hopes to be counted among the righteous.

The emphasis in verses 4–5 is on the righteous, those who seek God, and the context is the request that the righteous will continually rejoice and praise God as great
out of the experience of divine deliverance. The conclusion of the prayer confesses
dependence on divine help and deliverance. The prayer ends with the plea that this
help may come without delay, for the need is pressing. The encounter with the saving action of YHWH determines life and death in the Hebrew scriptures, and this
prayer urgently seeks that salvation in the midst of oppression. The psalmist's confession of faith is that YHWH is the one who can make life different and deliver the
faithful from the oppression of those who seek evil – as opposed to those who seek
YHWH. Psalm 70 is a prayer of "lucid brevity" but of the fervent expression of need
for divine help. In one sense, the prayer is all the petitioner has.

A Closer Look: God's Covenant Obligation

This brief prayer illustrates a number of the elements of individual lament psalms. The preceding commentary suggests that the term in the heading could suggest that the prayer invites God to remember the covenant and thus deliver those faithful to the covenant relationship. Ancient Israel's faith tradition centers on the confession that YHWH initiated a covenant relationship with this community. The community nurtured the historical memory of the covenant with YHWH as the God who comes to deliver them. Underlying the petition in Psalm 70 is the reality that the faithful petitioner is not enjoying the fruits of the covenant relationship but is rather enduring suffering and oppression at the hands of enemies. The petition is that God will act as the covenant God and deliver the faithful before it is too late and the oppressors destroy those faithful to the covenant. The petitioner confesses covenant faith and pleads with God to act like the covenant God and deliver the petitioner from the crisis at hand. The language of petition is central to the dialogue of covenant. The prayer operates with the hope that YHWH as the covenant God will hear and embrace the pain of the petitioner and come to deliver the petitioner in this genuine crisis of life and faith. The plea urgently seeks God's life-giving help.

PSALM 71

¹ In you, O LORD, I take refuge;
   let me never be put to shame.
² In your righteousness deliver me and rescue me;
   incline your ear to me and save me.
³ Be to me a rock of refuge,
   a strong fortress, to save me,
   for you are my rock and my fortress.

⁴ Rescue me, O my God, from the hand of the wicked,
   from the grasp of the unjust and cruel.
⁵ For you, O LORD, are my hope,
   my trust, O LORD, from my youth.
⁶ Upon you I have leaned from my birth;
   it was you who took me from my mother's womb.
My praise is continually of you.

⁷ I have been like a portent to many,
    but you are my strong refuge.
⁸ My mouth is filled with your praise,
    and with your glory all day long.
⁹ Do not cast me off in the time of old age;
    do not forsake me when my strength is spent.
¹⁰ For my enemies speak concerning me,
    and those who watch for my life consult together.
¹¹ They say, 'Pursue and seize that person
    whom God has forsaken,
    for there is no one to deliver.'

¹² O God, do not be far from me;
    O my God, make haste to help me!
¹³ Let my accusers be put to shame and consumed;
    let those who seek to hurt me
    be covered with scorn and disgrace.
¹⁴ But I will hope continually,
    and will praise you yet more and more.
¹⁵ My mouth will tell of your righteous acts,
    of your deeds of salvation all day long,
    though their number is past my knowledge.
¹⁶ I will come praising the mighty deeds of the Lord God,
    I will praise your righteousness, yours alone.

¹⁷ O God, from my youth you have taught me,
    and I still proclaim your wondrous deeds.
¹⁸ So even to old age and grey hairs,
    O God, do not forsake me,
until I proclaim your might
    to all the generations to come.
Your power ¹⁹and your righteousness, O God,
    reach the high heavens.

You who have done great things,
    O God, who is like you?
²⁰ You who have made me see many troubles and calamities
    will revive me again;
from the depths of the earth
    you will bring me up again.

²¹ You will increase my honor,
   and comfort me once again.

²² I will also praise you with the harp
   for your faithfulness, O my God;
I will sing praises to you with the lyre,
   O Holy One of Israel.
²³ My lips will shout for joy
   when I sing praises to you;
   my soul also, which you have rescued.
²⁴ All day long my tongue will talk of your righteous help,
for those who tried to do me harm
   have been put to shame, and disgraced.

Psalm 71 requires a great deal of its readers. The poetry makes sudden shifts, and the various elements characteristic of the psalmist's prayers are used in a variety of ways in this psalm. The psalm moves back and forth between petition and the expression of trust, and that movement seems to add to the urgency of the prayer. The prayer comes in three identifiable sections (vv. 1–8, 9–13, and 14–24), each containing both petition and expressions of hope. Enemies also appear in each section. The psalm's final section moves to a greater emphasis on hope. The psalm is a prayer for help from an individual "I" who is portrayed as elderly, is pursued by enemies, and is likely ill. The language of the psalm is associated with temple worship and its protection. This exposition of the psalm takes it as a unified composition, with the subject being strong apprehension about what will come next in life.

A Closer Look: Links to Psalm 70

Psalm 71 is the only psalm in Book II (Psalms 42–72) without a superscription, assuming that Psalms 42 and 43 were originally one poem. The commentary on Psalm 70 noted that there are a number of connections between that psalm and Psalm 71. The two psalms share terms for shame and confusion (Pss 70:2, 3; 71:13, 24) and terms for deliverance and salvation. The two texts describe enemies in similar ways, and there is a sense of urgency in both prayers (Pss 70:1, 5; 71:12). Praise also continues in both psalms. The two texts are related, and there is a basis for reading them together. There is also a basis for suggesting that the poet in Psalm 71 is familiar with the poetic tradition in ancient Israel and has drawn on other psalms in constructing this prayer. Crenshaw points to Psalms 22, 31, 35, 36, 38, and 40 as sources.[155]

---

[155] J. L. Crenshaw, *Psalms* (2001), 153.

The psalm's opening section, verses 1–8, is replete with language familiar to readers of the individual lament psalms. The opening plea portrays God as "rock of refuge" and fortress, and so the plea is for refuge. The plea is based on divine righteousness. God's righteousness has to do with YHWH's actions to initiate a right relationship with the worshiping community, and so the plea of the petitioner is for YHWH to act again out of that righteousness and bring protection for this faithful one. The opening petitions and characteristics of God seem to multiply in the first three verses and move quickly to the additional plea for rescue in verse 4, where the enemies enter the picture. They are portrayed as wicked, unjust, and cruel. This petitioner has continually counted on the divine faithfulness and continues to do that in the face of oppression and trouble. Using the image of the midwife (v. 6), the speaker recounts the praise of God from birth to the present. The hope is for that praise to continue into the future; the praise is in response to divine faithfulness.

Verse 7 is noteworthy, with its affirmation that the petitioner has been "a portent to many." The traditional reading of this text would suggest that the petitioner has been a sign that warns many. If the speaker is sick, others may take that as an indication of divine judgment and avoid someone who has become a symbol of danger and trouble to come. The enemies would point to this person as one under God's judgment. A portent or sign is itself ambiguous, however. A portent could be a sign of divine favor, and the speaker prays that God will act to bring protection so that the speaker becomes a sign of God's refuge in the congregation. The poetry suggests that the speaker is in momentous distress and yet petitions God for help in the context of a lifetime of experience that nurtures hope.

The psalm's first reference to "old age" comes at the beginning of a renewal of petition in verses 9–13. The plea is that God will not forsake this faithful one as age and vulnerability advance. Enemies lie in wait and plot against the speaker. They sense vulnerability and have come to the conclusion that the protecting God has forsaken this one and that they can immediately seize what is left of life for this one who is fading. The petition is that God "not be far" but rather be present to bring refuge and to bring justice for the petitioner and for those who seek to hurt the petitioner.

The prayer, both in this section and in its opening plea, uses the language of honor and shame. To be shamed and dishonored in ancient culture was a terrible loss; it broke relationships that contributed much to wholeness in life. To be shamed in the community meant a loss of value and a loss of a significant part of life. As already indicated, it may be that the community had come to the view that the petitioner was under divine judgment and dishonor, as evidenced by illness. They forsook this person who was in crisis, and that isolation was tantamount to loss of life. Therefore this person fervently petitions God for help and refuge.

Although it may well be the case that the petitioner is sick and elderly, that should not limit the appropriation of the prayer only to those who are old and sick. All readers of the Psalms are aging, and communities may also move toward vulnerability. The prayer is in a broad sense about the need for God and the refuge God can provide. Every person of faith can identify with the sense of being forsaken and left at the mercy of oppressors.

With the final section of the psalm, verses 14–24, the mood becomes predominantly hopeful. These verses begin with hope and praise, and verse 15 combines the themes of God's righteousness and God's saving deeds. As suggested earlier, the righteousness of YHWH is revealed in the salvation history, the mighty acts of God that bring the community into a right relationship with God and thus with each other. The psalm celebrates and narrates those deeds as the salvation history of this community. The psalm declares those mighty acts as a way of teaching this historical memory to the community and its future generations. The petitioner has learned the tradition of the salvation history and seeks to teach others. The one who is praying speaks of this historical memory in terms beyond the imagination. This history is a long-standing one, the tradition of narrating the history in worship and in the community is a long-standing one, and this worshiper's attention to that memory is also long-standing. The prayer is that God will allow this faithful one to continue to sing praise and thanksgiving as a way to bear witness to these mighty acts of God in the past and the mighty act of God in the present to bring protection for this oppressed one.

The concluding verses of the psalm demonstrate its connection to worship. Hope begins to pile on hope. God has brought "troubles and calamities," but there is now hope for "honor and comfort" and blessing from this same God. Psalm 71 is both intensely personal and public. The context of the plea from this faithful one who is older is worship. Hope becomes dominant at the end of the psalm because there has been a reversal of fortune. Those who sought shame for the petitioner now experience shame themselves instead. The confession of the psalm is that God has made justice possible and brought refuge for this one who prays.

Bridging the Horizons: Faith in Covenant Promises

The petitioner in Psalm 71 has been taught for a lifetime that YHWH is the covenant God who delivers and creates a community that makes possible wholeness of life. It is in this God and this covenant relationship that the speaker trusts and hopes. The petition is that God will bring to fruition precisely these covenant promises that the faith tradition has taught. In this way, the petition seeks to integrate lived experience and the received faith tradition. It operates out of the hope that this faith will become reality for this one who has been faithful for a lifetime. This speaker has had a long-standing relationship with the covenant God and with the faith tradition. This petition is part of the honest dialogue that nurtures that relationship. The psalm expresses a genuine vulnerability and fear of being forgotten and left to the mercy of bloodthirsty enemies. The even greater fear is to be forsaken by God and thus left without options. God is the one who initiates a relationship with "deeds of saving," so all depends on this God. The psalm is clear that there is trouble in life and that trouble is pressing, but the context of the petition is still hope and faith, crafted over a long life and including at its center an honest dialogue strikingly absent from most contemporary modes of worship.

PSALM 72 – OF SOLOMON

¹ Give the king your justice, O God,
   and your righteousness to a king's son.
² May he judge your people with righteousness,
   and your poor with justice.
³ May the mountains yield prosperity for the people,
   and the hills, in righteousness.
⁴ May he defend the cause of the poor of the people,
   give deliverance to the needy,
   and crush the oppressor.

⁵ May he live while the sun endures,
   and as long as the moon, throughout all generations.
⁶ May he be like rain that falls on the mown grass,
   like showers that water the earth.
⁷ In his days may righteousness flourish
   and peace abound, until the moon is no more.

⁸ May he have dominion from sea to sea,
   and from the River to the ends of the earth.
⁹ May his foes bow down before him,
   and his enemies lick the dust.
¹⁰ May the kings of Tarshish and of the isles
    render him tribute,

may the kings of Sheba and Seba
  bring gifts.
[11] May all kings fall down before him,
  all nations give him service.

[12] For he delivers the needy when they call,
  the poor and those who have no helper.
[13] He has pity on the weak and the needy,
  and saves the lives of the needy.
[14] From oppression and violence he redeems their life;
  and precious is their blood in his sight.

[15] Long may he live!
  May gold of Sheba be given to him.
May prayer be made for him continually,
  and blessings invoked for him all day long.
[16] May there be abundance of grain in the land;
  may it wave on the tops of the mountains;
  may its fruit be like Lebanon;
and may people blossom in the cities
  like the grass of the field.
[17] May his name endure for ever,
  his fame continue as long as the sun.
May all nations be blessed in him;
  may they pronounce him happy.

[18] Blessed be the LORD, the God of Israel,
  who alone does wondrous things.
[19] Blessed be his glorious name for ever;
  may his glory fill the whole earth. Amen and Amen.

[20] The prayers of David son of Jesse are ended.

Three matters are evident in reading this psalm. First, it is among the "royal psalms" that reflect the crucial role of the Davidic king in the theology and practice of the Jerusalem temple. It is clear that the king is a pivot point for theology and for the connection between theological claim and socioeconomic policy. Second, this is one of only two psalms that by superscription is linked to Solomon (see Psalm 127). If, as seems likely, Solomon is a prime reference point in the Old Testament for both the celebration and the critique of kingship, then we may take this Solomonic reference as a broad concern for monarchy in the faith of Israel.[156] Third, this psalm concludes Book II of the Psalter, after which the Psalter moves on in Book III to public trouble (Psalms 74, 79) and loss (Psalm 89), and in Books IV and V the praise of YHWH, making human kingship much less prominent.[157]

This psalm moves in a regular rhythm between *covenantal imperatives* addressed to the king and *divine promises* made to the king that are conditioned by these imperatives. The covenantal imperatives are stated in verses 1–4 and 12–14. These verses state the quite ancient Near Eastern conviction, much older than Israel's royal theology, that the king has a responsibility to govern such that a viable political and economic infrastructure is maintained for all members of the community. Specifically, the king has a responsibility to support and sustain the life of the poor and the marginal when they have no resources by which to sustain themselves. The psalm envisions a quite assertive, initiative-taking royal government on behalf of the poor and the needy.

In verses 1–4, the royal mandate, mouthed by Israel but taken as a divine imperative, is to maintain *justice* and *righteousness* for the poor, the needy, and the oppressed.[158] Evidently the notion of justice and righteousness has to do with economic maintenance and surely with the maintenance of an independent judiciary that would not be merely an exploitative tool of the powerful. Thus the verbs in verse 4, "defend, deliver, crush," surely concern a viable court system in which the marginal can expect reliable redress from the rapaciousness of an acquisitive society (see Deut 16:18–20; 17:8–13; 2 Chr 19:4–11).

The same active role of monarchy is urged in verses 12–14. The king, it is affirmed or perhaps anticipated, is the one who acts decisively on behalf of the poor and the needy, with economic policies that protect the poor and vulnerable from rapacious economic forces, and in solidarity that sustains them. These verses amount to a powerful assertion that the Davidic government – surely offered in the tradition as a model government – is to be proactive in its economic policies, which would curb the acquisitiveness of a socially irresponsible economy that pursued only the freedom of what we would now term "the market."

These two rhetorical units in verses 1–4 and 12–14 are situated amid great lyrical affirmations concerning the expansive well-being and success of the central government. Verses 5–7 portray the faithful king in hyperbolic language, linking the king to the life-giving processes of creation. This is followed in verses 8–11 by a lyrical expectation of military expansionism that has immense economic implications

---

156 See W. Brueggemann, *Solomon* (2005).
157 Christopher R. Seitz, "Royal Presence in the Canonical Books of Isaiah and Psalms," in Christopher R. Seitz, *Word Without End: The Old Testament as Abiding Theological Witness* (Grand Rapids, MI: Eerdmans, 1998), 150–167.
158 See Enrique Nardoni, *Rise Up, O Judge: A Study of Justice in the Biblical World* (Peabody, MA: Hendrickson, 2004).

for the prosperity of the realm. This lyrical assertion hopes for the defeat of all adversaries and competitors as far as the Euphrates River and thus a vision of "Greater Israel" that continues as an ideological force even in the imagination of some contemporary "Zionists." The defeat of military competitors perhaps alludes to something like Ps 2:10–11, in which the enemies of "God's son" are dramatically embraced. Because *money* follows the *army*, this lyrical anticipation imagines great communal prosperity. See more explicitly the narrative account of the visit of the Queen of Sheba in 1 Kgs 10:1–13 and, more generally, Isa 64:12, wherein Jerusalem becomes the trade center of the world. Notice in Isa 60:10 a reference to Tarshish, as in our verse 10. This vision of luxuriant prosperity is reiterated in verses 15–17, again with an exaggerated sense of the economic significance of the king and another allusion to the economy.

The juxtaposition of verses 1–4 and 12–14 concerning *care for the vulnerable by the regime* and verses 5–7, 8–11, and 15–17 envisioning *extravagant well-being for the regime* constitutes the central claim and affirmation of the psalm. These two accents are placed next to each other, but without any explicit connection. Without a clear link, however, we are surely free to conclude that it is *care for the poor* that becomes the basis for *economic prosperity* in the realm. The unstated but surely implied negative counterpoint is the recognition that neglect of the poor through economic indifference will inevitably lead to military failure and economic collapse. This link is elemental for a biblical understanding of royal practice and polity. What is outlined here in grand doxological fashion is made concrete in Jeremiah's oracle concerning monarchy, wherein the son Jehoiakim is accused of "unrighteousness" and "injustice" (Jer 22:13–14), whereas his father, Josiah, is celebrated as a king who did "justice and righteousness" toward "the poor and the needy." As a consequence of this policy, "it was well with him" (Jer 22:15–16). This link, generically asserted but connected to specific cases, is a prime claim of the Bible concerning the practice of public power.

Verses 18–20 constitute a doxology and conclusion designed for the end of the entire Book II (Psalms 42–72) and do not pertain to this psalm in particular.

Bridging the Horizons: The Bad Shepherd

What is offered in this psalm concerning the practice of royal power is matched in the negative assertion of Ezekiel:

Mortal, prophesy against the shepherds of Israel: prophesy, and say to them – to the shepherds; Thus says the Lord God: Ah, you shepherds of Israel who have been feeding yourselves! You eat the fat, you clothe yourselves with the wool, you slaughter the fatlings; but you do not feed the sheep. You have not strengthened the weak, you have not healed the sick, you have not bound up the injured, you have not brought back the strayed, you have not sought the lost, but with force and harshness you have ruled them. So they were scattered, because there was no shepherd; and scattered, they became food for all the wild animals. My sheep were scattered, they wandered over all the mountains and on every high hill; my sheep were scattered over all the face of the earth, with no one to search or seek for them. (Ezek 34:2–6)

The kings (shepherds) in Jerusalem are said to be the cause of exile ("scattered") because they looked to their private well-being at the same time that they neglected the public good. The fact that our psalm is explicitly linked to Solomon suggests that Solomon is exposed by this psalm as the king who failed the litmus test of care for the poor and whose government thereby collapsed in a tax revolt (see 1 Kgs 12:1–19).

Bridging the Horizons: Public Power

This psalm would seem to be a passionate lyrical statement of a commitment of socioeconomic justice as the foundation of right rule. David Jobling, however, has argued to the contrary that the psalm is a liturgical cover that makes noble sounds but is in fact designed to voice an ideology that condones the real practice of an acquisitive economy that in fact exploits the poor.[159]

If the connection of this psalm to Ezekiel 34 suggested earlier is a legitimate one, we may in Christian reading suggest that the social imperatives on the lips of Jesus in Matthew 25, for example, are a commendation of the same responsible exercise of power on behalf of the neighborhood:

Then the king will say to those at his right hand, "Come, you that are blessed by my Father, inherit the kingdom prepared for you from the foundation of the world; for I was hungry and you gave me food, I was thirsty and you gave me something to drink, I was a stranger and you welcomed me, I was naked and you gave me clothing, I was sick and you took care of me, I was in prison and you visited me." (Matt 25:34–36)

This conviction permits the recognition that this teaching that subverts a self-serving use of public power is recurring and sustained in biblical tradition and seeks to counter the uncritical practice of self-aggrandizement.

Whereas David Jobling sees this psalm as an ideological cover, Walter Houston has in fact made a compelling case that this psalm does indeed call public power in Israel to account:

Nevertheless, there is no reason to doubt that monarchic rule was exploitative, and that state officials were in the forefront of those fleecing the peasants....

---

[159] David Jobling, "Deconstruction and the Political Agenda of Biblical Texts: A Jamesonian Reading of Psalm 72," *Semeia* 59 (1992): 95–127.

Clearly Psalm 72 is not like an escapist novel, blotting out the real world of greedy officials, extravagant courts, and compromised rulers but not having any relation to it. The world it creates does have a relation to the real world, and as a work of literature it enables us to see that world in a new light.... At all events, Psalm 72 still challenges rulers to heed its call: that authority is only valid when based on care for the poor; that the humblest have first claim on state resources of power and money; that unless they defend the oppressed and repress the oppressor, they have no claim to any of the privileges that go with authority. It is a challenge never likely to be out of date.[160]

PSALM 73 – A PSALM OF ASAPH

[1] Truly God is good to the upright,
  to those who are pure in heart.
[2] But as for me, my feet had almost stumbled;
  my steps had nearly slipped.
[3] For I was envious of the arrogant;
  I saw the prosperity of the wicked.

[4] For they have no pain;
  their bodies are sound and sleek.
[5] They are not in trouble as others are;
  they are not plagued like other people.
[6] Therefore pride is their necklace;
  violence covers them like a garment.
[7] Their eyes swell out with fatness;
  their hearts overflow with follies.
[8] They scoff and speak with malice;
  loftily they threaten oppression.
[9] They set their mouths against heaven,
  and their tongues range over the earth.

[10] Therefore the people turn and praise them,
  and find no fault in them.

---

[160] Walter Houston, "The King's Preferential Opinion for the Poor: Rhetoric, Ideology and Ethics in Psalm 72," *Biblical Interpretation* 7 (1999): 355, 361–362.

¹¹ And they say, 'How can God know?
  Is there knowledge in the Most High?'
¹² Such are the wicked;
  always at ease, they increase in riches.
¹³ All in vain I have kept my heart clean
  and washed my hands in innocence.
¹⁴ For all day long I have been plagued,
  and am punished every morning.

¹⁵ If I had said, 'I will talk on in this way',
  I would have been untrue to the circle of your children.
¹⁶ But when I thought how to understand this,
  it seemed to me a wearisome task,
¹⁷ until I went into the sanctuary of God;
  then I perceived their end.
¹⁸ Truly you set them in slippery places;
  you make them fall to ruin.
¹⁹ How they are destroyed in a moment,
  swept away utterly by terrors!
²⁰ They are like a dream when one awakes;
  on awaking you despise their phantoms.

²¹ When my soul was embittered,
  when I was pricked in heart,
²² I was stupid and ignorant;
  I was like a brute beast toward you.
²³ Nevertheless I am continually with you;
  you hold my right hand.
²⁴ You guide me with your counsel,
  and afterwards you will receive me with honor.
²⁵ Whom have I in heaven but you?
  And there is nothing on earth that I desire other than you.
²⁶ My flesh and my heart may fail,
  but God is the strength of my heart and my portion for ever.

²⁷ Indeed, those who are far from you will perish;
  you put an end to those who are false to you.
²⁸ But for me it is good to be near God;
  I have made the LORD God my refuge,
  to tell of all your works.

This psalm, which opens Book III of the Psalter (Psalms 73–89), reflects on the claim of a disciplined life of faith and the temptation to a self-serving autonomy that rejects the restraints and disciplines of covenantal life. Thus it articulates the prime *either/or* of biblical faith, which is especially voiced in the tradition of Deuteronomy (see Deut 30:15–20).

The core claim of Torah faith is articulated in verse 1. God is good to and does good for the pure in heart; that is, for the Torah-keepers. Notice that in the first line the Hebrew text has "good to Israel" rather than "good to the upright." With this phrasing, it is clear that this psalm has in purview the community of faith grounded in covenant committed to covenantal responsibility.

The psalmist is thoroughly grounded in the Torah teaching that *God's blessing* comes to those *who obey Torah*. The life of Torah obedience, however, is restrictive and out of keeping with more attractive social options that focus on the satiation of the self. Verses 2–4 provide a rumination on the seductive alternative to Torah obedience that is so dramatically on exhibit in the lives of "the wicked, the arrogant" (v. 3). They know none of the restrictions of a life of Torah but live in their self-indulgent freedom. They are full of themselves, enjoy good health, and in general are cynical toward the old restrictions of Torah (v. 11). The speaker, moreover, having discerned the attractive power of the alternative, almost fell into that alternative (v. 2); he entertained the thought that the rigors of Torah obedience are "in vain" (v. 13). The psalmist is sorely tempted to give up Torah faith for this attractive alternative. Only at the last moment does he have a jolt of awareness that such an alternative would be a betrayal of everything he treasures and a scandal to his community of Torah practice (v. 15).

In the midst of this rumination, the psalm turns abruptly in verse 17 with its dramatic "until." The turn, in the horizon of the psalmist, comes about because of a visit to "the sanctuary," an act of worship that sharply refocuses life and causes the psalmist to return to the sober reality of his identity within his Torah community. The psalm is laconic about what happened in the sanctuary, but by verse 18 the psalmist is able to reenvision his entire existence and to reperceive the true destiny of those whom he has envied so much. He can see that the lives of the self-indulgent have no staying power but in fact will soon evaporate without a trace. They have done nothing significant with their lives and have made no remembered contributions to the life of the community. The psalmist thus comes to see and to confess that his own attraction to this destructive alternative was an act of "bitterness, stupidity, and ignorance" (vv. 21–22).

In a stark recognition of his true identity as a child of Torah and adherence to the God of covenant, the speaker now utters a powerful "nevertheless" whereby he is drawn back into the truth of his faith (v. 23). In some of the most compelling words of faith in the Psalter, the psalmist concedes that commitment to YHWH is all that counts in the end and all that is his true desire (vv. 23–26). He has been seduced into "gaining the world" and "forfeiting his life" (Matt 16:26). But now, with his sobered and recovered vision of faith, he sees that *nearness to God* is the goal of his life; any self-serving alternative simply cannot be sustained. In the end, the psalmist returns to the elemental faith claim of verse 1. It is telling that the term "good" occurs in verse 1 and again in verse 28. In verse 1, the "good" that God does is material prosperity, but by verse 28 the "goodness" celebrated is intimate communion with God.

Bridging the Horizons: Communion or Commodity

This psalm is among the most powerful concerning simple covenantal piety that refuses the grand lures of a self-indulgent security. The two sections of the psalm, verses 2–14 and verses 18–28, which are joined through the jolt of verse 17, demonstrate the "two ways" so poignant in Torah piety (see Psalm 1). The "two ways," which require a choice, continue to confront those who practice covenantal faith. Covenantal faith teaches that *communion* with God – and derivatively solidarity with one's neighbor – constitutes the true goal of human existence. The alternative, now offered among us in the market economy, is the endless pursuit of *commodities* that promise to make us safe and happy.

In simple and uncompromising fashion, the psalm attests that eventually this either/or cannot be avoided, nor can accommodation between them be reached. The choice of *communion* or *commodity* touches every phase of contemporary life, all the way from personal investment in the community to public policy that indicates support for or opposition to the neighborhood. The choice is always made again every time there is recourse to "the sanctuary" for a clear vision that is undisturbed by the dream of commodities. This psalm states with uncompromising clarity the teaching that looms large in Jesus' Sermon on the Mount:

No one can serve two masters; for a slave will either hate the one and love the other, or be devoted to the one and despise the other. You cannot serve God and wealth. (Matt 6:24)

PSALM 74 – A MASKIL OF ASAPH

¹ O God, why do you cast us off for ever?
Why does your anger smoke against the sheep of your pasture?
² Remember your congregation, which you acquired long ago,
which you redeemed to be the tribe of your heritage.
Remember Mount Zion, where you came to dwell.

³ Direct your steps to the perpetual ruins;
  the enemy has destroyed everything in the sanctuary.

⁴ Your foes have roared within your holy place;
  they set up their emblems there.
⁵ At the upper entrance they hacked
  the wooden trellis with axes.
⁶ And then, with hatchets and hammers,
  they smashed all its carved work.
⁷ They set your sanctuary on fire;
  they desecrated the dwelling-place of your name,
  bringing it to the ground.
⁸ They said to themselves, 'We will utterly subdue them';
  they burned all the meeting-places of God in the land.

⁹ We do not see our emblems;
  there is no longer any prophet,
  and there is no one among us who knows how long.
¹⁰ How long, O God, is the foe to scoff?
  Is the enemy to revile your name for ever?
¹¹ Why do you hold back your hand;
  why do you keep your hand in your bosom?

¹² Yet God my King is from of old,
  working salvation in the earth.
¹³ You divided the sea by your might;
  you broke the heads of the dragons in the waters.
¹⁴ You crushed the heads of Leviathan;
  you gave him as food for the creatures of the wilderness.
¹⁵ You cut openings for springs and torrents;
  you dried up ever-flowing streams.
¹⁶ Yours is the day, yours also the night;
  you established the luminaries and the sun.
¹⁷ You have fixed all the bounds of the earth;
  you made summer and winter.

¹⁸ Remember this, O Lord, how the enemy scoffs,
  and an impious people reviles your name.
¹⁹ Do not deliver the soul of your dove to the wild animals;
  do not forget the life of your poor for ever.

²⁰ Have regard for your covenant,
  for the dark places of the land are full of the haunts of violence.
²¹ Do not let the downtrodden be put to shame;
  let the poor and needy praise your name.
²² Rise up, O God, plead your cause;
  remember how the impious scoff at you all day long.
²³ Do not forget the clamour of your foes,
  the uproar of your adversaries that goes up continually.

Psalm 74 is a community lament growing out of the fall of Jerusalem (587/6 BCE) and the destruction of the temple. It was perhaps composed for services of grief over the defeat. Three perspectives will help readers with this text. First, the temple was the center of the universe, and the center of life for ancient Israel. The destruction of the temple meant that the center was gone; life as this community had known it was no more. There was now no place to achieve atonement in human relationships and in the divine–human relationship. The symbols of order and justice have collapsed. The center of the life-giving divine presence is no more. The destruction of the temple was far more than the leveling of a treasured building. It meant the end of ancient Israel's treasured life, and thus Psalm 74 is an urgent cry of anguish.

Second, the sequence of the poem is an important interpretive clue. Verses 1–11, framed by questions, offer an urgent petition that God see the flattened sanctuary and do something about it. The community understands that God has rejected the worshiping community. Verses 12–17, in great contrast, praise God as creator and king. The hope is that God will re-create the worshiping community, and so this section serves to persuade God to answer the community's petition. Verses 18–23 conclude the psalm with strong petitions that God act for the sake of this community. The psalm consists of *petition and complaint*, the two persistent markers of prayers for help in the Psalter, with the striking section of praise shaped into that structure.

Third, Psalm 74 is the second of the collection of the psalms of Asaph (Psalms 73–83) that begins Book III of the Psalter. Psalm 73 narrated an individual's crisis of Torah faith, a crisis resolved in "the sanctuary of God" (v. 17). Psalm 74 continues in urgently narrating a crisis, now that of the community tied to the obliteration of Zion/Jerusalem and especially its temple. The centrality of the temple in the resolution of the crisis of faith in Psalm 73 makes the destruction of the temple even more disturbing.

Verses 1–11. The psalm begins with questions characteristic of the prayers of the Psalter: Why has God forsaken this congregation ("the sheep of your pasture") tied to God from its creation in the Exodus event? The urgent questioning leads quickly to the petition that God "remember" this people and its long history and relationship with this God, and remember Mount Zion, the sanctuary where this God has come to dwell with this congregation. It was God who initiated the relationship with this flock, which has demonstrated divine faithfulness to the relationship. Now the worshiping community is shocked and bereaved, for it appears that God has rejected them. The hope is that God will see the rotting ruins of the sanctuary and act on behalf of ancient Israel. The psalm then movingly envisions the obliteration of the sacred place by the marauding enemies. First, they set up their symbols of power as an act of victory and of desecration of the sanctuary. Then, with their instruments of destruction, they smashed the beauty of this place of worship and burned the temple to the ground. The destruction was so complete that they also burned down "all the meeting places of God in the land." The Babylonians sought to wipe from the face of Zion any sign of this congregation's salvation history. What is more, the community complains that there are no directions – not even from the prophets – for how to move forward in this historic crisis.

Verses 10–11 then return to the form of questioning with which the psalm began: Why does God allow the enemy to desecrate the holy place? How long will the enemy triumph with glee? Why does God not act on behalf of the congregation? The interrogatives "why" and "how long" have the same effect and are central to the rhetoric of ancient Israel's prayers for help. The divine "hand" or power echoes the Exodus tradition central to Israel's historical memory. Then God saw the oppression of Israel and came to deliver the Israelites. Why does God not act in this grave new crisis? The questions that frame this first part of the psalm suggest that the purpose of these verses is not simply to describe for God what has happened in Zion but to move God to act on behalf of the worshiping community. Both God's place and God's people have been desecrated; it is as if they are no more. How long will God allow this chaos to continue? The prayer narrates the destruction of the temple as an assault on God. Is God no longer king? With these searching questions, the covenant community holds God accountable for the covenant promises of steadfast love and faithfulness. The intensity of the language in this first part of the psalm and the frequent use of the second-person pronoun suggest that the congregation fiercely holds onto the covenant relationship and urgently seeks God's direction and help.

Verses 12–17. The contrast between the questions in verses 10–11 and the affirmation in verse 12 may well bring a sudden jolt to readers. After the intense questioning in the first part of the psalm, verse 12 portrays God as king from of old and as the king who brings salvation. The reference is not to the Exodus tradition, however, but to creation traditions. This section narrates God's work in bringing order out of chaos to create life. The creatures of the watery chaos, the dragons and Leviathan, are tamed. The text brings to memory the creation of the heavens and the earth, the sea and the dry land, light and the seasons, all the necessities for life. The poetry brings to mind Genesis 1 and other ancient Near Eastern creation traditions. These verses confess that God from of old created by defeating the powers of chaos and creating order and life. The dragons of chaos in these verses are parallel to the invaders of the land and the temple portrayed in verses 1–11. The connection between the sections is that the community now faces life-threatening powers of chaos. God has of old demonstrated the power to tame such creatures of chaos and thus create order and hope. The community's prayer is that God will again bring wholeness of life out of chaos.

Verses 18–23. The psalm's concluding section moves back to the petition in the imperative and jussive mode. The plea is for God to "remember" the triumph and scoffing of this enemy who has violated the sacred sanctuary and defeated its congregation. The congregation is portrayed as "your dove," "your poor," "the downtrodden," and "the poor and needy." The plea is that the dove, the sacrificial offering of the poor, not be sacrificed to wild animals and that God attend to the needs of the congregation. At present, the Babylonians oppress "the poor," but the Israelites will not roll over and easily give in to the power politics of the day. Their confession of faith is that Israel has a special relationship with YHWH, whom they urge to act as King YHWH. This section of the psalm puts the issue explicitly in terms of the covenant relationship between YHWH and ancient Israel. God initiated that relationship, and the plea in Psalm 74 is for God to honor the commitments of that relationship and bring hope out of the current chaos. The land now holds darkness and violence; the covenant God can act to bring peace and hope. The concluding petition appeals to divine self-interest. God's reign is being mocked by the invaders, who seek to destroy the land and people and the reputation of the covenant God. Psalm 74 pleads for God to remember the covenant promise of divine action, for the witness to God's power to deliver is now fading.

A Closer Look: Noah

The reference to Israel as "your dove" (v. 19) in the context of a petition that God "remember" brings to mind the flood narrative in Genesis 6–9. The center and turning point of that narrative is at the beginning of Chapter 8:

But God remembered Noah and all the wild animals and all the domestic animals that were with him in the Ark. And God made a wind blow over the earth, and the waters subsided. (Gen 8:1)

In that tradition, Psalm 74 pleads with God to "remember" the congregation and Mount Zion and to remember the injustice done by the invaders. God's remembering would bring hope in this crisis.

Bridging the Horizons: A Prayer in Gravest Crisis

Psalm 74 is a powerful prayer in the face of ancient Israel's gravest public crisis. Jerusalem has fallen, and the temple, the central symbol of the gift of life for this community, lies in ruins. The angst is palpable in this prayer that cajoles God to deal with the crisis. The prayer petitions the covenant God to act in the tradition of the Creation, in which God brought order and life out of chaos. In the midst of this disaster, the community pleads with God to act on behalf of the community and on behalf of the divine reputation. Given this social setting, it is not surprising that the petition is intensely honest. The worshiping community calls YHWH to attend to this new assertion of chaos in the form of the violation of Zion/Jerusalem. Such is the task of the covenant God. The impact of the poem is that Zion – the place of divine presence and revelation – is lost but God is not. The psalm persistently and candidly addresses this God, so the loss narrated is grievous indeed but not final, because God can still be addressed, even from the grip of the powers of chaos. The psalm is a persuasive and honest address to God as a model of prayer in worship. In this public claim of pain, ancient Israel seeks to encounter the only truly life-giving one in all of creation.

PSALM 75 – TO THE LEADER: DO NOT DESTROY. A PSALM OF ASAPH. A SONG

¹ We give thanks to you, O God;
   we give thanks; your name is near.
People tell of your wondrous deeds.

² At the set time that I appoint
   I will judge with equity.
³ When the earth totters, with all its inhabitants,
   it is I who keep its pillars steady.
      Selah
⁴ I say to the boastful, 'Do not boast',
   and to the wicked, 'Do not lift up your horn;
⁵ do not lift up your horn on high,
   or speak with insolent neck.'

⁶ For not from the east or from the west
   and not from the wilderness comes lifting up;
⁷ but it is God who executes judgment,
   putting down one and lifting up another.
⁸ For in the hand of the Lord there is a cup
   with foaming wine, well mixed;

he will pour a draught from it,
  and all the wicked of the earth
  shall drain it down to the dregs.
⁹ But I will rejoice for ever;
  I will sing praises to the God of Jacob.

¹⁰ All the horns of the wicked I will cut off,
  but the horns of the righteous shall be exalted.

Psalm 75 comes in a form that is not the most familiar to readers of the Psalter. It includes characteristics of prophetic judgment, divine speech, thanksgiving, and instruction. The sequence of the poetry will help readers navigate the text. The psalm begins with thanksgiving and then shifts to direct speech from God. Apparently the oracular utterance concludes with verse 6, and the remainder of the psalm is a response to and confirmation of this word. Verses 1 and 9 suggest a context of praise and thanksgiving to the God who brings the justice articulated in the oracle, so the psalm likely originated in relation to a public worship setting tied to divine judgment and justice, perhaps a celebration and proclamation of the reign of God. The poem does not suggest the identity of its speaker. A liturgist leads the congregation in encountering divine judgment and justice as an affirmation of hope that the encounter makes possible. Such a call to faith has a prophetic tone. Perhaps this suggestion of structure and context will help readers grapple with this rather enigmatic poem.

A Closer Look: Reading Psalms Together

Psalm 75 is the third in a collection of psalms of Asaph (Psalms 73–83) at the beginning of Book III of the Psalter. The opening verse of Psalm 75 and its "wondrous deeds" echoes the end of Psalm 73. These deeds bring justice on the arrogant; the arrogant are also the source of the trouble in Psalm 73. When reading Psalms 73–75 in sequence, one also realizes that Psalm 75 sounds like a response to the concluding section of Psalm 74 and its petitions. The question of divine rule and justice is at the core of these three psalms that begin this Asaphite collection. Psalm 75 affirms the divine justice. Many interpreters would tie this collection of psalms to a time related to exile.

Verses 1–5. The psalm opens with the liturgist speaking a word of thanksgiving on behalf of the congregation. The nearness of the divine name suggests that God is present and active, as demonstrated in the "wondrous deeds" in the last line of verse 1. The paradigm of such deeds in the liturgical memory of Israel is in the Exodus narrative. This memory elicits from the community a sense of hope and a response of thanksgiving for the salvation history.

The psalm suddenly shifts to the first-person singular with verse 2, and it becomes clear fairly quickly that the voice is the divine voice. This oracular word likely continues through verse 5, because God is referred to in the third person in the following verses. The oracle gives the psalm a prophetic dimension but does not require a cult prophet to deliver it. Priests also delivered oracles; perhaps the liturgist continues to speak. Verses 2–5 proclaim that God judges with justice and so preserves creation, keeping "its pillars steady" and thus preserving the order that makes life possible. God created the world and sustains it with justice; creation and God's reign cohere. It is God, rather than those who consider themselves strong and seek to control society, who balances the scales of justice. The horn is a symbol of power, and so the wicked here are arrogant power mongers who presume that they have the ability to determine the course of life. Such power rightfully stands only with the divine creator and judge. Beyond that portrayal in verses 4–5, the psalm does not identify the wicked. These arrogant ones could be within the community of ancient Israel or they could be from other nations, such as Babylon, perhaps reflecting the exilic context of the psalms of Asaph. Habakkuk portrays Babylon as arrogant. These braggarts trust in themselves and thereby deny the reign of God. The purpose of the oracle is to proclaim divine rule and justice as determining the future; that word could bring hope to the community.

Verses 6–10. In the concluding verses of the psalm (vv. 6–10), the liturgist articulates a response to the oracle as a way of emphasizing its significance for the congregation. God – rather than self-sufficient humans – brings about just judgment. These verses emphasize this message in a variety of ways. The first is that the judgment does not originate from a geographical area – east, west, or wilderness. So, empires such as Babylon or Egypt do not bring judgment; that is the prerogative of the living God. That judgment brings justice to both the wicked and the righteous, and is not far away. A second image in these verses is the cup of divine wrath. This cup is in God's hand and holds foaming wine; the wicked will drink all of it. That is, the wicked will experience the full impact of divine wrath. That hope brings rejoicing for the speaker (v. 9). The psalm's final verse brings a poetic summary as a final affirmation of divine judgment as proclaimed in the oracle. The righteous, those faithful to their relationship with God, will find exaltation, but the power ("horns") of the wicked will come to naught. This last verse seems to be an addition to the oracular word from God that explicitly articulates its import for the congregation. This last section of the psalm instructs the congregation based on the oracle in verses 2–5.

Some readers will be uncomfortable with the proclamation of divine judgment on the wicked in Psalm 75. Perhaps a better way of thinking about the issue is in terms of justice. God is the one who will adjudicate human history; the psalm envisions a world in which divine justice reigns. That affirmation brings a word of hope for the congregation in Psalm 75. Some have suggested that the setting of the psalms of Asaph (Psalms 73–83) is tied to the exile, and such a word of hope would fit well with that context – a community waiting and hoping for justice. The psalm envisions divine justice in the divine timetable.

Bridging the Horizons: Nothing to Fear

Individual and corporate anxiety typifies contemporary Western culture. The echo of Franklin Delano Roosevelt's exhortation that "We have nothing to fear but fear itself" resounds, and yet fear characterizes much of the U.S. response to the rest of the world. There is much talk of security and especially of national security. Just such a context provides the basis for Psalm 75. The congregation portrayed in the poem is waiting for the reign of God to come to realization and therefore waiting for justice. That waiting brings anxiety and insecurity, and thus human efforts at security for the future of society. Military and economic fortresses and isolation from the world become the order of the day. At the base of these efforts is the sense that human efforts can ensure security. Some societies even claim divine sanction for these efforts. The Psalms in general and Psalm 75 in particular are skeptical about such efforts. Securing the future is finally a matter in God's hands. God will sort out the wicked and the righteous and work out the implications. Marvin Tate indicates that Psalm 75 uses three images to press trust in God's justice: God steadies the pillars of the earth (v. 3); the wicked will drink the cup of God's wrath (v. 8); and the horns of the wicked will be cut off (vv. 4–5, 10).[161] In the face of injustice and opposition, these images contribute to an artful poetic affirmation of the reign of God. Read in that way, this enigmatic poem can become a powerful resource of faith in our own world, which seems to totter.

PSALM 76 – TO THE LEADER: WITH STRINGED INSTRUMENTS. A PSALM OF ASAPH. A SONG

¹ In Judah God is known,
   his name is great in Israel.
² His abode has been established in Salem,
   his dwelling-place in Zion.
³ There he broke the flashing arrows,
   the shield, the sword, and the weapons of war.
      Selah

---

[161] M. E. Tate, *Psalms 51–100* (1990), 259–260.

⁴ Glorious are you, more majestic
   than the everlasting mountains.
⁵ The stout-hearted were stripped of their spoil;
   they sank into sleep;
none of the troops
   was able to lift a hand.
⁶ At your rebuke, O God of Jacob,
   both rider and horse lay stunned.

⁷ But you indeed are awesome!
   Who can stand before you
   when once your anger is roused?
⁸ From the heavens you uttered judgment
   the earth feared and was still
⁹ when God rose up to establish judgment,
   to save all the oppressed of the earth.
        Selah

¹⁰ Human wrath serves only to praise you,
    when you bind the last bit of your wrath around you.
¹¹ Make vows to the Lᴏʀᴅ your God, and perform them;
    let all who are around him bring gifts
    to the one who is awesome,
¹² who cuts off the spirit of princes,
    who inspires fear in the kings of the earth.

This psalm celebrates the *awesomeness* of God evidenced in great military power (vv. 7, 11). The psalm is a great act of praise that celebrates and relies on the wonder, majesty, and power of God. This doxological exuberance is articulated amid two subthemes. First, this is a "Song of Zion" that celebrates the temple in Jerusalem as the residence of God and as the place whence comes God's singular power and decisive rule in the earth. Thus even in Amos 1:2 it is "from Zion" that YHWH's judgment on the nations is enunciated by the prophet. God's dwelling place is in "Salem" (v. 2), a parallel to "Zion." In the final form of the text there is a reference to *Jerusalem* that speaks of the temple as the source of *shalom*, a clear reference to the name of the great temple builder, Solomon. All these terms – *Salem, Jerusalem, shalom,* and *Solomon* – are of course the same and in their several uses connect well-being that is received both as a gift of God and as a result of God's unchallenged governance.

The second theme alongside the temple theme is that the God who resides in the Jerusalem temple is a great war God who from that place wins decisive victories in the world: "The God of Israel smashes all implements of war – all symbols of human arrogance. He defeats the *mlky-'rs*, the leaders of chaos. But God's frightening judgment becomes public knowledge from the place of his presence."[162]

It is this God from the Jerusalem temple who breaks weapons and disarms all powers that resist the rule of YHWH, both the primordial powers of chaos and the historical enemies of Israel (v. 2). In verses 5–6, the humiliating defeat of the enemy is described; at the direction of YHWH, all the weapons of the enemy are reduced to nothing (see Ps 46:8–9; Isa 9:5). Thus the disarmament of the enemies is a great act of violent power in the interest of subsequent peace and order. Verse 10 suggests that earthly turmoil, likely military challenge, is simply an opportunity for the God of the temple to show forth power and dominion, and thereby to be glorified among the nations. Such a military challenge, according to the poem, constitutes no real threat at all, for this is a God who scoffs at such challenges from the nations that are after all only God's recalcitrant subjects; but for all of their recalcitrance, they are nonetheless God's subjects (see Psalm 2).[163]

Out of great military victory, the "supreme commander" in the Jerusalem temple holds court and dispenses justice (vv. 8–9). When YHWH has demonstrated supreme military power, all challenges are settled, and all creatures, all nations, and all competing powers are reduced to attentive silence. All await the verdicts of this God, for all know that behind God's judicial authority stands a demonstrated military capacity to enforce dictums. The outcome of such a solemn judicial meeting is that God gives decrees that are on behalf of the oppressed.[164] Most remarkably, this cosmic vision, with the Jerusalem temple at its epicenter, concerns "all the oppressed of the earth." At this great moment, the temple and its divine resident have transcended the particularity of Israel and work justice for the vulnerable against all earthly powers of oppression and exploitation. Thus the vision of a world under God's justice is an extraordinary claim made against all aggressive powers everywhere in the world. The temple, in this imagery, is a visible, concrete citadel of world justice; the God who dwells there is the proponent and enforcer of justice for all of the oppressed.

There are, we suggest, two ways in which we may construe the claims of temple presence, military victory, and world justice. On the one hand, we may take a quite "supernaturalist view" of the warrior God whose violent military capacity is used to create a viable human community of justice. Such a view would deal primarily

---

[162] H.-J. Kraus, *Psalms 60–150* (1988), 111.

[163] See Walter Brueggemann, "Pharaoh As Vassal: A Study in Political Metaphor," *CBQ* 57 (1995): 27–51.

[164] The same sort of judicial meeting presided over by God for the sake of the weak and the poor is reported in Psalm 82.

in liturgical-poetic imagination and would present an imaginative reconstrual of the world. On the other hand, we remember that the Jerusalem temple, abode of the creator God, is the royal chapel of the Davidic king. On that basis, we might imagine that the Davidic king receives from such liturgical articulation the warrant and legitimacy to fight the wars of Judah with a claim of divine mission for cosmic justice. This interpretation would take the liturgical act as ideological legitimization for political and military activity. To be sure, the king is nowhere mentioned here, and such a view requires an interpretive maneuver, but not one that is very venturesome.

Either way, directly or through human mediation, the God celebrated here is capable of wondrous deeds. These deeds are celebrated as the transformation of a violently contested human community into a community of justice with guarantees of life for the powerless who are oppressed.

Bridging the Horizons: Human Rights

The claim of this psalm that the God who resides in the Jerusalem temple has made a decree to protect all the oppressed of the earth leads to important contemporary ethical claims. Those ethical claims are nowhere more fully articulated than in the Helsinki Universal Declaration of Human Rights of 1948. Although other grounds may be cited for human rights in other theological and religious traditions, in the biblical tradition and derivative Jewish and Christian traditions it is exactly this claim for the God of the temple that is the ultimate theological guarantee of all human rights. The ethic envisioned in temple theology is not limited to Israel but pertains to all human communities and therefore to all public policy.

Bridging the Horizons: Liberation Theology

The decree concerning the protection of the oppressed in this psalm provides a theological foundation for the program of liberation theology and its articulation of "God's preferential option for the poor." The church's common preoccupation with private and individual sins has caused a lack of awareness about structural public sin. Speaking from a Roman Catholic perspective about God's preferential option for the poor, Donal Dorr writes:

An option for the poor does mean the rejection of an evil system and of bad *structures* in society. The Church has always insisted that people make an "option against sin". In recent years theologians and Church leaders have come to realise more clearly that this should include an option against what is called "social sin". One aspect of social sin is the embodiment of injustice in the unequal distribution of wealth and power in the world. Informed Church leaders are becoming more aware that in today's world (especially), great wealth and power are very often linked to injustice – either in the way they are acquired or in the refusal to share them with others. Christians are now being helped to see tha[t] against sin includes an option against embodied injustice – and therefore in favour of the victims of injustice. Correctly understood, an "option for the poor" is simply one aspect of an "option against sin". If we opt to resist injustice we must be opposed to the process of impoverishment and the systems that promote poverty.[165]

PSALM 77 – TO THE LEADER: ACCORDING TO JEDUTHUN. OF ASAPH. A PSALM

¹ I cry aloud to God,
   aloud to God, that he may hear me.
² In the day of my trouble I seek the LORD;
   in the night my hand is stretched out without wearying;
   my soul refuses to be comforted.
³ I think of God, and I moan;
   I meditate, and my spirit faints.
        Selah

⁴ You keep my eyelids from closing;
   I am so troubled that I cannot speak.
⁵ I consider the days of old,
   and remember the years of long ago.
⁶ I commune with my heart in the night;
   I meditate and search my spirit:
⁷ 'Will the LORD spurn for ever,
   and never again be favorable?
⁸ Has his steadfast love ceased for ever?
   Are his promises at an end for all time?
⁹ Has God forgotten to be gracious?
   Has he in anger shut up his compassion?'
        Selah

---

[165] Donal Door, *Option For the Poor: A Hundred Years of Vatican Social Teaching* (Maryknoll, NY: Orbis Books, 1983), 243–244.

¹⁰ And I say, 'It is my grief
   that the right hand of the Most High has changed.'

¹¹ I will call to mind the deeds of the Lᴏʀᴅ;
   I will remember your wonders of old.
¹² I will meditate on all your work,
   and muse on your mighty deeds.
¹³ Your way, O God, is holy.
   What god is so great as our God?
¹⁴ You are the God who works wonders;
   you have displayed your might among the peoples.
¹⁵ With your strong arm you redeemed your people,
   the descendants of Jacob and Joseph.
       Selah

¹⁶ When the waters saw you, O God,
   when the waters saw you, they were afraid;
   the very deep trembled.
¹⁷ The clouds poured out water;
   the skies thundered;
   your arrows flashed on every side.
¹⁸ The crash of your thunder was in the whirlwind;
   your lightnings lit up the world;
   the earth trembled and shook.
¹⁹ Your way was through the sea,
   your path, through the mighty waters;
   yet your footprints were unseen.
²⁰ You led your people like a flock
   by the hand of Moses and Aaron.

Psalm 77 is a solemn complaint (vv. 1–10) that culminates in a recital of the saving
memory of Israel (vv. 11–20). In the first half of the psalm, the characteristic elements of the complaint are expressed. The complaint begins with a cry of address
to God, asking God to hear (and therefore to answer in saving power) (vv. 1–2). But
although the address is to God, in fact the psalmist is completely preoccupied with
his own sorry state. That preoccupation with self is evident in the recurrence of the
first-person pronouns:

   my trouble,
   I seek,
   my hand,
   my soul,

I think,
I moan,
I meditate,
my spirit.

Although the prayer is addressed to God, the self remains the center of attention.

Verse 4 begins a new rhetorical unit with a "you" statement, accusing God of preventing sleep (v. 4a). But the poetry reverts to "I" statements in verses 4b–6. Only now the psalmist focuses not on present trouble but on an act of remembering and insomnia. Instead of counting sheep, the poet recounts ancient miracles wrought by God. The psalmist, in the dread of wakefulness, asks a series of questions that probe the character of God:

- Will YHWH spurn the psalmist forever?
- Has YHWH ceased to be faithful?
- Are YHWH's promises null and void?
- Has YHWH forgotten to be gracious?
- Has YHWH's anger terminated compassion?

Terrien observes that with these questions the psalmist is questioning the "catechism of the covenant" in a way that is "near-blasphemy."[166] The psalmist, thoroughly grounded in Israel's memory, appeals in these questions to the big words of faith: *steadfast love, promises, grace, compassion*. The questions do not receive an answer, and we may not be sure of the answer we are to infer. Perhaps the intended answer is an affirmation of YHWH's fidelity:

- No, YHWH will not spurn the psalmist forever.
- No, YHWH's fidelity has not halted.
- No, YHWH's promises are not null and void.
- No, YHWH has not forgotten graciousness.
- No, YHWH's anger has not vetoed compassion.

If that is the intended answer, then the psalmist affirms the truth of YHWH for his community. Marvin Tate suggests that the questions are not in fact resolved in the latter part of the psalm and that "no" is a possible answer to be inferred.[167]

But that *truth of YHWH* in which the psalmist is well schooled must yield to his *experience of dread and helplessness*, which is outlined in verses 1–4. In that case, the correct answer might be "yes":

- Yes, YHWH spurns.
- Yes, YHWH has stopped being faithful.

---

[166] S. Terrien, *Psalms* (2003), 555.
[167] M. E. Tate, *Psalms 51–100* (1990), 275–276.

- Yes, YHWH's promises are null and void.
- Yes, YHWH is not always gracious.
- Yes, YHWH's anger defeats compassion.

Both answers are available, depending on whether the focus is on *Israel's narrative faith* or the speaker's *described experience*. The clue to the "right answer" seems to be given in verse 10:

> And I say, "It is my grief
>   that the right hand of the Most
>   High has changed." (Ps 77:10)

The *Most High* (the most sweeping nomenclature available for the high God of creation) has changed; the power (right hand) of the high God has been altered. This would seem to suggest that the God of fidelity, grace, and compassion no longer has the capacity to save. Thus, in the middle of the night of insomnia, the troubled psalmist engages in "compulsive rumination" that is beyond containment or management. With all such nighttime disturbances, the psalmist may vacillate, entertaining variously, even simultaneously, the *no* of the tradition and the *yes* of experience. The nighttime rumination surely leaves the psalmist bewildered and exhausted.

But then, after verse 10, there is a long pause and a resumption of remembering, only this time of a very different type. What follows in verses 11–20 may indicate that *tradition* has reconstrued *experience*. Already in verse 5 the psalmist has returned to the tradition. Now, in verse 11, the psalmist "calls to mind, remembers, mediates, muses"; the subject is YHWH's "mighty deeds" that constitute the core memory of faith, a series of transformative, inexplicable miracles that leave Israel dazzled and capable only of doxology.

The psalm now focuses on normative faith claims, ponders the incomparability of God the Most High (v. 13), recalls the "wonders" of the past (v. 14), alludes to the old ancestral promises (v. 15), and then focuses singularly on the Exodus event (vv. 16–20). The poetry is a dramatic characterization of the way in which the storm God caused the earth to tremble (vv. 16–18), divided the waters of the sea to permit an exit to freedom (v. 19), and authorized Moses and Aaron to lead God's people into the wilderness (v. 20). The psalm ends rather abruptly, as though the review is complete. Or perhaps we imagine that this troubled insomniac has fallen asleep, consoled by the memory of his community.

The interesting and difficult matter of the psalm is the relationship between the complaint in verses 1–10 and the narrative recital (vv. 11–20). The psalm itself sets the two components side by side without relating them to each other. Since the narrative memory follows the complaint and the psalmist never returns to the complaint at the conclusion of the psalm, we may judge that the psalmist found resolution for his complaint by reengaging the communal memory. In the complaint itself, the psalmist certainly speaks as an Israelite but is nonetheless obsessively focused on himself. The complaint is saturated with "I, my, myself." In the narrative memory, by contrast, the first-person references have disappeared. This is not because the self disappears but because the self is repositioned in the community. The psalmist comes to see that the miracle of the Exodus deliverance pertains to him as to all Israelites. He as a member of the community of Israel is a subject of Exodus emancipation. He is brought to a new freedom by the wondrous power of God. If we imagine the Passover liturgy that asks, "Why is this night different from all other nights?" the psalmist knows the difference because he now walks amid his community "through the mighty waters." In retrospect, it is now clear that the questions of verses 7–9 are all to be answered in the negative:

- No, God will not spurn the psalmist forever.
- No, God's steadfast love has not ceased.
- No, God's promises have not been annulled.
- No, God has not forgotten to be gracious.
- No, God's anger has not shut up compassion.

By reengaging the defining memory of Israel, this psalmist now knows steadfast love, grace, and compassion. God has not changed on the big issues of fidelity. The life of the psalmist is in acute circumstances; God answers through the palpable contemporaneity of the tradition.

A Closer Look: Does God Change?

The psalm pivots on verse 10, which raises the acute question about whether God does change. Behind that question here, as in the book of Job, is the tension between the solidness of the tradition and the acuteness of experience. But a close reading of the remembered tradition of Israel would also indicate to the psalmist that the God of Israel is indeed a God of dynamism but does change and reposition in relationship to the world and in relationship to Israel. Although the doxology of verses 11–20 attests to God's abiding fidelity, the psalm is honest enough to voice the reality that lived experience does lead sometimes to the conclusion that God has changed and has departed fidelity. It is important in the study of this psalm as a pastoral resource not to resolve the question quickly, easily, or obviously. Here, as in many traditions of the Old Testament, the lived experience of the believer and the believing community must be honored even in the face of the tradition.

PSALM 78 – A MASKIL OF ASAPH

¹ Give ear, O my people, to my teaching;
   incline your ears to the words of my mouth.
² I will open my mouth in a parable;
   I will utter dark sayings from of old,
³ things that we have heard and known,
   that our ancestors have told us.
⁴ We will not hide them from their children;
   we will tell to the coming generation
the glorious deeds of the LORD, and his might,
   and the wonders that he has done.

⁵ He established a decree in Jacob,
   and appointed a law in Israel,
which he commanded our ancestors
   to teach to their children;
⁶ that the next generation might know them,
   the children yet unborn,
and rise up and tell them to their children,
⁷ so that they should set their hope in God,
and not forget the works of God,
   but keep his commandments;
⁸ and that they should not be like their ancestors,
   a stubborn and rebellious generation,
a generation whose heart was not steadfast,
   whose spirit was not faithful to God.

⁹ The Ephraimites, armed with the bow,
   turned back on the day of battle.
¹⁰ They did not keep God's covenant,
   but refused to walk according to his law.
¹¹ They forgot what he had done,
   and the miracles that he had shown them.
¹² In the sight of their ancestors he worked marvels
   in the land of Egypt, in the fields of Zoan.
¹³ He divided the sea and let them pass through it,
   and made the waters stand like a heap.
¹⁴ In the daytime he led them with a cloud,
   and all night long with a fiery light.

[15] He split rocks open in the wilderness,
   and gave them drink abundantly as from the deep.
[16] He made streams come out of the rock,
   and caused waters to flow down like rivers.

[17] Yet they sinned still more against him,
   rebelling against the Most High in the desert.
[18] They tested God in their heart
   by demanding the food they craved.
[19] They spoke against God, saying,
   'Can God spread a table in the wilderness?
[20] Even though he struck the rock so that water gushed out
   and torrents overflowed,
can he also give bread,
   or provide meat for his people?'

[21] Therefore, when the LORD heard, he was full of rage;
   a fire was kindled against Jacob,
   his anger mounted against Israel,
[22] because they had no faith in God,
   and did not trust his saving power.
[23] Yet he commanded the skies above,
   and opened the doors of heaven;
[24] he rained down on them manna to eat,
   and gave them the grain of heaven.
[25] Mortals ate of the bread of angels;
   he sent them food in abundance.
[26] He caused the east wind to blow in the heavens,
   and by his power he led out the south wind;
[27] he rained flesh upon them like dust,
   winged birds like the sand of the seas;
[28] he let them fall within their camp,
   all around their dwellings.
[29] And they ate and were well filled,
   for he gave them what they craved.
[30] But before they had satisfied their craving,
   while the food was still in their mouths,
[31] the anger of God rose against them
   and he killed the strongest of them,
   and laid low the flower of Israel.

³² In spite of all this they still sinned;
they did not believe in his wonders.
³³ So he made their days vanish like a breath,
and their years in terror.
³⁴ When he killed them, they sought for him;
they repented and sought God earnestly.
³⁵ They remembered that God was their rock,
the Most High God their redeemer.
³⁶ But they flattered him with their mouths;
they lied to him with their tongues.
³⁷ Their heart was not steadfast toward him;
they were not true to his covenant.
³⁸ Yet he, being compassionate,
forgave their iniquity,
and did not destroy them;
often he restrained his anger,
and did not stir up all his wrath.
³⁹ He remembered that they were but flesh,
a wind that passes and does not come again.
⁴⁰ How often they rebelled against him in the wilderness
and grieved him in the desert!
⁴¹ They tested God again and again,
and provoked the Holy One of Israel.
⁴² They did not keep in mind his power,
or the day when he redeemed them from the foe;
⁴³ when he displayed his signs in Egypt,
and his miracles in the fields of Zoan.
⁴⁴ He turned their rivers to blood,
so that they could not drink of their streams.
⁴⁵ He sent among them swarms of flies, which devoured them,
and frogs, which destroyed them.
⁴⁶ He gave their crops to the caterpillar,
and the fruit of their labor to the locust.
⁴⁷ He destroyed their vines with hail,
and their sycamores with frost.
⁴⁸ He gave over their cattle to the hail,
and their flocks to thunderbolts.
⁴⁹ He let loose on them his fierce anger,
wrath, indignation, and distress,
a company of destroying angels.
⁵⁰ He made a path for his anger;

he did not spare them from death,
but gave their lives over to the plague.
51 He struck all the firstborn in Egypt,
the first issue of their strength in the tents of Ham.
52 Then he led out his people like sheep,
and guided them in the wilderness like a flock.
53 He led them in safety, so that they were not afraid;
but the sea overwhelmed their enemies.
54 And he brought them to his holy hill,
to the mountain that his right hand had won.
55 He drove out nations before them;
he apportioned them for a possession
and settled the tribes of Israel in their tents.

56 Yet they tested the Most High God,
and rebelled against him.
They did not observe his decrees,
57 but turned away and were faithless like their ancestors;
they twisted like a treacherous bow.
58 For they provoked him to anger with their high places;
they moved him to jealousy with their idols.
59 When God heard, he was full of wrath,
and he utterly rejected Israel.
60 He abandoned his dwelling at Shiloh,
the tent where he dwelt among mortals,
61 and delivered his power to captivity,
his glory to the hand of the foe.
62 He gave his people to the sword,
and vented his wrath on his heritage.
63 Fire devoured their young men,
and their girls had no marriage song.
64 Their priests fell by the sword,
and their widows made no lamentation.
65 Then the LORD awoke as from sleep,
like a warrior shouting because of wine.
66 He put his adversaries to rout;
he put them to everlasting disgrace.

67 He rejected the tent of Joseph,
he did not choose the tribe of Ephraim;
68 but he chose the tribe of Judah,

Mount Zion, which he loves.
⁶⁹ He built his sanctuary like the high heavens,
   like the earth, which he has founded for ever.
⁷⁰ He chose his servant David,
   and took him from the sheepfolds;
⁷¹ from tending the nursing ewes he brought him
   to be the shepherd of his people Jacob,
   of Israel, his inheritance.
⁷² With upright heart he tended them,
   and guided them with skilful hand.

Psalm 78 is a lengthy poetic narration of ancient Israel's historical traditions. The opening of the psalm suggests that the psalm has connections with ancient Israel's wisdom teachers. The psalm is a didactic poem based on the historical traditions of the faith. That would fit with the label of *Maskil*, a term with wisdom connections, in the psalm's heading. The poem recounts history from a clear perspective, so that the current congregation can learn the lessons of history. The psalm is a kind of poetic sermon based on history. A number of interpreters have suggested a three-part structure for the psalm.[168] Verses 1–11 introduce the poem and articulate its purpose. Two recitals of history follow. Each includes accounts of divine generosity toward the faith community of ancient Israel, human rebellion, divine response in judgment, and a reconciliation in the relationship. Verses 12–39 concentrate on the wilderness traditions, and verses 40–72 emphasize the Exodus from Egypt and the move to the land. This structure will guide the exposition that follows.

A Closer Look: The Importance of Memory

The recital of ancient Israel's community memory is central to Psalm 78; the text rehearses the memory so that the community can learn from it and pass it on to future generations. Memory is one of the themes of the psalms of Asaph (Psalms 73–83); in particular, this theme continues from Psalm 77. There memory has something of an ambiguous presence. In Psalm 78, however, memory has a clear function in warning the community to learn from its history. In the recital of memory there is hope for the future.

The psalm's opening section, verses 1–11, makes clear that the text has a didactic purpose; the call is for the community to learn the lessons of history. Instructive are

---

[168] J. L. Mays, *Psalms* (1994), 255–256; J. C. McCann, Jr., "Book of Psalms," in L. E. Keck et al. (eds.), *The New Interpreter's Bible*, vol. 4 (1996), 990; M. E. Tate, *Psalms 51–100* (1990), 287.

the terms the text itself uses as labels for the psalm. In verse 1, "torah" is the term used in its broad sense of teaching, direction, or instruction, here used parallel to "words of my mouth." In verse 5, "torah" has to do with particular commands and ordinances. Parables and riddles also characterize the psalm; these also are words associated with wisdom and instruction. The psalm's historical recital is a riddle in the sense that it reveals the continuing mystery of divine grace and human frailty. The psalm creates the historical memory of the mighty acts of God, which, when remembered, bring great wonder. This salvation history calls each generation to respond to the divine call for faithfulness. Psalm 78 seeks to pass this memory on to the next generation so they might see its power for its day. The recitation is more than a description of the past; it is a rehearsal of the past so that the present and future might be wondrous. The psalm is more than information; it is the experience of a drama that calls for response from the congregation.

Verses 5–11 characterize the historical tradition specifically in terms of covenant, with the terms "covenant" and "torah" used as parallels in verse 10. YHWH initiated a covenant relationship with the faith community of ancient Israel and, as a gracious gift, gave them "torah" as a means of faithful response. That covenant relationship is to be passed on to each new generation in the community. Fullness of life is found in living out this covenant relationship, and so the future depends on remembering it in every generation. Ancestors forgot the covenant relationship (vv. 8, 11) based on the mighty acts of God. Ephraim, the major tribe of the Northern Kingdom, is singled out for retreating in battle. No specific event is indicated. The psalm operates from the perspective of Judah, the Southern Kingdom, and its Davidic dynasty as the faithful covenant partners. The psalm's view is that the Northern Kingdom of Israel continually broke the covenant with YHWH. This first part of the psalm articulates its purpose in terms of warning and thereby prefigures much of what is to follow in the historical recitals. The clear call is not to be like the faithless ancestors but to hear the history of the faith tradition and live by it: keep the covenant faithfully, for therein is wholeness of life.

The first major recital of history, verses 12–39, focuses on the wilderness traditions. Already the people have forgotten the mighty acts of God they witnessed in Egypt, "in the fields of Zoan." Zoan is a city in northern Egypt, though in the biblical tradition there is no recounting of events there. The psalm recounts the Exodus from Egypt with the crossing of the sea on dry ground and then the people being led by the cloud by day and the fire by night. God provided them with water in the wilderness, even water from rocks. Even in the face of such liberation and provisions, the people still rebelled against God in the wilderness, as recounted in the books of Exodus and Numbers. God had provided water, but could God provide bread and meat? Apparently the people did not yet trust God. In this recounting of historical memory, it appears that the people have forgotten the wondrous deeds of the Most High God, deeds that initiated their journey and their relationship.

The poem recounts God's pained response of anger against this faithless wilderness generation (vv. 21–22). Still, God provided manna from the heavens, described as "the grain of heaven" and "the bread of angels," in abundance. Then God provided birds for food until the people were well satisfied. Along with these provisions, however, there were still consequences from the wilderness rebellions. The narrative portions of the Hebrew scriptures recount in texts like Numbers 11 the encounter with death reflected in Ps 78:31, 34. Still the people rebelled, so their years became a terror. Then they remembered their liberator, though – to judge from verses 36–37 – their repentance was halfhearted. They spoke the necessary words to God but did not really live out their covenant relationship. YHWH, remembering human frailty ("that they were but flesh," v. 39), continued to restrain anger and be merciful and forgiving in the tradition of the confession in Exod 34:6–7.

The second major historical recital, in verses 40–72, again recounts the Exodus from Egypt and the journey to the land. It begins by summarizing again the rebellions in the wilderness to provide a transition back to the deliverance from Egypt by way of divine signs and wonders. The focus is on the plague traditions; the narrative account is in Exodus 7–12. First there was the turning of the river to blood and then the plagues of insects and frogs. Caterpillars and locusts then appeared, followed by hail and thunderstorms. The culmination of the tradition is the death of the firstborn. The plagues are portrayed in the psalm as expressions of fierce divine anger. Then God brought the people out of Egyptian bondage and through the wilderness and into the land promised to their ancestors. Even with the people in the land, they continued to rebel against the one who brought them out of bondage. This rebellion, "like their ancestor," is characterized as idolatry, and divine wrath was the consequence (vv. 58–59). The destruction of the sanctuary at Shiloh demonstrated the divine abandonment of the people. They were given over to the power of the sword and defeated. The "glory" in verse 61 is a reference to the Ark of the Covenant and its capture in the defeat narrated in 1 Samuel 4. Defeat was the order of the day.

Suddenly, verses 65–66 recount in stunning imagery that YHWH awoke like an intoxicated warrior and routed the foe. The divine warrior brought victory to Judah and Mount Zion, in contrast to the Northern Kingdom of Israel (Joseph/Ephraim). God was present with the people on Mount Zion, with the Davidic kings ruling in Jerusalem as the representatives of YHWH. David and his descendants brought hope and stability to the congregation. The psalm's perspective is clearly that of a Davidic Jerusalem of the Southern Kingdom.

Bridging the Horizons: Learning from the Past

Psalm 78 embodies the rehearsal of the story of faith for the worshiping community. It passes on the faith tradition of the ancestors. The poem thus serves a central educational purpose for communities of faith. In this psalm, the recital of history is not so much about passing along information as it is about learning the lessons of that history; that didactic purpose shapes the historical recital. Memory serves hope for the present and future. The historical recitals in Psalm 78 focus on two mistakes of past generations: (1) lack of trust in God to provide in the wilderness and (2) idolatry. Both mistakes reject the living God and the covenant relationship between God and the faith community of ancient Israel. Both have to do with the loss of memory, with forgetting the relationship that gives identity and hope.

The element of Psalm 78 that will trouble some readers is the imagery of divine wrath. The psalm typifies the tension between divine judgment and grace. The recital of salvation history holds out the hope that the people can reorient life and learn the lesson of the faithlessness of earlier generations and live out of divine grace and covenant identity and hope. The honest recitals of history in Psalm 78 make it clear that the people of God encounter judgment in life, but the confession of ancient Israel in the Psalter is that the divine anger endures for a moment while the divine favor endures for a lifetime. To put the matter in other words, God's "no" to the community is always in the context of God's "yes" to the community.

PSALM 79 – A PSALM OF ASAPH

¹ O God, the nations have come into your inheritance;
    they have defiled your holy temple;
    they have laid Jerusalem in ruins.
² They have given the bodies of your servants
    to the birds of the air for food,
    the flesh of your faithful to the wild animals of the earth.
³ They have poured out their blood like water
    all around Jerusalem,
    and there was no one to bury them.
⁴ We have become a taunt to our neighbors,
    mocked and derided by those around us.

⁵ How long, O LORD? Will you be angry for ever?
    Will your jealous wrath burn like fire?
⁶ Pour out your anger on the nations
    that do not know you,

and on the kingdoms
   that do not call on your name.
⁷ For they have devoured Jacob
   and laid waste his habitation.

⁸ Do not remember against us the iniquities of our ancestors;
   let your compassion come speedily to meet us,
   for we are brought very low.
⁹ Help us, O God of our salvation,
   for the glory of your name;
deliver us, and forgive our sins,
   for your name's sake.
¹⁰ Why should the nations say,
   'Where is their God?'
Let the avenging of the outpoured blood of your servants
   be known among the nations before our eyes.

¹¹ Let the groans of the prisoners come before you;
   according to your great power preserve those doomed to die.
¹² Return sevenfold into the bosom of our neighbors
   the taunts with which they taunted you, O LORD!
¹³ Then we your people, the flock of your pasture,
   will give thanks to you for ever;
   from generation to generation we will recount your praise.

The "Songs of Zion" (Psalms 46, 48, and 76), grounded in the liturgy of YHWH's presence in the Jerusalem temple as in 1 Kgs 8:1–13, assumed the full presence of YHWH in Jerusalem. From that affirmation, the guaranteed protection and safety of the temple in the city to perpetuity was also assumed. That conviction, moreover, was reinforced by the miraculous rescue of the city from the threat of the Assyrians, reflected in Isa 37:33–35, 36–38. The city and the temple were taken to be guaranteed beyond all the threats and vagaries of the historical process.

In the end, however, that theological conviction that had become ideological certitude could not restrain or veto the jeopardy that arises in the midst of history, for in fact – fact in the face of theological conviction – the city and the temple were razed by the Babylonian armies, armies that were able to do a century later what the Assyrian armies had been unable to accomplish (2 Kgs 25:8–21; Jer 39:1–10). The holy city was destroyed and the temple of Presence was burned. The assumed inviolability of Jerusalem turned out to be no longer credible.

Psalm 79 is a poem of anger and grief at the loss of Jerusalem and its temple, a poem that lives in the context of the artistic limits of the book of Lamentations. The poem as communal lament falls into two conventional parts, *complaint* (vv. 1–5) and *petition* (vv. 6–12), followed by an anticipated resolution of grief in *praise* and anger in *thanks* (v. 13).

The complaint is a characteristic description of the wretchedness of the situation left in the wake of the Babylonian armies (vv. 1–5). The most noticeable rhetorical feature in verses 1–3 is the recurrence of the pronoun "you," addressed to YHWH, thus articulating that the primary loss is for YHWH, whose city and temple this is. The pronouns reflect the characteristic rhetorical strategy of establishing in the complaint that the loss is the loss *for YHWH*, and consequently YHWH can be expected to respond. The complaint builds from the adjective "defiled" (v. 1), referring to foreign contamination that renders the holy site unsuitable for divine habitation. The outcome of such profanation is that Israel is physically exposed to death (vv. 2–3) and culturally exposed to shame (v. 4). In verse 5, interestingly, the devastation is linked to YHWH's anger, so the blame for the disaster is not singularly against Babylon but also against YHWH, who has violated YHWH's own temple.

In verses 6–12, the prayer turns to a series of petitions, interspersed with a corresponding series of motivations that reinforce the imperatives addressed to YHWH. The positive imperatives ask YHWH to punish the perpetrators of defilement vigorously and brutally. In the midst of these petitions, verse 8 is a curious confession of sin that suggests that the divine anger in verse 5 is warranted. That confession, however, is in the service of a plea for compassion and help. The motif of shame voiced in verse 4 is reiterated in verse 10a in the mocking of Israel and its God.

The petitions are reinforced by motivations in verses 7, 8b, and 9b. What strikes one the most, however, is the unrestrained hunger for vengeance against the perpetrators (vv. 10–12). Here there is nothing of the notion that YHWH has acted in anger as in verse 5 or that Israel is guilty as in verse 8. Here it is all about the unbearable violence of Babylon and the need for direct, brutal retaliation against the empire. The appeal for sevenfold vengeance is reminiscent of the words of Lamech in Gen 4:23–24, a vengeance that is total, and appropriate to the initial violation. But clearly the assault is felt to be more than military and political. In fact, the destruction touches Israel's most elemental symbolic embodiment of a sense of identity, and so the vengeance is commensurate with the profound sense of loss.

Not until verse 13 does the psalm turn toward a resolution with the "then" of praise and thanks. The unrelieved hatred and unrestrained zeal of the psalm may by verse 13 be satiated, but it is clear that any satisfaction now embraced is not focused on forgiveness or on trust but on the satisfaction that comes from total fulfillment of a thirst for vengeance. The psalm, still inside temple ideology, assumes that YHWH is as zealous for the Lord's house as Israel is. Such an assumption, of course, must be kept unqualified by the thought of verse 5 and verse 8, that YHWH is implicated in the destruction or that Israel is guilty. The thirst for vengeance is a cry of righteous indignation rooted in an assumed innocence that has been wrongly violated.

A Closer Look: Wild Justice

Such a cry of vengeance seems morally objectionable in modern bourgeois culture. But such a hunger for vengeance is evident everywhere, even in the contemporary world, both in terms of personal yearning to see the perpetrator punished and in the public arena in terms of those who assault established order. Susan Jacoby has written of "wild justice," the kind of justice that takes retaliation into its own hands when it believes that ordered structures of society do not deliver adequate vengeance.[169] The use of this psalm does not permit us any air of moral superiority in the modern world, for in fact the raw nerve of vengeance is alive and well among us as it was in that ancient context.

Bridging the Horizons: Not So Remote

This psalm may strike the contemporary reader as remote from our own religious life. In addition to the fact that Judaism, in its liturgical practice, still observes the memory of the destruction of Jerusalem, we may suggest that in U.S. society the violent attack against the United States on "9/11" has something of the same emotional/moral significance that the destruction of Judah has for this psalm. The "terrorists" in the 9/11 assault attacked the central symbols of U.S. national "imperial" identity – the World Trade Center and the Pentagon – which function not unlike the temple in ancient Jerusalem. The response to 9/11 in the United States, moreover, included the same thirst for vengeance as this psalm does in response to 587 BCE. This is not to justify such contemporary responses but to observe that the psalm, in its toxic rhetoric, is not remote from our own public life. To be sure, other societies have suffered in like measure, some of them at the hands of U.S. power, notably in Hiroshima and in Dresden. For readers of this psalm in the United States, however, the analogy to 9/11 is illuminating and makes the edginess so evident in this psalm immediately accessible.

Bridging the Horizons: A Strategy for Seeking Justice

The thirst for vengeance in the psalm, as in Gen 4:23–24, is surely objectionable among us. Eric Zenger, however, has made a compelling case that such a thirst for vengeance is in fact a strategy for seeking justice.[170] The "sevenfold" reference in verse 12, moreover, calls the reader's attention to the teaching of forgiveness,

---

[169] Susan Jacoby, *Wild Justice: The Evolution of Revenge* (New York: Harper and Row, 1983).
[170] E. Zenger, *God of Vengeance* (1996).

which appeals to the same mathematics, only in the opposite direction (see Matt 18:22). Such a reversal from *sevenfold vengeance* to *sevenfold forgiveness* is nowhere on the horizon of this psalm because the shame and pain are still too palpable, as they often are when vengeance is raw and unresolved.

PSALM 80 – TO THE LEADER: ON LILIES, A COVENANT. OF ASAPH. A PSALM

¹ Give ear, O Shepherd of Israel,
   you who lead Joseph like a flock!
You who are enthroned upon the cherubim, shine forth
² before Ephraim and Benjamin and Manasseh.
Stir up your might,
   and come to save us!

³ Restore us, O God;
   let your face shine, that we may be saved.

⁴ O LORD God of hosts,
   how long will you be angry with your people's prayers?
⁵ You have fed them with the bread of tears,
   and given them tears to drink in full measure.
⁶ You make us the scorn of our neighbors;
   our enemies laugh among themselves.

⁷ Restore us, O God of hosts;
   let your face shine, that we may be saved.

⁸ You brought a vine out of Egypt;
   you drove out the nations and planted it.
⁹ You cleared the ground for it;
   it took deep root and filled the land.
¹⁰ The mountains were covered with its shade,
   the mighty cedars with its branches;
¹¹ it sent out its branches to the sea,

and its shoots to the River.
¹² Why then have you broken down its walls,
    so that all who pass along the way pluck its fruit?
¹³ The boar from the forest ravages it,
    and all that move in the field feed on it.

¹⁴ Turn again, O God of hosts;
    look down from heaven, and see;
have regard for this vine,
¹⁵   the stock that your right hand planted.
¹⁶ They have burned it with fire, they have cut it down;
    may they perish at the rebuke of your countenance.
¹⁷ But let your hand be upon the one at your right hand,
    the one whom you made strong for yourself.
¹⁸ Then we will never turn back from you;
    give us life, and we will call on your name.

¹⁹ Restore us, O Lᴏʀᴅ God of hosts;
    let your face shine, that we may be saved.

This psalm is a pathos-filled lament concerning a public devastation, perhaps with reference to the destruction of Jerusalem. It is dominated by the threefold refrain of verses 3, 7, and 19. That refrain voices a direct imperative asking God to give life in a circumstance of suffering and death. The God addressed, moreover, is "the Lord of hosts"; that is, the God of massive military capability. The refrain concludes with a wish for the face (life-giving presence) of God that echoes the old, priestly blessing of Num 6:22–26.

Where that petitionary refrain recurs, it is variously situated in the conventions of the complaint psalm. Verses 1–2, reinforced by the refrain of verse 3, are a petition that follows an extended address to God. The address identifies God as "shepherd of Israel," the one who will guard, protect, and seek Israel's good (see Psalm 23; Ezek 34:11–16). That shepherd God, moreover, is situated on a throne amid the cherubim in the Jerusalem temple (see 1 Kgs 6:23–28). Reference to the cherubim is no doubt an allusion to the Ark of the Covenant, which is understood as a throne for this powerful God. It is the mighty God of the temple, pledged to Israel, who is addressed here.

The petition in verses 1–3 is followed by a complaint in verses 4–6, again reinforced by the refrain in verse 7. The petition acknowledges that the current trouble is rooted in God's anger – an acknowledgment that comes close to a tacit confession of sin; that anger is implemented according to the "you" statements of verses 5 and 6. James Mays observes that "the prayer concentrates with a single focus on one thing and one thing alone – the divine "Thou."[171] God is directly responsible for the dire circumstances of Israel.

At this point, the psalm pauses in an unusual way in order to review the history of Israel with YHWH. Verses 8–11 detail the "saving history" of Israel with a metaphorical "vine." With this imagery, the psalm recalls the Exodus (v. 8a), the settlement of the land that displaced other peoples (vv. 8–9), and the prospering of Israel in the land of promises (vv. 10–11). The review is designed, rhetorically, in order to prepare for the "why then?" of verse 12 that attributes the current disorder to YHWH. The alleged action of YHWH in verse 12 is a stunning contradiction of the memory of verses 8–11. The God who loved and created Israel is now its destroyer. God has reversed field completely and given Israel over to destructive occupiers ("boars"). The movement from the positive memory to the current disaster is reminiscent of the song of the vineyard in Isa 5:1–7.

Thus verses 12–13 attest to the failure, loss, and misery of Israel. In turn, that situation evokes a vigorous appeal to God in verses 14–17 asking God to again reverse field and "have regard" again for the people now abandoned. That imperative address to YHWH, "turn," is reinforced in verse 16 with another descriptive complaint. The appeal in verse 17 would seem to be a reference to a king in Israel, asking God to support the king in efforts at political restoration. That allusion to kingship, however, is quite soft and without specificity. In any case, the psalm assumes that YHWH is able to and eventually will restore this people that has been abased by defeat and devastation. The "they" of verse 3 remains unidentified, yet another example of the way in which the laments of Israel variously fault YHWH (vv. 5–6) or the enemy (v. 16) with enacting the devastation. Either way, appeal is made to YHWH for restoration, for Israel has no alternative source of help.

As in Psalm 79, the "then" of verse 18 anticipates a time of well-being that will be caused by YHWH's restoration, enacted in a way that answers Israel's prayer. The promise of the "then" nicely corresponds to the plea of verse 14. YHWH is asked to "turn back" in order to restore Israel. Israel promises never to "turn away" from loyalty to YHWH. The double use of "turn" is reminiscent of Jer 3:1–4:4, Jer 8:4–6, and the uses in Ps 90:3, 13. In its most desperate moment, Israel appeals to YHWH, completely confident of a good future from YHWH, if only YHWH can be moved to action.

This psalm exhibits a sustained encounter of Israel with YHWH. It is YHWH who caused defeat for Israel (vv. 5–6) and may yet turn (v. 14). The one who may yet turn is the God who creates and then judges Israel (vv. 8–13). In the end, the psalm exhibits a confident trust in YHWH, who can create a future and who may yet be the good shepherd. Israel has no alternative and therefore entrusts itself to the very God who has "broken down its walls." The God who judges is the God who will save! It is this God whom Israel trusts in every season of its life!

[171] J. L. Mays, *Psalms* (1994), 264.

PSALM 81 – TO THE LEADER: ACCORDING TO THE GITTITH. OF ASAPH

¹ Sing aloud to God our strength;
 shout for joy to the God of Jacob.
² Raise a song, sound the tambourine,
 the sweet lyre with the harp.
³ Blow the trumpet at the new moon,
 at the full moon, on our festal day.
⁴ For it is a statute for Israel,
 an ordinance of the God of Jacob.
⁵ He made it a decree in Joseph,
 when he went out over the land of Egypt.

I hear a voice I had not known:
⁶ 'I relieved your shoulder of the burden;
 your hands were freed from the basket.
⁷ In distress you called, and I rescued you;
 I answered you in the secret place of thunder;
 I tested you at the waters of Meribah.
  Selah
⁸ Hear, O my people, while I admonish you;
 O Israel, if you would but listen to me!
⁹ There shall be no strange god among you;
 you shall not bow down to a foreign god.
¹⁰ I am the LORD your God,
 who brought you up out of the land of Egypt.
 Open your mouth wide and I will fill it.

¹¹ 'But my people did not listen to my voice;
 Israel would not submit to me.
¹² So I gave them over to their stubborn hearts,
 to follow their own counsels.
¹³ O that my people would listen to me,
 that Israel would walk in my ways!
¹⁴ Then I would quickly subdue their enemies,
 and turn my hand against their foes.
¹⁵ Those who hate the LORD would cringe before him,
 and their doom would last for ever.

¹⁶ I would feed you with the finest of the wheat,
and with honey from the rock I would satisfy you."

The traditional interpretive issues of type, setting, and structure are of particular interest in Psalm 81. The text begins with the praise of God and moves to an exhortation to hear God's instruction, so the psalm is best classified as a hymn of praise that includes a prophetic warning. The elements are similar to those in Psalms 50 and 95. Psalm 81 suggests a festival background. The blowing of the trumpets in verse 3 could well refer to that act at New Year's and the festal complex for the autumn that included Tabernacles, the Day of Atonement, and New Year's (Rosh Hashanah). Many commentators connect the psalm with the festival as established in Torah texts (Lev 23:23–36, 39–43; Deut 16:13–15). The psalm celebrates God's strength used on behalf of ancient Israel and then calls for a response of loyalty from the community, a response that has been absent. So, in the context of praise, the psalm calls for a renewal of the relationship between the covenant partners YHWH and ancient Israel. In terms of literary structure, verses 1–5 constitute the praise of God; the last line of verse 5 marks the transition to a prophetic warning in the form of direct divine speech; that is, an oracle. There are two parts to the oracle. The first (vv. 6–10) reminds the people of God's benevolent history with them and the second (vv. 11–16) portrays the people's faithlessness and calls for the renewal of the covenant relationship.

Psalm 81 is a part of the psalms of Asaph (Psalms 73–83). The two previous psalms are both laments of the community; Psalm 80 recounts the history of ancient Israel and petitions God to restore the community. Psalm 81 also attends to historical memory, but then moves in a rather different direction by calling the people to hear and respond to God's teaching as a way toward renewal.

The opening verses (vv. 1–5) of the psalm set the context as the praise of God. The text begins with the imperative call to praise: sing aloud, shout for joy, raise a song, sound the various instruments of praise, and blow the shofar. The forms of praise are singing, shouting, and making music with tambourine, lyre, harp, and trumpet. The praise is in the classic psalmic style of a call to praise followed by the reason for the praise, in this case designated with the particle *kî*, meaning "for" or "because," at the beginning of verse 4. The reason for praise is connected with divine "statute," "ordinance," and "decree," and verse 5 connects that instruction to the experience of deliverance from Egypt. The verse may refer to the Passover narrative, but it likely brings to mind for the community the whole experience of the Exodus and God's powerful conflict with the Egyptian Empire and its gods. The mighty acts of God on behalf of this faith community call for enthusiastic praise. The reason for joyful praise implies the divine claim on the people. God brought them out of bondage and created them as a covenant people, and so gave them life as the people of YHWH. The allusions to divine instruction provide a transition to the remainder of the psalm.

Historical memory pervades Psalm 81. God's title is the God of Jacob/Israel. The reference to Joseph suggests a connection with the northern tribes, and the psalm later holds connections to Sinai. Clearly now, however, the psalm is tied to the Jerusalem temple and festival celebrations there. Zion is the place of divine presence, and from there God instructs.

The concluding line of verse 5 is unusual. Apparently the liturgist hears an unknown voice, the divine voice, and that introduces the oracle in verses 6–16. The oracle begins with a lesson (vv. 6–10) on the salvation history centered on the Exodus from Egypt. The "burden" and "basket" of verse 6 refer to the bondage in Egypt from which God liberated the community. The psalm characterizes that memory in terms of the honest dialogue of faith: Israel cried out and God heard, came, and delivered (Exod 3:7–9). The last line of verse 7 refers to the Massah/Meribah incident in Exod 17:1–7 (see also Num 20:9–13; Deut 6:16; Pss 95:8–9; 106:32–33), where the people complain that there is no water. The dominant historical tradition is that the quarrelsome people tested God at Massah/Meribah, but Psalm 81 suggests that God tested Israel. Then the divine oracle calls on Israel to hear/listen. That seems to be the central theme of the psalm: "Hear, O Israel." God heard the people when they cried out in bondage and brought them out of Egypt. Now the call is for the people to hear; that is, to take to heart the divine instruction and find life in following it.

The particular instruction in this part of the oracle is the first commandment of the Decalogue: Israel is to worship no other gods. "Strange" or "foreign" gods are the idols of the surrounding nations. Verse 10 then recounts the prologue to the Decalogue indicating that YHWH their God brought them out of bondage in Egypt. This God who gave them life is the only God who can give life, and thus commands them to avoid other deities. The concluding line of verse 10 articulates a divine promise of filling an open mouth. Perhaps the reference is to food (see v. 16) or to the praise of God, alluding to verses 1–5. This first part of the oracle centers on the mighty acts of God to give ancient Israel life. The commands in verses 8–9 are surrounded by the recounting of the salvation history.

The concluding portion of the oracle (vv. 11–16) refers to the people in such a way as to assume the community memory recounted in the psalm's first ten verses. YHWH refers to Israel as "my people" in verses 8, 11, and 13. They are "my people" even when they are not listening to YHWH. This God had already initiated a covenant relationship with the people, and so they were already "my people." They have not lived that way, however. Their history with God is characterized by faithlessness. They have neither listened to God nor lived by divine instruction. Hearkening unto the divine voice and appropriating the divine instruction together lead to fullness of life, but Israel listened to their own words and lived in their own ways by following other gods. Even with this history, God now calls the congregation to listen and to live by God's covenant instruction. The renewal of this relationship is still possible for "my people."

This last section of the psalm has a lamenting tone. It is as if God grieves over the covenant disloyalty of the people. Their disloyalty is in terms of not listening. Still, Psalm 81 calls the people now to renew their relationship with YHWH by listening. Listening to God is central to the identity of Israel, and that theme seems to be the central one of this psalm. So the congregation envisioned in this psalm is at a point of deciding whether they will listen to God and renew their covenant relationship. The psalm sets a context similar to the book of Deuteronomy and the historical books based on it; see especially Deut 30:15–20. In a renewed relationship, the community will see the defeat of its enemies, who are also God's enemies, and encounter the blessings of a full life. The conclusion of the psalm holds out the blessings of covenant faithfulness. The psalm places before the community a life-determining decision.

A Closer Look: Memory and Hope

Memory is central to Psalm 81. The psalm recounts the community's history and seems to follow structures of covenant in the recounting. YHWH initiated this relationship with the deliverance from slavery in Egypt. The people are then called to respond by way of the divine covenant instruction, or *torah*, and there are consequences to their decision. So central to the covenant response is the act of listening to God. The sequence of the covenant structure is telling. The people do not follow divine instruction in order to become people of God but rather because they are already "my people"; that is, they live by way of *torah*. The Deuteronomic understanding of covenant seems to be in mind in Psalm 81. The famous Deut 6:4–9 calls the people to listen to the only living God and live accordingly: "Hear, O Israel." The first commandment of the Decalogue voices the same call with the injunction to worship only YHWH, who liberated them from Egyptian slavery. The consequences of Israel's past decisions are narrated in unmistakable ways in the book of Judges. They go after other gods and then suffer the consequences of servitude to other nations. Still, when they cry to God, God hears and helps them. In Psalm 81, the oracle suggests that God is not interested in dwelling on the past and Israel's history of disloyalty but rather on learning the lesson of history and moving beyond it to a new era of hearing. A new life and a renewed covenant are possible through listening to the divine voice. That is the hope of the psalm.

Bridging the Horizons: A Call to Faithfulness

The preceding exposition has noted the liturgical context envisioned in Psalm 81. The text begins by enthusiastically calling the community to celebrate the mighty acts of God to deliver. Then the liturgist moves to proclaim a divine

oracle. The praise of God in this psalm is not an empty "feel good" emotional-
ism; it includes a call to faithfulness. Praise and faithfulness are tied together in
the life of hearing God. People are inundated with many competing voices in
contemporary culture. The militant consumerism of society seeks to drown out
all the other voices and determine the path of life. Psalm 81 is a call to listen to
the divine voice (vv. 8 and 13) and live in line with its call. Christian tradition
in the New Testament renews that call to live in line with the reign of God as
revealed in Jesus Christ as the way of life.

PSALM 82 – A PSALM OF ASAPH

¹ God has taken his place in the divine council;
    in the midst of the gods he holds judgment:
² 'How long will you judge unjustly
    and show partiality to the wicked?
        Selah
³ Give justice to the weak and the orphan;
    maintain the right of the lowly and the destitute.
⁴ Rescue the weak and the needy;
    deliver them from the hand of the wicked.'

⁵ They have neither knowledge nor understanding,
    they walk around in darkness;
    all the foundations of the earth are shaken.

⁶ I say, 'You are gods,
    children of the Most High, all of you;
⁷ nevertheless, you shall die like mortals,
    and fall like any prince.'

⁸ Rise up, O God, judge the earth;
    for all the nations belong to you!

This psalm operates with mythopoetic assumptions common in Israel's world of
polytheism. It describes (imagines) a courtroom scene in the heavenly realm where
the gods dwell. The scene imagined is one in which the "high God" calls other
gods (godlets, angels) to accountability. The scene is called a "divine council," a

meeting place of many gods. In this scenario, the high God conducts an inquiry to determine the criteria for a real "godness" and to determine which gods may in fact qualify as real gods. Thus the court convenes (v. 1). The presiding judge of the court, the high creator God who is the God of Israel, functions as prosecutor and instructor of lesser gods, who are subject to the will of the presiding judge (vv. 2–4). The speech of the judge begins in verse 2 with two accusatory questions; the lesser gods have been unjust and favored the wicked, who characteristically are also the powerful and the wealthy. The judge does not wait for a response to the questions but proceeds immediately to instruct those "in the dock" in the proper role of a god. That proper role, so defining for Israel's faith and ethics, is to be guardian, protector, and guarantor of the vulnerable – the weak, the widow, the orphan, the lowly, the destitute – all those who lack the resources to sustain and protect themselves. In this instance, the text, in the mouth of the high God, provides criteria for the reliable "godness" of God. Godness consists in care for the vulnerable.

Quickly the instruction of verses 3–4 leads to a *verdict* in verse 5 and a *sentence* in verse 6. The verdict is that the lesser gods lack wisdom and understanding, and by their actions of injustice they have destabilized the world. The world depends for its order on the performance of justice on the earth and in heaven, and these gods have reneged on that assignment (v. 5). Therefore, gods who are phony and who do not perform as gods are sentenced to death (vv. 6–7). The high God is a sovereign who will not tolerate lesser gods who stray from the divine program for the cosmos. Thus the psalm imagines the destruction of the gods – and by implication human agents and social practices – that are aligned against the will of God in the practice of injustice. Such gods have no future and warrant no allegiance or obedience in the practice of the community.

By the end of verse 7, the dramatic, imaginative performance of the heavenly court is completed. The court is adjourned with the verdict of "guilty." Verse 8 speaks in another voice. This is a human voice, surely an Israelite voice of one who has observed the drama of the trial and has noted the happy outcome. On the basis of a reliable characterization of godness – justice! – the human speaker utters a petition to the judge: Rise up! Rise up and perform your judicial function in the human community. It is established that the high God cares about justice. Now the appeal of Israel is that the god who gives such a ruling needs to be active in the world over which this god presides in order that justice for the vulnerable should characterize the whole earth.

A Closer Look: A Heavenly Court Scene

This imaginative scenario in the psalm may strike a current reader as odd because of the heavenly court and because of the assumption of polytheism and contestation among the gods. Nevertheless, this imaginative imagery is pervasive in the Old Testament. The Old Testament did not easily arrive at monotheism.[172] Once one grants the assumption of polytheism, the contest for adjudication among the gods becomes inescapable. But the surprising matter is that the criterion for adjudication among the gods is precisely justice for the vulnerable.

From this it is easy to see, on the one hand, that the gospel narratives of the New Testament attest to the claim that Jesus is "of God," for Jesus' characteristic actions are for the poor and the needy. Jesus does the things that God does, and so in the end is confessed by the church as "true God."

On the other hand, this characterization of God is crucial for the church's confession of "God's preferential option for the poor." Whereas the condemned show "partiality" to the wicked, the true God, it is asserted, is to show partiality toward the poor and the weak. In this way, the requirement of the gods is congruent with the core requirement of Israel to care for the vulnerable. God, like Israel, is held to that standard of justice.

A Closer Look: The Heavenly Company

The literature on the divine council can be consulted through the work of Patrick Miller and Theodore Mullen.[173] It is to be noted, however, that this language also permeates the hymnody of the church, with its great vision of the heavenly company. Whereas the two hymns that we cite here celebrate in awed obedience, the psalm imagines the same company of heaven to be recalcitrant against the will of the high God for justice:

Ye watchers and ye holy ones,
Bright seraphs, cherubim, and thrones,
Raise the glad strain, Alleluia!
Cry out, dominions, prince-doms, powers,
Virtues, archangels, angels' choirs,
Alleluia! Alleluia!
O higher than the cherubim,
More glorious than the seraphim,

---

[172] On the complex issue of the emergence of monotheism in ancient Israel, see Mark S. Smith, *The Origins of Biblical Monotheism: Israel's Polytheistic Background and the Ugaritic Texts* (Oxford: Oxford University Press, 2003); and Patrick D. Miller, *The Religion of Ancient Israel* (Louisville, KY: Westminster John Knox Press, 2000), Chapter 1.

[173] Patrick D. Miller, Jr., *Genesis 1–11: Studies in Structure & Theme* (JSOTSup 8; Sheffield: Sheffield Department of Biblical Studies, 1978), Chapter 1; and E. Theodore Mullen, *The Divine Council in Canaanite and Early Hebrew Literature* (Chico, CA: Scholars Press, 1980).

Lead their praises, Alleluia!
Thou bearer of the eternal Word,
Most gracious, magnify the Lord,
Alleluia! Alleluia![174]

* * *

King of kings, yet born of Mary,
As of old on earth He stood,
Lord of lords, in human vesture,
In the body and the blood,
He will give to all the faithful
His own self for heavenly food.
Rank on rank the host of heaven
Spreads its vanguard on the way,
As the Light of Light descendeth
From the realms of endless day,
That the powers of hell may vanish
As the darkness clears away.
At His feet the six-winged seraph;
Cherubim, with sleepless eye,
Veil their faces to the presence,
As with cease-less voice they cry,
Alleluia, Alleluia, Alleluia, Lord Most High![175]

Bridging the Horizons: Poem for the Oppressed

Hugo Assmann has shown the way in which the issue of false gods who operate on phony mandates is pertinent to contemporary life. His poetry arises in
the context of a liberation hermeneutic but is completely congruent with the
psalm:

The God of the Rich and the God of the Poor Are Not the Same God

But it so happens that this history
     of Jewish monotheism
  is not always told correctly,
  because right there in Israel
  the one God,
     the God of liberation for slaves,
  again became a rallying point

---

[174] "Ye Watchers and Ye Holy Ones," by John Athelstan Laurie Riley.
[175] "Let All Mortal Flesh Keep Silence," from the Liturgy of St. James.

of oppressors against oppressed
(and only now and then
    of the oppressed against oppressors).
At this point God is thought to have reasoned:
    "They did not understand that time,
    they have not yet understood the side that I took.
    So, I shall take sides
        once and for all,
        definitively."[176]

*   *   *

The true idolatry
    is not that of nonbelievers,
is not that of atheists
    (who are often those who
    destroy idols
    and are fighting against idols).
Idols are
    the gods of oppression.
Idols are
    the shining fetishes
    with divine names
    and broad smiles,
        with creeds,
        with worship,
        with prayers,
        with laws,
        with sacred and divine power,
                    power to oppress,
                    power to exploit,
                    power to kill.
The dominators,
the idolatrous,
    will never make the mistake
        of declaring themselves atheists
        (of their idols) –
    God, Homeland, and Family,
    Tradition, Family, and Property.
The family that prays together stays together
        without work,
        without food,

---

[176] Hugo Assmann, in Pablo Richard (ed.), *The Idols of Death and the God of Life* (Maryknoll, NY: Orbis Books, 1983), 202–203.

      without housing,
        without good health.
   In God we Trust. Amen.[177]

PSALM 83 – A SONG. A PSALM OF ASAPH

¹ O God, do not keep silence;
  do not hold your peace or be still, O God!
² Even now your enemies are in tumult;
  those who hate you have raised their heads.
³ They lay crafty plans against your people;
  they consult together against those you protect.
⁴ They say, 'Come, let us wipe them out as a nation;
  let the name of Israel be remembered no more.'
⁵ They conspire with one accord;
  against you they make a covenant –
⁶ the tents of Edom and the Ishmaelites,
  Moab and the Hagrites,
⁷ Gebal and Ammon and Amalek,
  Philistia with the inhabitants of Tyre;
⁸ Assyria also has joined them;
  they are the strong arm of the children of Lot.
     Selah

⁹ Do to them as you did to Midian,
  as to Sisera and Jabin at the Wadi Kishon,
¹⁰ who were destroyed at En-dor,
  who became dung for the ground.
¹¹ Make their nobles like Oreb and Zeeb,
  all their princes like Zebah and Zalmunna,
¹² who said, 'Let us take the pastures of God
  for our own possession.'

¹³ O my God, make them like whirling dust,
  like chaff before the wind.

---

[177] H. Assmann, in P. Richard (ed.), *Idols of Death and the God of Life* (1983), 204–205.

¹⁴ As fire consumes the forest,
   as the flame sets the mountains ablaze,
¹⁵ so pursue them with your tempest
   and terrify them with your hurricane.
¹⁶ Fill their faces with shame,
   so that they may seek your name, O Lord.
¹⁷ Let them be put to shame and dismayed for ever;
   let them perish in disgrace.
¹⁸ Let them know that you alone,
   whose name is the Lord,
   are the Most High over all the earth.

Book III of the Psalter includes several community laments, of which Psalm 83 is a good example. Readers can imagine the psalm used in an ancient liturgical setting in which worship leaders pray for God to deliver the community from oppressive enemies round about. The list of enemies appears to be a summary list of enemies of YHWH and ancient Israel, and so it is difficult to assign a particular crisis or date as background for the prayer. The psalm exemplifies the category of community laments. It begins with an opening plea and moves to *complaint*, painting a picture of a crisis with major emphasis on the enemies. The enemies are nations surrounding Israel, and so this community fears for its future and the future of YHWH's story with Israel. Then the psalm moves to *petition* that God will defeat the enemies and deliver this congregation. The petitions intensify as the psalm comes to a close. Verses 1–8 focus on complaint and are followed by petitions in two parts (vv. 9–12 and 13–18). Historical memory is central to the psalm.

A Closer Look: A Conclusion to the Psalms of Asaph

Psalm 83 concludes the collection of psalms of Asaph (Psalms 73–83) that begins Book III. The collection begins with Psalm 73 and issues of divine justice for the individual; Psalm 83 concludes the collection by raising similar issues for the community. The psalm also has connections with Psalm 82, which ends with the call for God to judge the earth. Psalm 83 ends with a prayer that even the enemies of Israel will know that the Most High reigns "over all the earth." The psalm lists "the nations" (Ps 82:8) and prays that they will all come under the rule of the Most High, a divine title emphasizing divine rule. This theme of divine judgment characterizes the psalms of Asaph.

Ancient Israel's prayer is characterized by complaint and petition. The psalm begins in verses 1–8 with an opening plea but moves to *complaint* centered on the enemies. The crisis has been going on for some time, and there has been nothing but silence from God. The first verse emphasizes the divine name (*ĕlōhîm*) by using it in the vocative to begin and end the plea that God not remain silent. The divine silence is in contrast to the "tumult" caused by the enemies. The prayer opens with the plea for God's engagement with the worshiping community in the midst of this raucous attack from enemies. The portrayal of the enemies in verses 2–5 brings to mind the portrayal in Psalm 2. Such enemies of the divine king and the community pervade the congregation's prayers for help in the Psalter. Opposition to God's purposes continues without end as enemies conspire and plot against God and God's people. Verses 2 and 5, beginning with an emphatic particle, emphasize opposition to God, whereas verses 3–4 emphasize opposition to ancient Israel. Verse 5 uses the language of covenant; the enemies "cut a covenant" to formalize their conspiracy against God and Israel. The purpose put in the mouth of the enemies in verse 4 is to destroy Israel. That would end Israel's witness to divine engagement with the congregation and in turn divine engagement with history on a broader scale. The complaint suggests that the divine reputation and reign are at stake in this crisis. The complaint uses very persuasive poetry.

The naming of the enemies in verses 6–8 is rather unusual in the lament psalms. Tate suggests that the listing of ten enemy nations is a summary for the sake of the liturgy and represents enemies that surround Israel from the south to the north in the Transjordan and then over to Phoenicia and back down the coast to the Philistines.[178] The number of enemies also suggests the dire straits Israel faces in this crisis and thus the need for divine help. The nations listed are known in the biblical tradition though they are not elsewhere listed as members of an enemy alliance. Two names are not common. The Hagrites are named in 1 Chronicles 5 as a group in the northern Transjordan, and Gebal is often identified as the city of Byblos on the coast of Lebanon. Genesis 19:36–38 identifies "the children of Lot" as the Moabites and Edomites, strengthened by the powerful armies of Assyria.

With verse 9, the psalm shifts from complaint to *petition*. The plea is that God will do to this list of enemies just what God has done to enemies in the past. Psalm 83 continues to call on Israel's historical memory, especially in the Deuteronomic tradition. The psalm alludes to narratives in Judges 4–8 and Gideon's defeat of Midian and the Midianite leaders Oreb, Zeeb, Zebah, and Zalmunna, as well as the defeat of the Canaanites Jabin and Sisera at the Wadi Kishon. The psalm alludes to the mighty acts of God in ancient Israel's historical memory to bolster the petition for divine action to destroy the enemies, and their leaders, listed in the psalm's complaint. Verse 12 quotes the enemies as claiming the purpose of taking over God's pastures, the pasture lands for God's flock Israel; that purpose is in line with the portrayal of the enemies in verses 1–8. They seek to attack God and seek to destroy God's covenant partner Israel. This petition in verses 9–12 that God act against the enemies seeks deliverance for Israel. The faith tradition characterizes YHWH as the

---

[178] M. E. Tate, *Psalms 51–100* (1990), 345, 347; see also J. L. Mays, *Psalms* (1994), 272.

one who tamed chaos and brought order and also as the one who delivered Israel from slavery in Egypt to create the covenant people. The petition calls for this historical tradition to come to fruition in the current crisis.

Verses 9–12 call to mind the mighty acts of God in history to envision the defeat of historical enemies. Verses 13–18 call on powerful destructions in nature as a basis for petitions for divine help. In verse 13, the petition is that the enemies will be blown away like chaff or like dust (or tumbleweed) that the wind blows away. Verse 14 hopes that the enemies will be consumed by fire and in verse 15 by storm and hurricane. The plea is for quick and full destruction of the enemies, bringing shame and disgrace on these oppressive enemies. Interestingly, the psalm concludes with a universal note. Verse 16 articulates a motive for the shaming of the enemies as the hope that they will seek God, and the psalm's concluding verse petitions that the nations will come to know that YHWH the Most High rules "over all the earth." The summary petition then is that the reign of God will become manifest.

Bridging the Horizons: An Honest Struggle

Psalm 83 is not a favorite prayer for contemporary use. It is, however, an example of prayer in the midst of a crisis for the community. The prayer is both honest and specific, probably reasons for its lack of use in contemporary communities. In a straightforward style, the psalm publicly claims the pain of the trouble and places it with God in characteristic forms of complaint and petition. So the psalm exemplifies the honest dialogue of faith and thus teaches about prayer and faith. The explicit honesty of the prayer will trouble some contemporary readers. The petitions against enemies are addressed to the divine warrior and so raise the problem of imprecations against enemies that arises in a number of psalms.

The Psalms make it clear that people of God are called to oppose injustice and evil in the world and that powers who oppose God, God's purposes, and God's communities pervade life. One of the difficulties with the imprecatory psalms is that it is simple for any community to assume that their enemies are God's enemies. Psalm 83 suggests a candid look at life and a candid dialogue with God. Some injustices and evil are clear and are to be opposed and included in the dialogue with God. Other issues are not so clear and are to become a part of the honest struggle with God in prayer. It is also worth repeating that verses 16 and 18 suggest the hope that the enemies will come to know God and God's reign. That motivation suggests a context for human opposition to evil. Although the psalm is plainly in opposition to the enemies, it suggests that any final decisions about enemies lie with the Most High, who reigns "over all the earth." The psalm does not encourage violence or personal vengeance but suggests that the final reality in this dialogue is the justice and reign of God. Communities that appropriate prayers such as Psalm 83 can then learn to stand for justice and the reign of God.

PSALM 84 – TO THE LEADER: ACCORDING TO THE GITTITH. OF THE KORAHITES. A PSALM

¹ How lovely is your dwelling place,
  O Lord of hosts!
² My soul longs, indeed it faints
  for the courts of the Lord;
my heart and my flesh sing for joy
  to the living God.

³ Even the sparrow finds a home,
  and the swallow a nest for herself,
  where she may lay her young,
at your altars, O Lord of hosts,
  my King and my God.
⁴ Happy are those who live in your house,
  ever singing your praise.
    Selah

⁵ Happy are those whose strength is in you,
  in whose heart are the highways to Zion.
⁶ As they go through the valley of Baca
  they make it a place of springs;
  the early rain also covers it with pools.
⁷ They go from strength to strength;
  the God of gods will be seen in Zion.

⁸ O Lord God of hosts, hear my prayer;
  give ear, O God of Jacob!
    Selah
⁹ Behold our shield, O God;
  look on the face of your anointed.

¹⁰ For a day in your courts is better
  than a thousand elsewhere.
I would rather be a doorkeeper in the house of my God
  than live in the tents of wickedness.
¹¹ For the Lord God is a sun and shield;
  he bestows favor and honor.

No good thing does the LORD withhold
   from those who walk uprightly.
¹² O LORD of hosts,
   happy is everyone who trusts in you.

The Zion songs (Psalms 46, 48, 76, 84, 87, and 122) celebrate the divine presence
in Zion, the Jerusalem temple. From that sacred place, YHWH gives life to the
community. This psalm articulates anticipation of being in that place and envisions
arriving there. Most interpreters suggest that the psalm reflects a pilgrimage to a
temple festival either at the beginning of the pilgrimage or at the point of arrival
at the temple. The speaker may well envision standing at the gates of the holy city
and thus arriving in Jerusalem, seeing the sanctuary, and celebrating its significance. The psalm reflects worship in Jerusalem during the Davidic monarchy. The
movement of the psalm is simple but important. Its beginning and end (vv. 1–4 and
10–12) anticipate entering the temple for the powerful experience of worship. Verses
5–7 reflect back on the journey toward the sanctuary, and verses 8–9 voice a petition
on behalf of YHWH's anointed.

A Closer Look: A Korahite Psalm

The heading of Psalm 84 places it among the psalms of the Korahites. The psalms
of Asaph and the Elohistic Psalter come to an end with Psalm 83. The first collection of Korahite psalms is in Psalms 42–49 in Book II of the Hebrew Psalter.
Psalms 84–85 and 87–88 are also part of this collection, and are included in Book
III. Korah was the leader of a guild of psalmists. Psalm 84 brings to mind the
first Korahite psalms, Psalms 42–43, with the images that anticipate worship in
the sanctuary and with the yearning to encounter the divine presence. Michael
Goulder has proposed a setting for the psalms of the Korahites – the autumn
festival at the sanctuary of Dan in the Northern Kingdom in the tenth through
the ninth centuries BCE.[179] The proposal is highly speculative, and whereas the
Korahite psalms use a variety of traditions, including those from the Northern
Kingdom, Psalm 84 is clearly attached to the Jerusalem cult.

Verses 1–4. The psalm begins with an exclamation of the beauty of the place of
YHWH's tabernacling presence. The speaker expresses powerful anticipation of
worship there; it may well be that the city or temple comes into view and the poetry
envisions the joy of that moment. It is the divine presence that makes the place and
its worship so powerful. The yearning and anticipation are strong. Verse 3 uses the

---

[179] M. D. Goulder, *The Psalms of the Sons of Korah: A Study in the Psalter* (JSOTSup 20;
Sheffield: JSOT, 1982).

image of small birds to articulate the care of this one who is called king: even the sparrow and swallow will find places to nest in the courts of YHWH. The powerful divine king provides safety and shelter in this holy place. How joyful it would be to lodge forever in the sanctuary and continually sing praise to the God who gives life. The anticipation is for the joy of worship and the protection of the divine presence for those on pilgrimage to worship on Zion.

A Closer Look: YHWH of Armies

The divine title "Lord of Hosts" is used in Ps 84:1, 3, 8, and 12. A literal rendering would be "YHWH of armies," with the armies or hosts referring to the angelic heavenly hosts, the heavenly hosts of sun, moon, and stars, or the hosts of Israel's armies. The title suggests the great God of military might and victory, who is powerfully present on Zion.

Verses 5–7. Verses 4 and 5 begin with a term that introduces a beatitude ("Happy are"). It has connections with Old Testament wisdom traditions and introduces an observation on life. The observations here relate to worship on Zion. Those who anticipate a pilgrimage to worship and those who are in worship and sing praises to YHWH and find strength in the divine presence know joy in life. Verses 5–7 reflect on the journey to Zion. As the people move through the pilgrimage to the place of special divine presence, they see renewal along the way from the refreshing rains. They move "from strength to strength," and the anticipation grows. The journey may be long and difficult, but the anticipation of encountering the presence of God in Zion brings hope and expectation.

Verses 8–9. These verses voice a petition for God's anointed, the king. The Davidic king is God's representative chosen to rule over the people in Jerusalem and therefore the one who guarantees justice in the community and speaks God's word to the community. So the king is "our shield," and the petitioner prays for God's support of this leader of the community. In the Psalter, petition is a characteristic mode of speech for those who anticipate the encounter with the divine in worship.

Verses 10–12. Verse 10 affirms the familiar view that one day in the temple precincts is far better than a thousand days anywhere else. Anticipation of an encounter with the divine presence is again in view, and the psalm beams that the shortest time and the minimum way of enjoying the presence of God is incomparably superior to the pleasure of the greatest opulence. A lowly position in the sanctuary is far superior to the highest position among the wicked. "The tents of wickedness" suggest not a specific place but any setting in which the guide is service of the self rather than service of God. The divine presence provides the light and warmth of the sun and the protection of the shield (see v. 9), and so it provides nurture for abundant life. Verses 10–11 have in view a holistic view of life; whole, healthy, complete life in all its dimensions. The conclusion of verse 11 ties this life to integrity. Encounter with the divine presence in worship can make possible an integration of the various dimensions of life and its hopes. The final verse of the psalm returns to the form of a beatitude (see vv. 4–5), articulating the hope that trust in the divine presence will bring joy.

A Closer Look: Sacrament

Psalm 84 is about the presence of YHWH on Zion. The book of Psalms, in several places, anticipates encountering the divine presence in worship:

> One thing I asked of the Lord, that will I seek after:
> to live in the house of the Lord all the days of my life,
> to behold the beauty of the Lord and to inquire in his temple. (Ps 27:4)

> My soul thirsts for God, for the living God.
> When shall I come and behold the face of God? (Ps 42:2)

The speaker in Psalm 84 anticipates the temple worship event. These texts make it clear that it is the encounter with the divine presence that makes the event and the place so significant, so these texts yearn for that life-giving event. The actions in worship and the place become visible means of encountering the wholeness of life that only YHWH can give. In Christian tradition, the language of sacrament fits the experience. These events are public events of pilgrimage and festival and thus are communal and not private events. These festival events, and their pilgrimages, can center the community and its faithful to make possible life as God has created and blessed it. Psalm 84 and the other Zion songs express anticipation of these occasions. The anticipation comes out of reflection in preparation for the powerful experience of worship. In Psalm 84, that reflection leads to a petition for the leader of the community.

PSALM 85 – TO THE LEADER. OF THE KORAHITES. A PSALM

¹ LORD, you were favorable to your land;
  you restored the fortunes of Jacob.
² You forgave the iniquity of your people;
  you pardoned all their sin.
  Selah

³ You withdrew all your wrath;
   you turned from your hot anger.

⁴ Restore us again, O God of our salvation,
   and put away your indignation toward us.
⁵ Will you be angry with us for ever?
   Will you prolong your anger to all generations?
⁶ Will you not revive us again,
   so that your people may rejoice in you?
⁷ Show us your steadfast love, O LORD,
   and grant us your salvation.

⁸ Let me hear what God the LORD will speak,
   for he will speak peace to his people,
   to his faithful, to those who turn to him in their hearts.
⁹ Surely his salvation is at hand for those who fear him,
   that his glory may dwell in our land.

¹⁰ Steadfast love and faithfulness will meet;
   righteousness and peace will kiss each other.
¹¹ Faithfulness will spring up from the ground,
   and righteousness will look down from the sky.
¹² The LORD will give what is good,
   and our land will yield its increase.
¹³ Righteousness will go before him,
   and will make a path for his steps.

This psalm is an offer of a prayer that confidently anticipates a positive, world-transforming response to prayer from God. It is a lament because it acknowledges alienation from God in verses 4–7, but it has none of the "edgy" elements of accusation and imperative that so often occur in this genre of prayer. It is rather a very straightforward act of piety that trusts God and awaits God's good pleasure.

Before uttering its petition in verses 4–7, the prayer addresses YHWH and makes five "you statements" concerning God that evidence YHWH's past graciousness (vv. 1–3). Perhaps these statements are to remind YHWH of past acts of generosity as in Ps 22:3–5. More likely they are simply testimony of the grounds on which the following petitions are based. In this remembrance, it is recalled that YHWH has in the past transformed Israel's life by way of forgiveness and pardon, which has overridden all of YHWH's anger and wrath. In sum, these verses are an assertion that YHWH is a God who forgives.

On the basis of that confident memory, the psalm now seeks forgiveness by issuing four imperative prayers around the verbs "restore, put away, show, grant" (vv.
4–7). In the midst of these imperatives grounded in past divine mercy, the psalmist
addresses three questions concerning YHWH:

Will you be angry forever?
Will YHWH prolong anger?
Will YHWH revive us again?

The answers, offered in hope, are provided in verses 1–3:

- No, YHWH will not be angry forever.
- No, YHWH will not prolong anger.
- Yes, YHWH will revive us again.

The confidence with which these questions are asked – with answers implied – is
grounded in the very character of YHWH. YHWH is not a God who remains in
alienation but is a God, as Israel knows from its past, who is seeking restoration of
the covenant with Israel and therefore restoration of Israel to its land.

In verse 8, the psalm turns; the psalmist has said what needs to be said and now
awaits the divine response. The wait is made in complete confidence, for the psalmist already knows from the past what God will say. It will be a word of well-being
(*shalom*) that is available to those who are faithful to YHWH. And because YHWH
will speak *shalom*, salvation will come to Israel and divine presence (glory) will be
reestablished in the land after a season of alienation. It is commonly assumed that
this verse and what follows are the verses of a single speaker, perhaps a creden-
tialed religious leader, who responds to Israel's questions in verses 5–6. This speaker
promises *shalom* and so is to be reckoned as one of the "*shalom* promisers" who is
rooted in Jerusalem theology and who anticipates that God is the guarantor of well-
being for the community.

The remainder of the psalm is a remarkable act of assurance. Although verses
10–13 might be taken as a divine oracle of assurance (salvation oracle) that responds
to the preceding petition, there is no indication that this is divine utterance. Indeed
YHWH is spoken of in the third person. This is rather a continuation of the statement of confidence on the part of the petitioners that began in verse 8. In this statement of confidence in YHWH's good intentions, the petitioners imagine a world of
complete harmony and reconciliation and speak about the coming world of well-
being as a gift of YHWH. This speech is accomplished by using the great terms of
covenant fidelity. The reconciliation sought between Israel and God is dramatically
voiced as harmony between steadfast love (*ḥesed*) and faithfulness (*amunah*). These
two initial terms in verse 10 constitute a recurring word pair in the Old Testament
that speaks of YHWH's utter fidelity, which is peculiarly known in the Jerusalem

establishment (see Ps 89:14, 24, 33). That word pair, so familiar in Scripture, is followed by a rather curious word pair, righteousness (*sedeqah*) and peace (*shalom*). These terms do not usually come together, but both speak of a completely harmonized world as a gift of God. In verse 11, the poem picks up the terms from verse 10 and arranges them in a new pair, faithfulness (*amunah*) and righteousness (*sedeqah*). In the end, all four terms in verse 10 are rough synonyms for well-being in creation grounded in the reliability of the creator who saves. The creation theme is accented in verse 12 as an anticipation of a productive agricultural environment. The verse may well refer back to verse 1, which looks to a recovering economy in the land. The final verse is a reiteration of what has gone before.

This psalm reflects a moment of renewal, restoration, and revival of community that is completely the gift of God. The petitioner is one who has complete confidence that YHWH is willing and able to enact such newness and waits in confidence for its appearance. The hope and expectation of this prayer are an anticipation of "the Lord's Prayer," the familiar Christian prayer that prays for the coming of God's kingdom on earth as it is in heaven. Thus it is an act of immense hope that is completely assured of God's goodness, which will be established in the earth. The petitioner refuses to let present circumstances erode confidence about God's future.

A Closer Look: YHWH's Utter Fidelity

The word pair that introduces the culminating vision of well-being in verses 10–13 – steadfast love and faithfulness – YHWH's utter fidelity, recurs often. It is of special interest that this word pair is no doubt behind the familiar words of Jn 1:14, "full of *grace* and *truth*." Thus Christ is attested in the Gospel of John as one with fidelity to restore and revive failed creation.

A Closer Look: The Kingdom of God Has Come Near

The convergence of terms in verses 10–13 characterizes a fully reconciled community in a fully reconciled creation. This cluster of terms is an act of outlining "the kingdom of God," the way the world will be when YHWH's rule is fully embodied. In Christian reading, it is pertinent that the comment of John the Baptist is that the kingdom of God is "at hand," at the threshold and about to arrive (Mk 1:14). The early church moreover attested to its arrival in Jesus' several acts of restorative fidelity. In the psalm, Israel already knows that the kingdom of God is "come near"; Israel can trace out its embodiment in transformed social and cosmic relationships.

Bridging the Horizons: *Babette's Feast*

In *Babette's Feast* by Isak Dinesen, verse 10 becomes a mantra for the general, who comes as an outsider, to name the newness that is given in the midst of feasting:

"Man, my friends," said General Loewenhielm, "is frail and foolish. We have all of us been told that grace is to be found in the universe. But in our human foolishness and shortsightedness we imagine divine grace to be finite. For this reason we tremble...." Never till now had the General stated that he trembled; he was genuinely surprised and even shocked at hearing his own voice proclaim the fact. "We tremble before making our choice in life, and after having made it again tremble in fear of having chosen wrong. But the moment comes when our eyes are opened, and we see and realize that grace is infinite. Grace, my friends, demands nothing from us but that we shall await it with confidence and acknowledge it in gratitude. Grace, brothers, makes no conditions and singles out none of us in particular; grace takes us all to its bosom and proclaims general amnesty. See! That which we have chosen is given us, and that which we have refused is, also and at the same time, granted us. Ay, that which we have rejected is poured upon us abundantly. For mercy and truth have met together, and righteousness and bliss have kissed one another!"[180]

In the end, we are able to see that the feast served by Babette is indeed an instance of the arrival of God's new rule of *shalom*. The fact that the "new governance" arrives in the form of a feast of course gives force for Christians to a Eucharistic theology that regards "the feast of gratitude" as a harbinger of the new rule to come.

A Closer Look: A *Shalom* **Prophet**

The voice that speaks God's *shalom* in verses 8–13 may be a "*shalom* prophet" of the kind that is condemned as a lackey of the Jerusalem establishment in Jer 6:13–15, Jer 8:10–12, and Ezek 13:8–16. It is the case, however, that the prophetic message of *shalom* on occasion is not dishonest ideology but is in fact the good news of God's rule. That surely is how this psalm is intended to be read; the voice of the *shalom* prophet is a welcome one to a community that has petitioned for restoration and salvation.

---

[180] Isak Dinesen, *Babette's Feast and Other Anecdotes of Destiny* (New York: Vintage Books, 1988), 40–41.

PSALM 86 – A PRAYER OF DAVID

¹ Incline your ear, O Lᴏʀᴅ, and answer me,
for I am poor and needy.
² Preserve my life, for I am devoted to you;
save your servant who trusts in you.
You are my God; ³be gracious to me, O Lᴏʀᴅ,
for to you do I cry all day long.
⁴ Gladden the soul of your servant,
for to you, O Lᴏʀᴅ, I lift up my soul.
⁵ For you, O Lᴏʀᴅ, are good and forgiving,
abounding in steadfast love to all who call on you.
⁶ Give ear, O Lᴏʀᴅ, to my prayer;
listen to my cry of supplication.
⁷ In the day of my trouble I call on you,
for you will answer me.

⁸ There is none like you among the gods, O Lᴏʀᴅ,
nor are there any works like yours.
⁹ All the nations you have made shall come
and bow down before you, O Lᴏʀᴅ,
and shall glorify your name.
¹⁰ For you are great and do wondrous things;
you alone are God.
¹¹ Teach me your way, O Lᴏʀᴅ,
that I may walk in your truth;
give me an undivided heart to revere your name.
¹² I give thanks to you, O Lᴏʀᴅ my God, with my whole heart,
and I will glorify your name for ever.
¹³ For great is your steadfast love toward me;
you have delivered my soul from the depths of Sheol.

¹⁴ O God, the insolent rise up against me;
a band of ruffians seeks my life,
and they do not set you before them.
¹⁵ But you, O Lᴏʀᴅ, are a God merciful and gracious,
slow to anger and abounding in steadfast love and faithfulness.
¹⁶ Turn to me and be gracious to me;
give your strength to your servant;

save the child of your serving-maid.
¹⁷ Show me a sign of your favor,
so that those who hate me may see it and be put to shame,
because you, Lord, have helped me and comforted me.

Psalm 86 is a typical psalm of complaint, except that it offers intriguing complexities in its rhetorical development. Verses 1–7 feature primarily a series of petitions, reinforced by motivational clauses in verses 1, 2, 3, 4, and 7, each introduced by "for." In these petitions, the psalmist seeks refuge, protection, and rescue, for the psalmist is completely without resources.

At the conclusion of the psalm, in verses 16–17, there is another series of petitions that again seek rescue. The latter series reaches a rhetorical climax in verse 17 with the preposition "so that" (in Hebrew a *waw* consecutive). The hope of the petitioner is to shame his adversaries. These adversaries have been identified in verse 14 as "ruffians" and "insolent." They are marked by their general dismissal of YHWH, a complete contrast to the speaker, who adheres closely to YHWH. Thus even the designation of the adversary seeks to draw God into the fray, for adversaries are an affront to YHWH just as they are a threat to the speaker. They will be shamed – and the petitioner enhanced – when all concede that the God of all comfort helps the one who is utterly helpless. Thus the petitions in verses 1–7 and verses 16–17 bespeak *deep need* that is matched by *deep confidence*. Calvin comments that "*trust or confidence in God . . . is the mother of all true religion.*"[181]

The complexity of this psalm, which we have not observed in many other psalms of lament and complaint, is that in the middle portion of the psalm, verses 8–15 (anticipated in verses 2b and 5), we find a series of strong "*you*" statements addressed directly to YHWH. These statements are not accusations against YHWH but rather doxologies that celebrate and enhance YHWH. This psalm features no less than six independent pronouns "you" (*attah*) that state, apart from the verb, a strong appeal to God, who is directly addressed.[182] As far as we are aware, there is no other psalm with such a heavy and sustained accent on "thou." As a result, what is most interesting about this psalm is not the complaint and petition of "I," the speaker, but rather the affirmation made of YHWH with the pronoun in verses 2, 5, 10 (twice), 15, and 17. In these utterances, the psalmist turns away from his own desperate plight and refocuses on YHWH, who is the grounds of all hope and new possibilities:

- In verse 2, "you [*attah*] are my God." In contrast to the insolent in verse 14, the speaker is completely committed to and reliant on YHWH, utterly "devoted" to YHWH.

[181] J. Calvin, *Commentary on the Psalms*, vol. 3 (1979), 381.
[182] On the patterned recurrence of this pronoun, see J. C. McCann, Jr., "Book of Psalms," in L. E. Keck et al. (eds.), *The New Interpreter's Bible*, vol. 4 (1996), 1020; and S. Terrien, *Psalms* (2003), 618–619.

- In verse 5, YHWH is characterized as "good and forgiving" (see Ps 85:2), with abundant *hesed*. YHWH is celebrated as generous and utterly reliable. The recurring use of the word "forgive" is most unusual and constitutes a major accent in this psalm.
- In verse 10, following the "formula of incomparability" in verse 8, YHWH is celebrated as a doer of "wonders," the kinds of miracles of transformation sought by this petitioner, and then, in the second line of the verse, "God alone."[183] Thus the confession builds from verse 2, "you are my God," to verse 8, "God incomparable," to verse 10, "God alone." There is no other source of hope for well-being.

In verse 15, this "you" statement comes to fullness as the psalm quotes the classic characterization of YHWH from Exod 34:6–7, using Israel's best vocabulary for divine fidelity, offering five terms and culminating in the primary word pair "a steadfast love and faithfulness" that we saw in Ps 85:10.

Finally, in verse 17, this one who is steadfast, incomparable, and "God alone" is the God of all comfort, who will answer the prayer and act on behalf of the petitioner. Thus, all of the great claims made for YHWH now come down to the specificity of action for this lowly servant in need. Even this "child of a servant girl" does not doubt that the incomparable God can and will be attentive to this voice of need, hope, and faith.

This psalm concerns a person in need who is able to announce himself as a legitimate petitioner before the God of life, like whom there is no other. Remarkably, the desperate needs of "I" are displaced by confident trust in "thou." The self is overwhelmed and immersed in the glorious truth of the "thou," who has the capacity to heal and restore the "I" of the petitioner.

This intimate transaction between incommensurate partners is fully reflected and articulated in this pattern of pronouns. The "I" of petition is taken with full seriousness, but the hope of the "I" is to have doxological lips that are fully occupied by the "thou" of power and fidelity. It is no wonder that the psalm ends in confidence. It is no wonder, moreover, that the "I" knows and relies fully on this intimate and undoubted source of help and comfort. This is a truth not doubted in this community of prayer, but never comprehended by the company of the cynical in verse 14, who do not "set you [God] before them."

A Closer Look: Communal Theology and Personal Faith

The affirmation of YHWH in verse 15, echoed by the other "you" statements of the psalm, quotes from and relies on the normative creedal confession or Exod

---

183 On the "formula of incomparability," see W. Brueggemann, *Theology of the Old Testament* (1997), 139–144.

34:6–7, a text used variously elsewhere in Scripture.[184] Thus the psalmist prays not only out of primal need and primal conviction but out of the deep truth of the community of faith. The whole of that communal confession is here mobilized in an intimately pastoral way. The usage evidences the way in which communal theology and intimate, personal faith depend on each other.

Bridging the Horizons: That I Belong to My Faithful Savior

This intimate confession of the handmaiden here attests to the primary claims of Israel's faith. That faith eventually becomes the grounds of the first question and the first answer of the Heidelberg Catechism:

Question: What is your only source of comfort and strength in this age and in the age to come?
Answer: That I belong to my faithful Savior Jesus Christ.

This theological formulation of course is Christologically put in the church's confession. Mutatis mutandis, however, the petition in this psalm and the affirmation of the catechism come to the same point: "that I belong to my faithful Savior." The psalm, like the catechism, knows the single source of comfort in the face of every tribulation. No wonder the "thou" of God prevails over the need of "I"!

PSALM 87 – OF THE KORAHITES. A PSALM. A SONG

¹ On the holy mount stands the city he founded;
² the LORD loves the gates of Zion
more than all the dwellings of Jacob.
³ Glorious things are spoken of you,
O city of God.
Selah

⁴ Among those who know me I mention Rahab and Babylon;
Philistia too, and Tyre, with Ethiopia
'This one was born there,' they say.

---

[184] W. Brueggemann, *Theology of the Old Testament* (1997), 215–218.

⁵ And of Zion it shall be said,
  'This one and that one were born in it';
  for the Most High himself will establish it.
⁶ The LORD records, as he registers the peoples,
  'This one was born there.'
     Selah

⁷ Singers and dancers alike say,
  'All my springs are in you.'

This poem is brief and rather enigmatic, but it is a fascinating reflection as part of the faith expressed in the book of Psalms. The structure of the psalm is not easy to follow. Perhaps a helpful way to read the text is to take it in two parts. The first three verses introduce the poem and celebrate Zion's significance as the city of God. The remainder of the psalm articulates the city's worldwide significance. Mark Smith has discerned a structure in verses 3–7 tied to prepositions and adverbs:

A "in you" (v. 3)
  B "there" (v. 4)
    C "in her" (v. 5)
  B' "there" (v. 6)
A' "in you" (v. 7)[185]

This proposal puts verse 5 at the center of the poem, with its affirmation that YHWH has established Zion. Still, the sequence of the text will not be easy to follow. The psalm begins with YHWH's love for Zion. The psalm then moves to divine speech in which God proclaims that other nations will know God and be given birthrights from Zion. The text is thus an interesting expression of the universal dimension of the Hebrew scriptures though still tied to Zion as the center. From Zion YHWH grants and nurtures life.

Psalm 87 is a Zion song and celebrates the city and its significance. This special place of divine presence is central in Book III of the Hebrew Psalter (Psalms 73–89). Psalm 84, another Zion song, also celebrates the sacred place. The destruction of the place also plays heavily in Book III and again demonstrates the centrality of Zion. Psalm 86:9 envisions a setting in which all nations as God's creations will come and bow down before YHWH and give glory to the divine name. This next poem, Psalm 87, envisions just such an event. With the "gates of Zion" (v. 2) and singers and dancers in the concluding verse, a liturgical procession into the sanctuary may be the setting envisioned.

---

[185] Mark Smith, "The Structure of Psalm LXXXVII," *VT* 38 (1988): 357.

The psalm opens with a vision of the city established on God's holy mountain. The divine origin of the holy place and the sanctuary are at the center of the psalm's concern. Zion is the special place of divine presence and care, even above other places. "The gates of Zion" specifies the place, and the emphasis is on the divine origin of the place rather than its human origin. The city makes visible YHWH's presence in this place. The voice of the poet introduces the theme of the poem in verses 1–3 – Zion. The founding and sacred nature of the place are divine actions and therefore notable. This remarkable opening vision of Zion brings a response of "glorious things" spoken of Zion. "The poet stands on the top of Mount Zion, absorbed in thought. What he sees and what he thinks takes shape in his mind under the impression of the festive mood that surges round him everywhere, and becomes a song of praise glorifying Jerusalem, the Holy City of God."[186] Verse 3 provides the transition to the remainder of the poem.

With verse 4, the psalm moves to direct divine speech and the proclamation that Rahab, Babylon, Philistia, Tyre, and Ethiopia "know me." The list includes traditional enemies of ancient Israel. Tate suggests that Rahab stands for Egypt and Babylon for the Mesopotamian powers, thus indicating the two major empires in the ancient Near East.[187] The Philistines and Phoenicians (Tyre) are closer but lesser powers, and Ethiopia (Cush) is distant. These nations have threatened Israel but here they are born in Zion. Other psalms suggest the defeat of these nations, so this positive proclamation about them may come as a surprise to readers. Verse 4 is the beginning of a roll call in which YHWH is claiming the nations. The universal horizon of Psalm 87 is remarkable. It is part of an emphasis in various texts in the Hebrew scriptures. The ancestors were called to bring blessing to the nations (Gen 12:1–3), and the universal dimensions of Isaiah 40–55 are well known. Psalm 87 proclaims that these nations were born in Zion. It could be that Zion is here pictured as a mother, but the scene appears to be more of a roll call of those included among the citizens of Zion. The poetic image becomes the proclamation of the liturgy that God's purposes are universal and include other peoples. That reading is preferable to understanding the psalm in terms of the Jewish Diaspora. The voice of the poet returns in verses 5–6 with this poetic image of the roll call of peoples who are counted as citizens of Zion. The concluding verse of the psalm is cryptic but is perhaps envisioning a joyful procession to Zion of people singing and dancing because Zion provides the food and drink to nurture full living for all peoples just as springs nurture life. The divine presence in the holy place blesses life.

Psalm 87 is a bit enigmatic, but it appears to be a remarkable poem in the Hebrew Psalter. YHWH claims the nations for the life-giving city of God. Zion was a geo-

---

[186] Artur Weiser, *The Psalms: A Commentary*, trans. H. Hartwell (OTL; Philadelphia: Westminster, 1962), 581.
[187] M. E. Tate, *Psalms 51–100* (1990), 391.

political reality for a period, but this psalm suggests more in terms of faith. Perhaps the perspective reflects the fact that other psalms in Book III mourn the destruction of Jerusalem/Zion. Psalm 87 is one of the texts in the Hebrew canon that includes the nations in divine hopes for the human community. In verse 4, YHWH declares that the nations "know me." The verb suggests an intimate, personal knowledge. In this text, that knowledge begins with the divine initiative of bringing these peoples into the citizenship of Zion. It is more than adoption; they were "born there." God created all peoples. With Zion as the center of divine presence, all peoples were then born there. It is a striking poetic image. Christian readings may associate this universal perspective of divine engagement with the world with the New Testament and the Pauline mission to the Gentiles (Eph 3:1–13), or the image of the new Jerusalem in the book of Revelation that includes all peoples.

PSALM 88 – A SONG. A PSALM OF THE KORAHITES. TO THE LEADER: ACCORDING TO MAHALATH LEANNOTH. A MASKIL OF HEMAN THE EZRAHITE

¹ O LORD, God of my salvation,
  when, at night, I cry out in your presence,
² let my prayer come before you;
  incline your ear to my cry.

³ For my soul is full of troubles,
  and my life draws near to Sheol.
⁴ I am counted among those who go down to the Pit;
  I am like those who have no help,
⁵ like those forsaken among the dead,
  like the slain that lie in the grave,
like those whom you remember no more,
  for they are cut off from your hand.
⁶ You have put me in the depths of the Pit,
  in the regions dark and deep.
⁷ Your wrath lies heavy upon me,
  and you overwhelm me with all your waves.
    Selah

⁸ You have caused my companions to shun me;
  you have made me a thing of horror to them.

I am shut in so that I cannot escape;
⁹ my eye grows dim through sorrow.
Every day I call on you, O Lᴏʀᴅ;
 I spread out my hands to you.
¹⁰ Do you work wonders for the dead?
 Do the shades rise up to praise you?
  Selah
¹¹ Is your steadfast love declared in the grave,
 or your faithfulness in Abaddon?
¹² Are your wonders known in the darkness,
 or your saving help in the land of forgetfulness?

¹³ But I, O Lᴏʀᴅ, cry out to you;
 in the morning my prayer comes before you.
¹⁴ O Lᴏʀᴅ, why do you cast me off?
 Why do you hide your face from me?
¹⁵ Wretched and close to death from my youth up,
 I suffer your terrors; I am desperate.
¹⁶ Your wrath has swept over me;
 your dread assaults destroy me.
¹⁷ They surround me like a flood all day long;
 from all sides they close in on me.
¹⁸ You have caused friend and neighbor to shun me;
 my companions are in darkness.

Psalm 88 is a peculiar theological *treasure* in the Psalter or a peculiar *problem* for theological interpretation, depending on how one views the remarkable rhetoric of the psalm. This psalm follows the familiar pattern of many psalms of complaint, and includes rhetorical acts of petition, complaint, and motivation. It is like many psalms, except that in one particularly notorious matter it is quite distinct from all the others. In many psalms discussed herein, we have seen that laments and complaints are almost always *answered*; the several prayers of Israel characteristically end in satisfied resolution expressed as praise and thanks. But not here! Here the prayer goes unanswered, even though the prayer is Israel's voice of urgent need, deep crisis, and passionate address to YHWH. The prayer is unanswered – YHWH never speaks or appears. The speaker receives no signal of engagement or concern on the part of the deity.

The prayer is organized around three statements of urgent petition, each of which names the deity in direct address and asserts that the prayer of need has been offered passionately and repeatedly over time:

O Lord, God of my salvation,
  when, at night, I *cry out* in your presence, let my prayer come before you;
  incline your ear to *my cry*. (Ps 88:1–2)
  * * *

Every day *I call* on you, O Lord;
  I spread out my hands to you. (Ps 88:9b, c)
  * * *

But I, O Lord, *cry out* to you;
  in the morning my prayer comes before you. (Ps 88:13)

The speaker trusts YHWH's capacity and has no doubt that if YHWH were to answer, all would be well. The reiterated reference to "cry, prayer, cry, call, cry" (with a rich, differentiated vocabulary) reflects both urgent need and deep trust in YHWH.

The poetic material that fills out the psalm between these verses of "cry" offers conventional themes of lament prayers but with remarkable intensity. The complaint of verses 3–9a is a familiar description of trouble that is designed to move YHWH to caring action. The rhetoric follows two patterns. On the one hand, in verses 3–5 and 8c–9a, the speaker simply describes a situation of acute vulnerability and powerlessness that pushes one to the edge of death. The statement teems with the vocabulary of weakness and death: "trouble, Sheol, pit, forsaken, slain, cut off." But in verses 6–8b the rhetoric shifts so that this is no longer description but accusation addressed to "you," to YHWH, who has caused the precarious situation of the speaker. These verses in fact accuse YHWH of infidelity and of betraying the trust and confidence of the psalmist. Thus the speaker grieves over not only a *threat* to life but a sense of *abandonment* by the very one on whom he counted. The conclusion is that the speaker suffers acute social isolation, left abandoned by God and, consequently, by neighbors.

After the reference to the repeated cry in verse 9b–c, verses 10–12 ask a series of six rhetorical questions that function as a motivation to YHWH. The purpose of the questions is to establish that the suffering and death of the speaker have direct and devastating consequences for YHWH. There is as much at stake for YHWH in this impending death as for the one who suffers and utters the questions. The assumed and required answer to all six questions is "No":

- No, YHWH's miracles are not performed for dead people, so YHWH must act before it is too late.
- No, dead people do not praise YHWH; if YHWH wants to be praised, YHWH will need to act soon to save them.
- No, YHWH's steadfast love is not celebrated among the dead.
- No, YHWH's fidelity is not appreciated by the dead.

▪ No, YHWH's miracles are not acknowledged in the realm of the dead.
▪ No, YHWH's past saving deeds are not remembered in death.

All of the questions have the same point. Yes, YHWH is God of the living, and if YHWH wants to be taken seriously, then YHWH must keep the speaker among the living, for the realm of death is the limit of YHWH's governance.

These six questions exhibit the courage and daring of Israel at prayer, and presume to appeal to YHWH's own self-interest. Frank-Lothar Hossfeld and Erich Zenger comment:

YHWH should recognize that his own interest must prevent him from dismissing the petitioner to Sheol ahead of time; if he did so, he would rob himself of a worshiper and a witness to his power. Here alone are helpful, praiseworthy actions and characteristics of YHWH named: *wonders, care, faithfulness, justice*; here alone does YHWH's power appear as bright and glorious in contrast to the dark underworld.[188]

Terrien goes even further to suggest that the psalm dares to mock and tease God:

The patient attempts to mock God himself in two ironic questions: "Wouldst thou make wonders for the dead?" and "Do the shades arise to praise thee?" (v. 11 cd).

God would not think of performing marvels to entertain the dead in their ennui. How could they react emotionally and intellectually to divine acts of prodigy since they have been deprived of human sensitivity or consciousness: they are immobile and have lost all possibility of knowing.

Would God perform a miracle and bring the dead back to life so that he might enjoy the thrill of an actor delighting an audience? The second question offers additional zest to man's teasing of God: the shades or ghosts do not rise to praise! The poet is reaching a theological ultimate when his wit implies that God enjoys being praised.

It is as if the poet states that the dead become nothing, and he is ready to address coarsely the Master of life and death with "The joke is on thee. Thou are a loser!"[189]

There is no doubt that these questions exhibit the psalmist, and in larger consequence Israel, ready to engage in playful but serious gamesmanship with YHWH.

Evidently, the motivational questions have not moved YHWH to act, because in verse 13 the cry of need is reiterated. Thus this unanswered cry is followed, in verses 14–18, with more complaints that accuse YHWH not only of inactivity but of aggressive deprivation that makes the life of the speaker unlivable. The themes of verses 3–9a are reiterated, and the psalmist concludes with an unresolved awareness of lethal "darkness" where the abandoned, shamed speaker must now exist.

---

[188] F.-L. Hossfeld and E. Zenger, *Psalms 2* (2005), 392.
[189] S. Terrien, *Psalms* (2003), 628.

This prayer is an honest acknowledgment in ancient Israel that prayers sometimes remain unanswered. YHWH is unmoved by urgent need and intense petition.

This is the honest experience of every person of authentic faith. YHWH is not a wishing well or an automaton that delivers on demand. At the very least, we may take this psalm as attestation of Israel's candor about God and before God, and yet the reiteration of verses 1–2, 9, and 13 also attests that unanswered prayer does not lead to lack of faith, or silence, or resignation. It leads rather to more urgent, vigorous petition, for Israel has no alternative source of help.

Bridging the Horizons: Unanswered Prayer

Israel is able to be honest in this psalm about unanswered prayer – and to include such prayer in its canonical collection of prayers – because it understands that prayer is a transaction between two free covenanted partners, both of whom operate toward the other in freedom. Such a sense of prayer means that Israel's proper task is to be engaged in truthful ways; its task is not to explain (or explain away) the silence and unresponsiveness of God, which are taken as a dimension of YHWH's inscrutable and awesome freedom. The experience of unanswered prayer – known in the contemporary world as in the ancient world – is most fully dramatized in the book of Job, where Job wants, more than anything, *to be heard* by the Holy One (Job 23:3; 31:35). Eventually, as the poem of Job develops, Job is *heard but disregarded* in that the answer he receives from the Lord of the whirlwind is no answer to his petition but an exhibit of divine power and awesomeness (Job 38–41). The conclusion of the poem of Job in the Old Testament makes clear that the issue of unanswered prayer – with its implied or stated awareness of YHWH's lack of faithfulness toward Israel – was acknowledged and struggled with in ancient Israel.

When Christians ponder the silence of God in the face of human need, they are drawn to the cross of Jesus and to the dread reality of Friday crucifixion. There is no doubt, as the gospel narratives evidence, that on that Friday of YHWH's deepest need and abandonment, a need expressed by Jesus' quoting of Ps 22:1, YHWH is silent and absent (Matt 27:46; Mk 15:34). The death of Jesus happens in a context of divine abandonment and is taken by the church as the quintessence of the divine reality through which all other experiences of divine absence are to be understood. Augustine reads Psalm 88 as a description of Christ's suffering, though Calvin concludes, against Augustine, that such an interpretation "has no connection with the meaning of the passage."[190]

In the contemporary world, unanswered prayer continues to be a deep point of faith. In the end, the church prays with Jesus that God's will – and not

---

[190] J. Calvin, *Commentary on the Psalms*, vol. 3 (1979), 409.

ours – should be done (Matt 26:39). But now as then, faith finds divine unresponsiveness in the face of deep need in the most intimate and unbearable moments of crisis. Beyond such absences known by honest faith in every congregation, the twentieth century has known fully about God's absence in the face of acute public violence, noticeably a sequence of genocides of which the Jewish *shoah* is the most prominent. The writing of Elie Wiesel looks deeply into that absence but with no more resolution than the psalmist can offer.

It is clear that the God of the Bible is no reliable antidote to evil, even though in our deepest need we make petition of the most simple, direct, and demanding kind. Therefore the large rational issue of theodicy looms in critical reflection, but biblical interpretation must take care not to seek explanations for the unexplainable.[191] The silence of God properly evokes not explanation but a rich blend of patient waiting and impatient demand. It is the case that the most brutal of genocides and the most intimate pastoral crisis are of a piece. In such needful emergencies, we are most mindful, as was the psalmist, of a need for God. But we are left, as was the psalmist, waiting, praying more intensely but mostly without resolution. It is an act of faith, in such circumstances, to continue fervent prayer. Care must be taken, tempting as it is, not to trade off the sustained work of petition for the more attractive work of rational explanation. The psalmist engages in no such explanation, knowing that explanation is no useful trade-off for a relation of demanding faithful utterance, even when the transaction does not yield existential or intellectual satisfaction.[192]

PSALM 89 – A MASKIL OF ETHAN THE EZRAHITE

[1] I will sing of your steadfast love, O LORD, for ever;
with my mouth I will proclaim your faithfulness to all generations.
[2] I declare that your steadfast love is established for ever;
your faithfulness is as firm as the heavens.

[3] You said, 'I have made a covenant with my chosen one,
I have sworn to my servant David:

---

[191] See Terrence W. Tilley, *The Evils of Theodicy* (Eugene, OR: Wipf and Stock, 2000).
[192] William Styron, *Sophie's Choice* (Toronto: Bantam Books, 1979), 614–615, utilizes Psalm 88 as a "prescription for my torment" by the lead character, Stingo. Styron and the woman on the bus understand that *voiced pain to God* matters in unbearable situations, even when there is no response.

⁴ "I will establish your descendants for ever,
   and build your throne for all generations." '
      Selah

⁵ Let the heavens praise your wonders, O Lord,
   your faithfulness in the assembly of the holy ones.
⁶ For who in the skies can be compared to the Lord?
   Who among the heavenly beings is like the Lord,
⁷ a God feared in the council of the holy ones,
   great and awesome above all that are around him?
⁸ O Lord God of hosts,
   who is as mighty as you, O Lord?
   Your faithfulness surrounds you.
⁹ You rule the raging of the sea;
   when its waves rise, you still them.
¹⁰ You crushed Rahab like a carcass;
   you scattered your enemies with your mighty arm.
¹¹ The heavens are yours, the earth also is yours;
   the world and all that is in it – you have founded them.
¹² The north and the south – you created them;
   Tabor and Hermon joyously praise your name.
¹³ You have a mighty arm;
   strong is your hand, high your right hand.
¹⁴ Righteousness and justice are the foundation of your throne;
   steadfast love and faithfulness go before you.
¹⁵ Happy are the people who know the festal shout,
   who walk, O Lord, in the light of your countenance;
¹⁶ they exult in your name all day long,
   and extol your righteousness.
¹⁷ For you are the glory of their strength;
   by your favor our horn is exalted.
¹⁸ For our shield belongs to the Lord,
   our king to the Holy One of Israel.

¹⁹ Then you spoke in a vision to your faithful one, and said:
   'I have set the crown on one who is mighty,
   I have exalted one chosen from the people.
²⁰ I have found my servant David;
   with my holy oil I have anointed him;
²¹ my hand shall always remain with him;

my arm also shall strengthen him.
22 The enemy shall not outwit him,
   the wicked shall not humble him.
23 I will crush his foes before him
   and strike down those who hate him.
24 My faithfulness and steadfast love shall be with him;
   and in my name his horn shall be exalted.
25 I will set his hand on the sea
   and his right hand on the rivers.
26 He shall cry to me, "You are my Father,
   my God, and the Rock of my salvation!"
27 I will make him the firstborn,
   the highest of the kings of the earth.
28 For-ever I will keep my steadfast love for him,
   and my covenant with him will stand firm.
29 I will establish his line for ever,
   and his throne as long as the heavens endure.
30 If his children forsake my law
   and do not walk according to my ordinances,
31 if they violate my statutes
   and do not keep my commandments,
32 then I will punish their transgression with the rod
   and their iniquity with scourges;
33 but I will not remove from him my steadfast love,
   or be false to my faithfulness.
34 I will not violate my covenant,
   or alter the word that went forth from my lips.
35 Once and for all I have sworn by my holiness;
   I will not lie to David.
36 His line shall continue for ever,
   and his throne endure before me like the sun.
37 It shall be established for ever like the moon,
   an enduring witness in the skies.'
         Selah

38 But now you have spurned and rejected him;
   you are full of wrath against your anointed.
39 You have renounced the covenant with your servant;
   you have defiled his crown in the dust.
40 You have broken through all his walls;

you have laid his strongholds in ruins.
41 All who pass by plunder him;
   he has become the scorn of his neighbors.
42 You have exalted the right hand of his foes;
   you have made all his enemies rejoice.
43 Moreover, you have turned back the edge of his sword,
   and you have not supported him in battle.
44 You have removed the sceptre from his hand,
   and hurled his throne to the ground.
45 You have cut short the days of his youth;
   you have covered him with shame.
      Selah

46 How long, O LORD? Will you hide yourself for ever?
   How long will your wrath burn like fire?
47 Remember how short my time is –
   for what vanity you have created all mortals!
48 Who can live and never see death?
   Who can escape the power of Sheol?
      Selah

49 LORD, where is your steadfast love of old,
   which by your faithfulness you swore to David?
50 Remember, O LORD, how your servant is taunted;
   how I bear in my bosom the insults of the peoples,
51 with which your enemies taunt, O LORD,
   with which they taunted the footsteps of your anointed.

52 Blessed be the LORD for ever. Amen and Amen.

This psalm is a liturgical assertion of the divine founding of the Davidic dynasty (vv. 1–37) and a protest against the failure of that divinely guaranteed institution (vv. 38–51). The concluding doxology of verse 52 serves as a summary act of praise for all of Book III (Psalms 73–89) and does not pertain in any direct way to this particular psalm.

The Davidic monarchy that dominated the life and imagination of Israel from 1000 to 587 BCE was definitive for the Jerusalem temple liturgy; the monarchy is reckoned to be not simply a political achievement (which it was) but a strategy of YHWH's governance of the world whereby the Davidic king is YHWH's regent to maintain order and justice in creation.

The theme of verses 1–37, to effect political legitimacy through theological claim, is the assertion of YHWH's promise to David and his heirs. The twin themes of verses 1–37 are announced in verses 1–4. First, the primal theme of YHWH's fidelity is sounded in verses 1–2, twice using the word pair *ḥesed* and *amunah*, steadfast love and faithfulness, or alternatively "grace and truth." This affirmation is the bottom line of Israel's theological confession; here YHWH's fidelity is as reliable as the surety of creation, for this is none other than the creator God. Second, this affirmation of divine fidelity that is the core of Israel's doxological practice is, in verses 3–4, directed to David and his dynasty. Here and in what follows the psalm renders in poetic form the foundational divine promise to David in 2 Sam 7:1–16. As a subset of the covenant YHWH has made with Israel at Sinai, a particular covenantal commitment is made to David whereby the dynasty is assured of God's own reliability.

With two themes established, the remainder of verses 5–37 introduces rich variations on the themes. In verses 5–14, the doxology celebrates YHWH's fidelity in the cosmic arena of the pluriform reality of the gods. Among the several gods in "the assembly of the holy ones," it is YHWH who is recognized as peculiarly faithful (v. 5). Indeed none of the divine council can match YHWH's character (see Psalm 82). The "formula of incomparability" in verse 8 would seem to focus on YHWH's might, but then quickly moves again to YHWH's "faithfulness." This incomparable, faithful power of YHWH is acknowledged in the work of creation, for YHWH has turned cosmic disorder to order and has made an ordered life in the world possible (vv. 9–13). This section concludes in verse 14, wherein the word pair "steadfast love and faithfulness" is accompanied by a second word pair, "righteousness and justice." The cluster of terms, reminiscent of Ps 85:10–11, signifies an ordered, safe, joyous world that YHWH guarantees.

As a response to this wondrous doxological affirmation, verses 15–18 exhibit Israel in the temple making a response to YHWH's incomparability. It is YHWH, "our king," who rules in Jerusalem, who is worshiped in the Jerusalem temple, and who will – in the following verses – guarantee the human king as a regent for YHWH's unchallenged governance of the world.

Verses 1–2 celebrate YHWH and then in verses 3–4 turn to David in the same way the Yahwistic doxology of verses 5–18 turns to David in verse 19. It is YHWH, in a series of first-person acts of empowerment, who has authorized and anointed David (vv. 19–21). YHWH is totally committed to the Davidic house. As a consequence, the Jerusalem monarchy will prosper in war and be utterly successful and prosperous in every way (vv. 22–27). In verse 28, our familiar word pair is again sounded (here "steadfast love" is rendered in the NRSV as "stand firm"). In verses 29–33, the divine claim to this human institution is asserted with an acknowledgment of possible alienation and punishment that is congruent with 2 Samuel 7. The dynasty is "forever"; that is, for all thinkable future generations (v. 28). The double "if" in verses 30–31 followed by "then" in verse 31 indicates that waywardness in violation of the covenant will indeed provoke divine wrath. That "if-then" reality,

however, is overridden in verse 33 with the "nevertheless" of unconditional commitment, again with the terms "steadfast love and faithfulness." The anticipated
punishment of verse 32 is serious, but it is not covenant-threatening. Underneath
every possible alienation to come, the abiding divine favor toward David is beyond
interruption. The conclusion of this affirmation in verses 34–36 grows powerfully
lyrical, so that the doxology leads to an extreme assertion to show that the God–
David connection is transcendent beyond question and beyond all of the vagaries
of history. YHWH will keep the covenant to David – YHWH is a truth-teller and
will not be false to David:

The promise to the dynasty is as sure as creation (v. 37).

It would be grand and reassuring if the psalm ended at verse 37, and perhaps in some
liturgical recitals this was the ending of the song of praise. But of course the psalm does
not end here. Abruptly, the psalm continues with a stunning "and now" in verse 38. It
is as though overriding circumstances disrupt the happy piety of the temple singers
by insisting that historical reality be faced. The circumstance of crisis in verses 38–51
powerfully and frontally contradicts the happy assurances of the foregoing:

Those words of recrimination challenge the veracity of God.... The psalmist
explodes into a sort of blasphemous accusation. He does not hesitate to contradict
the reiteration of the divine promise with his fateful "But!" (v. 39).... The theology
of protest is now a theology of blasphemy. The psalmist does not become an atheist:
he is the antagonist of God.[193]

Now the psalmist engages in truth-telling toward and against YHWH. This truth-
telling is a long complaint against the fickleness of YHWH. The "you" statements of
verses 38–45, not unlike those of Ps 44:9–14, accuse YHWH of causing the suffering
and humiliation of Israel. The rhetorical power of this series of "you" statements is
that they contrast so completely with the affirmations in the "you" form of verses
9–13. Now the God who was celebrated as powerful and faithful is identified as a
ruthlessly destructive agent in the life of Jerusalem. Although this characterization
may plausibly relate to a number of low moments in the course of the monarchy, it is
most likely that the reference is to 587 BCE and the destruction of Jerusalem. Whereas
that crisis was caused by Babylonian armies, in poetic articulation the destruction of
Jerusalem is directly accomplished by YHWH in YHWH's own lack of fidelity.

Given that experience of the city and the dynasty that was established by and
guaranteed by YHWH, the lament continues in verses 46–48 with a series of questions that articulate an unbearable circumstance and in verse 47 lead to a question
that we may take as the pivot point of the entire psalm. In light of the frequent use
of the word pair *ḥesed* and *amunah* in affirmative ways in what has gone before,
now the two terms are reiterated, this time with a stunning awareness that there
is no fidelity from YHWH. YHWH has defaulted on YHWH's own promise, and

---

[193] S. Terrien, *Psalms* (2003), 637–638.

that default has placed the dynasty and the city in an unbearable and unacceptable condition. The question posed to YHWH is in fact an accusation; all of the great doxological claims of verses 1–37 turn out to be a charade. There is no divine fidelity. Only at the end, anticipated in verse 47 and now fully voiced in Psalm 50, is one petition voiced: *remember*. Remember how much Jerusalem suffers; and behind that implicitly, remember your promises to king and city. There the psalm ends. There is no resolve, no assurance, no divine response. Jerusalem is left with its indignant assault on the God who has failed. God's *ḥesed* turned out to be unreliable. God's faithfulness, in this disaster, turned out to be an illusion. The doxological affirmation in verse 52 is at best curious. We may imagine that after verses 38–51, Israel can do doxology, but only with clenched teeth.

The juxtaposition of verses 1–37 and verses 38–51 poses a massive question for faith, the very question characteristically posed in Israel. The two units are placed according to the "and now" of verse 38. That rhetorical device characteristically functions in the Old Testament to connect a *memory* and a *present circumstance*. The device requires that memory – in this case, the memory of YHWH's fidelity – come to terms with present circumstances. The frequent use of the terms *ḥesed* and *amunah* is no doubt rooted in the ancient dynastic promise. In this psalm, however, it turns out that the frequent use of these terms is a setup for posing the deep question of verse 49. It turns out that the many affirmations of divine fidelity are a rhetorical ploy to make the question of the absence of divine fidelity all the more stark and demanding.

The question posed moreover receives no answer, not even a hint of an answer, nor a clue about divine response, nor a trace of YHWH's readiness to reengage Israel as a God of fidelity. The psalm permits the new edge of circumstance to persist and finally to dominate the psalm without resolution.

The psalm pertains to the Davidic promise in particular. In the faith of Judaism and eventually in the faith of the church, the promise is transposed into expectations of a coming messiah, a son of David. In messianic expectation, neither Jews nor Christians can let the unanswered question of the psalm be the last word. As a result, the hope of Jews and Christians is a defining part of faith, but that hope lies well beyond the purview of this psalm. If, however, we stay with the psalm itself, it is unmistakably clear that the psalm leaves things short of the resolution offered in conventional faith, either Jewish or Christian. One way to receive this reality in a Christian context is to let the promise be placed in jeopardy by Good Friday and the crucifixion as it was by the destruction of Jerusalem. If we Christians do not too quickly rush to Easter, we may hear in this psalm the "Saturday voice of faith" that is waiting, that is honest, and that refuses to let faith trump lived reality.[194] In the Christian context, Easter, of course, overcomes the defeat of Friday and the waiting

194 Walter Brueggemann, "Reading From the Day 'In Between'," in Tod Linafelt (ed.), *A Shadow of Glory: Reading the New Testament After the Holocaust* (London: Routledge, 2002), 105–116.

of Saturday. But such overcoming must not come too soon, and clearly does not receive voice in this psalm.

Thus, in the Jewish tradition concerning David and in the derivative Christian tradition, we may see in this psalm both *the deep resolve* to affirm God's trustworthiness and the *deep candor* that will not engage in denial about lived reality in order to protect God's reputation. Taking both *resolve* and *candor* together, there is a waiting, the outcome of which is not given ahead of time.

A Closer Look: The Covenant with David

God's covenant with David has been understood in recent scholarship in two ways. First, it is common to judge that the Sinai covenant assures God's fidelity to Israel *on the condition* of Torah obedience. By contrast, the covenant made with David is viewed as *unconditional* because YHWH is sworn not to remove YHWH's ḥesed from David. (In addition to 2 Samuel 7, see 2 Sam 23:5.) The latter text refers to "an everlasting covenant," one not to be disrupted by the vagaries of history. Jon Levenson has made a case that although there is some tension between the covenants of Sinai and David, they can be understood as components of the same general affirmation of faith:

There is much of value in the thinking of the school that focuses upon the disjuncture of the two covenant traditions. As we saw at length in Parts 1 and 2, the two derive from different Near Eastern antecedents, and, as we saw above, they can come into conflict, as in 1 Kings 8. On the other hand, it is an overstatement to present them as always standing in sharp and irreconcilable antithesis. We have already noted that Davidic circles were quite capable of accepting and redacting literature that had originally no place for David but a central place for Moses, for example, the book of Hosea. There may be a tension in the final product of such redaction, but the tension was tolerable to the proponents of Judean royalism. Not always did one covenant yield to the other. Furthermore, it is important to remember that the Davidic covenant as presented in both 2 Sam 7:14 and Ps 89:31–38 would seem to presuppose obligation by the Sinaitic pact.[195]

Second, Moshe Weinfeld has argued that the Davidic covenant, unlike that of Sinai, is modeled after a land grant.[196] In that administrative practice, a sovereign lord was free to reassign land as he chose and could freely assign land to a favorite subject. In this imagery, David receives his "kingdom" as a unilateral act of divine

[195] Jon D. Levenson, *Sinai and Zion: An Entry Into the Jewish Bible* (New York: Winston Press, 1985), 213.

[196] Moshe Weinfeld, "The Covenant of Grant in the Old Testament and in the Ancient Near East," *JAOS* 90 (1970): 184–203.

generosity, with David cast as a favorite subject of YHWH. This clearly is an image that is very different from the bilateral covenant of Mount Sinai.

Bridging the Horizons: The Expectation of a Davidic King

There can be no doubt that the Davidic monarchy was disrupted by the Babylonian incursion into Jerusalem in 587 BCE. To that extent, verses 38–51 reflect historical reality. There is also no doubt that the hope for and agitation for restoration of the monarchy continued in the exilic and postexilic periods after that disruption. But such restoration was not to be permitted by the governing empires, first Babylon and then Persia. The expectation remained alive, however, as is evident in Jer 23:5–6, Jer 33:14–16, and Ezek 34:23–24. Eventually this hope became politically "unrealistic," but continued with enormous theological force. It was eventually pushed into the long-term future, but the hope never lost its poignant, political dimension. It is an enduring expectation of restoration that operates in the New Testament when Jesus is asked by John the Baptist, "Are you the one who is to come, or are we to wait for another?" (Luke 7:20).

This remarkable dimension of the expectation of a coming king (messiah) is that as political possibility waned, the capacity for hope grounded in YHWH's fidelity persisted. Although our psalm itself has no answer to the question of verse 49, in the long run both Judaism and Christianity have bet on YHWH's *ḥesed* against the circumstances of lived history.

PSALM 90 – A PRAYER OF MOSES, THE MAN OF GOD

¹ Lord, you have been our dwelling-place
   in all generations.
² Before the mountains were brought forth,
   or ever you had formed the earth and the world,
   from everlasting to everlasting you are God.

³ You turn us back to dust,
   and say, 'Turn back, you mortals.'
⁴ For a thousand years in your sight
   are like yesterday when it is past,
   or like a watch in the night.

⁵ You sweep them away; they are like a dream,
   like grass that is renewed in the morning;

⁶ in the morning it flourishes and is renewed;
     in the evening it fades and withers.

⁷ For we are consumed by your anger;
     by your wrath we are overwhelmed.
⁸ You have set our iniquities before you,
     our secret sins in the light of your countenance.

⁹ For all our days pass away under your wrath;
     our years come to an end like a sigh.
¹⁰ The days of our life are seventy years,
      or perhaps eighty, if we are strong;
even then their span is only toil and trouble;
      they are soon gone, and we fly away.

¹¹ Who considers the power of your anger?
      Your wrath is as great as the fear that is due to you.
¹² So teach us to count our days
      that we may gain a wise heart.

¹³ Turn, O Lord! How long?
      Have compassion on your servants!
¹⁴ Satisfy us in the morning with your steadfast love,
      so that we may rejoice and be glad all our days.
¹⁵ Make us glad for as many days as you have afflicted us,
      and for as many years as we have seen evil.
¹⁶ Let your work be manifest to your servants,
      and your glorious power to their children.
¹⁷ Let the favor of the Lord our God be upon us,
      and prosper for us the work of our hands –
      O prosper the work of our hands!

In times of crisis, the community of ancient Israel would gather at the sacred place. Led by their priests and other leaders, the community would fervently articulate their crisis in prayer to YHWH in order to seek YHWH's intervention and deliverance from the crisis at hand. That is the kind of setting from which the community lament of Psalm 90 arose. Most commentators relate the prayer to distress in the postexilic community. The prayer consists of two major sections. The first (vv. 1–12) contrasts divine permanence with human frailty as a basis for lament. The second and concluding section (vv. 13–17) focuses on petition.

This community lament begins Book IV of the Psalter (Psalms 90–106) and is the only psalm associated with Moses in its superscription. Marvin Tate has explored the connections between Psalm 90 and various Mosaic texts in the Pentateuch.[197] Readers of the Psalter will recognize that prayers lamenting the destruction of Zion/Jerusalem are prominent in Book III (Psalms 73–89) and that Psalm 89 concludes with the unresolved petition in the face of the divine rejection of the Davidic covenant. Therefore the placement of this "Prayer of Moses" is noteworthy. The superscription to Psalm 90 takes readers back to the time prior to the kingdom of David, to the time prior to the building of the Jerusalem temple, to the time of "Moses, the man of God." There was no monarchy and there was no temple; the people were not yet in the land they had been promised. And yet Israel was engaged in a relationship with YHWH and in giving shape to that relationship. Connecting the prayer to Moses suggests that the psalm responds to the question of the fall of Jerusalem by going back to a time when the community's relationship with YHWH shaped the life of Israel but was not mediated by temple and king.

It is not unusual in the Psalter for lament psalms to reflect on the significance of the crisis at hand and thus take on a didactic and generalizing tendency. That move is noticeable in Psalm 90. The opening and closing of the poem make it clear that Israel's only genuine source of hope in the crisis is YHWH. In fact, the psalm begins with a word of praise as it addresses God. God has been "our dwelling-place" through the generations. The term suggests a place of help and refuge. This gift of a "home" comes from God, who was even before the creation. This God who always was has through the years provided protection for the community. Verses 1–2 focus on stability: God has been a reliable refuge for this faith community for generations. Even before there was a world, there was God, and so God's view is the view of the creator, in which a thousand years is only a day or a night (v. 4). In contrast to all that stability and permanence is the brevity of human life. Humans are like dreams or like grass that is renewed with the morning dew but then fades and withers in the evening; it lasts only a day. Time suggests the human frailty and the limited nature of human life. From dust humans come, and to dust they return. The divine–human contrast is central to verses 1–6, especially as seen in the themes of time and its passage.

In the context of the brevity of the human experience, the psalm moves in verses 7–12 to complaint. In the brief and precarious experience of this people, they complain that they are overwhelmed by divine wrath. It is only the disobedience of the people that YHWH sees, and thus they experience the oppression of the divine frown. With verse 9, the poet returns to the passage of time in human life and suggests that, under divine anger, years feel like a groan or a sigh. The length of human life is set at 70 or 80 years at best, and even those years are filled with trouble and woe. With the blink of an eye, a life is gone. The section then ends with the petition for wisdom to be able to reflect on such a short life and to be able to live it fully. For the Hebrew, the heart was the center of the will or intellect, and so "a wise heart"

---

[197] M. E. Tate, *Psalms 51–100* (1990), 438.

would help people deal with the frail and brief life before them. The wisdom reflection in this petition emphasizes the trouble of life, and the plea is for the ability to deal with the reality of a frail and brief life. In the experience of Israel, this reflection likely is associated with the experience of exile and its aftermath. The psalm makes it clear that humans do not control life with any contrived technique or skill. Rather, YHWH is the one who has created and gives life.

Verses 13–17 conclude the psalm by moving to the traditional psalmic style of petition. The hope is to restore the relationship of YHWH as "dwelling-place" (v. 1), and so the petition is for God to relent or turn around and have compassion on the servant ancient Israel. The term used for the request for God to relent is the traditional term for repenting. The psalm asks God to repent or turn around and have compassion. It is followed by the traditional question of lament: "How long?" Israel's hope is to rejoice and praise God, and so the community petitions for YHWH's "steadfast love." Israel's life and future depend on that gracious and compassionate gift. Verse 15 returns to the theme of time with the petition that YHWH grant the people as many days and years of joy as days and years of trouble. The hope is for glorious divine intervention on behalf of this generation and the next. The concluding petition is for divine favor so that fruitfulness may come from the community's work. The psalm ends with the repetition of that petition. The strong concluding petition seems to carry an expectant tone. Perhaps the trouble and woe of exile provides the background for this petition for a future of hope and thriving.

Bridging the Horizons: A Petition for Wisdom

Psalm 90 puts together a variety of perspectives on the human experience. Human frailty and divine anger result in a petition for the gift of divine help. Both Israel's experience of exile and the generalized human experience are part of the picture. The petition is for the wisdom to discern the significance of the human experience and for God's gift of fruitful work in life. The psalm seems to suggest a connection between sin and death, but there is no clarity on the suggestion. There is praise of the creator, reflection on the permanence of God, and reflection on the brevity of human life. The focus seems to be, however, on petition, that the creator not overlook the brief human life and let it end in trouble but be gracious toward this frail human congregation.

In Christian tradition, an Isaac Watts hymn summarizes Psalm 90:

O God, our help in ages past,
our hope for years to come,
our shelter from the stormy blast
and our eternal home.
Be thou our guard while life shall last,
and our eternal home.

PSALM 91

¹ You who live in the shelter of the Most High,
   who abide in the shadow of the Almighty,
² will say to the LORD, 'My refuge and my fortress;
   my God, in whom I trust.'
³ For he will deliver you from the snare of the fowler
   and from the deadly pestilence;
⁴ he will cover you with his pinions,
   and under his wings you will find refuge;
   his faithfulness is a shield and buckler.
⁵ You will not fear the terror of the night,
   or the arrow that flies by day,
⁶ or the pestilence that stalks in darkness,
   or the destruction that wastes at noonday.

⁷ A thousand may fall at your side,
   ten thousand at your right hand,
   but it will not come near you.
⁸ You will only look with your eyes
   and see the punishment of the wicked.

⁹ Because you have made the LORD your refuge,
   the Most High your dwelling-place,
¹⁰ no evil shall befall you,
   no scourge come near your tent.

¹¹ For he will command his angels concerning you
   to guard you in all your ways.
¹² On their hands they will bear you up,
   so that you will not dash your foot against a stone.
¹³ You will tread on the lion and the adder,
   the young lion and the serpent you will trample under foot.
¹⁴ Those who love me, I will deliver;
   I will protect those who know my name.
¹⁵ When they call to me, I will answer them;
   I will be with them in trouble,
   I will rescue them and honor them.

¹⁶ With long life I will satisfy them,
  and show them my salvation.

Psalm 91 is without a superscription in the Hebrew text and closely follows Psalm 90. In a sense, Psalm 91 responds to the previous psalm with an assurance coming immediately after a petition that likely reflects the difficulties of exile. Psalms 90–92 form a cluster of psalms at the beginning of Book IV and focus on the theme of God's refuge in response to the crisis of the fall of the Davidic kingdom portrayed in Psalm 89, the conclusion of Book III.

Psalm 91 introduces its theme and the poem's characters of God and the speaker who enjoys divine refuge. Verses 3–13 then imagine divine protection in the face of a number of crises, and the psalm's final verses take the form of a divine oracle confirming God's favor for those who trust. The psalm's affirmation is that God is the source of refuge in the midst of trouble. There is some kind of trouble in the background, but it is difficult to specify. Perhaps the speaker seeks refuge from oppressors, or perhaps the problem has been sickness and the speaker has gone to the temple seeking refuge. Some would suggest that the speaker is the king facing enemies in battle. Tate suggests a postexilic setting, but it is difficult to identify the particular crisis with any confidence.[198] The psalm relates to an ancient setting of worship and seeks to nurture trust in the congregation. Befitting a psalm of trust, Psalm 91 praises God as worthy of the community's trust, worthy of being trusted with their lives.

The psalm begins with parallel lines addressing the believer who enjoys the refuge or shelter of the divine presence. Two divine names are used, *Elyon* and *Shaddai*, rendered traditionally as "Most High" and "Almighty" in the NRSV. The words of confession in verse 2 announce the theme of the psalm – God as refuge and fortress. The confession is about entrusting one's whole life to God. The image of divine refuge may have been closely associated with the temple as a place of sanctuary from oppressors or crises, but it no doubt took on a broader significance in the community's life. The believer looks to God for shelter in the face of threats, and so here in the context of the congregation God is refuge, an image that is familiar to readers of the book of Psalms.

The middle portion of the psalm envisions a number of troubles and the protection God provides in the face of them. The images are striking and portray quite a list of strong difficulties a believer could face in ancient Israel and that could produce considerable anxiety and fear. Immediately following the confession of trust in verse 2, the poet speaks of the threat of the hunter's trap and of "deadly pestilence." Verses 5–6 speak of terrors that come in the night and plague or disease that brazenly stalks around in the middle of the day. Verse 7 speaks

---

[198] M. E. Tate, *Psalms 51–100* (1990), 452–453.

of thousands falling at the side of the believer. Perhaps the scene is that of war –
verse 5 refers to "the arrow" – or perhaps all the death is the result of the plague.
Destruction threatens, but the psalm's confession of trust is that those who fall
are encountering "the punishment of the wicked." The threats carry a kind of
demonic tone. They are portrayed in terms of evil and scourge. In verse 13, the
images of sudden and menacing threats move to the animal world, with references to lions and snakes.

The balance to these images of destruction is a collection of images of divine
protection. In verse 4, the image is that of a mother bird sheltering her young with
feathers and wings. The image shifts to battle and portrays God's protection in terms
of armor and a shield in the last line of the verse. In verses 7–10, the evil does not
come near the believer's tent because of divine protection. The believer sees many
wicked come to their end, but the one who trusts in God has found a "dwelling-
place" in the shelter of divine protection. In verses 11–12, the image is of angels or
divine messengers who guard the path of the believer so that even hitting one's foot
on a rock can be avoided. Verse 13 concludes the section with victory over the threat
of lions and snakes. This brief attention to the imagery in verses 3–13 makes it clear
that this middle section of the psalm is a gripping portrayal of threat in the midst of
life and God's trustworthiness in the face of threat. Note the verbs in these verses.

> God will deliver you. (v. 3)
> God will cover you. (v. 4)
> You will not fear. (v. 5)
> You will only look and see the punishment. (v. 8)
> God will command angels to guard you. (v. 11)
> You will trample lion and snake under foot. (v. 13)

The poem articulates these images of divine protection in the face of danger as the
reason for the confession of trust in verse 2.

Verses 14–16 are in the form of first-person speech from God. The Most High
confirms that those in intimate relationship with God will be protected. Those who
call on God will be heard and delivered. These verses are in the tradition of the salvation oracle that promises deliverance and hope for the future. The verbs here are
in the first person and come in quick succession:

> I will deliver. (v. 14)
> I will protect. (v. 14)
> I will answer. (v. 15)
> I will be with them. (v. 15)
> I will rescue. (v. 15)
> I will honor. (v. 15)
> I will satisfy. (v. 16)
> I will show them my salvation. (v. 16)

Those who are on the receiving end of these divine acts are characterized as "those who love me," "those who know my name," and those who "call to me." These phrases suggest not simple acquaintance with the divine but an intimate relationship with God, an ongoing encounter with the divine.

The psalm's concluding verse calls to mind Psalm 90. The promise is that God will "satisfy" believers with long life and wholeness ("salvation") in that life. Psalm 90:14 both prays that God will "satisfy" and is concerned about the length of life. Psalm 90:16 uses the same verb in the petition that God will "let your work be manifest to your servants" that is found in the concluding affirmation in Psalm 91: "I will show them my salvation." This hopeful set of divine promises in Ps 91:14–16 responds to the petition in Psalm 90.

Bridging the Horizons: A Confession of Faith

Some contemporary readers will suggest that Psalm 91 promises that God will not allow any troubles to come on believers and may read the psalm as unrealistic and naive. Two comments are in order: (1) In Psalm 91, the divine refuge is in the face of considerable danger; and (2) the psalm is a poetic affirmation of God's trustworthiness and thus seeks to engender trust from the congregation. It is not a theological treatise that attempts to answer all the challenges to its confession and portrayal of divine protection. The psalm announces the theme of divine refuge and then carries out the theme with a list of life's dangers. God's protecting shadow comes in the midst of those dangers. The conclusion of the psalm confirms God's protection in the form of an oracle. The purpose of the poem is to encourage trust in God from the congregation. Although the psalm has a didactic tone about it, it is in the form of a confession of trust. The psalm is neither sermon nor lecture, but a confession of faith with the purpose of drawing hearers/readers into trust in God's refuge. It is striking that the divine titles "Most High" and "Almighty" are important in the psalm. This transcendent God initiates an intimate relationship with these believers and cares for them with the love of a mother bird. Such divine care is not limited by time or space.

PSALM 92 – A PSALM. A SONG FOR THE SABBATH DAY

¹ It is good to give thanks to the LORD,
   to sing praises to your name, O Most High;
² to declare your steadfast love in the morning,
   and your faithfulness by night,

³ to the music of the lute and the harp,
  to the melody of the lyre.
⁴ For you, O LORD, have made me glad by your work;
  at the works of your hands I sing for joy.

⁵ How great are your works, O LORD!
  Your thoughts are very deep!
⁶ The dullard cannot know,
  the stupid cannot understand this:
⁷ though the wicked sprout like grass
  and all evildoers flourish,
they are doomed to destruction for ever,
⁸ but you, O LORD, are on high for ever.
⁹ For your enemies, O LORD,
  for your enemies shall perish;
  all evildoers shall be scattered.

¹⁰ But you have exalted my horn like that of the wild ox;
  you have poured over me fresh oil.
¹¹ My eyes have seen the downfall of my enemies;
  my ears have heard the doom of my evil assailants.

¹² The righteous flourish like the palm tree,
  and grow like a cedar in Lebanon.
¹³ They are planted in the house of the LORD;
  they flourish in the courts of our God.
¹⁴ In old age they still produce fruit;
  they are always green and full of sap,
¹⁵ showing that the LORD is upright;
  he is my rock, and there is no unrighteousness in him.

Psalm 92 is a thanksgiving psalm, giving thanks for the mighty acts of YHWH, including the defeat of enemies. The psalm offers thanks and encourages faith in YHWH on the part of the congregation. The poem begins with praise and thanksgiving to God followed by the narration of the defeat of evildoers. The contrast in the latter part of the psalm is the flourishing of the righteous. Commentators take a variety of views on what constitutes the parts of the psalm, but a three-part structure seems to be the best option, with verses 1–6 expressing praise and thanksgiving to God with the reason articulated. Verses 7–11 focus on the enemies and verses 12–15 on hope for the community.

A Closer Look: A Psalm for the Sabbath

The psalm's superscription connects the text with the Sabbath, and this is the only psalm assigned to that day in the Hebrew Psalter.[199] The text was likely an appropriate expression of thanksgiving for a variety of settings and came to be associated with the Sabbath. The Sabbath is clearly central to the Hebrew scriptures, so it is not a surprise that it has a place in a psalm heading, but the specific connection with Psalm 92 is not clear. There is nothing specific to the Sabbath in the body of the text. The psalm articulates prayer and worship, themes appropriate to the Sabbath, and affirms the divine order of creation and the moral order of life. These themes mesh well with the priestly creation account in Gen 1:1–2:3, where the Sabbath first appears in the Hebrew canon. Perhaps those themes connected the psalm with the Sabbath for the scribal editors of the Psalter.

A Closer Look: A Psalm Cluster

Psalms 90–92 form a cluster at the beginning of Book IV of the Psalter (Psalms 90–106). Psalm 92:1 addresses YHWH as *Elyon*, Most High, a divine title also important in Psalm 91. The steadfast love and faithfulness of YHWH are important in all three psalms, and measures of time appear in all three. The hope that the faithful will enjoy fruitful lives also comes to the fore in the three texts. In addition, Psalms 91 and 92 are concerned with evildoers. McCann suggests that these three psalms at the beginning of Book IV form a "response to the theological crisis posed by the exile and especially articulated in Book III."[200]

Verses 1–6. The psalm begins by commending the offering of praise and thanksgiving to God. Claus Westermann has shown that thanksgiving in the Psalter has to do with narrating God's acts of deliverance.[201] In Psalm 92, the first works listed are the loyal love and trustworthiness of YHWH. These terms are rendered in the NRSV as "steadfast love" and "faithfulness," terms familiar to readers of the Psalter. The speaker will recount such gracious divine acts morning and night. Craig

---

[199] Tate notes that the Septuagint assigns seven psalms for the Sabbath week – Psalms 24, 48, 82, 94, 81, 93, and 92 – in this order for each of the days. According to Tate, Psalm 92 was likely selected for this liturgical use earlier than the others, "being used with the *tamid* offering on sabbaths, or other sabbath worship, in the post-exilic temple in Jerusalem." See M. E. Tate, *Psalms 51–100* (1990), 465.
[200] J. C. McCann, Jr., "Book of Psalms," in L. E. Keck et al. (eds.), *The New Interpreter's Bible*, vol. 4 (1996), 1051.
[201] C. Westermann, *Praise and Lament in the Psalms*, trans. Keith R. Crim and Richard N. Soulen (1981).

Broyles suggests that the reference to morning and night implies a connection with the morning and evening temple offerings.[202] Praise and thanksgiving would accompany the offerings, sung to the music of lute, harp, and lyre, in the gladness of worship. The beginning of verse 4 signals to readers that the reason for the thanksgiving is to follow. It is articulated in the broadest terms of the work of YHWH, "the works of your hands." YHWH's works and thoughts are portrayed as very great and deep, and to occasion much singing with joy. In contrast to the worshiper who sings with joy is the dullard or fool who does not see or fathom the mighty acts of God. Because such blockheads "do not get it," they miss the joy of thanksgiving initiated by God's mighty acts.

Verses 7–11. The remainder of the psalm recounts the mighty acts of God in contrasting directions. The first emphasis has to do with the wicked. Verse 7 suggests that the wicked may sprout and appear to flourish like green grass, but they will inevitably wither. Indeed, they will perish and scatter (v. 9). This picture of the wicked contrasts with the exaltation of YHWH "for ever." What is more, YHWH has "exalted" the strength of the singer. The horn is a symbol of strength, and the image continues with the reference to a wild ox ready for battle. Perhaps preparation of the ox is in view in the problematic second line of verse 10. The singer has seen and heard "the downfall of my enemies." The fall of evildoers is the reason for thanksgiving in this section of the poem. The sequence of the account of the enemies is noteworthy. The initial reference in verse 7 is to "wicked" and "evildoers." Verse 9 portrays them as YHWH's enemies and evildoers. In verse 11, the singer characterizes them as "my enemies" and "my evil assailant." The description of God's enemies is the starting point rather than the singer's personal feelings about the opponents. The moral order of creation in which evil rebounds on the head of the foolish is the focus of the song. These comments do not solve the problem of how contemporary readers deal with the presence of enemies in the book of Psalms, but they do provide some context for that conversation.

Verses 12–15. The concluding verses of Psalm 92 move to the worshiping community and portray it with images from nature. The righteous are those living in faithful relationship with YHWH, and they will "flourish like the palm tree" and grow like the cedars of Lebanon. Palms were luxuriant plants, and the cedars of Lebanon were known for their strength and height. Further, the righteous "are planted in the house of the Lord" and flourish there. In the ancient Near East, especially in Egypt, gardens are often connected with sanctuaries to symbolize the nurturing of life in places of divine presence. That presence provides the sustenance for plants to grow and prosper. The image is of the continuing fruitful life of the righteous. This evidence confirms the psalm's conclusion that YHWH is righteous. God initiates the relationship with the faithful and nurtures them as their just refuge. The singer has

---

[202] C. C. Broyles, *Psalms* (1999), 364.

then rejoiced in the fall of the wicked and in the flourishing of the righteous as an expression of praise and thanksgiving.

Bridging the Horizons: Security

"Security" is a persistent word in contemporary Western culture. There is much talk of national security and of security in one's home. There is also much talk of emotional security. Most things currently associated with security come from human strength or economic or military power, from human constructions. Psalm 92 makes the remarkable suggestion that security might be in God rather than in humans. The psalm praises and thanks God for the fall of the wicked and the flourishing of the righteous. Such a confession is central to the faith of the worshiping community reflected in the Psalms.

PSALM 93

¹ The LORD is king, he is robed in majesty;
  the LORD is robed, he is girded with strength.
He has established the world; it shall never be moved;
² your throne is established from of old;
  you are from everlasting.

³ The floods have lifted up, O LORD,
  the floods have lifted up their voice;
  the floods lift up their roaring.
⁴ More majestic than the thunders of mighty waters,
  more majestic than the waves of the sea,
  majestic on high is the LORD!

⁵ Your decrees are very sure;
  holiness befits your house,
    O LORD, for evermore.

Psalm 93 is a hymn of praise celebrating the reign of YHWH. Most commentators agree that the psalm comes from a festival setting in the time of the Davidic kingdom in Jerusalem. The nature of the festival occasioned great debate in twentieth-century Psalms scholarship. Sigmund Mowinckel is the primary figure in this debate; he constructed an Enthronement Festival as part of the complex of fall festivals in ancient Jerusalem.[203] The Jerusalem cult reenacted the enthronement of YHWH as king as a sign of stability for the new year to come. Hans-Joachim Kraus and Artur Weiser also envisioned a festival, but Kraus argued that it celebrated the choice of Zion as the place of divine presence and the Davidic line as the rulers there.[204] Weiser argued for a covenant-renewal festival.[205] Others agreed that the festival celebrated the kingship of YHWH but objected to Mowinckel's language of enthronement. Marvin Tate has reviewed more recent scholarship on the issue and has come to the conclusion that there is sufficient evidence to support a festival celebration of the rule of YHWH, especially over the powers of chaos, as part of the fall festivals in ancient Jerusalem, but that we cannot know the details of the festival.[206] Psalm 93 comes from such a festival setting. It begins with the acclamation of YHWH as king and then emphasizes the taming of the primordial powers of chaos. The psalm concludes with an affirmation of the trustworthiness of YHWH's decrees. The poem's shifts in person might provide help in seeing its structure and imagining its liturgical setting. The leader of worship voices the first verse about YHWH, and the choir responds with verses 2–3 addressing YHWH. The leader again speaks in verse 4, and the choir responds with the concluding verse.

Psalm 93 begins a cluster of psalms (Psalms 93–100) that is central to the whole book. McCann calls Psalms 93 and 95–99 the theological heart of the Psalter.[207] The psalms celebrate the reign of YHWH, perhaps in response to the crisis of exile, especially as portrayed in Book III of the Psalter (Psalms 73–89). Affinities with the exilic prophetic voice of Isaiah 40–55 are also often suggested. Psalm 93 also has connections with the preceding psalm.[208] Of particular note is the confession in Ps 92:8 that YHWH is "on high for ever"; that affirmation fits well with the portrayal of King YHWH in Psalm 93.

A Closer Look: YHWH Is King

The psalm's opening phrase is *YHWH mālāk*, rendered in the NRSV as "The Lord is king." *Mālāk* is a verb, and so we suggest a rendering of "YHWH rules" or "YHWH reigns." The phrase has been central to the debate over the liturgical setting of the psalm. Mowinckel argues that the phrase should be translated "YHWH has become king" and fits an enthronement ritual. The alternative is "YHWH is king" as an indication of an unchanging condition. The point is

---

[203] S. Mowinckel, *The Psalms in Israel's Worship*, vol. 1 (1962), 113–114.

[204] H.-J. Kraus, *Psalms 60–150* (1988), 233–236.

[205] A. Weiser, *The Psalms* (1962), 617.

[206] M. E. Tate, *Psalms 51–100* (1990), 474–481.

[207] J. C. McCann, Jr., "Book of Psalms," in L. E. Keck et al. (eds.), *The New Interpreter's Bible*, vol. 4 (1996), 1053.

[208] See M. E. Tate, *Psalms 51–100* (1990), 474–478, who suggests that Psalms 92–94 form a cluster.

that YHWH is already king and does not need to be enthroned. Repeatedly
enthroning YHWH could suggest the cycles of nature emphasized in other
religions in the ancient Near East.[209] The beginning verses of Psalm 93 suggest
that YHWH has been king from of old, but the liturgical setting is more significant than that statement suggests. The phrase could well be an enthronement acclamation, but that does not assume that YHWH was not king and
now suddenly is somehow. It rather reenacts and celebrates the acclamation
for the festival congregation. The psalmic proclamation that YHWH reigns
makes the confession present and formative for the congregation. An example from Christian tradition is the Easter affirmation "Christ the Lord is risen
today." The proclamation confesses that Christ the Lord was raised on the first
Easter Sunday morning; it also brings the confession to life for contemporary
congregations.

The psalm's opening phrase announces the theme of the reign of YHWH.
The emphasis is that it is YHWH who reigns as king, robed in royal garments,
majesty, and strength. The words picture this divine king robed in majesty and
power. This king created the world and reigns over it; it is established and stable,
a witness to the divine rule. The choir response affirms that YHWH's throne is
"from of old" and that the victorious divine warrior tames the forces of chaos.
YHWH reigns, and thus the order of creation remains established. The hymnic
words provide assurance that chaos will not reassert itself and bring instability or catastrophe. The portrayal of chaos continues with the floods that raise
their voice and roar. The setting is the battle with the powers of chaos that
would undo the order of creation, but it is King YHWH who has tamed these
forces of disorder. One could interpret verse 3 as suggesting that the waters
threaten YHWH or that the waters praise YHWH, but in either case it is clear
that YHWH is greater than the waters of chaos. The proclamation of the liturgist in verse 4 is that YHWH rules above the mighty waves; the creation has
been established and remains established. The taming of the seas bears witness
to the divine kingship. Psalm 93 begins by acclaiming YHWH's reign and then
portrays the battle with the forces of chaos, so the divine king is present and
active on behalf of the creation and the congregation. Here the powers of chaos
are represented with the mighty waters; in other texts, the opposing powers are
historicized.

The psalm's concluding response from the choir proclaims that King YHWH's
decrees are trustworthy, perhaps a reference to the decrees of verses 1–4. These
reliable decrees are proclaimed in the liturgy of the sanctuary. The sanctuary is

---

[209] H.-J. Kraus, *Psalms 60–150* (1988), 232–233; and J. C. McCann, Jr., "Book of Psalms," in
L. E. Keck et al. (eds.), *The New Interpreter's Bible*, vol. 4 (1996), 1053.

symbolic of the divine throne room, and from there the divine king proclaims decisions or ordinances for governing the community's social and religious life. In that way, the sanctuary, the Jerusalem temple, becomes a source of divine blessing.

Bridging the Horizons: Chaos Knocking at the Door

Psalm 93 proclaims and celebrates the reign of YHWH. After the fall of the Jerusalem temple and the Davidic monarchy, the ancient faith community lived in a world with chaos knocking at the door. Many would describe the contemporary world in just that way. In such a setting, the proclamation of the reign of God with its talk of stability and trustworthy decrees becomes both difficult and essential. The psalm's proclamation seems out of step with the world, but the Psalms suggest the possibility of creating a world by way of liturgical experience. The call is to remember the ancient acclamation that God reigns and makes life possible. With that memory, the congregation can live into that hope, as if God rules, and they can find a home with nurture for hope and wholeness in this world with chaos knocking at the door.

PSALM 94

¹ O Lord, you God of vengeance,
   you God of vengeance, shine forth!
² Rise up, O judge of the earth;
   give to the proud what they deserve!
³ O Lord, how long shall the wicked,
   how long shall the wicked exult?

⁴ They pour out their arrogant words;
   all the evildoers boast.
⁵ They crush your people, O Lord,
   and afflict your heritage.
⁶ They kill the widow and the stranger,
   they murder the orphan,
⁷ and they say, 'The Lord does not see;
   the God of Jacob does not perceive.'

⁸ Understand, O dullest of the people;
  fools, when will you be wise?
⁹ He who planted the ear, does he not hear?
He who formed the eye, does he not see?
¹⁰ He who disciplines the nations,
he who teaches knowledge to humankind,
    does he not chastise?
¹¹ The LORD knows our thoughts,
  that they are but an empty breath.

¹² Happy are those whom you discipline, O LORD,
  and whom you teach out of your law,
¹³ giving them respite from days of trouble,
  until a pit is dug for the wicked.
¹⁴ For the LORD will not forsake his people;
  he will not abandon his heritage;
¹⁵ for justice will return to the righteous,
  and all the upright in heart will follow it.

¹⁶ Who rises up for me against the wicked?
  Who stands up for me against evildoers?
¹⁷ If the LORD had not been my help,
  my soul would soon have lived in the land of silence.
¹⁸ When I thought, 'My foot is slipping',
  your steadfast love, O LORD, held me up.
¹⁹ When the cares of my heart are many,
  your consolations cheer my soul.
²⁰ Can wicked rulers be allied with you,
  those who contrive mischief by statute?
²¹ They band together against the life of the righteous,
  and condemn the innocent to death.
²² But the LORD has become my stronghold,
  and my God the rock of my refuge.
²³ He will repay them for their iniquity
  and wipe them out for their wickedness;
  the LORD our God will wipe them out.

This psalm, for the most part not well known, is a powerful statement of trust in YHWH, constituted by three quite distinct rhetorical units: verses 1–7, 8–15, and 16–23. The sum of the three parts is readiness to trust in and rely on YHWH in the face of great, unmanageable adversity.

The first rhetorical unit in verses 1–7 follows the familiar contours of a lament; verses 1–2 voice a *petition* followed by an extended *complaint*. The petition addressed to YHWH asks YHWH to "rise up" and retaliate against the adversaries of the speaker. The petition is grounded in the conviction that God will act decisively – and of necessity savagely – to assert and maintain divine sovereignty over the earth. This "vengeance," as in Deuteronomy 32:35, is understood not as wild violence but as measured action commensurate with the legitimacy of God's rule. The plea for vengeance as a manifestation of YHWH's rule on the earth is a characteristic petition in Israel. The expected action of YHWH, to be sure, is indeed violent. When taken inside the frame of reference of covenantal faith, each assertion of divine power is seen to be appropriate and is given ready theological justification even now:

As poetic prayers, the psalms of vengeance are a passionate clinging to God when everything really speaks *against* God. For that reason they can rightly be called *psalms of zeal*, to the extent that in them passion for God is aflame in the midst of the ashes of doubt about God and despair over human beings. These psalms are the expression of a longing that evil, and evil people, may not have the last word in history, for this world and its history belong to God. Thus, to use theological terminology, these psalms are realized theodicy: They affirm God by surrendering the last word *to God*. They give *to God* not only their lament about their desperate situation, but also the right to judge the originators of that situation. They leave *everything* in God's hands, even feelings of hatred and aggression.

These psalms do not arise from the well-tempered psychological state of people from whom every scrap of sensitivity and emotion has been driven out. On the contrary, they are serious about the fundamental biblical conviction that in prayer we may say everything, literally everything, if only we say it to GOD, who is our father and mother.[210]

The background of the theological use of "avenge/vengeance" in Israel is not in the emotion of a hate reaction but in the sphere of legal custom. "Vengeance" was an act to enforce or restore justice where the regular legal processes were not competent or had failed. As an activity of the Lord, it was understood as a function of God's rule as the king who has right and responsibility to restore the order of things and to vindicate his authority.[211]

Viewed outside that frame of reference, from the perspective of the adversary for example, the hoped-for divine intrusion is seen to be unrestrained violence that is disproportionate to the affront and, consequently, an immense problem in the context of a compassionate covenantalism.

210 E. Zenger, *God of Vengeance* (1996), 79.
211 J. L. Mays, *Psalms* (1994), 302–303.

The extremity of the petition is justified in the psalm by the labeling of the adversary. The adversary is identified as "the proud," who imagine themselves as autonomous and not responsive to the divine will (v. 2), as the "wicked" who mock the Torah requirements (v. 3), and as "evildoers" who caused, perhaps by secret manipulation, distress in the community (v. 4). The intention of the combination of verses 5–6 and verse 7 shows the way in which Israel is capable of acute social analysis. Verse 7 exposes the theological dismissal of divine rule, for "without God everything is possible." But the attributed articulation of verse 7 is given concrete social reality in the actions of the social abuse of the vulnerable in verses 5–6. YHWH is understood to be the source of protection for the weak; when YHWH is not taken seriously, the weak are put at risk. Thus the speaker seeks YHWH's reengagement in the social process whereby the weak and vulnerable, no doubt including the speaker, can have safety and dignity. "Vengeance" thus is divine action against the rapacious strong in the interest of the weak, who are always at risk. As James Kugel has seen, this petition in the Psalter is appropriate to YHWH's elemental commitment to hear the cry of the weak: "But we ought not to lose sight of our particular focus. It says that hearing the victim's cry is a god's duty and God's duty. It says that if that job is not properly performed, the very foundations of the earth will shake."[212] And for that elemental commitment, the psalmist prays in unqualified confidence.

In verses 8–15, the middle portion of the psalm, the *voice of instruction* displaces the *voice of prayer*. The psalmist becomes teacher and now addresses the "blind fools" in the community. This addressee may be either the proud and arrogant named earlier who resist YHWH, or maybe other weak ones, such as the psalmist, who do not trust YHWH enough to make daring petitions. Either way, the psalmist knows that if the others took YHWH with the same seriousness as he does, everything would be different: the strong might not be outrageously rapacious; the weak might not be timid and therefore have courage to invoke YHWH. Verses 9–10 feature, in the form of rhetorical questions, a series of convictions about YHWH: God hears, God sees, God disciplines (*ysr*), God teaches (*lmd*), God chastises (*ykh*). The answer to all of these questions is *yes*. Yes, YHWH exercises governance and none can evade YHWH's exacting sovereignty. All are called to account, and only the most foolish imagine themselves immune to that oversight and discipline. On the basis of these affirmations, YHWH is now explicitly named in verse 11 following a series of pronouns. YHWH is the one who knows human thoughts, plans, and intentions. But all such human posturings – like the kind practiced in verses 5–11 by the wicked – are futile and have no reality. Human autonomy is an illusion before YHWH's surveillance.

Therefore, says the teacher in the cadences of the sapiential tradition, the ones chastised (*ysr*) and taught (*lmd*) by YHWH are fortunate indeed (v. 12). They are

---

[212] James L. Kugel, *The God of Old: Inside the Lost World of the Bible* (New York: Free Press, 2003), 124.

lucky because such attunement to the will of YHWH gives sustenance to the abused until the wicked are done in by YHWH (v. 13). Thus those in the same circumstances as the psalmist are to be glad for YHWH and not excessively shaped by the "thoughts" of the wicked, who in this instance seem to be so powerful and pervasive. Such human thought is an illusion that has no standing in a world governed by YHWH. This is indeed a daring affirmation, simply declaring that the threats of evildoers against widow, stranger, and orphan do not in the end constitute a substantive threat. And the reason, given in verses 14–15 and introduced by a double "for," is that YHWH is faithful and will stay in solidarity with "his people, his inheritance" (here especially widows, orphans, and sojourners) until justice prevails. Thus verses 8–15 are a defiant reassurance that the vulnerable are in fact safe because YHWH's purpose of justice will prevail.

On the basis of this remarkable insistence, the psalm ends with a ringing statement of confident trust (vv. 16–23). In verses 15–16, the psalmist again names the "wicked" and "evildoers," and acknowledges their deep threat before which the psalmist himself has no resources. Without resources, however, the psalmist – and all the vulnerable – can rely on YHWH's steadfast love, *ḥesed*, (v. 18) and consolation (v. 19), which produce joy. The rule of YHWH is a powerful antidote to the threat of an exploitative society.

In a second wave of petition, verses 19–20, like verses 16–17, ponder the wicked who assail the innocent. (The terms "innocent" and "righteous" are in parallel, which suggests that the reference is to Torah-keepers who are judged free of social affront.) The reality of the wicked and evildoers, however, is abruptly interrupted by the "but" of verse 22, which, in parallel to verses 18–19, asserts YHWH as "strength" and "refuge." YHWH will do to them what the vulnerable psalmist cannot do; YHWH will repay them and wipe them out. In verses 22–23, the psalm returns in confidence to the initial petition of verse 1. YHWH will take vengeance; YHWH will rise up to judge. YHWH will act, and all will be well for the righteous innocent. The world is under YHWH's sure governance. If the world were without YHWH – that is, with only the God who "does not see" (v. 7) – then the wicked would prevail and be able to exploit the innocent without limit. If there were no such God, widows and orphans – like this psalmist – would be hopeless, without resources. The point of the psalm, however, is to refute such a possibility. The world is very much "with God," who sees, knows, and judges. For that reason, finally asserted here, the hopeless can hope for justice. Conversely, the unjust, the wicked, may expect judgment and termination, consignment to "a pit."

A Closer Look: YHWH's Active Governance

In this meditative poem, there is a juxtaposition between *usurpatious social power* and the alternative reality *of YHWH's active governance*. The problem in making such a religious claim of course is that the competing claims are not commensurate. YHWH's claim is highly theological, and the work of the wicked is concrete and visible. Unless the claim for YHWH that dominates this psalm is simply otherworldly, palliative talk, then YHWH's governance must also be concrete and visible. Thus it is most likely that the psalm implies social *praxis* as the mode of YHWH's vengeance; that is, redress through human agency and human institutions. One clear example of such concrete praxis of YHWH's preferential option for "widow, orphan, and sojourner" (v. 6), who constitute YHWH's "people, inheritance" (v. 14), is the affirmation concerning King Josiah in Jeremiah:

Did not your father eat and drink
and do justice and righteousness?
Then it was well with him.
He judged the cause of the poor and needy;
then it was well.
Is not this to know me?
says the Lord. (Jer 22:15b–16)

It is, in this case, through *royal policy* that YHWH's will and YHWH's social redress come to concrete fruition. The psalm itself is silent on the matter, but Israel's ethical reflection characteristically expects YHWH's will for justice to be humanly enacted. Liturgically there is no such reflection on human agency, and the psalm appeals singularly to YHWH's own agency. But surely the interface of usurpatious social power and YHWH's active governance may be mediated in terms of such human agency. This mediation is exactly the work of "the righteous" who do YHWH's will in the world.

Bridging the Horizons: The Happiness of the Chastised

The sapiential instruction of verses 10–13, with its focus on *the happiness of the chastised*, has an echo (or parallel) in Job:

How happy is the one whom God reproves;
therefore do not despise the discipline
of the Almighty. (Job 5:17)

Not unlike the psalmist, Eliphaz asserts that YHWH's governance is equitable, reliable, and good. Those disciplined in instruction by YHWH maintain a life-giving connection that the autonomous can never know. As is well known, Job finds this instruction small comfort. We may imagine that even in this psalm the blind and foolish who are addressed here also find the assurance difficult to accept. The psalmist himself, however, finishes with such complete confidence in YHWH.

PSALM 95

¹ O come, let us sing to the LORD;
    let us make a joyful noise to the rock of our salvation!
² Let us come into his presence with thanksgiving;
    let us make a joyful noise to him with songs of praise!
³ For the LORD is a great God,
    and a great King above all gods.
⁴ In his hand are the depths of the earth;
    the heights of the mountains are his also.
⁵ The sea is his, for he made it,
    and the dry land, which his hands have formed.

⁶ O come, let us worship and bow down,
    let us kneel before the LORD, our Maker!
⁷ For he is our God,
    and we are the people of his pasture,
    and the sheep of his hand.

O that today you would listen to his voice!
⁸ Do not harden your hearts, as at Meribah,
    as on the day at Massah in the wilderness,
⁹ when your ancestors tested me,
    and put me to the proof, though they had seen my work.
¹⁰ For forty years I loathed that generation
    and said, 'They are a people whose hearts go astray,
    and they do not regard my ways.'
¹¹ Therefore in my anger I swore,
    'They shall not enter my rest.'

This psalm consists of two quite distinct parts. The first part is well known and familiarly used as a "call to worship" (vv. 1–7a). The second part is stringent in its admonition, which is known and used hardly at all among us (vv. 7b–11).

The first part of the psalm is a summons to praise and to join a liturgical procession into the cultic presence (vv. 1–7a). It is divided into two parts, each part following a standard doxological pattern of *summons and reason*. In verses 1–5, the summons to praise begins in an imperative followed by four jussive verbs, all of which are called praise. The reasons for praise begin in verse 3 with a *kî* ("for"), a conventional marker in doxologies. The reason for praise is the enthronement of the creator God, who presides over the divine council of "all gods" and is the one who made, maintains, and governs all parts of creation: the depths, the heights, the sea, and the dry land.

Thus Israel is invited to participate in a celebration of the creation, to be dazzled by the splendor of all creation, which the creator holds in his hand.

A shorter echo of verses 1–5 is given in verses 6–7a, with the same doxological pattern of summons and reason. The summons in verse 6 again begins with an imperative, this time with three jussives concerning the God who is "our maker." In light of verses 3–5, we might expect this action of YHWH to refer to creation. But in the reasons introduced by "for" in verse 7, the reference is to the people of the covenant, who enjoy an intimate relationship to YHWH as the people of the covenant, as the sheep of the one shepherd.

The twice-repeated pattern of summons and reason in verses 1–5 and 6–7a imagines Israel going to worship, giving bodily, visible testimony of adherence to YHWH as the God who is gladly trusted in and relied on. The two reasons given for praise, creation (vv. 1–5) and covenant (vv. 6–7a), are very different, but together constitute the total range of YHWH in Israel's life as *creator* and *redeemer*.

The second half of the psalm is commonly reckoned to be a "prophetic address" and has close affinities to Psalms 50 and 81 (vv. 7b–11). In these verses, Israel has joyously arrived at worship, but then it is addressed by a prophetic voice that warns that a commitment to this God is no casual matter. The summons – not unlike the initial summons at Sinai (Exod 19:5) and the familiar Deuteronomic summons (Deut 6:4) – is that Israel should *listen*; that is, it should turn its interest away from itself and its concerns and allow them to be addressed by the will and purpose of YHWH.[213] The purpose of worship in verses 1–7a is not warm, fuzzy communion. Worship is to be addressed by the Torah requirements of the God of Sinai and so be set on a course of intentional, covenantal obedience.

The obedience to which Israel is summoned in verse 7a is then contrasted, at some length, with the narrative recall of Israel's notorious disobedience in the wilderness just after the departure from Egypt (Exod 17:1–7; Num 20:1–13). It is recalled that in the wilderness Israel was without resources. In that emergency, Israel did not trust YHWH but in a panic of anxiety resisted Moses, doubted YHWH, and sought other alternative securities of its own making. The failure to trust YHWH is the central motif of these narratives; the voice in the psalm summons contemporary Israel in its own "today" *not* to replicate that ancient infidelity.

That memory of negativity, moreover, culminates in verse 11 with the powerful awareness that none of the rebellious generation made it to the promised land. It will be recalled, from the book of Numbers, that only Caleb and Joshua of that generation made it to the end of the journey, and that is because they were championed as the true *listeners* who trusted and obeyed YHWH and relied completely on YHWH's presence and promise (Num 14:22–24). The exception of Caleb and Joshua, of course, is not voiced in the psalm, where the accent is on unrelieved rejection. Verse 7 holds out the option of listening

---

[213] S. Dean McBride, "The Yoke of the Kingdom: An Exposition of Deuteronomy 6:4–5," *Interpretation* 27 (1973): 273–306.

obedience and the hope that it may now be possible, as it was not in that ancient narrative.

The two parts of the psalm do not easily cohere and in church practice have been completely divided, so that the hard saying in verses 7b–11 has been eliminated in practice. Without these verses, verses 1–7a permit worship to be imagined as a benign, agreeable meeting between a generous God and responsive people. But imagine how the tone of worship in verses 1–7a would be changed if the warning of verses 7b–11 were characteristically included as a part of the call to worship! Thus the congregation is on notice that worship is not "fun and games" in which everything remains business as usual. Worship becomes sober and urgent because everything is at stake in hearing YHWH's radical call to trust and obedience. Israel may still be dazzled about creation and covenant, but it now knows that the creator-redeemer God calls Israel – and the church – from benign autonomy to a deep trust. Such trust becomes the prerequisite to entering into YHWH 's good, promised future.

A Closer Look: The God of Israel Is the Creator

It is likely that verses 1–5 and verses 6–7a are remnants of independent liturgical scripts. But the fact that they come together in the psalm is worth notice. The grounds for praise in the two units are, respectively, *God the Creator* (vv. 3–5) and *God the Redeemer of Israel* (v. 7a). The interface between the two reflects the fundamental conviction of the Old Testament that the *God of Israel* is *the creator of the world*. It is not always easy in practice to hold the two claims together as they are here and in Israel's faith. It is the temptation of more conservative Christians to so emphasize God's work of salvation through the particularity of the gospel that the larger vista of creation is often lost or at least disregarded. Conversely, more liberal Christians, embarrassed by the "scandal of particularity," tend to focus on the universal claim of creation to the neglect of the concreteness of redemption.

A Closer Look: Obedience to Enter In

The unity of the psalm combines verses 1–7a and verses 7b–11, the first part lyrical in affirmation, the second part harsh and demanding. That unity, however, is crucial, for it affirms that relationship to YHWH, creator and savior of Israel, consists not simply in glad doxological praise but in hearing and obeying (see Exod 24:3, 7).

The upshot of verses 7b–11 is to indicate that entrance into worship, like entrance into the promised land, is dependent on an alternative obedience. The psalm concludes, negatively, that none of the rebels in the wilderness entered the land of promise. In his analysis of the book of Numbers, Dennis Olson sees Joshua and Caleb as wondrous exceptions to that negative judgment.[214] They are consequently an exception to the rule and constitute the continuity that runs from the generation of the wilderness to the generation of the promised land. As the two exemplify, hearing that leads to serious obedience is possible.

Bridging the Horizons: Promised Rest

Gerhard von Rad has usefully reflected on the appeal of Psalm 95 in the Letter to the Hebrews. Psalm 95:7b–11 is quoted in Heb 3:7–11; Ps 95:7b in Heb 3:15; Ps 95:11 in Heb 4:3; and Ps 95:7b in Heb 4:7. Such wide appeal of this part of the psalm treats the rest of the psalm in terms of well-being and security for the faithful in the face of persecution and social jeopardy caused by their faith. The psalm functions as an appeal to disciplined, determined obedience in the face of such risk.

Von Rad has noticed how the writer of the Letter to the Hebrews has juxtaposed references to Psalm 95 with references to Gen 2:1–4a. Of this juxtaposition, von Rad comments:

These are the two proof-texts which the author of the *Epistle to the Hebrews* has welded together! The simple fact that he can do so is an indication of the scope of the promised rest of the New Testament. This rest is an eschatological expectation, a fulfilment of the prophecies of redemption, an entering into that rest which there has always been, from the beginning, with God. In the fulfilment of this hope the whole purpose of creation and the whole purpose of redemption are reunited. Such is the insight vouchsafed to the writer in the simple juxtaposition of these two texts![215]

PSALM 96

[1] O sing to the LORD a new song;
  sing to the LORD, all the earth.
[2] Sing to the LORD, bless his name;
  tell of his salvation from day to day.

---

214 Dennis T. Olson, *The Death of the Old and the Birth of the New: The Framework of the Book of Numbers and the Pentateuch* (Chico, CA: Scholars Press, 1985).
215 G. von Rad, *Problem of the Hexateuch and Other Essays* (1966), 102.

³ Declare his glory among the nations,
  his marvelous works among all the peoples.
⁴ For great is the Lord, and greatly to be praised;
  he is to be revered above all gods.
⁵ For all the gods of the peoples are idols,
  but the Lord made the heavens.
⁶ Honor and majesty are before him;
  strength and beauty are in his sanctuary.

⁷ Ascribe to the Lord, O families of the peoples,
  ascribe to the Lord glory and strength.
⁸ Ascribe to the Lord the glory due his name;
  bring an offering, and come into his courts.
⁹ Worship the Lord in holy splendour;
  tremble before him, all the earth.

¹⁰ Say among the nations, 'The Lord is king!
   The world is firmly established; it shall never be moved.
   He will judge the peoples with equity.'
¹¹ Let the heavens be glad, and let the earth rejoice;
   let the sea roar, and all that fills it;
¹² let the field exult, and everything in it.
Then shall all the trees of the forest sing for joy
¹³ before the Lord; for he is coming,
   for he is coming to judge the earth.
He will judge the world with righteousness,
   and the peoples with his truth.

This psalm, along with Psalms 47, 93, 97, 98, and 99, constitutes a corpus of psalms that celebrate the enthronement of YHWH as king over all creation and king over the other gods. It is plausible, but not proven, that a liturgical drama of divine enthronement occurred annually in the Jerusalem temple. If such a drama was enacted, then this psalm, along with the others indicated, was perhaps a script for that liturgy.

The psalm begins in characteristic hymnic fashion with a *summons* to praise followed by *reasons* for praise (vv. 1–6). The summons is constituted by six imperative verbs in verses 1–3; note especially the fifth verb, "tell" (*bsr*), which means to narrate the victory of God. This verb characteristically refers to an announcement of good news from God and therefore is rendered in Christian usage as "gospel" (see Isa 40:9–11; 57:6). The summons is followed by reasons for praise in verses 4–6, introduced by the characteristic preposition "for." The reason for praise is that YHWH is God above all gods, the presiding officer in the divine council, to whom all of the other gods have submitted, either willingly or by conquest. Erhard Gerstenberger comments on the defeat of the other gods:

"All the gods ('ĕlōhîm) of the nations are 'nobodies' (elîlîm)" (v. 5a). Israelite polemics against "strange" gods are the outcome of a prolonged battle for survival in a multireligious, autocratic imperium (cf. Isa 40:18–25; 44:9–20). To claim superiority for Yahweh was the only means of defense against the Babylonian and Persian oppressors. Some of the Yahweh-kingship psalms indulge in this kind of refutation of foreign powers, being, as it were, documents of this crucial age (cf. Pss 93:3–4; 95:3; 97:7, 9); but few of them ridicule deities of other people as does v. 5 (cf. only 97:7).[216]

In a contest of the gods, it is beyond doubt that the creator God has the capacity to "make new," whereas other gods have no such generative power and can be dismissed as empty frauds; that is, as idols. Verse 6 is a conclusion of this hymnic unit, confirming that this great God alone merits praise and glad submissiveness.

Verses 7–9 are a second vigorous summons to praise, again addressed to all people. These verses are a quotation from Ps 29:1–2, with two important changes. First, the summons to praise is now addressed to "the families of all the peoples"; that is, to all the nations that have been on Israel's horizon since Gen 12:3. It is imagined that the Jerusalem temple is the great gathering point for all peoples who now worship the creator God YHWH. This vocative, moreover, is contrasted with the vocative of Ps 29:1 that summons "sons of God" to praise; that is, members of the divine council. The change brings the drama of worship down to earth as the concern of human subjects. The second change from Ps 29:1–2 is the addition of two imperatives, "bring an offering" and "tremble before him." Both new summonses add to the gravitas of the worship encounter and to the awesomeness of entering into the presence of YHWH.

Verse 10 enunciates what we judge to be the quintessential "gospel announcement" of the entire Old Testament, that the nations are summoned to acknowledge YHWH as fully sovereign on earth. The global horizon of this psalm is already evident in the vista of verses 1–3 – "all the earth," "among the nations," "all the peoples" – and is reinforced in verses 7–9 by "families of the peoples" and "all the earth." The imaginative reach of the Jerusalem liturgy is well beyond Israel, a fact evidenced in the prophetic vision of Isa 2:2–4 and Mi 4:1–4, as well as in the prophetic Oracles Against the Nations that are said in Amos 1:2 to be uttered "from Zion, from Jerusalem."

The claim made in this gospel announcement of verse 10 is that YHWH is sovereign over all. The formula "YHWH is king" is even more interesting and worth

---

[216] E. S. Gerstenberger, *Psalms, Part 2, and Lamentations* (2001), 188.

attention since Sigmund Mowinckel has offered a hypothesis of liturgical enactment. Mowinckel proposes to translate the passage as "YHWH has just [in this
liturgical action] become king."[217] The impact of the hypothesis is that the liturgy
itself is "effective" in enacting, performing, and dramatizing YHWH's rule. Such
a liturgical realism is a challenge to some Protestants, who fear a kind of magic
in such enactment, except that in church tradition both the birth of Jesus and his
resurrection are, in the hymnody of the church, understood as happening "today"
in the wonder of worship. Thus we at least entertain the thought that the psalm, and
others like it, is a performance of that of which they speak.

The outcome of such enthronement of the creator God as unchallenged
sovereign is to secure the order, stability, justice, and well-being of the earth (vv.
10b–12). Thus the destabilizing force of chaos is tamed so that creation cannot
"totter" (v. 10b). In response to the new gift of order, all creatures – heaven, earth,
the sea, its inhabitants, the field, and the trees – celebrate and welcome the new
regime. All these creatures know that the power of chaos – in the form of pollu-
tion, chemical destruction, and deforestation – works havoc in creation, and now
the havoc of chaos will stop. Thus the liturgy can imagine all of heaven and earth
rejoicing in the new rule of YHWH, and so the worshiping congregation joins with
all creation in acknowledging the new rule that makes the world safe and whole.

Verse 13 concludes with an anticipation that YHWH's rule will be extended over
all the earth. That new rule, unlike the old regime of chaos, will be characterized by
righteousness and by YHWH's reliable fidelity. The dominant metaphor is judicial;
the divine judge will sort out, punish, and reward all in the interest of a new general
well-being.

If the hymn is understood performatively, then we may imagine that the community that departs the liturgy does so with a new assurance about the world, and
therefore is gladly committed to a new obedience that is commensurate with the
new rule.

A Closer Look: A Variety of Contexts

The liturgical hypothesis of Mowinckel is by no means uncontested. Alternatives
to a present-tense cultic enactment of divine sovereignty are (a) that the psalm
pertains to a specific historical crisis, plausibly in the postexilic period, or (b)
that the expectation of YHWH's rule is eschatological, so that the faithful pray
for the coming of YHWH's kingdom "on earth as in heaven." Mays and McCann
rightly observe that these three alternative interpretations are not mutually

---

[217] See the most recent discussion of Mowinckel's hypothesis by J. J. M. Roberts, "The
Enthronement of YHWH and David: The Abiding Theological Significance of the Kingship
Language of the Psalms," *CBQ* 64, no. 4 (2002): 675–686.

exclusive.[218] In any case, important parallels between the psalm and the poetry of Isaiah 40–55 are to be noticed and taken into account. The citation of the psalm in 1 Chr 16:23–33, moreover, indicates that the psalm was a ready resource for worship in Israel in a variety of different contexts.

Bridging the Horizons: Announcing the Rule of God

Two terms merit particular attention. First, the "new song" is about new reality (v. 1). Second, the verb "tell" most likely means to tell "the news," which in the church is rendered as "gospel" (v. 2). The interface of *new* and *gospel* means to announce (enact?) the new rule of God. From this it is an easy interpretive maneuver in Christian usage to relate the newness of the gospel to the proclamation of the kingdom of God and the utterance of Jesus in Mk 1:14–15. It is for that reason that the psalm is widely used in the church during the Christmas and Epiphany seasons.

PSALM 97

1 The LORD is king! Let the earth rejoice;
  let the many coastlands be glad!
2 Clouds and thick darkness are all around him;
  righteousness and justice are the foundation of his throne.
3 Fire goes before him,
  and consumes his adversaries on every side.
4 His lightnings light up the world;
  the earth sees and trembles.
5 The mountains melt like wax before the LORD,
  before the LORD of all the earth.
6 The heavens proclaim his righteousness;
  and all the peoples behold his glory.
7 All worshippers of images are put to shame,
  those who make their boast in worthless idols;
  all gods bow down before him.
8 Zion hears and is glad,

---

[218] J. L. Mays, *Psalms* (1994), 309; and J. C. McCann, Jr., "Book of Psalms," in L. E. Keck et al. (eds.), *The New Interpreter's Bible*, vol. 4 (1996), 1065.

and the towns of Judah rejoice,
because of your judgments, O God.
⁹ For you, O Lord, are most high over all the earth;
you are exalted far above all gods.

¹⁰ The Lord loves those who hate evil;
he guards the lives of his faithful;
he rescues them from the hand of the wicked.
¹¹ Light dawns for the righteous,
and joy for the upright in heart.
¹² Rejoice in the Lord, O you righteous,
and give thanks to his holy name!

This psalm, along with Psalms 47, 93, 96, 98, and 99, celebrates the kingship of YHWH. The prime theological claim of this psalm is in the first verse. As we have seen in Psalm 96, it is possible that the initial assertion can be rendered "YHWH has just become king" in this moment of liturgical enactment. In any case, the initial response to the "gospel news" of divine rule is celebration on the part of all creation (v. 1). After that, the psalm develops the theme of divine kingship in three quite distinct rhetorical units.

Verses 2–5 characterize the cataclysmic coming of YHWH in a forceful, even violent *theophany*. In Old Testament theophanic reports, there are remnants of a storm god, in this case with clouds, fire, and lightning, which cause immense upheaval. Of particular interest are two notations in verse 2. First, "thick darkness" may indicate an environment of cultic presence that preserves the divine mystery so that the theophany may be understood within the temple. Second, the reference to "righteousness and justice" is curious in this context and may be understood as a liturgic-prophetic effort to stamp generic theophanic language in a specifically Yahwistic way. This sort of theophany is rooted, for Israel, in Sinai (Exod 19:16–25; see also Ps 18:7–15), but now that drama has been transferred in the imaginative practice of Israel from Sinai to Zion. In any case, the newly acknowledged king comes with dramatic notice so that all of the earth (and the coastlands) can see that the creation is under new management!

Verses 6–9 constitute a dramatic *doxological response* to the coming of the great king in theophany. The juxtaposition of "heavens" and "all peoples" indicates that all of creation praises YHWH; YHWH's righteousness, which bodes well for the earth; and YHWH's glory, which trumps all other gods (v. 6). Because of YHWH's glory, the gods are defeated and no idol can make a claim to legitimacy (v. 7). Because of YHWH's *righteousness*, all of Israel – Zion and Judah – rejoices in confidence that the world is rightly ordered (v. 8). Verse 9 draws a doxological conclusion that is precisely commensurate with verse 6. In the first line, *the earth* recognizes YHWH's exaltation; in the second line, the gods in heaven are submissive. Thus these verses indicate the totality of all reality in praise:

v. 6 heaven – all peoples righteousness – glory
   v. 7 the gods and the worshipers submit to the *glory*
   v. 8 Israel rejoices in *righteousness*
v. 9 most high in heaven – exalted over the gods

Israel's faith, however, characteristically moves from the cosmic and universal to the particular and historical. In verses 10–12, the great claims of *creation* are brought down to the specificity of *covenant*. Verses 10–11 describe the Torah-keeping, covenant-practicing Israelites, who "hate evil" and are "faithful, righteous, upright." They are the ones of all creation to whom YHWH is particularly and attentively committed (see Exod 19:5–6). They are the ones whose lives are filled with joy, safety, light, and security. It is no wonder that, of all creation, the Torah-keepers are the ones who rejoice and give thanks (v. 12).

In sum, the kingship of YHWH as guarantor of reality is expressed in three ways:

- the dramatic entry of King YHWH into power (vv. 2–5);
- the doxology of heaven and earth toward this king, marked by glory and righteousness (vv. 6–9);
- the assurance of the faithful in Israel, who obey the king and who respond in gratitude (vv. 10–12).

The doxology of Israel exegetes the wondrous rule of YHWH, wherein all reality is made secure.

Bridging the Horizons: The Birth of a King

For obvious reasons, the church has found Psalm 97 to be a particularly important resource for both the Christmas and Epiphany seasons. The church celebrates the kingship of Jesus and is able to appropriate this psalm in a Christological way. Such usage reminds us that the celebration of the kingship of Jesus is not a maudlin or romantic festival about a little baby but is rather about the embodiment of God's own rule of justice and righteousness on earth, which causes the angels in heaven to sing their praise to YHWH.

PSALM 98 – A PSALM

¹ O sing to the LORD a new song,
   for he has done marvelous things.
His right hand and his holy arm

have gained him victory.
² The LORD has made known his victory;
he has revealed his vindication in the sight of the nations.
³ He has remembered his steadfast love and faithfulness
to the house of Israel.
All the ends of the earth have seen
the victory of our God.

⁴ Make a joyful noise to the LORD, all the earth;
break forth into joyous song and sing praises.
⁵ Sing praises to the LORD with the lyre,
with the lyre and the sound of melody.
⁶ With trumpets and the sound of the horn
make a joyful noise before the King, the LORD.

⁷ Let the sea roar, and all that fills it;
the world and those who live in it.
⁸ Let the floods clap their hands;
let the hills sing together for joy
⁹ at the presence of the LORD, for he is coming
to judge the earth.
He will judge the world with righteousness,
and the peoples with equity.

Psalm 98 continues a series of hymns (Psalms 93–100) on the reign of YHWH.
These psalms likely come from a common festival setting that focuses on the divine
kingship, as noted in the treatments of the preceding texts. The festival celebrated
and reenacted the enthronement of YHWH over all the earth for the sake of order
and justice. The structure, vocabulary, and theme of Psalm 98 are particularly similar to those of Psalm 96. The predicative style of praise, characteristic of the hymns
in the Psalter, in which first the community is called to praise and then there follows
a reason for the praise, comes to the fore in Psalm 98. That pattern occurs twice in
the psalm. The text begins with a call to praise that is followed by the reason: God's
mighty acts of salvation from Israel's history (vv. 1–3). The verses that follow renew
the call to praise for all creation. The reason comes in the psalm's final verse: the
coming of YHWH as judge of the earth.

A Closer Look: Remembering God's Loyalty

Psalm 98 is part of the collection of psalms that celebrate the reign of YHWH
and is also part of Book IV (Psalms 90–106) and its response to the crisis of exile

articulated at the end of Book III (Psalms 73–89). Psalm 89:49, at the conclusion of Book III, poses a sad question: Where is the divine steadfast love and
faithfulness of old promised to David and his line? The petition is for YHWH
to remember the defeated exilic community. Psalm 98:3 provides a response to
that question from Psalm 89: YHWH "has remembered his steadfast love and
faithfulness to the house of Israel." There has, however, been a shift of context.
Psalm 89 concludes with a concern for "your anointed." Psalm 90 begins Book
IV with a "Prayer of Moses," and the acts of steadfast love and faithfulness that
YHWH has remembered clearly include in Psalm 98 the traditions of deliverance in the Exodus and the wilderness. These mighty acts demonstrating loyal
love and trustworthiness were prior to the Davidic covenant, which is central
to the prayer at the end of Book III. In the face of the fall of Jerusalem and the
Davidic kingdom, Psalm 98 and the other enthronement psalms press the congregation to renew the kingship of YHWH. This divine kingship is understood
as originating in the time prior to the line of David. The psalm encourages the
congregation to move forward with their trustworthy ruler YHWH.

Characteristic of the psalms that celebrate the reign of YHWH, Psalm 98 calls
the congregation to sing a new song. The rehearsal and claiming of the kingship
of YHWH bring a new orientation to life and so call for a new song. This opening call to sing praises is followed immediately by a reason with the characteristic
particle *kî* ("for/because"): God's marvelous and wondrous acts. The "right hand"
and "holy arm" suggest the root metaphor of Israel's historical memory, the deliverance from slavery in Egypt. Exodus 15:6, 12 celebrate that deliverance by the
"right hand" of YHWH in the Song of Miriam/Moses. A number of commentators
also note connections with Isaiah 40–55 and the promise of a return from exile.[219]
There the promise is of a new exodus. God's victories on behalf of the faith community of ancient Israel are not limited to the Exodus and the new exodus but also
include various manifestations of God's mighty acts on behalf of the community
and revealed to the nations. God is zealous for the salvation of the community, and
these acts of salvation are seen "to the ends of the earth." So God has acted on behalf
of Israel as the mighty divine warrior, *and* the purpose of this salvation history is
to reveal divine salvation and righteousness (rendered as "victory" and "vindication" in v. 2 in the NRSV) to all peoples. Ancient Israel's historical memory relates
to the reign of God over all creation. The psalm partakes of the tradition in which
Israel's purpose is to bring blessing to the nations (Gen 12:1–3). God's steadfast love
and faithfulness toward Israel have implications for all nations, and so the victories

[219] H.-J. Kraus, *Psalms 60–150* (1988), 263–264; J. C. McCann, Jr., "Book of Psalms," in L. E.
Keck et al. (eds.), *The New Interpreter's Bible*, vol. 4 (1996), 1072; and C. C. Broyles, *Psalms*
(1999), 381.

of the divine warrior are revealed for all to see. YHWH has remembered the commitments of loyalty and faithfulness and is working to fulfill them; that claim has marvelous implications for Israel and for all of creation. It is therefore no wonder that the psalm begins with a call for the congregation to sing a new song to this one who brings peoples out of bondage.

With verse 4, Psalm 98 launches into a renewed call to praise with great enthusiasm. The imperatives artfully demonstrate the enthusiasm: make a joyful noise, break forth into joyous song, sing praises, sing praises, and make a joyful noise. The psalm also lists the instruments of praise as lyre, trumpet, and horn. The end of verse 6 comes back to the focus of this group of hymns – the kingship of YHWH. This exuberant praise comes before the king of creation and of history. Verses 4–6 articulate an extensive call to praise with music, singing, and shouting. This call likely embodies with much joy the ancient enactment of the enthronement of YHWH in the Jerusalem cult, with its festival processions and symbols of the divine presence and activity in the world. The call to praise signals various ways to praise YHWH that are open to all.

The renewed call of praise in verses 7–8 broadens the call to all creation, in line with Psalm 96, though with different participants. The psalm here alludes to the creation tradition of the divine king defeating the powers of chaos and bringing order to the world and the community. The sea "and all that fills it" as well as the world and its inhabitants are now called to join in the praise of the divine king. The floods are called to applaud and the hills to sing. This remarkable call to praise might seem outlandish in a world characterized by the scientific method, but the poetic vision is that all creation will join in the praise of King YHWH. King YHWH "is coming to judge the earth," and thus praise from floods and hills becomes possible. This judgment will reveal God's "righteousness," the same term used in verse 2 (rendered as "vindication" in the NRSV), and God's justice. In a world with chaos knocking at the door, the promise brings hope. The threat of chaos becomes a new exodus to order and wholeness of life. The psalm implies that God's salvation history on behalf of one faith community has to do with the bringing of justice and the restoration of order for the whole of creation. No wonder the hymn shouts its call to praise.

Bridging the Horizons: An Unlikely Pair

The form of Psalm 98 moves in at least two directions. The first is that the praise of God is full-throated; it is uninhibited. The second is that this uninhibited praise is of important depth and richness. Among contemporary Christian communities, these directions are often incompatible. Some communities exhibit considerable substance in their worship but little joy or enthusiasm in the praise of God. Others show great enthusiasm but little substance. This psalm expresses powerful reasons for praising God – Israel's historical memory and God's coming to bring justice. The psalm weds the emotion and the intellect, both of which are vital to the praise of God. The psalm also weds the universal and the particular. It celebrates the kingship of YHWH and reminds the community that its historical memory of the mighty acts of King YHWH is for the sake of all peoples and all creation. The psalm begins with the particular salvation history of Israel and concludes with hope of justice for the entire world because of the advent of King YHWH. The world is turned in a new direction because of King YHWH's involvement, and so the world and the congregation are called to a new song. The psalm includes both the memory of God's mighty acts on behalf of the community and the reminder that these mighty acts have implications for all creation. Again, some contemporary worshiping communities focus on nurturing faith within the community; others emphasize the power of faith for the world beyond. Psalm 98 suggests that the journey inward and the journey outward are both essential to the full worship of the divine king.

PSALM 99

¹ The LORD is king; let the peoples tremble!
  He sits enthroned upon the cherubim; let the earth quake!
² The LORD is great in Zion;
  he is exalted over all the peoples.
³ Let them praise your great and awesome name.
  Holy is he!
⁴ Mighty King, lover of justice,
  you have established equity;
you have executed justice
  and righteousness in Jacob.
⁵ Extol the LORD our God;
  worship at his footstool.
  Holy is he!

⁶ Moses and Aaron were among his priests,
  Samuel also was among those who called on his name.
  They cried to the LORD, and he answered them.
⁷ He spoke to them in the pillar of cloud;
  they kept his decrees,
  and the statutes that he gave them.

⁸ O LORD our God, you answered them;
   you were a forgiving God to them,
   but an avenger of their wrongdoings.
⁹ Extol the LORD our God,
   and worship at his holy mountain;
   for the LORD our God is holy.

Psalm 99 is one of the hymns of praise often categorized as an enthronement psalm because it celebrates the kingship of YHWH. The text begins with the phrase "YHWH reigns," rendered in the NRSV as "The Lord is king," a hallmark of the cluster of psalms (Psalms 93–100) that emphasize the divine kingship in this section of the Hebrew Psalter. Psalm 99 is distinct in the cluster in having a poetic structure that is slightly more complex. Verses 5 and 9 function as a refrain to delimit the sections of the poem. The repetition of "Holy is he!" in verses 3 and 5 also indicates the parts of that section of the poem: verses 1–3 focus on YHWH's reign over Zion and over all peoples; verses 4–5 focus on divine justice. Verses 6–9 narrate the tradition of divine answers to those who prayed as part of the salvation history treasured in Israel's memory and imagination.

Another distinction in Psalm 99 is the attention given to ancient Israel's historical traditions. The Jerusalem cult traditions are clear in the psalm and reflect the festival setting in which YHWH's enthronement is reenacted for the congregation as a way of envisioning life with YHWH as creator and king. The connection to the liturgical setting common to the enthronement psalms that celebrate the reign of God (Psalms 93–100) is clear enough. In this psalm, the cultic setting becomes a context for remembering historical covenant traditions. McCann points to a number of verbal connections between Psalm 99 and Exod 15:1–18,[220] the song of Miriam/Moses that celebrates the divine deliverance at sea during the Exodus from slavery in Egypt, a manifestation of the kingship of YHWH that is central to ancient Israel's historical memory. Marvin Tate describes Book IV of the Psalter (Psalms 90–106) as a "Moses Book."[221] The book refers to Moses six times (Pss 99:6; 103:7; 105:26; 106:16, 23, 32) in addition to the superscription of Psalm 90. Psalms 99:6; 105:26; and 106:16 include Aaron.

These allusions suggest a connection to the wilderness traditions. Careful readers of the Psalter will remember that the conclusion of Book III in Psalm 89 narrated the destruction of the Davidic kingdom. The allusions to Mosaic traditions in Book IV imply a new setting in the wilderness of exile and its aftermath. As indicated earlier, Psalm 99 likely originated in the preexilic Jerusalem cult, but in Book IV of the Psalter the text has now found a new context tied to Moses traditions. In the second

²²⁰ J. C. McCann, Jr., "Book of Psalms," in L. E. Keck et al. (eds.), *The New Interpreter's Bible*, vol. 4 (1996), 1074–1075.
²²¹ M. E. Tate, *Psalms 51–100* (1990), xxvi.

wilderness experience, the affirmation of YHWH as the king who brings justice is transforming for the community of exile and its troubling aftermath.

Verses 1–5. The refrain-like verse 5 marks the first section of the poem, which begins with the exclamation characteristic of the enthronement psalms: "YHWH reigns." Further, YHWH is enthroned on the cherubim, the winged creatures with the Ark of the Covenant. The Jerusalem cult tradition proclaimed that YHWH is invisibly enthroned above the Ark and thus reigns from Zion. The divine kingship is not limited to ancient Israel, however, but extends to all peoples. Enthronement in Zion suggests the earthly sacred place marking divine rule and power, but the enthronement psalms make it clear that YHWH's reign is universal. All of creation and its peoples hear the call to tremble and quake, and to praise the "great and awesome" divine king whose name indicates the divine presence.

A Closer Look: Set Apart Is He

The phrase "Holy is he!" at the end of verse 3 and the end of verse 5 marks the distinct parts of this section of the psalm. The Hebrew notion of holiness has to do with being set apart. YHWH is set apart in the sense of being incomparable, different, unlike any other. This God is not set apart *from* the world, however, but rather set apart *to* the world. YHWH relates to the world unlike any other divine king. In turn, ancient Israel is called to be holy or set apart to YHWH. Holiness is thus not a separatist stance but a relational stance. YHWH relates to the world in a distinct way, and Israel is called to reflect that stance.

The distinction of YHWH in verses 4–5 has to do with justice and righteousness in Jacob/Israel. The section concludes in verse 5 with a call to worship YHWH at the footstool – that is, at the Ark in the Jerusalem temple – and concludes again with the exclamation "Holy is he!" Verse 4 fits the notion of holiness as a relational stance in characterizing King YHWH as one who establishes justice in the community. Justice in that sense included protecting the powerless, like the orphans and widows, from oppression by the powerful. Later in the psalm, YHWH answers prayers and forgives. Although the opening section of the psalm calls for a trembling response to the divine king, this God is clearly still fully engaged with the community in efforts toward order and wholeness. The psalm calls the community to embrace life with YHWH as king and thus to find ways in daily life to embody justice and integrity in all aspects of community life.

Verses 6–9. The psalm's second section focuses on Israel's historical traditions, with Moses, Aaron, and Samuel as those who "cried to the Lord." Moses famously and profoundly interceded on behalf of the people after the golden calf incident in Exodus 32–34, and Aaron interceded during the plague narrated in Numbers 16. Samuel prayed on behalf of the people in 1 Samuel 7 and 12; Samuel also fiercely stood for the kingship of YHWH, the focus of this psalm. The psalm suggests that Moses, Aaron, and Samuel demonstrated a pattern of interceding for the people and that God would answer them. As mediators between YHWH and the people, these three also should embody the justice emphasized in Psalm 99. Moses and Aaron encountered the revelation of God "in the pillar of cloud" in the wilderness; perhaps the inclusion of Samuel here refers to smoke from the altar at Shiloh, where his call is placed in 1 Samuel 3. These three leaders from Israel's history are here remembered for their powerful prayer and for hearing the voice of God. They responded with lives embracing YHWH's "decrees" and "statutes," so Moses, Aaron, and Samuel are examples of those involved in the dialogue of faith central to ancient Israel and central to the traditions of the covenant relationship between YHWH and Israel. Verse 8 repeats that YHWH answered Moses, Aaron, and Samuel as a God who was both merciful in forgiving them and as a God who held them accountable for any "wrongdoings." The tradition of YHWH as one who both forgives and judges is in line with the famous confession in Exod 34:6–7, very much part of ancient Israel's covenant traditions. Both the forgiving and the just judgment serve redemptive purposes.

The psalm concludes with a renewed call to extol and worship this holy king at the holy mountain. To extol means to lift up and praise YHWH as king. The concluding call repeats the refrain of verse 5, and the same root word for "extol" occurs in verse 2. The psalm calls the congregation to praise this God revealed in worship and history.

Bridging the Horizons: Imagining Life with YHWH

Psalm 99 characterizes YHWH in terms of both the particular and the universal. YHWH is enthroned in Zion and is the one who establishes justice for all of creation. The creator and ruler of creation also acts in both mercy and justice. This complex characterization of the divine typifies the Hebrew scriptures and is central for a full view of God in the contemporary world. In their current literary setting in Book IV of the Psalter, the enthronement psalms powerfully assert the kingship of this YHWH in the context of the praise of worship. "As such this grouping stands as the 'answer' to the problem posed in Ps 89 as to the apparent failure of the Davidic covenant with which Books One–Three are primarily concerned."[222] Psalm 99 is distinctive in characterizing YHWH as the one who answered the prayers of Moses, Aaron, and Samuel and thus was the divine king long before the Davidic kingdom in ancient Jerusalem. The psalm's historical emphasis shapes its significance. The song's liturgical power makes it possible for the community to imagine again life with YHWH as king, a life centered on the honest dialogue of

---

[222] G. H. Wilson, *Editing of the Hebrew Psalter* (1985), 215.

faith and the establishment of justice and mercy as exemplified in both the community's cultic traditions and its historical traditions. Remembering that reality in the festival liturgy could inspire the community to see such a life as the truly real and to live into that reality and hope in establishing ways of justice, mercy, and integrity in the community's life even in the face of a world overwhelmed with the chaos of exile and its aftermath. This liturgical function of memory and imagination is still the central act for contemporary communities of faith.

PSALM 100 – A PSALM OF THANKSGIVING

¹ Make a joyful noise to the LORD, all the earth.
² Worship the LORD with gladness;
  come into his presence with singing.

³ Know that the LORD is God.
  It is he that made us, and we are his;
  we are his people, and the sheep of his pasture.

⁴ Enter his gates with thanksgiving,
  and his courts with praise.
  Give thanks to him, bless his name.

⁵ For the LORD is good;
  his steadfast love endures for ever,
  and his faithfulness to all generations.

Psalm 100 is one of the texts in the Psalter that is so familiar to readers that it is difficult to find a fresh perspective on it. It is brief, though its language is lively and its theme profound. The psalm is a hymn of praise that uses imperatives to summon the community to worship. The text exemplifies the standard structure of the descriptive praise of God in the Psalms, with the imperative call to praise followed by the reason for the praise. That structure occurs twice in Psalm 100, with the universal call to praise in verses 1–2, which is given a rationale in the latter part of verse 3. Verse 4 then renews the call to praise, followed by the motivation in the psalm's final verse.[223]

---

[223] J. L. Mays, *Psalms* (1994), 317. Mays understands the structure to occur only once, with verse 5 providing the reason for the praise called for in verses 1–4.

The psalm's poetic voice is likely that of a liturgist or choir calling the community to praise. The language of the psalm suggests a liturgical setting. A procession into worship with the purpose of praise and thanksgiving is the most common suggestion. Although the text fits the beginning of worship, it could be a portion of a larger liturgical setting.

Attentive readers of the Psalter will realize that Psalm 100 shares much of the vocabulary of the enthronement psalms collected just before it in Book IV (Psalms 90–106). Psalm 100 uses royal language in relation to the divine king. Both McCann and Tate note connections with Psalm 95 and suggest that Psalms 95 and 100 constitute the frame around Psalms 96–99 as a collection of psalms celebrating the kingship of YHWH.[224] That view can be expanded a bit. The cluster of Psalms 93–100 relates to the kingship of YHWH, and Psalm 100 serves as an appropriate conclusion to the cluster.

The psalm begins with an imperative calling "all the earth" to the praise of God. The liturgical setting becomes clear in verse 2 with the call to enter the sanctuary for worship. The verbs are telling. The imperative in verse 1 suggests a shout of praise; the verb in the first line of verse 2 is literally "serve," though the NRSV understandably renders it as "worship." The verb connotes both worship and obedience – terms that fit the appropriate response to the divine king. Israel is called to worship and serve King YHWH rather than other gods or national rulers. Verse 2 calls the community to gather at the sanctuary for worship of the divine king, but the call also has political implications. The community's focus is YHWH as the living God, as opposed to other empires and their deities. The psalm also makes it clear that human rulers in Israel are not to be worshiped.

The imperative at the beginning of verse 3 – the verse at the center of the poem – shifts from the more common verbs associated with praise in worship to "know." The verb suggests more than knowing about YHWH. It rather has to do with recognizing that the community belongs to YHWH; that is the reason given for the worship of the divine king. Israel belongs to YHWH, who is both their creator and their shepherd. The shepherd image connotes royalty in the ancient Near East. The confession that YHWH "made us" could refer to both the creation of the world and the creation of the community in its salvation history. In these first verses, Psalm 100 serves as a public proclamation that YHWH is the living God, the creator and liberator who rules Israel and "all the earth." This proclamation is a fitting liturgical response to YHWH's acts and presence within the worshiping community. God made this people and continues to guide them to fullness of life. The psalm is a liturgical articulation of the first commandment; Israel worships no other king but YHWH. The first three verses have moved from a universal call to praise to a reason for praise centering on the life-giving relationship between YHWH and Israel.

---

[224] J. C. McCann, Jr., "Book of Psalms," in L. E. Keck et al. (eds.), *The New Interpreter's Bible*, vol. 4 (1996), 1077; and M. E. Tate, *Psalms 51–100* (1990), 535.

This psalm, in line with a number of the hymns of praise, articulates both particular and universal theological perspectives. It is part of the tradition in the Hebrew scriptures that understands YHWH's engagement with Israel to be for the sake of "all the earth." Ancient Israel's purpose as people of YHWH is to be a blessing for all the peoples of the earth (Gen 12:1–3). In that way, the story of God within the faith community of ancient Israel is tied to all peoples and to the future of all creation.

The footnote to verse 3 in the NRSV indicates a textual issue of note. A rendering of the standard Hebrew text is reflected in the footnote: "Know that YHWH, this one, is God, the one who made us and not we ourselves." Those who preserved the text also include in the margin an alternative reading from several Hebrew manuscripts and Greek texts: "Know that YHWH, this one, is God, the one who made us, the one to whom we belong." That rendering is the basis of the NRSV translation and appears to be the stronger textual tradition.

Verse 4 renews the summons to praise with a bit more specificity, calling the community to come into the sanctuary with thanksgiving and blessing of the divine name. The verse again reflects the liturgical setting; it concludes the use of seven imperatives calling the community to worship – make a joyful noise, worship, come, know, enter, give thanks, and bless. It may well be that this renewed summons to praise sparked the psalm's scribal superscription: "A Psalm of thanksgiving." In the Hebrew Psalter, to give thanks is to confess or declare how God has come to deliver and been present to bless. The act of thanksgiving constitutes the narrative praise of God and the blessing of the divine name as a response to God's involvement in the world on behalf of the community. The psalm's concluding verse offers the reasons for the praise called for in verse 4. The reasons use terms loaded with significance in the Hebrew Psalter – YHWH's goodness, steadfast love, and faithfulness. God continues to be present with the community and provides for fullness of life. The confession of the continuation of YHWH's loyal love and trustworthiness toward the community summarizes much of the narrative of the Hebrew scriptures and is a central confession of the faith of the Psalter.

Bridging the Horizons: Called to Worship

Psalm 100 is well known as a joyful and enthusiastic call to worship. The psalm partakes of no restrained formula; the opening imperative calls for a shout of joy in anticipation of the encounter with the divine in worship in the sanctuary as a sacred place of divine presence. The psalm's language is familiar in contemporary worship services, but often those settings miss the active nature of the psalm's verbs, such as entering through gates or into courts and singing. The psalm calls for such profound and uninhibited praise because this God is the one who has given life to ancient Israel and to "all the earth" and continues to nurture both. God is both creator/liberator and the one who gives guidance and provides for life. In turn, the psalm calls for a response of praise and gratitude, in both worship and life, which would constitute knowing that YHWH is God (v. 3).

PSALM 101 – OF DAVID. A PSALM

¹ I will sing of loyalty and of justice;
   to you, O LORD, I will sing.
² I will study the way that is blameless.
   When shall I attain it?

I will walk with integrity of heart
   within my house;
³ I will not set before my eyes
   anything that is base.

I hate the work of those who fall away;
   it shall not cling to me.
⁴ Perverseness of heart shall be far from me;
   I will know nothing of evil.

⁵ One who secretly slanders a neighbor
   I will destroy.
A haughty look and an arrogant heart
   I will not tolerate.

⁶ I will look with favor on the faithful in the land,
   so that they may live with me;
whoever walks in the way that is blameless
   shall minister to me.

⁷ No one who practices deceit
   shall remain in my house;
no one who utters lies
   shall continue in my presence.

⁸ **Morning by morning I will destroy**
all the wicked in the land,
cutting off all evildoers
from the city of the LORD.

This psalm is commonly reckoned among the royal psalms. The king in Jerusalem is generally taken to be the speaker. The psalm consists of a pledge to be a good and faithful king, providing some specificity about the conduct and policies that consti-tute good governance. The psalm is dominated by first-person pronouns, indicating the royal resolve to reflect the will and purpose of YHWH. The first-person state-ments may be taken as a list of practices the king will avoid, plus a few positives about right conduct.

The first verses set the tone for what follows. On the one hand, "singing loy-alty (*ḥesed*) and justice" suggests a liturgical, public act of commitment to YHWH's own sense of faithfulness and wise governance. Such a public act might have been a coronation. On the other hand, "I will study" indicates a reflective stance about the right substance of governance. The king will ponder ways in which to embody integrity, communal solidarity, and equitable administration. The list that follows concerns the several distortions of conduct that will detract from or violate faith-ful integrity. These distractions include what is base, bad company that will cause a "falling away" in disobedience, perverseness, evil, slander, arrogance, deceit, lies, wickedness, and evildoing. This is a standard list that reflects the required Torah commitments already voiced at the outset in Psalm 1. That is, the king is held to account for the same conduct that applies to every member of the Torah commu-nity. Only now those requirements are drawn closer to the exercise of governance. The sum of the list concerns whatever diminishes the solidarity of the neighbor-hood in which members are bound to each other in respect and honor.

This resolve to shun potentially destructive behavior and associations is inter-rupted in verse 6 by a positive statement concerning the faithful, who will be the king's allies and valued public. It is remarkable that except for "loyalty" and "justice" in verse 1, there is nothing here of the "justice and righteousness" that Psalm 72 would lead us to expect. On offer is a king who will be vigilant to order society with neighborly regard and to avoid all the seductions and distortions of power.

Much interpretation of this psalm takes it simply as a list of resolutions for the good exercise of royal power. This reading of the psalm is challenged, however, if we give priority to the question of verse 2, "When will you come to me?" (Note the poor translation of the question in the NRSV.) If we permit this question that the king asks of God to determine the whole of the psalm, then we may take it that the psalm is in fact an urgent petition to God, that God's faithful generosity should establish a better societal order. The bid of the king is that God should come visibly and bring a new order to the realm of the king. The several pledges of the king's recital that we have already noted function as *motivations* to move God to act in the king's favor. The list of "moral virtues" is thereby transposed, in this political context, into grounds from which to expect and hope for divine action and divine favor. What is otherwise rather abstract is seen to be an intense covenantal transaction whereby the king is a suppliant before a God who has good gifts to give and on whom the public order finally depends. This petition is an acknowledgment by the king that his governance is at best penultimate; it awaits the new governance of YHWH. It is clear that in Israel such complaints as this question function as acts of hope, in full expectation that God will answer and give what is needed. The motivations expressed as royal resolves provide grounds for YHWH to do what is asked.

A Closer Look: A Model King

If we take the psalm in a more conventional way as a description of a "model king," we may see that this psalm reflects and stands in the midst of Israel's rather stable and consistent inventory of the "virtues" of covenantal fidelity. These various inventories affirm what is constant with a variety of nuances, but they stay with the main points of neighborly solidarity that refuses self-serving advantage. The inventory appears, for example, in Psalms 15 and 24 in what are taken as norms for admission to worship. The most complete list is in Job 31, wherein Job recites his behavior as a model of neighborly fidelity. It is not a far stretch to suggest that the king in this psalm and Job in his recital are much alike, both powerful persons with social responsibility and great freedom about how to deploy that power. Both voices attest to discipline, obligation, intentionality, and a readiness for a responsible life in the neighborhood.

A Closer Look: Persuading YHWH

If we permit the question in verse 2 ("When will you come to me?") to govern our reading, then we see the "list of virtues" as a motivation designed to evoke God's positive response to royal need. The recital of Job in Job 31, moreover, performs the same function in the larger drama of the book. The Psalms are variously filled with such motivations, in the context of complaint and petition, which seek to give God reasons to answer prayers and to intervene on behalf of the petitioner:

In the broadest sort of way, they tend either to draw attention to some feature of *God's nature and character* or to lift up some aspect of *the situation of the petitioner(s)*. There are also a number of motive clauses that point to *the relationship between God and the petitioner(s)* as a reason for God's response.[225]

---

[225] P. D. Miller, *They Cried to the Lord* (1994) 116.

In this case, the motivation concerns the relation of king and God wherein the king is presented as a faithful, obedient subject of YHWH to whom YHWH may be expected to "come to me" in response to the petition. This motivation, like many in the Psalter, discloses Israel's capacity to persuade, crowd, or cajole YHWH into answering prayers. Among the possible motivations, as in this psalm, is a statement of innocence, indicating that God has an obligation to answer in response to human fidelity. Other cases of the same statement of innocence are found in Ps 35:13 and in Ps 7:3–5, where the statement is in the same form as that of Job 31. Thus the single question in Psalm 101 opens the way to see that this is an intense covenantal transaction in which the speaker has an urgent need that is congruent with his ethical resolve.

Bridging the Horizons: An Act of Hope

The question of verse 2 is an act of hope. The king knows that the rule of God's faithfulness and justice is not yet established. But the king passionately trusts that this new rule will come. Thus Terrien concludes: "A great void lies behind the begging for presence! A new age will create a new society."[226] Such an act of intense hope is a characteristic practice of faith. In the New Testament, the church is taught to pray: "Your kingdom come" (Matt 6:10). And the church in its celebration of the Eucharist will regularly assert that it "proclaims the Lord's death until he come."

The practice of insistent hope (and therefore a critique of present circumstances) is an acute countercultural activity of faith. In an overly affluent commodity society like the current United States, there is a great temptation to embrace "realized eschatology" in the conviction that it does not get any better than this. Such self-congratulatory satisfaction is the antithesis of hope. Or conversely, when one realizes that all of the achievements of a commodity society do not bring joy, one may end in despair, realizing that all of this is not enough. Both self-satisfaction and despair are enemies of hope. It is a work of faith to be vigilant and alert to live in expectation for what God will yet give. The psalm is authorization to address God with compelling reasons that God should not delay in bringing in an economy of peace and justice.

But of course the faithful know that such hope is not a casual, haphazard enterprise. Such hope requires readiness and discipline. Thus, in his parable, Jesus teaches, using the image of the bridesmaids, that there must be readiness for God's newness (Matt 25:1–13). Long before the parable, the king in our psalm avows his readiness for God's coming. In petitioning for God's newness, the disciplines of neighborly integrity are urgently required. The king who waits in

---

[226] S. Terrien, *Psalms* (2003), 694.

readiness may ask "When?" The calculus of *readiness and hope* is a primary occupation of faith, done well by those who practice integrity in the public domain.

PSALM 102 – A PRAYER OF ONE AFFLICTED, WHEN FAINT AND PLEADING BEFORE THE LORD

¹ Hear my prayer, O LORD;
 let my cry come to you.
² Do not hide your face from me
 on the day of my distress.
Incline your ear to me;
 answer me speedily on the day when I call.

³ For my days pass away like smoke,
 and my bones burn like a furnace.
⁴ My heart is stricken and withered like grass;
 I am too wasted to eat my bread.
⁵ Because of my loud groaning
 my bones cling to my skin.
⁶ I am like an owl of the wilderness,
 like a little owl of the waste places.
⁷ I lie awake;
 I am like a lonely bird on the housetop.
⁸ All day long my enemies taunt me;
 those who deride me use my name for a curse.
⁹ For I eat ashes like bread,
 and mingle tears with my drink,
¹⁰ because of your indignation and anger;
 for you have lifted me up and thrown me aside.
¹¹ My days are like an evening shadow;
 I wither away like grass.

¹² But you, O LORD, are enthroned for ever;
 your name endures to all generations.
¹³ You will rise up and have compassion on Zion,
 for it is time to favor it;
 the appointed time has come.

¹⁴ For your servants hold its stones dear,
and have pity on its dust.
¹⁵ The nations will fear the name of the Lᴏʀᴅ,
and all the kings of the earth your glory.
¹⁶ For the Lᴏʀᴅ will build up Zion;
he will appear in his glory.
¹⁷ He will regard the prayer of the destitute,
and will not despise their prayer.

¹⁸ Let this be recorded for a generation to come,
so that a people yet unborn may praise the Lᴏʀᴅ:
¹⁹ that he looked down from his holy height,
from heaven the Lᴏʀᴅ looked at the earth,
²⁰ to hear the groans of the prisoners,
to set free those who were doomed to die;
²¹ so that the name of the Lᴏʀᴅ may be declared in Zion,
and his praise in Jerusalem,
²² when peoples gather together,
and kingdoms, to worship the Lᴏʀᴅ.

²³ He has broken my strength in mid-course;
he has shortened my days.
²⁴ 'O my God,' I say, 'do not take me away
at the mid-point of my life,
you whose years endure
throughout all generations.'

²⁵ Long ago you laid the foundation of the earth,
and the heavens are the work of your hands.
²⁶ They will perish, but you endure;
they will all wear out like a garment.
You change them like clothing, and they pass away;
²⁷ but you are the same, and your years have no end.
²⁸ The children of your servants shall live secure;
their offspring shall be established in your presence.

Psalm 102 consists of three poetic sections: verses 1–11 take the form of a prayer for help, verses 12–22 affirm YHWH's reign, and verses 23–28 combine the themes of the first two sections in a conclusion. Initially the psalm fits the form of a prayer for help, but it varies considerably from that form as it moves beyond the first section.

Attempts to construct an ancient setting for the psalm vary considerably. Mowinckel and Eaton associate the psalm with the new year festival and perhaps the voice of the king.[227] The language of the first section of the psalm could well come from a setting of severe illness, but the images could also be applied in a variety of life crises. Others would emphasize the second section of the psalm and suggest that the setting has to do with the fall of Jerusalem and understand the prayer to come from the exile and to seek restoration for the community.[228] Perhaps an individual prayer in the first eleven verses has become the basis for a prayer of the community in an exilic setting. The psalm has varied parts, but its unity seems clear.[229] Its individual and corporate dimensions are related, and the motif of time runs through the whole poem. The best approach is to consider the lament in the first section and then follow the poem's sequence to consider its full import.

Another approach to the matter of context is to consider the psalm in its literary setting of Book IV (Psalms 90–106) of the Psalter. The psalm asserts the kingship of YHWH, the central proclamation of Psalms 93–100. It also returns to themes of the book's first psalm. Psalm 90 emphasizes human transience and divine permanence, divine judgment, and the hope that God makes possible.[230] These themes continue in Psalm 103. The connections to the beginning of Book IV suggest to readers that the conclusion to the book is beginning.

The first section of Psalm 102, verses 1–11, is a prayer for help, with an opening plea in verses 1–2 characteristic of individual laments. The plea is that YHWH will hear and be present in this time of crisis and cry for help. This opening section of the psalm is a clear example of the petition and complaint that characterize the prayers in the Psalter. The use of "days" in verses 3 and 11 and the image of withering grass in verses 4 and 11 frame the prayer that continues in the first section of the psalm. "Day" also occurs in verses 2 and 8. The images in this section emphasize the crisis portrayed by the speaker and begin to articulate the brevity and frailty of human life. The bones, the heart, and the skin burn, wither, and pass away. Life lasts no longer than smoke scattered by the wind. The images are stunning and continue unabated. The petitioner is like a tiny bird on a housetop or one who is alone in the wilderness. The body is so weak that even bread cannot be eaten. Groans become the food of life; verse 9 speaks of ashes for food and tears for drink. To make matters worse, enemies continually mock the petitioner, who is living the trouble and woe of divine absence and thus feels divine judgment. Days wither away like grass in the heat of the desert and are as impermanent as a shadow. The imagery and language of verses 1–11 are characteristic of the prayers of individuals in crisis in the Psalter.

---

[227] S. Mowinckel, *The Psalms in Israel's Worship*, vol. 1 (1962), 221; and J. H. Eaton, *Kingship and the Psalms* (1986), 80–81.

[228] C. C. Broyles, *Psalms* (1999), 390; and J. C. McCann, Jr., "Book of Psalms," in L. E. Keck et al. (eds.), *The New Interpreter's Bible*, vol. 4 (1996), 1086.

[229] See J. L. Mays, *Psalms* (1994), 323–324.

[230] G. H. Wilson, *Editing of the Hebrew Psalter* (1985), 218.

The language elicits strong responses from hearers/readers. It could certainly articulate the crisis of one who is terminally ill, but it could also adapt to a variety of settings in life understood as extreme settings of trouble and woe.

The second section of Psalm 102, verses 12–22, begins with a signal of emphatic contrast: "But you."[231] The contrast is between human impermanence and the permanence of YHWH's kingship. YHWH is enthroned throughout all the generations. The divine name (reputation) as creator and king is not frail and brief like the days of frail humans but lasts "forever." That confession of faith in verse 12 leads the poet to envision the divine king's restoration of Zion, the center of the divine presence within the community. The hope is that the time of restoration is at hand, in contrast to the miserable days of the petitioner narrated in the first section of the psalm. The community holds dear the sacred place, and the poet envisions a renewal of YHWH's presence and activity in Zion in response to the community's pleadings. This renewal will bear witness to future generations of God's great care for the community of Zion, and the witness will extend to "all the kings of the earth." This renewal from God will bring hope to those in despair, and the response of thanksgiving narrating this salvific action will make it possible for the nations to understand and come to worship YHWH as king.

The background for this section of the psalm would appear to be the destruction of Jerusalem in the sixth century BCE. Its sequence is noteworthy. It confesses the kingship of YHWH and then portrays the coming restoration of Zion as a divine act followed by the responding praise of the community. A plea that YHWH will restore Zion underlies these verses; that seems to be the function of this section in the poem. Also striking is the contrast with the misery of the petitioner in the psalm's first section, verses 1–11, and in turn the contrast between human transience and divine eternality. These first two sections of the psalm make it clear that both the individual petitioner and the community are in dire need of divine help. The question is what the divine king will bring.

The psalm's third section, verses 23–28, brings the themes of the psalm together. Verse 23 returns to the petitioner's cry for help amid brief and frail "days." The plea is that God will not cut life short and remove this one from the worshiping community. Verse 24 again appeals to God's endurance "throughout all generations" as a basis for the prayer for deliverance from premature death. This theme continues as the poem's concluding verses return to affirmations of YHWH's reign. God created long ago and continues to endure and will continue to reign even beyond the life of the creation. Nature changes but YHWH endures. The confession of the continuing reign of God leads to the poem's concluding word of hope. God's servants, the worshiping community, will find security even in the face of chaos and calamity as portrayed in this psalm. God will restore Zion, and God will be present to bless

---

[231] The beginning of verse 12 illustrates Westermann's *waw* adversative; see C. Westermann, *Praise and Lament in the Psalms* (1981), 70.

"throughout all the generations." This third section of the psalm brings together the themes of the first two. Based on a creation theology centered on the reign of YHWH and characteristic of Book IV of the Psalter, the psalm moves from a desperate cry for help to a vision of hope and finally to an echo of the prayer for help and an expression of hope.

A Closer Look: First Commentary

The psalm's superscription is distinct in the Psalter and provides important clues for readers of the text. The petitioner is said to be among the "afflicted," the lowly or needy who seek YHWH's help. The petitioner is "faint," without strength, and pours out a powerful plea for divine assistance. The heading becomes a kind of first commentary on the psalm and suggests that readers pray the prayer as a cry from one in need of God's help.

Bridging the Horizons: A Model Prayer

Psalm 102 weaves together both the individual and the community. Prayers from both come to full expression. Genuine faith does not allow any privatization. Corporate prayer and individual prayer are equally urgent, and the voices of both individual and community are fully present.

The psalm is about integrating reality and faith. The confession of ancient Israel is that YHWH reigns and yet the petitioner is not enjoying the fullness of life. How does the confession that YHWH is king square with the petitioner's crisis and with the community's trauma in the face of Zion's fall? The confession of divine kingship becomes the basis for the cry that YHWH might bring hope out of crisis. The psalm serves as a model prayer – as its superscription suggests – in seeking to put lived experience together with received tradition. It is a fine example of prayer as the honest dialogue of faith.

The psalm insists on the reign of YHWH even in the face of extreme crisis. The confession of YHWH as king, central to Book IV of the Psalter, persists, and the psalm brings that affirmation into dialogue with the trouble at hand. Psalm 102 does not lightly affirm the divine reign but rather brings it into honest and urgent connection with the current crisis. The psalm takes a straightforward view of life. It confesses the tenets of the received faith of creation and Zion theology as a means of articulating a hope for the worshiping community in the face of defeat, a hope found in the living God. The worship this psalm reflects relates to the whole of life.

PSALM 103 – OF DAVID

¹ Bless the LORD, O my soul,
  and all that is within me,
  bless his holy name.
² Bless the LORD, O my soul,
  and do not forget all his benefits –
³ who forgives all your iniquity,
  who heals all your diseases,
⁴ who redeems your life from the Pit,
  who crowns you with steadfast love and mercy,
⁵ who satisfies you with good as long as you live
  so that your youth is renewed like the eagle's.

⁶ The LORD works vindication
  and justice for all who are oppressed.
⁷ He made known his ways to Moses,
  his acts to the people of Israel.
⁸ The LORD is merciful and gracious,
  slow to anger and abounding in steadfast love.
⁹ He will not always accuse,
  nor will he keep his anger for ever.
¹⁰ He does not deal with us according to our sins,
  nor repay us according to our iniquities.
¹¹ For as the heavens are high above the earth,
  so great is his steadfast love toward those who fear him;
¹² as far as the east is from the west,
  so far he removes our transgressions from us.
¹³ As a father has compassion for his children,
  so the LORD has compassion for those who fear him.
¹⁴ For he knows how we were made;
  he remembers that we are dust.

¹⁵ As for mortals, their days are like grass;
  they flourish like a flower of the field;
¹⁶ for the wind passes over it, and it is gone,
  and its place knows it no more.
¹⁷ But the steadfast love of the LORD is from everlasting to everlasting
  on those who fear him,

and his righteousness to children's children,
¹⁸ to those who keep his covenant
and remember to do his commandments.

¹⁹ The LORD has established his throne in the heavens,
and his kingdom rules over all.
²⁰ Bless the LORD, O you his angels,
you mighty ones who do his bidding,
obedient to his spoken word.
²¹ Bless the LORD, all his hosts,
his ministers that do his will.
²² Bless the LORD, all his works,
in all places of his dominion.
Bless the LORD, O my soul.

Psalm 103 is one of the favorites among the hymns of praise; its opening words are familiar to worshipers. The psalm incorporates elements of hymns of praise and individual songs of thanksgiving. The praise follows the classic form of the Psalter, with the call to praise followed by reasons for the praise. The summons to praise in Psalm 103 is unusual in that it is a self-exhortation, but the context is still that of corporate worship. The psalm would fit well in a worship context in which the congregation offers praise and thanksgiving as a setting for individuals to express gratitude for deliverance from crises and for the bringing of offerings. The psalm exhibits the three classic parts of a hymn of praise: introduction, body, and conclusion. The opening summons to praise is in verses 1–5; the concluding verses 19–22 renew and expand the call to praise. The introduction and conclusion emphasize God's full involvement in the world with the repetition of "all." "All" of the divine works elicit an uninhibited response of praise and thanksgiving. The body of the hymn is in two parts (vv. 6–14 and 15–18), each focusing on a characterization of YHWH.

A Closer Look: Remembering Moses – A Way Past Exile

Book IV of the Hebrew Psalter (Psalms 90–106) is shaped as a response to the crisis of exile articulated pointedly in Psalm 89 at the end of Book III. Book IV calls readers to consider the time prior to the Davidic kingdom, the time of Moses, and to confess and appropriate the steadfast love of YHWH prior to the promise to David as a way to move forward in the face of the despair of exile. Psalm 103 makes an important contribution to that purpose; verse 7 ties the revelation of YHWH's compassion to Moses. McCann also suggests that Psalms 101–102 recount the losses of defeat and exile, the loss of monarchy, temple, and land. Psalm 103 responds with the praise hoped for in Ps 102:12–22.[232] The psalm clearly continues themes from its predecessor: divine permanence and human transience, and divine justice and compassion.

The opening words of Psalm 103 are both familiar and unusual. Verses 1–2 constitute the psalm's opening call to praise in the form of an exhortation to bless YHWH. The speaker calls on the self or person within (*nepeš*), traditionally rendered as "soul" in the NRSV, to bless YHWH and the name of YHWH, which is like no other. The psalm's opening and closing lines are identical and frame the poem. The frame can be expanded to the opening summons to praise in verses 1–2 and the closing verses 20–22, all of which emphasize the verb "bless." The verb carries an association with the knee and with kneeling before the one who gives life. The kneeling or blessing is a response to God's gift of blessing. The opening of the psalm calls the self and all the selves in the congregation to bless YHWH by remembering the benefits YHWH has given to make life possible. YHWH is the source of life. This praise and thanksgiving will contribute to the worship of the community. The psalm includes both individual and community in its call to praise as a part of worship, an act that is by definition corporate in the Hebrew scriptures. So the voice is likely that of a liturgist singing on behalf of the gathered congregation to offer praise and thanksgiving in response to all God's beneficent gifts.

Verses 3–5 then recount the gifts in the classic participial form of the praise of God in the Psalms. By recounting these divine acts, the congregation will remember or "not forget all his benefits." The verbs used to describe the divine acts are characteristic of the acts of deliverance from the crises portrayed in the lament psalms:

who forgives;
who heals;
who redeems;
who crowns;
who satisfies.

YHWH delivers the faithful from the Pit and moves them to the shelter of divine refuge; persons who were gripped by the power of death find new life. In portraying the divine gifts, verse 4 calls on two terms loaded with significance in ancient Israel's confessions – steadfast love and mercy. God's love does not change with external circumstances, and that love is like the love of a mother for her child. God renews the life of those who cry out in need. Verses 1–5 are classic hymnic confessions in the Psalms.

---

[232] J. C. McCann, Jr., "Book of Psalms," in L. E. Keck et al. (eds.), *The New Interpreter's Bible*, vol. 4 (1996), 1091.

The body of the hymn continues the recounting of the mighty acts of YHWH in the participial style of praise. Verse 6 characterizes the acts in terms of righteousness ("vindication") and justice for those in need. God acts to bring the community and those in it to a right relationship with the divine and just relationships with each other. With verse 7, the liturgist moves explicitly to Israel's historical memory and the revelation to Moses. The broad category of divine "benefits" is now attached to the historical revelation. The text for this poetic rehearsal is Exod 34:6–7, and the psalm quotes in verse 8 the positive pole of the famous confession:

The Lord is merciful and gracious,
slow to anger and abounding in steadfast love. (v. 8)

The emphasis is on the gifts of God characterized in terms of gracious mercy and loyal love.

The verses that follow expound this confession of faith with analogies, first in the negative. YHWH's anger and accusations do not last forever, and YHWH does not deal with the faithful "according to our sins." Verses 11–14 move the analogies to the positive in classic Hebrew poetic style, with verses 11 and 14 both beginning with "For/Because" and verses 12 and 13 each beginning with comparisons. YHWH's steadfast love is so vast that it brings about even the removal of sin. The poetic images emphasize the divine compassion in stunning ways. YHWH does not calculate by human standards but by way of unchanging love. God is not a calculating God in the way humans would use that term but operates out of immeasurable and transforming compassion and grace. God remembers the frailty of humans and so is compassionate. The confession in Exod 34:6–7 includes poles of both mercy and justice. The emphasis in Psalm 103 is on mercy, but the justice of YHWH is not absent. Verses 11 and 13 tie God's mercy to "those who fear him," those trusting and obeying YHWH. The context of the divine mercy is the relationship between YHWH and ancient Israel. This first part of the body of Psalm 103 (vv. 6–14) portrays a remarkably compassionate God.

The body of the hymn concludes in verses 15–18 with a contrast familiar from Psalm 102, the contrast between divine permanence and human transience. Humans flourish like grass or flowers but then are blown away by the wind; the contrast is with YHWH's steadfast love, which endures "from everlasting to everlasting." The term "steadfast love" (*ḥesed*) is used in verses 4, 8, 11, and 17. Those who keep the covenant with YHWH encounter the divine gifts of steadfast love and righteousness. In verse 14, YHWH remembers human frailty and is thus compassionate. In verse 18, those who remember to live in covenant faithfulness enjoy a relationship born of divine loyal love. The emphasis of the contrast between God's eternality and human frailty in verses 15–18 is the continuity of the divine steadfast love for the covenant community.

The psalm's concluding verses begin with an affirmation of YHWH's rule "over all." Such a confession of faith is central to Book IV of the Psalter. Based on the confession, Psalm 103 concludes with a renewed call to praise. First the angels or messengers are called to praise and then the hosts, perhaps the angelic hosts or the heavenly hosts of sun, moon, and stars. In the concluding verse, God's works are summoned to praise in all places, for God's reign reaches all places. The psalm then ends as it began: "Bless the Lord, O my soul." The psalm centers on the compassion and steadfast love of YHWH in relating to the faithful and to all of creation; the only proper response is uninhibited praise and thanksgiving.

The psalm's frame is the call to bless YHWH. The body of the psalm makes it clear that this blessing offered to YHWH is based on prior divine actions and presence. The basis for this poetic structure is Exod 34:6–7 and the first part of the confession there, which characterizes YHWH as "merciful and gracious, slow to anger and abounding in steadfast love." In its current place in Book IV of the Psalter, Psalm 103 calls on that part of ancient Israel's historical memory to speak to the crisis of exile. Exiles might well presume that the divine anger will endure, but Psalm 103 intones a different and surprising way of God in the world. The divine acts center on steadfast love and mercy. Psalm 103 stuns those in the chaos of exile with the proclamation that YHWH acts out of compassion rather than a precise moral calculus. Divine generosity far outlasts the encounter with divine wrath.

Bridging the Horizons: A God of Generous Compassion

McCann suggests that Psalm 103 is an ideal text to counter the notion that the God revealed in the Hebrew scriptures is a God of wrath and judgment.[233] The psalm acknowledges the tension between divine justice and mercy, but settles on the side of generous compassion and appeals to Israel's historical memory in so doing. The story of the covenant is based in divine compassion.

PSALM 104

¹ Bless the LORD, O my soul.
O LORD my God, you are very great.
You are clothed with honor and majesty,
² wrapped in light as with a garment.
You stretch out the heavens like a tent,
³ you set the beams of your chambers on the waters,

---

233 J. C. McCann, Jr., "Book of Psalms," in L. E. Keck et al. (eds.), *The New Interpreter's Bible*, vol. 4 (1996), 1093.

you make the clouds your chariot,
  you ride on the wings of the wind,
⁴ you make the winds your messengers,
  fire and flame your ministers.

⁵ You set the earth on its foundations,
  so that it shall never be shaken.
⁶ You cover it with the deep as with a garment;
  the waters stood above the mountains.
⁷ At your rebuke they flee;
  at the sound of your thunder they take to flight.
⁸ They rose up to the mountains, ran down to the valleys
  to the place that you appointed for them.
⁹ You set a boundary that they may not pass,
  so that they might not again cover the earth.

¹⁰ You make springs gush forth in the valleys;
  they flow between the hills,
¹¹ giving drink to every wild animal;
  the wild asses quench their thirst.
¹² By the streams the birds of the air have their habitation;
  they sing among the branches.
¹³ From your lofty abode you water the mountains;
  the earth is satisfied with the fruit of your work.

¹⁴ You cause the grass to grow for the cattle,
  and plants for people to use,
to bring forth food from the earth,
¹⁵ and wine to gladden the human heart,
oil to make the face shine,
  and bread to strengthen the human heart.
¹⁶ The trees of the LORD are watered abundantly,
  the cedars of Lebanon that he planted.
¹⁷ In them the birds build their nests;
  the stork has its home in the fir trees.
¹⁸ The high mountains are for the wild goats;
  the rocks are a refuge for the coneys.
¹⁹ You have made the moon to mark the seasons;
  the sun knows its time for setting.
²⁰ You make darkness, and it is night,

when all the animals of the forest come creeping out.
21 The young lions roar for their prey,
   seeking their food from God.
22 When the sun rises, they withdraw
   and lie down in their dens.
23 People go out to their work
   and to their labor until the evening.

24 O LORD, how manifold are your works!
   In wisdom you have made them all;
   the earth is full of your creatures.
25 Yonder is the sea, great and wide,
   creeping things innumerable are there,
   living things both small and great.
26 There go the ships,
   and Leviathan that you formed to sport in it.

27 These all look to you
   to give them their food in due season;
28 when you give to them, they gather it up;
   when you open your hand, they are filled with good things.
29 When you hide your face, they are dismayed;
   when you take away their breath, they die
   and return to their dust.
30 When you send forth your spirit, they are created;
   and you renew the face of the ground.

31 May the glory of the LORD endure for ever;
   may the LORD rejoice in his works –
32 who looks on the earth and it trembles,
   who touches the mountains and they smoke.
33 I will sing to the LORD as long as I live;
   I will sing praise to my God while I have being.
34 May my meditation be pleasing to him,
   for I rejoice in the LORD.
35 Let sinners be consumed from the earth,
   and let the wicked be no more.
Bless the LORD, O my soul.
Praise the LORD!

It is a great misfortune that *creation* as a theme of biblical faith has in contemporary usage been skewed into explanatory modes. That modernist attempt to compete with science through "creationism" (or "intelligent design") misses the point of the theological theme, which on its own terms is never explanatory but is character-istically *doxological*. Psalm 104 is a prime example of the way in which Israel – in hymnic modes – responds to the generative, life-giving power of creation and refers the wonder of creation back to the faithful power of the creator. Although the psalm has Egyptian parallels and reflects an older generic theology of creation, it has been made, through the traditioning process, into a vehicle for Israel's Yahwistic faith.

The psalm begins with a summons to the self to turn fully ("bless") to YHWH, ceding self in celebrative affirmation to YHWH (v. 1). The psalm concludes with the same summons to bless and thank (v. 35). After the summons, YHWH is named as "my God" and exuberantly affirmed. After the naming of YHWH in verse 1, the psalm then proceeds to give a long, glad inventory of all facets of creation that are credited to the creator God (vv. 2–23). This long section on creation without mention of the creator is bracketed by references to YHWH in verse 1 and in verse 24 that draw a doxological conclusion. (The exception is the mention of "trees of YHWH" in verse 16, but that mention of YHWH is not rhetorically or structurally important to the poem.)

The psalmist is smitten with the beauty, awesomeness, generativity, and ordered coherence of creation as guaranteed by the creator. Everything is in its place as part of a coherent, life-giving system. The inventory begins in verses 2–9 with a series of "you" statements crediting the basic structure of creation to the wondrous power of the creator. It is "you" who has done it all! These verses reflect a conventional view in the ancient world of the cosmos – heavens above, water beneath, earth well ordered with the mountains and valleys rightly apportioned. It is YHWH who has set a boundary on the waters so that the earth is a safe place protected from the threat of chaos. The setting of boundaries is reflected in Jer 5:22 but also in Mk 4:34, wherein Jesus is credited with doing the work of the creator.

After elaborating the macrostructure of the whole world, the psalmist ponders the abundance of creation resulting from the good supply of water in springs and streams (vv. 10–19). The Bible is set in an arid climate; for that reason, an abundance of water is indeed a wondrous gift of YHWH. The well-watered earth is a welcome habitat for all creatures: grass for cattle to eat, trees for birds' nests, mountains where wild goats can graze. The bringing forth of life-sustaining food is featured in the celebration of *oil, wine,* and *bread* as the elemental produce of the earth, all made possible by water. Calvin refers to this produce as "God's superabundant liberality."[234]

This long inventory concludes with the right ordering of "the times" (vv. 19–23). "Everything in its time" is reflected in the orbits of the sun and moon, of day and

[234] J. Calvin, *Commentary on the Psalms*, vol. 4 (1979), 155.

night. The result is that animals of prey and human beings do not get in each other's way, because the animals work the night shift while the human community sleeps.

The lyrical effect of this long inventory is celebration for the macrostructure (vv. 2–9), the abundant creation (vv. 10–18), and the well-ordered times (vv. 19–23). This entire recital of the splendor of creation leads to a second naming of the name of the creator God, "O Lord" (v. 24). This verse is a retrospective on the fullness of creation.

After this initial inventory culminating in doxology, the psalm offers in turn three quite concrete and compelling images (vv. 25–30). First, the sea (the great "deep" of v. 6) is a full place, full of creatures, ships, and Leviathan, the great sea monster (vv. 25–26). The Old Testament is characteristically leery of the threat of the sea as a vehicle for chaos and disorder. But here the evil monster of disorder is tamed and is reduced to a toy for YHWH's enjoyment (v. 26).[235] YHWH is not threatened by chaos but has reduced it to a vehicle for YHWH's own amusement (see Job 40:15–24). This playful attitude toward the "many waters" is itself an assurance that the order of creation is not under threat. Second, verses 27–28 attest to the generativity of creation. It is YHWH's good hand that feeds all creation, with the emphasis on "all." This statement, closely paralleled in Ps 145:15–16, amounts to a table prayer in which YHWH is thanked for food. It is likely that the best *theology of creation* is voiced exactly in the prayers that ponder that all food that sustains life is a gift.

Third, verses 29–30 affirm that the world lives by the breath of God. The term "breath" in verse 29 and the term "spirit" in verse 30 are the same Hebrew word, *ruaḥ*; the juxtaposition of the two asserts that the world is, moment by moment, dependent on the life-giving presence and power of YHWH. The creator holds the power of generativity on which the world depends, for the world does not have of itself the power of life. Thus YHWH's breathing matters decisively, as though YHWH were a great, reliable iron lung. These last two themes of *food* in verses 27–28 and *breath* in 29–30 attest to the complete dependence that creation has on the creator.

The psalm concludes with a glad doxology to YHWH, who looks at the earth and touches the mountains, and they respond as YHWH's creatures (vv. 31–34). The psalmist is overwhelmed by the wonder of it all, which is attributed to YHWH. In these verses, the psalm returns to the first-person singular verbs with which verse 1 was articulated. This glad affirmation, however, is jolted and interrupted in verse 35 by a warning against "sinners and the wicked." We do not expect such a conclusion in such a lyrical doxology. This reference, however, draws an old poem, perhaps of Egyptian origin, into the orbit of Israel's faith. The beauty and wonder of creation are not autonomous realities but are derived from YHWH. This means, in turn, that they are not unconditional but belong in the conditionality of Torah requirements. Thus the final verse constitutes a warning against exploitative use of creation that disregards the will and intention of the creator (v. 35). In a quite inchoate way, this

[235] See J. D. Levenson, *Creation and the Persistence of Evil* (1988), 17.

verse provides a mandate for care for the environment and a stricture against its careless, destructive use.

Bridging the Horizons: Wine, Oil, and Bread

The elemental gifts of creation named in verse 15 – wine, oil, and bread – are singled out in this psalm and are perhaps the substance of verses 27–28, concerning "food." It is also worth noting that this same triad – wine, oil, and bread – constitutes the characteristic stuff of sacramental life in the practice of the church. The sacraments use the most elemental signs of creation as attestations that creation is freighted with the gift of life from God in all its fullness.

Bridging the Horizons: Environmentalism

This psalm, as J. Clinton McCann notes, provides a basis for environmentalism:

The poet who wrote Psalm 104 was an environmentalist. The psalmist knew about the intricate interconnectedness and subtle interdependence of air, soil, water, plants, and animals, including humans. The psalmist knew the truth revealed in the etymological connection between the Hebrew word for "humanity" (אדם *'ādām*) and the word for "ground" (המדא *ădāmāh*): Human beings really are creatures of the earth. The same truth is revealed in the etymological connection between the English word *human* and the Latin word *humus*, "soil." But, as it were, we have forgotten our roots, both etymological and physical.[236]

As McCann sees, moreover, this environmentalism is rooted not in anxious self-concern but in praise of the creator. This is environmentalism that is theologically focused:

Taking the psalmist as an example, we would have to conclude that concern for the environment begins with praising God. To be sure, this sounds hopelessly simplistic, scientifically and technologically naive. But such a starting point – and its underlying conviction that the world belongs to God – is the only thing that will dislodge our arrogant assumption that *we* can *save* the world, as if it were ours to save! In biblical terms, salvation means life, and in biblical terms, the world does not need to be saved. God has already done that! Psalm 104 affirms that God has made every arrangement and provision for the life of the world.... The environmental crisis will be addressed by nothing short of praising God, exalting God, and humbling ourselves.[237]

---

[236] J. C. McCann, Jr., "Book of Psalms," in L. E. Keck et al. (eds.), *The New Interpreter's Bible*, vol. 4 (1996), 1099.
[237] J. C. McCann, Jr., "Book of Psalms," in L. E. Keck et al. (eds.), *The New Interpreter's Bible*, vol. 4 (1996), 1100.

Bridging the Horizons: Nature As Creation

In a recent study, Alister McGrath has shown the way in which "nature" is to be understood as "creation," as dependent on and referred back to the creator:

The Christian understanding of creation leads directly to the conclusion that there is a correspondence – the degree of which requires clarification – between the works of God and the being of God. Creation and redemption are not merely interconnected within the economy of salvation; they can each be argued to embody the character of God.... A Christian doctrine of creation affirms a congruence between the moral ordering of creation – including humanity as the height of that creation – and the mind of God.[238]

Well before McGrath, moreover, Calvin clearly articulated the cruciality of creation faith: "The world did not originate from itself, consequently, the whole order of nature depends on nothing else than his appointment, by which each element has its own peculiar property."[239]

This affirmation clearly has a defining pastoral agenda of comfort and assurance, a treasure in a world under anxious threat:

Nor is the language of the prophet to be viewed merely as an exhortation to give thanks to God; it is also intended to strengthen our confidence in regard to the future, that we may not live in the world in a state of constant fear and anxiety, as we must have done had not God testified that he has given the earth for a habitation to men.[240]

PSALM 105

1 O give thanks to the LORD, call on his name,
    make known his deeds among the peoples.
2 Sing to him, sing praises to him;
    tell of all his wonderful works.
3 Glory in his holy name;
    let the hearts of those who seek the LORD rejoice.
4 Seek the LORD and his strength;
    seek his presence continually.

---

[238] Alister E. McGrath, *A Scientific Theology: I Nature* (Grand Rapids, MI: Eerdmans, 2001), 193, 217.
[239] J. Calvin, *Commentary on the Psalms*, vol. 4 (1979), 149.
[240] J. Calvin, *Commentary on the Psalms*, vol. 4 (1979), 149.

⁵ Remember the wonderful works he has done,
   his miracles, and the judgments he has uttered,
⁶ O offspring of his servant Abraham,
   children of Jacob, his chosen ones.

⁷ He is the LORD our God;
   his judgments are in all the earth.
⁸ He is mindful of his covenant for ever,
   of the word that he commanded, for a thousand generations,
⁹ the covenant that he made with Abraham,
   his sworn promise to Isaac,
¹⁰ which he confirmed to Jacob as a statute,
    to Israel as an everlasting covenant,
¹¹ saying, 'To you I will give the land of Canaan
    as your portion for an inheritance.'

¹² When they were few in number,
    of little account, and strangers in it,
¹³ wandering from nation to nation,
    from one kingdom to another people,
¹⁴ he allowed no one to oppress them;
    he rebuked kings on their account,
¹⁵ saying, 'Do not touch my anointed ones;
    do my prophets no harm.'

¹⁶ When he summoned famine against the land,
    and broke every staff of bread,
¹⁷ he had sent a man ahead of them,
    Joseph, who was sold as a slave.
¹⁸ His feet were hurt with fetters,
    his neck was put in a collar of iron;
¹⁹ until what he had said came to pass,
    the word of the LORD kept testing him.
²⁰ The king sent and released him;
    the ruler of the peoples set him free.
²¹ He made him lord of his house,
    and ruler of all his possessions,
²² to instruct his officials at his pleasure,
    and to teach his elders wisdom.

²³ Then Israel came to Egypt;
　　Jacob lived as an alien in the land of Ham.
²⁴ And the LORD made his people very fruitful,
　　and made them stronger than their foes,
²⁵ whose hearts he then turned to hate his people,
　　to deal craftily with his servants.

²⁶ He sent his servant Moses,
　　and Aaron whom he had chosen.
²⁷ They performed his signs among them,
　　and miracles in the land of Ham.
²⁸ He sent darkness, and made the land dark;
　　they rebelled against his words.
²⁹ He turned their waters into blood,
　　and caused their fish to die.
³⁰ Their land swarmed with frogs,
　　even in the chambers of their kings.
³¹ He spoke, and there came swarms of flies,
　　and gnats throughout their country.
³² He gave them hail for rain,
　　and lightning that flashed through their land.
³³ He struck their vines and fig trees,
　　and shattered the trees of their country.
³⁴ He spoke, and the locusts came,
　　and young locusts without number;
³⁵ they devoured all the vegetation in their land,
　　and ate up the fruit of their ground.
³⁶ He struck down all the firstborn in their land,
　　the first issue of all their strength.

³⁷ Then he brought Israel out with silver and gold,
　　and there was no one among their tribes who stumbled.
³⁸ Egypt was glad when they departed,
　　for dread of them had fallen upon it.
³⁹ He spread a cloud for a covering,
　　and fire to give light by night.
⁴⁰ They asked, and he brought quails,
　　and gave them food from heaven in abundance.
⁴¹ He opened the rock, and water gushed out;
　　it flowed through the desert like a river.

[42] For he remembered his holy promise,
and Abraham, his servant.

[43] So he brought his people out with joy,
his chosen ones with singing.
[44] He gave them the lands of the nations,
and they took possession of the wealth of the peoples,
[45] that they might keep his statutes
and observe his laws.
Praise the LORD!

Psalm 105 – along with Psalms 78, 106, 135, and 136 – features Israel remembering and reciting its past with YHWH. Although this stylized recital may, in different articulations, serve different liturgical purposes, in this case it is to provide a
grounding for obedience to Torah commands (v. 45). The defining scholarship on
this psalm and this genre of historical recital is the work of Gerhard von Rad, who
hypothesized that the extended recitals grow out of the initial succinct liturgical
"credo" that voices the fundamental commitments of Israel.[241] Although von Rad's
casting of the matter is no longer fully accepted, his hypothesis helps us nonetheless
to understand the genre that exhibits Israel celebrating and giving thanks for the
miracles of YHWH that constitute its life in the world.

The psalm is divided into three parts: a doxological introduction (vv. 1–6), an
extended inventory of divine miracles expressed in narrative form (vv. 7–44), and a
brief but decisive conclusion (v. 45). The introduction is a characteristic summons
to praise that is dominated by a series of imperatives, all of which focus Israel's attention on YHWH. The particular subject of thanks and praise is "deeds" (v. 1), "wonderful works" (v. 2), and "wonderful works, miracles" (v. 5). These terms all bespeak
an action that is beyond human capacity or explanation that depends only on the
inscrutable power of YHWH. Martin Buber has defined these miracles as happen-
ings that have "abiding astonishment."[242] The miraculous events remembered here
were clearly acts of "abiding astonishment"; in generation after generation, Israel
continues to return to these old events for the sake of refreshed astonishment and
gratitude. After a long series of imperatives, the summons is a vocative (v. 6). The
summons is addressed to those who count Abraham and Jacob as their ancestors.
The appeal to Abraham is definitional, for in verses 7–11 and again in the conclusion
of verses 42–44, the focus is on Abraham as a carrier of the promise (see also Luke

---

[241] G. von Rad, *Problem of the Hexateuch and Other Essays* (1966), 8–13.
[242] The phrase is from Martin Buber, *Moses: The Revelation and Covenant* (Atlantic
Highlands, NJ: Humanities Press International, 1988), 75. See Walter Brueggemann,
Abiding Astonishment: Psalms, Modernity, and the Making of History (Louisville, KY:
Westminster John Knox Press, 1991).

1:55). Thus, to summon the children of Abraham is to situate them, in this act of praise, as continuing carriers of the divine promise.

The body of the psalm that names the miracle follows, as von Rad had seen, the general sequence of the Pentateuch, Israel's normative memory: Abraham (vv. 7–16), Joseph (vv. 16–25), Moses and the plagues (vv. 26–36), the wilderness sojourn (vv. 37–41), and finally land entry (vv. 42–44). The whole is apprehended, as von Rad had seen, as promise and fulfillment. The present congregation of Israel in every generation understands itself within the arc of promise on the way to fulfillment.

The key issue in the Abraham material is that YHWH has made an "everlasting covenant" with Abraham that contains the promise of land (vv. 10–11). The promise of the land is an abiding divine commitment on which there will be no default. Verses 12–15 reiterate the way in which YHWH has protected this vulnerable people on its way in its long season of landlessness. The focus on Abraham causes Isaac and Jacob to be mentioned only incidentally, but in the Genesis narrative the land promise is clearly reiterated and resworn in each successive generation (Gen 26:4; 28:13–15).

The second focus is on Joseph, which is something of a surprise because the Joseph narrative is seldom prominent in the Old Testament tradition (vv. 16–22). These verses closely reflect the Genesis narrative of Genesis 37–50. The Joseph narrative is an account of the way in which a "nobody" of an Israelite rose from slavery in the empire to become "Lord of Pharaoh's house," the administrator of the entire imperial apparatus (see Gen 47:13). In the Genesis narrative, as well as here, this rise to power and prominence is understood as an act of YHWH's hidden, providential governance, all in the interest of the well-being of Israel (see Gen 45:1–8). The addendum to the Joseph material in verses 23–24 refers to Gen 46:1–27 concerning the arrival of all Israel in Egypt. It is affirmed that Israel in Egypt was "exceedingly fruitful"; that is, carriers of the generative abundance of creation (see Exod 1:7). Verse 25 of the psalm ominously anticipates the coming oppression that will be the venue for the Exodus deliverance.

In verse 26, the psalm turns from the memory of the Genesis ancestors to the Exodus narrative. The Exodus account in verses 26–36 attends to Moses but is preoccupied with the retelling of the plague narrative of Exodus 7–12. In its narrative account and here in the song, the recital is surely

> that you may tell your children and grandchildren how I have made fools of the Egyptians and what signs I have done among them – so that you may know that I am the Lord. (Exod 10:2)

It is important that the grandchildren – and all Israel – know that YHWH is Lord of history and deliverer of Israel.

This plague recital is dominated by first-person verbs with YHWH, "he," as the subject of all the enactments. The note on "they rebelled" in verse 28 is a reference to Pharaoh, who is reckoned in Israel to be a subject of YHWH's will but is now a recalcitrant subject who is in rebellion against divine governance. The accomplishment of the Exodus with stolen silverware from the empire (v. 37; see Exod 3:22; 11:2; 12:35) opens the account of the wilderness sojourn (vv. 37–41). The recital attests to YHWH's presence and guidance (v. 39) and the wonders of food and water given in the wilderness, attested in Exodus 17. Here, as in every part of the recital, Israel is sustained and led on by YHWH's goodness when it had no capacity for the maintenance of its own life.

Finally, in verses 42–44, the psalm returns to the reference to Abraham (vv. 6, 7–11) and the land promises. Thus the promise (v. 11) and the fulfillment (v. 44) provide the envelope for the entire memory of Israel.

The conclusion of the psalm is introduced by "that" or "so that" (v. 45). That is, the miracles that give Israel life and identity are performed in the first instant – and subsequently remembered and recited – for a single purpose in every generation. That purpose is that Israel should obey *torah*, should keep (*smr*), and observe (*nsr*). The connection between *recital* and *command* is that *miracle* provides both the grounding motivation and the horizon of command to which Israel will respond. The mandate is not at all coercive but assumes that *thanks* for *miracles* will result in glad, responsive obedience. The miracles evoke answer, and in answering each generation becomes the new generation of miracles. Thus the claim of an "eternal covenant" was designed precisely to counter the experience and trauma of discontinuity faced by the community. It is most plausible that, as Moshe Weinfeld has proposed, the grant to Abraham and subsequently to David was in fact a land grant whereby the owner-ruler of the land could freely and unilaterally assign land to a favorite subject.[243] In this psalm, Abraham and all of his descendants are the recipients of such a land grant. The claim of an eternal covenant of the land grant and this entire psalm is precisely a lyrical doxological antidote to the crisis of exile. Its conclusion is an assertion that the recipients of the guaranteed land are then subject to obedience to the giver of the land.

Bridging the Horizons: The Promise of Land

There is no doubt that the promise of the land grant to Israel through the eternal covenant with YHWH functions as an enormous assurance to a jeopardized people and a source of identity and hope during that jeopardy. It is also the case, as Michael Prior has made so clear, that the unconditional promise of land easily turns into ideology that justifies policies of aggressive violence for reasons of state.[244] Such usage is undoubtedly an interpretive mistake in the tradition. In some forms of contemporary Zionism, such a claim for the people of the

---

[243] M. Weinfeld, "Covenant Grant in the Old Testament and in the Ancient Near East," *JAOS* 90 (1970): 184–203.
[244] Michael Prior, *Zionism and the State of Israel: A Moral Enquiry* (New York: Routledge, 1999); and Michael Prior, *The Bible and Colonialism: A Moral Critique* (Sheffield: Sheffield Academic Press, 1997).

covenant has been turned into an ideological foundation for some policies in the contemporary state of Israel. This is, of course, a misreading of the psalm, but it is a misreading that is readily available. There is no doubt, moreover, that this same promise of land has served many imperialist and expansionist states in the West. See, for example, David Gunn and his exposé of the British seizure of New Zealand through such a land promise.[245] Terrien has shrewdly observed that this statement of a guaranteed land was "in a time of royal and priestly agonies"; such an unconditional guarantee, Terrien proposes, represented the "mentality of Jeremiah's enemies," perhaps among them Hananiah.[246]

A Closer Look: The Monarchy and the Land Promise

The citation of this psalm in 1 Chr 16:8–22 is a marvelous example of the way in which the Jerusalem monarchy made liturgical and surely ideological use of old land promises. In this version of the psalm, it is as though the psalm pertained directly and precisely to the expansionist commitments of the Davidic regime.

PSALM 106

1   Praise the LORD!
    O give thanks to the LORD, for he is good;
    for his steadfast love endures for ever.
2   Who can utter the mighty doings of the LORD,
    or declare all his praise?
3   Happy are those who observe justice,
    who do righteousness at all times.

4   Remember me, O LORD, when you show favor to your people;
    help me when you deliver them;
5   that I may see the prosperity of your chosen ones,
    that I may rejoice in the gladness of your nation,
    that I may glory in your heritage.

---

[245] David M. Gunn, "Colonialism and the Vagaries of Scripture: Te Kooti in Canaan (A Story of Bible and the Dispossession of Aotearoa/New Zealand)," in Tod Linafelt and Timothy K. Beal (eds.), *God in the Fray: A Tribute to Walter Brueggemann* (Minneapolis: Fortress Press, 1998), 127–142.

[246] S. Terrien, *Psalms* (2003), 725.

⁶ Both we and our ancestors have sinned;
  we have committed iniquity, have done wickedly.
⁷ Our ancestors, when they were in Egypt,
  did not consider your wonderful works;
they did not remember the abundance of your steadfast love,
  but rebelled against the Most High at the Red Sea.
⁸ Yet he saved them for his name's sake,
  so that he might make known his mighty power.
⁹ He rebuked the Red Sea, and it became dry;
  he led them through the deep as through a desert.
¹⁰ So he saved them from the hand of the foe,
  and delivered them from the hand of the enemy.
¹¹ The waters covered their adversaries;
  not one of them was left.
¹² Then they believed his words;
  they sang his praise.

¹³ But they soon forgot his works;
  they did not wait for his counsel.
¹⁴ But they had a wanton craving in the wilderness,
  and put God to the test in the desert;
¹⁵ he gave them what they asked,
  but sent a wasting disease among them.

¹⁶ They were jealous of Moses in the camp,
  and of Aaron, the holy one of the LORD.
¹⁷ The earth opened and swallowed up Dathan,
  and covered the faction of Abiram.
¹⁸ Fire also broke out in their company;
  the flame burned up the wicked.

¹⁹ They made a calf at Horeb
  and worshipped a cast image.
²⁰ They exchanged the glory of God
  for the image of an ox that eats grass.
²¹ They forgot God, their Saviour,
  who had done great things in Egypt,
²² wondrous works in the land of Ham,
  and awesome deeds by the Red Sea.
²³ Therefore he said he would destroy them –

    had not Moses, his chosen one,
stood in the breach before him,
    to turn away his wrath from destroying them.
24 Then they despised the pleasant land,
    having no faith in his promise.
25 They grumbled in their tents,
    and did not obey the voice of the LORD.
26 Therefore he raised his hand and swore to them
    that he would make them fall in the wilderness,
27 and would disperse their descendants among the nations,
    scattering them over the lands.

28 Then they attached themselves to the Baal of Peor,
    and ate sacrifices offered to the dead;
29 they provoked the LORD to anger with their deeds,
    and a plague broke out among them.
30 Then Phinehas stood up and interceded,
    and the plague was stopped.
31 And that has been reckoned to him as righteousness
    from generation to generation for ever.

32 They angered the LORD at the waters of Meribah,
    and it went ill with Moses on their account;
33 for they made his spirit bitter,
    and he spoke words that were rash.

34 They did not destroy the peoples
    as the LORD commanded them,
35 but they mingled with the nations
    and learned to do as they did.
36 They served their idols,
    which became a snare to them.
37 They sacrificed their sons
    and their daughters to the demons;
38 they poured out innocent blood,
    the blood of their sons and daughters,
whom they sacrificed to the idols of Canaan;
    and the land was polluted with blood.
39 Thus they became unclean by their acts,
    and prostituted themselves in their doings.

⁴⁰ Then the anger of the LORD was kindled against his people,
    and he abhorred his heritage;
⁴¹ he gave them into the hand of the nations,
    so that those who hated them ruled over them.
⁴² Their enemies oppressed them,
    and they were brought into subjection under their power.
⁴³ Many times he delivered them,
    but they were rebellious in their purposes,
    and were brought low through their iniquity.
⁴⁴ Nevertheless, he regarded their distress
    when he heard their cry.
⁴⁵ For their sake he remembered his covenant,
    and showed compassion according to the abundance of his steadfast love.
⁴⁶ He caused them to be pitied
    by all who held them captive.

⁴⁷ Save us, O LORD our God,
    and gather us from among the nations,
that we may give thanks to your holy name
    and glory in your praise.

⁴⁸ Blessed be the LORD, the God of Israel,
    from everlasting to everlasting.
And let all the people say, 'Amen.'
    Praise the LORD!

The opening of Psalm 106 leads readers to expect a hymn of praise. Then, however, the psalm transitions to narrating the history of ancient Israel as a way of confessing sin rather than offering praise. Some interpreters have thus taken the psalm as a community lament, but perhaps a more helpful category is that of historical psalm. Based on the recounting of history, the psalm confesses sin and pleads for help. The beginning and ending of the psalm provide a frame for the historical recital in the body of the psalm. The frame and body do not fit together easily. The psalm begins (vv. 1–6) with a summons to praise in familiar language and then moves quickly to petition and confession of sin. The remainder of the text emphasizes historical recital in terms of Israel's pervasive iniquity first related to the Exodus from Egypt, especially at the sea (vv. 7–12), then in the wilderness (vv. 13–33), and concluding on the land (vv. 34–48).

Psalms 105 and 106 are closely related. They begin with a similar imperative call to praise, and both psalms recount the history of ancient Israel. The historical recital in the two texts is different, however, and attends to different parts of the history. Psalm 106 remembers the mighty acts of YHWH, but its focus is on the acts of Israel, which are less than glorious; the texts tell different sides of the story. Psalm 106 concludes Book IV of the Psalter (Psalms 90–106). The text reflects the crisis of exile that is so present in this collection of psalms and petitions for help in the midst of the crisis. The psalm also leads to the first poem in Book V (Psalms 107–150); Psalm 107 responds positively to the petition in Ps 106:47. The two texts also begin in similar ways. 1 Chronicles 16:35–36 appropriates Ps 106:47–48 as the conclusion to praise offered from Psalms 96, 105, and 106 on the occasion of David's bringing the Ark of the Covenant to Jerusalem.

Psalm 106 begins with a summons to praise in language used at the beginning of Psalm 107 and in the historical recital in Psalm 136. The opening words and the rhetorical question in verse 2 suggest that the mighty acts of YHWH and the corresponding praise are so massive as to overwhelm worshipers. However, those who live in line with the dazzling divine works (that is, those who are faithful to the covenant partnership with YHWH) are those who find wholeness in life. Verse 3 uses "justice" and "righteousness" to characterize this relationship. Verses 4–5 speak in the first person a petition that YHWH will "help me" when God delivers the community so that the speaker will partake of the joy and fullness of life found by this community of God's people. These opening verses suggest that the psalm relates to both individual and community.

Verse 6 makes the transition to the body of the psalm by moving to a confession of iniquity committed by both ancestors and the present congregation. The verse uses three verbs for sin – "sinned," "committed iniquity," and "done wickedly" – to show how pervasive the reality was. This verse begins the contrast with the emphasis on the mighty acts of YHWH central to Psalm 105; Psalm 106 emphasizes the failure of the community to respond positively to those mighty acts. In some ways, the tension between the divine promises and purposes and the waywardness of the people constitutes the core of Israel's story. The move from the opening verse of Psalm 106, with its call to praise, to the confession of sin in verse 6 takes place quickly and requires the full attention of readers. Kraus suggests that it may be that the community responds out of a consciousness of sin and suffering when hearing the call to praise.[247] The opening call to praise and the body of the psalm do not fit together easily; perhaps the community confesses sin and pleads for deliverance from the trauma of exile so that they can offer praise and thanksgiving to God.

Psalm 106 is about memory. Verse 4 asks for God to "remember me." In verse 7, the speaker declares that the ancestors did not remember the "wonderful works" of YHWH that showed "steadfast love" for the people. In the liberation from slavery in Egypt, when Israel came to the sea with Pharaoh's army in hot pursuit, they forgot in the face of the threat that YHWH had done mighty acts for them in bringing them out of Egypt and forgot that this powerful YHWH was with them. Yet YHWH

---

[247] H.-J. Kraus, *Psalms 60–150* (1988), 317.

delivered them from the hand of the Egyptian military-industrial complex. Israel came through the sea on dry ground, but the Egyptian army was stuck and drowned as the water returned. In response to this act of deliverance, the people offered praise and thanksgiving. The psalm refers to the story in Exodus 14–15. Psalm 106:8, however, alludes to the entire story of the liberation from Egypt and especially the narrative of the plagues. The purpose of these mighty acts goes beyond the liberation of Israel and even beyond its covenant relationship with YHWH. The full purpose of the narrative has to do with divine revelation: "so that he might make known his mighty power." The reputation ("name") and revelation of God have implications for all creation and for all peoples. The divine relationship with Israel has to do with blessings for all the nations. The focus of Psalm 106 is Israel's failure, but that narrative is always in the broader context of YHWH's covenant ways with this people, which relate to all peoples.

The historical recital continues with a catalog of Israel's memory lapses in the wilderness.

1. Verses 13–15 relate to various wilderness accounts in which the people put God to the test for food and water. God "gave them what they asked," but the result was a plague; Numbers 11 recounts such a result. Verses 14–15 stand in considerable contrast with Ps 105:40–43; the emphasis in Psalm 106 is Israel's rebellion.

2. Verses 16–18 allude to the rebellion in Numbers 16. The psalm refers to Dathan and Abiram; the text in Numbers also refers to Korah. The rebellion was against the leadership of Moses and Aaron and in turn YHWH.

3. Verses 19–23 focus on the rebellion of the golden calf in Exodus 32–34. Israel had again forgotten YHWH and the mighty acts that brought them out of slavery and worshiped a "cast image" rather than the living God. It was only Moses' remarkable intercession with YHWH that saved the people.

4. Verses 24–27 allude to the story of the spies who entered that land of promise and the failure of the people to trust the promise. That wilderness generation died in rebellion and did not see the promise fulfilled.

5. Verses 28–33 refer to Numbers 25 and the idolatry recounted there. The intercession of Phinehas delivered the community from the resulting plague. Verses 32–33 suggest that Moses was infected with bitterness as a result of the people's rebellions and so also died in the wilderness. The allusion is to the story at Meribah in Numbers 20.

The concluding section of the psalm recounts the history of sin when the people entered the land of promise. They were enticed by the people of Canaan into idol worship and even into human sacrifice. This unfaithfulness in the covenant relationship likely alludes to the narratives of early Israel in Joshua and Judges. The historical pattern recounted there is of continued covenant faithlessness followed by subservience to other peoples. Israel continued to cry out to God, and God heard and remembered the covenant and acted out of compassion. This concluding historical account leads to a petition that God will again hear and come to save Israel from the trauma at hand, the trauma of exile, so that the community can again offer praise and thanksgiving to God. The psalm operates from an analogy between Israel's history and the current crisis of exile. Israel experienced trouble and woe as punishment for breaking the covenant, but when they cried out to YHWH, the divine compassion followed. The frame of the history of disobedience in Psalm 106 is the persistence of YHWH's steadfast love. The psalm's concluding verse is the benediction to Book IV of the Psalter.

Bridging the Horizons: In the Interim

Psalm 106 operates from analogy:

The psalmist speaks as heir of the Pentateuch and the Deuteronomic history, and weaves their themes into the fabric of the penitence of the postexilic community. He stands too in the interim period foretold by the preexilic prophets, between God's judgment and salvation of the covenant people. He is able to recreate a cultic representation of the past to fit contemporary needs, to be the vehicle of both deep repentance and prayerful hope.[248]

The analogy is still pertinent. Contemporary communities of faith live in that interim period and continue to forget divine acts of compassion. The proclamation of Psalm 106 is that in such contexts the divine grace persists. Both the human pattern of unfaithfulness to the relationship with God and the surprising divine pattern of continuing steadfast love pervade the histories of faith communities in the traditions of Judaism and Christianity and continue with contemporary faith communities. Contemporary communities of faith can thus continue to pray the petition in Ps 106:47 that God will save so that the community can offer praise and thanksgiving to this one whose "steadfast love endures for ever."

PSALM 107

1 O give thanks to the LORD, for he is good;
   for his steadfast love endures for ever.
2 Let the redeemed of the LORD say so,

[248] Leslie C. Allen, *Psalms 101–150*, 2nd edition (WBC 21; Dallas: Word Books, 2002), 74.

those he redeemed from trouble
³ and gathered in from the lands,
   from the east and from the west,
   from the north and from the south.

⁴ Some wandered in desert wastes,
   finding no way to an inhabited town;
⁵ hungry and thirsty,
   their soul fainted within them.
⁶ Then they cried to the LORD in their trouble,
   and he delivered them from their distress;
⁷ he led them by a straight way,
   until they reached an inhabited town.
⁸ Let them thank the LORD for his steadfast love,
   for his wonderful works to humankind.
⁹ For he satisfies the thirsty,
   and the hungry he fills with good things.

¹⁰ Some sat in darkness and in gloom,
   prisoners in misery and in irons,
¹¹ for they had rebelled against the words of God,
   and spurned the counsel of the Most High.
¹² Their hearts were bowed down with hard labor;
   they fell down, with no one to help.
¹³ Then they cried to the LORD in their trouble,
   and he saved them from their distress;
¹⁴ he brought them out of darkness and gloom,
   and broke their bonds asunder.
¹⁵ Let them thank the LORD for his steadfast love,
   for his wonderful works to humankind.
¹⁶ For he shatters the doors of bronze,
   and cuts in two the bars of iron.

¹⁷ Some were sick through their sinful ways,
   and because of their iniquities endured affliction;
¹⁸ they loathed any kind of food,
   and they drew near to the gates of death.
¹⁹ Then they cried to the LORD in their trouble,
   and he saved them from their distress;
²⁰ he sent out his word and healed them,

and delivered them from destruction.
²¹ Let them thank the LORD for his steadfast love,
for his wonderful works to humankind.
²² And let them offer thanksgiving sacrifices,
and tell of his deeds with songs of joy.

²³ Some went down to the sea in ships,
doing business on the mighty waters;
²⁴ they saw the deeds of the LORD,
his wondrous works in the deep.
²⁵ For he commanded and raised the stormy wind,
which lifted up the waves of the sea.
²⁶ They mounted up to heaven, they went down to the depths;
their courage melted away in their calamity;
²⁷ they reeled and staggered like drunkards,
and were at their wits' end.
²⁸ Then they cried to the LORD in their trouble,
and he brought them out from their distress;
²⁹ he made the storm be still,
and the waves of the sea were hushed.
³⁰ Then they were glad because they had quiet,
and he brought them to their desired haven.
³¹ Let them thank the LORD for his steadfast love,
for his wonderful works to humankind.
³² Let them extol him in the congregation of the people,
and praise him in the assembly of the elders.

³³ He turns rivers into a desert,
springs of water into thirsty ground,
³⁴ a fruitful land into a salty waste,
because of the wickedness of its inhabitants.
³⁵ He turns a desert into pools of water,
a parched land into springs of water.
³⁶ And there he lets the hungry live,
and they establish a town to live in;
³⁷ they sow fields, and plant vineyards,
and get a fruitful yield.
³⁸ By his blessing they multiply greatly,
and he does not let their cattle decrease.

³⁹ When they are diminished and brought low
   through oppression, trouble, and sorrow,
⁴⁰ he pours contempt on princes
   and makes them wander in trackless wastes;
⁴¹ but he raises up the needy out of distress,
   and makes their families like flocks.
⁴² The upright see it and are glad;
   and all wickedness stops its mouth.
⁴³ Let those who are wise give heed to these things,
   and consider the steadfast love of the LORD.

Psalm 107 is the fullest, clearest example of a song of thanksgiving in which the speaker identifies a particular, nameable gift from God for which gratitude is voiced. Such particularity in *thanks* is in contrast to *praise*, which tends to be generic and much less tied to a particular experience.

The psalm can be readily divided into three parts:

- Verses 1–3 constitute an introductory summons to thanks that imagines all of "the redeemed" gathering home in God's goodness.
- Verses 4–32 provide four case studies in divine rescue that evoke a response of thanks.
- Verses 33–43 offer a summary reflection on God's generous governance that tilts toward the didactic.

The initial summons of verse 1 brings together the proposed human act of *thanks* and the substance for which Israel is grateful, divine *steadfast love*. That, briefly stated, is the sum of Israel's grateful faith. The beneficiaries of God's steadfast love can attest to the particular ways in which God's actions have been reliable. The term "gather" in verse 3 may suggest a postexilic setting, for the term often refers to the gathering of scattered Jews after the exile. See the triple use of the term in just this way in Isa 56:8.

The long middle section of the psalm provides four examples of *divine rescue and transformation* that attest to YHWH's *fidelity* and that evoke Israel's *gratitude* (vv. 4–32). The particular descriptions of trouble vary from case to case, and may be taken as representative of the contexts of complaint and need in which Israel turns to YHWH. In each case, the final verse offers a reprise on the particularity of divine intervention.

In verses 4–9, the case concerns being lost in the desert and coming close to death. Here, as in each case, the pivot point is the *cry* of need and the response of *rescue* (v. 6). The cry reflects Israel's characteristic practice of complaint, but prior to that the cry is the natural and inescapable act of persons in need who are at the end of their own resources (see Exod 2:23–25). The cry is an admission of need, an exhaustion of self-sufficiency, and a readiness for dependence.

Most remarkably, the cry is followed immediately by a divine response: "He delivered them." The two terms "cry" and "deliver" allow between them no space, no pause, no anxiety, no bargaining, and no uncertainty. It is almost, as the poet says, that God answers "before they call" (Isa 65:24). Not quite, of course, but the rhetoric exhibits an alert readiness on the part of God. That immediate divine effectiveness leads to a transformation of circumstances that in turn leads to thanks for steadfast love, a reiteration of the terms of verse 1. The divine response to desert wanderings is a case of steadfast love. The rhetoric advances to characterize the divine act as a "wonderful work," as a miracle that lies outside the capacity and understanding of Israel. The term "wonderful work" bespeaks the generous sovereignty of YHWH, which outruns every conventional discernment of reality. It is an inventory of such "wonders" that constitutes the fund of faith for Israel. And now Israel can add this "miracle" concerning desert wanderings to its repertoire (see Ps 105:39–41; on the inventory, see Ps 145:4–7). Verse 9 adds a reprise that looks back to this particular rescue.

In verses 10–32, we are offered three more cases of acute need and gracious divine intervention: prison (vv. 10–16), sickness (vv. 17–22), and a storm at sea (vv. 23–32). Although the particulars of the several crises vary, the stylized narrative remains the same in terms of *trouble* of a particular kind, *cry, deliverance,* and *thanksgiving.* In each case, the cry is promptly followed by a divine response. And in each case there is *thanks* for *steadfast love* and for a *wonderful work.* In the third and fourth cases, there is a fuller articulation of human response to divine attentiveness. Whereas "thanks" is rendered in each of the four cases, in verse 22 thanks is more fully enacted as "thanksgiving sacrifices"; that is, as a material offering. It may be that the same liturgical gesture is implied in the three other cases, but it is stated only here. In verse 32, moreover, the thanks of the rescued is augmented, as is often the case in resolved complaints in the book of Psalms, by the fuller praise of the congregation, which joins in celebration with the ones delivered. Both *the thank offering* and *the congregational praise* remind us that these wondrous transformative transactions are never private; they are always situated in a congregational context among those who know and trust the narrative of divine fidelity.

The psalm concludes in a more generic fashion in verses 33–43. The double use of "he turns" in verses 33 and 35 attests to the sovereign rule of the creator who continues to reduce rivers to deserts (in order to punish the wicked) and to transform deserts to rivers (in order that creation may prosper). God does indeed have "the whole world in his hands," and rules over it to punish and restore. The double theme is echoed by "bring low" and "raise up" to assert that human life is situated in a providential context where the ultimate decisions are from God's own hand; at the same time, God's predisposition is attuned to human choice and human conduct. Thus even this strong affirmation of divine sovereignty refers to a sturdy Deuteronomic theology of blessing and curse in which human choice to some great extent determines God's gift of a future (see Deut 30:15–120). It is clear that there is some tension between this rigorous theology of blessing and curse (vv. 33–43) and the case studies of verses 4–32, which more fully accent divine generosity. The more rigorous verses at the end of the psalm have suggested to some interpreters that these verses are a later addition to the psalm, reflecting a later division of the community into the wicked and the righteous. At the very least, these verses reflect a somewhat different accent; they bear witness to the contested issues in Israel's faith concerning *divine requirement* and *divine generosity*, a contestation that always continues.

The psalm concludes in verse 43 with a reminder that the experience of divine governance can be instructive. One can learn, on reflection, that one does not live in a morally indifferent or morally permissive world but in a world where the God who hears and saves is also the God who commands.

A Closer Look: To Thank

The main body of the psalm is dominated by the motif of *thank*, which occurs in each of the four cases, only in the third, in verse 22, it is "sacrifice of thanksgiving." The word "thank" itself (*ydh*) often means to "confess" or to narrate. Although the usage may refer to *narration of sin and guilt*, as in Neh 1:6 and Neh 9:2, it can also mean to *narrate one's gratitude* by retelling the story of need and rescue. Thus the narrative can concern sin that evokes repentance and hopefully forgiveness, or deliverance that evokes joy and thanks. Thus, to thank is to give a verbal account of that for which one is grateful. In a thank offering, however, the narrative is accompanied by a material presentation of something of worth (see Lev 7:11–14).

Thus thank properly concerns both *utterance and gesture*, or as we might say in the Christian tradition, "word and sacrament."

A Closer Look: Divine Freedom and Divine Responsiveness

The concluding verses, with an accent on divine sovereignty, are somewhat removed from the main body of the psalm. In the conclusion, the double "turn" of divine action (vv. 31, 35) and the "contempt/raise up" in verses 39–41 reflect Israel's pervasive conviction that YHWH, in YHWH's freedom, disposes of worldly affairs according to God's own inclination. This motif is evident in the Song of Hannah:

The Lord kills and brings to life;
He brings down to Sheol and raises up,
The Lord makes poor and makes rich;
He brings low, and he also exalts.

He raises up the poor from the dust;
He lifts the needy from the ash heap,
to make them sit with princes
And inherit a seat of honor. (1 Sam 2:6–8)

The same conviction receives later reiteration:

I form light and create darkness,
I make weal and create woe;
I the Lord do all these things. (Isa 45:7; see Isa 43:13; Job 5:18)

The accent on *divine freedom* in verses 33–43 and on *divine responsiveness* in verses 4–32 are both the subject of Israel's thanks and praise. Neither responsiveness without freedom nor freedom without responsiveness would lead to gladness. But Israel, in its thanksgiving and doxology, bears witness to this convergence that makes for life. The gift of life concerns particular persons rescued in their need; it also concerns the full, generous functioning of creation:

By his blessing they multiply greatly,
And he does not let their cattle decrease. (v. 38)

Bridging the Horizons: A Thankful Response

The impetus for life with YHWH in ancient Israel is most characteristically thanks. For that reason, Israel endlessly recited the *inventory of acts of divine fidelity* and probed for the right responses in gratitude. The defining quality of gratitude is an ongoing summons in our contemporary life as well. On the one hand, gratitude keeps faith simple and concrete and not overly abstract:

All we really have is Israel's concrete, *todah* witness to its faith that God was involved with a people in the events *todah* thankfully recites. We must finally understand, if we are to understand the Old Testament at all, that contact with God is made as a people lives a *todah* life, not as the finally true, abstract dogma is apprehended by the human mind.[249]

On the other hand, gratitude calls us away from the modern illusion of self-sufficiency:

Thus the message is diametrically opposed to what much of contemporary North American culture teaches people. In modern culture, maturity is often measured by how *self*-sufficient we are. We are taught that we earn what we have (see vv.

---

[249] Harvey H. Guthrie, Jr., *Theology as Thanksgiving: From Israel's Psalms to the Church's Eucharist* (New York: Seabury Press, 1981), 69.

4–9); we are taught that we must pull ourselves up by our bootstraps when we are down (see vv. 10–16); we are taught that wisdom is getting ahead in whatever way we can manage without getting caught (see vv. 17–22); we are taught that our security results from careful planning, investment, and management (see vv. 23–32). In short, we are taught to be self-made persons – no need to cry to God for help, and consequently no need to thank God for anything. Seldom, if ever, does it occur to us that human life depends on God. Thus the message of Psalm 107 is simple but radical: There is ultimately no such thing as self-sufficiency, for human life depends on God.[250]

George Stroup exposits Christian gratitude as the ultimate practice of faith:

Christian gratitude is shaped and determined by its object – that to which gratitude is directed – that is, God. And just as there is no other reality that is like God, so too Christian gratitude differs from all other forms of gratitude. It is a giving thanks by human beings in response to who God is and what God does. Gratitude, or human thanksgiving, is a never fully adequate response to the prior giving of God.[251]

Eventually a Christian exposition of thanks must come to the Eucharist (the term means "thanks"). In the liturgical formula, it is said: "It is very meet, right, and our bounden duty to give God thanks and praise." That is an odd way to live; it is, however, the way of all those who know the one who delivers from hunger, sickness, prison, shipwreck, and every form of failed life. No wonder the folks in the psalm have tales to tell and offerings to bring! By them we are drawn into the generosity of God, which evokes gratitude.

PSALM 108 – A SONG. A PSALM OF DAVID

¹ My heart is steadfast, O God, my heart is steadfast;
   I will sing and make melody.
   Awake, my soul!
² Awake, O harp and lyre!
   I will awake the dawn.
³ I will give thanks to you, O LORD, among the peoples,

---

[250] J. C. McCann, Jr., "Book of Psalms," in L. E. Keck et al. (eds.), *The New Interpreter's Bible*, vol. 4 (1996), 1119.
[251] G. W. Stroup, *Before God* (2004), 146.

and I will sing praises to you among the nations.
4 For your steadfast love is higher than the heavens,
and your faithfulness reaches to the clouds.

5 Be exalted, O God, above the heavens,
and let your glory be over all the earth.
6 Give victory with your right hand, and answer me,
so that those whom you love may be rescued.
7 God has promised in his sanctuary:
'With exultation I will divide up Shechem,
and portion out the Vale of Succoth.
8 Gilead is mine; Manasseh is mine;
Ephraim is my helmet;
Judah is my sceptre.
9 Moab is my wash-basin;
on Edom I hurl my shoe;
over Philistia I shout in triumph.'

10 Who will bring me to the fortified city?
Who will lead me to Edom?
11 Have you not rejected us, O God?
You do not go out, O God, with our armies.
12 O grant us help against the foe,
for human help is worthless.
13 With God we shall do valiantly;
it is he who will tread down our foes.

Psalm 108 is a combination of Ps 57:7–11 and Ps 60:5–12 into a new prayer. The resulting new prayer gives thanks for the return from exile but also prays on behalf of the community. The psalm begins with a vow of praise and thanksgiving (vv. 1–4), apparently in anticipation of divine help. Verses 5–9 petition for God to demonstrate steadfast love in helping the community; the latter part of the petition offers hope in the form of an oracle. The final section of the psalm (vv. 10–13) again petitions on behalf of the community, which is staring into the face of death, and concludes with a word of hope. The commentaries on Psalms 57 and 60 offer fuller expositions.

A Closer Look: A Combination Psalm

Most interpreters agree that Psalms 57 and 60 are prior compositions, but it is not clear how the parts of those psalms came together to make Psalm 108. McCann points out that Ps 108:5–6 has become part of a petition that is drawn from both Psalms 57 and 60.[252] The combining of parts from previous psalms to construct a new prayer suggests part of the process by which the Psalter came together. Psalm 108 fits its literary setting in Book V of the Psalter (Psalms 107–150). Psalm 107 celebrates divine assistance and calls for praise and thanksgiving to God for the return from exile; Psalm 108 continues in the mode of praise and thanksgiving. Psalm 108 also has some connections with its predecessor in the use of "give thanks" in verse 3 and "steadfast love" in verse 4; compare Ps 107:1, 8, 15, 21, 31, and 43. Psalm 108:3 reflects the exilic setting put at the end of Book III in Psalm 89 and continuing through Book IV. Psalm 108 is the first of three Davidic psalms near the beginning of Book V.

Verses 1–4. The psalm begins with a full-throated vow of praise and thanksgiving to God. The liturgist promises to sing praise even to the point of waking the dawn. This praise is set among the peoples and nations and will come from the self and from the accompanying instruments. The first three verses articulate the classic vow of thanksgiving, followed in verse 4 with the reason: the divine steadfast love and faithfulness. These realities are so pervasive as to be into the clouds and beyond the heavens. The singer is among the nations, but the divine loyal love and trustworthiness are ever present.

Verses 5–9. Verse 5 concludes the quotation from Psalm 57, where the sequence is the more familiar move from petition to vow of praise. Psalm 108 begins with the vow and moves to a petition that urges God to bring judgment that is fitting for the king of all creation. When God brings that judgment, it will mean deliverance for the community and for the liturgist. The petition assumes that trouble and woe are at hand, so the enactment of the divine steadfast love and faithfulness is still anticipated. The divine response to the petition comes in verses 7–9. God remains sovereign over ancient Israelite territory, including Shechem, Succoth, and Gilead; both Ephraim (the Northern Kingdom) and Judah are included. God also reigns over Israel's traditional enemies of Moab, Edom, and Philistia. The images in verse 9 are images of victory over these foes.

Verses 10–13. The final section of the psalm returns to petition; God's deliverance is still anticipated. The section begins with the question of who will lead the people into battle. The hope is that God will, but crisis is still the present reality. Verse 11 well fits a context of exile. The plea is for divine help since "human help is worthless." The final verse is an affirmation of hope that the divine king, not human armies, will bring rescue. The presence of Edom as a primary foe in verses 9–10 also fits the exilic setting, for Edom was often blamed for collaborating in the defeat of Jerusalem.

---

[252] J. C. McCann, Jr., "Book of Psalms," in L. E. Keck et al. (eds.), *The New Interpreter's Bible*, vol. 4 (1996), 1121. See also H.-J. Kraus, *Psalms 60–150* (1988), 333; and J. L. Mays, *Psalms* (1994), 347–348.

Therefore, the psalm moves from a vow of praise and thanksgiving "among the nations" to a petition that God's presence and activity come to bear "over all the earth." The second part of the psalm offers a petition in the face of crisis with an oracular promise of divine victory and a concluding word of hope in divine help.

Bridging the Horizons: Changing Contexts

The composition of Psalm 108 suggests the vitality of texts in Scripture. Two earlier poetic pieces are brought together in a new context. Scriptures are often appropriated for changed contexts. The poetic pieces were applied to the crisis of exile in Psalm 108, and the new psalm continues to be tied to contemporary contexts for communities of faith. The prayer operates out of Israel's fullest confession – confidence in the divine steadfast love and faithfulness – and seeks a renewal of that reality. The exiles had experienced divine judgment and here are reminded of divine help. The psalm is cynical about any human rescue, and so eschews any sense of self-sufficiency, but steadfastly holds to the power of divine loyalty and trustworthiness.

PSALM 109 – TO THE LEADER. OF DAVID. A PSALM

1 Do not be silent, O God of my praise.
2 For wicked and deceitful mouths are opened against me,
   speaking against me with lying tongues.
3 They beset me with words of hate,
   and attack me without cause.
4 In return for my love they accuse me,
   even while I make prayer for them.
5 So they reward me evil for good,
   and hatred for my love.

6 They say, 'Appoint a wicked man against him;
   let an accuser stand on his right.
7 When he is tried, let him be found guilty;
   let his prayer be counted as sin.
8 May his days be few;
   may another seize his position.

9 May his children be orphans,
   and his wife a widow.
10 May his children wander about and beg;
   may they be driven out of the ruins they inhabit.
11 May the creditor seize all that he has;
   may strangers plunder the fruits of his toil.
12 May there be no one to do him a kindness,
   nor anyone to pity his orphaned children.
13 May his posterity be cut off;
   may his name be blotted out in the second generation.
14 May the iniquity of his father be remembered before the Lord,
   and do not let the sin of his mother be blotted out.
15 Let them be before the Lord continually,
   and may his memory be cut off from the earth.
16 For he did not remember to show kindness,
   but pursued the poor and needy
   and the broken-hearted to their death.
17 He loved to curse; let curses come on him.
   He did not like blessing; may it be far from him.
18 He clothed himself with cursing as his coat,
   may it soak into his body like water,
   like oil into his bones.
19 May it be like a garment that he wraps around himself,
   like a belt that he wears every day.'

20 May that be the reward of my accusers from the Lord,
   of those who speak evil against my life.
21 But you, O Lord my Lord,
   act on my behalf for your name's sake;
   because your steadfast love is good, deliver me.
22 For I am poor and needy,
   and my heart is pierced within me.
23 I am gone like a shadow at evening;
   I am shaken off like a locust.
24 My knees are weak through fasting;
   my body has become gaunt.
25 I am an object of scorn to my accusers;
   when they see me, they shake their heads.

26 Help me, O Lord my God!

Save me according to your steadfast love.
²⁷ Let them know that this is your hand;
you, O LORD, have done it.
²⁸ Let them curse, but you will bless.
Let my assailants be put to shame; may your servant be glad.
²⁹ May my accusers be clothed with dishonor;
may they be wrapped in their own shame as in a mantle.
³⁰ With my mouth I will give great thanks to the LORD;
I will praise him in the midst of the throng.
³¹ For he stands at the right hand of the needy,
to save them from those who would condemn them to death.

Psalm 109 is the most difficult and most embarrassing psalm for conventional piety, for its central portion is a raw bid for vengeance from God toward one's adversaries (vv. 6–20). That long articulation of unfiltered yearning is framed by an introduction that gives cause for the bid for vengeance (vv. 1–5) and by a concluding prayer as the psalmist turns from malevolence to confident trust in YHWH (vv. 21–31).

At the outset, the psalmist asks God to break the silence and intervene in an unbearable social situation (v. 1). Verses 2–5 characterize the trouble to which God should attend; namely, a context of vicious, destructive slander against the person of the psalmist. The appeal to God would seem to be judicial, so it is God the judge who is asked to sort out and punish the guilty who diminished the life of the speaker.

The thirst for vengeance (vv. 6–20) is introduced in verse 6, which poses one of the most interesting textual-interpretive questions in the entire Psalter. It is conventional – as in the NRSV – to begin the section with "they say," thus putting the long thirst for vengeance in the mouth of the adversary of the psalmist. In this reading, it is the adversary who thinks and speaks such ignoble statements. These verses then would be an example of "words of hate," which the adversary is accused of using (v. 3), for what follows verse 6 are indeed "words of hate." This interpretive view is championed by Krauss and Lohfink. The adversary shrewdly does not insert the words "they say" but rather lets a colon at the end of verse 5 turn all that follows into a long quotation.²⁵³

The problem with this translation, which appears so innocent in the English Bible, is that there is no textual support in the Hebrew for the words "they say."²⁵⁴ Without these words, verses 6–20 are a continuation of the speech of the psalmist from verses 1–5. To follow the Hebrew is to make the psalmist the one who says

²⁵³ H.-J. Kraus, *Psalms 60–150* (1988), 338; and Norbert Lohfink, *In the Shadow of Your Wings: New Readings of Great Texts from the Bible* (Collegeville, MN: Liturgical Press, 2003), 124–125.
²⁵⁴ E. S. Gerstenberger, *Psalms, Part 2, and Lamentations* (2001), 257–259.

these hard, embarrassing wishes in verses 6–20. Our own reading, then, is to follow the Hebrew text and to permit the psalmist to be the speaker of these lines.

Perhaps the most interesting issue for reflection is why this translation tradition has intervened to remove these words from the psalmist and to reassign them to the adversary. I suspect that it is because "nice people" (faithful people "like us") should not think or say such things, so the liberty of the translator amounts to censorship. Or perhaps more subtly, the psalmist, in verses 21–31, will voice a trusting prayer, and it is thought to be incongruous for such a person of trust to speak such hate. But such a judgment wants to make a split – or place a protective wall – between hate and faith when in fact most of us know that in the midst of our confidence in God we find ourselves available on occasion for such less honorable self-announcement.

Thus we proceed here on the assumption that verses 6–20 are the voice of the psalmist, who has experienced the social destructiveness of the adversary and urges the righteous God to punish the adversary appropriately. The accusation against the adversary is in verses 16–18a, introduced by the usual preposition, "for." The adversary is accused of – guilty of? – a lack of *ḥesed* (kindness) that will enhance the neighborhood. Given an absence of neighborly solidarity, it is no surprise that such a person will engage in the socially destructive behavior that is detailed in these verses. Without *ḥesed*, the poor and the needy are exploited, an example of economic rapaciousness. The accent on "curse" (*qll*) means that the adversary has engaged in speech, as well as action, to belittle other members of the community, no doubt the psalmist included. Thus the indictment is against a person who is diminished or a danger to the community by refusing to act in solidarity.

It is because of this elemental and intolerable attitude toward the community that the psalmist seeks the elimination of such a person from the community. The petition to God asks that God should appoint a hard judge who has a reputation for firm and vigorous punishment of the guilty (v. 6). The psalmist is prepared to assume that the adversary is guilty of destructive behavior (v. 7) and so suggests to God appropriate punishment, namely purgation from the community.

The hope of retaliation from God is that the adversary may be socially humiliated and brought to an early death, that he may be an economic failure, and that his family life among those families who perennially hold land and therefore hold social power will be terminated. Perhaps the most telling position is in verse 12, a bid that the adversary should be shown *ḥesed* (kindness) by no one else in the community, for without measures of human solidarity from others we cannot prosper in a closed and intimate community. We should especially observe the double use of *ḥesed*: in verse 16, the adversary is accused of a lack of *ḥesed*, and in verse 12 the psalmist prays that the adversary should receive no *ḥesed* in the community. Thus the wish is precisely commensurate with the affront in the conviction that without *ḥesed* the adversary is sure to suffer the kind of trouble and humiliation that he has caused for others, including the psalmist.

It is as if by verse 20 the urgent expression of a negative hope has run its course. The psalmist has "gotten it all out." As a result, in verse 21, the speaker turns abruptly from a petition to YHWH for vengeance to an assertion: "But you YHWH my God." It is as though the speaker has concluded that in the end there is no satisfaction to come from engagement with the adversary, even in shrill accusation. Now, in a completely new direction of rhetoric, the speaker turns from hate to trust and appeals to YHWH's own *ḥesed* (steadfast love) as grounds for a new possibility. The speaker is "poor and needy" (v. 22), exactly like one who has been pursued by the adversary (v. 16). The poor and needy turn to YHWH as their only source of succor. Verses 22–26, in typical fashion, state the complaint about one's sorry, desperate situation, and verse 26 returns to the petition of verse 21, again addressed to "YHWH my God" and again appealing to YHWH's *ḥesed*. In verses 27–29, the prayer briefly echoes the long implication of verses 6–20. But as the psalm reaches its conclusion, the speaker finishes with great confidence in YHWH, certain to voice *thanks* and *praise* (v. 30). Such confidence is grounded in the certitude that YHWH stands alongside the needy to save them from those like the adversary.

We may notice two recurring terms in this psalm. First, the one who speaks is among the "needy" and is a speaker for them (v. 22). On the one hand, the adversary exploits the needy (v. 16), but, on the other hand, YHWH is in solidarity with the needy (v. 31). The threefold use of the term nicely plots the triangle of speaker-adversary-YHWH amid the crisis of social vulnerability. Second, the psalmist knows that *ḥesed* is the glue that makes communal life possible.[255] The lack of *ḥesed* is the primary accusation against the adversary (v. 16) and thus is matched by a petition for no *ḥesed* for the adversary (v. 12). In the end, moreover, the psalmist knows that *ḥesed* is found only in YHWH (vv. 21, 26), for it is YHWH who makes a viable community possible. In the end, this psalm is a meditation on YHWH's steadfast love. That divine propensity, however, is inescapably situated in the human and deathly reality of human community. The psalmist dares to insist not only on candor about social hurt but also that the readiness of God for reliable relationships matters in concrete human affairs.

Bridging the Horizons: An Embarrassing Psalm

The "embarrassment" of this psalm is the thirst for vengeance, and the greater "embarrassment" is that this thirst for vengeance is precisely in the midst of a deep affirmation of faith in YHWH. The psalm is a reflection on a thirst for vengeance that is an affront to many Christians, who find such a matter "sub-Christian."

---

[255] See Walter Brueggemann, "Psalm 109: Three Times 'Steadfast Love,'" *Word & World* 5 (1985): 144–154.

This psalm, however, does not urge anyone to thirst for vengeance. Rather it takes seriously the reality that many in fact thirst for vengeance, including many Christians. The psalm may be acutely pertinent to contemporary society, for we live in a society deeply geared toward vengeance. This reality is unmistakably evident in harsh communal punishment, including capital punishment, in the extremity of "road rage," in all sorts of "economic reforms" that reflect vengeance toward the poor, and no doubt in an aggressive military policy that is based on a desire to punish those with whom we disagree. All of this public threat is matched, of course, by domestic violence toward women and children, as though brutality is a primary method for resolving problems in social relationships.

We have suggested that such a thirst for vengeance, when palpably powerful, needs to be acknowledged. It can be dealt with in only three ways:

1. Vengeance can be enacted, as it often is among us, in violent ways.
2. Vengeance can be denied, in which case it will crop up in other destructive ways when least intended.
3. Vengeance can be articulated to YHWH, who is indeed "the God of vengeance" (Deut 32:39; Psalm 94).[256]

This latter, we propose, is what is accomplished through this psalm. The unrestrained expression is addressed to YHWH, from whom no secret can be hid. There is no evidence that the speaker enacted any violence, but rather only voiced it. We take this psalm to be a practical model for the voicing of such wishes in a safe place where the threat is heard, taken seriously and honored, and then left safely in God's hands. A God worthy of such prayer cannot be a "warm, fuzzy God" but must be one who is respected and taken seriously as an engaged, moral arbiter on behalf of the vulnerable. It is the speaker's capacity to trust such a God that permits a turn in verse 21 from hate to trust. We submit that this psalm is a model for much needed pastoral practice of *hate honored and relinquished* in a society that lives always at the brink of enacted violence. What the psalmist does is to "take it to the Lord in prayer."

Bridging the Horizons: Calvin's Critique

This psalm provides the opportunity for a critique of a society that regards vengeance as self-evidently legitimate. Calvin takes a very dim view of the sort of vengeance that is voiced in this psalm and offers a shrewd critique:

---

[256] Walter Brueggemann, *Praying the Psalms* (Winona, MN: Saint Mary's Press, 1982), 67–80.

In proportion to the amount of self-esteem which a man possesses, is he so enamoured with his own interests as to rush headlong upon revenge. Hence it comes to pass, that the more a person is devoted to selfishness, he will be the more immoderately addicted to the advancement of his own individual interests. This desire for the promotion of personal interest gives birth to another species of vice. For no one wishes to be avenged upon his enemies because that such a thing would be right and equitable, but because it is the means of gratifying his own spiteful propensity. Some, indeed, make a pretext of righteousness and equity in the matter, but the spirit of malignity, by which they are inflamed, effaces every trace of justice, and blinds their minds.[257]

This insight of Calvin, moreover, is echoed in the eloquent judgment of Terrien:

It is here that the theology of the cross might and should intervene. The supplication of authentic Christianity – not, alas, of historical Christendom, neither ecclesiastical nor sectarian – must remain, "Father, forgive them, for they know not what they do" (Luke 23:34). In spite of the violence of his words, produced by his fear and even his terror, the psalmist prays with a supreme confidence. The man's faith at length overcomes his language.[258]

It is of course the case that forgiveness is nowhere on the horizon of this psalm. It is our judgment that the *full voicing of vengeance* is a necessary prerequisite to a move to *forgiveness*. But that move lives beyond this psalm.

Bridging the Horizons: A Psalm Overheard

It is possible to think that such a psalm of vengeance is itself to be taken at face value as an act of prayer. It is also possible, as is often the case, to take the psalm as a cathartic psychological act. A third possible way to take the psalm is as an act of social power, as detailed by Gerald Sheppard. Sheppard suggests that such psalms were designed to be "overheard" both by the enemy and by supporters in the community. Sheppard suggests that if the enemy is "indirectly addressed" in these prayers, the enemy is situated as:

These prayers are not portrayed as silent agonies, but complaints and indictments shared with an audience to which the enemies belong. Applying this insight to the psalms, I find three principal ways in which the enemy is indirectly addressed in these prayers: (1) as someone whom the psalmist, through

---

[257] J. Calvin, *Commentary on the Psalms*, vol. 4 (1979), 275–276.
[258] S. Terrien, *Psalms* (2003), 748.

overheard prayer, implicitly exposes in public and from whom protection is now sought; (2) through indictments or threats against the enemy; and (3) by harsh commands, advice, or instruction given to the enemy, often in hope for the conversion of the enemy.[259]

It is fully possible that these several uses – theological, psychological, and sociological – are not mutually exclusive.

PSALM 110 – OF DAVID. A PSALM

[1] The LORD says to my lord,
'Sit at my right hand
until I make your enemies your footstool.'

[2] The LORD sends out from Zion
your mighty sceptre.
Rule in the midst of your foes.
[3] Your people will offer themselves willingly
on the day you lead your forces
on the holy mountains.
From the womb of the morning,
like dew, your youth will come to you.
[4] The LORD has sworn and will not change his mind,
'You are a priest for ever according to the order of Melchizedek.'

[5] The LORD is at your right hand;
he will shatter kings on the day of his wrath.
[6] He will execute judgment among the nations,
filling them with corpses;
he will shatter heads
over the wide earth.
[7] He will drink from the stream by the path;
therefore he will lift up his head.

---

[259] Gerald T. Sheppard, "'Enemies' and the Politics of Prayer in the Book of Psalms," in David Jobling et al. (eds.), *The Bible and the Politics of Exegesis* (Cleveland: Pilgrim Press, 1991), 73.

Psalm 110 is a royal psalm; beyond that basic classification, there is a lot of variety in the interpretation of this brief poem. The psalm likely comes from Jerusalem and the time of the Davidic monarchy. It is best to consider the text in two parts (vv. 1–3 and 4–7), though the text is enigmatic at points. Each part takes the form of a divine oracle that is then expanded. Both oracles proclaim the defeat of the king's enemies. The most likely setting for the origin of the psalm is the Davidic king's coronation; that setting connects the text with Psalm 2 and the promise there of the defeat of the king's enemies. Allen takes a more historical view, associating the psalm with David's capture of Jerusalem and accession to the throne.[260] Others would suggest a setting of preparing for war or celebrating victory in battle. For readers following the sequential shape of the Psalter, as we will discuss, Psalm 110 appears after the fall of the Davidic monarchy in Psalm 89 and in a sense reaffirms royal hopes.

The opening of the first part of the psalm, verses 1–3, is a formula of revelation. The speaker, perhaps the court poet in the context of coronation ceremonies for the Davidic king, pronounces an oracle, a word in direct speech from YHWH. The traditional rendering of the divine name can cause awkwardness in English; the opening line announces that YHWH speaks to my ruler – the king. What YHWH speaks to the king is the call to sit at YHWH's right hand, a place of honor and power as YHWH's chosen representative to rule over the people in Jerusalem. YHWH will bring victory over the king's enemies, "make your enemies your footstool." The footstool is also likely an allusion to the Ark of the Covenant as YHWH's footstool, so the opening oracle follows the Davidic royal ideology. Just as YHWH is the divine king over all creation, so is the Davidic king YHWH's representative, who will rule over those who oppose YHWH and the kingdom. The right hand is clearly a place of honor and rule here, but the use of the phrase in Psalm 109 is also noteworthy. In Ps 109:31, the divine king stands at the right hand of the oppressed, whereas at the beginning of Psalm 110 the Davidic king sits at the right hand of YHWH. The implication is that, as YHWH's representative, the king is the one to make divine protection of the needy a reality.[261] Psalm 109:6 also speaks of the wicked accuser "on his right," perhaps suggesting that the position can be corrupted and used unjustly. The opening of Psalm 110 makes clear that it is YHWH who is "the power behind the throne"; the Davidic king represents the divine king. So, this opening oracle includes both promise and limit. The earthly king is in a position of honor and will enjoy victory over opponents, but the king's ruler is YHWH, from whom any authority derives.

Verses 2–3 articulate implications of the oracular word in verse 1. The king rules from Zion/Jerusalem with the "mighty scepter," the symbol of royal authority. The psalm makes it clear that the king and kingdom face enemies, but the king also

[260] L. C. Allen, *Psalms 101–150* (2002), 114–115.
[261] J. C. McCann, Jr., "Book of Psalms," in L. E. Keck et al. (eds.), *The New Interpreter's Bible*, vol. 4 (1996), 1130.

enjoys divine authorization. YHWH sends for the scepter. Verse 3 is somewhat
enigmatic. Its first part suggests that those in the kingdom offer themselves in willing service either on the day of coronation or in preparation for battle against enemies. The second part of the verse may refer to the remarkable birth of the king,[262]
but the renewal and hope of morning and dew, and youth, may reflect needs in the
preparation for battle. The decisive divine word that begins the psalm is expanded
in verses 2–3.

The second part of the psalm, verses 4–7, begins with another announcement
of an oracular word that is sure and firm. Likely the addressee of the oracle is still
the Davidic king, and the proclamation is that the king is installed as a priest. In
Jerusalem, the king's roles included priestly functions as leader of the cult. The
reference to Melchizedek relates to Genesis 14; the name associates the king with
righteousness. The expansion of the oracle in verses 5–7 begins with YHWH, now
at the king's right hand, bringing victory in battle and authorizing the king's rule.
The divine ruler brings judgment by defeating and shattering nations "over the
wide earth." Verses 5–6 bring to mind the historical tradition of the great victories YHWH brought the people in early Israel. YHWH gloriously defeated those
who opposed the covenant people; in Psalm 110 YHWH promises such victories
for the ruler of the covenant people. The psalm's concluding verse is also somewhat
enigmatic. There is likely a shift of the pronoun referent to the earthly king, and
with victory comes the lifting of the head. With victory in hand, the king can stop
and drink refreshing waters from the stream. Some commentators associate the
drinking from the stream with a coronation ritual of drinking renewing water from
the spring of Gihon (1 Kgs 1:38) in Jerusalem.[263] The second oracle ties the king to
priestly duties, but the expansion in verses 5–7, in the tradition of Psalm 2, returns
to the theme of divine authorization of Davidic rule and victory over those who
oppose YHWH and YHWH's anointed.

Bridging the Horizons: Changing Hope

Psalm 110 centers on two oracular words that proclaim divine authorization of
the priestly Davidic king. In the sequence of the Psalter, this text comes after
the fall of the Davidic kingdom at the end of Book III (Psalm 89). The Psalter
was also brought together after the destruction of Jerusalem and the trauma
of exile. Those realities suggest that the community understood Psalm 110 in
terms of hopes for the restoration of the monarchy or at least some kind of hope
that YHWH was not finished with the faith community of ancient Israel. The
psalm is about concrete manifestations of YHWH's reign among the people.

---

[262] H.-J. Kraus, *Psalms 60–150* (1988), 350.
[263] H.-J. Kraus, *Psalms 60–150* (1988), 352; and C. C. Broyles, *Psalms* (1999), 415.

Eventually any hopes of restoration of the kingdom shifted to the future and messianic hopes. Christian traditions understand that hope to come to fruition in New Testament proclamation. The New Testament alludes to Psalm 110 in Matt 22:41–46; Mk 12:35–37; Luke 20:41–44; Acts 2:29–36; and Heb 1:5–14. Psalm 110 is one of the important texts used to argue for Jesus as the messiah in New Testament texts. The risen Christ sits at the right hand of God and fulfills the messianic expectation. King Jesus' gracious messianic rule is cast in terms of justice and faith for those in need as the hallmarks of the reign of God.

PSALM 111

¹ Praise the LORD!
I will give thanks to the LORD with my whole heart,
    in the company of the upright, in the congregation.
² Great are the works of the LORD,
    studied by all who delight in them.
³ Full of honor and majesty is his work,
    and his righteousness endures for ever.
⁴ He has gained renown by his wonderful deeds;
    the LORD is gracious and merciful.
⁵ He provides food for those who fear him;
    he is ever mindful of his covenant.
⁶ He has shown his people the power of his works,
    in giving them the heritage of the nations.
⁷ The works of his hands are faithful and just;
    all his precepts are trustworthy.
⁸ They are established for ever and ever,
    to be performed with faithfulness and uprightness.
⁹ He sent redemption to his people;
    he has commanded his covenant for ever.
    Holy and awesome is his name.
¹⁰ The fear of the LORD is the beginning of wisdom;
    all those who practice it have a good understanding.
    His praise endures forever.

Psalm 111 is an alphabetic acrostic, with each line beginning with the successive letter of the Hebrew alphabet. The form provided a compositional structure for the poet; it also suggests something of the completeness of the poem – A to Z. The acrostic form and the psalm's concluding verse associate the composition with wisdom, but the poem has several elements. Its beginning and ending suggest that the poem is a hymn of praise. The historical memory of God's mighty acts and the covenant instruction are also important in the poem. It was likely used in congregational worship as a hymn of praise that includes didactic elements; perhaps that perspective offers the best starting point. The ten verses are of a piece. The first three verses begin with praise and emphasize the mighty acts of God. The recounting of these acts in ancient Israel's historical memory continues through the remainder of the poem, which concludes with a wisdom comment. A number of commentators would date the psalm after the return from exile.

A Closer Look: The Mighty Acts of God

Psalms 111 and 112, both alphabetic acrostics, are connected; both begin with *Hallelujah!* Psalm 111 emphasizes the mighty acts of God, and Psalm 112 the response of the community and its consequences.[264] Book V of the Hebrew Psalter (Psalms 107–150) begins with the call to thanksgiving to YHWH in Psalm 107, a call that continues in Psalms 111–112. The context suggests that the return from exile continues the tradition of YHWH's mighty acts. Psalms 107, 111, and 112 also include wisdom elements, suggesting that even though praise endures, the crisis of exile calls for reflection.

The psalm begins with *Hallelujah!* as an opening call to praise outside the alphabetic acrostic structure. The intensity of the poem is clear from its beginning. The liturgist expresses the purpose of offering thanksgiving to YHWH when the congregation is gathered and to do so "with my whole heart." In Hebrew, the heart is the seat of the mind or will, and so the speaker anticipates bringing the whole self to the act of praise in the midst of worship. Praise and worship are not private matters but include the self in the context of the worshiping community. The reason for praise in Psalm 111 is the mighty acts of God; verse 2 announces the theme. The root word of the term used there, "works," occurs five times in the psalm (vv. 2, 4, 6, 8, and 10). The psalm suggests that the congregation both "delight in" these works and study them; the congregation can again be dazzled by this memory. The works are full of "honor," "majesty," and "righteousness." The terms suggest that the purpose of the divine acts is to bring the community into a right relationship with YHWH.

---

[264] See J. C. McCann, Jr., "Book of Psalms," in L. E. Keck et al. (eds.), *The New Interpreter's Bible*, vol. 4 (1996), 1133. See also H.-J. Kraus, *Psalms 60–150* (1988), 357, who characterizes Psalms 111, 112, and 113 as a group of hallelujah psalms since each begins with the term; Psalm 113 concludes with it.

The opening verses of Psalm 111 celebrate the mighty acts of God and suggest a response of delight and reflection rather than the burden of obligation. The broad scope of YHWH's mighty acts in the first verses of the psalm moves to focus on the covenant relationship.

Verse 4 labels the works of YHWH as "wonderful deeds" and begins to bring to mind the salvation history of God's liberation and establishment of the faith community of ancient Israel. The name, reputation, or memory of YHWH crafted in these wondrous deeds is of one who "is gracious and merciful." Those terms call to mind the formative confession of faith in Exod 34:6–7 of YHWH as one who graciously renews the covenant partnership with ancient Israel. "Merciful" comes from a term suggesting the womb-love of the mother who has given birth to the children of Israel. The context of covenant often includes the narration of the mighty acts of God. The mighty acts include the provision of food and the gift of "the heritage of the nations," the land. The paradigmatic narrative of YHWH's mighty acts for this community is the liberation from slavery in Egypt and the difficult journey through the wilderness to the land promised to the ancestors. Verse 7 labels these works as "faithful and just." Then the historical recital continues with attention to the divine "precepts." The term is about the covenant instruction given to the community as a basis for living. Such covenant living is labeled as "faithfulness and uprightness." Verse 9 then offers a brief summary of the covenant relationship.

> He sent redemption to his people;
> he has commanded his covenant forever. (v. 9)

YHWH has been faithful and asks faithfulness in response; the covenant relationship is both gift and task. This God is "holy," like no other, and the psalm delights in this God and in the memory of the beneficent acts this God has accomplished for the faith community. The holiness and awesomeness of God are intended not to create distance from the congregation but to call the people to acknowledge and explore these acts of salvation in both worship and in living.

Psalm 111 operates in the tradition of ancient Israel's salvation history and emphasizes the connection between the tradition of the mighty acts of God and God's covenant instruction. Hearing the historical memory also suggests meditating on the narrative and both worshiping and living into the covenant relationship. The salvation history created and shaped the community, and God continues to sustain the community. The psalm weds the salvation history and covenant instruction, and thus is a fine example of the covenant theology characteristic of the Hebrew canon. It recites the historical narrative in ancient Israel's traditional terms. That narrative of divine acts initiated the covenant partnership with ancient Israel. God liberated the people from slavery and called them to respond by way of the covenant instruction that is *torah*. In doing so, the community continues to find wholeness of life. The concluding verse of Psalm 111 characterizes such covenant faithfulness as "the fear of the Lord." The verse ties the salvation history to the Hebrew wisdom tradition, not the most common connection in the Hebrew canon. According to Ps 111:10, in covenant faithfulness is found wisdom and understanding, both gifts from YHWH. The concluding line of the psalm then frames the entire composition with an allusion to the psalm's first line and placing the composition in the context of the continuing praise of God.

Bridging the Horizons: Emotion and Intellect

Psalm 111 is a model of the combination of powerful emotion and intellectual reflection characteristic of the Hebrew Psalter. The psalm begins with a full-throated call to praise and thanksgiving and delights in the mighty acts of God. The emotional quality of the language is strong and vibrant. The psalm also urges study and reflection on those mighty acts, and on the covenant relationship and its words, in its conclusion to the tradition of wisdom, the Hebrew intellectual tradition. The tie of covenant and wisdom is not common in the Hebrew scriptures. The poem also includes both individual and community in the heart of its perspective. The speaker "with my whole heart" will give thanks in the company of the congregation (v. 1). In this worship setting, which weds emotion and intellect, the psalm also articulates important theological perspectives on the covenant. The psalm suggests that identity-forming theological perspectives are best gained, crafted, and sustained in the context of a worshiping community. Psalm 111 stunningly recites dimensions of the theology of the Hebrew scriptures in the context of the praise of God.

PSALM 112

¹ Praise the LORD!
  Happy are those who fear the LORD,
  who greatly delight in his commandments.
² Their descendants will be mighty in the land;
  the generation of the upright will be blessed.
³ Wealth and riches are in their houses,
  and their righteousness endures for ever.
⁴ They rise in the darkness as a light for the upright;
  they are gracious, merciful, and righteous.
⁵ It is well with those who deal generously and lend,
  who conduct their affairs with justice.
⁶ For the righteous will never be moved;

they will be remembered for ever.
⁷ They are not afraid of evil tidings;
   their hearts are firm, secure in the LORD.
⁸ Their hearts are steady, they will not be afraid;
   in the end they will look in triumph on their foes.
⁹ They have distributed freely, they have given to the poor;
   their righteousness endures for ever;
   their horn is exalted in honor.
¹⁰ The wicked see it and are angry;
   they gnash their teeth and melt away;
   the desire of the wicked comes to nothing.

Psalm 112 is a good example of a didactic or wisdom psalm. Like the wise teachers who crafted Proverbs, the teacher who crafted Psalm 112 has observed life and passes on lessons for full living. It is helpful to read the psalm in terms of a teacher addressing students in poetry. The psalm is a compact piece of poetry that commends a wise lifestyle to the reader. The treatment here will set a context for the psalm and then read through its portrait of the righteous.

Psalm 112 is a sequel to Psalm 111; both texts are alphabetic acrostics with the poetic lines beginning with successive letters of the Hebrew alphabet. The psalms also share words and phrases: "Righteousness endures forever" occurs in Ps 111:3 and Ps 112:3, 9. The setting of that phrase illustrates the relationship between the texts. Psalm 112 presses the praise of YHWH in Psalm 111 to issues about living wisely. "The fear of the Lord" in the concluding verse of Psalm 111 becomes the hallmark of the lifestyle commended in Psalm 112. The characterizations of YHWH in Psalm 111 become the characteristics of those who revere YHWH in Psalm 112. Considering Psalms 111 and 112 as sequels is most helpful to the interpreter. Mays and McCann have also noted connections between Psalm 112 and Psalm 1.[265] Both psalms are extended beatitudes, both delight in YHWH's *torah*, and both articulate the blessing of the righteous and the futility of the wicked. McCann takes Psalm 112 to be a restatement of Psalm 1 in the context of the trauma of exile and its aftermath, as is appropriate to the setting in Books IV and V of the Psalter (Psalms 90–106 and 107–150).

Psalm 112 begins with hallelujah as a call to praise, as do Psalms 111 and 113, and Psalm 113 concludes in the same way. The first line of the alphabetic acrostic begins with the same word that begins the Hebrew Psalter as the beginning of the beatitude form – 'ašrê. The traditional rendering of the term is "blessed," but that translation has been used less in recent years because there is another Hebrew term for "blessed" – *bārûk* – and that term is a cultic term suggesting the priestly blessing,

---

[265] J. L. Mays, *Psalms* (1994), 360; and J. C. McCann, Jr., "Book of Psalms," in L. E. Keck et al. (eds.), *The New Interpreter's Bible*, vol. 4 (1996), 1135–1136.

a different connotation from the term beginning Psalm 112. The NRSV and other translations have thus moved to a rendering of "happy." Given the current connotation of that English word in terms of satisfaction with external circumstances, that rendering appears to be an unhappy one. The Hebrew term carries a much more profound sense of the basics of a lifestyle. One suggestion for a translation is "joyful," but that term also carries cultic connotations; another suggestion is "contented," but that seems rather tame. The sense of the Hebrew term is that living the lifestyle the psalm urges, a lifestyle of integrity, brings about wholeness. The term *shalom* suggests a life where all the parts fit together well. The person's life journey, inward and outward, fits together and constitutes healthy living.

Psalm 112 portrays such people as "those who fear the Lord." Fear in this context does not suggest intimidation or "being afraid" in the way that phrase is often used in contemporary discourse. The parallel poetic line portrays these people as those who "delight in his commandments." The verb carries the sense of reverence or awe. The wisdom context suggests that those who "fear YHWH" are those who live in line with the created order and who delight in the guidance of divine instruction that shapes and enriches their days. The psalm's opening verse announces the theme, which is then expounded in the remainder of the poem. The righteous lifestyle is not limited to one generation but enjoys continuity into the future. The commended lifestyle is not a private one but extends to the whole family and to the community. In this lifestyle are found "wealth and riches" (v. 3). Notice that the parallel poetic line uses the term "righteousness." The sense of the poetry is not that of contemporary preachers of prosperity but a life that is counted as a gift from the creator and used to initiate and sustain faithful relationships. The psalm is commending a quality of life rather than a brute materialism. Those living faithfully contribute to a community of integrity and are portrayed in verse 4 as "gracious, merciful, and righteous," perhaps with an echo of the famous confession in Exod 34:6–7 portraying YHWH as gracious and merciful; see Psalm 111. These terms connote much of ancient Israel's faith, characterizing the faithful as those who are generous, who love with the love of a mother who has given birth, and who craft relationships of fidelity. Verse 5 speaks clearly of generosity and does so in terms of justice.

Verse 6 is a kind of summary of the righteous lifestyle and recalls language from the end of Psalm 15 in characterizing the righteous as those who "will never be moved." Again, the sense of the poetic portrait of the righteous is not that of unending material wealth and health but a confession that YHWH and YHWH's instruction are stable and bring stability to faithful living. Psalm 112 paints a portrait of "those who fear the Lord" not in terms of cowering before a punishing God but in terms of those who revere and worship the creator and delight in the creator's guidance for living, manifested in faithful relationships – with God and with other people. There is no legalism here but a portrait that commends living faithfully.

YHWH has created and sustains the world and life in it, and has tamed the powers of chaos. That confession makes it possible for the righteous to deal with "evil tidings" and a society that is in disorder. Stability is based in God's stability and leads to faith that the divine purpose will in the end come to fruition. Malicious gossip does not destroy a lifestyle of integrity and trust in the divine purpose. Those who continue to contribute to a healthy community operate out of trust in the divine loyalty; therein is their hope for stability. Verse 9 summarizes the lifestyle yet again in terms of generosity, stability, and well-being. The psalm's final verse articulates the contrast with the wicked, who are angered by the well-being of the righteous. The wicked are not stable but waste their energy trying feverishly to maintain their grip on an acquisitive lifestyle that fades away. Psalm 112 operates from the Hebrew wisdom tradition that observes life and passes on those observations. Life may not always go as planned for those living well, but what sustains such people of faith are the kinds of hopes articulated in Psalm 112: God initiates relationships of fidelity and justice, and supports such a lifestyle.

Interpreters of Psalm 112 have noted connections to Psalm 1, but by the time readers of the Psalter reach Psalm 112 the literary setting has shifted. Those who shaped the final books of the Psalter have faced the crisis of exile and its aftermath. Remarkably, the teacher in Psalm 112 affirms the wise lifestyle of Psalm 1 but now in a setting of severe trouble. Hope comes not in external circumstances but in trustworthiness and loyalty deriving from the creator. Divine guidance for living also comes from that reality. Psalm 112 commends a wise lifestyle and perspective that nurtures hope, even in the face of "evil tidings."

Bridging the Horizons: The Importance of Context

The reading of Psalm 112 herein suggests that context is central for interpretation. The context of readers in contemporary Western culture may well lead to a reading of the text in terms of works of righteousness or in terms of a proclamation that grants material prosperity and health to members of a community of faith. Readers may take the psalm to be a naive articulation of an exact moral calculus and may read Psalm 1 in a similar way. The response to the reading may be to embrace a contemporary "gospel" of prosperity, or it may be to dismiss the psalm as outmoded and misguided. The commentary here has taken a more nuanced approach to the text. The context is the Hebrew wisdom tradition and an artful alphabetic acrostic from a teacher who has learned about life and as a result in this poetic form commends a lifestyle in line with YHWH's created order. The lifestyle is based on integrity, both in terms of justice and in terms of lives being wholly integrated. The lifestyle finds hope not in self-confidence or in feverish effort but in faithful relationships initiated and sustained by the creator. The psalm imparts divine guidance for living. Such relationships and guidance can offer stability in the face of chaos. That nuanced reading of the psalm leads to a different response than those mentioned from contemporary society.

PSALM 113

¹ Praise the LORD!
Praise, O servants of the LORD;
    praise the name of the LORD.

² Blessed be the name of the LORD
    from this time on and for evermore.
³ From the rising of the sun to its setting
    the name of the LORD is to be praised.
⁴ The LORD is high above all nations,
    and his glory above the heavens.

⁵ Who is like the LORD our God,
    who is seated on high,
⁶ who looks far down
    on the heavens and the earth?
⁷ He raises the poor from the dust,
    and lifts the needy from the ash heap,
⁸ to make them sit with princes,
    with the princes of his people.
⁹ He gives the barren woman a home,
    making her the joyous mother of children.
Praise the LORD!

This psalm follows the conventional pattern of a hymn, being divided into a summons (vv. 1–3) and reasons for praise (vv. 4–9), with a concluding acclamation of
praise – "hallelujah!" – that matches the initial "hallelujah" of verse 1. This envelope
of "hallelujah" at its beginning and end begins a modest cluster of Psalms, Psalms
113–118, that bear the marks of "hallelujah" and are commonly reckoned to be a corpus that focuses around that theme of unfettered praise toward YHWH. Whereas
the pattern of the psalm is conventional, the reasons for praise are distinctive in a
quite complex and spectacular way.

The summons to praise in verses 1–3 begins with a "hallelujah" followed by four
summonses, "Praise, praise, praise, bless," and finally, in verse 3, an assurance that
the name of YHWH will be praised. The only vocative is "servants of YHWH" in
verse 1, presumably all those who adhere to YHWH. The juxtaposition of verses
3–4 indicates that all the earth will offer praise to YHWH, in every time (v. 2) and
in every place (v. 3). Although this hymn may be offered in the temple, its read-

ing imagines it to be only part of the great cosmic lyric of acclamation to YHWH celebrating what Terrien calls the "super cosmic majesty of YHWH."[266]

The reasons for praise begin in verse 4, where we may imagine a "for" to introduce the new hymnic maneuver. The first reason for praise in verse 4 is that YHWH is elevated above all creation. The rhetoric assumes a cosmic enthronement of YHWH over heaven and earth and, by implication, over all the gods assembled in the divine council. From the unchallenged splendor and sovereignty of verse 4, the psalmist in verses 5–6 can issue, in the form of a rhetorical question, *a formula of incomparability*.[267] There is no God like YHWH! There is no God like YHWH enthroned in splendor and majesty. But then verses 7–9 give substance to the incomparability of YHWH. It distinguishes YHWH from all other gods not only in power but unrivaled divine power deployed in a quite specific way. Whereas the formula of incomparability in verses 5–6 looks back to verse 4 and celebrates majestic power, it also looks forward in verses 7–9 to the specific use of that power. YHWH is the subject of a series of verbs that bespeak radical social upheaval: YHWH raises, YHWH lifts, YHWH makes, YHWH gives. YHWH, the incomparable sovereign over all reality, is allied with the poor, the needy, and the barren women, all those who are without social power in an economy of demand organized in patriarchal ways. The poor who have no power now have the staying power of YHWH on their behalf. The needy who live in humiliation now have YHWH to give them social standing to make them, in terms of social capacity, an equal to princes. The barren woman who is humiliated in a patriarchal society now, by the mercy of YHWH, is given a home and the joy of motherhood. The commentators regularly notice the juxtaposition of majesty in verse 5 and the descent of YHWH in verses 7–9 into the needfulness of the earth. McCann nicely summarizes the verbs:

Verses 5b–9 are bound grammatically by the fact that each of the six verbal forms is *hiphil*, a causative form of the verb. A more literal translation captures the effect: God "makes God's self high in order to sit" (v. 5b), "makes God's self low in order to see" (v. 6a), "causes the poor to arise" (v. 7a), "makes exalted the needy ... to cause them to sit with princes" (vv. 7b–8a), "makes a home" (v. 9a). In short, God is active. God's character is known, and God is to be praised (vv. 1–5a), because God makes particular things happen (vv. 5b–9).[268]

And before McCann, Calvin commented:

The prophet strengthens his position for the celebration of God's praises, by contrasting the height of his glory and power with his unbounded goodness. Not that

---

[266] S. Terrien, *Psalms* (2003), 763.
[267] See W. Brueggemann, *Theology of the Old Testament* (1997), 139–144.
[268] J. C. McCann, Jr., "Book of Psalms," in L. E. Keck et al. (eds.), *The New Interpreter's Bible*, vol. 4 (1996), 1139.

his goodness can be separated from his glory; but this distinction is made out of regard to men, who would not be able to endure his majesty were he not kindly to humble himself, and gently and kindly draw us towards him. The amount is, that God's dwelling above the heavens, at such a distance from us, does not prevent him from showing himself to be near at hand, and plainly providing for our welfare.[269]

It is no wonder that the psalm ends in "hallelujah," a great doxology that is on the lips of the poor, the needy, the barren, and all those who are raised by the power of YHWH to new life. The doxology never explains. It only attests what Israel knows. YHWH is indeed incomparable, unlike any other in power, unlike any other in compassion, able to deploy power for the sake of social transformation. No wonder all adherents to YHWH must sing without restraint; the new life to which the hopeless are raised is indeed a miracle. Doxology is the only proper response to the inscrutable transformative power of YHWH that is visible in the world.

A Closer Look: YHWH's Name

In verses 1, 2, and 3, it is not only YHWH who is celebrated but also "YHWH's name." The name constitutes both a particular form of the presence of YHWH in Deuteronomic theology and a title that enunciates peculiar and unrivaled power both before the gods in heaven and before the creatures on earth. It is this name before which every knee should bow (see Isa 45:23).

A Closer Look: Poor, Needy, Barren Women

The rescue of the triad of the wretched – poor, needy, barren women – is characteristic in the hymnody of Israel. Particular reference should be made to the Song of Hannah in 1 Sam 2:5–8. Hannah, in a clear parallel, sings of the same transformation. That rendering of reality, moreover, is echoed and reiterated in the Song of Mary in Luke 1:52–53. There is no doubt that this revolutionary celebration of YHWH became the leitmotif of the Gospel according to Luke and extends into the book of Acts, where it is the church, congruent with its risen Lord, that turns the world upside down (Acts 17:6). The psalms, long before the church, asserted that it is YHWH who causes social inversions and the empowerment of the powerless.

The juxtaposition of verse 4 and verses 7–9 attests in remarkable ways that the incomparability of YHWH is constituted at the same time by a *power on high* and *compassion below*. That juxtaposition is voiced in the remarkable statement

---

[269] J. Calvin, *Commentary on the Psalms*, vol. 4 (1979), 333.

in Deuteronomy wherein YHWH is celebrated as "God of Gods" (as in v. 4 of the psalm) and yet is the one who attends to the vulnerable (as in Ps 13:7–9):

> For the Lord your God is God of gods and Lord of lords, the great God, mighty and awesome, who is not partial and takes no bribe, who executes justice for the orphan and the widow, and who loves the strangers, providing them food and clothing. (Deut 10:17–18)

The juxtaposition of power and transformative compassion defines the faith of Israel and, derivatively, the work of Jesus in the narrative memory of the church (see Luke 7:22).

PSALM 114

¹ When Israel went out from Egypt,
    the house of Jacob from a people of strange language,
² Judah became God's sanctuary,
    Israel his dominion.

³ The sea looked and fled;
    Jordan turned back.
⁴ The mountains skipped like rams,
    the hills like lambs.

⁵ Why is it, O sea, that you flee?
    O Jordan, that you turn back?
⁶ O mountains, that you skip like rams?
    O hills, like lambs?

⁷ Tremble, O earth, at the presence of the LORD,
    at the presence of the God of Jacob,
⁸ who turns the rock into a pool of water,
    the flint into a spring of water.

This psalm celebrates the power of YHWH in narrative fashion, but it bears none of the marks of the conventional hymn of praise. The psalm begins with a succinct narrative account of Israel's primal memory, namely the *Exodus* and the *choice of Israel* to be God's people and place of presence (vv. 1–2). Verse 2 allows that because of Israel's departure from Egypt – an event here not directly credited to YHWH – Israel/Judah enjoys special status.

The middle portion of the psalm is divided into two parts, a narrative report (vv. 3–4) and a taunt-song based on that narrative (vv. 5–6). The reference to the Exodus in verse 1 leads to a focus on the Exodus deliverance and the dividing of the waters necessary for the Exodus departure. Conversely, the Exodus event in verse 3 is placed parallel to the stopping of the waters of the Jordan, an event said in Jo 4:23 to be "as" the Exodus event. Thus, verse 3 appeals to the old "credo tradition." Verse 4, however, offers a very different image of the destabilization of mountains and hills, both said to totter like an unstable animal. It is not evident that this imagery relates directly to the Exodus or to the crossing of the Jordan. More likely, verse 4 is an appeal to a creation tradition wherein the creator God reorders all of creation and brings it under his sovereignty. Thus verses 3–4 would seem to bring to an interface *the Exodus memory* and *the creation traditions*.[270]

Verses 5–6 play on verses 3–4 and mention the same four elements of creation – the sea, the Jordan, mountains, and hills. In each case, however, the mentioned element of creation is placed in a rhetorical question that in fact resituates the elements of creation. The sea is mocked for fleeing before YHWH as in verse 3. So also the Jordan is mocked for its retreat before YHWH. The mountains are shamed for slipping into instability, and the hills are as feeble as a lamb. On all counts, the creaturely elements are unable to withstand the force and intention of the creator God. The interface of historical memory and mythic imagery led Terrien to comment:

[T]he vestige of the mythical Monster who was vanquished at creation, according to ancient Near Eastern beliefs, is addressed ironically as a coward. The Jordan turns back as a defeated army in retreat. The mountains, the very symbol of solidity, behave like rams, and the hills like lambs. Nature bows before the people of God. The universe is both demythicized and remythicized in order that the singers may celebrate the power of Yahweh.[271]

Thus the taunting is in fact a way of emphasizing YHWH as powerful and intentional, and capable of imposing his will on all creation.

The narrative of verses 3–4 and the derivative taunt of verses 5–6 lead to the imperative plus a vocative in verse 7, wherein God is referred to explicitly for the

---

[270] On the relation of these two theological themes, see Frank Moore Cross, *Canaanite Myth and Hebrew Epic: Essays on the History of the Religion of Israel* (Cambridge, MA: Harvard University Press, 1973), 121–144; and Terence E. Fretheim, *God and the World in the Old Testament: A Relational Theology of Creation* (Nashville, TN: Abingdon Press, 2005), 109–126.

[271] S. Terrien, *Psalms* (2003), 769. See also E. S. Gerstenberger, *Psalms, Part 2, and Lamentations* (2001), 282–283, on the close parallels to this ironic mocking in the epic of Baal.

first time. The imperative verb "tremble" addresses "the earth." The earth is summoned to quake before the theophanic coming of YHWH and the consequent rule of YHWH, and thereby to acknowledge that all the earth is subject to this rule. Then, in verses 7–8, when it is asked before whom creation trembles or what the creator is like, the answer is the narrative of verses 7–8 that is addressed in a vocative to the listener. The one who evokes fear and terror is the one who turns a rock to water. The verse alludes to the miracle of Exod 17:1–7, wherein YHWH, via Moses, can do better than obtain blood from a turnip. The appeal to Exodus 17 causes verses 7–8 to form a rhetorical envelope with verses 1–2 around the Exodus-wilderness sequence. But inside the envelope of verses 1–2 and 7–8, attention is given to YHWH's rescue of Israel and YHWH's continuing fidelity toward Israel. The sum of all these parts is the assertion of YHWH's great power, which has been evident in the life of Israel. All of creation is to observe the miracles wrought by YHWH in Israel; on that basis, all creation is to acknowledge YHWH's sovereignty. Everything depends on YHWH's capacity to *turn*; YHWH is the one who *turns* mourning to dancing, who *turns* sadness to joy, who *turns* death to life, who *turns* slavery to freedom. It is no wonder that all of creation must heed this creator God, whose primal turning is to the benefit and enhancement of Israel.

A Closer Look: Exodus and Creation

A reader of this psalm may pay particular attention to the way in which the artistic skill of the psalmist blends together the specificity of the Exodus sequence in Israel and the largeness of the creation myth that is attested in Canaanite religion. Although scholars have spent a great deal of energy sorting this out and over the last generation have given priority to the historical, in fact one cannot and should not choose between the two. It is exactly the wonder of Israel's doxology that *cosmic myth* and *historical particularity* are sounded in the same cadences. Israel knows about the particularity of its miracles from YHWH; it also knows that these miracles are incidents in the larger scheme of the wonder of all of creation under the sovereignty of YHWH.

PSALM 115

1 Not to us, O LORD, not to us, but to your name give glory,
  for the sake of your steadfast love and your faithfulness.
2 Why should the nations say,
  'Where is their God?'

3 Our God is in the heavens;
  he does whatever he pleases.
4 Their idols are silver and gold,
  the work of human hands.
5 They have mouths, but do not speak;
  eyes, but do not see.
6 They have ears, but do not hear;
  noses, but do not smell.
7 They have hands, but do not feel;
  feet, but do not walk;
  they make no sound in their throats.
8 Those who make them are like them;
  so are all who trust in them.

9 O Israel, trust in the Lord!
  He is their help and their shield.
10 O house of Aaron, trust in the Lord!
  He is their help and their shield.
11 You who fear the Lord, trust in the Lord!
  He is their help and their shield.

12 The Lord has been mindful of us; he will bless us;
  he will bless the house of Israel;
  he will bless the house of Aaron;
13 he will bless those who fear the Lord,
  both small and great.

14 May the Lord give you increase,
  both you and your children.
15 May you be blessed by the Lord,
  who made heaven and earth.

16 The heavens are the Lord's heavens,
  but the earth he has given to human beings.
17 The dead do not praise the Lord,
  nor do any that go down into silence.
18 But we will bless the Lord
  from this time on and for evermore.
Praise the Lord!

Psalm 115 is a poem with a variety of dimensions and thus has been interpreted in a variety of ways. The poem does not fit the usual classifications of psalms. It includes praise and lament and the call to trust in YHWH. The psalm implies liturgical use, perhaps in a festival, but gives little specificity there. At times, the poem addresses YHWH in the second or third person; at other times, it addresses Israel in the first, second, or third person. Perhaps the best route is to interpret the psalm in terms of praise because it appears as part of the collection called the Hallel (Psalms 113–118), so named because all these psalms focus on *hallelujah*. The psalm's beginning and end also frame the poem in that context. The structure of the poem is also not easy to delineate; perhaps the intensity of the poem pushes beyond traditional interpretive categories. The textual tradition seems to reflect the varied interpretations of the psalm. Some texts combine Psalms 114 and 115. Some begin a new poem at Ps 115:12. Allen has suggested a poetic structure for our extant Psalm 115 that emphasizes verses 9–11.[272]

> A   Verses 1–4. A Plea to the Omnipotent God
>   B   Verses 5–8. A Disavowal of Idol Worship
>   C   Verses 9–11. Calls to Trust in YHWH
>   B'   Verses 12–13. Assurances of Blessing
> A'   Verses 14–18. Priestly Blessing; Communal Promise of Praise

Allen's proposal with its emphasis on verses 9–11 provides a good starting point. The psalm's content suggests some modification. Verses 1–2 and 16–18 shape the poem in terms of divine transcendence. Verses 3–8 contrast YHWH with the idols as a way to emphasize YHWH's acts; verses 12–15 also focus on YHWH's engagement on behalf of Israel. A modified chiastic structure then seems to fit, with the emphasis still on the central verses 9–11 and their call to trust.

A Closer Look: Crisis of Exile

A number of interpreters suggest that the psalm's polemic against idolatry supports a postexilic date; the proclamation of the text fits a world in which nations trust the gods they have made. The use of "steadfast love" and "faithfulness" in the first verse also echoes the importance of those terms at the beginning of Book V (Psalms 107–150). McCann suggests that Psalm 115 is "congruent with the apparent purpose of Book V to address the crisis of exile and its aftermath."[273] These matters of background are helpful for the interpreter, though they are implicit in the text, where the emphasis is on the theological more than the historical.

---

[272] L. C. Allen, *Psalms 101–150* (2002), 147.
[273] J. C. McCann, Jr., "Book of Psalms," in L. E. Keck et al. (eds.), *The New Interpreter's Bible*, vol. 4 (1996), 1144.

The unusual grammar in the psalm's opening verse, as reflected in the NRSV rendering, emphasizes that the glory goes not to the community but to the divine name, reputation, and presence. That reputation comes from the manifestation of "steadfast love" and "faithfulness," a central word pair for the faith confessed in the Psalter. The confession in the first verse seems to partake of both lament and praise traditions in the Psalms and implies that YHWH's glory fills all creation. The opening confession leads to a rhetorical question in verse 2: Why should the nations question the presence of Israel's God? Verses 1–2 set the opening frame for the poem.

Verse 3 affirms that "our God is in the heavens," not limited to the heavens but reigning over all creation from the heavenly throne room. The second line of the verse emphasizes the affirmation highlighting the divine freedom, power, and delight (as opposed to arbitrariness). The affirmation sets a contrast with other national deities and leads to the ridiculing of the idols in the following verses. These images of silver and gold are made by human hands. They have mouths and eyes, but do not speak or see. They have ears and noses, but do not hear or smell. They have hands and feet, but do not feel or walk. They make no sound. This tradition of the ridiculing of the idols is part of the Hebrew canon, especially in the Psalms and Prophets. Idols are made by human hands and so are not living things, and yet they are worshiped. Verse 8 provides an arresting conclusion to this part of the psalm: those who make these idols and worship them become like them – lifeless. Because of the skill with which they are crafted, the idols give every appearance of life, but they are in reality without life, in contrast to the living God YHWH. The makers of the idols seek to create life, but they are limited by their own humanity. As their own handiwork, their deities reflect themselves. They seek glory but will in the end face defeat and emptiness. The polemic in verses 3–8 sets the contrast with YHWH, who is present and active for Jacob/Israel.

The affirmations in the first part of Psalm 115 lead to the central section, verses 9–11, and the call to trust in YHWH as help and shield. The call is put in a three-part structure: to Israel, the house of Aaron, and those who are faithful to YHWH. So the call includes both the congregation and the priests. The call is to trust based on the divine "steadfast love and faithfulness" (v. 1). This community knows the tradition of God as help and shield in the midst of trouble and woe. The psalm brings that memory to the present again for the congregation and so calls on hearers/readers to trust, to live based on the historical memory the community has with the living God, in contrast to the idols made by human hands. Israel's God is present and active and has demonstrated trustworthiness.

Verses 12–15 continue the threefold address to the house of Israel, the house of Aaron, and "those who fear the Lord." YHWH has remembered ("been mindful of") the whole congregation – people and priests – and been present to bless them; that is, to provide the vibrancy to grow and thrive in the world. This gift is to all in the congregation, "both great and small." This confession of faith leads to the priestly prayer in verses 14–15 that the YHWH "who made heaven and earth" will bless the community and their children.

The affirmation of YHWH as creator in verse 15 leads to the beginning of the psalm's conclusion, verses 16–18 – the heavens belong to YHWH. Verse 16 calls to mind the priestly creation account in Genesis 1. In that account, woman and man are created in the image of God in order to take care of the earth, just as God takes care of all creation. That seems to be the perspective in the second line of the verse. Humans are God's representatives, who are responsible for the earth as opposed to being authorized to exploit the earth. Verse 17 reflects the characteristic view of death in the Hebrew scriptures. The dead go to Sheol, the netherworld or world of the dead, and are no more. The descriptions of Sheol suggest that the dead become like zombies wandering in the underworld in silence. They have no voice for praise, in contrast to the congregation of ancient Israel, which praises the creator in response to the life-giving divine presence and activity on behalf of the community. The beginning of verse 18 – "But we" – emphasizes the contrast, just as the syntax at the beginning of the psalm indicated emphasis: "Not to us." The psalm begins and ends with the community, but it is a community that looks beyond itself to YHWH and the praise of YHWH. "Glory" is a manifestation of the divine presence and activity in the world, and the community sings in full voice of that glory in the present and into the future. The psalm ends with the renewed summons to praise, *hallelujah*. Psalm 115 sets a model for the community based on their relationship with YHWH. This living God initiates a relationship with them by way of divine presence and activity, and the community will continue to hope that the memory of this salvation history will invade the present and will make life possible now and in the future. That confession of faith is in contrast to those who worship idols; this congregation will have no part of idol worship but will trust in the maker of heaven and earth.

A Closer Look: The Living God

The central part of Psalm 115 focuses on the call to trust in YHWH as the living God. The sense of the verb "trust" has to do with structuring life based on a relationship with God. The psalm's confession is that God has been shown to be worthy of that trust and that God's powerful care does not waver through the twists and turns of life. The psalm's confession brings to mind the beginning of the Decalogue and the call to worship of the living God who liberated Israel from slavery and to reject any graven images. Images gave a fixed point of contact and could well lead to the presumption that the makers of idols could manipulate and control them just as they made them and moved them. The living God of ancient Israel is not limited to an image and so cannot be manipulated. This God YHWH, however, has demonstrated the ongoing purpose of bringing blessing and deliverance to the faith community of ancient Israel. The

narrative of the community's salvation history provides a basis for the psalm's
call to trust. New Testament tradition continued this emphasis, for example, in
the model prayer's call to hallow God, "who is in the heavens" (v. 3) and to whom
"the kingdom, the power, and the glory" belong. This ancient call to trust in the
living God may seem foreign to readers in contemporary Western culture – a
consumerist society that bows at the feet of human control with the purpose of
making possible the pursuit of happiness. Psalm 115 portrays life as a gift from
the creator, and so calls for living based on gratitude and trust in this living God;
therein is the basis for integrity and hope.

PSALM 116

¹ I love the LORD, because he has heard
  my voice and my supplications.
² Because he inclined his ear to me,
  therefore I will call on him as long as I live.
³ The snares of death encompassed me;
  the pangs of Sheol laid hold on me;
  I suffered distress and anguish.
⁴ Then I called on the name of the LORD:
  'O LORD, I pray, save my life!'

⁵ Gracious is the LORD, and righteous;
  our God is merciful.
⁶ The LORD protects the simple;
  when I was brought low, he saved me.
⁷ Return, O my soul, to your rest,
  for the LORD has dealt bountifully with you.

⁸ For you have delivered my soul from death,
  my eyes from tears,
  my feet from stumbling.
⁹ I walk before the LORD
  in the land of the living.
¹⁰ I kept my faith, even when I said,
  'I am greatly afflicted';
¹¹ I said in my consternation,
  'Everyone is a liar.'

¹² What shall I return to the LORD
   for all his bounty to me?
¹³ I will lift up the cup of salvation
   and call on the name of the LORD,
¹⁴ I will pay my vows to the LORD
   in the presence of all his people.
¹⁵ Precious in the sight of the LORD
   is the death of his faithful ones.
¹⁶ O LORD, I am your servant;
   I am your servant, the child of your serving-maid.
   You have loosed my bonds.
¹⁷ I will offer to you a thanksgiving sacrifice
   and call on the name of the LORD.
¹⁸ I will pay my vows to the LORD
   in the presence of all his people,
¹⁹ in the courts of the house of the LORD,
   in your midst, O Jerusalem.
Praise the LORD!

Psalm 116 is a psalm of thanksgiving from one in the community of faith who expresses praise and gratitude for deliverance from life-threatening trouble. The poetic language of such psalms is characteristically open for use in a variety of settings. Another way to put the matter is that the psalm is adaptable for life and worship in various contexts. The psalm gives indications of liturgical use in services of thanksgiving and a connection with sacrifice. Thanksgiving psalms narrate the deliverance from trouble and declare this testimony to the congregation; in that sense, the psalm is a particular kind of praise. As a psalm of praise, Psalm 116 has been included in the Hallel, a collection associated with the term *hallelujah* (Psalms 113–118). The text has connections with Psalm 115, with references to Sheol, eyes, and feet. Psalms of thanksgiving traditionally begin with a statement of the purpose for giving thanks and praise to God, then narrate the deliverance, and close with a renewed vow of praise; Psalm 30 provides a clear example. Psalm 116 includes these elements, but its poetic structure is a bit more complex. The Greek and Latin textual traditions divide the psalm into two: verses 1–9 and 10–19. The psalm's structure is not easy to discern, but the reading here will follow Mays's suggestion of a poem with a narrative of deliverance at its heart.[274] Verses 13–14 and 17–18, with their repetition of vows of thanksgiving in the style of a refrain, provide structural markers, and Mays suggests that verse 7 also concludes a section. The characteristic form of the thanksgiving psalm appears in verses 1–7, and the additional sections build

---

[274] J. L. Mays, *Psalms* (1994), 368–369.

from there to focus on gathering in the sanctuary with the worshiping community to offer gratitude and sacrifice to YHWH as the one who comes to deliver. Each section of the psalm (vv. 1–7, 8–14, and 15–19) includes a narrative of salvation as well as praise and thanksgiving in worship.

Verses 1–7. The psalm begins with the confession "I love the Lord" growing out of the salvation narrative the psalm reports. The opening reflects the basic theological tradition of the thanksgiving psalms that YHWH is one who hears and responds by coming to deliver when petitioners cry out in distress. The opening confession of love for YHWH is unusual in the Psalter but grows out of this encounter with divine deliverance. The psalm's first two verses articulate the purpose of offering praise and thanksgiving to YHWH as the one who comes to deliver in the ongoing dialogue of faith. The following verses tell the story of the crisis, petition, and deliverance. The speaker comes from the perspective of one who has been helped in the midst of trouble, and so delight in YHWH as the God of mercy and salvation is front and center. The psalm portrays the crisis in terms characteristic of lament and thanksgiving psalms. The petitioner was gripped by the power of death, trapped, distressed, and anguished, and so cried out to YHWH. Sheol is the realm of the dead, the underworld. The view of death that typifies the Hebrew scriptures is that at death people descended to Sheol, sometimes named the Pit. Sheol is a place of no return, a prison that offers no release. Sheol can also be portrayed as the power of death that invades life and diminishes it. The petitioner in Psalm 116 has suffered a sojourn in Sheol gripped by the power of death, with the fullness of life diminished. Death has stalked this person of faith and brought severe anguish.

The psalms of thanksgiving dazzle readers with narratives of liberation from this deathly power that has "encompassed" those who bear witness in these psalms. It is YHWH who brings this amazing deliverance. Verses 5–6 rehearse this narrative of divine deliverance of this one; the summary is one sentence: "When I was brought low, he saved me." God brought this one up from the encounter with Sheol and death back to wholeness in the land of the living. The psalm thus celebrates YHWH as "gracious," "righteous," and "merciful," powerful adjectives for YHWH in the faith tradition of ancient Israel. The narrative of salvation demonstrates these characteristics. In line with the thanksgiving psalm's confession, verse 7 is not the standard conclusion to the form. The speaker calls the self back to rest, fullness of life, and trust, based on God's remarkable act of salvation. The verse calls to mind the inner dialogue of Psalms 42–43. The concluding line of verse 7 is also similar to the concluding line of Psalm 13, a lament psalm. The frame of this first section of Psalm 116 has some particular characteristics, but its confession is clearly in line with the theological traditions of the lament and thanksgiving psalms. The remarkable central narrative is in verse 6: "When I was brought low, he saved me."

Verses 8–14. The psalm of thanksgiving continues and builds with further narration of the divine rescue. Walking "in the land of the living," in the community that makes possible full living, can now be a reality because God has delivered from death, tears, and stumbling. God answered the prayer for help, and so wholeness of life is now possible again. The psalmist had cried out to God; verse 10 makes it clear that the raw honesty of prayer in the midst of trouble is included in the sphere of faith. Verse 11 would suggest, however, that others may not have been supportive. Perhaps others in the tradition of Job's dialogue partners or the enemies in the lament psalms saw the crisis as divine judgment. The speaker in Psalm 116 is now fully alive, however, and grateful to God. And so the question arises as to how best to express gratitude to God for this great act of benevolence. The psalm suggests lifting "the cup of salvation" and fulfilling the vow of thanksgiving. The image of the cup likely came from practices of sacrifice and a drink offering of wine in the community's worship. The story is of how God came to deliver the worshiper from the power of death, and so the worshiper expresses gratitude with an offering to the one responsible. Calling "on the name of the Lord" is the characteristic response of faith in crisis and in thanksgiving (vv. 4, 13, and 17). Words and acts of thanksgiving in worship grow organically from the miraculous story of rescue.

Verses 15–19. Psalm 116 exhibits a structure of intensification as it builds yet again to a third expression of thanksgiving. The opening verse of this section seems a bit awkward in the NRSV rendering. The sense is not that God is pleased when faithful believers die but rather that God finds their deaths costly. The psalm makes it clear that God acts to rescue petitioners and so does not enjoy their death but seeks full life for them. In fact, the self-description in verse 16 suggests a close relationship between YHWH and the one offering this prayer. The speaker recounts for the third time in Psalm 116 the basic narrative of rescue from the power of death: "You have loosed my bonds." The response is a sacrifice of thanksgiving and the testimony of how God has come to deliver the speaker from trouble and woe. Perhaps the psalm itself will become the words that accompany the sacrifice as the worshiper fulfills the vow of thanksgiving in worship in the sanctuary, identified in the end as the temple in Jerusalem. The sacrifice and narrative are the characteristic responses of thanksgiving in worship. The psalm concludes with the renewed call to praise – *hallelujah*.

Psalm 116 articulates praise and thanksgiving to YHWH for rescue from a crisis in the life of a worshiper and encourages the congregation to enter the experience and also offer gratitude. As is characteristic of thanksgiving psalms, the poem offers thanks by telling the story of trouble, petition, and deliverance. The story is about the God who comes to deliver, and the psalm seeks to involve the congregation in the narrative and thereby facilitate an encounter for the community with this God and express gratitude in word and deed.

A Closer Look: The Hallel

Psalm 116 is part of the psalm collection called the Hallel, which was used at Passover. The cup of salvation (v. 13) became part of the festival and its recital of the narrative of deliverance from Egyptian bondage. The New Testament writers appropriated the story, so it is not surprising that the cup of salvation came to be associated with the Eucharist in Christian tradition. "Eucharist" means thanksgiving, so the psalm fits that setting. It is often associated with Maundy Thursday and the lifting of the cup as an indication that the crucifixion and resurrection of Jesus are at hand.[275] Such a use of the image in Christian tradition brings a new interpretation of thanksgiving for deliverance.

PSALM 117

¹ Praise the LORD, all you nations!
  Extol him, all you peoples!
² For great is his steadfast love toward us,
  and the faithfulness of the LORD endures for ever.
Praise the LORD!

This psalm, the briefest of them all, offers everything that is needed for praise of God, who is creator and savior. The basic structure of praise, so clear here, consists of a *summons* to praise expressed as a vocative imperative and *reasons* for praise, characteristically introduced by the preposition "for" ("because"). In this psalm, the summons is voiced in two imperatives, "praise, extol," and the vocative address is to "all you nations, all you peoples." The enterprise of Israel at praise can include, or imagine, all peoples of the earth joining in praise of YHWH.

The reasons given for such exuberance express Israel's oldest, deepest theological conviction, that YHWH has been experienced in the life of Israel and in the life of the world as steadfast and faithful. The two terms *hesed* and *'emeth* constitute a defining word pair in Israel's rhetoric that is likely rooted in the stylized recital of Exod 34:6–7. YHWH is celebrated as a positive agent in a destabilized world, as a reliable partner in a world of fickleness and transience. The psalm concludes with a final reiteration of the initial summons.

The tension between the "universal" summons and the Israelite reason is often noted and constitutes the major point of interpretation in the psalm. Kraus, quoting Martin Achard, judges that the inclusiveness of the summons attests that "Israel

---

275 J. C. McCann, Jr., "Book of Psalms," in L. E. Keck et al. (eds.), *The New Interpreter's Bible*, vol. 4 (1996), 1149.

is not the end of the revelation of the Old Testament, it is the instrument which its God has chosen for manifesting his glory."[276] Such a verdict utilizes Israel's experience of divine fidelity (and its attestation to that fidelity) as a way of recruiting other nations into the wonder of God's glory. Thus the psalm pushes beyond the singing community that sings to this God as its own.

A Closer Look: Strong Enough to Effect Its Purpose

The only surprising word in this psalm is the term rendered "great" (see Ps 103:11). That translation might suggest largeness or majesty, but the term in fact bespeaks might or strength, often with a military connotation; that is, enough strength to work one's will. In this psalm, then, YHWH's steadfast love is strong enough to effect its purpose, namely the well-being and security of Israel and, by implication, the well-being and security of the nations. It is not enough that YHWH should be faithful. Israel celebrates a divine faithfulness that is effective against every threat.

A Closer Look: Romans 15

In Romans 15, Paul is concluding his complex argument about how the God of the Jews is indeed the God of the Gentiles as well. He asserts that Gentiles might glorify God for his mercy (Rom 15:9), just what they are summoned to do in this psalm. Paul takes the vocative summons of the psalm seriously and sees that this praise cannot be contained in a more parochial environment. What follows in Rom 15:9–12 is a series of Old Testament quotations, all of which attend to the Gentiles. Verse 11 in particular is likely a quotation from this psalm, so Paul has mobilized the psalm as an attestation to his argument that the God of mercy is the God of all peoples. Paul makes a point of what might be passed over in the psalm as a phrase of incidental or even careless doxological rhetoric. In Paul's purview, the vocative becomes a pivot point in resituating the fidelity of God in world history.

Bridging the Horizons: Transcending Particularities

This large vision of Israel's worship of YHWH and the tension of "universalism and particularism" are at the heart of this psalm. The tension between "the chosen people" (Israel, the church, and most recently the United States) and other peoples

---

[276] H.-J. Kraus, *Psalms 60–150* (1988), 391.

is now an acute practical political problem that has a theological dimension in how the "Christian West" is to relate to non-Christian civilization.

That deep and as yet unresolved issue is given artful expression in the famous vision of all peoples streaming to Jerusalem, where they will learn peace and beat their weapons into artifacts of peace (Isa 2:2–4; Mi 4:1–4). The imagery envisions all peoples praising YHWH and submitting to YHWH. Micah's version of this poem, however, adds a curious verse that we may notice:

For all the peoples walk,
Each in the name of its god,
But we will walk in the name of the Lord our God
Forever and ever. (Mi 4:5)

This verse suggests all peoples are in the procession to a peace-generating Jerusalem, but still with their own theological particularity, "in the name of its God." No doubt Psalm 117 is a venue for continued work and reflection about the character of YHWH vis-à-vis other peoples and the privilege of the chosen in a worldwide hallelujah. One dare imagine that exuberant praise (without self-reference) might be a way of transcending truculent particularities. Patrick Kavanaugh judges:

To go on the grand tour
A man must be free
From self-necessity.[277]

Praise amid "all the peoples" is a grand tour. In order to participate, every particularity, including that of Israel, must get beyond self-necessity. Psalm 117 invites us to a grand tour of the God of fidelity, who outstrips every self-necessity.

PSALM 118

¹ O give thanks to the Lord, for he is good;
his steadfast love endures for ever!

² Let Israel say,
'His steadfast love endures for ever.'

---

[277] Patrick Kavanaugh, "The Self Slaved," quoted in Daniel W. Hardy and David R. Ford, *Praising and Knowing God* (Philadelphia: Westminster Press, 1985), 83.

³ Let the house of Aaron say,
  'His steadfast love endures for ever.'
⁴ Let those who fear the LORD say,
  'His steadfast love endures for ever.'

⁵ Out of my distress I called on the LORD;
  the LORD answered me and set me in a broad place.
⁶ With the LORD on my side I do not fear.
  What can mortals do to me?
⁷ The LORD is on my side to help me;
  I shall look in triumph on those who hate me.
⁸ It is better to take refuge in the LORD
  than to put confidence in mortals.
⁹ It is better to take refuge in the LORD
  than to put confidence in princes.

¹⁰ All nations surrounded me;
   in the name of the LORD I cut them off!
¹¹ They surrounded me, surrounded me on every side;
   in the name of the LORD I cut them off!
¹² They surrounded me like bees;
   they blazed like a fire of thorns;
   in the name of the LORD I cut them off!
¹³ I was pushed hard, so that I was falling,
   but the LORD helped me.
¹⁴ The LORD is my strength and my might;
   he has become my salvation.

¹⁵ There are glad songs of victory in the tents of the righteous:
'The right hand of the LORD does valiantly;
¹⁶ the right hand of the LORD is exalted;
   the right hand of the LORD does valiantly.'
¹⁷ I shall not die, but I shall live,
   and recount the deeds of the LORD.
¹⁸ The LORD has punished me severely,
   but he did not give me over to death.

¹⁹ Open to me the gates of righteousness,
   that I may enter through them
   and give thanks to the LORD.

²⁰ This is the gate of the Lord;
   the righteous shall enter through it.

²¹ I thank you that you have answered me
   and have become my salvation.
²² The stone that the builders rejected
   has become the chief cornerstone.
²³ This is the Lord's doing;
   it is marvelous in our eyes.
²⁴ This is the day that the Lord has made;
   let us rejoice and be glad in it.
²⁵ Save us, we beseech you, O Lord!
   O Lord, we beseech you, give us success!

²⁶ Blessed is the one who comes in the name of the Lord.
   We bless you from the house of the Lord.
²⁷ The Lord is God,
   and he has given us light.
Bind the festal procession with branches,
   up to the horns of the altar.

²⁸ You are my God, and I will give thanks to you;
   you are my God, I will extol you.

²⁹ O give thanks to the Lord, for he is good,
   for his steadfast love endures for ever.

Psalm 118 is a thanksgiving psalm from ancient Israel's worship, though the psalm contains a variety of elements and thus a variety of settings have been constructed for the text's ancient setting. Kraus suggests that the psalm was an entrance liturgy.[278] Worshipers gather for a festival and process with praise and thanksgiving followed by an antiphonal litany and singing. The composition is framed in verses 1–4 and 22–29 with the voices of worshipers; the verses in between narrate a person's deliverance as an example of thanksgiving. Allen agrees that the context is a processional liturgy but suggests that the thanksgiving comes from a royal victory in battle.[279] The psalm begins with a priestly voice but shifts to the king in verses 5–13. Much of the psalm is in the first-person singular, but the crisis portrayed seems to relate to the community and thus we have the suggestion of the king's voice representing

---

[278] H.-J. Kraus, *Psalms 60–150* (1988), 395.
[279] L. C. Allen, *Psalms 101–150* (2002), 165–166.

the people. The psalm also echoes ancient Israel's historical memory of the Exodus from Egypt and second exodus from exile.[280] The literary structure followed here considers the psalm in three parts. Verses 1–4 call the community to thanksgiving. Verses 5–18 narrate a divine rescue, also in three parts: verses 5–9 rehearse the rescue; verses 10–14 focus on the crisis; and verses 15–18 put the rescue in the context of ancient Israel's historical faith. Verses 19–29 conclude the celebration of the rescue.

A Closer Look: Weaving Hallelujahs Together

Psalm 118 concludes a collection of psalms of praise associated with *hallelujah* and called the Hallel – Psalms 113–118 – that was used during Passover. The psalm brings the collection to a fitting conclusion. It begins with reference to YHWH's "steadfast love," central to Psalm 117, and focuses on thanksgiving, central to Psalm 116. Psalm 118 also uses the threefold address to Israel, the house of Aaron, and those who revere YHWH, as found in Psalm 115. The text also remembers the Exodus experience, as does Psalm 114, and refers to princes, as does Psalm 113. Psalm 118 also echoes other texts: verse 5 recalls the "broad place" of Pss 18:19 and 31:8; verse 6 calls to mind the refrain of Ps 56:4, 11; and verse 14 recalls the beginning of the song of Miriam/Moses in Exod 15:2. McCann sets the broader literary context:

Book V begins by establishing a post-exilic perspective and by commending consideration of God's steadfast love. Not coincidentally perhaps, Psalm 118 begins and ends with the same verse that opens Book V (Ps 107:1), suggesting the possibility that Psalms 107–118 together offer a perspective from which to face the reality of continuing oppression: recollection of God's past activity as a basis for petition and grateful trust in God's future activity on behalf of the people.[281]

The first and last verses of Psalm 118 are the same and frame the composition by summoning the congregation to thanksgiving because YHWH is the God who provides for life and whose "steadfast love" endures into the future. The emphasis on YHWH's "steadfast love" characterizes the faith of the Psalter. The call to thanksgiving (vv. 1–4) continues by addressing priests and people with the three categories familiar from Psalm 115: Israel, house of Aaron, and "those who fear the Lord." Each group is called to confess that YHWH's loyal love endures into the future. The repetition indicates emphasis. The congregation's encounter with YHWH's unchanging love brings the response of praise and thanksgiving.

280 J. C. McCann, Jr., "Book of Psalms," in L. E. Keck et al. (eds.), *The New Interpreter's Bible*, vol. 4 (1996), 1153, provides a helpful summary of the issues.
281 J. C. McCann, Jr., "Book of Psalms," in L. E. Keck et al. (eds.), *The New Interpreter's Bible*, vol. 4 (1996), 1153–1154.

In verses 5–18, the voice of a person within the congregation narrates a demonstration of YHWH's steadfast love. Verse 5 articulates the basic narrative, and verses 6–9 suggest its implications. The petitioner was being strangled and constricted in distress, and YHWH brought about the rescue to "a broad place" where full breathing was possible. The confession is that YHWH heard the petition and came to deliver the petitioner. The experience brought the realization that God as refuge is far more powerful than any crisis and far more powerful than any human, even any human ruler. Fear can be a powerful reality, but refuge in God can bring hope, even in the face of such trauma.

Verses 10–14 continue the narrative of salvation, with an emphasis on the trouble and woe. "All nations surrounded" the petitioner on every side; the enemies are described as a swarm of bees and as a blazing fire. In the face of such fearsome enemies, the petitioner pleaded with YHWH and "the Lord helped me." The repeated line "in the name of the Lord I cut them off!" reflects the victory. Verse 14 calls on the community's historical memory, with an allusion to Exod 15:2 and the rejoicing over the deliverance at the sea in the exodus from slavery in Egypt. God's strength and might brought salvation for the people then and has done so now for the petitioner.

Verses 15–18 conclude this part of the psalm with continued references to the exodus from Egypt. The songs of thanksgiving ring out because of the victory wrought by YHWH's right hand. That is the language of the Exodus tradition. YHWH's right hand has brought the people out of bondage and now has in turn delivered the petitioner from distress, and the petitioner gives thanks in the congregation. There was trouble but no death; rather YHWH brought wholeness of life. This one has returned from the cusp of death and bears witness to the newness of life with this testimony in worship. The purpose of the psalm is to invite the congregation to enter the narrative and encounter again the God who comes to deliver and so renew the confession:

The Lord is my strength and my might;
he has become my salvation. (v. 14)

The survival of this threatening crisis is at the core of Psalm 118, which has been composed for a liturgy of thanksgiving. The identities of the petitioner and crisis remain open. Verses 10–12 could support the suggestion that the speaker is the king, as noted earlier, but the psalm is also adaptable to a variety of settings in which a faithful petitioner tells the story of salvation. Verse 9 does not take a positive view of princes, and the opponents in verses 1–2 could be outsiders. Perhaps it is best to say that the voice of the text is the liturgist representing the community and leave open the identification of the speaker and crisis. Some would date the psalm after the fall of the Davidic monarchy.[282]

[282] See C. C. Broyles, *Psalms* (1999), 438–439.

Verses 19–29 begin with a reference to the procession to worship for the purpose of thanksgiving to the God who comes to deliver. The voice is again the voice of the representative person of faith who has been rescued. This surprising rescue was an act of YHWH to bring life out of death and to renew the right relationship with the petitioner. The psalm then shifts to the voice of the community, where this rescue is received as a marvelous act of hope. Verse 25 then articulates a petition on behalf of the community; perhaps the community's crisis is not past. The import of verses 26–27 is obscure, but perhaps the reference is to the one who was delivered and that person's testimony of thanksgiving has brought renewed hope for the congregation, which celebrates now, even in the midst of a continuing time of trouble and petition. God has brought light, and the response is thanksgiving. The psalm concludes as it began, with a renewed call to praise and thanksgiving to the God who persistently brings good and mercy.

The open poetic language and varied traditions in Psalm 118 suggest that the composition is a kind of model prayer for the worshiping community. The petitioner voices need in the midst of trouble and celebrates the divine deliverance with thanksgiving as a witness to YHWH's involvement in the world and the community of faith. The individual story of salvation provides an example of God's beneficent engagement with the world.

A Closer Look: Triumphal Entry

The New Testament writers found Psalm 118 to be a beneficial text for portraying the work of Jesus in the world. All four gospel writers use Ps 118:25–26 when narrating the triumphal entry on Palm Sunday (Matt 21:1–11; Mk 11:1–11; Luke 19:28–40; Jn 12:12–19). Matthew 21:42 also quotes Ps 118:22–23. Christian tradition suggests that divine acts of salvation continued to fulfillment in the crucifixion and resurrection of Jesus, leading to renewed thanksgiving.

PSALM 119

¹ Happy are those whose way is blameless,
  who walk in the law of the LORD.
² Happy are those who keep his decrees,
  who seek him with their whole heart,
³ who also do no wrong,
  but walk in his ways.
⁴ You have commanded your precepts

to be kept diligently.
5 O that my ways may be steadfast
in keeping your statutes!
6 Then I shall not be put to shame,
having my eyes fixed on all your commandments.
7 I will praise you with an upright heart,
when I learn your righteous ordinances.
8 I will observe your statutes;
do not utterly forsake me.

9 How can young people keep their way pure?
By guarding it according to your word.
10 With my whole heart I seek you;
do not let me stray from your commandments.
11 I treasure your word in my heart,
so that I may not sin against you.
12 Blessed are you, O LORD;
teach me your statutes.
13 With my lips I declare
all the ordinances of your mouth.
14 I delight in the way of your decrees
as much as in all riches.
15 I will meditate on your precepts,
and fix my eyes on your ways.
16 I will delight in your statutes;
I will not forget your word.

17 Deal bountifully with your servant,
so that I may live and observe your word.
18 Open my eyes, so that I may behold
wondrous things out of your law.
19 I live as an alien in the land;
do not hide your commandments from me.
20 My soul is consumed with longing
for your ordinances at all times.
21 You rebuke the insolent, accursed ones,
who wander from your commandments;
22 take away from me their scorn and contempt,
for I have kept your decrees.
23 Even though princes sit plotting against me,

your servant will meditate on your statutes.
24 Your decrees are my delight,
   they are my counsellors.

25 My soul clings to the dust;
   revive me according to your word.
26 When I told of my ways, you answered me;
   teach me your statutes.
27 Make me understand the way of your precepts,
   and I will meditate on your wondrous works.
28 My soul melts away for sorrow;
   strengthen me according to your word.
29 Put false ways far from me;
   and graciously teach me your law.
30 I have chosen the way of faithfulness;
   I set your ordinances before me.
31 I cling to your decrees, O LORD;
   let me not be put to shame.
32 I run the way of your commandments,
   for you enlarge my understanding.

33 Teach me, O LORD, the way of your statutes,
   and I will observe it to the end.
34 Give me understanding, that I may keep your law
   and observe it with my whole heart.
35 Lead me in the path of your commandments,
   for I delight in it.
36 Turn my heart to your decrees,
   and not to selfish gain.
37 Turn my eyes from looking at vanities;
   give me life in your ways.
38 Confirm to your servant your promise,
   which is for those who fear you.
39 Turn away the disgrace that I dread,
   for your ordinances are good.
40 See, I have longed for your precepts;
   in your righteousness give me life.

41 Let your steadfast love come to me, O LORD,
   your salvation according to your promise.

⁴² Then I shall have an answer for those who taunt me,
for I trust in your word.
⁴³ Do not take the word of truth utterly out of my mouth,
for my hope is in your ordinances.
⁴⁴ I will keep your law continually,
for ever and ever.
⁴⁵ I shall walk at liberty,
for I have sought your precepts.
⁴⁶ I will also speak of your decrees before kings,
and shall not be put to shame;
⁴⁷ I find my delight in your commandments,
because I love them.
⁴⁸ I revere your commandments, which I love,
and I will meditate on your statutes.

⁴⁹ Remember your word to your servant,
in which you have made me hope.
⁵⁰ This is my comfort in my distress,
that your promise gives me life.
⁵¹ The arrogant utterly deride me,
but I do not turn away from your law.
⁵² When I think of your ordinances from of old,
I take comfort, O Lord.
⁵³ Hot indignation seizes me because of the wicked,
those who forsake your law.
⁵⁴ Your statutes have been my songs
wherever I make my home.
⁵⁵ I remember your name in the night, O Lord,
and keep your law.
⁵⁶ This blessing has fallen to me,
for I have kept your precepts.

⁵⁷ The Lord is my portion;
I promise to keep your words.
⁵⁸ I implore your favor with all my heart;
be gracious to me according to your promise.
⁵⁹ When I think of your ways,
I turn my feet to your decrees;
⁶⁰ I hurry and do not delay
to keep your commandments.

61 Though the cords of the wicked ensnare me,
    I do not forget your law.
62 At midnight I rise to praise you,
    because of your righteous ordinances.
63 I am a companion of all who fear you,
    of those who keep your precepts.
64 The earth, O LORD, is full of your steadfast love;
    teach me your statutes.

65 You have dealt well with your servant,
    O LORD, according to your word.
66 Teach me good judgment and knowledge,
    for I believe in your commandments.
67 Before I was humbled I went astray,
    but now I keep your word.
68 You are good and do good;
    teach me your statutes.
69 The arrogant smear me with lies,
    but with my whole heart I keep your precepts.
70 Their hearts are fat and gross,
    but I delight in your law.
71 It is good for me that I was humbled,
    so that I might learn your statutes.
72 The law of your mouth is better to me
    than thousands of gold and silver pieces.

73 Your hands have made and fashioned me;
    give me understanding that I may learn your commandments.
74 Those who fear you shall see me and rejoice,
    because I have hoped in your word.
75 I know, O LORD, that your judgments are right,
    and that in faithfulness you have humbled me.
76 Let your steadfast love become my comfort
    according to your promise to your servant.
77 Let your mercy come to me, that I may live;
    for your law is my delight.
78 Let the arrogant be put to shame,
    because they have subverted me with guile;
    as for me, I will meditate on your precepts.
79 Let those who fear you turn to me,

so that they may know your decrees.
80 May my heart be blameless in your statutes,
    so that I may not be put to shame.

81 My soul languishes for your salvation;
    I hope in your word.
82 My eyes fail with watching for your promise;
    I ask, 'When will you comfort me?'
83 For I have become like a wineskin in the smoke,
    yet I have not forgotten your statutes.
84 How long must your servant endure?
    When will you judge those who persecute me?
85 The arrogant have dug pitfalls for me;
    they flout your law.
86 All your commandments are enduring;
    I am persecuted without cause; help me!
87 They have almost made an end of me on earth;
    but I have not forsaken your precepts.
88 In your steadfast love spare my life,
    so that I may keep the decrees of your mouth.

89 The LORD exists for ever;
    your word is firmly fixed in heaven.
90 Your faithfulness endures to all generations;
    you have established the earth, and it stands fast.
91 By your appointment they stand today,
    for all things are your servants.
92 If your law had not been my delight,
    I would have perished in my misery.
93 I will never forget your precepts,
    for by them you have given me life.
94 I am yours; save me,
    for I have sought your precepts.
95 The wicked lie in wait to destroy me,
    but I consider your decrees.
96 I have seen a limit to all perfection,
    but your commandment is exceedingly broad.

97 Oh, how I love your law!
    It is my meditation all day long.

⁹⁸ Your commandment makes me wiser than my enemies,
       for it is always with me.
⁹⁹ I have more understanding than all my teachers,
       for your decrees are my meditation.
¹⁰⁰ I understand more than the aged,
       for I keep your precepts.
¹⁰¹ I hold back my feet from every evil way,
       in order to keep your word.
¹⁰² I do not turn away from your ordinances,
       for you have taught me.
¹⁰³ How sweet are your words to my taste,
       sweeter than honey to my mouth!
¹⁰⁴ Through your precepts I get understanding;
       therefore I hate every false way.

¹⁰⁵ Your word is a lamp to my feet
       and a light to my path.
¹⁰⁶ I have sworn an oath and confirmed it,
       to observe your righteous ordinances.
¹⁰⁷ I am severely afflicted;
       give me life, O LORD, according to your word.
¹⁰⁸ Accept my offerings of praise, O LORD,
       and teach me your ordinances.
¹⁰⁹ I hold my life in my hand continually,
       but I do not forget your law.
¹¹⁰ The wicked have laid a snare for me,
       but I do not stray from your precepts.
¹¹¹ Your decrees are my heritage for ever;
       they are the joy of my heart.
¹¹² I incline my heart to perform your statutes
       for ever, to the end.

¹¹³ I hate the double-minded,
       but I love your law.
¹¹⁴ You are my hiding-place and my shield;
       I hope in your word.
¹¹⁵ Go away from me, you evildoers,
       that I may keep the commandments of my God.
¹¹⁶ Uphold me according to your promise, that I may live,
       and let me not be put to shame in my hope.

[117] Hold me up, that I may be safe
     and have regard for your statutes continually.
[118] You spurn all who go astray from your statutes;
     for their cunning is in vain.
[119] All the wicked of the earth you count as dross;
     therefore I love your decrees.
[120] My flesh trembles for fear of you,
     and I am afraid of your judgments.

[121] I have done what is just and right;
     do not leave me to my oppressors.
[122] Guarantee your servant's well-being;
     do not let the godless oppress me.
[123] My eyes fail from watching for your salvation,
     and for the fulfilment of your righteous promise.
[124] Deal with your servant according to your steadfast love,
     and teach me your statutes.
[125] I am your servant; give me understanding,
     so that I may know your decrees.
[126] It is time for the LORD to act,
     for your law has been broken.
[127] Truly I love your commandments
     more than gold, more than fine gold.
[128] Truly I direct my steps by all your precepts;
     I hate every false way.

[129] Your decrees are wonderful;
     therefore my soul keeps them.
[130] The unfolding of your words gives light;
     it imparts understanding to the simple.
[131] With open mouth I pant,
     because I long for your commandments.
[132] Turn to me and be gracious to me,
     as is your custom toward those who love your name.
[133] Keep my steps steady according to your promise,
     and never let iniquity have dominion over me.
[134] Redeem me from human oppression,
     that I may keep your precepts.
[135] Make your face shine upon your servant,
     and teach me your statutes.

136 My eyes shed streams of tears
    because your law is not kept.

137 You are righteous, O Lord,
    and your judgments are right.
138 You have appointed your decrees in righteousness
    and in all faithfulness.
139 My zeal consumes me
    because my foes forget your words.
140 Your promise is well tried,
    and your servant loves it.
141 I am small and despised,
    yet I do not forget your precepts.
142 Your righteousness is an everlasting righteousness,
    and your law is the truth.
143 Trouble and anguish have come upon me,
    but your commandments are my delight.
144 Your decrees are righteous for ever;
    give me understanding that I may live.

145 With my whole heart I cry; answer me, O Lord.
    I will keep your statutes.
146 I cry to you; save me,
    that I may observe your decrees.
147 I rise before dawn and cry for help;
    I put my hope in your words.
148 My eyes are awake before each watch of the night,
    that I may meditate on your promise.
149 In your steadfast love hear my voice;
    O Lord, in your justice preserve my life.
150 Those who persecute me with evil purpose draw near;
    they are far from your law.
151 Yet you are near, O Lord,
    and all your commandments are true.
152 Long ago I learned from your decrees
    that you have established them for ever.

153 Look on my misery and rescue me,
    for I do not forget your law.
154 Plead my cause and redeem me;

give me life according to your promise.
¹⁵⁵ Salvation is far from the wicked,
  for they do not seek your statutes.
¹⁵⁶ Great is your mercy, O Lord;
  give me life according to your justice.
¹⁵⁷ Many are my persecutors and my adversaries,
  yet I do not swerve from your decrees.
¹⁵⁸ I look at the faithless with disgust,
  because they do not keep your commands.
¹⁵⁹ Consider how I love your precepts;
  preserve my life according to your steadfast love.
¹⁶⁰ The sum of your word is truth;
  and every one of your righteous ordinances endures for ever.

¹⁶¹ Princes persecute me without cause,
  but my heart stands in awe of your words.
¹⁶² I rejoice at your word
  like one who finds great spoil.
¹⁶³ I hate and abhor falsehood,
  but I love your law.
¹⁶⁴ Seven times a day I praise you
  for your righteous ordinances.
¹⁶⁵ Great peace have those who love your law;
  nothing can make them stumble.
¹⁶⁶ I hope for your salvation, O Lord,
  and I fulfil your commandments.
¹⁶⁷ My soul keeps your decrees;
  I love them exceedingly.
¹⁶⁸ I keep your precepts and decrees,
  for all my ways are before you.

¹⁶⁹ Let my cry come before you, O Lord;
  give me understanding according to your word.
¹⁷⁰ Let my supplication come before you;
  deliver me according to your promise.
¹⁷¹ My lips will pour forth praise,
  because you teach me your statutes.
¹⁷² My tongue will sing of your promise,
  for all your commandments are right.
¹⁷³ Let your hand be ready to help me,

for I have chosen your precepts.

174 I long for your salvation, O LORD,
and your law is my delight.
175 Let me live that I may praise you,
and let your ordinances help me.
176 I have gone astray like a lost sheep; seek out your servant,
for I do not forget your commandments.

Psalm 119 is of course the longest psalm; it is also notoriously rated to be boring, repetitious, and without plot development. Calvin comments on the nature of this psalm: "As this psalm treats of various matters, it is difficult to give an epitome of its contents.... In short, he frequently passes from one topic to another, and prosecutes no one particular subject continuously."[283] Such features as "boring, repetitious, and without plot development," however, need to be reassessed in light of the structure of the psalm and its apparent pedagogic intention. It is rightly seen by James Mays and Patrick Miller to be a psalm of Torah piety; that is, a testimony and instruction concerning the wisdom, healthiness, and fidelity that belong to a life rooted in response to the commands and instructions of Israel's Torah.[284] It is likely that this pattern of poetry is designed to be comprehensive and all-inclusive; that is, voicing everything on the subject from A to Z. In this case, that means everything that can be said about Torah piety.[285]

The didactic device for this testimony and instruction is an acrostic pattern whereby each line begins, in succession, with a letter of the alphabet, thus moving through the alphabet from A to Z; that is, from aleph to taw. (In popular song, this acrostic device is known from the swoon song of the 1950s, "'A,' you're adorable, 'B,' you're so beautiful, 'C,' you're a cutey full of charms....") The Old Testament features a number of such acrostic poems, but none that are recognizable in translation.

Given that general pattern, however, Psalm 119 is nonetheless distinctive because it offers an eightfold acrostic pattern; that is, each of the first eight verses begin with aleph, the first letter of the Hebrew alphabet, and on through the alphabet, eight lines per letter. Since there are twenty-two letters in the Hebrew alphabet, the outcome is eight times twenty-two, or 176 verses. That is why the psalm is so long. Because the central passion of the psalm is a resolution to adhere to Torah commands and to benefit from such adherence, we can see why the psalm is so repetitive. The central truth of Torah obedience cannot be said too often. The repetition

---

283 J. Calvin, *Psalms*, 398.
284 James Luther Mays, "The Place of Torah-Psalms in the Psalter," *JBL* 106 (1987): 3–12; and Patrick D. Miller, *Israelite Religion and Biblical Theology: Collected Essays* (JSOTSup 267; Sheffield: Sheffield Academic Press, 2000), 319–336.
285 See Norman K. Gottwald, *Studies in the Book of Lamentations* (SBT; Chicago: Alec Allenson, 1954), 23–32.

of the psalm makes it possible for this psalmist to echo the primal claim of Psalm 1, though many times over. As we have seen, Psalm 1 is an introduction to the entire Psalter and intends that all parts of the Psalter should be read with reference to Torah piety. Thus Ps 119:1–2 echoes the beginning of Ps 1:1, both of which affirm that Torah obedience is the route to a whole and joyous life. The connection of Psalms 1 and 119 is strong and visible enough that Claus Westermann, for example, can propose that at some point in the development of the Psalter these two psalms constituted the beginning and the end of the collection.[286]

It is not possible here to review all of the rich aspects of this long instruction. We may single out two recurring accents that look beyond and beneath a simple ethics of obedience. First, Torah instruction is taken in the psalm as attestation not only to the will of YHWH but also to the fidelity of YHWH, which provides the matrix in which commands are given to Israel. Thus the psalmist can speak of YHWH's steadfast love (vv. 64, 76, 88, 124), YHWH's mercy (vv. 76, 156), YHWH's graciousness (v. 132), YHWH's righteousness (v. 142), and YHWH's justice (v. 156). It becomes clear that the intention of the psalmist is not to give a formal code of commands but to focus on the faithful person of YHWH, who gives YHWH's own self in this relationship of command and obedience.

Second, the psalmist regularly petitions YHWH for the gift of life, which is given through YHWH's promise (vv. 17, 25, 37, 40, 50, 88, 93, 107, 149, 159, 175). It is clear that obedience to Torah is not an automatic trigger for "life" but that "life" is a gift of YHWH's own self in faithful commitment to Israel and to this psalmist.

The outcome of these observations is to see that Torah piety does not consist in the flat response of obedience to a code of commands. Rather, Torah obedience is a full existence of trust in and loyalty to a covenant partner, trust and loyalty that are embodied in obedience to instruction but that bespeak an interpersonal, interactive communion and not simply compliance with a set of rules.

It is clear that Torah piety in general and in this psalm in particular view adherence to Torah instruction as the alternative to a life of autonomous self-serving and self-sufficiency that can only end in self-destruction. The alternative to this glad practice of obedience is "false ways" (v. 29), "selfish gain" (v. 36), "vanity" (v. 37), "disgrace" (v. 39), "shame" (v. 46), "arrogance" (vv. 51, 69, 78, 85), and being "wicked" (vv. 53, 95) – all forms of *social failure* in the context of a covenantal community. The psalmist has a dread of falling out of the relationship of fidelity and knows that outside fidelity there lies only misery and humiliation. Now it might be thought that the shaming of such *autonomy* would lead to a deadly *conformity* to command, and Christian caricature of this psalm has often suggested as much. There is not, however, any such flat conformity in this psalm, or in the tradition of Deuteronomy that stands behind it. It is clear, rather, that the Torah tradition of Deuteronomy – and

---

[286] C. Westermann, *Praise and Lament in the Psalms* (1981), 252–253.

consequently of the Psalter – is constituted by a lively and imaginative practice of interpretation that keeps Torah current and open and deeply related to the real circumstances of life. It is clear that the psalm is much more aware of *the threat of autonomy* than the alternative *threat of conformity*, but that is likely because the Torah tradition, when rightly practiced, included no such flat conformity.

The offer of Torah piety as an alternative to *self-destructive autonomy* is an act and pertinent word in our current consumer culture, even though it must be articulated so that it is not heard as a new legalism. It is clear that the rising younger generation in U.S. society knows how to produce lots of wealth. It is far less clear that it knows how to produce (or receive) meaning or wisdom. Thus the teaching of Torah piety, albeit with imaginative openness, is a genuine opportunity to offer an alternative and a countercommunity to the rat race of commodity, which can only end in loss and defeat. There is little doubt that in his own context of postexilic Judaism, the psalmist understood himself to be a voice for an alternative community that cherished and entertained a radically humane covenantal ethic. That same urgency for a radical covenantal ethic rooted in fidelity is as urgent now as it was then.

It is the great *hope* of the psalmist to avoid the trap of autonomy. The psalmist imagines Torah to yield not a life of narrow conformity but a life spacious in self-regard and neighborly love:

I shall walk at liberty,
for I have sought your precepts. (Ps 119:45)

When an interpretation of this psalm moves beyond caricature, especially in conventional Christian practice, the psalm has remarkable contemporaneity in a fast, money-chasing society that has lost its way in brutality, vulgarity, and abuse. The psalm voices the ringing conviction that it could be otherwise!

Bridging the Horizons: Legalism?

Very much Christian piety and Christian interpretation has caricatured and thereby dismissed this psalm and Torah piety in general as so much "Jewish legalism." Such an unfortunate and eventually disastrous misreading of this psalm and Jewish piety in general is grounded in an ill-conceived contrast of *grace and law* that has been generally rooted in a misunderstanding of Paul's "theology of grace."[287] That long-standing misreading contrasted a Christian notion of "unconditional grace" with an ungraced Jewish legalism dismissed as "law." Such a misreading fails to notice – a failure produced by a faulty reading

---

[287] See Krister Stendahl, "The Apostle Paul and the Introspective Conscience of the West," in Krister Stendahl, *Paul Among Jesus and Christians* (Philadelphia: Fortress Press, 1989), 78–96.

lens – that this psalm appeals to and relies on YHWH's gracious gift of life. The phrase "covenantal nomism" posed by E. P. Sanders helps to situate the instruction of Torah in the context of covenantal fidelity, and therefore obviously the perspective of this psalm and Judaism in general.[288] A widespread contemporary rapprochement of Jews and Christians now permits a new opening for Christian understanding of Jewish notions of Torah. A wondrous by-product of such a new understanding is, of course, a fresh sense of the claims of Christian faith as well. Attention to Jewish interpretive maneuvers in such a rapprochement is evidenced in the recent manifesto [dibru emut]. Psalm 119 might well function as a case study in the long history of misunderstanding that is now happily being redressed. From this psalm and from Judaism more generally, Christians in a postmodern environment might learn again about a life-giving alternative to the hopeless pursuit of autonomy.

Bridging the Horizons: A Cliff Note for Life

One of the authors (Brueggemann) may be permitted a personal reference. In his tradition of faith, confirmands at age thirteen were given a "confirmation verse" by the pastor. His pastor, in his case his father, gave him as his confirmation verse – a Cliff Note for his life:

Your word is a lamp to my feet
and a light to my path. (Ps 119:105)

This verse has proved to be exactly the right note for him as he knows, in retrospect, that he was destined to become a student of Scripture.

Beyond that personal reference, however, this verse may form a leitmotif in a pluralistic culture. It affirms that the biblical tradition is an adequate, reliable guide to the pilgrimage of human life. The polemical dimension of the claim made for the word is a refutation of the claims of "rival scrolls"; for example, the writings of Adam Smith, Karl Marx, Charles Darwin, Carl Jung, or whoever. Beyond the polemic, the positive affirmation is the insistence that an *agency of fidelity* is at the center of reality and that *responding fidelity* is the source of well-being, joy, and liberty for all of human life. This is an enormous claim amid many competing offers of "meaning" in a postmodern world. The psalm asks only that attention be paid to the *cost* and to the *joy* of this scroll tradition.

---

[288] E. P. Sanders, *Paul and Palestinian Judaism* (Philadelphia: Fortress Press, 1977), 511–515 and passim.

PSALM 120 – A SONG OF ASCENTS

¹ In my distress I cry to the LORD,
  that he may answer me:
² 'Deliver me, O LORD,
  from lying lips,
  from a deceitful tongue.'

³ What shall be given to you?
  And what more shall be done to you,
  you deceitful tongue?
⁴ A warrior's sharp arrows,
  with glowing coals of the broom tree!

⁵ Woe is me, that I am an alien in Meshech,
  that I must live among the tents of Kedar.
⁶ Too long have I had my dwelling
  among those who hate peace.
⁷ I am for peace;
  but when I speak,
  they are for war.

Psalm 120 begins a series of fifteen psalms (Psalms 120–134) that bear the superscription "Psalm of Ascent." It is likely that these fifteen psalms constitute an earlier collection used in a particular liturgical community. Most plausibly the collection was used liturgically by pilgrims who were on their way to the Jerusalem temple. Although that hypothesis may explain the collection, it is important to notice the particularity of each of the psalms, as each touches the concrete life of the community at worship.

This psalm is a lament that articulates a petition to YHWH (vv. 1–2), addresses the adversary with a negative wish (curse?) (vv. 3–4), and concludes with a description of the situation of risk and threat (vv. 5–7).

The petition in verses 1–2 twice names YHWH and voices the petitionary imperative "deliver." In a small, face-to-face community, the power of slander and destructive speech is enormous. Here the psalmist is put at risk by such speech and asks YHWH to counteract that jeopardy.

In verses 3–4, the psalmist addresses those who practice the "deceitful tongue" and imagines out loud what punishment they deserve and will be given. This statement relies on the conviction that there is answerability in YHWH's world, wherein such destructive, antineighborly talk cannot be done with impunity. The psalmist, in his abhorrence of his adversary, proposes the punishment of arrows and hot coals. We may notice that the zealous wish for retaliation is vicious and concrete, but the petition in verses 1–2 leaves the matter in YHWH's hands.

The concluding complaint (vv. 5–7) is a statement of self-pity in which the psalmist describes for YHWH a life exposed without secure habitat. References to "Meshech" and "Kedar" are completely enigmatic but perhaps refer to exposed terrain of a wilderness variety that offers no safe place for one at the brink of "homelessness." Gerstenberger suggests that the references are not concrete but appeal to old labels for a "legendary inhumane people":

In my opinion, it is futile to speculate about the historicity and geographical location of such hostile tribes. Arguing from the very nature of psalm texts that were used by many people in succeeding generations (see "Introduction to Psalms"), one must admit that any possible reference to a concrete situation must have acquired symbolic value in order to stay meaningful to the users of the text. We may surmise, therefore, that the complaint gives voice proverbially to how much a given suppliant is suffering from ostracism among his or her neighbors, all the more so whenever a foreigner becomes the target of communal disdain. Here could be hidden a special subtlety: a member of the Israelite/Jewish community formally complains about some legendary inhumane people who do not let a stranger live in peace. But he or she does so within the community where the prayer was certainly used.[289]

The psalm concludes with a self-recommendation as an advocate for social harmony (*shalom*) that is refused by those who prefer aggressive hostility. There is some irony in the fact that this "peacemaker" in verse 4 appeals to weaponry in his wish for revenge. The last verse sets before YHWH the conduct of "I" and "they" as a motivation for divine response and intervention.

Bridging the Horizons: Homelessness

Although this psalm may be the voice of pilgrimage, the governing metaphor of "alien" (*ger*) in verse 5 suggests one at risk of homelessness without a safe social environment. The psalm may make powerful contact with contemporary life if we focus on the image of *homelessness* and lack of a safe place. In the first instance, our society, especially urban society, grows more and more brutal and dangerous. Among those now exposed to assaulting human power are the many immigrants who lack resources and social protection. This prayer may be the voice of all such vulnerable persons. But beyond that, the strangeness of the new

---

[289] E. S. Gerstenberger, *Psalms, Part 2, and Lamentations* (2001), 319.

postindustrial world of the Information Age drives many people to a sense of "homelessness," even in the midst of a settled environment. This psalm is the voice of faith in an environment of risk and displacement. It trusts YHWH in that risk, but speaks with candor about the exposure to danger, which is real and concrete. In the life and faith of Judaism, the *exile* – as experience and as defining memory – seems a proper matrix for the psalm.

PSALM 121 – A SONG OF ASCENTS

¹ I lift up my eyes to the hills –
  from where will my help come?
² My help comes from the LORD,
    who made heaven and earth.

³ He will not let your foot be moved;
  he who keeps you will not slumber.
⁴ He who keeps Israel
    will neither slumber nor sleep.

⁵ The LORD is your keeper;
    the LORD is your shade at your right hand.
⁶ The sun shall not strike you by day,
    nor the moon by night.

⁷ The LORD will keep you from all evil;
  he will keep your life.
⁸ The LORD will keep
  your going out and your coming in
    from this time on and for evermore.

This psalm, along with Psalm 23, is our best-loved psalm. It is a song for pilgrims under way to the temple in Jerusalem who are passing through ominous terrain. The question of verse 1 does not imagine that YHWH is one who dwells in the mountains. Rather the hills are filled with threat and danger that evoke for the pilgrims the question of "help" (v. 1). There is little agreement among interpreters on the particularity of the question: "By the *mountains*, the Prophet means whatever is great or excellent in the world; and the lesson he teaches is, that we ought to account all such favour as nothing."[290] Terrien asks:

> Was it that the poet, before undertaking his pilgrimage to Jerusalem, dwelt in a region of sharp cliffs, ravines, and caverns that concealed wild animals and even robbers, and that the pilgrimage itself passed through mountainous and dangerous defiles?[291]

(An alternative understanding of the mountains is that the reference is to the hilly location of Zion and the temple.) The remainder of the psalm is an answer to the question of verse 1 (vv. 2–8).

The simple, direct, unambiguous answer in verse 2 is that YHWH is the single, necessary, all-sufficient source of help who in this case will give protection. The primary qualifier for the name of YHWH is that this is the creator God, the one who has power and purpose enough to create all that is. As creator of "heaven and earth," moreover, YHWH is surely sovereign over "the hills," even if they seem full of threat. The threat is more than overmatched by the creator, who is full of power and glory (see the parallel in Ps 91:4–6).

The following verses exposit the character of YHWH, the creator God (vv. 3–8). In verses 3–4, YHWH is referred to only by pronoun. YHWH is credited with three characteristics: (a) YHWH protects the path of the pilgrims; (b) YHWH is vigilant and does not sleep; and (c) YHWH is endlessly awake and attentive. These three statements, of course closely in parallel, fill out the content of the term "help." This is the God who is "a very present help in time of trouble" (Ps 46:1). This is the keeper, the one who guards, protects, preserves, and keeps safe. Thus, in verse 4 the question of verse 1 is fully answered.

In verses 5–8, more statements are made concerning YHWH, only now YHWH is explicitly named four times. For this rhetorical unit, verse 5 reiterates the primary claim of verses 3–4: YHWH is "keeper." YHWH is like a shade tree to protect travelers from the heat of the sun; the poetic parallel of the moon is added in context, for one does not need to be protected from the moon. If this parallelism is rather a poetic device, then the sun and moon may be regarded, as often interpreted, as demonic forces that are subject to the rule of YHWH. In our judgment, such an interpretation is not necessary; it is easy enough to stay with the concrete dangers that are all around the pilgrims.

From the specificity of sun and moon, verses 7–8 make a more general claim. Now YHWH protects the traveler from "all evil," from every possible threat. It is

---

[290] John Calvin, *Commentary on the Book of Psalms*, vol. 5 (Grand Rapids, MI: Baker, 1979), 63–64.

[291] S. Terrien, *Psalms* (2003), 811.

YHWH who keeps one's life safe, even in dangerous circumstances. Verse 8 continues a rhetorical pattern that amounts to a benediction for travel. The traveler is safe departing and arriving, and all along the way.

This psalm voices a simple, direct confidence in YHWH. The term "keep" (along with "help") governs the poetry and gives content to the name of YHWH. The recurrence of the term "keep" attests to the abiding, complete trustworthiness of the presence of YHWH in every season of risk.

Bridging the Horizons: The Vigilance of YHWH

It is conventional to take the affirmation of this psalmist at face value: God is endlessly vigilant. Such an affirmation is a source of great assurance. In lived reality, however, alongside these words might be set Isa 51:9, 17, which summons YHWH to vigilance and action; the reason for the summons is that YHWH is not endlessly awake and vigilant. In the dramatic presentation of Israel's faith, YHWH is a God who may indeed sleep and who requires attentiveness to be awakened. The statement of Isaiah 51 does not readily conform to conventional faith, but it is a candid recognition that YHWH cannot always be credited with attentive care.[292]

Bridging the Horizons: The Lord Bless You and Keep You

Such trust as voiced in this psalm is at the center of the life of faith. James Mays nicely connects this faith to the confession of the Heidelberg Catechism.[293] Trust in YHWH is not some great abstraction but in fact has to do with God's attentive care for the fullness of the pilgrim person and the pilgrim community. It should be noted, moreover, that this psalm, in its trust in YHWH, has rhetorical parallels to the familiar benediction of Num 6:24–26. When the priest assures that the "Lord will bless you and keep you," the *keeping* is the vigilant protection of YHWH that is reflected in this psalm.

---

[292] J. D. Levenson, *Creation and the Persistence of Evil* (1988), has exposited the texts that indicate YHWH is not fully established in sovereignty. For that reason, there are urgent appeals that YHWH should "awaken" (Pss 7:6; 44:23; 59:5).

[293] J. L. Mays, *Psalms* (1994), 391–392.

PSALM 122 – A SONG OF ASCENTS. OF DAVID

¹ I was glad when they said to me,
  'Let us go to the house of the LORD!'
² Our feet are standing
  within your gates, O Jerusalem.

³ Jerusalem – built as a city
  that is bound firmly together.
⁴ To it the tribes go up,
  the tribes of the LORD,
  as was decreed for Israel,
  to give thanks to the name of the LORD.
⁵ For there the thrones for judgment were set up,
  the thrones of the house of David.

⁶ Pray for the peace of Jerusalem:
  'May they prosper who love you.
⁷ Peace be within your walls,
  and security within your towers.'
⁸ For the sake of my relatives and friends
  I will say, 'Peace be within you.'
⁹ For the sake of the house of the LORD our God,
  I will seek your good.

Of all the "psalms of ascent" (Psalms 120–134), Psalm 122 most directly serves the conventional hypothesis that these psalms were designed for pilgrims on their way to a festival in the Jerusalem temple. The psalm is a reflection on the wonder of Jerusalem – city, monarchy, temple – which became and remained a focal point of Israel's imagination (see Ps 137:5–6). It is of defining importance that the name Jerusalem has within it the term *shalom*, so that the city can be imagined as a seat of *shalom*, a gift of God to Israel and eventually a gift of God to all nations (see Isa 2:2–4).

The psalm begins with a familiar expression of delight about approaching the city, an anticipation of entry into its wonders as a place of beauty and divine presence (vv. 1–2). Verses 3–5 constitute a distinct piece of rhetoric, a reflection on the city, seemingly in a voice other than that of the glad worshipper of verses 1–2. It is affirmed that the city is the goal of Israelite pilgrimage, likely reflecting a well-established practice of festival pilgrimage by those who lived a distance from the city (see Deut 14:22–27), and that the purpose of the journey is to give thanks to the divine name. The reference to "the name" likely suggests a Deuteronomic notion of divine presence, wherein YHWH dwells in heaven but is committed in a palpable way to the temple (see 1 Kgs 8:30). "Thanks" concerns regular performance of both an utterance of gratitude and a material offering as a sign of gratitude. The act of thanksgiving is Israel's public, material, visible affirmation that it lives by the gifts of YHWH, who creates a material abundance and who saves Israel in its crisis of need. The act of thanksgiving is the quintessential act of ceding life back to God, who has given it. The explicit reason for thanks in this instance is the Davidic "thrones of justice" that are constituted there. The monarchy has a primary function as judicial arbiter to assure a proper ordering of security. As we have seen in Psalm 72, that throne of justice is to assure that the weak, needy, and vulnerable have a reliable advocate and resources for sustenance in the world of aggressive acquisitiveness. In such texts as Jer 22:3 and Jer 23:5–6, it is anticipated that the monarchy will guarantee equitable well-being in the time to come in order to fend off social as well as cosmic forces of chaos. Israel in Jerusalem has much for which to give thanks.

The psalm concludes with prayers for the well-being (peace) of Jerusalem (vv. 6–9). The imperative of verse 6a is perhaps a priestly liturgical invitation to prayer that is followed by a regularly used prayer uttered by the grateful worshipers. It is a prayer for the well-being of the city, its king, and its temple, a prayer for the safety and protection of the city, which was characteristically exposed to military threats. The reiteration of "*shalom*" and the hope for "good" for the city indicate the centrality of the city for the well-being of all of society.

A Closer Look: Jerusalem the Epicenter of the World

The symbolic, liturgical, and eventually eschatological claims for Jerusalem are completely disproportionate to the historical reality of the city. (In Christian tradition, a like statement could be made concerning the historical Jesus and the imaginative Christological freight assigned to the historical figure.) There is no doubt that these claims for Jerusalem are largely generated by the royal temple Jerusalem establishment itself, its poets and priests being to some extent in the service of the political establishment.

The most sweeping claim made for the city is a well-known prophetic oracle of Isa 2:2–4 and Mi 4:1–4 that envisions Jerusalem as the epicenter of the world of nations, a place for Torah instruction of the nations, and a place from which comes the disarmament of the world. The greatest expectation of the city is the vision of "the new Jerusalem" in Isa 65:17–25, a vision echoed in Rev 21:22. It is important in Isa 65:17–25 to see that the *shalom* of the city is indeed an expectation of a socioeconomic infrastructure in this world that permits a viable and sustainable human community. The vision of Isa 65:17–25, clearly a postexilic hope, is intimately linked to the affirmation that the Jerusalem temple will be a welcoming place for all – not unlike Isa 2:2–4 – "a house of prayer for all peoples" (Isa 56:7; see Matt 21:13).

Bridging the Horizons: A City of Peace?

The wondrous claim of *shalom* for Jerusalem continues to reverberate in the present time in the "Abrahamic communities" of Jews, Christians, and Muslims. That expectation inescapably clashes with the "fact on the ground" that Jerusalem is a place of primal contentiousness that makes the world a violent and unsafe place. As is characteristic in the Old Testament, the incongruity between *faithful imagination* and *facts on the ground* is an incongruity that is to be honestly faced without denial or cover-up. To be sure, such contestation and hostility over the holy city are nowhere present in the psalm itself, but they need to be front and center when we ponder the psalm. It is the case that the hope of Israel characteristically contradicts our conventional practices and invites penitence. This psalm – and its deep claims for the city – invites a reform away from self-serving ideology that legitimates violence. The psalm thus stands as a summons to sanity that is rooted in gratitude, an alternative to contemporary insanity, which is grounded in narrow and self-centered images of tribal and ideological futures.

Bridging the Horizons: Prayers for Jerusalem and Babylon

Psalm 122 is clearly a prayer for the *shalom* of the city. This usage calls to mind the famous letter of Jeremiah to the exiles in Jer 29:4–10. In verse 7, the prophet counsels the deportees to "seek the *welfare* of the city where I have sent you in exile, and pray to the Lord on its behalf, for in its *welfare* you will find your *welfare*." The word "welfare" of course renders the Hebrew *shalom*; the prophet is exhorting the deportees to pray for the *shalom* of the city of Babylon. Thus we may notice that in the two texts together there are prayers for the city of Jerusalem and subsequently prayers for the city of Babylon. Babylon is no substitute for Jerusalem, but the double usage does indicate the intensely urban focus of this psalm tradition. The city is the focal point of order and possibility in this society as in every society.

PSALM 123 – A SONG OF ASCENTS

[1] To you I lift up my eyes,
   O you who are enthroned in the heavens!
[2] As the eyes of servants
   look to the hand of their master,
   as the eyes of a maid

to the hand of her mistress,
so our eyes look to the LORD our God,
until he has mercy upon us.

3 Have mercy upon us, O LORD, have mercy upon us,
for we have had more than enough of contempt.
4 Our soul has had more than its fill
of the scorn of those who are at ease,
of the contempt of the proud.

This psalm is one of the loveliest prayers in all of Scripture, simple and direct, trust-ing and confident, spoken out of need and in much hope. It begins abruptly, "To you," but the name of YHWH is not uttered until the end of the long second verse. In this piety, however, there is little need to name the God addressed, so direct and obvious is the connection between the one who prays and the one who is addressed. Before God is named, God is characterized as the one enthroned in the heavens, the creator who presides over the assembly of gods in heaven (see Psalm 82). Thus, in a simple utterance, the prayer appeals to the entire liturgical drama of divine enthronement so central to the Jerusalem temple (see the psalms of enthronement, Psalms 93 and 96–99).

Having alluded to kingship, verse 2 utters the counterterm, "servant." The rela-tionship of the two characters in this prayer is servant to king. The verse ponders that relationship according to human analogies: servant to master, maid to mistress. The verse is organized around "as … as … so." The two uses of "as" offer analogues.[294] How is it that a servant looks at a master? How does a maid look in the face of a mistress? Here there is no suspicion, no fear, no dread, no resentment; otherwise the analogue would not work in the prayer. Rather, the look is one of gladness, awe, dependence, and glad submissiveness that is rooted in trust. The servant knows that his life is safe in the governance of the master. (Such an image, of course, is not politically correct and, taken at face value, would encourage questions concerning the enslaved. Taken in context, however, the imagery bespeaks glad reliance on the master.)

The "so" at the end of verse 2 now names "YHWH our God"; the look is one of hope that awaits mercy. The master may be busy, elsewhere preoccupied and dis-tracted, but the petitioner is patient and knows that in due course the master will exhibit mercy. It is this mercy that is the grounds of the prayer and the basis for the relationship. YHWH is indeed a God of mercy:

The Lord passed before him, and proclaimed,
"The Lord, the Lord,

---

294 On "as" as the "copula of imagination," see Garrett Green, *Imagining God: Theology and the Religious Imagination* (San Francisco: Harper and Row, 1989), 73, 140, and passim.

a God merciful and gracious,
slow to anger,
and abounding in steadfast love
    and faithfulness." (Exod 34:6)

The term "mercy" signifies unconditional regard for, love that is completely gratu-
itous. The master gives himself over to the well-being of the servant.

It is on the basis of verses 1–2 and this relationship of awaited mercy that the
petition of verses 3–4 can now be uttered. The petition in verse 3a utters the word
"mercy" two more times in the name of YHWH yet again, so that the petition
of verse 3a nears the praise of verse 2a. The reason for the petition in verse 3a is
given in verses 3b–4, introduced, characteristically, by "for." The reason mercy is
now required is that the speaker – and his ilk, for the prayer is for "us" – have had
more than their fill of contempt and scorn. The rhetoric of verses 3b–4 matches the
substance twice. It is "filled to abundance" or "satiated," and three times uses the
two terms for derogation. The speaker voices an urgent petition out of unbearable
humiliation.

We may learn more about that contempt and scorn by noting the descriptive
phrase "those who are at ease." Reference to the same term in the more familiar
passage of Amos 6:1 suggests that the reference is to the economically affluent who
are arrogant, self-indulgent, and indifferent to those who have less. Calvin comments on those who treat the speaker with contempt: "The epithet *proud* is justly
applied to the same persons who are described as *rich*; for wealth engenders pride
of heart."[295]

The usage thus suggests an exploited "servant class" by those

who lie on beds of ivory,
    and lounge on their couches,
and eat lambs from the flock,
    and calves from the stall;
who sing idle songs to the sound of the harp,
    and like David improvise on instruments of music;
who drink wine from bowls,
    and anoint themselves with the finest oils,
    but are not grieved over the ruin of Joseph! (Amos 6:4–6)

The actions are of those

who oppress the poor,
who crush the needy. (Amos 4:1)

The prayer is the voice of a servant class that looks to an alternative "master."
What a way to think of prayer, as a recharacterization of social relationships with

---

[295] J. Calvin, *Commentary on the Psalms*, vol. 5 (1979), 82.

the new character YHWH, God of mercy, as the defining reference. Thus the prayer presents the humiliated turning from the ones who are at ease to the one "enthroned in heaven," a turn that means a *departure from contempt* and *embrace of mercy*. The God of mercy thus is presented as the alternative and antidote to unbearable relationships and social inequity. Although the psalm does not say so, we imagine that "mercy" here is not only a divine attribute and intention but also a matter of practice by adherents of YHWH, who will not engage in scorn and contempt toward the needy. The prayer is an immense act of hope, a conviction that demeaning social relationships are not the norm and need not endure. The voice of such hope grows out of urgent need, but the grounds of such hope is in the one addressed, the God of all hope, who will, sooner or later, turn the world to well-being, even for those whom the world holds in contempt.

Bridging the Horizons: The God of All Mercy

The tax collector in Luke 18:13 in utter humiliation "would not even look up to heaven." Our psalmist, unlike the man in the parable of Jesus, dares to look to heaven, not because he is worthy but because he knows that the master to whom he looks is merciful. Thus the breaking of humiliation is the capacity to look in expectation, a capacity that is grounded in the God of all mercy.

Bridging the Horizons: Generative Grace

Concerning "our eyes" that look to God in expectation of mercy, attention may be given to a narrative by Isak Dinesen. During her time in Africa, she employed and worked with a number of locals who lived in an oral culture. Dinesen recounts that one of her workers, Jogona Kanyagga, told her a long tale of his life that Dinesen wrote down and then read back to him. She reports that when she read the story back to him and read out his name,

he swiftly turned his face to me, and gave me a great fierce flaming glance, so exuberant with laughter that it changed the old man into a boy, into the very symbol of youth. Again as I had finished the document and was reading out his name, where it figured as a verification below his thumbmark, the vital direct glance was repeated, this time deepened and calmed, with a new dignity.

Such a glance did Adam give the Lord when He formed him out of the dust, and breathed into his nostrils the breath of life, and man became a living soul. I had created him and shown him himself: Jogona Kanyagga of life everlasting.[296]

---

[296] Isak Dinesen, "A Shooting Accident on the Farm," in Isak Dinesen, *Out of Africa and Shadows on the Grass* (New York: Random House, 1985), 126.

Jogona Kanyagga had the look of gratitude like the look of Adam, a look of new life when one reflects one's existence back to the source of powerful generativity. Such is the look of the psalmist turned toward the God of mercy.

PSALM 124 – A SONG OF ASCENTS. OF DAVID

¹ If it had not been the LORD who was on our side
– let Israel now say –
² if it had not been the LORD who was on our side,
when our enemies attacked us,
³ then they would have swallowed us up alive,
when their anger was kindled against us;
⁴ then the flood would have swept us away,
the torrent would have gone over us;
⁵ then over us would have gone
the raging waters.

⁶ Blessed be the LORD,
who has not given us
as prey to their teeth.
⁷ We have escaped like a bird
from the snare of the fowlers;
the snare is broken,
and we have escaped.
⁸ Our help is in the name of the LORD,
who made heaven and earth.

The center of this psalm is the blessing voiced to YHWH (praise and thanks) because YHWH has rescued Israel from a situation of great risk (vv. 7–8). Prior to this affirmation of YHWH, the psalm begins in a wondrously structured "if-then" worst-case scenario (vv. 1–5). The psalm concludes with a stereotypical acclamation of YHWH (v. 8).

The beginning of the psalm is a meditation on what the fate of Israel would have been had it not been accompanied by YHWH (vv. 1–5): "If the God of Israel even for only a moment turned away from his chosen people, they would be cast into total destruction by their voracious, lurking enemies."[297] The purpose of these

---

[297] H.-J. Kraus, *Psalms 60–150* (1988), 442.

verses is not to entertain such a dismal option but in fact to reject it as an empty risk because YHWH is faithful. The rhetoric is organized around two "if" clauses (vv. 1–2), the consequence of which is stated in three "then" clauses (vv. 3–5). The "if" that is entertained and only by inference rejected is the prospect that YHWH would not have been actively in solidarity with Israel. It is scarcely a thinkable condition in Israel, but for rhetorical effect the psalm entertains that option. In verse 2, it is worth noting that the term rendered in the NRSV as "enemies" is in fact *'adam*; that is, any human agent. It appears in context that "the man" refers to a military threat, perhaps the sort of threat visited by Sennacherib (2 Kgs 18:13), Nebuchadnezzar (2 Kgs 24:10), or any imperial intruder.

The imagined consequence of being abandoned by YHWH is stated in two quite distinct images (vv. 3–5). First, without YHWH the enemy would have swallowed up Israel like a mighty hungry monster, and Israel would have been helpless. Second, the intruder would be a force not unlike the surging of chaotic waters, before which Israel would be helpless. That is, without YHWH, Israel is completely vulnerable, without resources, and sure to be done in.

In the quick rhetorical turn of verse 6, however, that scenario is totally rejected. It is not true that YHWH was not on our side, and therefore the threat of monsters or chaotic waters is in fact no real threat at all. After pondering this impossible possibility, the psalm comes to its Yahwistic sense and affirms YHWH (vv. 6–7). YHWH has not been absent, negligent, passive, or silent; YHWH has not "handed over" Israel to such threats. The reference to the teeth of a predator in verse 6 perhaps alludes back to the imagery of verse 3. But Israel had escaped from the trap or snare "like a bird." This language may echo the arrogant claim of Sennacherib that he had Hezekiah and Israel shut up in Jerusalem (under siege) "like a bird in a cage."[298]

But the siege laid by the Assyrians could not hold, because YHWH would not let it happen. *"'adam"* (any intruding force) will of course know that it is stronger than any Israelite capacity (see, for example, Isa 36:8), but such intruders characteristically miscalculate because they do not reckon with YHWH, who stands by Israel and makes Israel safe. It is entirely plausible that this psalm refers to a particular deliverance; in psalm usage, however, such a statement can be reused in many crises and eventually become a stereotypical affirmation of YHWH's powerful fidelity. Israel is safe, even in an ominous world that is notoriously unsafe and full of threats.

Verse 8, a close parallel to Ps 121:2, is a conventional liturgical formula. It is nonetheless completely appropriate in this setting. The creator of heaven and earth is enormously powerful and exercises sovereignty over the nations. That claim of governance, however, becomes visibly effective in specific, nameable crises, the kinds

---

[298] This is a famous phrase of boasting that was left in the recovered documentation of Sennacherib when he was at the height of his military domination. Great military powers do tend to boast, as for example President George W. Bush's quite premature assertion in Iraq, "mission accomplished."

of crises reflected in the body of the psalm. The *creator God*, known by an *Exodus name*, is indeed "help," precisely for this people that is helpless in the face of the enemy: "To profess that God is our fundamental help means to profess that we are not sufficient to create and secure our own lives and futures. In short, we need help.... Discipleship and servanthood (see Ps 123:2) really begin with the profession that we owe our very lives to God (see Mark 8:34–35)."[299]

The outcome of this psalm is not unlike the great psalms of enthronement (Psalms 93 and 96–99) and the prophetic oracles of YHWH's intervention (Jer 50:9–10; Isa 41:25). The world cannot be rightly discerned without the hidden but completely reliable governance of YHWH. The creator is the one who saves, and "*adam*" must fully come to terms with that decisive reality.

PSALM 125 – A SONG OF ASCENTS

¹ Those who trust in the Lord are like Mount Zion,
  which cannot be moved, but abides for ever.
² As the mountains surround Jerusalem,
  so the Lord surrounds his people,
  from this time on and for evermore.
³ For the sceptre of wickedness shall not rest
  on the land allotted to the righteous,
  so that the righteous may not stretch out
  their hands to do wrong.
⁴ Do good, O Lord, to those who are good,
  and to those who are upright in their hearts.
⁵ But those who turn aside to their own crooked ways
  the Lord will lead away with evildoers.
  Peace be upon Israel!

Psalm 125 is a statement of profound trust in YHWH articulated according to the imagery of Jerusalem. The psalm begins with two analogues between *the faithful* and *the city of Jerusalem* (vv. 1–2) and states the twofold consequence of YHWH's protection of city and land (v. 3). The psalm concludes with a statement that is part petition and part instruction (vv. 4–5), followed by a benediction over the people of YHWH (v. 5c).

---

[299] J. C. McCann, Jr., "Book of Psalms," in L. E. Keck et al. (eds.), *The New Interpreter's Bible*, vol. 4 (1996), 1191.

The psalm begins with two analogies that affirm the *known reality* of Jerusalem and then imagine the *less known reality* of the faithful. Jerusalem cannot be "moved" (see Psalm 46); that is, destabilized and made insecure. Indeed, it is a primary claim of the Songs of Zion, as in Psalm 46, that Jerusalem is guaranteed to be safe against every threat, whether military incursion or cosmic upheaval:

> Therefore we will not fear,
> > though the earth should change,
> though the mountains shake in
> > the heart of the sea;
> though its waters roar and foam,
> though the mountains tremble
> > with its tumult.
> There is a river whose streams
> > make glad the city of God,
> the holy habitation of the Most High.
> God is in the midst of the city;
> > it shall not be moved;
> God will help it when the
> > morning dawns. (Ps 46:2–5)

Now it is suggested that those who trust in YHWH are like Jerusalem: secure, immovable, and utterly safe. And that guarantee is "forever!"

Jerusalem is *surrounded by mountains*. Anyone (in Israel) can see that; now it is affirmed that YHWH's people are *surrounded* in a like manner by YHWH's protective fidelity, and that guarantee as well is "forever." The poetic reasoning is from city to people: the people as safe, treasured, and protected as the city surely is.

Verse 3 states an outcome of that affirmation. (We take it as an outcome, but verse 3 could also be the cause of the statement of well-being in verses 1–2, for the introductory particle "*kî*" ["for"] is ambiguous. Verse 3 could begin "because" or "surely" in the sense of the consequence. We take the latter reading, but a causative interpretation is also possible.) Either way, it is asserted that the "scepter of wickedness" will not abide in the land, apparently an assurance of no foreign occupiers. Such a claim belongs to Jerusalem theology, but it is surely contradicted by some of the experience of the city and by the prophetic oracles concerning YHWH's mobilization of foreigners against the city. The city is safe against such intruders; as a consequence, the people of Israel will not do evil. Thus the reassurance is "like king, like people": no bad kings, ergo, no destructive people. Verse 3 traces the practical result of the assurance of verses 1–2.

Verses 4–5b constitute a quite distinct rhetorical unit. Verse 4 begins as a petition, only *good* for the *good*; that is, an urging to YHWH to be faithful and generous toward the Torah-keepers. Conversely, the parallel statement in verse 5 concerning those who "turn aside" (from Torah obedience) is not expressed as a parallel petition but in fact is an assurance that the disobedient will indeed be punished. This is an odd rhetorical interface between petition and instruction, but the choice of rhetorical articulation makes sense: the obedient ask for divine favor that is due them; they are, moreover, so assured of their merit of YHWH's goodness that they trust completely that YHWH will punish the "crooked." "Evildoers" are totally under judgment, and now the "crooked" have the same fate as the evildoers. Those who "trust in the Lord" (v. 1) have confidence in YHWH's equitable governance and therefore in the moral coherence of their world, over which YHWH presides. Thus, "trust in YHWH" is not simply a personal relationship but is confidence in the reliability of the moral world over which YHWH presides, confidence that YHWH's world is a safe place in which to act in "righteousness" (v. 3).

The psalm concludes with a benediction *of shalom*, a conventional preoccupation of the psalms of ascent (see Pss 120:7; 122:6–8). Israel yearns for a safe place of well-being; Jerusalem is the place where such well-being is promised and is known to be available.

A Closer Look: The Taproot of Unconditional Grace

Like the psalms of ascent generally, this psalm appeals to the Zion theological tradition that is reflected in the Songs of Zion, especially Psalm 46.[300] That tradition voiced a complete assurance of a safe, ordered creation rooted in YHWH's sovereignty and enacted liturgically through the Davidic monarchy. It is no stretch to conclude that this *unconditionality* of YHWH's guarantee is the taproot of what became *unconditional grace* in later Pauline theology. Here the same truth is concretely offered in a quite practical voice.

For that reason, it is all the more starchy that verses 4–5b, by contrast, voice a demanding Torah either/or that is rooted in the Sinai tradition of covenant. Thus the psalm exhibits the way in which major traditions quite distinct from each other are mobilized together in a fresh configuration of *assurance and demand*, or as is better said in German, *Gabe und Aufgabe*.

PSALM 126 – A SONG OF ASCENTS

[1] When the LORD restored the fortunes of Zion,
we were like those who dream.
[2] Then our mouth was filled with laughter,

---

[300] On Zion theology, see Ben C. Ollenburger, *Zion, the City of the Great King: A Theological Symbol of the Jerusalem Cult* (JSOTSup 41; Sheffield: Sheffield Academic Press, 1987).

and our tongue with shouts of joy;
  then it was said among the nations,
  'The Lord has done great things for them.'
³ The Lord has done great things for us,
  and we rejoiced.

⁴ Restore our fortunes, O Lord,
  like the watercourses in the Negeb.
⁵ May those who sow in tears
  reap with shouts of joy.
⁶ Those who go out weeping,
  bearing the seed for sowing,
  shall come home with shouts of joy,
  carrying their sheaves.

The distinguishing rhetorical feature of this psalm is the double use of the phrase "restore the fortunes" in verses 1 and 4, each time the two Hebrew words with the name of YHWH. The two uses mark the psalm as two quite distinct units, verses 1–3 as a celebrative memory of YHWH's transformative act for the sake of Jerusalem and verses 4–6 as a petition that YHWH would now, again, perform such a transformative act.

The celebrative memory of verses 1–3 lacks specificity; it could, however, refer to any rescue of Jerusalem, perhaps from the siege of Jerusalem by Sennacherib in 701 BCE (see Isa 37:36–38), or more likely the return of the deported to Jerusalem in the sixth and fifth centuries BCE. In any case, that wondrous act of restoration evokes a threefold response of gladness. First, it seemed like a dream, so unreal, so impossible, so beyond explanation, even beyond anticipation. But of course that is in the nature of YHWH's rescue miracles; outside the purview of YHWH, such wonders seem like a fantasy – except in this case it is a lived reality! Second, at the first "then," subsequent to the deliverance, the people of Israel were filled with joy and offered glad songs of thanksgiving. It is credible to think that the joyous lyrics of Isaiah 40–55 are an embodiment of the songs of joy that are here mentioned. Note especially the "new song" in Isa 42:10, a new song for a new historical beginning! Third, the second "then" is that the other nations watched this magnificent restoration of Jerusalem and were dazzled by it. Not only were they dazzled but, as is often the case in the Old Testament, they practiced good Yahwistic theology. They can recognize and give praise to YHWH, the God known in the world as the worker of wonders. Thus the restoration of Jerusalem evokes a glad response from the entire international community. It is sometimes the case that the nations are summoned to praise YHWH (Pss 117:1; 100:1), but here they are not summoned. Rather, the response of the nations is spontaneous, so overwhelming is the act of restoration itself.

The first part of the psalm concludes with Israel's reprise in verse 3. Israel confirms the acclamation of the nations that YHWH has done "great things." Thus the term "great things" is on the lips of the nations and in the mouth of Israel. The term occurs regularly as a reference to a miracle, a transformative act of which only YHWH is capable.

The second half of the psalm (vv. 4–6), by appeal to the celebration just concluded, can now petition YHWH for one more such wondrous restoration. Two images are used to make the bid for a divine miracle. The first reference is to *'ph* (watercourses) in the Negeb, perhaps a reference to the deep gulleys that run dry except in the season of great rain. In this imagery, it is the gift of rain that constitutes a "great thing," so the appeal to YHWH may be in the face of an enormous drought, for it is YHWH the rainmaker who gives or withholds rain (see Jer 3:3 and the curse of drought in Jer 26:19–20).

The second, more elaborate imagery is within the range of agricultural references but is a rather complex articulation (vv. 5–6). The contrast is, on the one hand, "sow in tears," "go out weeping," and "bearing seed for sowing," thus utilizing the planting season as one of loss, sadness, and deprivation. On the other hand, the second side of the image is "reap with shouts of joy," "come home with shouts of joy," and "carry the sheaves." The phrases yield a triple pattern:

- sow ... reap,
- weep ... shouts of joy,
- go out ... come home.

The poetry is too lean to give specificity or even to evidence the connection between the several motifs. It is clear that the first set (sow, weep, go out) is negative and the second set (reap, shouts of joy, come home) is positive. The hoped-for move from the one to the other is by the anticipated action of YHWH, who, by restorative activity, will accomplish one more "great thing." The imagery perhaps is a prayer for rain in the season of drought:

They need ever-recurring rhythms of renewal that come like the seasonal freshets that make the dry watercourses of the Negeb run with water. The prayer for that renewal uses a contrasting correlation between weeping/sowing and reaping/laughing. The contrast between tears and laughter represents the change sought (e.g., 30:5). In the old religious myths of Ugarit and Egypt, seedtime was associated with the death of the god of fertility, and harvest was associated with his revival. The ancient tradition seems to have created an association of sowing with grief and of joy with harvest.[301]

Related to that might be hopeless sowing in drought and ample harvest after rain. But the imagery is quite supple, so it might refer to the "going out" of deportation

---

[301] J. L. Mays, *Psalms* (1994), 400.

and "coming home" of homecoming. It belongs to the imaginative character of the poetry to be open to more than one reading.

In the end, the double use of "restore fortunes" in verses 1 and 4 makes clear that in both *celebrative memory* and *urgent appeal* it is YHWH's capacity for transformative miracles that is the center of attention. Here speaks a people who lack resources of their own and count completely on the good and powerful inclination of YHWH. It is YHWH alone who is the giver of all newness by which Israel lives. Because the imagery is agricultural, the prayer makes the larger claim that it is YHWH, the giver of all seasons, who sustains creation (Gen 8:22).

A Closer Look: *Shavot*

The word *shavot*, which occurs in verses 1 and 4, is a technical term that refers to a complete reversal of fortune that is wrought by the inscrutable power of God. The word can be used quite generically, as in Job 42:10 for the reversal of the destiny of Job by the faithfulness of God. The word is peculiarly utilized in exilic texts to refer to the homecoming of the Jews from deportation brought about by the power of God (see Jer 30:18; 31:23; 32:44; 33:11, 26).

Bridging the Horizons: Agricultural Wonder

The imagery of *sowing and sadness* and *reaping and joy* calls to mind the imagery of Jesus' teaching, "except a grain of seed fall into the ground ..." (Jn 12:24). The appeal of such teaching reflected in this psalm is to a simple agricultural wonder, one recognized by every schoolchild who plants a bean seed in a Styrofoam cup and waits for new life. In the teaching of Jesus, this agricultural imagery clearly refers to his own resurrection, the gift of new life out of death. In the Old Testament, moreover, the imagery of resurrection is utilized to refer to exile and homecoming (see Ezek 37:1–14). Thus we may take a range of references in relationship to the imagery of the psalm that voice the core claim of both Judaism and Christianity. In every such reference, the gap between being dead in the ground and alive in the world is occupied only by the doer of "great things." Israel and the church gladly attest to this doer of "great things."

PSALM 127 – A SONG OF ASCENTS. OF SOLOMON

[1] Unless the LORD builds the house,
  those who build it labor in vain.
  Unless the LORD guards the city,

the guard keeps watch in vain.
2 It is in vain that you rise up early
    and go late to rest,
    eating the bread of anxious toil;
      for he gives sleep to his beloved.

3 Sons are indeed a heritage from the LORD,
    the fruit of the womb a reward.
4 Like arrows in the hand of a warrior
    are the sons of one's youth.
5 Happy is the man who has
    his quiver full of them.
  He shall not be put to shame
    when he speaks with his enemies in the gate.

Psalm 127 consists of two parts, with the theme of work done in futility in verses 1–2 and the theme of sons as blessings in verses 3–5. Because of the references to family, Kraus suggests that the psalm was a wisdom text related to the beginning of a new family.[302] Psalm 127 has been included in the Songs of Ascents (Psalms 120–134) and tied to Solomon in its superscription. The reference to Solomon ties the psalm to wisdom and to the building of the temple. The psalm would suggest that achievements in life, even the achievements of the great King Solomon, are "in vain" without YHWH's participation. In the Songs of Ascents, "house" most often refers to the temple (including v. 1) or the line of David, "sons" to the line of David, and "city" to Jerusalem. It is likely that this poem about daily work and family has been included in a collection tied to pilgrimage to the sacred city of Jerusalem and thus been interpreted in that light. In its current setting in the Psalter, Psalm 127 is connected with the building of Zion/Jerusalem and the temple, as well as with the Davidic monarchy.

A Closer Look: A Pivot Psalm

Psalm 127 is the eighth of the Songs of Ascents and so falls at the middle of the collection. McCann suggests that it is a kind of pivot in the collection.[303] The needs of the people in the midst of a hostile world are at the fore in the first part of this group of psalms. Psalm 127 continues to encourage trust in YHWH as the key to full living but also moves toward joy in life. The remainder of this group

---

302 H.-J. Kraus, *Psalms 60–150* (1988), 453.
303 J. C. McCann, Jr., "Book of Psalms," in L. E. Keck et al. (eds.), *The New Interpreter's Bible*, vol. 4 (1996), 1197.

of psalms moves in a positive direction. Psalm 128 also continues themes from Psalm 127: daily work and family.

The opening verses of Psalm 127 display a poetic characteristic of the Songs of Ascents: stairstep parallelism in which phrases are repeated as the poetic lines move forward. The verses suggest three labor activities that are carried out in futility unless they include divine involvement: house building, guarding a city, and "anxious toil." A house could refer to a family or a building. The initial wisdom setting recounted earlier in terms of family and community would suggest that a family's lasting accomplishments are blessings from God. The psalm does not imply that human effort is wasted but suggests putting such effort in the context of the creator's engagement with the world. One could approach the daily tasks of building a family/house or guarding a city, or the unending efforts of a workaholic, in an autonomous fashion focusing only on one's own efforts, but the psalm suggests that all those efforts will come to no good end unless they are undertaken as part of God's purpose in the world. The sense of the last line of verse 2 is not clear. It could mean that YHWH grants rest, in contrast to the "anxious toil" with little sleep in the first part of the verse, or it could mean that God gives provisions for living while people sleep, which would then be gifts from YHWH.

As noted, the context in the Songs of Ascents suggests that the house building and city guarding are tied to Jerusalem and the temple (and the Davidic dynasty with the sons in vv. 3–5). The opening verses of the psalm then urge the view that the lives of families and of the community of ancient Israel will not come to fruition outside the context of YHWH's gracious blessing. The perspective applies to both audiences.

Verses 3–5 pursue the family theme in terms of sons. Verses 3–4 are in the form of a proverb and speak of sons as rewarding blessings, "a heritage from the Lord." "Heritage" often refers to the land as a gift from YHWH. The sons provide a future for the family or house. The image in verse 4 is of sons as arrows. The psalm's final verse begins with the form of a beatitude and ties the arrow image to that of a quiver. The wisdom view is that a quiver full of arrows – a house full of sons – symbolizes divine blessing and suggests influence in life. Conflicts at the city gate (the court) are more likely to end in favor of the one with sons as a sign of blessing and importance. Blessing from God ties the two parts of Psalm 127 together and provides one of the unifying themes in the Songs of Ascents. Daily labor and family life were central to the lived history of ancient Israel, as is the case in most societies. These basic endeavors are necessary for a community to thrive. The psalm's perspective is that the endeavors do not succeed from autonomous human effort but from work in the context of the gift of the creator. The psalm is a kind of poetic application of the wisdom perspective that reverence for God is where all wisdom begins – here in daily labor and family life and in ancient Israel's public life tied to Jerusalem, the temple, and the Davidic monarchy.

Pilgrims to Zion/Jerusalem go to the sacred city seeking YHWH's blessing. That is the context of the Songs of Ascents. Psalm 127 ties the blessing to daily life for families and for the community. Blessing in the Hebrew scriptures operates from the divine presence to provide the vibrancy to grow and thrive in the world. That blessing brings wholeness of life and hope for a future. The urging of this brief poem is not to reject the blessing but to embrace it in all of living.

Bridging the Horizons: A Self-Made Man

The father of one of the authors (Bellinger) was known in his small community as a "self-made man." That phrase is a staple of the American myth and usually refers to a person who has risen from a lower socioeconomic status and achieved a great deal. In the contemporary acquisitive American society, the achievements typically have to do with property and finances or with family and social status. The image of the workaholic continues to influence people in Western culture so that they might be successful and rich. The poetic picture in Ps 127:2 fits many in this culture well: "you rise up early and go late to rest, eating the bread of anxious toil." Many people in today's culture achieve remarkable things, but the notion that anyone is a "self-made man" is misguided. Many people and parts of society contribute to any person's success. Psalm 127 makes the further claim that lasting achievements are gifts from the creator. To declare autonomy from the creator would be to walk the path of the fool. The poet/teacher urges the perspective from experience that lasting contributions do not come solely from individual humans. Rather, the gifts of the creator and the contributions of the community typify all human successes. The fitting response to such gifts is gratitude. In the midst of a society characterized by militant consumerism, this poem still invites hearers and readers to consider again their approach to living.

PSALM 128 – A SONG OF ASCENTS

¹ Happy is everyone who fears the LORD,
    who walks in his ways.
² You shall eat the fruit of the labor of your hands;
    you shall be happy, and it shall go well with you.
³ Your wife will be like a fruitful vine
    within your house;
    your children will be like olive shoots
    around your table.
⁴ Thus shall the man be blessed
    who fears the LORD.

⁵ The Lord bless you from Zion.
  May you see the prosperity of Jerusalem
  all the days of your life.
⁶ May you see your children's children.
  Peace be upon Israel!

Interpreters have proposed a variety of structures for reading Psalm 128, a poem commonly associated with wisdom. The NRSV rendering sets the poem in three parts, related to work, family, and the sanctuary in Jerusalem. Another possibility is to take the opening verse as a beatitude, followed in verses 2–4 with the theme of work and family, with a concluding benediction in the final verses. Decisions about literary structure depend on the textual clues the interpreter follows. An important clue in this psalm is the repetition of "who fears the Lord" in verses 1 and 4. Readers could take the second occurrence of the phrase as the introduction to the second part of the psalm or could construe the first four verses as the first section framed by the phrase and verses 5–6 as a benediction.[304] The reading that follows will consider the first four verses together framed by the reference to those who fear YHWH, a central phrase of the wisdom tradition, and verses 5–6 as a concluding benediction. It may help readers to know, however, that other understandings of the psalm's structure are possible.

Although the psalm is often associated with wisdom, it seems to reflect a cultic background. As indicated, at least part of the psalm is in the form of a benediction pronounced by a leader in temple worship, perhaps at the conclusion of some type of festival. The blessing of a harvest would be a plausible suggestion, but the psalm provides little evidence on that question. In its current setting in the Psalter, the psalm is paired with Psalm 127. Both use the form of the beatitude, and both speak of YHWH's blessing in terms of work and family. Psalm 128 is the ninth of the Songs of Ascents (Psalms 120–134) and, along with other poems in the collection, refers to Zion and to peace. From this point in the collection, the psalms take a positive tone. As noted previously, the collection was associated with pilgrimage to Zion/Jerusalem.

The opening section of the psalm, verses 1–4, is framed by the phrase "those who fear the Lord." The first use of the phrase is in the form of a beatitude, in the style of the beginning of Psalm 1. The psalm's opening word is often rendered as "happy." In contemporary Western culture, "happy" often connotes pleasure with external circumstances, but that is not the sense of the Hebrew term. Other possible renderings are "joyful" or "contented." The term introduces an observation about living: one who walks or lives in ways in line with YHWH's purposes finds wholeness. Walking in YHWH's ways provides the parallel to the fear of YHWH in verse 1. In this phrase, "fear" is not about being intimidated or "shaking in your boots"

304 See J. C. McCann, Jr., "Book of Psalms," in L. E. Keck et al. (eds.), *The New Interpreter's Bible*, vol. 4 (1996), 1200; and C. C. Broyles, *Psalms* (1999), 463.

before the divine presence. It is rather about reverence or awe before YHWH, and the observation that whom one reveres, one obeys. To fear YHWH is to entrust all of life and hope to this one and follow the divine guidance. The perspective of the psalm is that such a decision about lifestyle makes a difference; living in line with YHWH's teaching brings a profound joy and completeness to life.

Verse 2 illustrates such a full life in terms of everyday work. In daily life, one sees this wholeness of life in operation. In the ancient world, labor was about growing food, and the enjoyment of that task was eating the fruits of one's labors. That is a good life in line with divine purposes and demonstrates its joy. A further illustration follows in verse 3, with a fruitful vine and an olive shoot applied to family life. The wife is compared to a vine with many clusters of grapes and the children to olive shoots, a symbol of strength and growth. These plants were common to the life of ancient Israel and provided for daily life. Verse 4 ties these illustrations of work and family back to YHWH's blessing. It is YHWH who is present to make possible the vibrancy to grow and live fully. The images used encourage pilgrims to see the hopes for full living and to see the daily joys of life in terms of divine blessing. This picture of blessing is in line with promises of the prophets beyond the trauma of exile (Amos 9:13–15; Isa 65:17–25).

The psalm concludes in verses 5–6 with a benediction, a blessing from God. The blessing comes from Zion, the sacred place of divine presence. The hopes for Jerusalem, the goal of the pilgrimage tied to the Songs of Ascents, come from the divine presence. The hope is for a long and full life for the city of Jerusalem and for the pilgrims. God is present to bring about powerful growth and full living. The completion of that blessing is put in terms of *shalom*, or peace, but not just as the absence of conflict. The hope is for the encounter with the reign of YHWH and the consequence of a healthy and full life for individuals and the community. The psalm suggests that such life comes from the creator who reigns from Zion and is found by living in line with the divine teaching. The blessing is thus a gift from YHWH rather than a human success, and is tied to both individuals and Israel; the two are bound together.

The psalm's conclusion is a benediction, a word of blessing at the conclusion of worship that carries the sense of worship from the sanctuary into daily living. So the blessing comes from Zion, the temple, as part of the power of worship, but then comes into all of life. The pilgrims thus receive a priestly blessing and hope to live out that blessing faithfully based on the encounter with YHWH in the sanctuary; they hope for a life that fits together in integrity, a life of peace.

Bridging the Horizons: A Holistic Blessing

Blessing in the Hebrew scriptures has to do with the divine presence making possible the power to grow and thrive in the world. It is very much related to daily life and work, and families and communities. Psalm 128 ties the divine blessing to worship, and the conclusion of the psalm illustrates the benediction taking the blessing into life, which is very much a part of the psalm in its references to labor, families, and wisdom. Wisdom ties the blessing to a life in line with God's purposes. The psalm's theological perspective – in line with the perspective of the Songs of Ascents and the Psalter – is not that those walking the journey of faith earn such divine blessing but that in embracing a faithful lifestyle as part of a community of faith pilgrims can find a path that fits together in integrity and wholeness. The psalm thus becomes a confession of trust in YHWH and a word of hope.

PSALM 129 – A SONG OF ASCENTS

¹ 'Often have they attacked me from my youth'
  – let Israel now say –
² 'often have they attacked me from my youth,
  yet they have not prevailed against me.
³ Those who plough ploughed on my back;
  they made their furrows long.'
⁴ The LORD is righteous;
  he has cut the cords of the wicked.
⁵ May all who hate Zion
  be put to shame and turned back.
⁶ Let them be like the grass on the housetops
  that withers before it grows up,
⁷ with which reapers do not fill their hands
  or binders of sheaves their arms,
⁸ while those who pass by do not say,
  'The blessing of the LORD be upon you!
  We bless you in the name of the LORD!'

Psalm 129 will not be familiar to many readers. Its interpretation is somewhat obscure and its tone less than positive. The psalm is often interpreted as a psalm of thanksgiving centered on verse 4. God has delivered the people, and the speaker narrates the experience or declares it to the congregation, to use Westermann's terms,[305] and the psalm is thus a particular kind of psalm of praise. Others would

---

[305] C. Westermann, *Praise and Lament in the Psalms* (1981).

suggest that the psalm is a petition or a psalm of confidence. One of the issues has to do with the translation of the verbs in verses 5–6. The verbs could be taken in a jussive sense and therefore as petitions, or as indicative imperfects and therefore as expressions of confidence. The verbs allow for both understandings, so some commentators have sought other interpretive clues. Allen interprets verses 5–6 in line with other psalm texts that also refer to "all" enemies and takes the verses as statements of confidence.[306] Broyles suggests that the absence of a direct address to YHWH in the psalm makes interpreting the verbs as petitions less likely.[307] The best option is to leave the interpretation open, thus making it possible for readers to relate the psalm to a variety of contexts. Verses 1–4 of the psalm recount the work of enemies, and verses 5–8 express petitions or statements of confidence. Agricultural images run through the psalm to unify it and are particularly striking in the second section.

Most interpreters would suggest that the psalm has a postexilic origin. The first part of the psalm uses the first common singular pronoun and thus seems to reflect the oppression of an individual. This rehearsal of an individual's memory of trouble and hope has been brought into the context of the community and its enemies, especially put in terms of Zion and its opponents. The psalm is now included in the Songs of Ascents (Psalms 120–134) and its context of pilgrimage to Zion/Jerusalem. The poetic voice is now the voice of the pilgrims to Zion.

The psalm begins with a rehearsal by an individual of a lifetime of oppression from enemies, and then the liturgist turns to the congregation and urges the repetition of that first line. In that way, the community joins in the complaint of this person about enemies. The complaint turns quickly to a confession of confidence at the end of verse 2 that the enemies have not succeeded. Enmity has been the common experience of this person "from my youth" and of the community. With the eyes of faith, however, they have confidence and hope because of YHWH's help. The shocking agricultural image in verse 3 suggests that the enemies have plowed long furrows in the back of the speaker. The picture is of cruel and inhuman treatment, but YHWH "has cut the cords of the wicked." The cords are apparently the ropes used in plowing the furrows in the back of this faithful one. YHWH has brought an end to the persecution and is therefore characterized as "righteous," the one who acts to bring about right relationships.

In verses 5–8, the voice of the community comes to the surface, and in verses 5–6 it expresses either petitions or confidence. The psalm could be appropriated in either circumstance. The enemies are now portrayed as haters of Zion, those who opposed the community. The poet includes in liturgy and prayer concern about those who hate Zion; there is no denial of the pain and difficulty of life here. The

---

[306] L. C. Allen, *Psalms 101–150* (2002), 247.
[307] C. C. Broyles, *Psalms* (1999), 466.

psalm embraces the public claiming of pain and brings it into the circle of faith. Enemies are at hand, and the psalm either prays for divine help in the midst of this trouble and woe or confesses confidence in YHWH in that context. The community puts its trouble to God and leaves it with the creator and redeemer. The enemies become YHWH's problem also, and this community understands that it lives by divine trustworthiness.

Verses 6–7 continue with agricultural imagery. Grass is said to take root on earthen roofs but does not find enough nourishment to grow. It withers, and so harvesters end up with empty hands and certainly no harvest of sheaves. What is more, those who pass by the harvesters do not speak YHWH's blessing on the harvest. The tone is one of imprecation, whether one takes the verbs in verses 5–6 as petitions or as confessions of confidence. The hope articulated in the psalm is that YHWH will bring the wicked oppressors of Zion to an end. The community has encountered strong oppression, and the language of this prayer reflects that trouble. In the end, the matter is left to the God of Zion, a place of hope and confidence for the congregation. The final verse articulates the blessing that is denied by those who see the harvester of withered grass. It is likely that the psalm ends with two parallel lines of the missed blessing, but some interpreters take the psalm's final line as a priestly blessing on the worshiping community.

A Closer Look: Haters of Zion

An individual voice is heard in Psalm 129 – in the Songs of Ascents – in the context of the congregation of pilgrims on the way to Jerusalem/Zion or who have already arrived there. The community of pilgrims continues to face strong opposition and confesses that. The psalm brings that enmity fully into the context of the community's relationship with YHWH, the God of Zion. This brief but powerful poem puts the question of these haters of Zion before the divine judge, who is present in Zion. The issue of the oppressors is taken to the divine judge as opposed to suggesting that the congregation take on the task of exacting vengeance. The psalm is honest and brings the imprecation of both individual and community before YHWH as a part of faith. The faith portrayed in the Psalter makes clear that there is opposition in life and brings that opposition fully into the relationship and dialogue with the God of Zion. Contemporary oppressed communities will identify with the psalm. The psalm also has connections with Psalm 130, a text that makes clear that opposition can also come from within persons of faith and the community of faith. That argues against an arrogant attitude about conflict, but Psalm 129 firmly puts these conflicts within the realm of faith.

PSALM 130 – A SONG OF ASCENTS

¹ Out of the depths I cry to you, O LORD.
² Lord, hear my voice!
  Let your ears be attentive
    to the voice of my supplications!

³ If you, O LORD, should mark iniquities,
  Lord, who could stand?
⁴ But there is forgiveness with you,
  so that you may be revered.

⁵ I wait for the LORD, my soul waits,
  and in his word I hope;
⁶ my soul waits for the LORD
  more than those who watch for the morning,
    more than those who watch for the morning.

⁷ O Israel, hope in the LORD!
  For with the LORD there is steadfast love,
  and with him is great power to redeem.
⁸ It is he who will redeem Israel
    from all its iniquities.

Psalm 130 is a fine example of a brief psalm that operates around a life crisis. It is not clear whether the crisis is past or present. If the perfect verbs in verses 1 and 5 are taken to refer to past events, the psalm would best be understood as one that narrates deliverance from trouble and in so doing offers praise to YHWH. Most interpreters, however, take the verbs to suggest a current crisis and so interpret the prayer as a petition in the midst of trouble. The verbs allow either interpretation, but the use of the imperative ("hear my voice!") and the jussive ("Let your ears be attentive") in verse 2 suggests that the most likely reading centers on petition. The psalm begins with a plea for hearing and a confession of sinfulness in the presence of the one who forgives sin. In verses 5–6, the speaker confesses faith in terms of waiting for God. The witness of the petitioner in verses 1–6 is then applied to the community in the concluding verses in urging the community to hope and to appropriate the faith espoused in the psalm. The psalm offers a model of faith in crisis and in that sense carries an instructional purpose as well as a liturgical one. The psalm fits well the liturgical setting envisioned in 1 Kgs 8:3–40, where ancient Israel prays for forgiveness in the sanctuary and the forgiveness leads to reverence for YHWH (v. 4). A postexilic date is often suggested for the psalm; perhaps the redemption of Israel (v. 8) has to do with return from exile.

A Closer Look: Confession and Petition

Psalm 130 is part of two collections. It is the eleventh poem in the Songs of Ascents (Psalms 120–134). Its confession of iniquities committed by the faithful provides a balance to the suffering of the faithful at the hands of persecutors in Psalm 129 and so provides a warning about an arrogant attitude readers might infer from the previous psalm. An emphasis on divine compassion continues in Psalm 131. Psalm 130 is also among the church's seven penitential psalms because of its awareness of human sinfulness and divine forgiveness. Its opening phrase is deeply entrenched in Christian tradition. The psalm does not overemphasize the confession of sin, but it clearly articulates the need for divine forgiveness.

Out of the very depths of human experience, the petitioner cries for a divine hearing:

The "depths" referred to are elsewhere always qualified as being "deep waters" (Ps 69:2, 14; Isa 51:10; Ezek 27:34), and thus belong to the familiar language of the cosmic threat posed by the primeval forces. Only here is the word found as an unqualified substantive, which may be grounds enough to regard it as having a special reference to the sense of sinfulness, which is taken up in verse 3.[308]

The poet has no secure place to stand and so cries out to YHWH for help while facing the threat of being overwhelmed by the waters of chaos. YHWH is the one who can forgive and rescue, as indicated in the moving verse 3. If YHWH kept account of all human iniquities, no one would survive, but YHWH is merciful and forgiving. The divine mercy allows the petitioner to stand before the divine presence in the mystery of worship. The popular understanding of such a confession among many contemporary readers would be that obedience to God could lead to forgiveness, but the sequence in verse 4 is the reverse. YHWH forgives, and the response is reverence for God. The petitioner worships God in reverence and gratitude in response to forgiveness. Psalm 130 moves from a sense of human sin to an awareness of divine forgiveness in its opening prayer in verses 1–4.

The petitioner has offered this prayer and in verses 5–6 waits for God's mercy to come to fruition. Morning was the time for deliverance from trouble, and the petitioner's waiting is compared to the waiting of the guards who watch for the morning. Waiting here is not impatiently watching the time pass. It is rather anticipating that divine forgiveness and a new beginning will come. Hope is at

---

[308] Alastair G. Hunter, *Psalms* (Old Testament Readings; London: Routledge, 1999), 218.

hand, and the waiting is a yearning for it to become reality. The waiting is in light of the promise.

In verses 7–8, the petitioner urges the congregation to appropriate the prayer in verses 1–6. The speaker turns to the members of the congregation in verse 7 to call them to the hope exemplified in verse 5. The basis of the hope is put in language familiar to readers of the Psalter – "steadfast love" and redemption. The confession of ancient Israel's faith tradition and of the petitioner in Psalm 130 is that YHWH's way is as one who keeps bringing this community back into fullness of life and thus a faithful relationship with the Redeemer and with the human community. YHWH's beneficence toward Israel does not wane. The concluding verse emphasizes with the pronoun that YHWH is the one who engages Israel in this way.

A Closer Look: Intensification and Expectation

With the use of repetition, Psalm 130 shapes a structure of intensification and expectation. The prayer is brief but put in arresting poetic form. The petitioner and the community look with anticipation into the hope of redemption at the conclusion of verse 8. That hope makes it possible for the speaker and the congregation to move through the encounter with the depths of chaos and to move toward hope and a fresh start. The petitioner begins with a plea that is dependent on divine mercy and calls for YHWH to give heed to the prayer. The psalm honestly confesses human frailty and sinfulness but finds hope in the forgiveness of YHWH. The psalm anticipates that YHWH can still be addressed in the depths of chaos; YHWH has not forsaken the petitioner or Israel. It is a minority voice in the book of Psalms, but it is clear that at times the encounter with the powers of chaos and death is the consequence of human iniquity. Psalm 130 exemplifies such a journey gripped by the power of death and announces that, even from the depths of such chaos, YHWH still hears the honest cries of the struggling person of faith. YHWH is never beyond hearing distance.

PSALM 131 – A SONG OF ASCENTS. OF DAVID

[1] O LORD, my heart is not lifted up,
   my eyes are not raised too high;
I do not occupy myself with things
   too great and too marvelous for me.
[2] But I have calmed and quieted my soul,
   like a weaned child with its mother;
   my soul is like the weaned child that is with me.

³ O Israel, hope in the Lᴏʀᴅ
from this time on and for evermore.

Psalm 131 is a brief poem expressing trust or confidence. The opening verses in the voice of the individual give expression to trust, and the final verse urges the congregation to take hold of that faith. Therefore, the psalm speaks in the voice of an individual in the context of the community in the same way that Psalm 130 does. Psalm 131 confesses trust and faith in YHWH and calls the community to such trust. The psalm uses repetition in the fashion characteristic of the Songs of Ascents (Psalms 120–134). The psalm's first two verses speak of humility and trust in YHWH, as does its predecessor Psalm 130. Psalm 131:3 also repeats Ps 130:7 to bring a further connection with the texts. The traditional setting of the Songs of Ascents is pilgrimage to Zion. The image of mother and child in Psalm 131 could fit that context and bring to mind the place of women in the sojourn.

Psalm 131 begins unusually with a triple negative. The heart is the seat of the intellect or will, so the first verse confesses that the mind or the will of the speaker is not beyond reason and verse 2 affirms the same of the speaker's view of life. The speaker's perspective is appropriately modest. The verse is not an expression of low self-esteem but simply the confession that the speaker is not arrogant and does not suffer from an exaggerated view of the self that leads to self-delusion and deception. This person of faith is rather calm and quiet. The second verse portrays the self-characterization with the imaginative image of a weaned child snuggled into the shoulder of a mother. The image of this satisfied and peaceful child on the mother's shoulder expresses the speaker's peace in the proper place in life under the care of a trustworthy God. The translation of the last line of verse 2 is somewhat obscure, as indicated by the note in the NRSV. "Like the weaned child upon me is my life" provides a satisfactory rendering. The comparison is to the peaceful and satisfied child. Hunter takes a very different view of the poetic image.[309] He suggests that the custom of the day included nursing children into their third year, and so a weaned child might well be fretful and fussy. In that case, the image would communicate a sense of tension and suspense, and Hunter suggests that is the impact of Psalms 130–131. That interpretation of the image does not fit the opening verse or closing verse of Psalm 131. The focus of the psalm is on the hope that trust in YHWH brings. The concluding verse summons the congregation to trust in YHWH in the present and future. That trust is at the heart of this brief poem.

A Closer Look: Mother and Child

The book of Psalms commends a life in faithful relationship with YHWH and the community of faith. In such relationships are found hope and fullness of life.

---

[309] A. G. Hunter, *Psalms* (1999), 219.

Such a life reflects YHWH's created order and provides a firm basis for the pilgrimage of faith. Psalm 131 urges the community to live based on God's ordering of the world and God's trustworthiness rather than the accomplishments of persons. This call applies to individuals and the community. The image of the child in verse 2 brings to mind the hope and trust as well as the honesty and questions of children. In these senses, the psalm portrays in poetry the life of faith. The image of mother and child adds to the poetic images used in the Psalms. McCann suggests that the poet was a woman and that the humility expressed in the opening verse might have been forced on her by a patriarchal culture.[310] That may be so; the psalm could suggest an early feminist perspective. The text uses the image of mother and child to portray a life of faith and hope in YHWH based on a trust in the divine presence that brings health and wholeness for the journey into the future.

PSALM 132 – A SONG OF ASCENTS

¹ O LORD, remember in David's favor
   all the hardships he endured;
² how he swore to the LORD
   and vowed to the Mighty One of Jacob,
³ 'I will not enter my house
   or get into my bed;
⁴ I will not give sleep to my eyes
   or slumber to my eyelids,
⁵ until I find a place for the LORD,
   a dwelling-place for the Mighty One of Jacob.'

⁶ We heard of it in Ephrathah;
   we found it in the fields of Jaar.
⁷ 'Let us go to his dwelling-place;
   let us worship at his footstool.'

⁸ Rise up, O LORD, and go to your resting-place,
   you and the ark of your might.

---

[310] J. C. McCann, Jr., "Book of Psalms," in L. E. Keck et al. (eds.), *The New Interpreter's Bible*, vol. 4 (1996), 1209.

⁹ Let your priests be clothed with righteousness,
    and let your faithful shout for joy.
¹⁰ For your servant David's sake
    do not turn away the face of your anointed one.

¹¹ The LORD swore to David a sure oath
    from which he will not turn back:
    'One of the sons of your body
    I will set on your throne.
¹² If your sons keep my covenant
    and my decrees that I shall teach them,
    their sons also, for evermore,
    shall sit on your throne.'

¹³ For the LORD has chosen Zion;
    he has desired it for his habitation:
¹⁴ 'This is my resting-place for ever;
    here I will reside, for I have desired it.
¹⁵ I will abundantly bless its provisions;
    I will satisfy its poor with bread.
¹⁶ Its priests I will clothe with salvation,
    and its faithful will shout for joy.
¹⁷ There I will cause a horn to sprout up for David;
    I have prepared a lamp for my anointed one.
¹⁸ His enemies I will clothe with disgrace,
    but on him, his crown will gleam.'

With references to the Davidic dynasty, the Jerusalem temple, and the Ark of the Covenant, Psalm 132 likely originated in Jerusalem in the time of the Davidic monarchy. The psalm is often connected to the cultic reenactment of 2 Samuel 6 – the narrative of David's bringing the Ark to Jerusalem. The psalm celebrates YHWH's choice of the Davidic dynasty and of Jerusalem/Zion as the central place of divine presence. Mowinckel reads the psalm in light of ancient Near Eastern practices.[311] The Babylonian gods, king, and priests would go in cultic procession to find and deliver the lost, dead, or imprisoned god. The cultic narrative in Israel says that David and his soldiers go in search of the Ark as the central symbol of YHWH's presence, find it, and provide a place for it in Zion.

---

[311] S. Mowinckel, *Psalms in Israel's Worship*, vol. 1 (1962), 276.

A Closer Look: The Chosen Dwelling

This psalm has been included in the Psalter among the Songs of Ascents (Psalms 120–134), likely a postexilic collection. The psalm is closely associated with Zion, the goal of the pilgrimage traditionally suggested as the setting of the collection. It provides a theological base for the pilgrimage by rehearsing YHWH's choice of Zion as the sacred place of the divine presence and the place from which YHWH's chosen one rules, as suggested in Ps 122:3–5. Psalm 132, however, is longer than the other psalms in the collection and different in the attention it gives the monarchy. Allen suggests that the psalm has a particular purpose in the collection that is tied to the hopes expressed for the community in Pss 130:7 and 131:3, a messianic hope from the promise to David and centered in Zion as the sacred place of YHWH's presence.[312] YHWH's hopes for the community await fulfillment, but Psalm 132 helps maintain these hopes by articulating them with reference to "the good old days" of the Kingdom of David. The psalm serves as a liturgy of memory and hope.

Psalm 132 is also an artfully crafted poem. The first part of the psalm is framed by petitions in verses 1 and 10. A narrative introduces a quotation from David in verses 3–5. Verse 6 then introduces another quotation, probably through verse 9. This section of the psalm focuses on David's efforts to find a resting place for YHWH; in so doing, David fulfills a vow. The second part of the psalm (vv. 11–18) echoes the first with parallel content and sequence. David makes a vow to YHWH in the first part; YHWH makes a vow to David in the second. Two narratives introduce quotations in both parts of the psalm. The first part of verse 11 introduces a quotation that runs through verse 12, and verse 13 introduces with narrative a quotation that completes the psalm.

The two parts also share vocabulary. Verse 11 echoes verses 1–2 with reference to YHWH, David, and the language of oaths, language that continues in verses 3–5 and in verse 12. Verses 8 and 14 refer to a resting place for YHWH, and verses 9 and 16 to priests and faithful ones and their clothing and shouts. Verses 10 and 17 refer to David as the anointed one. Interpreters have suggested other poetic structures for Psalm 132, perhaps seeing verses 9 and 16 as refrains,[313] but the echo between verses 1–10 and 11–18 suggests an artful poetic structure of petition and response. The hope in verses 1–10 anticipates fulfillment; verses 11–18 articulate a hope realized. Verses 9 and 16 illustrate the movement of the psalm. It will help to consider each part of the psalm in smaller units.

---

[312] L. C. Allen, *Psalms 101–150* (2002), 275.
[313] See A. G. Hunter, *Psalms* (1999), 224; and L. C. Allen, *Psalms 101–150* (2002), 264–266, 270.

Verses 1–5. The psalm begins with a prayer asking YHWH to remember positively the hardships David has seen. Perhaps the hardships include the efforts to find a "dwelling place" for YHWH. Verse 2 then introduces David's oath to "the Mighty One of Jacob." David has a place and will not rest until YHWH has a place. Such is the vow.

Verses 6–10. The scene shifts as verse 6 introduces in narrative form another quotation. "We" could suggest a chorus or the leaders of worship; they remember the events of hearing that the Ark of the Covenant, the primary symbol of YHWH's presence, was located in Jaar. They heard these things in Ephrathah, a location associated with David. Jaar is apparently another name for Kiriath-Jearim, referred to in 1 Samuel 4–6. Israel understood that YHWH was invisibly enthroned above the Ark, and so the call to worship at the footstool, the Ark, follows. Verse 8 alludes to the tradition in Num 10:35–36 of the Ark as the object of divine leadership into battle in the narrative of the Exodus from Egypt and the wilderness journey. The worshiping community now seeks a sacred sanctuary for the divine presence. The hope is that YHWH's priests will minister in line with the divine intent to bring the community into a right relationship with this life-giving presence and that those who live in fidelity to their relationship with YHWH will be able to "shout for joy." In verse 10, the frame of the first part of the poem returns to a petition that YHWH will remember David's acts of fidelity. The petition is that YHWH will not turn away but continue to be present with David, the divinely chosen one.

Verses 11–12. The beginning of the second part of the psalm, again in narrative form, introduces a quotation. The quotation is YHWH's sure promise to David and articulates in poetic form the Davidic covenant that David and his sons will rule over the people in Jerusalem as God's chosen representatives. This articulation makes it clear that David's descendants are to keep the covenant with YHWH; that will determine whether the dynasty endures.

Verses 13–18. Verse 13 also introduces a quotation to conclude the psalm. YHWH has chosen David and his descendants, and YHWH has chosen Jerusalem/Zion as a resting place, a sanctuary. This divine presence brings blessings, provisions for life, and hopes for a future. The mediators of such blessings are the priests robed in the hope of salvation, of wholeness in life. God delights in this choice of Zion as a "habitation." The concluding verses return to the promise to the Davidic line that YHWH will bring strength, hope, and a future. The promise brings hope for the whole community.

Psalm 132 is a prime example of Davidic theology. Zion is both the chosen place of the divine dwelling and the place of the throne of the line of David. Davidic rule is supported by the temple as the divine habitation, symbolized with the Ark of the Covenant there. Finding a resting place for YHWH is the central theme of the psalm, but it is the combination of Zion as YHWH's resting place and the choice of David as the anointed one that provides the structure to support the theme. In the first part of the psalm, David works on behalf of YHWH in the search for a sanctuary, whereas in the second part of the psalm YHWH promises the divine right of a faithful Davidic line. The psalm comes to a full conclusion with both the choice of Jerusalem/Zion as the divine dwelling place and the founding and support of David and his descendants on the throne in Jerusalem. Both YHWH and the Davidic line have a "habitation."

The community of pilgrims sings this song to affirm that YHWH has blessed them with leaders in the line of David based at the goal of the pilgrimage – Zion. The king's primary task is to establish justice as the order of the kingdom. The Davidic promise offers a future and hope for the pilgrims. The divine right of kings was often abused in ancient Jerusalem, but still the community sings of the royal ideal and its enduring hope. Zion is also chosen as the "habitation" of the divine presence, a sanctuary for the blessing of the pilgrims. Worship there is about encounter with this mysterious, life-giving presence. The psalm sings of renewal and of hope for this pilgrim community of faith.

PSALM 133 – A SONG OF ASCENTS

¹ How very good and pleasant it is
  when kindred live together in unity!
² It is like the precious oil on the head,
  running down upon the beard,
  on the beard of Aaron,
  running down over the collar of his robes.
³ It is like the dew of Hermon,
  which falls on the mountains of Zion.
  For there the LORD ordained his blessing,
  life for evermore.

Psalm 133 begins with a wisdom saying about how best to live; central to the saying is the notion of unity. It may well be that the saying originated in a family setting and commended the benefits of brothers living together in the family home. Verses 2 and 3 use similes to illustrate the simple proverb that begins the psalm. The similes add some depth of life experience in expanding the adjectives "good and pleasant" in verse 1. The psalm effectively uses poetic repetition. "Beard" occurs twice in verse 2, and the participle "going down" occurs three times in verses 2 and 3, concluding with the divine blessing coming down on the community. The psalm's conclusion summarizes while framing the poem with its opening line.

A Closer Look: A Family Journey

The repetition of Psalm 133 will be familiar to readers of the Songs of Ascents (Psalms 120–134). The psalm fits well in this collection. It focuses on Zion as the place of divine presence and blessing; that is a special emphasis of Psalm 122 and also occurs in Psalm 134. McCann notes that family imagery is also important in the collection (Pss 122:8; 127:3–5; 128:3, 6; 131:2).[314] Family is put in the broader context of the community of faith in the collection. In Psalm 133, a family saying has been brought into the context of a community on pilgrimage to Zion. The pilgrims are now kindred by virtue of their covenant relationship with YHWH. The themes of Zion, blessing, and community make the placement of the psalm near the end of the collection most appropriate.

The opening saying of the psalm extols the virtues of community with the adjectives "good and pleasant." The literal rendering of the term the NRSV translates as "kindred" is "brothers," so the saying may well come from a setting in which brothers lived together in the patriarchal home. Verses 2 and 3 illustrate the saying with similes and in so doing move to the broader context of the community at worship. The first image is of the precious anointing oil "running down" onto the beard of Aaron and then "running down" over the collar of the priestly robe. Readers of the Songs of Ascents may be reminded of the references to priestly clothing in Ps 132:9, 16 and the naming of the king as the anointed one in Ps 132:10, 17. The second simile moves from the high priest to the broader world of creation and the refreshing dew of Hermon in the heights running down to Mount Zion. Hunter suggests that Hermon could represent Mount Zaphon, the abode of the High God in the north, and so symbolize the divine dwelling place now in Zion.[315] The conclusion of the psalm relates to the blessing that comes down on the community on pilgrimage to Zion. The blessing endures well into the future. The divine presence powerfully encountered at Zion makes possible the vitality to grow and thrive in the world; such is the psalm's understanding of blessing.

Having arrived at the intended destination, the pilgrim community gathers as one family in Zion, and Psalm 133 celebrates the delight and goodness of the setting. The psalm's opening exclamation of delight in community is tied to the concluding word on divine blessing. The psalm's two images of oil and dew nurture this sense of the blessing and joy of community. The moist dew and the fragrant anointing oil conjure in the pilgrims' imaginations the sense of the gracious divine blessing coming down on them in this place, Zion. The use of the participle "coming down"

[314] J. C. McCann, Jr., "Book of Psalms," in L. E. Keck et al. (eds.), *The New Interpreter's Bible*, vol. 4 (1996), 1214.
[315] A. G. Hunter, *Psalms* (1999), 226.

three times suggests that hearers/readers look up to the heavens whence comes the divine help and blessing. The blessing flows down to the community from Mount Zion. The psalm operates from a proverbial wisdom stance suggesting that wholeness of life is encountered by way of the divine blessing from Zion and is lived in the community. The poem's images seek to flow into the imaginations of the pilgrims to encourage renewal of this kind of full living blessed by YHWH in Zion and enjoyed on the journey together.

PSALM 134 – A SONG OF ASCENTS

¹ Come, bless the LORD, all you servants of the LORD,
  who stand by night in the house of the LORD!
² Lift up your hands to the holy place,
  and bless the LORD.

³ May the LORD, maker of heaven and earth,
  bless you from Zion.

Psalm 134 is a hymn of praise beginning with the standard summons to praise; the standard reason for praise does not follow, however. What follows is a priestly benediction. The psalm seems to reflect cultic use, and praise could have been part of the cultic context from which the psalm originated. The psalm fits well the pronouncement of a priestly benediction on worshipers as they leave the sanctuary to which they have journeyed for festal celebrations and return to the rest of life. Verses 1 and 2 of the brief composition constitute a call to praise and are in a chiastic form with the imperative calls to "bless the Lord" framing two references to the sanctuary. In the psalm's final verse, it is YHWH who blesses, with the use of the same verb and the repetition of the divine name. The name YHWH occurs five times in the brief psalm along with the apposition "maker of heaven and earth" in verse 3 and references to blessing and to the place of worship in each verse. The psalm is brief but powerful.

A Closer Look: Destination Praise

Psalm 134 brings the collection of the Songs of Ascents (Psalms 120–134) to an appropriate conclusion, since the psalm has connections with other parts of the collection. Psalm 122 focuses on the house of worship, and the community blesses God in Psalm 124. YHWH blesses the people from Zion in Psalms 128,

132, and 133, and YHWH is referred to as maker of heaven and earth in Psalms 121 and 124. The reference to those "who stand by night" might also bring to mind the reference to YHWH as the one "who keeps Israel will neither slumber nor sleep" in Psalm 121. The call to praise in Psalm 134 is also similar to the call to praise at the beginning and end of Psalm 135. Psalm 133 emphasizes the unity of the gathered pilgrim community, and Psalm 134 calls that community to praise YHWH, which is the goal of the pilgrimage. So Psalm 134 brings this collection of pilgrimage songs to a fitting conclusion, emphasizing the goal of the journey in terms of praising YHWH and receiving YHWH's blessing.

The psalm's opening call is to "bless the Lord." The root of the verb has to do with knees and kneeling to acknowledge that YHWH is the one who reaches out to the community with the gift of life and blessing. The servants who are called to the act of praise may be priests and Levites but may also include others in the community who serve YHWH and who are in the sanctuary at night; the portrayals of the cult in Leviticus, for example, suggest that participation was likely broader than only that of priests and Levites. The lifting of the hands in verse 2 is an act of prayer, often tied to the sanctuary; see 1 Kgs 8:38. The emphatic summons to praise in verses 1 and 2 is followed by a priestly benediction in verse 3. It is YHWH, characterized as "maker of heaven and earth," who now gives the blessing, the power to grow and thrive in the world. The verse speaks the hope that from Zion this God will bless the pilgrim community. The purpose of the blessing is that the encounter with the divine presence in worship will go with the community to bring about wholeness in their ongoing lives. The Songs of Ascents frequently remind the community that this kind of blessing comes from the creator.

One of the hallmarks of Psalm 134 is the reciprocal nature of blessing: the community is called to bless YHWH, and the psalm concludes with a prayer that YHWH will bless the people.[316] YHWH the creator is strongly present on Zion and bequeaths blessings from there. YHWH blesses, and then the community reflects that blessing in acts of praise. Blessing is the power to grow and live fully in the world and is possible because of the divine presence. The movement of blessing is a mutual one and reflects the dialogue of a relationship in which both partners, YHWH and Israel, participate fully. The liturgist calls the community to praise in Psalm 134 and pronounces the divine blessing on the community. The concluding blessing speaks the hope that the presence and power of the creator will go with the worshiping community into all of life. This God focuses on the relationship with this pilgrim community and extends the loyal love and trustworthiness emphasized

[316] J. L. Mays, *Psalms* (1994), 414.

in the Psalter even to the point of risk. This God intensely present in Zion goes with the pilgrims into the fray of the rest of life.

A benediction is a beneficial word, a word that has the purpose of carrying the renewing power of the encounter with God in sanctuary worship into the rest of life:

We may perhaps imagine the pilgrims, who first encountered the formula "maker of heaven and earth" at the outset of the festival sequence in 121:2, now returning to their homes emboldened and encouraged by that final blessing: "May Yahweh, maker of heaven and earth, /bless you from Zion."[317]

Readers have followed this community on pilgrimage in the Songs of Ascents, and so we may also take this final blessing on "you" as a blessing on readers of the collection. Amen.

PSALM 135

¹ Praise the LORD!
   Praise the name of the LORD;
   give praise, O servants of the LORD,
² you that stand in the house of the LORD,
   in the courts of the house of our God.
³ Praise the LORD, for the LORD is good;
   sing to his name, for he is gracious.
⁴ For the LORD has chosen Jacob for himself,
   Israel as his own possession.

⁵ For I know that the LORD is great;
   our LORD is above all gods.
⁶ Whatever the LORD pleases he does,
   in heaven and on earth,
   in the seas and all deeps.
⁷ He it is who makes the clouds rise at the end of the earth;
   he makes lightnings for the rain
    and brings out the wind from his storehouses.

⁸ He it was who struck down the firstborn of Egypt,
   both human beings and animals;
⁹ he sent signs and wonders

---

[317] A. G. Hunter, *Psalms* (1999), 228.

into your midst, O Egypt,
  against Pharaoh and all his servants.
¹⁰ He struck down many nations
  and killed mighty kings –
¹¹ Sihon, king of the Amorites,
  and Og, king of Bashan,
  and all the kingdoms of Canaan –
¹² and gave their land as a heritage,
  a heritage to his people Israel.

¹³ Your name, O LORD, endures for ever,
  your renown, O LORD, throughout all ages.
¹⁴ For the LORD will vindicate his people,
  and have compassion on his servants.
¹⁵ The idols of the nations are silver and gold,
  the work of human hands.
¹⁶ They have mouths, but they do not speak;
  they have eyes, but they do not see;
¹⁷ they have ears, but they do not hear,
  and there is no breath in their mouths.
¹⁸ Those who make them
  and all who trust them
  shall become like them.
¹⁹ O house of Israel, bless the LORD!
  O house of Aaron, bless the LORD!
²⁰ O house of Levi, bless the LORD!
  You that fear the LORD, bless the LORD!
²¹ Blessed be the LORD from Zion,
  he who resides in Jerusalem.
  Praise the LORD!

In part, this psalm belongs to the genre of "historical recital" and has much in common with Psalms 78, 105, 106, and 136. As we shall see, however, it is a good bit more complex than those psalms, and is mostly given a coherent, artistic shape. This psalm is formed of five rhetorical units arranged in chiastic fashion:

vv. 1–4   summons to praise and acclamation of YHWH
  vv. 5–12   celebration of YHWH as creator redeemer
    vv. 13–14   affirmation of YHWH's name
  vv. 15–18   dismissal of the idols and their makers
vv. 19–21   summons to bless YHWH

The opening (vv. 1–4) and closing (vv. 19–21) sections make clear that this is a liturgical piece with priests and people engaged in "taking sides" for YHWH and against the idols. The substantive claim for YHWH (vv. 6–12) and the dismissal of the idols (vv. 15–18) constitute the primary "work" of the psalm, work that the worshiping community gladly accomplishes. At the center of the psalm (vv. 13–14), YHWH's name is acknowledged on the basis of the recital in verses 5–12 and in contrast to the idols, who, of course, have no name (vv. 15–18).

The psalm begins, in characteristic hymnic fashion, with a summons to praise supported by a series of reasons for praise. The summons consists of five imperatives – "praise, praise, praise, praise, sing" – with one vocative, "servants of YHWH who stand in the house of the Lord" (vv. 1–4). This vocative would seem, in the first instant, to be addressed to priestly groups, a notion supported by the reference to Aaron and Levi in verses 19–20. But of course the vocative comes to pertain to the entire community of Israel, all of whom are to join in doxological affirmation of YHWH.

The summons is supported in these verses by three reasons, each of which is introduced by "for" (*kî*):

> for YHWH is good;
> for YHWH is gracious;
> for YHWH has chosen Jacob/Israel.

The first two qualities of YHWH, of course affirmed everywhere in Israel, are given substance here. It is YHWH's *commitment to Israel* that constitutes the primary reason for praise. On that basis, it is certain that the summons to praise concerns all Israel, for Israel is to celebrate its own status as the recipient of YHWH's abiding favor. The term "own possession" is rendered *segulah* and looks back to the usage of Exod 19:5. The term refers to the personal, intimate treasure of a monarch who has much wealth but cherishes this special object. The object of praise, of course, is YHWH. Here, however, it is worth noticing that twice (vv. 1, 3) it is YHWH's *name* that is to be praised. As we shall see in verse 13, the name of YHWH here refers to honor, splendor, and majestic power that are rightly YHWH's, to which Israel subscribes and which other gods acknowledge, if not willingly then by default. The God to be praised is the God known everywhere as the powerful sovereign. What a wonder that the cosmic sovereign is peculiarly allied with Israel! Verse 5 begins with a fourth *kî* and could count as a fourth reason for praise. The rhetoric of verse 4 and what follows, however, is so different from what precedes it that we take it as a new rhetorical unit and render *kî* as "surely," as in "surely I know."

Israel is prepared to utter and publicly affirm what it knows most certainly (vv. 5–12). Here and only here in this psalm, there is a first-person singular speaker. This could, perhaps, be a line in a recital assigned to a leading priest; more likely, the "I" is an invitation that every Israelite take responsibility for what follows. This is what "we" all know!

Israel knows, and gladly proclaims, that YHWH is sovereign over all other gods (in a polytheistic world) and therefore can act freely everywhere in creation – in heaven and on earth – as all creation is YHWH's work and YHWH's realm of governance. Thus, verse 6 celebrates the accomplishments of YHWH the creator who governs not only heaven and earth but the chaotic waters beneath the earth as well. Verse 7 features the rainmaker God and echoes the claims of the divine cadences of the whirlwind speeches of Job (see Job 38–41). This is a God who answers to none!

The poetry moves abruptly in verse 8 from the horizon of creation to the particularity of Israel's normative memory. The recital begins by referring to the Exodus (vv. 8–9). It is plausible that the reference to "the sea and all deeps" in verse 6 provides an opening to the Exodus, for the Exodus is made possible because YHWH does indeed command the deeps and "divides the waters." As Terence Fretheim observes, the Exodus event itself is a performance of the powerful creator God.[318] The management of the waters of the Red Sea to bring about Israel's emancipation is evidence of the creator God who manages the chaotic waters. It is worth noting that in the "historical recital" of verses 8–12, YHWH is not once mentioned by name. By portrayal and by perfect verbs, the recital refers back to the initial reference to YHWH in verse 5. We might have expected the reiteration of the divine name here but, in liturgical cadence, YHWH as author and instigator of the great events is unmistakably clear. As YHWH has defeated the gods (v. 5) and the waters (v. 7), so YHWH easily defeats "Pharaoh and all his servants" (v. 9). The capacity of YHWH to govern continues in the narrative of verses 10–11 with reference to Sihon and Og and the initial entry into the land (see Num 21:21–35). The outcome of land entry, echoing verse 4, is that Israel receives the land of promise. This is the culmination of the entire account from creation on. Everything is for this purpose. As Israel is YHWH's treasured possession, so is the land of promise now Israel's great gift and treasure.

The recital of "sacred history" advances no further. Now the hymn breaks out in doxological conclusion (vv. 13–14). YHWH is addressed directly in acclamation. It is "your name" and "your faith" (renown) that stagger Israel with delight. YHWH has accomplished such wonders that they will always be remembered and celebrated. Verse 14, again introduced by "for" (*kî*) as in verses 4 and 12, shows that the wonder of YHWH is the miraculous emergence of Israel. The particularity of this confession is focused and intense, even while the largeness of creation and the governance "in heaven and on earth" are voiced.

Verses 13–14 represent the rhetorical climax of the poetry. It remains now to trace the implications of this affirmation of YHWH, an implication that already surfaced in verse 5. In that verse, there is a dismissive acknowledgment of "other gods." Now, in verses 15–18, the "other gods" are reduced to mere idols, empty

---

318 Terence E. Fretheim, "The Plagues As Ecological Signs of Historical Disaster," *JBL* 110 (1991): 385–396.

objects without life, power, or authority. The unmasking of the idols – no doubt including the would-be gods of the imperial powers – is a daring liturgical act not unlike the daring liturgical act of defying death (see 1 Cor 15:55). The idols are not *powers* but *products*, products of human wealth and human artistic imagination (see the details on production of the gods in Isa 44:8–20). As in the parallel dismissive recital of Ps 115:5–7, the dominant word in this recital is "not" – *not* speak, *not* see, *not* hear, *not* breathe! In every regard, the idols are without power, a total contrast to YHWH, who "does whatever he pleases." These idols do nothing, amount to nothing, and merit no attention and certainly no obedience. They have, moreover, no breath (*ruaḥ*), no capacity for life. Not much is made of that point here, but it may be noted that *ruaḥ* is used in verse 7 to mark the "wind" that YHWH commands; and of course it is the *ruaḥ* of YHWH that creates heaven and earth (Gen 1:2; see vv. 6–7 in this psalm) and the *ruaḥ* as wind that causes the Exodus waters to part (see Exodus 14:21; this psalm vv. 8–9). Thus YHWH is praised because YHWH has a life-giving, life-causing, life-transforming *ruaḥ*; the idols have none! Of course, in verse 18 those who bet on such lifeless objects are fated to lead a failed, futile life.

With the dismissal of the nongods in deference to the true God, the congregation reaches its climactic statement by returning to verses 1–4 (vv. 19–21). Now, instead of praise, the term is "bless," four times. All are called to enhance YHWH – the house of Israel, the house of Aaron, the house of Levi, all who fear YHWH. This fourfold summons is arranged chiastically:

(a) Israel
    (b) priests of Aaron
    (c) priests of Levi
(d) you that fear the Lord.

All praise, priests and people!

The outcome is that, by the end of the liturgy, YHWH is blessed. More than that, YHWH, who resides in Jerusalem, is blessed. The "Jerusalem angle" is quite subdued in this psalm, except that Jerusalem becomes a place where all hopes and fears of Israel are gathered around the creator who gives *ruaḥ* as creator and redeemer. It is no wonder that the symmetry of the fourfold blessing of YHWH that concludes the psalm causes the congregation once more to say "alleluia." That is Israel's last best word, which refers all of life back to its God in dazzled gratitude.

A Closer Look: YHWH's Reputation

The enhancement and protection of YHWH's name (reputation) is the work of doxology that seeks to magnify YHWH; that is, to make YHWH larger and more significant in the eyes of the other nations and the other gods. On this theme, see Exod 14:4, 17; Isa 42:8; 48:9–11; Ezek 36:22–32. Rolf Rendtorff comments on the Ezekiel text:

Here there is almost an echo of something like divine self-criticism, or more precisely: his insight that he cannot punish Israel without causing damage to himself and his name by association. If God wants to stay God, then he must remain God for Israel.[319]

Bridging the Horizons: Restraining Religious Patriotism

The peculiar claim of Israel amid the cosmic claim of creation is characteristic in the Psalter. Kept in perspective, such a "burst of religious patriotism" is not unexpected. Terrien, however, comments on the danger of such patriotism if it is left unrestrained:

When patriotism is founded on the motif of divine election and is not submitted to a religious and ethical judgment like those of the oracles of the great prophets, from Amos to Ezekiel, it quite easily descends into vulgar chauvinism. The universal mission becomes blurred and even nonexistent.[320]

Such a claim of exceptionalism might as well apply to the church, as Terrien has noted. Ours is a time when ethnic and patriotic zeal is enacted with enormous uncritical passion. This temptation to vulgar chauvinism might relate to the church when it becomes "an arrogant sect":

The Christian church became an arrogant sect when it took itself to be the New Israel, uniquely chosen and exclusive of other nations or religions. This hymn to the Creator of all humankind is marred, like other psalms of Zion, when it yields to the temptation of theological imperialism.[321]

And of course the same temptation may be applied to a nation-state. The current form of military aggressiveness on the part of the United States is a case in point; in U.S. civic religion, such adventurism enacted in violence is too readily understood as the action of God's chosen people in the world.

---

[319] Rolf Rendtorff, *The Canonical Hebrew Bible: A Theology of the Old Testament* (Leiden: Deo, 2005), 255.
[320] S. Terrien, *Psalms* (2003), 859.
[321] S. Terrien, *Psalms* (2003), 859.

PSALM 136

¹ O give thanks to the LORD, for he is good,
   for his steadfast love endures for ever.
² O give thanks to the God of gods,
   for his steadfast love endures for ever.
³ O give thanks to the LORD of lords,
      for his steadfast love endures for ever;

⁴ who alone does great wonders,
   for his steadfast love endures for ever;
⁵ who by understanding made the heavens,
   for his steadfast love endures for ever;
⁶ who spread out the earth on the waters,
   for his steadfast love endures for ever;
⁷ who made the great lights,
   for his steadfast love endures for ever;
⁸ the sun to rule over the day,
   for his steadfast love endures for ever;
⁹ the moon and stars to rule over the night,
   for his steadfast love endures for ever;
¹⁰ who struck Egypt through their firstborn,
    for his steadfast love endures for ever;
¹¹ and brought Israel out from among them,
    for his steadfast love endures for ever;
¹² with a strong hand and an outstretched arm,
    for his steadfast love endures for ever;
¹³ who divided the Red Sea in two,
    for his steadfast love endures for ever;
¹⁴ and made Israel pass through the midst of it,
    for his steadfast love endures for ever;
¹⁵ but overthrew Pharaoh and his army in the Red Sea,
    for his steadfast love endures for ever;
¹⁶ who led his people through the wilderness,
    for his steadfast love endures for ever;
¹⁷ who struck down great kings,
    for his steadfast love endures for ever;
¹⁸ and killed famous kings,
    for his steadfast love endures for ever;

¹⁹ Sihon, king of the Amorites,
   for his steadfast love endures for ever;
²⁰ and Og, king of Bashan,
   for his steadfast love endures for ever;
²¹ and gave their land as a heritage,
   for his steadfast love endures for ever;
²² a heritage to his servant Israel,
   for his steadfast love endures for ever.

²³ It is he who remembered us in our low estate,
   for his steadfast love endures for ever;
²⁴ and rescued us from our foes,
   for his steadfast love endures for ever;
²⁵ who gives food to all flesh,
   for his steadfast love endures for ever.

²⁶ O give thanks to the God of heaven,
   for his steadfast love endures for ever.

Psalm 136, twinned in canonical order with Psalm 135, is the purest expression of a song of "historical recital" (see other examples in Psalms 78, 105, and 106).[322] The psalm begins in verses 1–3 with a threefold summons to thank YHWH. There is no vocative, so the addressee is surely *all Israel*, and perhaps, beyond Israel, *all of creation*. In this special summons to gratitude, it is astonishing that the name of YHWH is sounded only once in the first summons and not again, for the doxological formulas "God of gods" and "Lord of lords" are used to refer to YHWH, who presides over all of the gods. This reticence about the divine name, moreover, is matched in the parallel conclusion in verse 26, where the divine name is not used. In the body of the psalm, which refers to YHWH's deed, moreover, the name is not again uttered. Once apparently is enough, for Israel in doxological mode knows full well who to thank.

The second line of each of the initial summonses in verses 1–3 – and subsequently in every verse of the psalm – is an affirmation and celebration of YHWH's abiding covenant loyalty. Thus YHWH is known in Israel as the fully reliable embodiment of fidelity; Israel's readiness to thank is exactly a match for divine *fidelity*. Thus the central dynamic of the YHWH–Israel relationship *is faithfulness* in every circumstance that evokes and requires a life of *gratitude*. In its thanks, Israel, at its best,

---

[322] See Gerhard von Rad, *From Genesis to Chronicles: Explorations in Old Testament Theology* (Minneapolis: Fortress Press, 2005), 7–10.

knows that YHWH's fidelity guarantees an ordered life of well-being that Israel could secure only as a gift.

The body of the psalm placed between the initial summons to *thank* (vv. 1–3) and the concluding summons to *thank* (vv. 26) gives an inventory of reasons for gratitude in Israel. Curiously, the divine name is not attached to any of the powerful verbs of transformation, most of which are given in an infinitive form with the subject understood from verse 1 as YHWH.

The middle body of the inventory divides into three distinct parts. The first part is a celebration of YHWH's wondrous works of creation that make an ordered life possible (vv. 4–9). The theme of the whole is that YHWH alone has done great "wonders," great actions that are inexplicable and impossible except by divine power. Verse 4 as an introduction intends that all that follows should be recognized as miracles, as divine acts that lie beyond human capacity or human comprehension. The characterization of the act of creation follows a conventional sequence of heavens (v. 5), earth (v. 6), and sun and moon that give stability and order to the whole (vv. 7–9). Only in verse 5 is it said that creation is an act of "understanding" (*tebunah*). The presentation of creation as an act of wisdom and understanding (*hocmah* and *tebunah*) is recognized in other doxologies (see Jer 10:12; 51:15). The term "wisdom" used in Jeremiah and the term "understanding" used in the psalm do not go very far toward the famous text of Prov 8:22–31 wherein "wisdom" is a co-agent of creation. The usage nonetheless moves in the same direction to make the claim that the world is wisely ordered for well-being, a claim that in Christian tradition eventuates in the affirmation of *logos* as a mark of creation (Jn 1:1). The notion is at most inchoate here; it is clear nonetheless that creation has an intentionality that is well beyond the exercise of raw divine power.

The whole creation – and each of its parts – is taken, in liturgical response in the second half of each verse, as a show of divine fidelity. The routinization and regularity of creation – in more recent times the grounds for science – is an act of fidelity, a claim reflected in the prophetic oracles of Jer 31:35–36, 37.[323]

The second, larger section of the main body of the psalm provides an inventory of the miracle of Israel's history and clearly follows what became the Pentateuchal narrative (vv. 10–22). Verses 10–15 remember the Exodus and the massive defeat of Pharaoh that made departure from slavery possible. The wilderness sojourn receives only one verse, and is governed by the comprehensive verb "led" with reference to all of the trials of hunger and thirst, dispute, and rebellion reflected in the wilderness narrative (v. 16). As in the Pentateuchal narrative, the wilderness reference in verse 16 (see Exodus 17–18 and Numbers 11–14) functions primarily to connect the Exodus (vv. 10–15; see Exodus 1–15) and the gift of the land (vv. 17–22; see Num 21:21–36 and Joshua 1–12). The conquest of the land, with particular

---

[323] On a theological sense of the regularity of creation as grounds for science, see Alister E. McGrath, *A Scientific Theology: Nature*, vol. 1 (Grand Rapids, MI: Eerdmans, 2001).

reference to Sihon and Og (see Ps 135:11), is credited fully to YHWH, without mention of the leadership of Joshua or the activity of Israel. As is characteristic in such
recitals, these verses exhibit no awkwardness about seizing land from an already
settled population. The conclusion of these verses twice reiterates the term "inheritance," which signifies not only occupation and settlement but proper legitimacy
as well. Thus the routine recital of Israel's past, in agreement with the succinct "cre-
dos," is *out of slavery* and *into land*. The entire act of deliverance and settlement is
accomplished, like creation in verse 4, by YHWH alone. The entire narrative reality,
moreover, is an awesome act of divine fidelity: YHWH has made good on the initial
promise to the slaves (Exod 3:8).

   After the recital of the wonder of creation (vv. 4–9) and saving history (vv. 10–22),
the psalm draws a reflective conclusion while still continuing the same refrain in
the second line (vv. 23–25). In this summary statement, verses 23–24 turn on the
term "save" (*prg*); YHWH remembers – perhaps from the Exodus – that Israel is
characteristically "no people," who depend completely on YHWH. Then finally, in
verse 25, the psalm returns to comment on creation; YHWH has created the world
as a reliable, food-producing system. It is no wonder that the psalm concludes with
one more statement of thanks. What else could be said after a summary of miracles,
each of which attests to complete divine fidelity?

A Closer Look: Praise, Thanks, and the Eucharist

It is quite remarkable that this comprehensive inventory of miracles is designed
in this psalm to evoke *thanks*. In many other psalms, the expected response is one
of praise, a more generic, less focused liturgical act. Harvey Guthrie has demonstrated the way in which thanks is a more elemental impulse than praise.[324]
Guthrie, moreover, traces this elemental praise in Israel to the Christian practice
of the Eucharist.[325] Indeed, the church's "Great Eucharistic Prayer," in cadence
and in substance, is not unlike this psalm.

Bridging the Horizons: Gratitude

George Stroup has nicely articulated the fact that *thanks* – gratitude – is the most
elemental response of faith to the good gifts of God. Stroup concludes:

The old life, turned away from God and neighbor, has passed away. It is no more.
For those who were dead to sin there is now new life before God and before

---

[324] Harvey H. Guthrie, *Theology As Thanksgiving: From Israel's Psalms to the Church's
Eucharist* (New York: Seabury Press, 1981).
[325] H. H. Guthrie, *Theology As Thanksgiving* (1981), 181–216.

neighbor. The "all this" is "from God"; it is God's free gift of God's good will to
sinners. God reconciles not only the world to himself but sinners to one another.
Having received this gift, the church, in gratitude for what has been given to it,
is in turn to give to the world by being reconciled to its neighbors. It is not the
church who reconciles. Ministries of social justice are based not on human good
will, but on human gratitude for God's good will in Jesus Christ.[326]

PSALM 137

¹ By the rivers of Babylon –
  there we sat down and there we wept
  when we remembered Zion.
² On the willows there
  we hung up our harps.
³ For there our captors
  asked us for songs,
  and our tormentors asked for mirth, saying,
   'Sing us one of the songs of Zion!'

⁴ How could we sing the Lord's song
  in a foreign land?
⁵ If I forget you, O Jerusalem,
  let my right hand wither!
⁶ Let my tongue cling to the roof of my mouth,
  if I do not remember you,
  if I do not set Jerusalem
  above my highest joy.

⁷ Remember, O Lord, against the Edomites
  the day of Jerusalem's fall,
  how they said, 'Tear it down! Tear it down!
  Down to its foundations!'
⁸ O daughter Babylon, you devastator!
  Happy shall they be who pay you back
  what you have done to us!

[326] G. W. Stroup, *Before God* (2004), 172.

⁹ Happy shall they be who take your little ones
   and dash them against the rock!

This unusual but finely honed text is a psalm packed with emotional freight and is often familiar to contemporary readers both because of its stunning beginning and its troubling ending. The psalm is distinct in questions of genre. It is commonly associated with community psalms of lament tied to the exile, but its structure does not follow typical patterns. It is strongly associated with Zion and so is sometimes considered along with the Songs of Zion. Perhaps it is helpful to read the text as a Song of Zion cast in terms of community lament over the loss of Zion, both Jerusalem and temple, and thus a setting in which no Songs of Zion can be sung. The memory of Zion comes to the fore in this gripping and raw expression of grief. *The sociohistorical setting of the psalm is ancient Israel's trauma of exile in Babylon.* The opening of the psalm brings that setting to the imagination; that vivid memory has caused Kraus to suggest that Psalm 137 is the only reliably dated psalm.[327] Still, with its typical open-ended poetic language, it is difficult to be very precise about the psalm's date or setting. It could reflect some kind of cultic setting or gatherings of the exiled community by the river in Babylon, or an even later memory of the trauma of exile in its aftermath.

English translations of Psalm 137 often suggest reading the psalm in three units of three verses each. The psalm likely consists of three units, but verse 4 goes with the opening unit, as suggested by Shimon Bar-Efrat.[328] The poetic voice in the first four verses is in the first-person plural and moves to the singular in verses 5–6. The psalm's final three verses constitute a new unit beginning with an imperative. Each unit concludes with a prepositional phrase.

A Closer Look: Literary Context

With a focus on Jerusalem, Psalm 137 echoes themes in the Songs of Ascents (Psalms 120–134), themes present in Psalms 135–137 that are without superscriptions. Books IV (Psalms 90–106) and V (Psalms 107–150) relate to the crisis of exile, and that setting is clearly present in the grief expressed in Psalm 137. The next collection of psalms, a collection of Davidic psalms (Psalms 138–145), also focuses on lament. There are particular connections with Ps 138:2, 5, and 7 with reference to the temple, singing, and enemies. Psalm 137 is an unusual text, but it fits in its current literary context.

---

[327] H.-J. Kraus, *Psalms 60–150* (1988), 501.
[328] Shimon Bar-Efrat, "Love of Zion: A Literary Interpretation of Psalm 137," in Mordechai Cogan, Barry L. Eichler, and Jeffrey H. Tigay (eds.), *Tehillah le-Mosha: Biblical and Judaic Studies in Honor of Moshe Greenberg* (Winona Lake, IN: Eisenbrauns, 1997), 3–11.

Verses 1–4. The psalm opens with an intense scene of grief tied to the trauma of exile in Babylon in the sixth century BCE. The setting is beside the canals between the Tigris and Euphrates in Babylon, but that memory yields quickly to the pressing memory of defeated Zion. This memory is not one that brings rejoicing with harps and songs but rather painful grief. The Babylonian captors intensify the grief with their mocking and taunting of this completely defeated enemy: "We want to hear you sing one of your famous songs of Zion now while you are defeated captives in this land of exile." There can now be no songs of Zion, but memory is a powerful capacity and actually brings to mind for this grieving community the worship of Zion in all its beauty and strength. Many of the psalms reflect this gracious and refreshing worship. For the exilic community, however, this mocking is not only a mocking of Israel; it is also a mocking of a defeated YHWH. The psalms also pose such a question from enemy nations: Where is their God now? (See Ps 115:2.) This community in an alien place expresses grief with a rhetorical question: How could we sing any of YHWH's songs in a foreign and idolatrous place? This opening unit glistens with the grief of laments and would lead one to expect further laments.

Verses 5–6. The theme of memory has taken the stage, however, and what follows is an oath of self-imprecation. McCann has noted a chiastic structure in these verses:

A – If (*'im*) I forget you, Jerusalem,
B – let my right hand wither!
B' – Let my tongue cling to the roof of my mouth
A' – if (*'im*) I do not remember you.[329]

The pledge is that forgetting Jerusalem might bring a withered right hand and a tongue clinging to the roof of the mouth. The hand would no longer be able to play the harp and the tongue no longer be able to sing the Songs of Zion. The memory is more precious than body or life. The psalm's stunning intention is that, in spite of the fact that the temple has been left in ruins and Jerusalem destroyed, the victorious captors will not control the memory and imagination of this community of exiles. Memory is a powerful weapon and can be sustained over the long haul and fuel resilience. So memory here might lead to hope tied to Zion. The taunting of the captors and the grieving memory of Zion might lead to something more.

Verses 7–9. The psalm's concluding unit begins with an address to YHWH pleading that YHWH will remember Edom's collaboration in the destruction of Jerusalem. The quotation serves to demonstrate Edomite cruelty when the city was defeated; see Obadiah 10–14 and Ezekiel 35 for the tradition of Edomite collusion in the routing of Jerusalem and killing of its inhabitants. Verse 8

---

[329] J. C. McCann, Jr., "Book of Psalms," in L. E. Keck et al. (eds.), *The New Interpreter's Bible*, vol. 4 (1996), 1227.

then addresses Babylon with an unusual example of a beatitude; the hope is that Babylon will encounter the "blessing" of the law of retaliation. Israel here engages in an act of hope for divine justice with blessing on those who do unto Babylon what Babylon has done to Jerusalem. The concluding verse reflects the warfare of that cultural setting and the practice of destroying the next generation of warriors. See 2 Kgs 8:12; Hos 10:14; 13:16; Na 3:10; and Isa 13:16 for references to the practice. The brutally honest conclusion of the psalm expresses an unrestrained faith in the justice of King YHWH.

The psalm moves from an intense expression of grief and silence through a determined vow of memory to this frightening blessing of cruel hopes against Babylon. The intense concluding section features three imperatives in verse 7, beginning with the address to YHWH, and calls for YHWH to remember the terrible injustices of Edom and Babylon and bring about a terrible justice on them. The psalm is an arresting example of a structure of intensification; it ends with a scalding beatitude. Psalm 137 steadfastly refuses to sing songs of Zion but laments instead. Still, the lamenters remember the songs of Zion and in that sense bring them to life. "The memory, the pledge to remember, and the call for God to remember in effect already actualize the remembrance. The anti-song of Zion makes possible the song of Zion."[330] Robert Alter notes:

The Psalms are of course poems written out of deep and often passionate faith. What I am proposing is that the poetic medium made it possible to articulate the emotional freight, the moral consequences, the altered perception of the world that flowed from this monotheistic belief, in compact verbal structures that could in some instances seem simplicity itself.[331]

A Closer Look: An Alternate Response

The conclusion of Psalm 137 is shocking for many contemporary readers. Often responses move in two very different directions. Some suggest that the blessing on vengeance is so abhorrent that it should not be considered as part of the revelation of Scripture. Others would find quick support for acting in vengeance on their enemies. Neither of those perspectives appreciates the full sense of the psalm. Certainly the social context of the origin of the psalm makes the text intelligible. Beyond that basic note, those who would read and pray the Psalms could consider a variety of angles of vision on Psalm 137:

1. The poetic voice of Psalm 137 is that of powerless exiles. They have encountered an immense defeat in which Zion, the center of life, has been left in

---

[330] William H. Bellinger, Jr., "Psalm 137: Memory and Poetry," *HBT* 27 (2005): 16.
[331] R. Alter, *Art of Biblical Poetry* (1985), 113.

ruins. They now have no place for worship, no place to effect atonement, and no leader to bring justice. Chaos has overwhelmed the order of creation. What is left is the raw wound of grief, and this psalm artfully and brutally brings the grief and hostility to expression. Those expressions seem to be necessary to make possible any move to hope. Psalm 137 voices the faithful anger of exiles as a base from which hope could emerge.

2. The context of war stands behind the psalm's ruthless hopes. The "little ones" (v. 9) are the future of an oppressive empire. Part of the hope at the end of the psalm is that the oppressive injustice of that empire will not see a future but will end.

3. The psalm constitutes a bold act of faith as it publicly claims pain and "takes it to the Lord." The brutally honest cry for vengeance in the midst of immense loss is then given over to the judge of all things. That becomes an act of hope in YHWH. The capacity to hand the issue to the creator and redeemer leaves space for memory and hope.[332]

The psalm's focus on memory comes in the remembered setting, the oath to remember, and the imperative call for YHWH to remember the injustice done to the community. The artful and powerful articulation of memory makes it possible for the hopes of Zion to endure. Fundamental to the poetic piece is the irony that singing of Zion is impossible and yet the psalm is in no way mute; it assures a future for Zion and its songs and so functions to nurture hope. One might say that this intense poem will not allow its readers and hearers to forget; its words bring Zion to life in memory, and it vows to remember and pleads with YHWH to remember the injustice done to Zion. The context of memory provides a path to read the psalm in terms of faith and hope. Its grief moves to anger, and the faithful act of anger from exiles may make it possible for the faith of those exiled from Zion to endure into the future.

PSALM 138 – OF DAVID

[1] I give you thanks, O Lord, with my whole heart;
before the gods I sing your praise;
[2] I bow down toward your holy temple
and give thanks to your name for your steadfast love and your faithfulness;
for you have exalted your name and your word

---

[332] See E. Zenger, *God of Vengeance?* (1996), 47–50.

above everything.
³ On the day I called, you answered me,
  you increased my strength of soul.

⁴ All the kings of the earth shall praise you, O Lᴏʀᴅ,
  for they have heard the words of your mouth.
⁵ They shall sing of the ways of the Lᴏʀᴅ,
  for great is the glory of the Lᴏʀᴅ.
⁶ For though the Lᴏʀᴅ is high, he regards the lowly;
  but the haughty he perceives from far away.

⁷ Though I walk in the midst of trouble,
  you preserve me against the wrath of my enemies;
you stretch out your hand,
  and your right hand delivers me.
⁸ The Lᴏʀᴅ will fulfil his purpose for me;
  your steadfast love, O Lᴏʀᴅ, endures for ever.
  Do not forsake the work of your hands.

"Psalm of thanksgiving" is the category most commentators choose in interpreting Psalm 138. The speaker prayed to God in the midst of crisis and now, having been delivered, sings in the sanctuary this song of thanksgiving to fulfill a vow made during the crisis. Some have taken the speaker to be the king, but the more common view is that the psalm reflects the aftermath of exile, with some ties to the prophecies of Isaiah 40–55. Verse 3 suggests that the speaker has been delivered, so this approach to the psalm finds support, though the conclusion of the psalm suggests that the crisis is not only in the past. Thanksgiving and petition in worship are the primary themes of the psalm; it echoes many other texts in the Psalter, especially in the first parts of the book. The psalm is an artful composition, especially calling on repetition and variation. "Your steadfast love" appears in the center of the first unit (vv. 1–3) and in the concluding verse. The psalm's concluding unit (vv. 7–8) echoes verse 3 and the account of the crisis there, giving a frame to the poem. The verb for giving thanks and the term "all" in the first unit are repeated in the second unit (vv. 4–6). The characteristic psalmic pattern of praise followed by a reason with the particle *kî* ("for, because") structures the psalm's middle unit, however, with the particle occurring three times; the divine name YHWH also occurs four times in those verses.

A Closer Look: Important Connections

The superscription simply indicates that Psalm 138 is a Davidic psalm. McCann has suggested that the text provides a transition between the Songs of Ascents

(Psalms 120–134) and its appendix (Psalms 135–137) and the Davidic collection (Psalms 138–145) that concludes Book V of the Psalter.[333] Singing of the ways of YHWH (v. 5), the temple (v. 2), and enemies (v. 7) suggests connections to Psalm 137. The psalm also exhibits connections to Psalms 135–136. The speaker begins by giving thanks to YHWH in line with the invitation at the beginning and end of Psalm 136. The refrain there emphasizes the divine "steadfast love," a theme in Ps 138:2, 8. The gods in verse 2 relate to Pss 135:5 and 136:2–3; YHWH's name in verse 2 relates to Ps 135:1, 3; and YHWH's greatness in verse 5 relates to Ps 135:5.

Psalms 138–145 form the final Davidic collection in the Psalter and begin to move toward a conclusion by summarizing the book's faith. Psalm 138 provides something of a summary of the thanksgiving in the book of Psalms; see Psalm 30 for a particularly clear example. The composition asks the community of hearers/readers to remember and experience again the steadfast love and trust-worthiness of YHWH as seen in the book of Psalms. YHWH is the living and acting God who comes to deliver, and so the community is called to rehearse the narrative of liberation for all to hear and see. The psalm confesses the faith of thanksgiving in this summary fashion, though it is clear that the confession still comes in a world filled with trouble and woe. Opposition to YHWH and those who worship YHWH is ever present but so are praise and thanksgiving in this worshiping community, for YHWH continues to hear their cries.

Verses 1–3. Giving thanks, singing praise, and bowing in worship are charac-teristic verbs of thanksgiving in the Psalter and Israel's cult, and are the focus of the beginning of Psalm 138. The substance of thanksgiving is the narration of a crisis, petition, and deliverance from YHWH. Verse 3 articulates the narrative in summary fashion. In the midst of trouble, the speaker cried out to YHWH and YHWH delivered so that the life of the speaker was emboldened or exalted with strength or refuge. That seems to be the sense of the conclusion of verse 3, though the text is difficult. The text at the end of verse 2 is also obscure. Still, the import of the psalm's first unit is clearly about YHWH's liberation from crisis; the words make up the testimony of the speaker. With "my whole heart" – the entirety of the speaker's intelligence and intention – the thanksgiving is voiced, and it comes in response to the divine steadfast love and faithfulness, a charac-teristic word pair in the Psalms. YHWH has again demonstrated that crisis does not diminish the divine commitment or trustworthiness. Verses 1–3 use the rich vocabulary of Israel's faith and worship; singing and praying, bowing, and giving thanks are all central acts at the place of the divine presence, the "holy temple." The pattern of a prayer for help followed by praise and thanksgiving pervades

---

[333] J. C. McCann, Jr., "Book of Psalms," in L. E. Keck et al. (eds.), *The New Interpreter's Bible*, vol. 4 (1996), 1231.

the Psalter and Israel's worship. Psalm 138 provides a kind of guide to the practice and significance of thanksgiving at the heart of temple worship.

Verses 4–6. The discussion of the first part of the psalm focused on the worship setting in Israel's tradition, but the psalm's first verse interestingly indicates that the praise is "before the gods." The term is *ĕlōhîm*, and so could be rendered "God," but the standard divine title in Psalm 138 is YHWH. With the reference to "all the kings of the earth" in verse 4, most interpreters take verse 1 to refer to the gods. Israel's thanksgiving becomes a witness of YHWH's deliverance before the gods and kings, and their nations. Kraus takes this perspective to reflect influence from the expansive message of Isaiah 40–55.[334] The middle unit of the psalm confesses that the kings of the nations will join in the thanksgiving to YHWH because they have heard the divine word and because they have seen the greatness of YHWH's glory. They have seen that YHWH is present and active in the world. It is a striking poetic affirmation of faith that the leaders of other nations will sing of the ways of YHWH. Readers may remember that in the preceding psalm even Israel cannot sing "the Lord's song" in another land. Liberation from crisis has a stunning effect on worship. YHWH, who is above all, comes down to those who are lowly and troubled and raises them up to new life – in contrast to the arrogant (v. 6), who will not publicly claim their pain and seek divine help. In a sense, Psalm 138 is a simple summary of Israel's faith, but it is still powerful, because it reflects faith in a world with chaos knocking at the door, likely in the aftermath of exile.

Verses 7–8. Enemies pervade the Psalter, and Psalm 138 is no exception. The crisis does not appear to be past. The divine hand/right hand is the means of rescue from trouble, and verse 7 is a confession of trust in YHWH as the one who delivers. The language of these concluding verses brings to mind the other laments and thanksgiving psalms. The psalm concludes with the hope that YHWH will continue to bring renewal in loyal love. The psalm's penultimate line echoes the refrain of Psalm 136. The community can trust that YHWH will bring hope out of crisis and thereby make thanksgiving and faith possible. The hope is that YHWH will continue to demonstrate this steadfast love in the life of this community. The conclusion of the psalm suggests that chaos persists. The congregation sings with a voice of thanksgiving and with a voice of petition. Trouble never disappears, but neither does YHWH. The divine right hand of deliverance continues to reach out to those in crisis and anxiety.

The praise and thanksgiving brought to poetic expression in the Psalms moves in a variety of directions. It responds to the God who embraces pain and so calls Israel to worship. It also testifies to the divine engagement with the world and in

---

[334] H.-J. Kraus, *Psalms 60–150* (1988), 506. See L. C. Allen, *Psalms 101–150* (2002), 313–314; and J. L. Mays, *Psalms* (1994), 424.

so doing bears witness to those beyond the congregation of Israel. The references
to gods and kings in Psalm 138 are noteworthy; the psalm includes a universal
dimension. The confession of thanksgiving in this psalm anticipates the conclusion of the Psalter's song of faith.

PSALM 139 – TO THE LEADER. OF DAVID. A PSALM

¹ O Lord, you have searched me and known me.
² You know when I sit down and when I rise up;
   you discern my thoughts from far away.
³ You search out my path and my lying down,
   and are acquainted with all my ways.
⁴ Even before a word is on my tongue,
   O Lord, you know it completely.
⁵ You hem me in, behind and before,
   and lay your hand upon me.
⁶ Such knowledge is too wonderful for me;
   it is so high that I cannot attain it.

⁷ Where can I go from your spirit?
   Or where can I flee from your presence?
⁸ If I ascend to heaven, you are there;
   if I make my bed in Sheol, you are there.
⁹ If I take the wings of the morning
   and settle at the farthest limits of the sea,
¹⁰ even there your hand shall lead me,
    and your right hand shall hold me fast.
¹¹ If I say, 'Surely the darkness shall cover me,
    and the light around me become night',
¹² even the darkness is not dark to you;
    the night is as bright as the day,
    for darkness is as light to you.

¹³ For it was you who formed my inward parts;
    you knit me together in my mother's womb.
¹⁴ I praise you, for I am fearfully and wonderfully made.
    Wonderful are your works;

that I know very well.
¹⁵ My frame was not hidden from you,
    when I was being made in secret,
    intricately woven in the depths of the earth.
¹⁶ Your eyes beheld my unformed substance.
    In your book were written
    all the days that were formed for me,
    when none of them as yet existed.
¹⁷ How weighty to me are your thoughts, O God!
    How vast is the sum of them!
¹⁸ I try to count them – they are more than the sand;
    I come to the end – I am still with you.

¹⁹ O that you would kill the wicked, O God,
    and that the bloodthirsty would depart from me –
²⁰ those who speak of you maliciously,
    and lift themselves up against you for evil!
²¹ Do I not hate those who hate you, O LORD?
    And do I not loathe those who rise up against you?
²² I hate them with perfect hatred;
    I count them my enemies.
²³ Search me, O God, and know my heart;
    test me and know my thoughts.
²⁴ See if there is any wicked way in me,
    and lead me in the way everlasting.

The dilemma for readers of Psalm 139 is how to connect the often-quoted beautiful poetic imagery of verses 1–18 with the shocking petition against enemies in verses 19–22. The difficulty is reflected in the attempts of form critics to delineate the psalm's type. Verses 1–18 exhibit a number of hymnic features, if in a meditative tone, in praise of the creator, who is ever present, and do so with poetic language that soars. The psalm's concluding unit (vv. 19–24) shifts to a petition, including strong imprecations against enemies. Allen suggests that false accusation is in the background, and so he takes the psalm as an expression of innocence: "an individual complaint in a developed form, prefaced by a long passage praising divine attributes which the sufferer finds relevant to his situation."[335] Most likely the setting reflected

335 L. C. Allen, *Psalms 101–150* (2002), 324, 330. H.-J. Kraus, *Psalms 60–150* (1988), 513, also understands murderous persecution by the wicked to be in the background of the psalm. C. C. Broyles, *Psalms* (1999), 484, interprets the text in terms of qualifications to enter the sanctuary, which include passing judgment on the wicked.

in the psalm's concluding unit has to do with false accusation, and the petitioner has come to the sanctuary to protest innocence and pray for help from the God who knows, sees, and examines. Verses 1–18 set the context for the petition.

The poem makes clear that YHWH stands as the judge of all creation. The psalm's concluding petition that YHWH "search me" and "test me" affirms that YHWH is the divine judge who brings justice. McCann has seen that the key root word in the psalm is "know" (vv. 1, 2, 4, 6, 14, 23).[336] YHWH's knowing runs through verses 1–18 and undergirds verses 19–24. Because YHWH knows the speaker completely and knows the enemies, the psalm concludes with the petition that YHWH bring justice in the midst of this crisis. Verses 1–18 are crafted with stunning poetic skill and soar with the reality of divine knowledge; verses 23–24 fit well with the style of the first parts of the psalm. Verses 19–22, however, bring readers back down to earth with the urgent petition for divine justice based on the divine knowledge the psalm praises. The judge of all the earth is the one who sees all of creation, who wills fullness of life and faith for the worshiping community, and who sees the oppressive opponents of that community. Psalm 139 then seeks justice from the divine judge. The exposition here will follow this interpretive path. Still, a comment by James Mays provides a wise proviso: "The psalm is a spiritual achievement that transcends the limits and functions of the usual types."[337]

Psalm 139 is part of the Psalter's final collection of Davidic psalms. Its place in Book V of the Psalter suggests a connection to the aftermath of exile. Although the psalm is rather different from Psalm 138, both texts focus on YHWH as present and trustworthy and attend to those who opposed the worshiping community. The fact that evil oppressors appear in Psalm 139 along with its stunning poetic portrayal of the divine presence reminds readers again that the actions of the wicked pervade the whole of the book of Psalms. Still, it is YHWH who judges all the earth.

The psalm's opening confession of faith (v. 1) is reflected in its concluding petition (v. 23). Verses 1–18 consist of three units: YHWH's searching the petitioner, being present to the speaker, and creating the speaker. Verses 17–18 bring this part of the psalm to a conclusion in summarizing fashion. Verses 19–24 come to the pressing matter of enemies and pray both for the destruction of these enemies and that God will search the speaker's "heart." Our consideration of the psalm will now look at each unit of the text with attention to its powerful poetic style.

Verses 1–6. The psalm's first poetic unit expands its opening affirmation: "YHWH, you have searched me and known me." The next group of verses enjoy that confession with remarkable poetic imagery. God knows the entire life of the speaker: sitting down, rising up, thinking, lying down, walking, and speaking. God examines and knows the speaker completely. The imagery is captivating and suggests that divine knowledge of this person is far beyond any human knowledge. It also

---

[336] J. C. McCann, Jr., "Book of Psalms," in L. E. Keck et al. (eds.), *The New Interpreter's Bible*, vol. 4 (1996), 1235.
[337] J. L. Mays, *Psalms* (1994), 427.

suggests that this person is very much the subject of YHWH's attention. Divine probing and knowing, actions attributed to the judge of all the earth, are central to these first verses. First- and second-person pronouns dominate these verses, suggesting that the relationship between YHWH and the speaker – the I–Thou relationship – is the central focus. The unit concludes with an inspiring affirmation of the place of humans as YHWH's creations, but that affirmation stands in some tension with other affirmations of human knowledge in the psalm, especially the kind of certainty about enemies articulated in the psalm's final unit.

Verses 7–12. Verse 7 articulates the focus of the second poetic unit in the form of a double question: the poetic "I" cannot escape the presence of YHWH. The imagery creatively affirms that YHWH is ever present as a guide in all places. YHWH is present in heaven above and in Sheol below, and even in "the farthest limits of the sea." The divine presence is more encompassing than the speaker can imagine; the poetic imagery is remarkable. The affirmation of the divine presence in Sheol, the place of the dead or the underworld, is most unusual. Most psalms portray Sheol as a place of divine absence. The poetic images do not stand as flat, literal propositions of doctrine but as poetic figures to affirm divine presence in the farthest heights and depths. Verses 11–12 suggest that, even when the speaker is surrounded by darkness, YHWH will see and be present to this one, for YHWH sees light even in the midst of darkness. As judge of all the earth, YHWH sees all.

Verses 13–18. The psalm has affirmed that YHWH is ever present. Verse 13 begins this poetic unit by affirming that YHWH was present at the beginning of the speaker's life. YHWH created this worshiper and from the beginning formed all the parts of the human body, so from the beginning YHWH has known this person who is "fearfully and wonderfully made." The life of the petitioner is written in the divine book of life, and every human day finds its significance in living in the ways of that book. Verses 17–18 bring the unit to a conclusion with the exclamation that YHWH's thoughts are beyond comprehension. God is indeed transcendent and yet still present. There is a tension in the psalm's poetry. These verses suggest that knowledge of YHWH is beyond comprehension, but the psalm is a portrayal of the divine engagement with this person of faith and of the divine ways in the world. The speaker possesses some knowledge of YHWH. The psalm's concluding unit consists of an urgent plea for YHWH to act in a certain way.

Verses 19–24. In a pattern that seems to fit much of Psalm 139, the first verse of the poetic unit speaks the petition expanded in the following verses. The prayer is an urgent plea that YHWH defeat the enemies and remove their injustice from the petitioner's world. The enemies are characterized as "bloodthirsty." They seek the lives of the faithful and speak maliciously of YHWH. Perhaps they also speak maliciously of the petitioner and thus are false accusers of some sort. In the context of the close I–Thou relationship so powerfully expressed in this psalm, the petitioner urges YHWH to make an end of these evil ones. They loathe YHWH and the faithful of the worshiping community, so the speaker confesses as an act of trust to hating and loathing these enemies of God and the faithful. The confession of trust in verse 22 takes the poetry to the shocking height of hating these enemies with a "perfect hatred." Perhaps "perfect" carries the sense of a full or complete hatred. The psalm's concluding words of petition echo the confession at the beginning of the poem and hope that YHWH will search and probe, and know the petitioner's intentions and inner thoughts. The petitioner hopes that YHWH will see that this faithful one is not among the evil ones who oppose God and will lead the speaker in the ways of faith. This concluding poetic unit also displays some tension in that the petitioner already knows who the evil ones are and hates them. No uncertainty is expressed about YHWH as the judge of all the earth, of the speaker's place in the community of faith, or the just action for YHWH to undertake. YHWH is the judge of all the earth. Still, the petitioner begs YHWH to "search me."

A Closer Look: Seek God's Order

The psalm articulates a kind of tension in that the speaker knows a lot, but the central confession of the text is that YHWH knows the speaker completely. The poem confesses a lot about YHWH and about the enemies, and the speaker stands confidently before YHWH as creator and judge of all the earth. The difficulty for readers is that the petition in verses 19–22 can be pressed to the extreme if not put in the context of the whole poem. Psalm 139 and the book of Psalms recognize the pervasive and destructive presence of evil in the world and oppose it clearly. This psalm and the Psalter also confess that there is only one judge of all the earth, and that judge is not a human being. A person's relationship to evil and injustice then becomes a matter of honest searching before the one divine judge in the context of the faith community. One's personal enemies are not simply counted as also enemies of God. The issue of unjust persons is to be navigated in the context of the I–Thou relationship with the divine judge who finally decides and to whom vengeance belongs. Perhaps the Hebrew wisdom tradition provides a helpful way to consider Psalm 139. God created the world and life, and placed order in it, and God continues to sustain and govern that order. The task of humans is to seek and find that order and live into it. YHWH is the creator and judge who knows humans and the one who grants judgment and mercy.

PSALM 140 – TO THE LEADER. A PSALM OF DAVID

¹ Deliver me, O Lᴏʀᴅ, from evildoers;
   protect me from those who are violent,
² who plan evil things in their minds

and stir up wars continually.
³ They make their tongue sharp as a snake's,
and under their lips is the venom of vipers.
    Selah

⁴ Guard me, O LORD, from the hands of the wicked;
protect me from the violent
who have planned my downfall.
⁵ The arrogant have hidden a trap for me,
and with cords they have spread a net;
along the road they have set snares for me.
    Selah

⁶ I say to the LORD, 'You are my God;
give ear, O LORD, to the voice of my supplications.'
⁷ O LORD, my Lord, my strong deliverer,
you have covered my head in the day of battle.
⁸ Do not grant, O LORD, the desires of the wicked;
do not further their evil plot.
    Selah

⁹ Those who surround me lift up their heads;
let the mischief of their lips overwhelm them!
¹⁰ Let burning coals fall on them!
Let them be flung into pits, no more to rise!
¹¹ Do not let the slanderer be established in the land;
let evil speedily hunt down the violent!
¹² I know that the LORD maintains the cause of the needy,
and executes justice for the poor.
¹³ Surely the righteous shall give thanks to your name;
the upright shall live in your presence.

Psalm 140 is an individual lament in which a faithful worshiper lodges a complaint in the sanctuary about false accusers. The standard lament elements are present: address to YHWH, portrayal of a crisis, petition, and a hopeful conclusion. The poetry is designed with repetition. McCann has noted that the terms "evil," "violent," "lips," and "wicked" in verses 1–4 are repeated in verses 8–11 in reverse order.[338]

---

[338] J. C. McCann, Jr., "Book of Psalms," in L. E. Keck et al. (eds.), *The New Interpreter's Bible*, vol. 4 (1996), 1239–1240.

The emphasis of the psalm is enemies in the context of petition. The first (vv. 1–5) and third (vv. 8–11) poetic units focus on the enemies with petitions for protection and deliverance. Those sections frame verses 6–7, which attend to the relationship between YHWH and the worshiper in the context of trust. The psalm's concluding unit (vv. 12–13) brings the text to a hopeful end. Psalm 140 is reminiscent of earlier laments in the Psalter, especially Psalms 57, 58, and 64, which also focus on enemies. The psalm is yet another reminder for readers of the Psalter that opposition to the divine purpose persists in life and that the psalmic movement of faith from crisis to hope persists even more.

Petition to YHWH in the face of opposition from enemies is the theme that concludes Psalm 139; it continues in Psalm 140. The poem expands the petition in Ps 139:19–22 but ends in the kind of hope articulated in the first parts of Psalm 139. Psalm 140 also initiates a series of classic lament psalms in the final collection of Davidic psalms (Psalms 138–145). The background appears to be a community facing the aftermath of exile. The collection begins with thanksgiving in Psalm 138 and concludes with praise in Psalm 145, providing a framework for the laments.

The psalm's opening poetic unit (vv. 1–5) begins directly with a petition to YHWH for deliverance and protection from enemies who are characterized as violent warmongers who do nothing but craft premeditated acts of oppression. Their speech is a weapon of violence compared to "the venom of vipers." The plea is for protection from the power ("hands of the wicked") of these malicious enemies who seek the demise of the petitioner. The unrelenting portrayal of the enemies in the context of petition continues in verse 5 with the use of hunting imagery. The comparison is to the ancient method of trapping an animal by way of a trap with a hidden net. The hunting imagery is employed in a number of psalms as a portrayal of plots against faithful worshipers. The imagery in this case reflects malicious accusations seeking to bring down the petitioner.

The context of petition continues in the psalm's second poetic unit (vv. 6–7) but with a focus on the relationship between YHWH and the petitioner. Verse 6 is a quotation of a petition from the speaker that YHWH will hear prayers for help. The quotation begins with the confession "You are my God" and thereby puts the I–Thou relationship at the center of attention. Verse 7 continues with the confession that YHWH is both my Lord and my strong deliverer; the personal pronouns emphasize the relationship. This unit of the psalm emphasizes faith and trust in the covenant God YHWH, who comes to deliver. Out of such confessions of faith come petitions in the midst of trouble and conflict. Psalm 140 is a call for God to demonstrate fidelity to the covenant promises. The covering of the head in battle in the conclusion of verse 7 is an image of protection in the face of violent opponents.

Verses 8–11 return to the key words from the first verses of the psalm, though in reverse order: "wicked," "lips," "evil," and "violent." The petition is similar to that at the beginning of the psalm, though put in the negative. Enemies continue to plot against the petitioner; this plot is the consuming desire of their lives. The hope of the faithful worshiper is that YHWH will thwart these conspiracies. Verse 9 moves the portrayal of the enemies to those who lift up their heads; they arrogantly presume that they will defeat the petitioner and enjoy victory. The remainder of the unit employs standard language of retribution. The plea is that the malicious words of the enemies will come back on them, that their evil will rebound on them and defeat them. The imagery continues in verse 10 with the hope that fiery coals will fall on the enemies and that they will fall into pits never to be seen again. The latter image may reflect the hope that the enemies will go down to Sheol, the realm of the dead. This powerful poetic imagery reflects the standard petitions for retribution in the Psalter. Hunting imagery reappears in verse 11 with the petition that a personified evil will hunt down the enemies and trap them so that their evil desires and acts will rebound on their heads. The urgent petition is that retributive justice will come and expose the false accusers and defeat them.

The psalm's concluding unit, verses 12–13, provides the characteristic hopeful conclusion to a lament psalm with an expression of certainty that YHWH hears and embraces the pain of the petitioner and comes with hope. Verse 12 confesses a central faith tenet for the psalmists – YHWH brings justice for those in need. God maintains a just order for the poor and needy, and that order is reflected in the retributive justice given to the wicked and in protection given to the falsely accused petitioner. The psalm concludes with a vow of praise and thanksgiving to this God who delivers. Those who "live in your presence" participate in worship that renews life and faith and live out that faith in the rest of their life. It is the "righteous" and the "upright" – those who work at a faithful relationship with YHWH demonstrated in just human relationships – who embrace this concluding word of hope for the congregation.

A Closer Look: Covenant Faith

Psalm 140 is a striking example of the covenant theology confessed in the Psalter. The psalm is the prayer of a faithful worshiper portrayed as persecuted and in need of the benefits of the covenant promise that YHWH is the God who comes to deliver. The Hebrew scriptures' covenant traditions characterize YHWH as the one who hears and embraces pain and intervenes on behalf of the righteous. The righteous are those who live in fidelity to the covenant relationship YHWH initiated. The petitioner in Psalm 140 stands in a crisis perpetrated by unrelenting scoundrels and thus turns to the trustworthy covenant God for help. The issue for the petitioner is justice promised in covenant faith and confessed in verse 12. That justice is now nowhere in sight, so the petition is for the judge of all the earth to "make it so." That juxtaposition of the received covenant faith tradition and the crisis of persecution at hand is the conflict that drives Psalm 140 and its petition. The confession of faith that YHWH brings justice stands in opposition to the current experience of the worshiper. The poem makes it unmistakable that evil and opposition to justice and faith pervade all of life; that perspective runs through the Psalter. The expression of that evil in Psalm 140 comes in the words and accusations of the enemies. At the same time, the psalm makes it clear that YHWH is the one who embraces pain and brings justice. The psalm's urging is that YHWH will do exactly that – establish justice and bring hope to the oppressed.

PSALM 141 – A PSALM OF DAVID

¹ I call upon you, O LORD; come quickly to me;
  give ear to my voice when I call to you.
² Let my prayer be counted as incense before you,
   and the lifting up of my hands as an evening sacrifice.

³ Set a guard over my mouth, O LORD;
  keep watch over the door of my lips.
⁴ Do not turn my heart to any evil,
  to busy myself with wicked deeds
  in company with those who work iniquity;
   do not let me eat of their delicacies.

⁵ Let the righteous strike me;
  let the faithful correct me.
  Never let the oil of the wicked anoint my head,
  for my prayer is continually against their wicked deeds.
⁶ When they are given over to those who shall condemn them,
  then they shall learn that my words were pleasant.
⁷ Like a rock that one breaks apart and shatters on the land,
   so shall their bones be strewn at the mouth of Sheol.

⁸ But my eyes are turned toward you, O God, my LORD;
  in you I seek refuge; do not leave me defenseless.
⁹ Keep me from the trap that they have laid for me,
  and from the snares of evildoers.
¹⁰ Let the wicked fall into their own nets,
   while I alone escape.

Psalms 140–143, individual lament psalms, are at the heart of the final Davidic collection (Psalms 138–145) in the Psalter. Psalm 141 is a petition from a worshiper but exhibits a more reflective tone and thus a wisdom dimension. The poetic structure is difficult to discern because of textual difficulties in verses 5–7. The note at the end of verse 7 in the NRSV indicates that the meaning of these verses is uncertain. The commentary on verses 5–7 here will deal with that issue, but it requires that any outline of the psalm's literary movement and interpretation be tentative. The psalm begins with an opening plea in the first two verses and continues in verses 3–5 with a petition for protection from the enticements of evil. The most common renderings of the psalm take verses 6–7 as retribution on the wicked and verses 8–10 as concluding petitions for protection. The ancient setting of this prayer was likely the sanctuary where a worshiper has brought a complaint; after participation in worship that included incense and sacrifice, this faithful one sought YHWH by way of petition.

A Closer Look: In the Aftermath of Exile

Psalm 141 is the fourth psalm in the final Davidic collection in the Psalter. The poem likely came from a setting in the community's worship and has now been placed in Book V (Psalms 107–150) and related to the community's struggles to come to terms with the aftermath of exile. The psalm thus likely reflects the struggle of an individual worshiper and – given its placement in the Psalter – the struggles of the second-temple community. Psalms 140, 141, and 142 are closely related and all are laments that have been placed in this Davidic collection in Book V. McCann notes verbal links between Psalms 140 and 141: "wicked" in Ps 140:4, 8 and in Ps 141:10; "righteous" in Ps 140:13 and Ps 141:5; "guard" in Ps 140:4 and "guard/keep" in Ps 141:3, 9; "lips" in Ps 140:3, 9 and Ps 141:3; "evil" in Ps 140:1, 2, 11 and Ps 141:4, 5; "my lord" in Ps 140:7 and Ps 141:8; and "traps, nets, snares" in Ps 140:5 and Ps 141:9. He also notes connections between Psalms 141 and 142: "refuge" in Ps 141:8 and Ps 142:5; "voice" in Ps 141:1 and Ps 142:1; "righteous" in Ps 141:5 and Ps 142:7; and "trap" in Ps 141:9 and Ps 142:3.[339]

The psalm begins with an opening plea in verses 1–2 in the first-person singular, pleading with YHWH to come quickly, for the need is urgent. The plea is that YHWH will hear the worshiper's voice. The second verse uses the offerings of both incense and sacrifices as images for the petition; the imagery may reflect the psalm's cultic background. The petitioner has witnessed the offering of both incense and sacrifices and prays that YHWH will accept this plea just as YHWH accepts these

---

[339] J. C. McCann, Jr., "Book of Psalms," in L. E. Keck et al. (eds.), *The New Interpreter's Bible*, vol. 4 (1996), 1243.

offerings. "The lifting up of my hands" is the posture of prayer and so parallels "my prayer" in verse 2. The personal pronouns suggest that the context of this opening plea is a close relationship with YHWH.

Verses 3–5 continue with a petition but move in a direction rather distinctive for the Psalms. The portrayal of the threat from enemies takes the form of enticement or entrapment rather than violence or accusation. The pervasive power of the enemies could become attractive. The prayer is that YHWH will keep the petitioner from indulging in evil behavior among the wicked. Verse 3 is often interpreted as a petition to keep the speaker from uttering evil words, but the mouth here could be the place where evil enters into the life of the petitioner. From these verses, it is easy to envision a speaker who at one time in the past had spoken and done evil in the company of the opponents but who now accompanies the righteous and seeks to stay with the community of faithful worshipers and so resist temptation. The plea is for divine help in that effort. The concluding line of verse 4 even uses the image of "delicacies" to refer to evil. With verse 5, readers begin to encounter difficulties of text and translation. The NRSV rendering suggests the hope that correction and reproof will come from other faithful worshipers, but it could also be that the discipline comes from YHWH, the Righteous One. The verse continues with a petition; the NRSV rendering takes the prayer to ask that the "workers of iniquity" not anoint the speaker with evil ways; others take the petition to articulate the hope that other believers will anoint the speaker.

The interpretation of verse 5 is problematic but appears to suggest that the petitioner continues to pray against evil deeds. Perhaps that context can help with the interpretation of verses 6–7, where the text is even more difficult. The most common rendering takes verse 6 as an announcement of judgment on the wicked and an exoneration of the petitioner. The wicked ones and their leaders will be shattered in this judgment and consigned to Sheol, the realm of the dead. In this interpretation, the verses express the hope that retribution will come on the wicked and that the petitioner will be spared. That reading of the verses seems plausible, but the text is difficult, so any interpretation must be tentative. Others take the breaking apart and shattering in verse 7 to refer to the petitioner and the just.

The psalm's conclusion (vv. 8–10) focuses on the contrast between the petitioner's intent and that of the opponents. The petitioner seeks YHWH and YHWH's refuge; the hope is for protection in the face of threats. Verses 9–10 use hunting imagery akin to that in Psalm 140. The enemies have laid traps and snares for the petitioner. The enemies continue to try to entice this faithful worshiper to join their wicked ways, and the plea is that YHWH will guard the speaker from those evil ways and relationships. The psalm concludes with the hope for retributive justice on the wicked, that they themselves will fall into the traps they have prepared and so endure the consequences of their evil ways. The petitioner seeks YHWH's refuge and protection from the wiles of the "workers of iniquity" to make possible an escape into the community of faith.

The faith articulated in Psalm 141 has a more introspective and reflective tone than is reflected in most psalms. The prayer confesses that the boundary between the faithful and the unfaithful is not always clear. The portrayal of the "workers of iniquity" is in terms of temptation or enticement. The prayer asks for divine help in avoiding those pitfalls. The intentions of humans can be uncertain, so the psalm appeals to divine faithfulness as central to a life of integrity. It was suggested earlier that this reflective tone has ties to wisdom traditions. The psalm portrays the wise or righteous person as one who is cautious about speech and conduct and who seeks to avoid those things that will lead to evil. The human will can be frail, so prayer and faith become central to the attitude commended in the prayer.

Bridging the Horizons: Deliver Us from Evil

The Psalms focus on the honest dialogue of faith in the midst of life and its struggles. The book characterizes the way of the righteous and the way of the wicked, and the consequences of the two lifestyles. Psalm 141 reflects an awareness of the difficulties people have in constructing those lives and so seeks divine help in the face of the temptations of evil. The psalm admits that the boundary between these two lifestyles is difficult to discern. That part of life requires reflection and careful discernment as part of a worshiping community. Candor and care characterize such a life; the support of a congregation is also central. Such a lifestyle, however, finally depends on the faithfulness of God. Christian tradition points to the Lord's Prayer for a central tenet of this psalm: "Lead us not into temptation but deliver us from evil."

PSALM 142 – A MASKIL OF DAVID. WHEN HE WAS IN THE CAVE. A PRAYER

¹ With my voice I cry to the LORD;
  with my voice I make supplication to the LORD.
² I pour out my complaint before him;
  I tell my trouble before him.
³ When my spirit is faint,
   you know my way.

  In the path where I walk
  they have hidden a trap for me.
⁴ Look on my right hand and see –

there is no one who takes notice of me;
no refuge remains to me;
 no one cares for me.

⁵ I cry to you, O LORD;
  I say, 'You are my refuge,
  my portion in the land of the living.'
⁶ Give heed to my cry,
  for I am brought very low.

  Save me from my persecutors,
  for they are too strong for me.
⁷ Bring me out of prison,
  so that I may give thanks to your name.
  The righteous will surround me,
  for you will deal bountifully with me.

Psalm 142 is a characteristic individual cry for help set in a series of lament psalms. The petitioner complains of being isolated and yet pursued by persecutors. The standard elements of the individual lament are present; the prayer is addressed to YHWH at the beginning, and then the petitioner portrays the crisis at hand in terms of a sense of isolation except for enemies. The cry for hearing and help brings petition to the fore in the psalm's two concluding verses. The psalm's conclusion is a brief expression of hope. The crisis centers on enemies who pursue this faithful worshiper to exhaustion and isolation. Forsaken by all others, this one cries to YHWH for help in the midst of a crisis described in verse 7 as a prison.

A Closer Look: Praying in Context

Psalm 142 appears in the final Davidic collection in the Hebrew Psalter. The psalm connects with other parts of the collection. It looks forward to Psalm 143 in that both psalms begin with "supplications" and calls for YHWH to "save me" in Ps 142:6 and Ps 143:9. The spirit faints in Ps 142:3 and Ps 143:4, and enemies pursue the petitioner in Ps 142:6 and Ps 143:3. The superscription to Psalm 142 includes a historical note referring to David's experience in "the cave." The most familiar such setting is the cave of En-gedi in 1 Samuel 24, but there is also the cave of Adullam in 1 Samuel 22. Mays suggests that the scribes who preserved the psalm sought a setting in David's life to fit the psalm.[340] The superscription

---

[340] J. L. Mays, *Psalms* (1994), 431. See also J. C. McCann, Jr., "Book of Psalms," in L. E. Keck et al. (eds.), *The New Interpreter's Bible*, vol. 4 (1996), 1246.

is not so much about the origin of the psalm as it is about a life setting in which readers can envision the praying of the psalm. It is significant that in this superscription, as in other such psalm superscriptions, David is not a grand and glorious king but is a representative person of faith struggling with the troubles of life. The superscription also labels the psalm as a "Maskil," a teaching poem or an artistic poem.

The psalm begins with a cry for help in the first-person singular. The cry is addressed to YHWH and is characterized as a "supplication" or "complaint" about "my trouble." The complaint is described in verses 1–2; direct address to YHWH comes in verse 3. The cry is a plaintive and honest one; the petitioner is in great trouble. The address then comes to YHWH, the one whom Israel's faith tradition portrays as embracing pain. The picture of the crisis begins in the latter part of verse 3 and continues with verse 4; enemies are at the center of the issue. The imagery is characteristic of the laments in this Davidic collection of psalms; much of it relates to hunting. The enemies have laid a trap for the petitioner, who realizes that there is no one at hand to help. No one cares or takes notice of the trouble. There is no refuge, and so the petitioner turns to ancient Israel's covenant God as the one who hears and helps. The crisis is one of persecution and loneliness.

The cry continues in verse 5 with an echo of Israel's faith tradition. The petitioner's self-quotation refers to YHWH as refuge and portion. Numbers 18:20 and Deut 10:9 indicate that priest and Levite do not have a set portion in the land of ancient Israel; YHWH is their portion – the source and provision of life for them. Psalm 142 portrays YHWH as "my refuge, my portion in the land of the living." Implicit in this confession is the hope that the petitioner will remain in the land of the living and not go down to the realm of death, Sheol. The isolation of this crisis is also very present, for now YHWH is the only support for the life of the petitioner. The speaker faces a life-threatening crisis and so turns to YHWH as Israel's divine covenant partner, who hears and embraces pain and comes to deliver. The psalm seeks to negotiate current experience in light of this faith tradition. God is the one who comes to deliver, and yet this person of faith is not being delivered. The prayer is thus a cry urging that God act on the hopes of the covenant relationship and bring help. Enemies are everywhere; they lie in wait. Personal resistance is no longer effective; only YHWH can save. The prayer is put in terms of release from prison in verse 7. Some take that reference literally; others take it as an image of being trapped and isolated, and helpless in this crisis.

The psalm's concluding lines tie the prayer for release from prison to a vow of praise. Rescue would make it possible for the petitioner to offer praise and thanksgiving in the congregation by narrating the crisis, prayer, and deliverance so that the community might also encounter this covenant hope that YHWH is the one who comes to deliver. The end of the psalm pictures the righteous surrounding the petitioner because of the divine act of salvation. Apparently this conclusion is a confession of faith; the crisis has not passed. What has changed is the petitioner's faith perspective; hope is now at hand. The hope is that this persecuted person of faith will be surrounded by the worshiping community and be able to give thanks because of YHWH's act of salvation. This cry for help ends in hope for "the righteous," those who live into a faithful relationship with YHWH and with the faith community; such a conclusion is characteristic of Israel's prayers.

Psalm 142 is a fine example of Israel's prayers for help in the Psalter. It portrays a crisis in representative terms and so provides a prayer for those who come to the sanctuary seeking divine help. The prayer is adaptable for many of the crises of life, which include enemies and isolation. The psalm also characterizes the movement of the Psalter as a whole from individual to community. Verse 4 portrays the crisis with "No one cares for me," but in the final verse the portrait is of the speaker surrounded by the righteous. The psalm also moves from "I cry to the Lord" in its first verse to giving thanks to YHWH's name in verse 7. The movement from complaint to thanksgiving and from individual to community is the movement of the Psalter as a whole. The movement from crisis to hope and the movement from individual to community are tightly interconnected. Psalm 142 exhibits the standard sequence of lament psalms: address to YHWH, complaint about trouble, petition, and a concluding word of hope. The psalm artfully portrays both trouble and faith. In this way, complaint and praise are also tightly interconnected. This psalm is characteristic of the laments of the Psalter, and its closing word centers on hope. The psalm articulates a crisis that tests ancient Israel's covenant faith and finds that it holds; YHWH is the one who embraces pain in the midst of the life of the congregation. Enemies persist, and YHWH continues to hear the plaintive cries of the faithful and continues to deliver, whether in the context of the aftermath of the exile in the sixth century BCE or later generations.

PSALM 143 – A PSALM OF DAVID

[1] Hear my prayer, O Lord;
  give ear to my supplications in your faithfulness;
  answer me in your righteousness.
[2] Do not enter into judgment with your servant,
   for no one living is righteous before you.

[3] For the enemy has pursued me,
  crushing my life to the ground,
  making me sit in darkness like those long dead.

⁴ Therefore my spirit faints within me;
   my heart within me is appalled.

⁵ I remember the days of old,
   I think about all your deeds,
   I meditate on the works of your hands.
⁶ I stretch out my hands to you;
   my soul thirsts for you like a parched land.
     Selah

⁷ Answer me quickly, O LORD;
   my spirit fails.
Do not hide your face from me,
   or I shall be like those who go down to the Pit.
⁸ Let me hear of your steadfast love in the morning,
   for in you I put my trust.
Teach me the way I should go,
   for to you I lift up my soul.

⁹ Save me, O LORD, from my enemies;
   I have fled to you for refuge.
¹⁰ Teach me to do your will,
   for you are my God.
   Let your good spirit lead me
   on a level path.

¹¹ For your name's sake, O LORD, preserve my life.
   In your righteousness bring me out of trouble.
¹² In your steadfast love cut off my enemies,
   and destroy all my adversaries,
   for I am your servant.

Psalm 143 is the last psalm of complaint in the Psalter, after which the Psalter concludes with a series of hymns (Psalms 144–150). This prayer of complaint is conventional in that it offers a series of *petitions* that are followed by *complaints* that describe the speaker's need and serve to reinforce the urgency of the petition. In our review of the psalm, we will notice four distinctive features that are embedded in the conventional form.

Petitions dominate the entire psalm:

Hear, give ear, answer (v. 1)
do not enter ... (v. 2)

answer, do not hide, let me hear (vv. 7–8)
save (v. 9)
let your spirit lead (v. 10)
preserve, bring me out (v. 11)
cut off, destroy (v. 12)

The speaker is in deep distress and claims enough entitlement to address YHWH in a demanding way.

The *complaint*, which characterizes for YHWH the circumstance of need, concerns a social situation of threat for which the speaker has no adequate resources (vv. 3–4, 6a, 7). The speaker lives, as is commonplace in these psalms, amid enemies (v. 3) and adversaries (v. 12) who place the speaker in jeopardy and near death. As a result, the speaker must throw himself completely on the good intentions of YHWH. The prayer seeks to motivate YHWH to act in positive ways that will extricate the speaker from an unbearable situation of risk. For that reason, the speaker positions himself before YHWH not only in need but in lyrical trust and confidence:

in you I put my trust . . .
to you I lift up my soul; (v. 8)
I have fled to you for refuge; (v. 9)
You are my God; (v. 10)
I am your servant. (v. 12)

These statements of trust come close to an ingratiating tone, suggesting that in response YHWH has some obligation to act on behalf of the speaker.

We may note four markers that give particularity to the psalm:

1.   At the beginning (v. 1) and at the conclusion (v. 11), the psalm appeals to the righteousness of YHWH, to YHWH's capacity to intervene in effective ways to support and sustain the one in need. The two uses provide an envelope for the entire psalm and show the reason why the speaker trusts YHWH, being fully confident of YHWH's capacity for rehabilitation. In verses 1–2, moreover, the psalm contrasts the effective righteousness of YHWH with the deficient righteousness of the speaker. This contrast between human righteousness and divine righteousness, with particular reference to this psalm, became a leitmotif for Martin Luther as he articulated an evangelical discernment of justification by the righteous. In that connection, it is verse 2 on the inadequacy of human righteousness that has caused this psalm to be slotted as one of the traditional "penitential psalms." Lindström, however, makes the judgment that verse 2 is an intrusion in the psalm and calls the reader away from the original affirmation of the psalm.[341]

---

[341]   F. Lindström, *Suffering and Sin* (1994), 122–126.

The readiness of the speaker to trust YHWH's righteousness is enforced by an appeal to YHWH's trustworthiness. In verse 1, righteousness stands in close parallel to "faithfulness" (*amunah*), YHWH's reliability. At the conclusion, YHWH's "righteousness" parallels YHWH's steadfastness (*ḥesed*), an account also sounded in the middle of the psalm at verse 8. Thus, the trustworthiness of YHWH is attested in the great words of Israel's faith:

righteousness, faithfulness; (v. 1)
steadfast love; (v. 8)
righteousness, steadfast love. (vv. 11–12)

The psalmist, like the psalm, is encompassed by a God who is his only source of comfort and strength.

2.   Although there are bits and pieces of other motivations offered to persuade YHWH to action, verses 5–6 are especially filled with resolve. They consist of four "I" statements, three of which refer to YHWH's past miracles and the final one, in verse 6, matching YHWH's past deeds to the speaker's present desperate circumstances. As with all such motivations, the intention is to move YHWH to act, for YHWH is perfectly capable of such action now as in the past.

3.   In verses 8 and 10, the motif of instruction is twice voiced. Grammatically the two verbs "cause to know me" and "teach" are imperatives not unlike all of the petitions. These two, however, function quite differently. As Mandolfo has seen elsewhere, there is a readiness on the part of the petitioner, when rescued, to begin to instruct others in obedience that properly belongs to YHWH.[342] Thus the psalmist is not only a *suppliant* but intends immediately to become a *witness* as well. The "way" and the "path" to be sought clearly refer to the commands of the Torah. This plea, in Calvinist terms, represents the "third use of the law." Those given new life by YHWH are prepared for obedience to the God who saves.

4.   The central phrase in verse 11, "for your name's sake," is of importance. After boldly issuing the several imperative petitions mentioned, the speaker acknowledges that he in fact has no compelling grounds for petition. Consequently, verse 11 makes quite a different appeal: do not preserve my life because I am needy or worthy but rather because it will enhance YHWH's own reputation. We have seen, for example, that YHWH's "name" (renown) is celebrated in Ps 135:13. Here appeal is to the same concern for YHWH's reputation. YHWH gains "points" in the presence of the other nations and the other gods for committing a powerful

---

[342] C. Mandolfo, *God in the Dock* (2002).

act of rescue. The nations are able to see the power and fidelity of YHWH so YHWH's distinctive character can be more fully appreciated and affirmed. The readiness of YHWH to act in order to enhance God's own righteousness is evident in Ezek 36:22, 32. Conversely, the warning about YHWH's reputation in Exod 32:12 and Num 14:13–16 functions for Moses as a positive motivation addressed to YHWH. Thus the psalmist, in a show of considerable chutzpah, stands in the prayer tradition of Israel and seeks to leverage YHWH by appealing to YHWH's own self-regard.

In this prayer, it is clear that Israel "pulls out all the stops" of need, urgency, and fidelity. In the end, however, beyond any attempt at manipulation, this prayer exhibits Israel's turning to its only hope, YHWH. The final appeal is filled with pathos: "I am your servant." The news is that YHWH, in righteousness, faithfulness, and steadfast love, has regard for his servant. In this transaction that evokes God's saving response, Israel speaks in deep, complete confidence: "It was entirely of God's free mercy that he looked for deliverance; for, had he brought forward anything of his own, the cause would not have been in God, and only in God."[343]

PSALM 144 – OF DAVID

[1] Blessed be the LORD, my rock,
   who trains my hands for war, and my fingers for battle;
[2] my rock and my fortress,
   my stronghold and my deliverer,
   my shield, in whom I take refuge,
     who subdues the peoples under me.

[3] O LORD, what are human beings that you regard them,
   or mortals that you think of them?
[4] They are like a breath;
     their days are like a passing shadow.

[5] Bow your heavens, O LORD, and come down;
   touch the mountains so that they smoke.
[6] Make the lightning flash and scatter them;
   send out your arrows and rout them.

---

[343] J. Calvin, *Commentary on the Book of Psalms*, vol. 5 (1979), 258.

7 Stretch out your hand from on high;
   set me free and rescue me from the mighty waters,
   from the hand of aliens,
8 whose mouths speak lies,
     and whose right hands are false.

9 I will sing a new song to you, O God;
   upon a ten-stringed harp I will play to you,
10 the one who gives victory to kings,
   who rescues his servant David.
11 Rescue me from the cruel sword,
   and deliver me from the hand of aliens,
   whose mouths speak lies,
   and whose right hands are false.

12 May our sons in their youth
   be like plants full grown,
   our daughters like corner pillars,
   cut for the building of a palace.
13 May our barns be filled
   with produce of every kind;
   may our sheep increase by thousands,
   by tens of thousands in our fields,
14 and may our cattle be heavy with young.
   May there be no breach in the walls, no exile,
   and no cry of distress in our streets.

15 Happy are the people to whom such blessings fall;
   happy are the people whose God is the LORD.

This psalm moves from "blessed" (*bārûk*) in verse 1 to "blessed" (*'ašrê*) in verse 15. The voice that speaks here is the Davidic king, as this psalm is reckoned as the tenth and final "royal psalm." Although the royal reference is not definitive, special attention should be paid to the way in which this psalm "rereads" Psalm 18. This psalm is divided into four distinct rhetorical units, each of which refers to God, three times by the name YHWH.

In verses 1–4, the psalm celebrates the work of YHWH in defense and protection, and notices that "Adam," by contrast, has no staying power and cannot protect anyone. Verses 1–2 are a royal attestation to the faithful power of YHWH, who is blessed, praised, and celebrated. The dominant rhetorical feature in these verses is the pronoun "my," which reflects the singular, preemptive claim of the king. YHWH is *my* rock, *my* steadfast love, *my* fortress, *my* stronghold, *my* deliverance, *my* shield, the one who brings military victory for the king and military defeat for the enemies of the king. This is the voice of a glad success.

In verse 3, the psalm ponders the contrast between YHWH and "Adam." "Adam," of course, refers to humanity, but it may also in context refer to human power and human capacity; that is, human military capacity to work its way and bring itself security. Verse 3 is clearly a quotation from Psalm 8. In Psalm 8, however, "man" is celebrated as the quintessential wonder of creation, whereas here "man" is seen to be without staying power or capacity. Notice should also be taken of the parallel phrasing of Job 7:17, only there the quotation concerns God's excessive attention to "man," who could use a respite from divine surveillance. In verse 3 of the present psalm, it is as if the king in Jerusalem acknowledges the limit, if not the futility, of his own military capacity. Human (royal) capacity is fragile and vulnerable.

In verses 5–8, the king addresses YHWH with a petition at the outset in verses 5–6, which is that YHWH should break the heavens open and intrude on the earth with a mighty theophanic entry. The verses describe the characteristic cataclysmic upheaval caused by the coming of God. In verse 7, however, the petition turns abruptly from such a generic description to a quite personal request that YHWH's hand of power should be mobilized on behalf of the king and his realm, which is apparently in dire straits. This more intimate request is in three verbs, "stretch out, set free, rescue." Apparently the king and his company are on the short end of a military confrontation, and the king has come to the limit of his capacity and faces defeat. That threat is described in two ways: first, as a threat of chaotic waters that cannot be resisted; and second, as an alien force – likely an invading army – that threatens the stability of the realm. A fuller characterization of such "aliens" is offered in Jeremiah, where the Babylonian armies are described in ominous terms:

> I am going to bring upon you
> > a nation from far away,
> > > O house of Israel,
> > > > says the Lord.
> It is an enduring nation,
> > it is an ancient nation,
> a nation whose language you do not know,
> > nor can you understand what they say.
> Their quiver is like an open tomb;
> > all of them are mighty warriors. (Jer 5:15–16)

This urgent petition gives force and specificity to the acknowledgment in verse 4 that "Adam" is like a breath and a passing shadow. More is required in such a situation of threat, and that more is YHWH, who, unlike the "king's own," is capable of liberation and rescue.

In verses 9–11, the psalm turns to praise – or to the promise of praise. The king promises a "new song," perhaps a specially commissioned anthem for the temple, in the wake of the anticipated divine victory. This pledge of praise may itself be taken as a declaration of praise, but more likely it is a vow of praise if and when victory is given. Therefore, for now the praise is being withheld until the victory is given. It is clear in verse 11 that the victory is not yet in hand, for the vow of praise here turns to a petition – "rescue, deliver" – the same as in verse 7. Indeed the characterization of the enemy in verse 11 reiterates the phrasing of verse 8, suggesting a conventional dismissive characterization of the adversary. Thus, the psalmist moves between *praise* and *petition*, precisely the place in which Israel always stands before YHWH: on the one hand *needful*, on the other hand *grateful*.

The psalm concludes in verses 12–15 with a prayer – or perhaps a wish, or a statement of royal intentionality – for the well-being of the entire realm. The plural pronoun "our" – used six times – refers not to the royal family but to the entire realm. The five nouns modified by the pronoun (omitting for now the final one, "streets") – sons, daughters, barns, sheep, cattle –summarize the complete material wealth and property of the realm. (See a like inventory in Jer 5:17.) Thus this is a wish, or a benediction, for the "good life" of the entire realm. Before the mention of YHWH in verse 18, these verses do not explicitly refer to YHWH. But YHWH as creator is everywhere implied; it is YHWH the creator who gives abundantly. Here the rhetoric mentions every kind of abundance, indicated by such terms as "full grown," "filled," "produce of every kind," and "heavy." The counterpoint to this positive vision of abundance is the hope that there will be no breach, no exile, no cry. The triad with the negative particle "no" (*'aîn*) creates a powerful contrast to the foregoing positive vision of prosperity.

Finally, verse 15 offers something of a concluding benediction, twice using the term "happy, blessed, fortunate" (*'ašrê*). The psalm envisions well-being that is a gift from God, the giver of every blessing. The psalm begins with *bārûk*, "bless," a theological word of praise and well-being. It concludes with *'ašrê* ("bless"), a term meaning material peace and prosperity. Israel knows, always, that *material prosperity* is rooted in *the truth of God*, the one who gives blessing. Thus the psalm traverses the ominous dangers of war, the threat of immeasurably difficult enemies, to a vision of well-being. The action of "peace and prosperity" is only possible from the creator God because the deliverer God has removed the threat and has made new life (and new song) available. Because the psalm is on the lips of the king, it is clear – even to the king – that the king is, at best, manager and administrator of the gifts of YHWH, not capable himself of generating gifts of either victory or prosperity. We may take this psalm as a reflection on the reality of the king as "Adam" (v. 3). Since the narrative account of Genesis 1–2, Adam has had a role in presiding over and managing YHWH's real estate, the earth. The king, however, is only the manager, a role quite dependent on the gifts of life, which only YHWH can give. Complete reliance on YHWH, voiced here, seems, among other things, to define the true and modest role of Adam. Consequently, the king will not do much – except to sing – a proper doxological acknowledgment of a true life before the giver of all life.

PSALM 145 – PRAISE. OF DAVID

¹ I will extol you, my God and King,
  and bless your name for ever and ever.
² Every day I will bless you,
  and praise your name for ever and ever.
³ Great is the LORD, and greatly to be praised;
   his greatness is unsearchable.

⁴ One generation shall laud your works to another,
  and shall declare your mighty acts.
⁵ On the glorious splendour of your majesty,
  and on your wondrous works, I will meditate.
⁶ The might of your awesome deeds shall be proclaimed,
  and I will declare your greatness.
⁷ They shall celebrate the fame of your abundant goodness,
   and shall sing aloud of your righteousness.

⁸ The LORD is gracious and merciful,
  slow to anger and abounding in steadfast love.
⁹ The LORD is good to all,
  and his compassion is over all that he has made.

¹⁰ All your works shall give thanks to you, O LORD,
  and all your faithful shall bless you.
¹¹ They shall speak of the glory of your kingdom,
  and tell of your power,
¹² to make known to all people your mighty deeds,
  and the glorious splendour of your kingdom.
¹³ Your kingdom is an everlasting kingdom,
  and your dominion endures throughout all generations.

  The LORD is faithful in all his words,
  and gracious in all his deeds.

¹⁴ The LORD upholds all who are falling,
   and raises up all who are bowed down.
¹⁵ The eyes of all look to you,
   and you give them their food in due season.
¹⁶ You open your hand,
   satisfying the desire of every living thing.
¹⁷ The LORD is just in all his ways,
   and kind in all his doings.
¹⁸ The LORD is near to all who call on him,
   to all who call on him in truth.
¹⁹ He fulfils the desire of all who fear him;
   he also hears their cry, and saves them.
²⁰ The LORD watches over all who love him,
   but all the wicked he will destroy.

²¹ My mouth will speak the praise of the LORD,
   and all flesh will bless his holy name for ever and ever.

Psalm 145 is both an alphabetic acrostic and a psalm of praise in worship. The beginning of the psalm is more in the style of an individual song of thanksgiving, and the first-person form continues through the poem, but the tone of the hymn pervades the psalm, which is likely tied to the temple. The blessing of the divine name in the psalm's first and last verses frames the poem, which exhibits a good bit of repetition. There are also some shifts in the poetry. YHWH is addressed in the second person in parts of the psalm and spoken about in the third person in other parts. That style reflects an alternation between the offering of praise and the characterization of YHWH by way of divine attributes. The exposition that follows will delineate four poetic units: verses 1–3, 4–9, 10–13, and 14–21. The first three units use the sequence of a declaration of intent to offer praise followed by a portrayal of YHWH. The sequence is reversed in the final unit, and the last verse characteristically renews the vow of praise.[344] That poetic structure is in addition to the alphabetic acrostic structure that further shapes the poem. The acrostic form suggests comprehensiveness in the poem, a theme in other dimensions of the psalm. Psalm 145 thus provides an example of sophisticated poetic art.

The psalm also concludes the final collection of Davidic psalms in the Hebrew Psalter. It is likely that the psalm concludes the body of Book V, with Psalms 146–150 providing a fivefold doxological conclusion to the Psalter. Mays suggests that Psalm

---

[344] See C. C. Broyles, *Psalms* (1999), 505–506; J. L. Mays, *Psalms* (1994), 438; J. C. McCann, Jr., "Book of Psalms," in L. E. Keck et al. (eds.), *The New Interpreter's Bible*, vol. 4 (1996), 1259.

145 is "the overture to the final movement of the Psalter."[345] The final five psalms all echo features and language in Psalm 145, and the concluding verse of Psalm 150 echoes the concluding verse of Psalm 145. Psalm 145 has been used frequently in both Judaism and Christianity, and is the only Davidic psalm whose superscription labels it as "praise."

Verses 1–3. The psalm begins with an immediate and intense declaration, in the first-person singular, of the intent to praise God. This praise is to take place every day and "forever and ever," a phrase used in each of the first two verses. YHWH is characterized as "my God and King," with the personal pronoun emphasizing the relationship. The verbs for praise are "extol" and "bless." The first has to do with lifting up the divine name and witness, and the second has to do with the knee and kneeling to acknowledge divine blessings received. The familiar verse 3 speaks of God in terms of incomprehensible greatness that calls for more praise.

Verses 4–9. Psalm 145 is a good example of a poetic structure of intensification as descriptions pile up. The next expression of praise has one generation declaring to the next the mighty acts of God so that the praise of God will continue into the future. Then the poem returns to a first-person vow to meditate on the wonderful works and greatness of God and then to proclaim the mighty acts of God. The praise bears witness to the divine presence and activity in the world and thus leads the generations to sing praise and thanksgiving to YHWH. This anticipation of celebrations of divine goodness leads to further characterizations of YHWH in verses 8–9. These verses echo the famous confession of faith in Exod 34:6–7, emphasizing the positive side of that confession. Grace, mercy, patience, steadfast love, goodness, and compassion are all characteristics of the divine king. The adjectives continue to pile up and the praise intensifies. The divine compassion is for all of creation. God provides fullness of life for all, and this psalm appropriates loaded vocabulary from Israel's faith tradition to portray YHWH's kingship over all creation. "My God and King" is over all and in all, and focuses on steadfast love.

Verses 10–13. The structure of intensification continues with the proclamation that all people and all of God's works will sing praise and thanksgiving to God. The verbs are "give thanks" and "bless." God's creatures and God's acts bear witness to the divine presence and activity; the glory of the divine king is seen in these mighty acts. These expressions of praise emphasize one dimension of Israel's praise – bearing witness to God's mighty acts so that all the people of the world may know them. YHWH's kingdom endures and continues through the generations. YHWH reigns over this "everlasting kingdom." This everlasting divine dominion over all brings to mind the conclusion of Psalm 22, with its emphasis on the divine kingship over all. The concluding line in the NRSV rendering of verse 13 is not in the Masoretic version of the Psalter, the standard Hebrew text. It has been provided from other Hebrew texts and other versions. Most English versions include the line because it supplies a line necessary for the alphabetic acrostic structure.

[345] J. L. Mays, *Psalms* (1994), 439.

Verses 14–21. The concluding line supplied in verse 13 speaks of divine trustworthiness and grace, and the portrayal of YHWH in this last poetic unit focuses on YHWH's support of the persecuted and liberation of the oppressed. The divine presence is the thing most needed for fullness in life; the creator makes provision for a full life. The psalm ties the divine presence to those who pray in truth. God hears the petitions of the faithful and cares for them. The contrast is with the wicked. The antithetic parallelism in verse 20 illustrates the contrast of the faithful with the wicked and their respective fates in life. The portrayal of YHWH in this concluding poetic unit is the longest descriptive part of the psalm and slows the pace for readers to meditate on the kindness and justice of YHWH in bringing hope to the faithful. The change of sequence in this unit (noted previously) to the priority of the portrayal of YHWH suggests emphasis on this section. The psalm's concluding verse articulates a brief but powerful vow of praise. The speaker and "all flesh" will praise YHWH. The vow provides a sudden crescendo of an ending to the poem. The complete alphabetic acrostic has come to an end. The comprehensiveness suggested by the acrostic structure is reflected in the seventeen occurrences of "all," most of them in this last poetic unit. The praise of God in Psalm 145 is unlimited and relates to all.

The kingship or dominion of YHWH is a central theme in Psalm 145. The root word *mālāk* for king is used four times in verses 11–13 to emphasize YHWH's reign. The psalm is a poetic portrayal of YHWH as king with a strong tie to creation language. YHWH is the creator who provides for life. Only verse 20 mentions "the wicked." The theme of the conflict with the powers of chaos does not appear in Psalm 145 as it does in other creation texts centering on the establishment of order by the divine creator king (Psalm 104, for example). Psalm 145 is a powerful expression of the praise of the divine king, especially when tied to the community that shaped Book V of the Psalter (Psalms 107–150), a community likely still struggling with the aftermath of exile. Their life is under threat, and yet the community explosively praises the divine creator and king. The concluding verse of Psalm 145 is likely the benediction of Book V, leading to the fivefold doxology concluding the Psalter (Psalms 146–150), and it is a resounding vow of praise:

> My mouth will speak the praise of the Lord,
> and all flesh will bless his holy name forever and ever. (v. 21)

PSALM 146

¹ Praise the LORD!
   Praise the LORD, O my soul!
² I will praise the LORD as long as I live;
   I will sing praises to my God all my life long.

³ Do not put your trust in princes,
  in mortals, in whom there is no help.
⁴ When their breath departs, they return to the earth;
  on that very day their plans perish.

⁵ Happy are those whose help is the God of Jacob,
  whose hope is in the Lord their God,
⁶ who made heaven and earth,
  the sea, and all that is in them;
  who keeps faith for ever;
⁷ who executes justice for the oppressed;
  who gives food to the hungry.

  The Lord sets the prisoners free;
⁸ the Lord opens the eyes of the blind.
  The Lord lifts up those who are bowed down;
  the Lord loves the righteous.
⁹ The Lord watches over the strangers;
  he upholds the orphan and the widow,
  but the way of the wicked he brings to ruin.

¹⁰ The Lord will reign for ever,
  your God, O Zion, for all generations.
Praise the Lord!

This psalm is a hymn of praise to YHWH that traces out the character of YHWH in some fullness and affirms the impact of YHWH's character on the life of the world. This psalm is framed in verses 1–2 and 10 by statements of praise that are sounded, surprisingly enough, in the first-person singular. This is a voice that can gladly attest to the decisive difference that YHWH makes in the world. The utterance of this voice is preoccupied with the question of Ps 121:1, "From where will my help come?"

The first answer given to that question is a negative one, eliminating one candidate for "help." In verses 3–4, in something of a didactic tone, the poem asserts that "princes" are of no help. In fact, the poetic parallelism in the NRSV is a bit misleading, for in Hebrew it is "princes ... son of man" ("mortals"); the second element of the parallel shows this to be an echo of Ps 8:4, "man ... son of man" (see Ps 144:3). Whereas Psalm 8 exalts human capacity, here the psalmist declares human capacity to be fragile, unreliable, and without staying power ... without breath, without life, without generative capacity, and consequently no help at all. The focus is not on humanity in general but on *powerful* humanity, the sort of folks who seem to be properly in charge and able to manage worldly affairs. No, says the psalm, they are not reliable!

But the dismissal of "princes ... son of man" is only a ploy. In verse 5, the psalmist nominates a second candidate for help, the one who in fact concerns him again in a sapiential mode with the use of the term "happy" (see Ps 144:15); the God of Jacob – promise-maker and covenant-keeper – is seen to be the true help. This use of "help" refers back to verse 3 and contrasts human capacity and divine capacity. Whereas human help is futile and helpless, the God of Jacob is indeed adequate, reliable grounds for hope. Adherents to YHWH can have complete confidence in the generative divine power that is at work in the world to bring all creation to a good end.

By verse 5b, the psalm moves out of a *didactic* mode that is designed to dismiss "human help" and into a *doxological* mode in order to celebrate the awesome help embodied in the person of YHWH. The affirmation *of hope in YHWH* in verse 5 is an entry point into doxology that is offered in two modes. First, in verses 6–7b, we are offered a series of participial statements, and then, in verses 7c–9, a second series of participles, only this time YHWH is explicitly named five times as the subject. Although the rhetoric is so different that YHWH is first implied and then named, all of the participles narrate the continuing and characteristic actions that are available everywhere all the time, because YHWH is the faithful sovereign who wills well-being for the world.

The series of participial, doxological statements begins in verse 6 with an affirmation of YHWH as creator, even of the sea (see Ps 104:25–26)! But the accompanying participial phrase, terse as it is, is even more crucial: "Who keeps faith forever!" Creation may be seen as a sign of YHWH's abiding fidelity, a point affirmed in Jer 31:35, 37; 33:25–26. Characteristically, in verse 7 the subject shifts from the stability of creation to the social reality of economic development; YHWH is decisively allied with the poor and hungry (see Ps 113:7–9; 1 Sam 2:7–8). This psalm does not link verse 7 to verse 6 in any specific way, but we may conclude that economic disparity is a violation of the ordering of creation, so the creator God intervenes in the economy to make it right.

In the series of participial statements that explicitly name YHWH, the recurring subject is the socially vulnerable and powerless who stand in need of an advocate: prisoners, the blind, the bowed down, strangers, widows, and orphans. This is indeed "God's preferential option" for the vulnerable and needy, the ones who are outsiders and who are kept outsiders in familiar economic arrangements in order to maintain a certain arrangement of social power and social possibilities. In this series, the fourth statement is peculiar: "YHWH loves the righteous." This statement is without exposition, but in context the affirmation perhaps refers to human agents, who, like YHWH, invest in the vulnerable who are just names, thus imitating YHWH's own social proclivity.

This terse statement about the righteous – on which see characteristic portrayals in Psalm 112 or Job 31 – illuminates the final statement of verse 9 concerning the

wicked. The reference to the "righteous" in verse 8 – those allied with YHWH's
work – is a perfect counterpoint to the "wicked" in verse 9, likely those who resist
YHWH's protection of the vulnerable; in fact, the wicked are those who practice
social policies and attitudes that produce and prey on the socially vulnerable. Thus
the wicked are not just the socially indifferent but those who actively generate more
vulnerable, needy, impotent people. This way of ordering the economy is anti-
YHWH, anticreation, and antisociety, and is bound to fail.

The good news of the psalm, after this wondrous affirmation of YHWH, is the
concluding doxological articulation of verse 10. YHWH will be king ... forever.
It follows that Yahwistic policy – resisted by the wicked and enacted by the righteous – is the "order of the day" for all days to come. The worshiping community
affirms and is assured that YHWH's policy of humility, fidelity, compassion, and
restoration is the normative ordering of the earth. It is the God worshiped in the
Jerusalem temple who guarantees, against every resistance and deterrence, that
these restorative measures will eventually succeed. The duration of "all generations"
in verse 10 matches "forever" in verse 6. This doxology states the truth of the creator, and therefore human creation will do well to sign on for such restorative activity: "You call the worlds into being ... and set before each one the ways of life and
death."[346] It is no wonder that the psalmist issues a final doxology: Halleluiah (v. 10)!
The affirmation is very good news; only the doomed wicked could think otherwise
and resist.

Bridging the Horizons: YHWH, Jesus, and the Marginalized

The catalog of YHWH's characteristic activities toward the vulnerable and dis-
inherited is echoed in Luke 7:22. In that narrative confrontation with John the
Baptist, Jesus is said to make a decisive difference in the lives of the marginal-
ized. In the context of the psalm, the gospel narrative makes the point that Jesus
does indeed do the work that is doxologically celebrated concerning YHWH.

PSALM 147

¹ Praise the Lord!
How good it is to sing praises to our God;
for he is gracious, and a song of praise is fitting.

346 United Church of Christ Statement of Faith, *The New Century Hymnal* (Cleveland: Pilgrim Press, 1995), 885.

2 The LORD builds up Jerusalem;
   he gathers the outcasts of Israel.
3 He heals the broken-hearted,
   and binds up their wounds.
4 He determines the number of the stars;
   he gives to all of them their names.
5 Great is our Lord, and abundant in power;
   his understanding is beyond measure.
6 The LORD lifts up the downtrodden;
   he casts the wicked to the ground.

7 Sing to the LORD with thanksgiving;
   make melody to our God on the lyre.
8 He covers the heavens with clouds,
   prepares rain for the earth,
   makes grass grow on the hills.
9 He gives to the animals their food,
   and to the young ravens when they cry.
10 His delight is not in the strength of the horse,
   nor his pleasure in the speed of a runner;
11 but the LORD takes pleasure in those who fear him,
   in those who hope in his steadfast love.

12 Praise the LORD, O Jerusalem!
   Praise your God, O Zion!
13 For he strengthens the bars of your gates;
   he blesses your children within you.
14 He grants peace within your borders;
   he fills you with the finest of wheat.
15 He sends out his command to the earth;
   his word runs swiftly.
16 He gives snow like wool;
   he scatters frost like ashes.
17 He hurls down hail like crumbs –
   who can stand before his cold?
18 He sends out his word, and melts them;
   he makes his wind blow, and the waters flow.
19 He declares his word to Jacob,
   his statutes and ordinances to Israel.
20 He has not dealt thus with any other nation;

they do not know his ordinances.
Praise the LORD!

Psalm 147 is a hymn of praise to YHWH, part of the group of doxologies that concludes the Psalter (Psalms 146–150). In fact, Psalm 147 is a combination of three hymns, each of which might, at some point in the tradition, have stood alone.

The first hymnic section (vv. 1–6) consists of a summons to praise (vv. 1a, b) and an extended series of reasons for praise introduced by "for" (*kî*) (vv. 1c–6). The key assertion is that YHWH is gracious, and the remainder of the unit supports that claim. The term rendered "gracious" (*na'îm*) is a peculiar one that suggests an anesthetic dimension of beauty. The rhetorical pattern of the list of reasons is somewhat irregular, with YHWH named three times (vv. 2, 5, 6). YHWH is characteristically the subject of active verbs, and the psalm celebrates YHWH's recurring actions. The statement of verse 3 would seem to refer to the reclamation of Jerusalem after 587 BCE and the return of deportees to Jerusalem, a statement suggested by the more general statement of verses 3 and 6. The "brokenhearted" and the "downtrodden" are not identified. Although the terms may be taken quite generically, in light of verse 2 the term more likely refers to deported Jews in the sixth century BCE. This is a reference to actions in the social arena that are supported by references to the power of God the creator, a large claim that culminates in the acclamation of verse 5 celebrating YHWH's power.

The second hymn in verses 7–11 again begins with a summons to praise and thanks (v. 7), followed by a series of reasons for praise (vv. 8–11). The reasons are not introduced by the usual preposition "for." Verses 8–9 celebrate the creator God, as does verse 4. The rhetoric changes in verses 10–11 to make a critical contrast between military power (strength of wars) and YHWH's divine power on behalf of those who are adherents of YHWH. The contrast between *armed power* and *YHWH's fidelity* is a recurring theme in the Psalter, no doubt because armed power was a continuing temptation for the Jerusalem establishment. This temptation is particularly reflected in the tradition of Isaiah (see Isa 7:9; 30:15–17). This psalmic theme asserts that victory does not always go to the strong and to the swift. The psalm vouches for something incalculable in the historical process that eventually is credited to YHWH (see Zech 4:6; Prov 21:30–31).

The third hymnic unit again begins with a double summons to praise, now for the first time with a double vocative (v. 12). This is followed by a series of reasons for praise introduced by "for" (vv. 13–20). The list of reasons begins with YHWH's attention to Israel in all of its particularity: "your gates, your children, your borders" (vv. 13–14). But then in verses 15–17 the list moves to a larger horizon and celebrates YHWH's mighty power as creator, the list being not unlike the great self-praise in the book of Job (see Job 38–41). In verse 18, the focus moves to YHWH's word and YHWH's wind that moved the psalmist to ponder YHWH's command to Israel (vv. 19–20). Thus the psalm moves easily from creation to the history of Israel, for the power of this same God is manifest in both arenas. The concluding acclamation of verse 20 likely pertains to the entire psalm and not simply to verses 12–20. As is the usual case, the psalm easily combines cosmic claims and the particularity of Israel. Although we might think of a tension in that process, no tension is signaled by the psalm itself. All of these realms stand together as a single realm over which YHWH presides in faithful sovereignty.

PSALM 148

¹ Praise the Lord!
Praise the Lord from the heavens;
    praise him in the heights!
² Praise him, all his angels;
    praise him, all his host!

³ Praise him, sun and moon;
    praise him, all you shining stars!
⁴ Praise him, you highest heavens,
    and you waters above the heavens!

⁵ Let them praise the name of the Lord,
    for he commanded and they were created.
⁶ He established them for ever and ever;
    he fixed their bounds, which cannot be passed.

⁷ Praise the Lord from the earth,
    you sea monsters and all deeps,
⁸ fire and hail, snow and frost,
    stormy wind fulfilling his command!

⁹ Mountains and all hills,
    fruit trees and all cedars!
¹⁰ Wild animals and all cattle,
    creeping things and flying birds!

¹¹ Kings of the earth and all peoples,
    princes and all rulers of the earth!
¹² Young men and women alike,
    old and young together!

¹³ Let them praise the name of the LORD,
   for his name alone is exalted;
   his glory is above earth and heaven.
¹⁴ He has raised up a horn for his people,
   praise for all his faithful,
   for the people of Israel who are close to him.
   Praise the LORD!

Psalm 148 is a hymn of praise from the community's worship. It begins in characteristic fashion with the imperative call to praise and moves to the basis for the
praise. It concludes with a renewed call to praise. That standard hymnic structure
of the summons to praise followed by the motivation for the praise is essential to
the text, but the balance of the parts is somewhat different in this hymn in that the
summons to praise is longer than the reason for it. The praise is in two movements:
from heaven in verses 1–6 and from earth in verses 7–14. Each part begins with
an extensive summons to praise; the basis for the praise follows. The movements
are parallel. In the first unit, the messengers and host of YHWH are first called to
praise, followed by a call to other objects in the heavens. In the second unit, the
sequence is different, with the first call to earthly creatures and objects in nature,
followed by the call to humans. The effect of the poetic structure is a universal call
to praise of the creator, who also cares for the worshiping community.

Psalm 148 is the third song in the fivefold doxology that concludes the Psalter
(Psalms 146–150). This text is related to Psalm 150 in that the elaborate summons to
praise takes up most of the psalm. McCann suggests that although Psalms 147 and
148 do not use the specific vocabulary of the kingship of God, they are framed by
psalms that do (Pss 146:10 and 149:2), and so he takes Psalm 148 to portray YHWH's
universal sovereignty, a theme he finds to be central to the Psalter.³⁴⁷

First Movement of Praise (vv. 1–6). The psalm begins and ends, as do all five of
the concluding songs of the Psalter, with the exclamation "Praise the Lord!" This
familiar imperative call to praise occurs eight times in verses 1–4. The number
of times the imperative is used in the first four verses and then the use of the
jussive of the verb expressing a request in verse 5 make this call to praise impossible to ignore, even overwhelming. In parallel to verse 7, the first verse delineates
the geography of praise. In this first poetic unit, the praise is in the heavens, the
heights. The summons then lists those who are summoned to praise. First come
YHWH's angels and host. The popular association of angels with wings, feathers,
and harps is not relevant. Angels are messengers; the parallel term likely refers to
the host of heavenly messengers, though the term can refer to the heavenly host of

---

³⁴⁷ J. C. McCann, Jr., "Book of Psalms," in L. E. Keck et al. (eds.), *The New Interpreter's Bible*,
   vol. 4 (1996), 1270.

sun, moon, and stars or to a military host. Next summoned to praise are objects of nature: sun, moon, stars, and sky. The cosmology includes the notion that rainwater comes from above and therefore must be above the sky that expands above. So the highest realms of creation are called to the praise of YHWH the creator. The modern scientific mindset might suggest that calling inanimate objects to praise is odd, but the song soars with poetic license to a powerful summons of all creation to the praise of YHWH.

The call from the heavens is to praise YHWH's "name" (v. 5), for the name is representative of YHWH. Verses 5–6 proclaim the basis of this call to praise. The reason is that God has created all those called to praise – the angels, heavenly host, sun, moon, stars, sky, and rain. YHWH created them by command, perhaps an allusion to Genesis 1 and the creation by divine fiat portrayed there. YHWH also set the order of creation and the place in it for all those called to praise. The parts of creation are established and ordered, and that order continues. The creator brought order out of chaos, a word of good news for the community that shaped the final parts of the Psalter and that continues to deal with the aftermath of exile.

Second Movement of Praise (vv. 7–14). Verse 7 begins anew with the same imperative call to praise – "Praise the Lord" – but this time from the earth. Now summoned to praise are the creatures of the deep and even the very depths of the seas. The list of those summoned to praise then includes other elements of nature – fire, hail, snow, frost, and wind. The references to snow, frost, and hail bring to mind Ps 147:16–17. The one who created by command (v. 5) continues to control the "stormy wind" with a command. The poetic imagery moves through the created order with references to mountains and hills and their fruit trees and cedar trees. All of these parts of nature are summoned to praise. Next on the list of those summoned are wild and domestic animals, creepy crawlers, and birds. The list of the various parts of creation is again perhaps an allusion to the priestly Creation account in Genesis 1. In verses 11–12, the summons moves to humans. This part of the list of those summoned begins with kings, princes, and "all rulers of the earth." The emphasis is on including all people in the call to praise, men and women, young and old, as well as rulers. The psalm's call to praise is universal, including both the human and the natural worlds.

Verse 13 uses the jussive mode ("Let them praise") to continue the call to praise, just as in verse 5, and thus makes the transition to the reason for praise. The basis for praise is in the incomparability of the divine name or reputation. YHWH's name and YHWH's glory are central manifestations of the divine presence and activity in the world, and they are exalted "above earth and heaven"; that is, above all. There is no one like YHWH. The final verse narrows the focus to the community of Israel, the community in a covenant relationship with the creator. "Horn" is usually a symbol of strength. At times the term is used in terms of David and his line as the anointed one, but here the reference appears to be broader in terms of the covenant community. God brings strength to them. The creator and divine king makes life possible for this community. Perhaps the reference is to the continuing divine presence and strength for the community, which continues to struggle with the aftermath of exile. The psalm ends as it began, with the imperative call to praise: "Praise the Lord!"

The poetic strategy of Psalm 148 is to pile one summons to praise on another. Repetition and variation lead readers and hearers to the overpowering sense of the summons of all everywhere to praise YHWH, who is creator and king and like no other. The emphasis is on creation, though the final verse includes the YHWH–Israel covenant relationship. There is no tension in including the universal and the particular in the psalm. The creator cares for Israel. All of creation is summoned to praise, including Israel, a community that has encountered pain and a community to whom King YHWH is committed.

A Closer Look: A Double Call to Praise

Psalm 148 is a kind of double call to sing praise, from heaven and from earth. The psalm constitutes an event of praise that declares YHWH to be creator and king of all creation. The lists of those called to praise bring to mind nature wisdom and its encyclopedic knowledge.[348] YHWH as creator has established the order of creation. That order is central to the basis for praise in verses 5–6. Verses 13–14 include as bases for praise the incomparability of YHWH and the election of Israel. The poet has left no stone unturned in the poetic call to the praise of YHWH. The entirety of creation and the covenant people, all humanity and the rest of creation, are summoned to join in singing praise to YHWH. The all-encompassing call to praise anticipates the final verse of the Psalter. Implicit in this universal summons to praise is a celebration of the reign of God, a central theme in the Psalms and good news to the psalm's singers, hearers, and readers.

PSALM 149

¹ Praise the LORD!
Sing to the LORD a new song,
  his praise in the assembly of the faithful.
² Let Israel be glad in its Maker;
  let the children of Zion rejoice in their King.

---

[348] See H.-J. Kraus, *Psalms 60–150* (1988), 564.

³ Let them praise his name with dancing,
　making melody to him with tambourine and lyre.
⁴ For the LORD takes pleasure in his people;
　he adorns the humble with victory.
⁵ Let the faithful exult in glory;
　let them sing for joy on their couches.
⁶ Let the high praises of God be in their throats
　and two-edged swords in their hands,
⁷ to execute vengeance on the nations
　and punishment on the peoples,
⁸ to bind their kings with fetters
　and their nobles with chains of iron,
⁹ to execute on them the judgment decreed.
　This is glory for all his faithful ones.
　Praise the LORD!

This psalm begins in verses 1–4 with a characteristic hymnic pattern, thus making it appropriate to the collection of hymns in Psalms 145–150 that conclude the Psalter. In verses 5–9, however, the psalm takes an unusual and unexpected turn that moves beyond the conventional logic of Israel's praise.

Verses 1–4 offer a familiar hymnic pattern of summonses (vv. 1–3) and reasons for praise (v. 4). The summons, after the initial "hallelujah," consists of imperative and jussive verbs that invite vigorous and active praise and that locate the praise among "the faithful" in the Jerusalem temple. As in Psalms 96 and 98, the "new song" is a celebration of the "maker and king" in Jerusalem, whether YHWH is always and everywhere king or has just been made king by liturgical generativity. Either way, Israel is invited to join in celebrative doxology.

The reason for the summons to praise in verse concerns YHWH's connection to Israel, so that "his people" in verse 4 are surely "the faithful" in verse 1. Not only is YHWH committed to this people, but YHWH acts to achieve victory (salvation: *ys'*) for the "humble," though the term is parallel to "his people." The two terms together in parallel suggest to the community that it is dependent on YHWH's powerful intervention and advocacy on its behalf, a commitment visibly and decisively enacted in the world. None of this is at all unusual.

In verses 5–6a, the poetry returns to the jussive form of verses 2–3. In verse 5, the "victory" of verse 4 is transposed into "glory" (*kabod*) that bespeaks a claim for the abiding *weightiness* of YHWH (see 1 Sam 5:6–7). In context, the usage would seem to refer to the *glory of God* and not the self-exaltation of Israel, except that in verse 6b the subject turns to become "two-edged swords in their hands." In that phrase, attention is abruptly turned from YHWH as the agent of victory to Israel's capacity to do battle. From this point into verses 7–9a, there are a series of three infinitive phrases concerning intended violent actions for which "the two-edged sword" is the tool of effectiveness. It is a sharp sword in the hands of Israel that will:

- execute vengeance and punishment;
- bind kings and nobles in shackles; and
- do justice.

These phrases portray an act of great savage power by which the adversaries of Israel are overpowered and punished, thus establishing the supremacy of *Israel's power* as a result of *YHWH's victory*. The psalm moves from a celebration of YHWH's power to an affirmation of Israel's military capacity.

This line of reasoning concludes in verse 9b with a recognition that this measure of military prowess is indeed the "claim to fame" (glory: *hdr*) of Israel. Now attention is focused completely on Israel's ability to accomplish such military success. The final "hallelujah" of verse 9c would seem to be a wistful attempt to return the impetus for well-being to YHWH, though in context we judge that effort to be anemic at best.

Thus the psalm that begins in conventional doxology to YHWH culminates in admiring affirmation of Israel's military capacity, which is not at all seen to be connected to the initial doxology. Anthony Ceresko has suggested that the psalm can be readily understood as reflecting Israel's primal traditions.[349] Thus verses 1–4 celebrate the remembered event of the *Exodus* and verses 6–9 recall the violent act of *possession of the land*. Such a strategic interpretation would keep the psalm focused on ancient memory rather than on contemporary strategy. But that still leaves the question of a doxology to YHWH or self-affirmation of Israel's military capacity.

The poetry in fact has both a celebration of YHWH's victory and an affirmation of Israel's capacity to subdue the adversary and take vengeance. A characteristic theology of radical grace and a notion of semipelagianism have caused conventional theology to pose *divine achievement* and *human capacity* as a radical either/ or. Clearly, however, Israel understands divine and human capacities as intimately intertwined. This is nowhere more clearly evident than in the Song of Deborah that acknowledges YHWH's victory in Jgs 5:11, where the poet reports on the triumphant singing of women at the village watering hole:

> there they repeat the *triumphs of the Lord*,
> the triumphs of his peasantry in Israel. (Jgs 5:11b, c)

In this poetry, the "triumphs" (*sdqth*) of YHWH and the "triumphs of his peasantry" are in parallel without any distinction between the two. It is clear in this case that the two are equated or taken as one and the same thing.

---

[349] Anthony R. Ceresko, "Psalm 149: Poetry, Themes [Exodus and Conquest], and Social Function," *Biblica* 67 (1986): 177–194.

So it is with this psalm. YHWH achieves the "victory." The effect of that victory, however, is that Israel may "execute, bind, and execute." Although the psalm speaks of the "glory" accomplished by YHWH (see Exod 14:4, 17), the conclusion drawn is that great remembered successes indicate Israel's "glory" (*hdr*). In the end, the hymn becomes, at the same time, a celebration of Israel's achievement. The "humble" effectively used power against their adversary. Praise moves close to self-affirmation and self-congratulation. Israel knows that the power of YHWH is continually connected to its own praxis of power.

Bridging the Horizons: The Temptation of Legitimation

This ready juxtaposition of praise to YHWH and exaltation of military power is a recurring liturgical-ideological practice when a nation is at war. The purpose of such a ready juxtaposition is to legitimate military action and to identify such action with the purposes of God.

This temptation is a palpable one, of course, in the Old Testament, where "church and state," "temple and monarchy," were so closely intertwined. In a directly derivative way, the same practice reappears in the contemporary United States, where chauvinism regularly and readily identifies national purpose with divine intention. Thus, in World War II, it was "Praise the Lord and pass the ammunition." In more recent U.S. military adventurism in the Mideast, it is recurringly "God Bless America," a compelling echo of Israel's ancient and theomilitary claim.

PSALM 150

¹ Praise the Lord!
  Praise God in his sanctuary;
  praise him in his mighty firmament!
² Praise him for his mighty deeds;
  praise him according to his surpassing greatness!

³ Praise him with trumpet sound;
  praise him with lute and harp!
⁴ Praise him with tambourine and dance;
  praise him with strings and pipe!
⁵ Praise him with clanging cymbals;
  praise him with loud clashing cymbals!

⁶ Let everything that breathes praise the LORD!
    Praise the LORD!

The final poem in the Hebrew Psalter is a hymn of praise for the worshiping congregation and consists of a series of summonses to praise. There are ten imperative calls and a final jussive (expressing a request) summons to praise YHWH. The
concluding verse identifies the addressees – "everything that breathes" – and verse
2 articulates the basis of the praise. The first two verses call to praise with a motivation. Verses 1–2 introduce the theme with the reason for praise. Verses 3–6 expand
the call to praise by listing instruments of praise. Verses 3–5 are structured in terms
of the instruments. The first line of verse 3 names one instrument, the trumpet.
Each of the next three lines lists two instruments, and verse 5 names the cymbals in
both of its parallel lines. The parallelism is one of intensification, with the second
line louder. In verse 6, the verb shifts to the jussive mode (expressing a request) and
brings the psalm to a climactic conclusion with its universal address. Within the
opening and closing frames of *hallelujah*, the uses of the divine name *El* in verse 1
and YHWH in verse 6 are also noteworthy as framing devices.

Psalm 150 is the fifth of the fivefold doxology of poems that concludes the Psalter;
each poem begins and ends with "hallelujah." It is often suggested that Psalm 150
serves as the doxology for both Book V (Psalms 107–150) and the entire book of
Psalms, but the more recent suggestion is that Ps 146:21 serves as the doxology for
Book V and Psalms 146–150 as the conclusion for the Psalter. Psalm 150:6 is reminiscent of Ps 146:21, perhaps supporting this view. Psalm 150 provides an intense
exclamation to conclude this final movement of the Psalter; it brings together the
preceding poems' calls to praise with music. The book of Psalms begins with a poem
that commends Torah as the way for living and ends with a composition that urges
praise of YHWH as central to that life.

The psalm begins and ends with the consistent call to praise in Psalms 146–150:
Hallelujah! The opening verse continues with the summons to praise *El* (God) in
both the sanctuary and the great "firmament," or sky. Praise is both for cultic settings and for all of creation; it is to be universal. The remainder of this text emphasizes the cultic setting. Verse 2 continues the call to praise and articulates reasons for
the praise. The standard hymnic pattern in the Psalter is the call to praise followed
by substantial reasons for the praise. The question is whether the congregation will
respond to the call, and so the poets craft bases for the praise. The first reason is the
summary reminder of the mighty acts of YHWH, a reference to the acts of the salvation history that constitute Israel's faith memory. The liberation from bondage in
Egypt is the defining act, but there is a history of such acts for this community, such
as guidance in the wilderness, acts of deliverance from enemies, and a new exodus
into hope out of exile. These acts have throughout ancient Israel's history called for
a response of praise. The second reason given is YHWH's "surpassing greatness."
God is creator, king, and liberator, and thus worthy of praise. The praise of God

in the Psalms is persistently substantive, and that is so in Psalm 150, with the basis for praise given in verse 2, though it is also clear that in this psalm the summons to praise dominates.

The concluding poetic unit (vv. 3–6) extends the call to praise and names the musical instruments to be used. A variety of instruments are to contribute to the praise of God. The opening line of verse 3 names the sound of the trumpet. Each of the following three lines lists two instruments in this symphony of praise: lute and harp, tambourine and dance, strings and pipes. Verse 5 lists cymbals twice. The instruments vary. They are loud and soft; there are wind, string, and percussion instruments, and human dance is included. The list ends with the crescendo of "loud clashing cymbals." Music is central to the congregation's praise as it speaks to both intellect and emotion. The framing of the psalm in terms of the summons to praise and the frequently repeated summons make it clear that all the singing and music of these instruments are directed to YHWH. The expanded call to praise in Psalm 150 is a fine example of the Hebrew poetic structures of intensification in the Psalms. The envisioned sounds of praise reach a climax in verse 5 and lead to the universal call to praise in verse 6. Each line in verses 1–5 gets slightly longer until "everything that breathes" is called to the enthusiastic praise of God. Breath indicates the vitality of life given by the creator to all creatures, and so the call to praise is universal. The change of the verb from imperative to jussive (expressing a request) also gives emphasis to the concluding verse, and the psalm ends as it began, with the ever-renewed call to praise – *hallelujah.* The praise of YHWH at the end of the Psalter is uninhibited.

"Every being is to fulfill his or her highest function by praising the creator."[350] The emphasis in Psalm 150 is not on the basis for praise but on the summons to praise. The psalm provides an open ending to the Psalter and sets the question for faith communities of whether they will fulfill the summons. When worshiping communities sing the praise of God, Psalm 150 has been answered fully and faithfully. And further, no one is barred from this praise; the summons is to all who breathe. The praise of God is both possible for all who have breath and of the highest order for "everything that breathes."

Bridging the Horizons: The Whole Duty of Humans

This stunning conclusion to the Psalter, with its explosive call to praise, brings to mind the confession that the whole duty of humans is to praise and enjoy God. The Psalter ends by calling all to enjoy God and to praise God with enthusiasm. That kind of praise is essential to the life of faith and its hope, and therefore the whole worshiping community is summoned to full-throated praise around the presence of God.

---

[350] L. C. Allen, *Psalms 101–150* (2002), 404.

Author Index

Biblical Texts Index

Subject Index

rmation can be obtained
esting.com
ISA
1222
0B/613